G000167998

Hong Kong

The Complete **Residents'** Guide

Passionately Publishing...

EXPLORER

Hong Kong Explorer 1st Edition   ISBN 13 - 978-976-8182-80-7   ISBN 10 - 976-8182-80-6

Copyright © Explorer Group Ltd 2007
All rights reserved.

Front Cover Photograph: Pete Maloney

Printed and bound by Emirates Printing Press, Dubai, United Arab Emirates.

Explorer Publishing & Distribution
PO Box 34275, Zomorrodah Bldg, Za'abeel Rd, Dubai
United Arab Emirates
Phone   (+971 4) 335 3520
Fax   (+971 4) 335 3529
Email   Info@Explorer-Publishing.com
Web   www.Explorer-Publishing.com

While every effort and care has been made to ensure the accuracy of the information
contained in this publication, the publisher cannot accept responsibility for any errors or
omissions it may contain.
No part of this publication may be reproduced, stored in a retrieval system, or transmitted,
in any form or by any means, electronic, mechanical, photocopying, recording or otherwise,
without the prior permission in writing of the publisher.

Welcome...

Congratulations, you hold in your hands the most comprehensive book available on life in Hong Kong. Now get ready, because whether you've lived here for a while or have just arrived (or indeed are planning the move), life is about to get a lot more interesting, as well as fun, stress-free and fulfilling. This complete residents' guide will arm you with insider knowledge on all aspects of life on and off the island, so even if you've barely stepped off the plane it won't be long before you're calling Hong Kong home...rather than calling home for help.

First up is **General Information** giving you a quick history lesson, some vital facts and figures, and introducing you to Hong Kong's culture and lifestyle. Then it's **Residents**, the mother of all chapters - literally, as this beauty will take care of everything. All the ins and outs, ups and downs and administrative necessities of setting up home are covered, from immigration procedures to finding work, residential areas to healthcare, and everything in between.

And of course it isn't all paperwork and no play. The **Exploring** chapter will take you on a journey around Hong Kong Island, Kowloon and the New Territories, highlighting the good, the bold and the unusual. There are also suggestions of weekend breaks and holiday hotspots from Hong Kong should you be planning a little sojourn. The playing continues with **Activities**, where every sport and hobby known to man (and woman, of course) has been covered, as well as spas and other pastimes that will ensure your well-being. From play to pay, the **Shopping** chapter tells you how far your money will go, whether you're splashing out in the malls or bargain hunting in the markets.

With so much administrative business taken care of, and some downtime pleasure mixed in, it's time for a celebration, and the **Going Out** chapter can point you in the right direction. Whether you want to sample the local cuisine or satisfy your appetite for a homeland dish, we have independently reviewed the best restaurants, cafes, bars and nightclubs. So, cheers to your new life in Hong Kong... just make sure you get out there and live it!

The Explorer Team

Explorer online

Life can move pretty fast so make sure you keep up at www.explorerpublishing.com. Register for updates on the latest happenings in your city, or let us know if there's anything we've missed out with our reader response form. You can also check out city info on various destinations around the world - whether you're planning a holiday or making your next big move, we've got it covered. All our titles, from residents' guides to mini visitors' guides, mini maps to photography books are available to purchase online so you need never be without us!

"It's that Volkswagen feeling!"
It Gets Me.

I can't quite say why I'm so madly attracted to my Volkswagen. It's like we share an uncommon passion. Sure, it feels so safe and sound on the road, while also looking sleek and styled on the outside. It also feels nice and comfortable on the inside, too!

But it's really more than all that. It's another dimension. A real connection – it's like a soul mate. I guess I can say it's the ONE for me. So why do I always go for a Volkswagen? Because it simply gets me.

For the love of automobiles

Hashim MM
AKA: Speedy Gonzales
They don't come much faster than Hashim – he's so speedy with his mouse that scientists are struggling to create a computer that can keep up with him. His nimble fingers leave his keyboard smouldering (he gets through three a week), and his go-faster stripes make him almost invisible to the naked eye when he moves.

Jane Roberts
AKA: The Oracle
After working in an undisclosed role in the government, Jane brought her super sleuth skills to Explorer. Whatever the question, she knows what, where, who, how and when, but her encyclopaedic knowledge is only impressive until you realise she just makes things up randomly.

Helen Spearman
AKA: Little Miss Sunshine
With her bubbly laugh and permanent smile, Helen is a much-needed ray of sunshine in the office when we're all grumpy and facing harrowing deadlines. It's almost impossible to think that she ever loses her temper or shows a dark side... although put her behind the wheel of a car, and you've got instant road rage.

Jayde Fernandes
AKA: Pop Idol
Jayde's idol is Britney Spears, and he recently shaved his head to show solidarity with the troubled star. When he's not checking his dome for stubble, or practising the dance moves to 'Baby One More Time' in front of the bathroom mirror, he actually manages to get some designing done.

Henry Hilos
AKA: The Quiet Man
Henry can rarely be seen from behind his large obstructive screen but when you do catch a glimpse you'll be sure to get a smile. Lighthearted Henry keeps all those glossy pages filled with pretty pictures for something to look at when you can't be bothered to read.

Kate Fox
AKA: Contacts Collector
Kate swooped into the office like the UK equivalent of Wonderwoman, minus the tights of course (it's much too hot for that), but armed with a superhuman marketing brain. Even though she 's just arrived, she is already a regular on the Dubai social scene - she is helping to blast Explorer into the stratosphere, one champagne-soaked networking party at a time.

Ieyad Charaf
AKA: Fashion Designer
When we hired Ieyad as a top designer, we didn't realise we'd be getting his designer tops too! By far the snappiest dresser in the office, you'd be hard-pressed to beat his impeccably ironed shirts.

Katie Drynan
AKA The Irish Deputy
Katie is a Jumeirah Jane in training, and has 35 sisters who take it in turns to work in the Explorer office while she enjoys testing all the beauty treatments available on the Beach Road. This Irish charmer met an oil tycoon in Paris, and they now spend the weekends digging very deep holes in their new garden.

Ingrid Cupido
AKA: The Karaoke Queen
Ingrid has a voice to match her starlet name. She'll put any Pop Idols to shame once behind the mike, and she's pretty nifty on a keyboard too. She keeps us all ticking over and was a very welcome relief for overworked staff. She certainly gets our vote if she decides to go pro; just remember you saw her here first.

Ivan Rodrigues
AKA: The Aviator
After making a mint in the airline market, Ivan came to Explorer where he works for pleasure, not money. That's his story, anyway. We know that he is actually a corporate spy from a rival company and that his multi-level spreadsheets are really elaborate codes designed to confuse us.

Kiran Melwani
AKA: Bow Selector
Like a modern-day Robin Hood (right down to the green tights and band of merry men), Kiran's mission in life is to distribute Explorer's wealth of knowledge to the fact-hungry readers of the world. Just make sure you never do anything to upset her – rumour has it she's a pretty mean shot with that bow and arrow.

Abdul Gafoor
AKA: Ace Circulator
After a successful stint on Ferrari's Formula One team Gafoor made a pitstop at our office and decided to stay. He has won our 'Most Cheerful Employee' award five years in a row – baffling, when you consider he spends so much time battling the traffic.

Andrea Fust
AKA: Mother Superior
By day Andrea is the most efficient manager in the world and by night she replaces the boardroom for her board and wows the pants off the dudes in Ski Dubai. Literally. Back in the office she definitely wears the trousers!

Ahmed Mainodin
AKA: Mystery Man
We can never recognise Ahmed because of his constantly changing facial hair. He waltzes in with big lambchop sideburns one day, a handlebar moustache the next, and a neatly trimmed goatee after that. So far we've had no objections to his hirsute chameleonisms, but we'll definitely draw the line at a monobrow.

Cherry Enriquez
AKA: Bean Counter
With the team's penchant for sweets and pastries, it's good to know we have Cherry on top of our accounting cake. The local confectioner is always paid on time, so we're guaranteed great gateaux for every special occasion.

Ajay Krishnan R
AKA: Web Wonder
Ajay's mum and dad knew he was going to be an IT genius when the found him reconfiguring his Commodore 64 at the tender age of 2. He went on to become the technology consultant on all three Matrix films, and counts Keanu as a close personal friend.

Claire England
AKA: Whip Cracker
No longer able to freeload off the fact that she once appeared in a Robbie Williams video, Claire now puts her creative skills to better use – looking up rude words in the dictionary! A child of English nobility, Claire is quite the lady – unless she's down at Jimmy Dix.

Alex Jeffries
AKA: Easy Rider
Alex is happiest when dressed in leather from head to toe with a humming machine between his thighs – just like any other motorbike enthusiast. Whenever he's not speeding along the Hatta Road at full throttle, he can be found at his beloved Mac, still dressed in leather.

David Quinn
AKA: Sharp Shooter
After a short stint as a children's TV presenter was robbed from David because he developed an allergy to sticky back plastic, he made his way to sandier pastures. Now that he's thinking outside the box, nothing gets past the man with the sharpest pencil in town.

Enrico Maullon
AKA: The Crooner
Frequently mistaken for his near-namesake Enrique Iglesias, Enrico decided to capitalise and is now a regular stand-in for the Latin heartthrob. If he's ever missing from the office, it usually means he's off performing for millions of adoring fans on another stadium tour of America.

Alistair MacKenzie
AKA: Media Mogul
If only Alistair could take the paperless office one step further and achieve the officeless office he would be the happiest publisher alive. Wireless access from a remote spot somewhere in the Hajar Mountains would suit this intrepid explorer – less traffic, lots of fresh air, and wearing sandals all day - the perfect work environment!

Firos Khan
AKA: Big Smiler
Previously a body double in kung fu movies, including several appearances in close up scenes for Steven Seagal's moustache. He also once tore down a restaurant with his bare hands after they served him a mild curry by mistake.

Freya Simpson Giles

Freya is a climatic refugee from England and long term resident of Hong Kong. After working as a freelance writer and editor for four years, she has recently set up her own business – Giles Publications. She lives at the beach with her husband, young daughter and a recently acquired three-legged dog. Her hobbies include travel, salsa and eating out.

Rehana Sheikh

Rehana is a 'permanent expat,' having lived in Hong Kong for 21 years. She writes on all aspects of living in the region and offers walks through country parks and tours to historical places. When she has free time she plays mahjong and hits the trails and paths – her footprints can be seen all over the hills and valleys of Hong Kong.

Lesley Croft

Lesley is a seasoned expat with first hand experience of arriving in a new country and not knowing where anything is. She has developed a phobia of cardboard boxes, having had 12 different addresses over the last 16 years. She arrived in Hong Kong, with aforementioned boxes, five years ago and since she unpacked them has no plans to move again. Famous last words!

Pete Spurrier

A disastrous expedition along the Silk Road led Pete Spurrier to an accidental arrival in Hong Kong in 1993. He has lived here ever since, writing and publishing on local culture, entertainment and travel. Hong Kong's outdoor attractions keep him busy: when not hiking up hills in typhoons, he likes to eat alfresco on the outlying islands.

Paul Kay and Victoria Burrows

Victoria is Welsh, but grew up in South Africa. In the four years she's been in Hong Kong, she's developed a passion for Chinese painting and steamed dumplings. She also loves books, shoes, deserts, tropical fish and travelling. Paul also lives and works in Hong Kong, where he spends his days longing for square sausage and dreaming of playing for Glasgow Rangers Football Club.

David Bellis and Ross Vermeer

David and Ross have followed similar paths since arriving in the late 1980s: from teaching English and working for peanuts, to moving on to better jobs, marrying local ladies and most recently starting families. Neither shows signs of leaving, saying that the worthy quest for decent dim sum and the perfect pint continues to give meaning to their time in Hong Kong.

Thanks...

The biggest thank you must go to the Hong Kong Explorer authors, whose tireless research, unfailing commitment and insider knowledge has ensured that this book is the most comprehensive guide to HK life available. Further thanks goes to Jodie for providing moral support and food parcels, Rania for her editing input and eclectic music, the MTR Corporation for their logo, and Hong Kong's hotels, malls, restaurants, bars, clubs and associations for sharing their info and images. Last but not least, thanks to everybody in the Explorer office for their support. We can all be very proud of this book.

Rafi VP
AKA: Party Trickster

After developing a rare allergy to sunlight in his teens, Rafi started to lose a few centimeters of height every year. He now stands just 30cm tall, and does his best work in our dingy basement wearing a pair of infrared goggles. His favourite party trick is to fold himself into a briefcase, and he was once sick in his hat.

Shyrell Tamayo
AKA: Fashion Princess

We've never seen Shyrell wearing the same thing twice – her clothes collection is so large that her husband has to keep all his things in a shoebox. She runs Designlab like clockwork, because being late for deadlines is SO last season.

Sunita Lakhiani
AKA: Designlass

Initially suspicious of having a female in their midst, the boys in Designlab now treat Sunita like one of their own. A big shame for her, because they treat each other pretty damn bad!

Roshni Ahuja
AKA: Bright Spark

Never failing to brighten up the office with her colourful get-up, Roshni definitely puts the 'it' in the IT department. She's a perennially pleasant, profound programmer with peerless panache, and she does her job with plenty of pep and piles of pizzazz.

Tim Binks
AKA: Class Clown

El Binksmeisterooney is such a sharp wit, he often has fellow Explorers gushing tea from their noses in convulsions of mirth. Years spent hiking across the Middle East have given him an encyclopedic knowledge of rock formations and elaborate hair.

Sean Kearns
AKA: The Tall Guy

Big Sean, as he's affectionately known, is so laid back he actually spends most of his time lying down (unless he's on a camping trip, when his ridiculously small tent forces him to sleep on his hands and knees). Despite the rest of us constantly tripping over his lanky frame, when the job requires someone who will work flat out, he always rises to the editorial occasion.

Tissy Varghese
AKA: PC Whisperer

With her soft voice and gentle touch, Tissy can whip even the wildest of PCs into submission. No matter how many times we spill coffee on our keyboards she never loses her temper – a real mystery, especially as she wakes at 3am every day to beat the Sharjah traffic.

Shabsir M
AKA: Sticky Wicket

Shabsir is a valuable player on the Indian national cricket team, so instead of working you'll usually find him autographing cricket balls for crazed fans around the world. We don't mind though – if ever a retailer is stumped because they run out of stock, he knocks them for six with his speedy delivery.

Tom Jordan
AKA: The True Professional

Explorer's resident thesp, Tom delivers lines almost as well as he cuts them. His early promise on the pantomime circuit was rewarded with an all-action role in hit UK drama Heartbeat. He's still living off the royalties – and the fact he shared a sandwich with Kenneth Branagh.

Shefeeq M
AKA: Rapper in Disguise

So new he's still got the wrapper on, Shefeeq was dragged into the Explorer office, forced to pose in front of a camera, and put to work in the design department. The poor chap only stopped by to ask for directions to Wadi Bih, but since we realised how efficient he is, we keep him chained to his desk.

Zainudheen Madathil
AKA: Map Master

Often confused with retired footballer Zinedine Zidane because of his dexterous displays and a bad head-butting habit, Zain tackles design with the mouse skills of a star striker. Maps are his goal and despite getting red-penned a few times, when he shoots, he scores.

Laura Zuffa
AKA: Travelling Salesgirl

Laura's passport is covered in more stamps than Kofi Annan's, and there isn't a city, country or continent that she won't travel to. With a smile that makes grown men weep, our girl on the frontlines always brings home the beef bacon.

Mohammed T
AKA: King of the Castle

T is Explorer's very own Bedouin warehouse dweller; under his caring charge all Explorer stock is kept in masterful order. Arrive uninvited and you'll find T, meditating on a pile of maps, amid an almost eerie sense of calm.

Mannie Lugtu
AKA: Distribution Demon

When the travelling circus rode into town, their master juggler Mannie decided to leave the Big Top and explore Dubai instead. He may have swapped his balls for our books but his juggling skills still come in handy.

Motaz Al Bunai
AKA: Car Salesman

Motaz starts every day with a tough decision, namely, which one of his fleet of exotic cars he's going to drive to work. If he ever takes a break from his delightful designing, he could always start his own second-hand car garage – Motaz's Motors.

Maricar Ong
AKA: Pocket Docket

A pint-sized dynamo of ruthless efficiency, Maricar gets the job done before anyone else notices it needed doing. If this most able assistant is absent for a moment, it sends a surge of blind panic through the Explorer ranks.

Noushad Madathil
AKA: Map Daddy

Where would Explorer be without the mercurial Madathil brothers? Lost in the Empty Quarter, that's where. Quieter than a mute dormouse, Noushad prefers to let his Photoshop layers, and brother Zain, do all the talking. A true Map Daddy.

Matt Farquharson
AKA: Hack Hunter

A career of tuppence-a-word hackery ended when Matt arrived in Dubai to cover a maggot wranglers' convention. He misguidedly thinks he's clever because he once wrote for some grown-up English papers.

Pamela Grist
AKA: Happy Snapper

If a picture can speak a thousand words then Pam's photos say a lot about her - through her lens she manages to find the beauty in everything – even this motley crew. And when the camera never lies, thankfully Photoshop can.

Mimi Stankova
AKA: Mind Controller

A master of mind control, Mimi's siren-like voice lulls people into doing whatever she asks. Her steely reserve and endless patience mean recalcitrant reporters and persistent PR people are putty in her hands, delivering whatever she wants, whenever she wants it.

Pete Maloney
AKA: Graphic Guru

Image conscious he may be, but when Pete has his designs on something you can bet he's gonna get it! He's the king of chat up lines, ladies – if he ever opens a conversation with 'D'you come here often?' then brace yourself for the Maloney magic.

Mohammed Sameer
AKA: Man in the Van

Known as MS, short for Microsoft, Sameer can pick apart a PC like a thief with a lock, which is why we keep him out of finance and pounding Dubai's roads in the unmissable Explorer van – so we can always spot him coming.

Rafi Jamal
AKA: Soap Star

After a walk on part in The Bold and the Beautiful, Rafi swapped the Hollywood Hills for the Hajar Mountains. Although he left the glitz behind, he still mingles with high society, moonlighting as a male gigolo and impressing Dubai's ladies with his fancy footwork.

MISSING
your favorite channels?

Please call
24-hour
sales hotline: **2888 0008** then press 1

or visit any of our PCCW shops
www.now-tv.com

Find them all on
now TV

Choose from over 120 fabulous channels:

A **PCCW** service

Residents' Guides

All you need to know about living, working and enjoying life in these exciting destinations

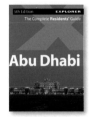

* Covers not final. Titles available Winter 2007.

Activity Guides

Drive, trek, dive and swim... life will never be boring again

Mini Guides
The perfect pocket-sized
Visitors' Guides

* Covers not final. Titles available Winter 2007.

Mini Maps
Wherever you are,
never get lost again

* Covers not final. Titles available Winter 2007.

Photography Books
Beautiful cities caught through the lens

Contents

Contents

moving?

relax.
we carry
the
load. SM

Door to door moving with Allied Pickfords

Allied Pickfords is one of the largest and most respected providers of moving services in the world, handling over 50,000 international moves every year.

We believe that nothing reduces stress more than trust, and each year thousands of families trust Allied Pickfords to move them. With over 800 offices in more than 40 countries, we're the specialists in international moving and have the ability to relocate you anywhere anytime. Move with Allied to Allied worldwide.

www.alliedpickfords.com

ALLIED PICKFORDS®
The Careful Movers™

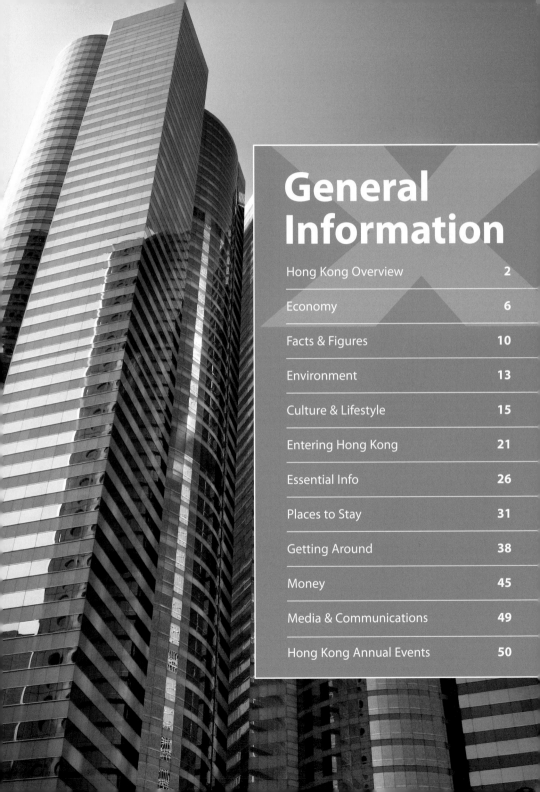

General Information

General Information

Geography

Hong Kong comprises a small, irregularly-shaped peninsula, plus a group of islands, covering just under 1,100 square kilometres of territory overall. Clinging to China's southern coast, it lies just within the Tropic of Cancer, looking out to the South China Sea. Hong Kong's only land 'border' is with mainland China. Although Hong Kong is now of course a part of China, it is cut off from the rest of country to maintain its status as a Special Administrative Region (hence its official name, the Hong Kong SAR).

The People's Republic of China

Sheung Shui

NEW TERRITORIES

Tuen Mun

Sha Tin

Tsuen Wan

KOWLOON

Lantau Island

HONG KONG ISLAND

Most people who haven't been to Hong Kong think of it as a city. This is a mistake, for two reasons. First, it ignores the 80% of Hong Kong's territory that is undeveloped, mountainous, and often strikingly beautiful. Second, since Hong Kong's population density is usually calculated using its overall area, it's easy to underestimate just how incredibly crowded its urban areas really are.

It's easiest to think of Hong Kong as divided into three parts: Hong Kong island, Kowloon, and the New Territories/outlying islands. The north side of Hong Kong island is home to the city's oldest urban areas, and it's still the financial and administrative centre. Its famous skyline is reproduced on innumerable postcards, holiday snapshots, and cheesy paintings.

The Kowloon peninsula lies about a mile away, directly across Hong Kong's shrinking but still heavily used deepwater harbour. Kowloon is home to most of Hong Kong's people, and it is blanketed by intense urban development. Its skyline was kept low

Hong Kong Fact Box

Coordinates – 22°15′ North 114°10′ East

Borders – The People's Republic of China

Total land area – 1,092 sq km

Total coastline – 955 km

Percentage of developed land – approx 20%

The view from The Peak

Hong Kong Overview

for many years because it lay on or near the flight path into the old Kai Tak Airport. But building restrictions have now been relaxed, and newly-constructed behemoths around Kowloon look eye-to-eye with their older brothers across the harbour.

The New Territories comprises the rest of Hong Kong's mainland. It is dotted with 'new towns', highly-planned suburban settlements comprising row after row of 40 to 60 storey residential tower blocks. But most of the New Territories is wild, with hiking trails, picnic areas and beaches providing plenty of opportunities to get outdoors. Hong Kong also lays claims to over 200 islands. Just a few are big enough to visit, but Lantau Island (Hong Kong's biggest island by far), Lamma Island, and Cheung Chau are worth it for their residential areas, tourist attractions and scenery.

Throughout Hong Kong the landscape is hilly to mountainous; Hong Kong's highest peak, Tai Mo Shan in the New Territories, measures 959m, while Hong Kong island's more famous Victoria Peak towers over the city at 552m. When Hong Kong was ceded to the British in the 19th century, the landscape had been almost stripped of trees, but large areas are now reforested.

History

The Distant Past

Archaeological studies show that parts of Hong Kong have been inhabited for at least five millennia. The area was incorporated into the Chinese empire in the Qin Dynasty, around 200BC. Ancient Hong Kong may originally have been a salt production and pearl fishing hub, but in the Tang Dynasty, around 1,000 years ago, trade took on a greater role. Hong Kong briefly played host to the court of the Southern Song Dynasty in the late 13th century, as the Mongols swept through China's northern reaches. In a foreshadowing of modern events, Hong Kong's population grew sharply in this era as refugees arrived seeking sanctuary from political upheaval to the north.

Contact with the West

The 16th century witnessed Hong Kong's growing contact with the west. Portuguese traders were the first to arrive, although they were expelled from Hong Kong and eventually set up shop across the Pearl River delta in Macau. The British East India Company arrived in southern China in 1699, and trade with the British empire developed quickly. Hong Kong was mostly bypassed in favour of Canton (modern Guangzhou) during these years, however, leaving some fishing villages and quite a few pirates.

The Birth of Modern Hong Kong

Modern Hong Kong is the offspring of the Opium War, fought between Britain and China between 1839 and 1842. Hong Kong island was ceded to the victorious British in the Treaty of Nanking. Another round of the Opium War broke out soon after, with a similar result: in 1860, under the Convention of Peking, the Kowloon Peninsula came under British rule. The New Territories were annexed via a 99-year lease in 1898, mostly to provide a defence buffer around the city.

During this time Hong Kong's rapidly expanding, trade-based economy fuelled the building of dockyards, warehouses and colonial villas. The population grew steadily, fed by a stream of migrant workers from Guangdong Province. Hong Kong then, like now, was famous for its urban density and transitory population.

Colonial Hong Kong was a hierarchical and segregated society, with sharp social divisions along racial lines. Yet its stable government and firm rule of law still attracted many Chinese immigrants seeking economic opportunity. It was also a hideout for fugitives; Sun Yat-sen, for example, came to Hong Kong several times after his efforts to reform Chinese society ran foul of authorities there.

Who Rules Hong Kong?

For most of its history, Hong Kong was left to its own devices. It was just too small and far away to warrant any attention from the Chinese Emperor in distant Beijing, or his representatives in nearby Guangzhou. These days, a Chief Executive and an 'elected' Legislative Council give Hong Kong some of the trappings of democracy, and an appearance of autonomy. Yet it is clear where the real power lies. When tough decisions must be made, politicians in Hong Kong look over their shoulders uneasily: what will Beijing say?

History Buffs

Those with an interest in Hong Kong's history should check out the Museums, Heritage & Culture section of the Exploring chapter, starting on p.164. The website of the Leisure and Cultural Services Department (www.lcsd.gov.hk) is also a good source of information on Hong Kong's museums and heritage sites.

War, and More War

After this long and relatively peaceful phase of expansion, World War II threw Hong Kong into chaos. The Japanese launched an invasion across the mainland border just hours after their attack on Pearl Harbour and, despite the brave and desperate defence of its armed forces, Hong Kong was not prepared to offer long-term resistance. The city fell on Christmas day, 1941. The following years of occupation were bleak, with mass rapes, the imprisonment of westerners in concentration camps, and economic collapse. Many of Hong Kong's Chinese residents were forcibly repatriated to China by the Japanese administration; Hong Kong's population of 1.6 million at the start of the war was reduced to just 500,000 by its end, depopulating much of the city. Hong Kong was finally returned to British control in August 1945, after the defeat of Japan.

The British government tried to stay neutral during the final phases of China's civil war, but the city's population was soon swelled by refugees escaping the 1949 communist victory. At this point, Chinese forces might easily have overrun Hong Kong, but then, as now, the mainland believed it was better off leaving Hong Kong's economy alone. Its value as a trade and finance centre was too great to compromise. Further waves of immigrants were set off by the Great Leap Forward and its ensuing famine in the late 1950s, and the Cultural Revolution of the mid 1960s.

Building the City

As Hong Kong became increasingly crowded and prosperous, the Hong Kong Government stepped up its attempts to provide the expanding population with social services and infrastructure. A massive public housing programme was catalysed by a catastrophic 1953 fire in one of Hong Kong's squatter settlements, and new public health and education programmes grew quickly.

For the next several decades, Hong Kong's economy grew continuously, often at a furious pace. Manufacturing dominated the post-war years, but a transition to a services-based economy was nearly complete by the 1990s.

The Lease Runs Out

In 1982, 15 years before the lease on the New Territories expired, a series of long and often acrimonious talks on Hong Kong's future began between the UK and Chinese governments. Chinese leader, Deng Xiao Ping, stood firm: nothing would do but the transfer of all of Hong Kong's territory to Chinese control. The British Government eventually acknowledged that it would be futile to attempt to retain Kowloon or Hong Kong island independently of the New Territories.

Aberdeen

Hong Kong Timeline

221BC	First mention of Hong Kong in Chinese records
16th century AD	Hong Kong comprises small villages; growing contacts with the west
1842	Treaty of Nanking cedes Hong Kong island to the British at conclusion of Opium War
1860	Convention of Peking adds the Kowloon peninsula to Hong Kong's territory
1899	The New Territories added via a 99-year lease
1920s	Period of unrest marked by Seamen's Strike in 1922
December 25, 1941	Hong Kong falls to invading Japanese army
August 1945	Hong Kong returned to British rule after Japanese surrender
1950s	Waves of immigrants from mainland China swell Hong Kong's population; social services and public housing greatly expanded
1960s	Population continues to grow along with economy; communist-led riots break out in 1967
1984	British Prime Minister Margaret Thatcher and Chinese Premier Zhao Ziyang sign the Joint Declaration ensuring Hong Kong's return to Chinese sovereignty in 1997
June 4, 1989	Tiananmen Square crackdown in Beijing sparks huge demonstrations in Hong Kong
1992-1995	Hong Kong's last Governor, Chris Patten, attempts to introduce democratic reforms, to decidedly mixed reactions
June 30-July 1, 1997	Hong Kong handover
October 1997-2003	Deep recession and high unemployment
March-June 2003	SARS crisis, everyone in Hong Kong wearing surgical masks
March 2005	Tung resigns as popularity drops; cites health reasons. Donald Tsang is named to serve out the remainder of Tung's term

An agreement was signed on December 19, 1984, stipulating that Hong Kong would become part of China under a 'one country; two systems' arrangement: that is, Hong Kong would retain its economic and social independence, and its common-law jurisprudence.

A period of upheaval followed the 1989 crackdown on pro-democracy students in Beijing's Tiananmen Square, heightening the tension in Hong Kong, and spurring many people to emigrate. Nevertheless, the Basic Law, a mini constitution for post-handover Hong Kong, was approved in 1990.

The handover itself was completed amidst much pomp and ceremony – and rain – at midnight on July 1, 1997.

The Post-Handover Years

Tung Chee Hwa, a wealthy shipping magnate, was selected as Hong Kong's first Chief Executive. His term of office started relatively well, but his administration was dogged by a combination of a severe economic recession (see Economy p.6) and a number of policy blunders. The 2003 SARS epidemic, which was centred in Hong Kong, was another significant setback. The massive pro-democracy march in Hong Kong on July 1, 2003 was widely seen as a vote of no confidence in Tung, but he stayed in office until tendering his resignation in March 2005.

Tung was replaced by his then Chief Secretary, Donald Tsang, who is known both for his trademark bow tie, and for his long career as a civil servant.

Hong Kong Overview

Hong Kong's economy has grown strongly in recent years, after suffering a deep recession in the late 1990s, and yet another slow-down in 2003 during the SARS epidemic. In 2005, Hong Kong's per-capita GDP was estimated at US$37,400.

Trade

Tax Status

Whether you live in Hong Kong or are just visiting, there is no VAT or sales tax on any purchases you make. The 2006/7 budget speech did indicate that the government was seriously considering introducing a Goods and Services Tax (GST) because Hong Kong's current sources of tax (salaries, profits, land premiums, investment) fluctuate too much to be relied on. A consultation period followed, but the government dropped the plans in the face of public opposition.

Throughout the first hundred years of British rule, trade with China was the bedrock of the local economy. Hong Kong's sheltered harbour and proximity to Canton (Guangzhou) placed it perfectly for handling the sea-bound trade between China and the rest of the world.

Trade is still an important part of the local economy: in 2005, Hong Kong was the world's second busiest container port (first place went to Singapore). The real threat to Hong Kong's trade, however, is the nearby mainland city of Shenzhen, currently the world number four. Its combination of good location and lower handling fees have increased its container traffic at a rate of around 20% per year, compared to single digit increases for Hong Kong.

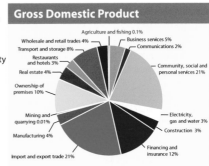

Gross Domestic Product

- Agriculture and fishing 0.1%
- Wholesale and retail trades 4%
- Business services 5%
- Transport and storage 8%
- Communications 2%
- Restaurants and hotels 3%
- Community, social and personal services 21%
- Real estate 4%
- Ownership of premises 10%
- Mining and quarrying 0.01%
- Electricity, gas and water 3%
- Construction 3%
- Manufacturing 4%
- Financing and insurance 12%
- Import and export trade 21%

Manufacturing

In the 1960s and 70s, manufacturing grew in importance, and the label 'Made in Hong Kong' was seen around the world. An unlikely combination of events triggered this rapid growth. First, large numbers of people from China streamed into Hong Kong. A small number of wealthy immigrants (mainly Shanghainese) brought the capital and experience needed to set up new manufacturing businesses. The penniless majority (many from Guangdong province) became cheap labour in the factories. At the same time, China's involvement in the Korean war put it under embargoes from both the US and United Nations, stifling Hong Kong's trading role.

This manufacturing boom soon faded, starting in late 1978, when China opened its doors to foreign investment. Hong Kong's manufacturers seized the chance to relocate their factories to Southern China, benefiting from lower cost land and labour. In 1991, manufacturing still accounted for 14.4% of Hong Kong's GDP, but by 2004 its share was just 4.1%.

Services

As manufacturing left Hong Kong, so the service sector (especially financial services) grew to take its place. The rapid growth in the 1980s and 90s means that today services make up over 90% of Hong Kong's GDP. The main components of these services are civil aviation, shipping, travel and tourism, trade-related services, and financial and banking services.

Continued Integration with China

Each stage of Hong Kong's economic development can be linked to events in mainland China, and this will continue to be the pattern for the future. Hong Kong's role as the provider of value-added services will be challenged as China develops, with Shanghai a worthy competitor. On the bright side, China's market for Hong Kong's services continues to expand, with the two economies growing ever more interconnected.

Income Tax
If you plan to work in Hong Kong, there is happier news. The maximum tax you'll pay on your salary is just 16% of the balance after all deductions have been claimed. And there is no capital gains tax, making Hong Kong a great place to start investing for your retirement.

Recent developments in this area include the conclusion of a free trade agreement with China; and the Closer Economic Partnership Arrangement (CEPA), which applies zero tariffs to all Hong Kong-origin goods and preferential treatment in 27 service sectors. Hong Kong, along with the Macau SAR, has also joined a new pan-Pearl River Delta trade block with nine Chinese provinces, which aims to lower trade barriers among members, standardise regulations, and improve infrastructure.

Employment

Unemployment inevitably rose during Hong Kong's 1997 - 2003 economic downturn, peaking at 8.6% in 2003. To appreciate how unusual this was, unemployment averaged just 2.5% in the 15 years leading up to 1997. The economic downturn also set off significant pay cuts in almost all sectors. The recovering economy has improved things; salaries started to increase again in 2005, and unemployment had fallen to 5.2% at the start of 2006. The recovery has not reached everyone though, with salaries for unskilled and semi-skilled workers remaining flat. This will be an ongoing problem as the economy moves further towards services that require a skilled workforce.

Tourism

Tourism contributes a significant chunk of the services revenues of Hong Kong's GDP. In 2005, Hong Kong received over $100 billion from inbound tourism – just over 7% of total GDP.

Tourism Site
The website of the Hong Kong Tourism Board (www.discover hongkong.com) is a good source of information on things to see and do during your time here.

In 2005, over 23 million people visited Hong Kong, almost double the 13 million that visited in 2000. Most of this increase can be traced back to the Chinese government's decision to make it easier for its citizens to visit Hong Kong: over the same 2000-2005 period, visitors from Mainland China have increased from 3.8 million to 12.5 million. Looking ahead, the Hong Kong Tourism Board (HKTB) says they aim to beat the UNWTO's forecast of Hong Kong attracting more than 56 million visitors a year by 2020. Despite the impressive growth listed above, it slowed significantly in 2005, so it is far from certain that they can meet that goal.

Who is the target visitor? Geographically, the HKTB tries to appeal to tourists from a broad mix of countries rather than focusing on one or two, thereby reducing the risk if one country's arrivals fall off. In terms of market segments, attracting more families and business visitors is seen as key to Hong Kong's future tourism success. Two developments which opened in 2005 targeted those segments: Disneyland (p.203) in September, then AsiaWorld-Expo (Hong Kong's largest exhibition and events complex) in December.

The HKTB is also trying to paint a much broader picture of the SAR's attractions, instead of relying on the simple 'food and shopping' themes they've used in the past. Again, they're reaching out to families, stressing educational experiences to augment the fun activities. The Hong Kong Wetland Park (p.6), which has recently opened, is a good example of this plan in action.

All these visitors need somewhere to stay. By the end of 2006, Hong Kong had 44,942 rooms provided in 123 hotels and 5,372 rooms provided in 484 tourist guesthouses. With occupancy rates steady at over 80%, extra capacity is clearly needed. The first steps have already been taken to meet this growing demand and over 20 hotels opened in 2005 and 2006 so there is plenty of choice for all visitors.

Typical Basic Monthly Salaries

Chief Financial Officer	$98,000
Regional HR Director	$95,000
Sales Director	$72,000
Finance Manager	$44,000
Regional Sales Manager	$42,000
HR Manager	$33,500
Credit Analyst, Corporate Banking	$23,000
Programmer	$18,500
Secretary to Executive	$17,500
Receptionist	$10,000

(Includes figures from Manpower, and from government websites)

Key Hong Kong Projects

It used to seem as though the Hong Kong shoreline moved on a yearly basis, with continual 'reclamation' of land from Hong Kong's harbour to build on. In recent years public opinion has turned against further reclamation, and the government has responded by shelving or scaling back several projects. Still, you'll see (and hear!) plenty of construction while in Hong Kong. Here are some of the larger projects underway.

Hong Kong – Zhuhai – Macau Bridge

www.hyd.gov.hk

Approval has been given for preparatory work to begin on this 30km bridge, but its final details are still unclear. The bridge will give Hong Kong a direct road link across the Pearl River to Macau and Zhuhai.

Completion: TBC

Lok Ma Chau Spur Line

www.kcrc.com

This line will provide a much-needed second rail crossing from Hong Kong into the Mainland. In 2005, the current railway crossing point at Lo Wu handled an average of 249,000 passenger trips a day – it's believed to be the busiest crossing point in the world.

Completion: 2007

Route 8, with Stonecutters Bridge

www.hyd.gov.hk

Although this new road will be less than 14km long, it will include the 1.6km long Stonecutters Bridge, three tunnels, and a 1.4km viaduct. The clear span of Stonecutters Bridge is 1,018m, making it one of the longest span cable-stayed bridges in the world.

Completion: 2009

SkyCity

www.hongkongairport.com

SkyCity is being built next to the present passenger terminal at Chek Lap Kok airport. SkyCity's AsiaWorld-Expo exhibition and events complex recently opened, and the second passenger terminal and SkyPlaza shopping centre was due to open in the first quarter of 2007. The complex will eventually include a second airport hotel, a nine hole golf course, office development, and a permanent cross-boundary ferry terminal.

Completion: 2010

West Island Line

www.mtr.com.hk

The Hong Kong government has approved the extension of the MTR's Island Line to the residential areas in Kennedy Town, at the western end of Hong Kong island. This new line is expected to eliminate the regular traffic jams that currently form on the roads running from this area into the Central business district.

Completion: 2010 (estimated)

West Kowloon Cultural District

www.hab.gov.hk/wkcd

This project started off as an idea to give Hong Kong a dose of culture, by building a complex of museums and performance venues on existing reclaimed land. The original plans (in particular a giant canopy) faced strong public opposition, however, and the project is now back at the consultation stage.

Completion: TBC

Mini Marvels

Explorer *Mini Visitors' Guides* are the perfect holiday companion. They are small enough to fit in your pocket but beautiful enough to inspire you to explore. With area information, detailed maps, visitors' information, restaurant and bar reviews, the lowdown on shopping and all the sights and sounds of the city these mini marvels are simply a holiday must.

8

International Relations

Hong Kong's international relations are unusual, based on its mixed parentage. Since 1997, China has been responsible for Hong Kong's defence and foreign affairs. But Hong Kong has also retained many aspects of its pre-97 autonomy, including independent membership in the World Trade Organization (WTO) and the Asia-Pacific Economic Cooperation (APEC) forum. Hong Kong also continues to be treated as a distinct customs territory separate from the Mainland, thereby maintaining its free port status.

Hong Kong is also responsible for economic relations with its trading partners. It has overseas Economic and Trade Offices in ten of the key trading partner countries. In return, foreign countries have kept their representation in Hong Kong, with 110 Consulates or Consulates-General located in Hong Kong. You won't find a single consular area in Hong Kong, but they are generally within easy reach of the main business district.

You'll also find this added autonomy in operation at the individual level. Many local residents have two passports, and both offer visa-free access to many more countries than the normal Chinese passport. All Chinese citizens holding Hong Kong permanent identity cards can apply for a Hong Kong SAR (HKSAR) passport. But, in another quirk of history, people holding BNO (British National Overseas) passports issued before 1997 may continue to use them, and renew them for life.

Government & Politics

The structure of Hong Kong's government is defined in 'The Basic Law of the Hong Kong Special Administrative Region' (The Basic Law). This in turn follows the agreements reached between Britain and China prior to the 1997 handover. The key point of those agreements is summarized as 'one country; two systems', meaning that, for at least 50 years after the handover, China agrees that Hong Kong's previous capitalist system and lifestyle will be left untouched.

As mentioned above, the Basic Law states that the Beijing government is responsible for Hong Kong's defence and foreign affairs. However, it also notes that Hong Kong will enjoy 'executive, legislative and independent judicial power, including that of final adjudication'.

The head of the executive branch of Hong Kong's government is the Chief Executive (CE). The first CE, Tung Chee Hwa, resigned in 2005, part-way through his second term. His replacement, Sir Donald Tsang, was the Chief Secretary in Tung's government. Tsang completed the remainder of Tung's second term, and then faced re-election in March 2007. The civil service comprises various departments that report to the Secretaries, who in turn report to the CE. Hong Kong's civil service is generally considered to be competent and relatively free from corruption. Transparency International's *Corruption Perceptions Index* for 2005, ranks Hong Kong as the world's 15th least corrupt country, out of a total of 158.

The legislative branch of government, the Legislative Council, has the power to enact laws; examine and approve budgets, taxation and public expenditure; and monitor the work of the Government. The council currently has 60 Members, with 30 Members returned by geographical constituencies through direct elections, and 30 Members by functional constituencies. The third and final branch of government is the judiciary. Hong Kong continues to follow the common law traditions established during British rule, and the strong rule of law is seen as one of Hong Kong's key attractions to businesses.

Political Correctness

Relations between Taipei and Beijing continue to have their ups and downs. As an outsider you'll probably want to steer clear of this whole issue, and avoid making references that can upset parties on either side. This is particularly a problem if you are working in a regional role, and have to refer to the region in speeches or in writing. The easiest way is to avoid using country names. For example, let's say you sell to a market that includes Beijing, Hong Kong, Shanghai and Taipei, and you need to list them in a report that will be sent to all four locations. Some people just stick to listing out the city names, while others use 'Greater China Region' to encompass them all.

Democracy

Don't be misled by the word 'election', as Hong Kong is still far from achieving full democracy. For example the CE is selected by an Election Committee of just 800 members, most of whom are elected by various sectors of the economy. The Basic Law says that the ultimate aim is the election of the CE and all members of the legislative council by universal suffrage, but determining when that will take place is the source of continued friction between the government and large sections of the public.

Population

Hong Kong's Census and Statistics Department recorded that Hong Kong's population was 6,970,800 at the end of 2005, compared with 5,522,200 in 1991. They project it will reach 8,380,000 by 2033.

The average household currently has 3.1 members; just over half (53.5%) live in property they own.

Before 1996, there were more males than females in Hong Kong. Since then the number of males per 1,000 females has dropped to 917. By 2033, they estimate only 698 males per 1,000 females. Reasons given for this imbalance include the large number of foreign domestic helpers (who are predominantly female), the movement of mainland wives into Hong Kong, and the fact that females outlive males.

The United Nations Development Programme survey in 2003 gave Hong Kong residents a life expectancy at birth of 81.6 years, ranking second in the world after Japan. By 2033, the local government predicts life expectancy at birth will be 82.5 years for males and 88 years for females.

Population by Nationality

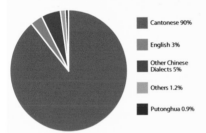

Population by Principal Language

Cantonese 90%
English 3%
Other Chinese Dialects 5%
Others 1.2%
Putonghua 0.9%

Education Levels

Lower Secondary 19%
Matriculation 9%
No schooling/ kindergarten 8%
Primary 21%
Tertiary: Degree course 13%
Tertiary: Non-degree course 4%
Upper Secondary 26%

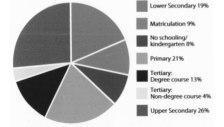

National Flag

Hong Kong's pre-1997 flag incorporated Britain's Union Jack, so it obviously had to be replaced. A competition to design a new flag was held, with a panel of judges selecting the winner from the thousands of entries submitted. Surprisingly, the winning design was rejected by the Chinese government, so a second more formal selection process had to follow.

The design that was finally adopted depicts Hong Kong's national flower, the bauhinia, on a red background. The flag shares themes with China's national flag, as each use the same shade of red, and each shows five stars.

You can see the flag outside many government buildings, or, if you are awake early, you can attend the public flag raising at the Golden Bauhinia Square outside the Hong Kong Convention & Exhibition Centre. The flag is raised each morning at 08:00, by five police officers. On the first day of the month there is more of a show, as the five officers wear ceremonial dress and are accompanied by a rifle escort team and the Police Silver band.

Local Time

Hong Kong is eight hours ahead of UCT (Universal Coordinated Time – formerly known as GMT). That means if it is 12:00 midday in Hong Kong it is 13:00 in Tokyo, 09:30 in Delhi, 04:00 in London, and 23:00 the previous day in New York. Hong Kong does not alter its clocks for daylight savings or summer time.

Social & Business Hours

Many companies' stated office hours are from 09:00 to 17:30, with an hour's break for lunch. You'll probably be directed to voicemail if you try calling an office outside

Time Zones

Athens	-6
Auckland	+4
Bangkok	-1
Beijing	0
Berlin	-7
Colombo	-2.5
Denver	-15
Dubai	-4
Dublin	-8
Jakarta	-1
Johannesburg	-6
Kuala Lumpur	0
London	-8
Los Angeles	-16
Mexico City/Dallas	-14
Moscow	-5
Mumbai	-2.5
New York	-13
Paris	-7
Perth	0
Rome	-7
Seoul	+1
Singapore	0
Sydney	+2
Taipei	0
Tokyo	+1
Toronto	-13

those times, but it is very likely there are people still working. Unless you are working in an administration role, you are more likely to leave the office between 18:00 and 19:00, and later times are not uncommon.

The local employment laws say that at least one in every seven days must be a rest day. Some industries follow that to the letter, with most restaurant staff working a six-day week. Office workers typically work a five, or five-and-a-half day week. On July 1 2006, the gradual introduction of a five-day working week for civil servants began. The plan was that over the following year many departments would phase out Saturday working by introducing extended working hours during the week. Departments whose services are widely offered to the public will remain open on Saturdays. This is expected to encourage more private sector firms to switch to a five-day week.

Most government offices are open between 09:00 and 17:00 Monday to Friday, and with the scrapping of Saturday working, many are now open earlier in the morning and later at night. Some do still open on Saturday mornings. If you plan to be first in line when the doors open, it is worth calling to check first. The website www.info.gov.hk/info/5day has details of the five-day week initiative, along with links to the various government departments concerned.

Shops in the Central district typically open from 10:00 to 19:00, closing after the office workers leave for home. In shopping areas such as Tsim Sha Tsui or Causeway Bay however, shops stay open till at least 20:00 or 21:00, and if you visit Mong Kok you'll find the streets are still busy and shops are open well past 22:00. Shops are open seven days a week.

Public Holidays

Hong Kong has 17 public holidays per year, helping make up for the generally stingy annual leave allowances local companies give. The holidays fall into three main groups. First come the Christian holidays of Christmas and Easter. Then there's a patriotic group including Labour Day, National Day, and the snappily-titled 'Hong Kong Special Administrative Region Establishment Day'. Finally, the bulk are traditional Chinese cultural holidays such as Lunar New Year and the Ching Ming festival, which have been celebrated in Chinese communities for hundreds if not thousands of years. These holidays are based on a traditional lunar calendar, so they move around year by year.

Some other points to think about:

- If a public holiday falls on a Sunday, the following Monday is given as the holiday instead. But if it falls on a Saturday and you work a five-day week, tough luck – you lose that holiday.

- The land borders to China are very busy around public holidays, and are best avoided.

- China has three 'Golden Week' national holidays per year, corresponding to the Hong Kong public holidays for the Lunar New Year, Labour Day, and National Day. During these weeks, basically all of China is on holiday at the same time. Choose another time of year to visit!

Public Holidays 2007

The first day of January	01-Jan
The day preceding Lunar New Year's Day	17-Feb
The second day of the Lunar New Year	19-Feb
The third day of the Lunar New Year	20-Feb
Ching Ming Festival	05-Apr
Good Friday	06-Apr
The day following Good Friday	07-Apr
Easter Monday	09-Apr
Labour Day	01-May
The Buddha's Birthday	24-May
Tuen Ng Festival	19-Jun
The day following Hong Kong Special Administrative Region Establishment Day	02-Jul
The day following Chinese Mid-Autumn Festival	26-Sep
National Day	01-Oct
Chung Yeung Festival	19-Oct
Christmas Day	25-Dec
The first weekday after Christmas Day	26-Dec

11

- Lunar New Year (more commonly known as Chinese New Year or just CNY) is the most important holiday in the Chinese calendar. It is the one time of year that most of Hong Kong's shops and businesses close, with many people travelling home to spend the time with their families.
- Two holidays you should make the effort to attend are the Tuen Ng Festival (more commonly known as the 'Dragon Boat Festival'), and the Mid-Autumn Festival. See Annual Events on p.50 for more details.

Photography

You won't be short of subjects to photograph, but as always use your common sense and in particular avoid taking pictures of any military installations or soldiers. For the general public the best approach is to ask permission first, though many people prefer to use a zoom lens and take photos anonymously from a discreet distance. People working in areas that see a lot of tourists (for example, certain markets) are most likely to object to having their photo taken. Occasionally – especially in villages that feature a tourist attraction – photography is allowed, but a small fee will be charged.

Temperature & Humidity

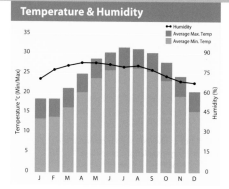

Rainfall

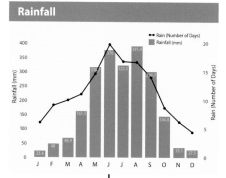

Climate

Although Hong Kong lies in the tropics, its climate is seasonal. These seasons break down differently however, from those in Europe or North America:

Winter comprises just January and February. A typical winter's day is cool – in the teens – with a light jacket needed. Most years see a couple of surges of cold air that drop temperatures below 10°C for a few days. When it does get cold though, it's really cold – Hong Kong buildings are not heated, so heavier jackets and sweaters are needed.

In spring (March to May), temperatures are mild – usually hanging around in the low to mid-20s – but it's frequently cloudy, foggy and humid. Most years, the rainy season really gets going in May.

Summer (June to September) is hot and very wet – it can rain off-and-on for days on end. There are sunny days, too, but wilting humidity is a constant. Daytime highs are typically in the low 30s, and night time temperatures drop only into the high 20s.

Autumn (October to December) is lovely, with clear days and lower humidity. Temperatures gradually drop from shirt-sleeve warmth in October to the crisp high teens in December.

Typhoons can strike Hong Kong anytime between April and November. Hong Kong's concrete and steel buildings stand up well to typhoons, but the city shuts down –most people get off work and are strongly encouraged to remain at home – when conditions seriously deteriorate and a 'number 8' signal or higher is hoisted. There are also rainstorm warnings issued when rainfall is so heavy it impedes transport; these usually don't last long enough to have much effect on day-to-day activities, but you might find yourself being delayed for an hour or two.

Flora & Fauna

Before you arrive in Hong Kong, you'll probably have seen the pictures of all the concrete and skyscrapers. Not the sort of place to go looking for a wide range of plants and animals? True, the city doesn't have such a broad variety, but less than one quarter of Hong Kong's area is considered urban or built-up – the rest is countryside.

Flora

Around 3,100 different species of flora have been recorded across Hong Kong, about 2,100 of which are native to the region. The plant life is typical of a subtropical region, though you'll also find some species from Southeast Asia right at the northern end of their distribution range. In older parts of the city you'll see magnificent banyan trees, with their roots snaking across the granite walls. In the winter months you'll also see bauhinia plants in flower in Hong Kong's parks.

Fauna

Larger animals resident in the Hong Kong countryside include barking deer, civet cats, squirrels, wild boar, Chinese Porcupines, Chinese Pangolins and Mongooses. Most of these animals are very shy, however, so if you are keen to see them, your best bet is to visit Kadoorie Farm (p.208), which displays several of Hong Kong's indigenous species as part of its conservation programme. If you enjoy hiking you'll certainly see some of the 300 species of butterflies and dragonflies that live locally, and on sunny days it is not uncommon to see snakes.

Birds

It won't be long before you notice large birds of prey circling above Hong Kong's harbour. These are Black-Eared Kites, and are also common above Hong Kong Island. They don't restrict their interest to wooded areas, and if you work near a window you'll likely see them swooping past your building. If you are a more serious birdwatcher, head for the Mai Po marshes. This area of wetlands is an important part of many birds' migrations from northern China, Mongolia and Siberia. Some species spend the winter in the Mai Po area, while others use it as a feeding and resting area before continuing their journey. The WWF reports that over 340 species of birds have been recorded in these wetlands.

Marine Life

The most eye-catching inhabitant of the local seas is the Chinese white dolphin. Despite its name, its actual colour is nearer to day-glo pink! Other surprises are that Hong Kong is also home to almost 1,000 species of fish, more species of coral than the Caribbean, and has a nesting site for Green Turtles on a beach on one of its outlying islands (p.177).

Protection

Hong Kong's government has departments committed to the environment, including the Environmental Protection Department, and the Agriculture, Fisheries and Conservation Department (AFCD). Yet pollution, and particularly air pollution, still makes a major dent in Hong Kong's quality of life. The Chief Executive summed up the problem in a March 2006 policy speech: 'Hong Kong is seeing fewer days of blue sky'.

Environmental Issues

What Can You Do?
Local voluntary organizations that tackle these issues include the WWF (www.wwf.org.hk), Clear the Air (www.cleartheair. org.hk), and Civic Exchange (www.civic-exchange.org).

Hong Kong faces many challenges, as you'd expect when so many people are squeezed into such a small area. The population has risen from under 500,000 to nearly seven million in the last hundred years, placing a strain on natural resources.

One of the earliest problems was the supply of enough fresh water. The British administration built reservoirs, but the problem was never really solved until water was piped from China. One side effect of the reservoir building is that very little construction was allowed in the catchment areas around the reservoirs, unintentionally forming mini-nature reserves.

Hong Kong's seawater has also faced its share of problems. The harbour between Hong Kong island and Kowloon is still not a place you would want to swim, but water quality has improved markedly since a major sewage treatment system was commissioned in 2001. Outside the harbour, the water quality at Hong Kong's beaches has also shown steady improvement, but still suffers after heavy rain when pollutants are washed into the sea. In open waters, there are concerns about the decline of Hong Kong's fish stocks. There are doubts whether the AFCD can successfully meet the two seemingly incompatible goals of developing the fishing trade, while at the same time conserving fishery resources.

Air pollution has got noticeably worse since the late 1990s, with smoggy days becoming increasingly regular. Southern China's rapid industrial development is identified as the source of the pollution, and you'll soon learn to tell which way the wind is blowing. On days when the wind is from the south, clean air blows in from the sea and all is clear. When the wind blows from the north, the smog descends. However pointing the finger of blame is not so straightforward, as Hong Kong is the largest external investor in South China, and many of the offending factories are owned by Hong Kong companies.

No Smoking

Hong Kong is following New York's lead and introducing strict no smoking laws across the city. Many entertainment venues, shopping malls and restaurants are already smoke-free but 2007 brings more sites where you could get fined up to $5,000 for lighting up. Public beaches, stadiums, lifts, public transport carriers , hospitals and even indoor areas of mahjong-tin kau premises are all now boasting fresh air but it's worth going to www.tobaccocontrol. gov.hk to see if any more have been added to the list.

Culture

Arrive in Hong Kong and you could be in any international city – a modern airport, a quick ride on an express train, then checking in to one of the international hotel chains. But then you notice a local storekeeper lighting incense sticks at a little shrine outside his shop. Or that friends head out to lunch with their parents every Sunday without fail. Or that you are gently scolded for not giving someone 'face'– and as the list grows longer, you realise that despite outward appearances, many things work differently here. The Confucian model still has a strong influence, with the family a very important part of local life. Parents expect – and usually receive – their children's respect, with many families getting together for meals several times a week. Children often live at home into their twenties and thirties, which can be a surprise to overseas visitors. You'll also feel Confucian currents if you are working in a Chinese-owned company. Many still use a paternal style of management, where 'father knows best'.

The Chinese view of health will seem very different too, though western medicine is widespread and most people (including doctors themselves) see no conflict in using the best of both. Visit a western doctor about flu, for example, and you'll likely leave with the usual medicines, plus instructions to buy a glass of hot cola with ginger to make you feel better! Where western medicine focuses on fixing things that are broken, the Chinese approach to health is much broader. For example, certain foods will be chosen or avoided depending on whether they are appropriate for the season and weather; or a home-cooked meal will often include a soup whose ingredients were chosen for their medicinal properties.

Finally, there are those beliefs that will seem superstitious to outsiders, but that are very natural for local residents. Many people place great faith in Feng Shui, for example. They consult a trusted master for advice on decisions from how to arrange furniture in a new house, to what is the best day to hold a wedding. This is not limited to family life, as many successful businesspeople and famous entertainers also consult a Feng Shui master when they are about to make big decisions, or if they have been facing unexpected problems. Hong Kong's temples also play a role, serving a steady stream of people who pray to the gods for help, or look for guidance on their fortunes.

Language

Other options **Language Schools** p.250, **Learning Chinese** p.155

The official languages of Hong Kong are Chinese and English, with spoken announcements typically repeated in both the Cantonese and Putonghua dialects of Chinese. In business, English is widely understood, though meetings will often use a mix of Chinese and English, depending on who is talking to whom. Note that although not everyone in a meeting will speak to you in English, you should assume that everyone can understand it to avoid any embarrassing situations.

Naming the Chinese Language

Chinese people all speak, read, and write Chinese - right? As you'll quickly find out, it's not that simple. In fact people in different Chinese regions speak distinct dialects. These are often so different as to be mutually incomprehensible. As transportation and communications improved, it therefore became more and more necessary for people in China's different regions to be able to communicate. A national language was needed. In the early 20th century it was decided that the Beijing dialect would be used as the foundation for this national language. Originally it was known as 'guoyu', literally 'national language'. After 1949, the name was changed to 'putonghua', or 'common language', while in the west it is commonly referred to as Mandarin. Although more Hong Kong people are learning putonghua for business, the Chinese you'll hear used for everyday life in Hong Kong continues to be Cantonese, the dialect of southern China.

Shops and restaurants in the business district and tourist areas will usually have English-speaking staff available, and English menus are available in most restaurants. If you venture out to the residential areas, or out of the city altogether, you may have more trouble finding an English speaker. Your best bet is to collar someone dressed in business clothes and ask if they speak English. If you are worried about finding your way (eg. when hiking in the countryside, or visiting a customer in a remote industrial estate) it's worth getting the address and directions written out in Chinese so you can show them to your taxi driver, or a helpful stranger.

So should you learn Chinese? Unfortunately, most foreigners find Chinese, and especially Cantonese, difficult to learn. Your first attempts to pronounce Cantonese words will almost surely be misunderstood, as it is a tonal language and also has sounds that are not commonly used in western languages. But if you plan to live here for a year or more, then persevere. Learning Cantonese will definitely give you a better understanding of life in Hong Kong, and a richer experience during your time here. For the words and phrases in the following table we've given a phonetic equivalent of the Cantonese, although it has to be said that you're not likely to be understood if you

Basic Cantonese

General

Please	mm goi
Thank you	mm goi
Thank you	doh jeh
How are you?	nei hou maa?
Very good; very well	hou hou

Accidents

Police	ging chaat
Driver's licence	che paai
A traffic accident	gaau tung sat si
Insurance	bou him

Taxi / Car Related

Stop	ting
Right	yau
Left	jaw
Go straight ahead	jik hoi
North	bak
South	laam
East	dung
West	sai
Intersection, turning	gaai hau
First	dai yat
Second	dai yi
Road	lou
Street	gaai
Roundabout	wui syun chiu
Traffic light	hung luk dang
Close to something	gan jue
Petrol station	yau jaam
Beach	saa taan
Mountain	saan
Airport	gei cheung
Hotel	jau dim
Ban	ngan hong
Restaurant	chaan teng
Go slowly	maan maan

Introduction

My name is...	ngoh giu...
What is your name?	nei giu mat-yeh meng a?
Where are you from?	nei hai bin dou lai?

Questions

How much?	gei do cheen ?
Where?	bin dou?
When?	gei si?
Which? Who?	bin go?
Why?	dim gaai?
What?	sam mo?
How do I get to...	ngoh dim hui...?

Greetings

Good morning	joe san
Goodbye	joi gin
You're welcome (lit. No need to be polite)	m saai haak hei
Excuse me; sorry	m hou yi si

Numbers

Zero	ling
One	yat
Two	yee
Three	saam
Four	sei
Five	ng
Six	luk
Seven	chat
Eight	baat
Nine	gau
Ten	sup
Hundred	baak
Thousand	cheen

Three to Know

If you are just visiting, a few easy phrases that will get a good response are: 'Joe san', meaning 'good morning'; a common greeting before lunch. 'Mm goi', meaning 'thank you', for small actions, eg. someone gives you change, or moves something out of your way. 'Doh jeh', also meaning 'thank you', but used when someone has given you a gift, or has really gone out of their way to help you.

try to pronounce them. You'll notice there are no entries for yes and no, as in Cantonese you ask and answer questions differently from English. The words 'yes' and 'no' are widely understood however, so just use those with a nod or shake of the head as appropriate.

Religion

Hong Kong residents are granted religious freedom by The Basic Law, and in practice Hong Kong is very tolerant of different religions. All of the world's major religions are represented here, with over 500,000 Christians, and strong Muslim, Hindu, Sikh and Jewish communities.

That leaves over six million people unaccounted for – so what do they believe? Locally, religious practice is a mish-mash of Buddhism, Taoism, and ancestor worship. Even Hong Kong's temples often contain a mix of Buddhist and Taoist deities.

Chinese Names

Chinese names are typically formed from three Chinese characters. The first character represents the family name, and is the same as their father's. The next two characters are their given name. Unlike most western names, a Chinese given name usually has a clear meaning, made up from two ordinary words. A lady's given name might be 'Happy Child', for example, while a man's might be 'Defender of the country'. Many local Chinese also have an English given name, likely given to them when they started school, or chosen themselves when they were older. English name choices can be very creative, so expect to encounter a few surprises during your time here.

Although these temples are often busy with tourists, you'll find they are still in very active use. You'll see people making offerings of incense and burning paper 'money', hoping for good fortune in return. Many temples also offer fortune-telling services, through use of 'chim', ie. a cup filled with small numbered sticks that's shaken until one of the sticks falls out. The stick is then taken to a temple attendant, who gives you a copy of the fortune that matches your number. These slips are often written in very old, flowery Chinese, so interpreting them is as much an art as actually getting the slip in the first place. Temples are busiest around Chinese New Year, when people come to seek good luck in the year ahead, and to try to discover what their fortunes will be over the next twelve months.

Hong Kong's long coastline means many local temples are dedicated to Tin Hau. Tin Hau is the goddess protecting seafarers, so every fishing village typically had a temple to her, located on the seashore so it was visible to boats entering and leaving the harbour. Today you'll find many of these temples are a long way from the sea, due to the repeated reclamation over the last 150 years. Apart from Tin Hau, other popular local deities include Kwun Yum (the Buddhist Goddess of Mercy), Pak Tai (Supreme Emperor of the Dark Heaven and local patron of the island of Cheung Chau) and Hung Shing (God of the South Seas and a weather prophet).

Places of Worship

Cathedral of the Immaculate Conception	www.catholic.org.hk	Central	2522 8212
Church of Jesus Christ of Latter-day Saints	www.lds.org.hk	Kowloon Tong	2339 8100
Community Church Hong Kong	www.cchk.net	Central	2551 6161
Kowloon Mosque	www.iuhk.org	Tsim Sha Tsui	2724 0095
Methodist International Church	www.mic-hk.org	Wan Chai	2575 7817
Ohel Leah Synagogue	www.ohelleah.org	Mid-Levels	2589 2621
St. Andrew's Church (Anglican Episcopal)	www.standrews.org.hk	Tsim Sha Tsui	2367 1478
St. John's Cathedral	www.stjohnscathedral.org.hk	Central	25234 157
The Vine Christian Fellowship	www.thevine.org.hk	Central	2573 0793
Union Church	www.unionchurchhk.org	Mid-Levels	2523 7247

17

Apart from the large temples, many Chinese homes have one or more small shrines. In particular, the oldest male of the family typically has the family god's shrine in his house. Festivals in spring and autumn celebrate the family's god, and their ancestors. On days when the family is expected to visit their ancestors' graves, local graveyards are very busy, with traffic jams on surrounding roads and long walks common. From time to time families also travel back to their home towns in Southern China to visit older ancestors' graves.

National Dress

Hong Kong has no real national dress to speak of. The people you see on the streets could have been transported from any international city. Of course it wasn't always like this. Photographs from the first half of the 20th century still show the average Hong Kong resident dressed very differently from the expats. Ladies would be wearing the figure-hugging cheongsam dress, or perhaps the looser jacket and trouser suit called the sam-foo. Men would wear mandarin-collar jackets with the long sleeves rolled up to reveal the double lining, or even full length gowns. These traditional clothes can still be seen in tourist settings, but typical residents now wear them just a few times in their lives, at special occasions such as weddings.

Red Bombs

You should know that presents are rarely given to couples who are getting married. Cash is preferred instead. The amount of cash you give depends on where the reception is being held, as it is assumed the cash will help cover the costs of the banquet. Expect to give around $500-$1,000, but ask a local friend or colleague for advice on the going rate. If you receive an invitation but are unable to attend, it is customary to send around $300 with your reply. In either case the notes should be as clean and new as possible, and enclosed in a lucky 'lai see' envelope. The fact that invitations are sent out in red envelopes, with their implicit demand for money attached, has led to their local nickname of 'red bombs'.

Hong Kong Weddings

If you spend several months in Hong Kong, there's a good chance you will be invited to at least one Chinese wedding. Wedding banquets are usually large affairs, with many friends, colleagues and family invited. Apart from the big dinner, there will often be slightly risqué games arranged by the couple's friends as entertainment after the meal. The goal is to embarrass the couple as much as possible, but it all passes off in good humour.

Although you will probably only see the banquet, and perhaps the registration, a Hong Kong wedding day is typically a long and busy one for the couple and their families. It begins in earnest when the groom and his groomsmen arrive at the bride's house to find the door locked and guarded by the bridesmaids. The groomsmen must face a series of challenges and negotiations before they are allowed to 'buy' entry to the house, and access to the bride. Then there will be prayers to the family gods, and serving tea to the wife's parents. Next the whole troupe move across town to the groom's parents' house to repeat the tea ceremony. There will often be a registration or church service in the middle of the day, followed by plenty of photos in a nearby park, then finally the banquet. If you take a stroll through Hong Kong Park you may see a selection of newlyweds posing for pictures.

Food & Drink

Other options **Eating Out** p.350

First a reminder – Chinese food in Hong Kong will taste different from your local Chinese restaurant at home. Sounds obvious, but this comes as a disappointment to some visitors. Once you get past this hurdle, Hong Kong's food is likely to be one of your happiest memories of time spent here.

Local Food

The majority of Hong Kong's residents hail from the Guangdong (Canton) region of southern China, so naturally Cantonese food is the most widely available. Dim sum (also called yum cha) is a popular style of Cantonese eating you should make sure to try during your stay. Dim sum are served in small portions, either in small bamboo baskets if steamed, or on plates if fried or baked. It's available from early morning through to early afternoon. For many older residents, dim sum with friends is a part of their daily ritual, usually after a visit to the market, or finishing their morning exercises. Smaller 'hole-in-the-wall' restaurants serve other Cantonese food such as roast meat with rice, or steamed/stewed food such as beef brisket, or prawn dumplings, served with noodles. These small shops are found all over Hong Kong, and are well worth a visit. There may be queues around 13:00 to 14:00, but outside these times you won't have any trouble finding a seat. As usual, space is at a premium, so expect to share a table if the restaurant is at all busy.

Near the bottom of the eatery food chain come the outside stalls, specialising in just a couple of dishes such as beef balls with noodles. The surroundings are very basic, but the stalls with the best reputations attract people from all over the city.

At the bottom you have the street vendors, selling a variety of deep fried foods from their push carts. Many Hong Kong people swear by this snack food, but you'll have to work out just how strong a stomach you have before deciding whether to take the plunge – marinated pig's ear, anyone?

Seafood

Seafood deserves a special mention, given Hong Kong's coastal location. Seafood restaurants in the city have large fish tanks installed, so you can point out your chosen fish as it swims past. It'll be whisked away for a rendezvous with a sharp knife and a hot wok, then return a few minutes later cooked in your favourite style. If you have time, skip the city restaurants and take a ferry to one of the restaurants on Cheung Chau or Lamma Island instead. The surroundings are more basic, but the outdoor setting, combined with fresh seafood and cold beer, make for an excellent meal.

Takeaway Tips

Long working hours and hectic social lives mean that not many people in Hong Kong have time to cook. Many dine out almost every night, but when it all gets too much, home delivery is another option. Once again Hong Kong shows that it is a true service society and delivery services are not limited to pizza restaurants and the odd curry house. In fact you can pick up delivery catalogues containing delivery menus from a couple of dozen restaurants. Pick one restaurant or mix and match. Be warned, the prices are elevated and there is also an added delivery charge. As with everything here, convenience comes at a cost. To get your copy of a catalogue, log on to any of the following; www.ringadinner.com, www.soho delivery.com.hk, www.diala dinner.com.hk.

19

Chinese Food

Of course 'Chinese food' covers a huge region and range of cuisines, and most are represented in Hong Kong. The big difference between north and south China is that the staple grain of the north is wheat, unlike the rice that grows in southern China. So with northern food you can expect more breads, pancakes and pastries. Peking Duck is an obvious example of northern food, but there are many other delicious dishes available. Northern food also tends to use more chilli than Cantonese cuisine, with SzeChuan dishes winning the prize for the most eye-watering.

Chopsticks

Chinese food is chopped up into bite-size pieces, designed for picking up with chopsticks and popping into your mouth. Well, in theory at least. If you're relatively new to chopsticks you'll find you drop as much on the table as you get to your mouth. Add in some forearm cramps after a long meal, and it can be enough to have you asking for a knife and fork. Persevere though – it won't be long before you're proficient, and the extra reach chopsticks give you makes it easier to grab what you want from across the table. You'll know you've made the grade when you can move slippery button mushrooms from dish to mouth without them pinging off into a neighbour's bowl.

Other Asian Food

Japanese sushi? Indian curries? Malaysian satay? Nepalese water buffalo? If you need a break from Chinese food there are plenty of other Asian countries' cuisines to try.

Western Food

You won't have any problem getting a fix of home cooking while you are here, but the choice of restaurants will be much smaller and the prices higher than eating local food. The exception is fast food, with McDonalds and KFC restaurants throughout the city. In the cheaper western restaurants be prepared for 'western' food that doesn't taste quite right, for example, Italian recipes which have been tweaked to match local tastes, just like Chinese food is at home. You'll also find this east-west mix produces some surprising combinations, such as a bowl of pasta swimming in a weak broth, topped with a slice of ham and a fried egg – for breakfast.

Extreme Food

If you're seeking the bungee-jump of the culinary world, you're in the right town. Stinky beancurd, congealed pig's blood, snake soup and chicken feet in black bean sauce will all exercise your powers of mind over matter. If you really can't stomach something, don't worry about politely refusing it. But as a general rule, it's a good idea to try new things first, and ask what they are later.

Eating at Home

If you'll be eating at home, expect to change your shopping habits. Limited room and a desire for fresh food mean many local people make daily visits to the market. This emphasis on freshness can make the local wet market a bit traumatic for the squeamish, though. Fish lie cut in half lengthwise, hearts beating and gills moving to prove their recent demise. Chickens can be bought live, then killed, plucked and prepared for you on the spot Even if you give the market's fish and poultry sections a miss, make sure you visit the fruit and veg section. Seasonal fruits are cheap and tasty, so expect to develop a taste for fruit you've heard of such as mangoes and lychees, together with some new favourites such as pomelo and longan (dragon's eyes).

Water

Hong Kong's drinking water is treated to the same level as in other developed countries, and is safe to drink as it leaves the water main. If a building's communal water tank is not well maintained, there is a small risk that water could be contaminated before it reaches the tap - but this should not be a problem in any modern hotel, office block or residential complex. In older buildings, the use of iron pipes can lead to rust-coloured water that is harmless, but looks dirty. Even though the tap water is safe, many Hong Kong residents boil it before drinking, or drink bottled water. Hong Kong does not suffer from water shortages, though before 1965 they were very common. Since then, water from the Dongjiang river in southern China has been piped to Hong Kong, and now makes up the bulk of fresh water consumed here.

Visas

Other options **Residence Visa** p.60, **Entry Visa** p.59

Hong Kong actively encourages tourism, so for most visitors, arrival is generally hassle-free.

Tourist Visas

Travellers from most western and Asian countries are granted a visa-free stay on arrival. The length of stay varies from country to country, with UK citizens getting the best deal at 180 days and citizens of most other western countries (including Europe, Australia, New Zealand and the United States) getting 90 days. Citizens of some Eastern European, Asian and Middle-Eastern countries get 30 or 14 days. The nationals of a number of former Soviet republics and some Asian and African countries require pre-approved visas to enter Hong Kong, so check your country's status carefully in the table on the website. You can find a full list of current tourist visa requirements at the Hong Kong Immigration Department's website www.immd.gov.hk/ ehtml/hkvisas_4.htm. If you have to apply for a Hong Kong tourist visa, the procedure is explained at www.immd.gov.hk/ehtml/topical_11.htm. Ironically, citizens of mainland China have a far more difficult time gaining access to Hong Kong, although restrictions have eased in recent years. Their visa arrangements are handled completely separately from citizens of other countries.

Work Visas

If getting into Hong Kong as a tourist is easy, securing a work visa isn't. Prior to 1997, British nationals could work in Hong Kong visa-free, but now all non-Hong Kong citizens must meet quite stringent requirements to be granted the right to be employed here. These requirements vary somewhat, but in general an individual must be sponsored for a work visa by an employer in Hong Kong, who must have proved to the Immigration Department that the job in question could not be filled by a Hong Kong resident. It's now quite difficult to simply show up in Hong Kong and hope to land a job, as your prospective employer will need to jump through the hoops with Immigration on your behalf.

Once you've got a reputable company sponsoring you, however, things are generally quite straightforward. Working visas are typically granted for the length of your employment contract, although they're rarely granted for more than two years at a time. If your company wants to keep you, and will say so in writing, renewal is almost always routine.

There has been some good news recently for expatriate families in Hong Kong. Until very recently, spouses of individuals holding work visas were themselves barred from working. This restriction has now been reversed, so if your spouse holds a valid Hong Kong work visa, you are free to search for employment as well without the need to apply for a separate working visa.

Hong Kong International Airport

Opened in 1998, Hong Kong International Airport was initially perceived as a disaster. It carried the burden of replacing the iconic Kai Tak Airport, which was simultaneously loved and loathed by most who passed through it. HKIA's location was controversial as it was built on a plot of land created by levelling an entire island, which angered environmentalists. It was also colossally expensive. HKIA's first few weeks of operations were plagued by logistical problems and extremely bad press. But to the credit of its staff, and its basically sound design, this debacle was turned around within about six months. HKIA is now regularly ranked as one of the world's best - and busiest - airports. Yet there are few long queues, especially once you're past your initial baggage check-in. Immigration and security checks run smoothly, even at peak hours. Baggage for arrivals often appears on carousels 10 or 15 minutes after your plane lands. And ground transport into the city is plentiful and well-organised. The airport's atmosphere is light and pleasant. Although the choice of restaurants and shopping is hardly inspired, it is fairly wide-ranging. There are duty-free shops for both those departing and those arriving.

In fact, the most common type of work visa in Hong Kong is that granted to domestic helpers, mostly from the Philippines and Indonesia, who are sponsored by the individuals or families who will be employing them. These contracts are always for two years, and domestic helpers are far more tightly restricted than other visa holders. They must live in their employers' homes, and they have no chance of gaining permanent residency in Hong Kong, no matter how many years they work here. If you are planning to employ a domestic helper in Hong Kong, you'll find all the information you need at www.jobs.gov.hk/eng/domestic/content.asp.

Information on all types of non-tourist visas is available from the Hong Kong Immigration website; this FAQ section is a good starting point: www.immd.gov.hk/ehtml/faq_hkv.htm.

Investment Visas

You can be granted a visa to run your own company in Hong Kong, but you'd better be prepared to prove your worth to the Immigration Department – and remember they're going to be interested strictly in your net worth, not your outstanding personal qualities and fascinating hobbies.

Student Visas

Visas are also granted for educational purposes, and the process is quite similar to that for work visas; again, the key is having institutional backing.

Permanent Residency in Hong Kong

Once you've worked in Hong Kong for seven consecutive years, and can prove your continuous presence, you can apply for permanent residency. This means you will no longer need a visa to work and live in Hong Kong. You will then also be eligible to apply for 'right of abode', a kind of sub-citizenship which includes most of the rights granted to full Hong Kong citizens, including voting, but which lapses if you leave Hong Kong for more than three years.

Electronic Immigration Clearance

Once you are granted a working visa and are resident in Hong Kong, you and your family members above 11 years old must obtain Hong Kong Identity Cards. These 'smart IDs' encode not only your immigration status, but can be used to gain access to other public services (such as libraries) and allow you to take advantage of self-service immigration clearance via the e-channels at the airport and Hong Kong's border crossings. The e-channel machines use fingerprint verification technology. For details of how to use the e-channels, and their location and opening hours, see the website www.immd.gov.hk/ehtml/20041216.htm.

Meet & Greet

Meeting people at Hong Kong airport is quite straightforward, with just one proviso – there are two main exit points for arriving passengers, imaginatively labelled A and B. If you're an arriving passenger you don't need to pay any attention to this distinction, but if you're picking someone up at the airport, you should check the arrivals board for the flight your party is on; it will indicate which exit those passengers will be using. While

New to Hong Kong?
Old China Hand?

Hong Kong's Friendliest
Online Community has
Something for Everyone!
www.geoexpat.com

Friendly Forums
Resource Directories
Free Classifieds
Business and Social Networking
Events Calendar
and
Lots of people just like YOU!

Geo
expat.com

Buy over 150,000
Books, CDs, DVDs,
Toys and Baby Products
from the comfort of your home
www.shopinhk.com

Unit 709, Cyberport 1,
100 Cyberport Road,
Pokfulam, Hong Kong
Phone: (852) 2989-9145
Email: sales@shopinhk.com

SHOPinHK

you are waiting in the greeting area at that exit, keep an eye on the large monitors showing who is arriving at the other exit, just in case!

Once you're out into the arrivals area, you'll find all the services and transport you'll need admirably organised and laid out right in front of you. Money changing and ATMs, tourist and hotel information, transport options and tickets – it's all there, and all easy to use. There are duty-free shops available when both departing and arriving in Hong Kong (although Hong Kong is a famously free port, there are high taxes on cigarettes, liquor and some other luxury items, so it's worth visiting duty-free if you're looking to humour your vices; see the customs section below for details). Staff at airport service counters will speak English, and generally try quite hard to help visitors. You can find a map of the airport's arrival hall facilities at www.hongkongairport.com.

A meet-and-assist service to help passengers from transport links to departure gates, and arrival gates to transport links, is available from the airport's ancillary services provider, Worldwide Flight Services. Their 24 hour hotline is 2261 2727.

Allowances
Non-Hong Kong residents are limited to bringing in:
• 200 cigarettes or 50 cigars or 250 grams of 'other manufactured tobacco'; and
• one litre of 'alcoholic liquor'.
Note that the limitations on those holding Hong Kong ID cards are even more stringent:
• 60 cigarettes or 15 cigars or 75 grams of other manufactured tobacco; and
• a single 750 ml bottle of 'still wine'.

Customs

Clearing customs at Hong Kong airport, ferry terminals, and land border stations usually constitutes a simple wave-through, although you may be pulled aside and asked where you're arriving from, and subsequently have your luggage searched. The usual naughty items – firearms, drugs, fireworks and endangered animals – are prohibited, but note that there are no restrictions on bringing in currencies and perfumes, and that carrying in food items is generally not a problem. You can find the full rundown at the Hong Kong Customs website, www.customs.gov.hk. The allowances for bringing alcohol and tobacco into Hong Kong are considered to be pretty low when compared to some other countries around the world, and are especially tight if you hold a Hong Kong ID card. The information on the left gives you an overview of what's allowed.

Leaving Hong Kong

Departing from Hong Kong airport is just as easy as arriving. Most airlines no longer require reconfirmation of flights out of Hong Kong, but it is still worth checking with your airline, especially if it's based in mainland China. As all flights from Hong Kong are 'international' (even those to the mainland require immigration clearance), passengers are always advised to arrive at the airport two hours in advance of their flights. You also have the option of checking in 'remotely' up to 24 hours before your flight at either of two airport express train stations, Hong Kong Station in Central, and Kowloon Station in west Kowloon. This can be a great way to get rid of your luggage if you are checking out of your hotel in the morning, but won't fly until the evening. Note that you can only use this service if you have bought a ticket for the Airport Express train. You can also check in the ordinary way at the airport for any flight. In all cases, immigration clearance is usually swift and uneventful.

If you are sending children alone on flights out of Hong Kong, the airport's ancillary services provider, Worldwide Flight Services (24-hour hotline +852 2261 2727) will escort your child from a ground transport pickup point to the departure hall and check-in, and to the departure gate. You can also arrange this service by asking your airline.

Your airline can also arrange an escorted wheelchair service, taking the passenger from the check-in counter through immigration to the departure gate. If you have elderly parents who are not confident travellers, this will make their journey a lot less stressful.

25

In Emergency

In an emergency, dial 999. This will connect you to the emergency services hotline. The telephone operators speak English, and handle emergency calls for the Police, Fire and Ambulance services. Fortunately, Hong Kong is a very safe city, so you are more likely to face less urgent problems. If that is the case, the front desk at your hotel is a good starting point to get help.

Health Problems

If your problem needs urgent and immediate attention, the emergency services hotline will arrange an ambulance to take you to a government hospital's accident and emergency department. There are many hospitals that provide 24 hour emergency and outpatient services, so if you are well enough to jump in a taxi you can make your own way to one. Remember to bring your passport and credit card to simplify admission. Well-known government hospitals include Queen Elizabeth in Kowloon and Queen Mary on Hong Kong island, while private hospitals include the Adventist and the Sanatorium on the island, and St Teresa's in Kowloon.

There are also many English-speaking general practitioners of western medicine in Hong Kong. Your hotel will likely have a doctor available on 24 hour call who can visit your room, or they can direct you to a nearby doctor's office.

Lost/Stolen Property

If you think you've left something in a taxi, there is a 24 hour hotline (1872 920) you can call that will broadcast your details to all taxi drivers. In any case, you'll need to report the loss or theft to the police. Call the general police hotline first (2527 7177) and they'll give you the details of the nearest station. Remember to notify your bank as soon as possible if you've lost credit cards, and to contact your local consulate if your passport is missing (see the table on p.27).

Also remember to make copies of all important documents (passport, visas, credit cards, insurance policies) before you start your trip, to speed up the reporting and replacement. It's a good idea to keep a set of copies in your hotel room safe, and another with a reliable friend or relative at home who can fax them to you if needed.

Health Requirements

You are not required to show any proof of vaccination before entering Hong Kong. If you are visiting for a city holiday, probably all you need to watch out for are mosquitoes. There is no malaria in Hong Kong, but there have been a handful of cases of dengue fever and Japanese encephalitis in the last five years. The chance of you catching either of these is close to zero, but in any case mosquito bites are a pain, so follow the standard guidelines of wearing light-coloured clothing and using insect repellent.

If you plan to work and live in Hong Kong for an extended period, it is typically recommended that you get vaccinations (or boosters) for Hepatitis A and B, Tetanus, Diptheria, Measles and Typhoid. Check with your regular healthcare provider before you leave home to get the latest information, preferably at least a month before you go, as some treatments need to be started before the trip begins.

Emergency Services	
Adventist Hospital	2574 6211
Emergency Services (Police, Fire, Ambulance)	999
The Hong Kong Sanatorium & Hospital	2572 0211
Police Hotline (non-emergency)	2527 7177
Queen Elizabeth Hospital	2710 2111
Queen Mary Hospital	2855 4111
St. Teresa's Hospital	2200 3434
Taxi Lost Property	187 2920

Going Postal
Hong Kong has an efficient postal service, for both local and overseas mail. For example, it costs $3 to send a postcard by airmail to Australia, the UK or US, and it will arrive in seven days or less. You can buy stamps at local post offices, or from the 7-Eleven and Circle-K chains of convenience stores. Most postal delivery is direct to your home address but the post office also offers PO boxes for rent at many of its branches. Smaller branches provide access to the boxes during normal office hours, while the 11 largest branches offer access seven days a week.

Bird Flu

Statisticians indicate that the world is due for another influenza epidemic, with a modified version of avian influenza ('bird flu') a likely candidate. It also appears that new strains of influenza that affect humans often originate from southern China, making it likely that Hong Kong would be one of the first large cities in the world to be exposed to the next epidemic. So should you avoid Hong Kong? Probably not. As the SARS outbreak showed, modern travel means these diseases will spread quickly around the world anyway.

Travel Insurance

Every overseas traveller should have travel insurance – just in case. If you are only visiting Hong Kong, you can probably take a basic plan without the expensive extras for extreme sports. You might wish there was insurance against overspending on your credit card, but otherwise you'll find it hard to sign up for anything risky here – no skiing or bungee-jumping, etc.

Embassies & Consulates

Be sure to call before visiting any of the consulates listed. The smaller offices may not open every day, and some are only open for two or three hours on those days.

Female Visitors

Women are unlikely to face problems with personal safety in Hong Kong, even those who are travelling alone.

Taxis and public transport are all safe to travel on as a single woman, even late into the evening. Similarly, streets stay busy until late at night, making it safe to be out and about. This feeling of safety is one of the highlights for many expats who move to Hong Kong.

Travelling with Children

Hong Kong is a mixed bag for families travelling with children. On the plus side, local culture is very family-centric. When you visit Chinese restaurants for Dim Sum, for example, many tables will have the full family present. Local restaurants are also so noisy that you don't have to worry about trying to keep your children quiet. As for facilities, you'll probably get a high chair without any trouble, but that's it. There are several western restaurants, such as Dan Ryan's (p.354), that make more of an effort, providing crayons and balloons to help keep the children amused.

In terms of child-friendly places to go, Ocean Park(p.203) and Disneyland (p.203) are the two obvious choices. In warm weather there are also plenty of public swimming pools and beaches to visit.

On the down-side, Hong Kong is a sunny, sweaty place in summer so sun hats, sun cream, and regular reminders to drink water are the order of the day. You might also want to leave the stroller at home if you have babies or toddlers. The crowded streets are difficult to navigate, so a baby carrier is often a better option. Finally, busy areas like Mong Kok and Causeway Bay should be avoided on days when the air pollution levels are high.

Embassies & Consulates

Country	Phone	Map
Australia	2827 8881	17-A2
Austria	2522 8086	16-E2
Bangladesh	2827 4278	17-A2
Belgium	2524 3111	16-E2
Canada	2810 4321	16-E2
China Visa Office	2827 1881	17-A2
Czech Republic	2802 2212	17-A2
Denmark	2827 8101	17-A2
Egypt	2827 0668	17-B2
Finland	2525 5385	17-A2
France	3196 6100	16-F2
Germany	2105 8788	16-F2
Great Britain	2901 3000	16-F2
Greece	2774 1682	16-F2
Iceland	2876 8888	17-E1
India	2528 4028	16-F2
Indonesia	2890 4421	17-B2
Ireland	2527 4897	16-E2
Israel	2821 7500	16-F2
Italy	2522 0033	16-E2
Japan	2522 1184	16-E2
Jordan	2524 0085	16-E2
Korea	2529 4141	16-F2
Lithuania	2522 2908	16-E2
Luxembourg	2877 1018	17-A2
Monaco	2893 0669	17-A2
Netherlands	2522 5127	16-E2
New Zealand	2877 4488	17-A2
Oman	2873 2177	14-B1
Pakistan	2827 1966	17-A2
Philippines	2823 8500	16-F2
Poland	2840 0814	16-F2
Portugal	2587 7182	16-E1
Russia	2877 7188	17-A2
Singapore	2527 2212	16-F2
Slovak Republic	2484 4568	6-A4
South Africa	2577 3279	17-A2
Spain	2525 3041	16-F2
Sri Lanka	2876 0828	16-F2
Sweden	2521 1212	16-E2
Switzerland	2522 7147	17-A2
Taiwan	2525 8315	16-F2
Thailand	2521 6481	16-F2
USA	2523 9011	16-E2
Vietnam	2591 4510	17-A2

Physically Challenged Visitors

Getting around Hong Kong in a wheelchair is a challenge. Crowded pavements, uneven surfaces, and the fact that crossing a road often means a subway or footbridge are some of the difficulties you will face. The recommended approach is to use a manual wheelchair and take a strong friend to help you up and down, rather than using an electric wheelchair.

There have been improvements, however, with newer buildings such as the airport well laid out for wheelchair access, and larger hotels also promoting wheelchair-friendly facilities. All MTR stations are officially 'accessible' but this can vary from simply taking a public lift, to 'wheelchair aid with staff assistance'. Many buses now have low floors to enable wheelchair access, but should be avoided at rush hour when there are simply too many people to get on board. Finally, taxis are a good choice as the wheelchair is carried free-of-charge and they can take you closer to your destination.

Dress

You'll see a very wide range of dress styles in Hong Kong. Admire the perfectly coiffured ladies out for afternoon tea and a spot of shopping, then see a delivery man cycle past wearing shorts, rubber boots, and nothing else. It's probably best to leave your boots at home though, and think 'smart-casual' when planning what to wear. In general, the dress sense here is a little smarter – and a little more conservative – than is the norm in the western world.

If you are here for business, men should wear a suit and tie, and women a jacket and skirt. Even in summer it is best to bring these with you, though once you know who you are working with you can follow their lead and often leave the jacket in your hotel. For leisure, daytime wear varies according to the season. In spring and autumn, wear light clothing in daytime, adding a sweater or light jacket in the evening. In summer, short sleeves, and shorts or skirts will be best, though if you'll be sitting inside for some time, for example in a cinema, bring a sweater or light jacket to combat the air-conditioning. It's

Hong Kong Useful Telephone Numbers	
Collect Calls	10010
Consumer Council	2929 2222
Department of Health	2961 8989
Directory Enquiries	1081
Emergency Service (Police, Fire, Ambulance)	999
General Police Enquiries	2527 7177
Hong Kong Immigration Department (24 hours)	2824 6111
Hong Kong International Airport, English (24 hours)	2181 0000
Hong Kong Tourism Board Visitor Hotline	2508 1234
Overseas IDD and Cardphone Enquiries	10013
RTHK's Service Hotline (Newsline)	2272 0000
Time & Temperature	18501
Weather	187 8066

worth picking up a light collapsible umbrella when you get here to protect you from summer's many rainy spells – any type of raincoat would quickly get unpleasantly sweaty. In winter it can get cold enough to need an overcoat.

At the beach or swimming pool, bikinis are common, but many local ladies still prefer a more modest one-piece. Topless or nude sunbathing is a definite no-no.

In the evening, it is rare to be expected to wear a tie, but it is still best to err on the smart side. Shoes, trousers (not jeans) and a shirt with a collar for men, and dresses for ladies, will get you into the majority of places, whereas sleeveless tops, flip-flops and shorts could see you turned away.

Dos & Don'ts

Please note that in an effort to make Hong Kong a cleaner place, there are on-the-spot fines of $1,500 for people caught spitting or littering. Otherwise, the local laws are based on the British system, so as long as you follow normal good behaviour, you'll be fine.

Crime & Safety

Other options **In Emergency** p.26

Hong Kong is a safe place to live and visit, with comparatively low crime rates. Although you are unlikely to experience any violent crime, you should be aware that pickpockets are known to operate at Hong Kong's tourist areas. Simple common-sense steps will minimise the chance of any problems:

- Leave as many valuables as possible in your hotel safe, or better still, leave them at home.
- Keep bags closed, and valuable items such as wallets, mobile phones, etc, out of sight.
- Keep wallets and bags in front of your body where you can see and feel them.
- Don't leave bags hanging on the backs of seats in restaurants. Instead keep them on your lap or, if they are too large, at your feet in front of you.

If you're visiting during summer, typhoons are another potential danger. The vast majority of these pass by with a few days of wind and rain, but little real damage. You may even start to wonder what all the fuss is about. But if you read about past typhoons, with a wind gust at 234km per hour in 1999, or sea levels 23 feet above normal in 1962, you'll realise that it is worth giving them due respect when the typhoon signal no. 8 or higher is hoisted.

Local Numbers

Apart from a few special cases for hotlines, all local residential, business and mobile telephone numbers are eight digits long. If you are calling a local number from within Hong Kong there is no need to add any area code. But if you are dialing a Hong Kong number from overseas, remember to add the 852 country code before the telephone number

First Impressions

Here are a few tips that may help when meeting people:

- On a business visit, bring a full box of business cards with you. Most people you meet in a business setting will pass you a card and expect yours in return, so you'll be surprised how many cards you'll get through. Cards are held in both hands as you give and receive them.
- On initial greetings, most people will shake hands briefly. It is likely to be softer than you are used to - leave the bone-crusher handshake you've been perfecting at home.
- Don't kiss (even a peck on the cheek) or hug someone unless you are very sure of your relationship. A handshake is as much body contact as most people will be comfortable with.
- Avoid gifts of clocks, watches, or white or yellow flowers, all of which have associations with funerals.

Police

The local police wear blue uniforms, and are armed with revolvers. Hong Kong has one of the highest police-to-population ratios in the world, so you'll often see them patrolling on foot. Traffic policemen patrolling on motorbikes are also widespread. The police on the street are generally approachable if you need simple help like directions, though their standard of English varies considerably. If you are the victim of a crime, you'll need to file a report at the local police station, which you can find by calling the hotline (2527 7177). Of course, in an emergency simply dial 999.

Make a Copy

Before travelling to Hong Kong, make copies of your essential documents and keep them in a safe place – either back home with friends or family, or in your hotel safe once you arrive. They will come in very handy if you're unfortunate enough to lose the originals.

Lost/Stolen Property

If you lose property, or it is stolen, you'll need to make a report to the local police station as quickly as possible. Ask your hotel or call the hotline (2527 7177) to find the location. If you think you left something in a taxi, call the taxi hotline (1872 920) and they will broadcast details to all drivers. For public transport, call the company's hotline for help.

Lost/Stolen Property	
Citybus Ltd	2873 0818
Hong Kong Tramways Ltd	2548 7102
Kowloon-Canton Railway Corporation	2929 3399
Mass Transit Railway (MTR) Corporation	2881 8888
New Lantau Bus Co (1973) Ltd	2984 9848
New World First Bus Services Ltd	2136 8888
New World First Ferry Services Ltd	2131 8181
The 'Star' Ferry Co Ltd	2367 7065
The Kowloon Motor Bus Co (1933) Ltd	2745 4466
The Peak Tramways Co Ltd	2522 0922

Remember also to cancel any missing credit cards by calling the relevant company: American Express (2811 6122), Mastercard (800 966 677), or Visa (800 900 782). You'll also need to contact your country's consulate if you have lost your passport. See p.27 for a list of embassies and consulates.

Finally, check your travel insurance policy to see how you should report the loss to them, and to make sure that you have all the documentation they will need to process your claim.

Tourist Information

The Hong Kong Tourism Board (HKTB) offers reliable help and information to visitors. They can answer questions about what to see, where to buy specific items, and how to get places. They also publish a variety of publications including 'what's on' listings and self-guided walking tours.

You can visit the HKTB offices on Hong Kong island in the Causeway Bay MTR station (near exit F), or in Kowloon at the Star Ferry concourse, Tsim Sha Tsui. Both are open daily 08:00 to 20:00. You can also call their multi-lingual hotline (2508 1234), available 09:00–18:00 daily, or visit their website at www.discoverhongkong.com.

Hong Kong Tourism Offices		
Australia	Sydney	+61 2 9283 3083
Canada	Toronto	+1 416 366 2389
China	Beijing	+86 10 8518 3778
	Chengdu	+86 28 8676 8768
	Guangzhou	+86 20 3758 9300
	Shanghai	+86 21 6385 1242
France	Paris	+33 1 4265 6664
Germany	Frankfurt	+49 69 959 1290
Head Office	Hong Kong	+852 2807 6543
India	New Delhi*	+91 11 2651 1423
Italy	Turin*	+39 011 669 0238
Japan	Osaka	+81 6 6229 9240
Japan	Tokyo	+81 3 5219 8288
Philippines	Manila*	+63 2 809 4479
Singapore	Singapore	+65 6336 5800
South Korea	Seoul*	+82 2 778 4403
Taiwan	Taipei*	+886 2 8789 2080
Thailand	Bangkok*	+66 2 634 2288
UK	London	+44 20 7533 7100
USA	Los Angeles	+1 310 208 4582
	New York	+1 212 421 3382
	San Francisco*	+1 415 781 4587

Hong Kong Tourist Info Abroad

The HKTB also has a network of offices and representatives around the world, promoting Hong Kong as a destination. Note that the representative offices (marked with an *) only handle enquiries from the travel trade and media, while the full offices also welcome inquiries from the general public.

Places to Stay

You'll find a wide range of accommodation available, from a bed in a backpacker dormitory to a luxury harbour-view suite with your own helicopter pad. Currently, there are 123 hotels and 484 guesthouses in Hong Kong, giving a total of 44,942 rooms. That seems like a lot, but Hong Kong also boasts one of the highest hotel occupancy rates in the world, meaning there is a good chance your preferred hotel will be full if you turn up without a booking. So, advance booking is strongly recommended. If that isn't an option, the Hong Kong Hotel Association operates counters by both exits A and B of the airport. They are clearly marked 'Hotel Reservation and Transportation', and staff there can help you find accommodation at one of their member hotels.

Hotels

Other options **Weekend Breaks** p.220

Electricity

The electrical system follows the UK standard (220 volts, 50Hz), and also uses the UK-style three pin plugs. Hong Kong's power supply is very reliable, and power cuts are almost unheard of.

Most of Hong Kong's hotels are grouped in the business and tourist areas around the harbour. In Kowloon, that means Tsim Sha Tsui, while on the island it's the strip from Central through to Causeway Bay. Recent years have seen hotels popping up in more remote areas; their rates can be cheaper, if you don't mind the extra travelling.

The Hong Kong Tourism Board claims that there is no need for any hotel star-rating system, as 'the laws of supply and demand have ensured that Hong Kong's hotels maintain the highest standards'. Dig a bit deeper and you'll find that internally they divide hotels into four categories – but don't make the results public.

Even within the same hotel you'll find a wide range of prices depending on the season, the size of the room, and the view. Ah, the view! If you are staying in one of the fancier hotels, it's worth paying the extra to get the harbour view – it's something you'll certainly remember from your trip. Make sure you get a room with a full harbour view though, as on lower floors you may just be getting a glimpse of the sea.

You should expect to pay less than the advertised nightly rate (rack rate). Booking as part of a package will often reduce costs, as can booking in advance through a hotel's website. Some websites adjust prices upwards as you get closer to the arrival date, and rooms get scarcer. It is also worth checking prices on third-party websites, though they often work in the opposite way to hotel websites, ie. their prices drop if you can take a last-minute deal. Finally, if you have to walk into a hotel to find a room, the sign showing the rack rate will probably give you a shock. Ask the staff what 'walk-in' specials they have on offer; unless they are absolutely full you'll usually be given a better price. And don't forget to check if quoted prices include the 13% tax.

Main Hotels

Name	Phone	Website	Map
Conrad Hong Kong	2521 3838	www.conradhotels.com	16-F2
Four Seasons	3196 8888	www.fourseasons.com/hongkong/	16-E1
Grand Hyatt	2584 7878	www.hongkong.grand.hyatt.com	17-A2
InterContinental Grand Stanford	2721 5161	www.hongkong.intercontinental.com	15-D4
InterContinental Hong Kong	2721 1211	www.hongkong-ic.intercontinental.com	15-D4
Island Shangri-La	2877 3838	www.shangri-la.com	16-F2
JW Marriott	2810 8366	www.marriott.com/hkgdt	16-F2
Kowloon Shangri-La	2721 2111	www.shangri-la.com/hongkong/kowloon/en	15-D4
The Landmark Mandarin Oriental	2132 0188	www.mandarinoriental.com	16-E2
Langham Hotel	2375 1133	http://hongkong.langhamhotels.com	15-C4
Langham Place Hotel	3552 3388	http://hongkong.langhamplacehotels.com	15-C2
Mandarin Oriental	2522 0111	www.mandarinoriental.com/hongkong	16-E2
The Peninsula	2920 2888	www.peninsula.com	15-D4
Ritz Carlton, Hong Kong	2877 6666	www.ritzcarlton.com/hotels/hong_kong	16-F2
Sheraton Hong Kong Hotel & Towers	2369 1111	www.starwoodhotels.com	15-D4

31

Main Hotels

Conrad Hong Kong

Pacific Place, 88 Queensway
Admiralty
🚇 Admiralty
Map 16-F2

2521 3838 | www.conradhotels.com

The hotel is built above the Pacific Place office and shopping complex. It has good transport connections, so a short ride in a taxi or on the MTR can get you to most of the places you'll want to go. Many of the rooms have excellent views of the peak or harbour. The Sunday brunch at the Brasserie on the Eighth restaurant is highly recommended.

Four Seasons

8 Finance St
Central
🚇 Central
Map 16-E1

3196 8888 | www.fourseasons.com/hongkong

The newest of Hong Kong's major hotels, the Four Seasons opened in 2005, and forms the final phase of the IFC development. In probably the best hotel location on Hong Kong island, it sits above the terminus of the airport express line right in the heart of Central. It's perfect for business, but a spa and two outdoor infinity pools overlooking the harbour make it a great place to relax as well.

Grand Hyatt

1 Harbour Rd
Wan Chai
🚇 Wan Chai
Map 17-A2

2584 7878 | www.hongkong.grand.hyatt.com

This hotel has an unusually large outdoor sports area for Hong Kong, including an 80m pool, tennis courts and a golf driving range. You'll also find a range of top-quality restaurants, and the recently re-opened JJ's nightclub. The Grand Hyatt is a popular choice when exhibitions and conferences are held at the neighbouring Hong Kong Convention & Exhibition Centre.

InterContinental Grand Stanford

70 Mody Rd
Tsim Sha Tsui
🚇 Tsim Sha Tsui
Map 15-D4

2721 5161 | www.hongkong.intercontinental.com

Located in Tsim Sha Tsui East, the hotel features 578 rooms and suites, half of which enjoy views over Victoria Harbour. Facilities include a rooftop heated swimming pool and a fitness centre, and there is a wide selection of dining outlets from Italian to regional Cantonese. The hotel also offers extensive banquet and conference facilities and a fully equipped business centre.

InterContinental Hong Kong

18 Salisbury Rd
Tsim Sha Tsui
🚇 Tsim Sha Tsui
Map 15-D4

2721 1211 | www.hongkong-ic.intercontinental.com

The InterContinental offers perfect views across the harbour to Hong Kong island's skyline, particularly impressive at night. Leisure facilities include an outdoor heated pool and the feng shui inspired I-Spa, and diners can enjoy the popular restaurant, SPOON. If you have something to celebrate, consider a night in the Presidential Suite, which boasts its own private infinity pool.

Pacific Place, 88
Queensway
Admiralty
🚇 *Admiralty*
Map 16-F2

Island Shangri-La

2877 3838 | *www.shangri-la.com*
The Shangri-La has a reputation for excellent service, whether you are staying for business or pleasure. From the hotel you have easy access to the Pacific Place complex if you want to be indoors, or if the weather is fine, you can stretch your legs in nearby Hong Kong Park. Inside the hotel, you can admire the world's largest Chinese silk painting, over 16 storeys high.

Pacific Place, 88
Queensway
Admiralty
🚇 *Admiralty*
Map 16-F2

JW Marriott

2810 8366 | *www.marriott.com/hkgdt*
Together with the Conrad and the Island Shangri-La, the JW Marriott is located above the Pacific Place complex. With 577 rooms and 25 suites offering views of the harbour, city or mountains, the hotel focuses on the needs of the business traveller. Facilities include 15 meeting rooms, six dining outlets, and a 24 hour health club to help fight the jetlag.

64 Mody Rd
Tsim Sha Tsui East
🚇 *Tsim Sha Tsui*
Map 15-D4

Kowloon Shangri-La

2721 2111 | *www.shangri-la.com/hongkong/kowloon/en*
A landmark on TST East's waterfront, the Kowloon Shangri-La has recently undergone significant renovation. Each of the 700 guest rooms and suites is furnished with either a king-sized bed or two double beds, and has floor-to-ceiling bay windows, offering either harbour or city views. There's a range of fine restaurants and bars, and state-of-the-art fitness facilities.

The Landmark
15 Queen's Rd
Central
🚇 *Central*
Map 16-E2

The Landmark Mandarin Oriental

2132 0188 | *www.mandarinoriental.com*
If you like high-tech gadgets, and a contemporary feel, then this hotel is a good choice. Two flat panel TVs in each of the 113 rooms and suites, plus the ability to plug your iPod into the room's sound system should help keep you entertained. The hotel also boasts an impressive spa covering two floors, and offering a wide range of treatments.

8 Peking Rd
Tsim Sha Tsui
🚇 *Tsim Sha Tsui*
Map 15-C4

Langham Hotel

2375 1133 | *http://hongkong.langhamhotels.com*
The Langham Hotel is just a five-minute walk from the Star Ferry pier, and is within easy reach of the MTR station and TST's commercial and entertainment options. The hotel has 495 rooms and suites, a Mediterranean-style rooftop swimming pool, and a 24 hour gym with sauna. There are six restaurants and a bar, a Grand Ballroom and five function rooms.

33

Langham Place
Mong Kok
🚇 *Mong Kok*
Map 15-C2

Langham Place Hotel

3552 3388 | http://hongkong.langhamplacehotels.com

Located in the heart of Kowloon, this hotel comprises 665 rooms and an array of facilities, including hotel-wide broadband connection, four restaurants, and five function rooms. The top three floors are home to the Chuan Spa, which specialises in traditional Chinese medicine while also offering international treatments and massage. There is a fitness studio and a heated rooftop swimming pool.

5 Connaught Rd
Central
🚇 *Central*
Map 16-E2

Mandarin Oriental

2522 0111 | www.mandarinoriental.com/hongkong

This hotel opened in 1963 and has built up a dedicated following of guests from around the world. The hotel recently underwent a complete renovation, and now offers 502 rooms and suites with either a harbour or city view. Leisure facilities include the Mandarin Spa, an indoor pool, and a fitness centre. Business visitors can take advantage of the business centre and the services of a dedicated 'IT butler'.

Salisbury Rd
Tsim Sha Tsui
🚇 *Tsim Sha Tsui*
Map 15-D4

The Peninsula

2920 2888 | www.peninsula.com

Probably the best-known hotel in Hong Kong, you'll want to visit the Peninsula even if you aren't staying here. High tea in the lobby, drinks at sunset in the Felix bar, or excellent French cuisine at Gaddi's, are all waiting to tempt you. To arrive in style you could use the helicopter shuttle service between the rooftop helipad and the airport, or perhaps let one of their fleet of Rolls Royces do the job.

3 Connaught Rd
Central
🚇 *Central*
Map 16-F2

Ritz-Carlton, Hong Kong

2877 6666 | www.ritzcarlton.com/hotels/hong_kong

The Ritz-Carlton is located in the heart of Hong Kong's main financial and business district, and is within walking distance of major shopping, entertainment and dining areas. Each of the 216 rooms has views of the harbour on one side, or skyscrapers and the Peak on the other. There are six restaurants, and leisure facilities include a heated outdoor pool and a hot tub overlooking the surrounding skyline.

20 Nathan Rd
Tsim Sha Tsui
🚇 *Tsim Sha Tsui*
Map 15-D4

Sheraton Hong Kong Hotel & Towers

2369 1111 | www.starwoodhotels.com

With 782 guest rooms and suites, many of which have a harbour view, this is something of a Hong Kong hotel heavyweight. Located in a prime position, the Sheraton offers easy access to the attractions of TST, the Star Ferry pier and the MTR station. The hotel has a fully-equipped health club with instructors, a spa, sauna, and massage facilities. There is also a serviced business centre.

Dry Cleaners p.74
Divorce Lawyers p.108

Written by residents, these unique guidebooks are packed with insider info, from arriving in a new destination to making it your home and everything in between.

Explorer Residents' Guides
We Know Where You Live

Abu Dhabi · Amsterdam · Bahrain · Barcelona · Dubai · Dublin · Geneva · Hong Kong · Kuwait
London · New York · New Zealand · Oman · Paris · Qatar · Shanghai · Singapore · Sydney

EXPLORER
www.explorerpublishing.com

Holiday Ideas

For details of resorts and hotels in Macau, Shenzhen and Zhuhai, and for suggestions of holiday destinations a little further afield, turn to p.217.

Resorts

Hong Kong is not really set up for resort vacations. If that is an important part of your holiday, there are several options within easy reach of Hong Kong. Macau is a popular getaway, with the new Las Vegas-style hotel and casino complexes offering glitz, and the Westin Resort is a popular choice for families. The sea around Macau is coffee-coloured from the river silt though, so if you are looking for picture-postcard white sand and blue sea, your closest getaways are Hainan Island in south China, or the Philippines. If you can stretch to it, Thailand, Malaysia, and Singapore are only a three-hour flight away.

Backpacking

Many backpackers travelling around Asia will spend at least some time in Hong Kong, often using it as the gateway to the China section of their travels. It can also be a good, safe place to recharge your batteries with some familiar food, if you find your health is suffering. If money is tight, the biggest risk of a visit to Hong Kong is to your wallet. A few nice meals, a couple of evenings at the local nightclubs, and you've probably spent a month's budget. It doesn't have to be that way though. Supermarkets are well stocked, and small local Chinese restaurants will fill you up for $30 or so. Check out happy-hour offers for drinks, or get a bottle or two of local beer with your meal. If you avoid taxis, public transport is inexpensive, and many attractions are free or inexpensive to visit. And just walking the streets is a highlight of the trip for many visitors - though you might struggle with the heat in summer.

Hotel Apartments

If you'll be staying for a month or more, say on a short-term contract, then serviced apartments are often a better choice than hotels. You can get similar facilities, including a pool, gym, etc, but in fully furnished accommodation that is more spacious and feels more like a home than a hotel room.

A serviced apartment can be a useful base for the first few months you are here, while you decide which part of town you'd like to live in. You can check the latest prices for the standard accommodation listed below on the websites provided. For deluxe accommodation you will probably need to contact the company for current prices, but you can expect to pay at least $30,000 per month, and over $100,000 for larger apartments.

Hotel Apartments

Deluxe	Phone	Area	Website
Four Seasons Place Hong Kong	3196 8228	Central	www.fsphk.com
Gateway Apartments	2118 8008	Tsim Sha Tsui	www.gatewayapartments.com.hk
Harbour Plaza Hong Kong	2996 8491	Hung Hom	www.harbour-plaza.com
Lanson Place Boutique Hotel & Residences	3477 6829	Causeway Bay	www.lansonplace.com
Pacific Place Apartments	2844 8361	Admiralty	www.pacificplace.com.hk
Standard			
151 and 163 Serviced Apartments	2511 5848	Wan Chai	www.nos151and163.com.hk
338 Apartment	2338 6388	Central	www.338apartment.com
Central 88	3472 2288	Central	www.central88.com
Eaton House Serviced Apartments	3182 7000	Happy Valley	www.langhamhotels.com/eatonhousehk
Excellent Court	6109 1111	Jordan	www.excellent-court.com.hk
Hong Kong Gold Coast	2457 0789	Tuen Mun	www.goldcoasthotel.com.hk
Ice House Serviced Apartments	2836 7333	Central	www.icehouse.com.hk
Portobello Lodge Serviced Apartments	2554 3527	Aberdeen	www.portobello.com.hk
Shama (Causeway Bay)	2522 3082	Causeway Bay	www.shama.com
Shama (Central)	2522 3082	Central	www.shama.com
Shama (Mid-Levels)	2522 3082	Mid-Levels	www.shama.com
Shama (SoHo)	2522 3082	SoHo	www.shama.com
Shama (Wan Chai)	2522 3082	Wan Chai	www.shama.com

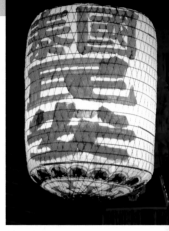

Guest Houses

If you are looking for budget accommodation and don't mind basic facilities, a guest house is another option. Make sure it is licensed (the government has a list at www.hadla.gov.hk), and that it is a 'Tourist Guesthouse'. The alternative is 'Local People Guesthouses', which are aimed at the China market. Chungking Mansions in Tsim Sha Tsui (TST) was traditionally the focal point for budget accommodation, but it is an old and crowded building. You are better off staying elsewhere, as there is plenty of choice. See the table below for some suggestions. In Causeway Bay, expect to pay $300 - 400 per night for a double room, while in Tsim Sha Tsui the rate is around $200 - 300 per night. Ask about discounts if you'll be staying a week or longer. Rooms have a small private toilet and shower, TV and air-conditioning. That's about all the facilities you should expect, though you may be surprised to find that all four listed below offer WiFi wireless internet!

Guest Houses			
Chung Kiu Inn	Causeway Bay	2895 3304	www.chungkiuinn.com.hk
Wang Fat Hostel	Causeway Bay	2895 1015	www.wangfathostel.com.hk
Cosmic Guest House	Tsim Sha Tsui	2369 6669	www.cosmicguesthouse.com
Man Hing Lung Hotel	Tsim Sha Tsui	2311 8807	www.manhinglung-hotel.com

Hotel Search

Follow the 'Accommodation' link on the Hong Kong Tourism Board's website (www.discover hongkong.com) to find details of places to stay.

Hostels

Several organisations operate hostels in Hong Kong, including the Youth Hostels Association (YHA). Most of the YHA's hostels are located in the countryside, so they are of limited interest to short-term visitors. The exception is the Mount Davis hostel (2788 1638, www.yha.org.hk), located at the top of a hill at the western end of Hong Kong island. Great views, low-cost (dormitory beds from $80 a night), but also rather inconvenient to get to and from.

If location is important, the best bargain is the YMCA's 'The Salisbury', in Tsim Sha Tsui (2268 7888, www.ymcahk.org.hk). It offers modern accommodation in the heart of the tourist area, with a bed in a four-person dormitory costing just $230 a night.

Campsites

Other options **Camping** p.233

If you're invited to join friends camping, don't rush out to buy a tent just yet. Locally, 'camping' means heading out of the city, but staying in a rented flat with air-conditioning, bathroom, etc. Camping in tents is called 'wild camping'.

Where to go for your wild camp? The government lists 37 approved camping sites, but it is unlikely anyone will complain if you pitch your tent in remote areas. A popular 'unofficial' site is Tai Long Wan, in the northeast New Territories, Hong Kong's most beautiful beach. Many people choose to camp right on the sand, though the best site is on a low headland that divides the bay into the two main beaches.

Winter is the best season for camping – there is less chance of rain and fewer mozzies – and the temperature is more comfortable. In general, expect to bring your own food and water, though at Tai Long Wan there are a couple of small stores that sell drinks and cooked food.

37

Getting Around

Other options **Exploring** p.164, **Maps** p.409

Hong Kong is a six-year-old boy's dream city – it's like the living book of Big Transport. Trains, buses, boats, and trams – even the world's longest escalators – move millions of people around the city each day. The fruits of decades' worth of massive infrastructure projects are everywhere. Traffic runs for miles, 50 feet above the ground on elevated highways. Three tunnels run beneath Hong Kong's harbour, and many more cut

through its mountainous interior. An entire island has been levelled to make space for the airport. Towering – and beautiful – bridges span deep-sea channels through which giant container ships pass.

At first, Hong Kong's frenetic and overpowering sense of movement may impress the casual observer, in much the same way as the sense of swarming anarchy one gets staring at an anthill. But with a little familiarity, this city's transport web is quickly tamed, as a great deal of order lies just below the disorienting surface.

Air

Other options **Meet & Greet** p.22

Since Hong Kong borders only mainland China, air travel is a big deal here – virtually all trips to destinations other than the mainland (and many trips there, too, for that matter) are by air.

Cross-Harbour Routes

Note that Citybus and First Bus cross-list each other's routes. If you're planning a cross-harbour trip, it's especially worthwhile checking if any tunnel buses are going your way. Remember that all three companies share the cross-harbour routes, so don't give up after checking just one.

Fortunately, Hong Kong has an airport built to match these needs. Hong Kong International Airport (HKIA), opened in 1998, and overcame some teething problems to quickly take a place among the world's best. It lies on the flattened remains of a small island, Chek Lap Kok, just north of Hong Kong's largest island, Lantau. There was originally just one huge terminal, with the upper floor dedicated to departures, the lower to arrivals, but Terminal Two was due to open in March 2007. There are big duty-free shops for both those departing and those arriving. HKIA is extremely busy, with around 750 flights a day provided by over 80 airlines. There are flights to most major cities, with direct-flight options usually available. With the advent of longer-range aircraft in recent years, even the east coast cities in North America are now reachable in one incredibly long haul (16 hours) from Hong Kong. You'll still need a stopover to make it to destinations in central and South America, and to many African cities, however.

Hong Kong is also home to a world-class airline, Cathay Pacific. Although Cathay doesn't fly into China itself (this job is relegated to its sister airline, Dragonair), they do fly to most major cities in Asia, North America, Europe and Australia.

Airport Trains and Buses

An extremely fast train, the Airport Express, runs from HKIA to stations in Kowloon and Central on Hong Kong island. Travel time into the city is just over 20 minutes. The platform for boarding the Airport Express is located right in the arrivals area of HKIA, and with ticket machines and counters scattered all around the airport, it's very convenient indeed if you're headed into the heart of the city. Note also that you can check in up to 24 hours in advance of your flight at the Airport Express stations, so long as you use the train to reach the airport when it's time for you to fly.

The Octopus Card

One of the best features of Hong Kong's public transport system is that all modes of transport - except taxis - can be paid for using the same stored-value card system, called the Octopus. Getting an Octopus card is almost mandatory for Hong Kong residents, and may well be worthwhile if you're visiting for more than a couple of days. They can also be used in convenience stores, supermarkets and some fast-food restaurants.

If your destination lies in other Hong Kong districts, however, your best bet for cheap transport may be an airbus. Several lines run into the city, covering most of the urban areas and new towns, and stopping near many hotels. The most useful routes are as follows:

• A11 To North Point Ferry Pier (via Central, Admiralty, Wan Chai and Causeway Bay)

• A21 Hung Hom KCR Station (via Mong Kok and Tsim Sha Tsui)

• A22 Lam Tin MTR Station (via Jordan Road, To Kwa Wan, Kowloon City and Kwun Tong)

• A31 Tsuen Wan (Discovery Park)

• A41 Sha Tin (Yu Chui Court)

Taxis are also readily available at HKIA; a ride into the city will cost around $250 to $300.

Airlines

Aeroflot Russian Int'l Airlines	2537 2611	www.aeroflot.org
Air Canada	2329 0973	www.aircanada.ca
Air China	2216 1088	www.airchina.com.cn
Air France	2180 2180	www.airfrance.com
Air India	2216 1088	www.airindia.com
Air New Zealand	2862 8988	www.airnewzealand.com.hk
Air Philippines	2216 1088	www.airphils.com
All Nippon Airways	2186 6038	www.ana.co.jp
American Airlines	2826 9102	www.aa.com
Bangkok Airways	2769 5255	www.bangkokair.com
British Airways	2216 1088	www.ba.com
Cathay Pacific	2747 1888	www.cathaypacific.com
China Airlines	2769 8391	www.china-airlines.com
China Eastern Airlines	2216 1088	www.ce-air.com
China Southern Airlines	2216 1088	www.cs-air.com
Continental Airlines	2180 2180	www.continental.com
Delta Airlines	2526 5875	www.delta.com
Dragonair	2180 2180	www.dragonair.com
EL AL Israel Airlines	2216 1088	www.elal.com
Emirates Airline	2216 1088	www.emirates.com
HongKong Express	3151 1800	www.hongkongexpress.com
Japan Airlines	2847 4567	www.jal.co.jp
Jetstar Asia	2216 1088	www.jetstarasia.com
KLM Royal Dutch Airlines	2180 2180	www.klm.com.hk
Korean Air	2769 7511	www.koreanair.com
Lufthansa	2868 2313	www.lufthansa.com
Malaysia Airlines	2525 2321	www.mas.com.my
Pakistan International Airlines	2366 4770	www.piac.com.pk
Philippine Airlines	2301 9300	www.pal.com.ph
Qantas	28229 000	www.qantas.com.au
Qatar Airways	2769 6032	www.qatarairways.com
Royal Brunei Airlines	2869 8608	www.bruneiair.com
Royal Jordanian	2861 1811	www.rja.com.jo
Royal Nepal Airlines	2769 6046	www.royalnepal.com
Singapore Airlines	2520 2233	www.singaporeair.com.hk
South African Airways	2877 3277	www.saa.co.za
Thai Airways	2876 6888	www.thaiair.com
United Airlines	2122 8256	www.unitedairlines.com.hk
US Airways	3110 3637	www.usairways.com
Vietnam Airlines	2810 6680	www.vietnamair.com.vn
Virgin Atlantic Airways	2532 6060	www.virgin-atlantic.com

The Star Ferry

Boat

Hong Kong's most famous transport link is the venerable Star Ferry, which sloshes back and forth between Hong Kong island and Kowloon in just about 10 minutes. You will take the Star Ferry if you visit Hong Kong – simple as that. But less picturesque – and much faster – ferries play a big part in Hong Kong's overall transport scheme, with multiple routes connecting the inhabited outlying islands, and a few spots in the New Territories, with the city. Most ferries these days are 'fast' ones, with fully enclosed, air-conditioned cabins, but some routes still mix in older 'slow' ferries with open decks that can be very pleasant for seeing a different face of Hong Kong.

Bus

Some crucial facts about Hong Kong's buses:

- Their coverage is remarkably wide. Many visitors and expatriates find Hong Kong's complex bus networks a bit intimidating and avoid using them. This is a mistake, because large – and interesting – parts of the SAR are not accessible from the MTR and other trains.
- Bus frequency is generally good. You rarely wait longer than 15 minutes, and much shorter waits are the norm.
- The buses are quite comfortable. Most are air-conditioned double-deckers.

There's no point trying to list out 'essential' routes: there are too many that you might find useful. You should instead bookmark all three major bus companies' websites, as all provide excellent route information (including photos of each individual bus stop) and route- and destination-search capacities:

- Kowloon Motor Bus (KMB) www.kmb.com.hk
- Citybus www.citybus.com.hk
- New World First Bus www.nwfb.com.hk

Car

Other options **Transportation** p.156

In a holdover from British rule, Hong Kong drives on the left-hand side of the road – unlike mainland China, which drives on the right – with roundabouts liberally employed in some parts of the city. Hong Kong's roads are generally orderly and well-maintained, and signage is adequate (with occasional irritating lapses). The speed limit is 50 kmph unless otherwise posted; it rises to 70-80 kmph in rural areas, where it is marked. There are just a few stretches of genuine 'highway'

Minibuses

No discussion of road transport in Hong Kong would be complete without mentioning the ubiquitous minibuses that run on just about every road in the SAR. There are two types: the cream-and-green ones follow set routes with more or less official 'stops', much like ordinary buses. The cream-and-red ones have more freedom; they generally follow a point-to-point route, but they can pick up and drop off passengers wherever they like, much as a taxi would. They may also vary their routes a bit depending on how full up they are. If you're a visitor, you're not likely to need to use minibuses often, but they come in very handy indeed if you're exploring rural areas.

Getting Around

where speeds of 100-110 kmph are allowed.
Hong Kong's roads often suffer from heavy congestion, particularly near the entrance to the most centrally-located cross-harbour tunnel. True gridlock is actually not that common, but accidents, construction and simple overcrowding can all cause long, frustrating delays. Driving in densely-populated districts such as Causeway Bay, Tsim Sha Tsui and Mong Kok is particularly stressful, as streets are often narrow and one-way, and crowds of pedestrians are everywhere. The Hong Kong Government is in fact pursuing a policy of increasing pedestrianisation in these areas.

Hong Kong has its fair share of lousy drivers, although the situation isn't nearly as bad as some expats will have you believe. There are problems with both overly-aggressive drivers looking to show off, and – ironically – with tentative, inexperienced drivers, as many people here take driving lessons and obtain licences without gaining much realistic driving experience.

Buying a Car

Longer-term Hong Kong residents face a motoring dilemma. A car at your disposal is useful and fun, especially for people who simply enjoy cars and driving, yet the disadvantages here are so extreme, and public transport is so good, that you may very well choose not to drive at all.

On the up side, in spite of frequent congestion, Hong Kong's roads are quite safe. Driving here is more like driving in a large western city than in most other Asian cities. It's also easy to pick up a cheap used car from departing expats who are rapidly liquidating their assets. And if you live or work in more remote parts of Hong Kong, especially in the New Territories, you may find driving saves you considerable time in commuting.

But for most Hong Kong people a car is strictly a status symbol – an almost pure luxury. Automotive costs are uniformly high: licensing (about $5,800 a year for cars with 1500-2500cc engines), taxation on new cars (can be almost equal to the price of the car), petrol (over $13 per litre), and renting a fixed parking space in a housing development (typically $2,000 - 3,000/month or more). Cross-harbour tunnel fees (ranging from around $20 - 40) also add up, and other tunnels in the New Territories charge fees, too. Journeys in and out of the urban centres by car are often slower than taking public transport, once time securing parking is figured in. And you'll be actively contributing to Hong Kong's already worrisome air pollution.

For most new residents, it's therefore worth delaying the purchase of a car by at least a month or two, and trying taxis and public transport first.

If you do decide to buy a car in Hong Kong, you're likely to be entitled to drive on your home country's licence for one year. After this point, you must hold a Hong Kong driver's licence. This is not as intimidating as it sounds, residents of most countries don't need to take a test and can pick up a Hong Kong licence – which is good for 10 years – simply by filling in a form and paying a fee (currently $900).

You will also need to secure third-party liability insurance, and licence and register your vehicle. Cars older than six years must be formally examined for emissions and roadworthiness prior to relicensing.

Driving Rules

Seatbelts are required for driver and all passengers, in front and back seats, and child safety seats are necessary for babies and toddlers. Talking on mobile phones while driving is prohibited (although this law is frequently flouted), but hands-free devices are legal. More information on vehicle regulations and licensing is available at the Transport Department's website: www.td.gov.hk. You may also find their Road User's Code useful for learning the rules of the road in Hong Kong.

Parking

Parking in Hong Kong is very rarely free, and most areas of the city have no street-level parking whatsoever. Most carparks are situated in the lower levels of residential buildings and shopping malls, or built as very cosy high-rise garages. Hourly costs are high, ranging from $8-10 per hour in outlying areas, up to $30 per hour or more in the heart of the city. One useful tactic is to look for shopping malls that offer two or three hours' free parking in return for spending a stipulated amount on the premises. Many restaurants also validate parking; it's always worth asking, if you've parked on site.

41

The Complete **Residents'** Guide

Licenced to Drive?

For information on driving licences and whether or not you're covered for driving in Hong Kong, turn to p.62 in the Residents section.

Hiring a Car

For tourists, hiring a car in Hong Kong is simply not advised. Roads are crowded and complex, parking is expensive, and public transport and taxis are all you'll need to see the city and its sights. Even if you're interested in hiking or other outdoor pursuits, a car will only be a burden.

Renting cars in Hong Kong is also very expensive, if any other disincentive is needed to convince you.

If you decide you really must rent a car, Hertz and Avis will be happy to take your money. You have few other choices. There are small local car rental agencies aplenty, but they're generally more interested in arranging tours and drivers. One you could try is Jubilee International (see table). Base rental prices range from about $500 – 700 per day for a compact car to $1,000 per day or more for a full-sized car. Weekly prices start at $2,500 for a compact, and $4,000 or more for a full-size.

Car Rental Agencies		
Avis	2890 6988	www.avis.com
Hertz Rent A Car	2525 1313	www.hertz.com
Jubilee International	2530 0530	www.jubilee.com.hk

Cycling

Other options **Cycling** p.236

If you come to Hong Kong expecting to see rivers of elegant black bicycles like the ones that flow through some other Chinese cities, you're in for a rude shock. Hong Kong must be one of the world's worst cities for bikers. It's true that recreational

cyclists are relatively common in the New Towns, as cycle-paths were part of the towns' design, and a few riders also brave rural roads at weekends. In Kowloon and Hong Kong however, the only cyclists you'll see are delivery men. Dressed in shorts, vest and flip-flops, a heavy load (even an entire pig carcass) dangling from their handlebars, they seem oblivious of the fact they're usually cycling the wrong way down a busy main road.

Taxi

Hong Kong is well-served by taxis. They're relatively cheap – the starting price in urban-area taxis is $15 – and even a very long trip, for example, from the airport into town, costs about $300. Unless it's raining or rush hour, taxis are easy to find, either at posted ranks, by hailing on the street, or by calling a dispatcher (see table; note that $5 is added to the fare for calling a taxi).

All Hong Kong taxis are metered, and although occasional scams are reported, Hong Kong cabbies are mostly reliable. All Hong Kong taxis are privately owned, some by a number of big companies, and others

42

by individual owner-operators who join associations. But they are heavily regulated, and their numbers strictly limited by government licensing.

Red-and-grey urban taxis can go anywhere in Hong Kong. There are also separate sets of taxis restricted to the New Territories (green) and Lantau Island (blue).

One Hong Kong taxi quirk to keep in mind is that urban drivers further divide themselves according to the side of the harbour they prefer to work on; that is, there are 'Hong Kong side', and 'Kowloon side' taxis. Generally drivers are happy to take you across the harbour, since it means a big fare, but some drivers may be reluctant if they're nearing the end of their shifts. When you do take a cross-harbour taxi ride, remember that, on top of the metered fare, you will have to pay double the tunnel fee: once to cross with you in the taxi, and once to get the driver back over to 'his side'. You can get by with paying a single tunnel fee by tracking down one of the special taxi ranks exclusively devoted to drivers looking to get back across the harbour.

Most taxi drivers will be able to understand your directions in English – if your destination is well-known, that is. But if it's not, it's best to get your destination written out for you in Chinese. Your hotel concierge will be happy to do this, as will Hong Kong-based business associates and friends. Broadly speaking, taxi drivers on Hong Kong side are more likely to speak competent English than those on Kowloon side, but there is great variation all around the city.

At the moment, Hong Kong taxis do not accept Octopus cards for payment, but it's just a matter of time until they do. Note that if you need a receipt from a Hong Kong taxi you can certainly get one, but you must ask for it. Just the word 'receipt' should get the required response, even if your driver doesn't speak much other English.

Taxi Companies

Abbo Taxi Owners' Association Ltd	2383 0168
Fraternity Public Car Radio Centre Ltd	2527 6324
Golden Link Taxi Owners & Drivers Assn Ltd	2571 2929
Happy Taxi Operator's Assn Ltd	2728 8281
HK & Kln Radio Car Owners Assn Ltd	2760 0455
Kln Taxi Radio Centre	2760 0412
NT Taxi Radio Serv Centre Ltd	2457 2266
NT Taxi-Call Serv Centre	2383 0899
Pak Kai Taxi Centre	2728 2281
Rights Of Taxi (Si Hai) Telecommunication Center Ltd	2697 4333
Sun Hing Taxi Radio Assn	2450 2288
The Taxi Operators Assn Ltd	2362 2337
Taxi Radio Call Centre	2391 9366
Taxicom Vehicle Owners Assn Ltd	2529 8822
United Friendship Taxi Owners & Drivers Assn Ltd	2760 0477
Urban Taxi-Call Serv Centre	2383 0180
Wing Lee Public Cars Co Ltd	2397 0922
Wing Tai Car Owners & Drivers Assn Ltd	2527 8524
Wing Tai Radio Taxi	2865 7398
Yellow Taxi Group Ltd	2675 7688

Train

The mostly-underground Mass Transit Railway (MTR) and above-ground Kowloon-Canton Railway (KCR) comprise the most visitor-friendly transport network in Hong Kong.

The MTR comprises five main lines, plus one short line dedicated to serving Hong Kong Disneyland. Most lines run underground, but in places the MTR comes hurtling out of hillsides and you're suddenly on elevated platforms running right through the city. Most of the core urban areas, on both Hong Kong island and Kowloon, are within ten minutes' walk of an MTR station. The MTR has built up a well-deserved reputation as one of the world's best public transport systems. Trains are spotless, bright and well air-conditioned, and run at minute-to-minute frequency at peak hours – you almost never have to wait more than five minutes. MTR stations are also clean and safe.

The KCR, comprising three main lines plus ancillary light rail and bus services, is primarily a suburban system, serving 'new towns' such as Sha Tin, Tai Po and Ma On

Discount Cabs
*Although there are
really no 'unofficial'
taxis in Hong Kong,
you may well be able
to wangle discounted
fares – usually around
20-30% off the metered
fare – on longer
journeys if you call any
of several covert
dispatching centres.
Since you won't find
these numbers in the
book, it's best to ask a
Hong Kong resident
who speaks Cantonese
for help. Note, however,
that this practice is
definitely against the
rules, and the Hong
Kong Government is
considering ways of
quashing it.*

Shan. The KCR's name is misleading: although its East Rail line runs on the same tracks that take express trains across the border to 'Canton' (now Guangzhou), KCR trains stop at the Lo Wu border station. Although the KCR isn't quite as swish as the MTR, it's still a fast, reliable service.

The major drawback to both of Hong Kong's trains systems can be summed up in two words: rush hour. The morning rush – 08:00 - 09:30 or so, is the worst, but trains do get crowded in the early evenings (18:00 - 19:00) as well.

Tram

Hong Kong's land-based transport icons are its trams, which are still used daily by thousands of people moving along the north side of Hong Kong island. They're not fast, or particularly comfortable, but they have undeniable charm and a great view from the front of the upper deck. For short journeys they're sometimes quicker than bus or train, and certainly far cheaper.

Walking

Other options **Hiking** p.247

Despite its heavy traffic and sometimes-noxious climate, Hong Kong can be quite walking-intensive. In many areas, above and below ground walkways are provided for pedestrians. Tsim Sha Tsui, one of the city's busiest districts, is now honeycombed with bright, pleasant pedestrian tunnels; you can walk for what seems like miles in comfort. Still, in no matter what part of the city, you'll often find yourself standing at large intersections awaiting the little green man's permission to cross the street. You should note that in many areas pavements get seriously congested, almost to the point of pedestrian gridlock, and that in parts of Hong Kong island 'walking' means 'climbing steps'. Getting 'up the hill' on the island is greatly aided however, by an extensive public escalator system that takes riders up from the central business district, through trendy SoHo's restaurants and pubs, and on up to the residential Mid-Levels. Walking is safe virtually everywhere in the city.

Tsing Ma Bridge

Money

Credit cards are widely accepted for payment in Hong Kong, especially Visa and Mastercard. In smaller stores, or for smaller purchases (say under $200), you may find that only cash is accepted, so if you're low on cash it's worth checking if the store or restaurant will take your card. Hotels and large stores in the tourist areas will often accept payment in other currencies, especially US$ and Chinese renminbi. Outside those areas, expect to use Hong Kong dollars.

Local Currency

Hong Kong's currency is the dollar, divided into 100 cents. Coins are available in 10c, 20c, 50c, $1, $2, $5, and $10 denominations. When the $10 coin was introduced, the $10 note was phased out. However a combination of deflation, and forgery problems with the $10 coin, means that the $10 note has been reinstated. Other notes available are the $20, $50, $100, $500 and $1,000. You can expect to see several different designs of each note during your visit, as three of the local banks (HSBC, Standard Chartered, and Bank of China) issue their own notes.

Main Banks

American Express	2811 1200	www.americanexpress.com.hk
Bank of America	2847 6567	www.bankofamerica.com.hk
Bank of China	2826 6888	www.bochk.com
Bank of East Asia	2912 1710	www.hkbea.com
Citibank	2868 8888	www.citibank.com
Dah Sing Bank	2507 8866	www.dahsing.com
Hang Seng	2825 5111	www.hangseng.com
HSBC ▶ p.109	2822 1111	www.hsbc.com.hk
International Bank of Asia	2842 6222	www.iba.com.hk
Lloyds TSB International ▶ p.47	2847 3000	www.lloydstsb.com.hk
Standard Chartered	2886 8888	www.standardchartered.com.hk

Although their designs differ, they all follow the same colour scheme, except... to add to the confusion, new $10 notes are purple and $50 notes green, but there are still older green $10 notes and purple $50 notes in circulation!

If you are visiting from the US, currency translation is straightforward as the HK$ has been pegged to the US$ since 1983, at the rate of HK$7.8 for every US$1.

Banks

Most banks have their head office in Central district on Hong Kong island, but you'll find sub-branches distributed throughout the built-up areas of Hong Kong. You'll find names you are familiar with such as HSBC, Citibank, and Bank of America, along with large local banks such as Hang Seng and Standard Chartered that may be new to you. All are internationally recognised, so you'll have no problems if you need to transfer money to and from home.

Banks are open from 09:00 to 16:30 Monday to Friday, and 09:00 to 12:30 on Saturdays. Note that smaller branches don't offer currency exchange services.

ATMs

You won't have to walk far to find an ATM. Bank branches have ATMs outside, every MTR station has them, and shopping malls usually have several too. You should not have any problem using your home bank's debit or credit card here, as local ATMs support the two global ATM networks, Cirrus and PLUS. Check your card to see which you use, then look for an ATM that shows the same logo. American Express cardholders can withdraw cash at any ATM showing the 'Jetco' logo.

Exchange Rates

Foreign Currency (FC)	1 Unit FC = x HK$	1 HK$ = x FC
Australia	6.19	0.16
Bahrain	20.79	0.05
Bangladesh	0.11	8.81
Canada	6.73	0.15
Cyprus	17.67	0.06
Denmark	1.38	0.72
Euro	10.28	0.10
India	0.18	5.67
Japan	0.06	15.51
Jordan	11.02	0.09
Kuwait	27.00	0.04
Malaysia	2.24	0.45
New Zealand	5.52	0.18
Oman	20.28	0.05
Pakistan	0.13	7.76
Philippines	0.16	6.15
Qatar	2.15	0.46
Saudi Arabia	0.27	3.75
Singapore	5.10	0.19
South Africa	1.10	0.91
Sri Lanka	0.07	13.93
Sweden	1.11	0.90
Switzerland	6.32	0.16
Thailand	0.23	4.29
UAE	2.13	0.47
UK	15.34	0.07
USA	7.81	0.13

* Rates correct at time of going to print

Money Exchanges

When you need to change money into local currency, there are several options, including banks, your hotel, or licensed money exchanges. Hotels typically offer the worst rates, taking around 7% of your money for the privilege of changing it. Banks are a safe bet, and charge around 2-3%, with good exchanges charging 1-2%. You can get better rates than these on popular currencies such as the US$, while relatively rare currencies will get you a worse rate.

Money exchanges are easy to find – just look for their brightly lit 'Change' signs; they're typically open from 09:30 – 19:30. However, beware the changers on main streets in the heart of the tourist areas (for example along Ashley Road in Tsim Sha Tsui), who can charge over 15%. So jot down your hotel's rates as a reference before you start, and be prepared to walk off the main streets to get a better deal. If this all sounds like too much trouble, using an ATM to withdraw money from your home bank's savings account is fast, available 24/7, and typically costs you only 2-3%.

Credit Cards

Using your credit card to pay often gets you a better effective exchange rate than changing money into a local currency and then paying cash. The exception is when you are bargaining for goods where the margins are low (eg. computers or electronic goods), since the shop may add an extra fee (typically around 3%) if you want to pay by credit card.

Some small restaurants and cafes may not accept credit cards, nor will many market stalls. Either bring enough cash with you to cover these, or check first that they accept your card before doing business.

If you are unlucky enough to lose your card, or it is stolen, be sure to inform the issuer immediately so you won't be liable for any further transactions. (see Lost/Stolen Property p.26)

Credit Card Fraud

Although it isn't common, you may be a victim of credit card fraud even though you still have the card in your possession, and you're not likely to know about it until your card is rejected when you try to make a purchase. If this happens to you, contact your home bank to check the card's balance and recent transactions. If the card's balance is used up, and there are transactions you don't recognise, assume your credit card has been 'skimmed' and copied. You should not be liable for the fraudulent transactions, but you will probably not be able to use that card again as your bank will want to issue you with a new one. When paying with your credit card, try to keep the card in sight at all times to avoid your card being skimmed.

46

International Account
Welcome to Hong Kong
from Lloyds TSB International

Our multi-currency International Account offers an impressive range of financial products and services that make it easy to live, work and travel worldwide.

We're always close at hand with telephone and Internet banking available 24/7, relationship managers who know and understand your individual requirements and a local office on hand to support you.

Benefits include:

- Choice of Offshore accounts in three currencies; sterling, US dollar and euro.

- No minimum balance required.

- Facility to carry out international money transfers over the phone and currency money transfers on the internet.*

- No £1 overseas transaction fee charged.

- Simple account opening process – just contact your local representative office, and they'll be pleased to help.

- Telephone banking and Internet banking are available 24/7, 365 days a year.

Any questions? Just contact us...

Call Louise Curtis **+852 2847 3936**
Or email **offshore@lloydstsbiom.com.hk**
or **louisecurtis@lloydstsb.com.hk**

Issued by the Hong Kong representative office of Lloyds TSB Offshore Limited, Suites 3901-04, Two Exchange Square, Central, Hong Kong. Registered Office: P.O. Box 160, 25 New Street, St. Helier, Jersey JE4 8RG which is its principal place of business. Registered in Jersey, No. 4029. The Isle of Man Branch of Lloyds TSB Offshore Limited is licensed by the Isle of Man Financial Supervision Commission to conduct banking and investment business and is registered with the Insurance and Pensions Authority in respect of General Business. Lloyds TSB Offshore Holdings Limited has registered the business name of Lloyds TSB International in Jersey and has licensed it to Lloyds TSB Offshore Limited. All Lloyds TSB Offshore International accounts will be opened in either the Jersey or Isle of Man branch of Lloyds TSB Offshore Limited based on your offshore residency, Jersey for Europe and the Isle of Man for the rest of the world.

Deposits are not covered by the UK Financial Services Compensation Scheme made under the Financial Services and Markets Act 2000. Deposits made with Lloyds TSB Offshore Limited, Isle of Man Branch are covered by the Depositors Compensation Scheme contained in the Isle of Man Banking Business (Compensation of Depositors) Regulations 1991. Lloyds TSB Offshore Limited is not an authorised institution within the meaning of the Banking Ordinance and is therefore not subject to the supervision of the Hong Kong Monetary Authority. The paid up capital and reserves of Lloyds TSB Offshore Limited are £301m as at 31st December 2005.

The information contained in this document does not constitute an invitation to make deposits or to provide any other products or services in any jurisdiction to any person to whom it is unlawful to make such an offer or solicitation in such jurisdiction. * There may be a charge for some of these services, for a full list of tariffs please ask for a tariff and rates sheet.

OB1285 11/06

Tipping

Tipping is not universally expected in Hong Kong, but always appreciated. The actual amount to tip varies according to who you are dealing with:

- Taxis – the driver will usually just round the fare up to the nearest dollar; in any case, that's all you need to pay.

- Hotel washroom attendants – they appreciate a small tip, say $2.

- Ordinary restaurants – let's say you pay for a $400 meal with a $500 note. You're surprised to see that the change comes back as a $50 and two $20 notes, plus some coins, ie. a $5, two $2s, and a $1. It isn't that the cashier didn't have a $100 note. Instead, she's guiding you in making a tip – in this case you take the notes and the $5 coin, and leave the small coins. Even when paying by credit card, local practice is just to round up to give a tip in the $5-$20 range. You really don't need to calculate the tip as a percentage of the total bill.

- Bellhops - give them $10 - $20 depending on the number of bags they are carrying for you.

- Salons - if you get a haircut, take a massage, or visit a beauty salon, a 5 - 10% tip will be welcomed, and you'll get an extra smile on your next visit.

- Hotel restaurants, and other upmarket restaurants – a 10% service charge will be added to the bill automatically, but it won't go to the staff. An extra 5-10% tip will be appreciated if you had good service – leave it as cash if you are paying by credit card, so that it goes to the waiters.

Sunset over Hong Kong and Lamma Island harbours

Newspapers/Magazines

Hong Kong's main English-language local newspaper is the *South China Morning Post*, or SCMP, priced at $7 a copy. The SCMP covers all areas you'd expect in a modern daily, with particular coverage of Hong Kong and China news. The other local English daily is *The Standard* ($6), which has more of a business focus. For international news with an Asian slant, choices include the *Asian Wall Street Journal*, *International Herald Tribune*, and *USA Today International*. Of course the bulk of the local newspapers are written in Chinese, with popular titles including the *Apple Daily*, *Oriental Daily*, *Hong Kong Economic Times*, and *Ming Pao*.

You shouldn't have any trouble finding a local newspaper, as there are newspaper stands on every busy pavement (that's most of them in Hong Kong), or you can buy one at any 7-Eleven or Circle K convenience store. The news stands at the Star Ferry piers in Central and Tsim Sha Tsui also have a good selection of overseas newspapers and magazines, as do the Bookazine (www.bookazine.com.hk) and Page One stores. The overseas newspapers they stock will typically be at least two days old though, so visiting these newspapers' websites could be an easier way to keep up to date with news from home. Finally, if you just like browsing (or if you're a cheapskate!), visit the fifth floor of the Hong Kong Central Library in Causeway Bay. You don't need a library card; just walk in and take your pick from current issues of 300 newspapers and 4,000 periodicals.

Books

Other options **Websites** p.49

If you're looking for something to read on the long flight to Hong Kong, two of James Clavell's novels (*Tai Pan* and *Noble House*) are set in Hong Kong. They are definitely fiction, but you'll also pick up a feel for life in Hong Kong, and its culture and customs. If you prefer non-fiction, Frank Walsh's *A History of Hong Kong* covers exactly what its title suggests, while Martin Booth's *Memoir Gweilo: Memories of a Hong Kong Childhood* is a charming tale of life in Hong Kong as a child in the 1950s. (In the USA, the book is titled *Golden Boy: Memories of a Hong Kong Childhood*). Many people also swear by Jan Morris's *Hong Kong*, but as it was written well before the handover, it may feel a bit dated.

Once you reach Hong Kong, pick up a copy of *HK Magazine*, a free weekly magazine with listings of what's on, together with general-interest articles and restaurant reviews. *BC Magazine* covers similar ground, with more emphasis on what's happening in the local bars, clubs and live music scene. You'll find both available at many bars, restaurants and bookshops.

The Whole World's Your Home

Explorer Residents' Guides are going global with new titles for locations as far flung as Dublin and New Zealand in the pipeline. So if you fancy living abroad check out the complete list of current and upcoming Explorer guides on our website *www.explorer publishing.com* Remember life's a trip...all you need to do is pick a destination.

Websites

Websites	
www.asia-city.com	What's on & restaurant reviews
www.cityline.com.hk	Cinema listings and online booking
www.discoverhongkong.com	Hong Kong Tourist Board's visitor website
www.foodbyweb.com.hk	Deliveries from your favourite restaurants
www.geoexpat.com ▶ p.23	Expat forums, classifieds, etc.
www.hkexpats.com	Expat forums, classifieds, etc.
www.hkoutdoors.com	Information about Hong Kong's countryside
www.info.gov.hk	Government portal, with links to departmental websites
www.scmp.com	Website of the South China Morning Post newspaper
www.thestandard.com.hk	Local Newspaper
www.underground.org.hk	Detailed weather information
www.yp.com.hk	Hong Kong Yellow Pages

The table lists some of the websites you're likely to find helpful during your visit. You can also check out some of the local expats' blogs for a more informal take on Hong Kong life – an internet search for 'Hong Kong blog' will quickly take you to the popular sites.

Hong Kong Annual Events

Ching Ming, and Chung Yeung Festivals

Various Locations
April & October (Lunar calendar date)

To visitors these are simply two public holidays that fall in spring and autumn. For locals, though, these are days to pay respects to their ancestors. Many families visit graveyards and older hillside graves to tidy them up and make offerings.

Chinese (Lunar) New Year

Various Locations
February (Lunar calendar date)

The biggest festival in the Chinese calendar, when everyone makes the effort to get home and spend it with their families. It's the one time of the year when Hong Kong feels quiet, with many shops and businesses closed. Major events held over the three-day holiday include a huge fireworks display over the harbour, and a street parade of floats, performers and marching bands from around the world.

Cheung Chau Bun Festival

Cheung Chau island
www.cheungchau.org
May (Lunar calendar date)

One of Hong Kong's unique events, this week-long festival culminates in a parade of costumed children on stilts, and a mad race to the top of bun-clad bamboo towers. The higher the bun, the greater the glory!

Cricket Sixes

Kowloon Cricket Club
www.hksixes.com
November

Your best chance to see international cricket in East Asia, the weekend-long Sixes is cricket's answer to the Rugby Sevens. As with the Sevens, the Sixes follows a format that encourages a faster, more entertaining game, attracting a wider audience than the usual cricket buffs.

Dragon Boat Festival

Various Seafront Locations
www.discoverhong kong.com
June (Lunar calendar date)

The official name is the 'Tuen Ng Festival', but you'll remember it as the dragon boat festival. Head to the seafront to see teams of around 20 sitting in slender dragon boats, paddling furiously to the beat of their drummers. Local races are held near fishing villages such as Aberdeen and Stanley, with the international races usually held a week or so later in Sha Tin. Check with the Tourist Board for the exact details of where and when to see them.

Hong Kong Arts Festival

Various Locations
www.hk.arts festival.org
February - March

Get a dose of culture at Hong Kong's main arts event. With a mix of overseas and local artists, and a variety of music, theatre, dance, popular entertainment and film programmes, you're sure to find something that catches your fancy.

Hong Kong Flower Show

Victoria Park
www.lcsd.gov. hk/green/hkfs
March

If you enjoy flowers, this is a colorful show of pot plants, flower arrangements and large landscape displays. If it inspires you to bring a little life into your apartment, there are also plenty of stalls ready to sell you their plants, with orchids especially popular.

Hong Kong International Film Festival

Various Locations
www.hkiff.org.hk
March - April

Film buff? Leave reality behind and indulge in over two weeks of cinema. Hollywood and indie, local and international, old and new. With several hundred films to choose from, there is a bit of everything. Warning – popular films are often sold out, so book early.

Hong Kong Marathon

Races start from
Tsim Sha Tsui
www.hkmarathon.com
February

The highlight for runners is the chance to run across the Tsing Ma suspension bridge, normally the roadway from the city to the airport. If running 26 miles in Hong Kong's polluted air seems like too much, there are also half marathon and 10K races held the same day.

Hong Kong Sevens

Hong Kong Stadium
www.hksevens.com
March

Considered the main event in the World Sevens Series, the Sevens offer a weekend of fast-paced, exciting rugby, attracting fans from around the world. Teams from 24 nations compete, including all the world's rugby majors. For many regular visitors, the close of play on the pitch each day marks the start of a long night – head to Wan Chai and Lan Kwai Fong to join the party.

Hong Kong World Festival

Tamar Site, Admiralty
www.hkworld
carnival.com
Until March

The largest mobile carnival and funfair in the world is in Hong Kong until March and features over 70 rides, rollercoasters and games. Open from 11.00 - 23.00 there is a variety of food, drink and merchandise available and guarantees a fun day for the family. Visit the website for location and ticket price details.

Horse Racing

Happy Valley
Racecourse & Sha Tin
Racecourse
www.hkjc.com
September - July

Whether or not you are a horse racing fan, you should visit the races at least once to see Hong Kong's passion for gambling in action. Races are held on Wednesdays, Saturdays and Sundays. Most weeks only have racing on one or two of those days, though, so check the fixtures calendar on their website to be sure. Major races include the Chinese New Year Race Meeting, the Hong Kong Derby, and the Queen Elizabeth II Cup.

International Arts Carnival

Various Locations
www.hkiac.gov.hk
July - August

Aimed at helping keep children busy over the summer vacation, there is fun for adults too. If your kids want to sit back and be entertained, there are performances by acrobats, and mime and comedy to choose from. If the performances inspire a more active approach, check the long list of workshops covering everything from mime and puppets to singing and clowning.

Lan Kwai Fong Julyfest

Lan Kwai Fong
www.lankwaifong.com
July

As Hong Kong's bar & club centre, you probably don't need an excuse to visit Lan Kwai Fong. Still, on this day things go that bit further, with stalls on the street serving food and drinks from lunchtime onwards. In the afternoon there is a variety of performances and competitions to keep you busy, with the party carrying on late into the night.

Mid-Autumn Festival

Various Locations
October (Lunar
calendar date)

The public holiday is the strangely named ' The day following Chinese Mid-Autumn Festival'. The reason is that on the evening of the actual festival children head to open spaces carrying lanterns, hoping to see the full moon. It's a late night for all, so the following day is a public holiday. It's a pretty sight to see all the lanterns lit up, so make the effort to get out for a walk in a park that evening – Victoria Park and the Peak are good bets.

Oxfam Trailwalker

MacLehose Trail
www.oxfamtrail
walker.org.hk
November

Teams of four aim to finish the 100km-long MacLehose hiking trail in under 48 hours. The fastest teams run it, and finish in under 14 hours. For most people the goal is simply to finish, regardless of the time taken. All teams are sponsored, raising money for Oxfam's various poverty alleviation and emergency relief projects.

MOTO**RAZR** *maxx V6*

Move faster with 3.5G HSDPA high speed mobile broadband, external touch music keys and a 2 mega-pixel camera with flash. **The new MOTORAZR maxx V6. Cutting-edge speed for cutting-edge style.**

hellomoto.com

AES INTERNATIONAL

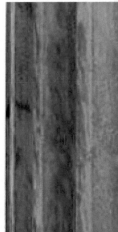

Individual Solutions...

...for individual clients

- Savings and Investments
- Offshore Banking
- Foreign Exchange
- Financial Planning
- Tax and Legal Advice
- Corporate Services

info@aesfinance.com   www.aesfinance.com

14 Rue Maunoir, 1207 Geneva, Switzerland, TEL:+41 22 534 9474

Residents

Residents

Overview

Think Hong Kong and a number of images may come to mind. It's where the old world meets the new, where high-rise buildings and neon outline a maze of a city milling with locals and dotted with expatriates. The gateway to China or a historic throwback to British Colonialism, the island is undeniably the behemoth of the Far East. Hong Kong is a number of things: a financial hub, a safe city with a low crime rate, a stunning amalgamation of culture and noise. The island has developed at an astounding rate and top quality health and education facilities and a developed infrastructure make it the kind of place you'd want to call home.

With a vibrant and burgeoning China across the border promising opportunities and new challenges, Hong Kong continues to attract new residents. Fear of China's control and interference after the 'handing over' in 1997 is a thing of the past.

Hong Kong is an exotic, attractive and exciting destination and seldom do people pass up the opportunity to move here. It's an attractive and exciting destination because of the many conveniences it offers. You can have a lifestyle that's a good mix of both East and West, and Hong Kong is one of the few places in Asia where people stay on and make it their permanent home, happily and contentedly.

Like any booming city, space here is like gold dust. Living in an apartment block may mean sacrificing room to swing a cat for proximity to the downtown area and of course some of the most breathtaking views, good amenities and well-managed housing. Lest we mislead you, Hong Kong carries hefty rent prices and expensive private schooling. The better schools often have long waiting lists, so do your research and plan ahead. The Asian Financial Crisis of 1997 took its toll as companies downsized and expatriate packages changed, but now, as the economy is picking up, expanding housing allowances and generous relocation packages are making a comeback.

Before You Arrive

So you're moving, congratulations and hooray! Be warned though, space is tight in Hong Kong, and with high humidity for much of the year it's not the best place to bring everything and your kitchen sink. What to bring and what to leave behind is every expat's dilemma. Another important thing is to tie up all your domestic business before you leave home. Here are some things to consider before you arrive:

- Double check you have all your documents and certificates attested, and make lots of copies
- Bring plenty of passport photos – you're going to need them
- Find out your tax status early so you don't get stung when you get home
- Get your finances in order, and make sure your bank is aware of your move
- Check the situation regarding pension payments
- Consider renting out your property in your home country, rather than selling
- One option is to buy an open return air ticket. That way you can go home for your

---

Urban Myths

Don't believe everything you hear:

Mandarin is the official language...
Not exactly – a good grasp of Mandarin will certainly get you far in China, and may better your chances in Hong Kong, but officially it's Cantonese (and English) that you need to be getting your tongue around.

Hong Kong is overcrowded and dirty...
Nope, not any more and it's down to the 2003 SARS (Severe Acute Respiratory System) outbreak, which forced a major clean up. The place is now practically squeaking.

Chinese people are rude...
This is a massive misconception and one that's normally wrongly picked up from the pace and tone of the language. The Chinese are actually incredibly friendly, hospitable and if they speak English, will have you nattering for ages, especially in Hong Kong.

---

holiday and re-buy a ticket from home – which is much cheaper than buying a ticket from Hong Kong

- Try and get your shipping done in advance so you're not waiting too long for your belongings when you get to your new home
- Get reports and transfer letters from your children's school. Some schools will be happy to send them straight to Hong Kong

Of course you could skip much of this fuss and fuddle by hiring a professional mover that will do all of this for you! (See Relocation Company numbers on p.110)

When You Arrive

Setting up home, finding your way around and meeting people in Hong Kong is not that big a challenge. This is an expat-friendly place where foreigners themselves have set up services and businesses designed to assist in every step of your new life, so you can go the easy route or turn this into a real adventure.

Here's some of the key issues you should be covering:

Residency/visas – if you are coming to Hong Kong to start a new job then your employer should arrange your visa (p.60). Once that is sorted you can then sponsor your dependents (p.60). Residents must then apply for a Hong Kong ID card (p.61).

Furnish your new home and get connected – for advice on furnishing your new place and getting the electric, gas, water, phone and TV connected, turn to the Setting Up Home section starting on p.110.

Motoring – if you plan to drive in Hong Kong then you'll need the correct licence (p.62), and you'll either be hiring (p.158) or buying (p.158) a car.

Register with your consulate – this is necessary for tax exemptions (if you qualify) and for any just-in-case safety scenarios. See p.27 for contact details.

Make friends – to help you settle into your new life there are plenty of social groups and associations that you can join. See p.262 for details.

Copious Copies

During the first few weeks in town you'll get through quite a few copies of your essential documents, as they're needed almost every time you apply for something. There are plenty of places for making copies of your documents, but the prices can vary from 50c to $2. On the second floor of the Immigration Tower in Wan Chai you can have copies made for $1 each.

Essential Documents

The most essential document for living and working in Hong Kong is your passport with a valid visa. This enables you to get resident status and qualifies you to apply for an identity card. If you are planning on getting a driver's licence then be sure to bring your current and valid licence from your home country.

If you are accompanying a spouse, you'll need your birth and marriage certificate in order to process your visa. All the necessary paperwork for you and your dependents, including birth certificates, marriage certificates, university certificates and affidavits may well have been submitted to the personnel department of your company who will apply for this visa for you and your family.

Hong Kong's flag

All documents to be submitted must be in English or Chinese. If they are not, then get them translated and certified by a relevant government agency or at your consulate before you leave your home country.

57

When You Leave

Leaving us already?! Be organised and cover all bases. Use our checklist as a starting point.

Some things to do at least a couple of months before you leave:

- Notify your landlord.
- Select a moving company and get a quote from several to compare prices.
- Determine the number of days needed for packing and then fix a date to start.
- Decide what you want to do with all your belongings. Make a list of the things you want to sell on, ship and store. The earlier you start selling things, or at least advertising, the better your chances of making some money back – you can sell anything in Hong Kong. Other expats prefer to buy used furniture and appliances, since many are here short term and are looking for a bargain.
- Make alternate accommodation arrangements for when the house is packed.
- Make an inventory of precious items like antiques and jewellery and have them valued for insurance purposes.
- Make an inventory of other household goods for insurance purposes.
- Make a list of things that will accompany you, to be packed separately.
- Advertise your sale items in magazines and newspapers, and email your friends and put notices in your building and supermarkets.
- Make arrangements for your pet to be exported home through pet companies.
- Notify phone, electricity and telephone companies about the disconnection date.
- Note down the number on your gas meter and the date of disconnection notice for all utilities so you are not charged for extra days.
- Collect all house keys to hand over to the landlord.
- Be sure to have the house cleaned up before you leave.
- Close your bank accounts and inform schools, doctors, dentists, clubs and organisations about your move.
- Cancel your newspaper and other subscriptions.
- Help your domestic help to find suitable employment.

Legislative Council Building

Immigration ◀
Department
*The Immigration
Department is located
in Immigration Tower,
7 Gloucester Road,
Wan Chai. Telephone
2829 3223.*

Entry Visa

Other options **Visas** p.21

The visa that you use to enter Hong Kong will depend on many factors, including whether you're here to visit, to work, or to join your spouse or parents (or children) as a dependant. One important point to remember is that your passport must be valid for six months or more to apply for any visa.

Examples of visas include:

- **Visit Visa** – citizens of several countries are allowed to visit Hong Kong and stay 'visa-free' for between seven and 180 days. These include the UK (180 days), Australia, France, Germany, Italy, Singapore, Spain, and the US (90 days), South Africa (30 days) and India and the Philippines (up to 14 days). A full list of nationalities and visa requirements can be found at www.immd.gov.hk/ehtml/hkvisas_4.htm. If you don't qualify for a visa-free stay then you can apply at the Chinese embassy or consulate in your home country, a friend or business contact in Hong Kong can sponsor you and apply for a visa on your behalf, or you can download form ID(E)936 from www.immd.gov.hk and mail it to the Immigration Department once completed. The application process can take up to four weeks, and once the visa is ready it will be posted to you. Note that people already in Hong Kong on a visitor's visa (irrespective of nationality) are not permitted to change to an employment visa without leaving and re-entering first.
- **Employment Visa** – if you are coming to Hong Kong to take up a new job then your employer should have taken care of all the paperwork before your arrival (p.56). Once you're here you should begin the process of applying for an ID card (p.61). As an employed resident you can then sponsor your dependants (p.60).
- **Dependant/Residency Visa** – this applies to the spouses and children (and sometimes parents) of Hong Kong residents. See p.60 for details.

Remember that visa requirements can change from time to time, so check with the Hong Kong Immigration Department or with the Chinese Embassy in your home country before applying.

Some companies and consultants that specialise in visas and immigration matters include Dearson Winyard International (3101 7616, www.dwiglobal.com), Emigré Asia Services (2783 7183) and Expat Strategies (2834 3100, www.expatstrategies.com). The Immigration Advice Centre number is 2801 7316.

Other Types of Entry Permit

- **Capital Investment Entrant Scheme** – applicants must have had net assets of not less than $6.5 million for at least two years before applying.
- **Domestic Help Visa** – valid for a two-year domestic work contract.
- **Entry for Investment Visa** – those setting up a business can get a visa, providing they fulfil certain criteria.
- **Freelancers' Visa** – valid for one year at a time, but you will need a sponsor, and you have to explain to the Immigration Department what you will be doing in Hong Kong.
- **HKSAR Travel Pass** – makes it easier for frequent business travellers to enter Hong Kong (holders can enter through the 'resident' channel at the airport).
- **Re-Entry Permits** – if non-permanent residents return within 12 months, residential status is unaffected. If it is over that period and the visa has expired, then a call to immigration is required.
- **Training Visa** – valid for up to one month, for people who cannot get similar training in their own country.
- **Working Holiday Scheme** – this scheme is between New Zealand, Australia and Ireland. It's valid for 12 months and can be used by applicants just the once.

59

Residence Visa

Other options **Visas** p.21

In Hong Kong there are two categories of 'expat' resident. Firstly, there are permanent residents who can live and work without a visa (but can't be away from Hong Kong for more three years). This permanent residence status is granted to people who have lived in Hong Kong continuously for seven years, and who fulfil certain requirements set by Immigration, such as proving you intend to make Hong Kong your home, you speak the language and so on. This isn't set in stone so be aware of changes and amendments.

The second type is the resident who has a straightforward employment visa that allows them to live and work in Hong Kong, and to sponsor a spouse and children. However, should that person lose their employment status, they also lose their visa.

Employment Visa

To get an employment visa you must have a job in a company that is willing to sponsor you and carry out the application process. The application will be submitted for you, and you're not required to be in the country. Your passport copy, birth certificate copy, attested degree certificates, the sponsoring company's employment letter and the relevant forms and fee will be submitted to the Immigration Department to start the process. The Immigration Department reviews the application and necessary documents to see that you have the relevant skills and experience for the job, and are sufficiently qualified with the necessary level of education. Before issuing an employment visa they will also consider your suitability for the job, how you'll contribute favourably to Hong Kong, and if that job can be filled from local sources. The Immigration Department will also ask for a confirmed offer of employment, and proof that the remuneration package includes salary, accommodation, medical and education allowances, as well as other benefits appropriate for professionals in Hong Kong. You'll also need to have a clean criminal record, and have lived abroad (outside of China and Macau) for one year or more.

The application process takes four to six weeks, after which an entry visa label will be issued to the sponsor (your employer) who should then send it to you, ready for your arrival in Hong Kong. Once you get your visa, you can apply for residency for your spouse and children under 18 (see below) and apply for your Hong Kong ID card (p.61).

Dependant Visa

A Hong Kong resident holding a work or business visa can apply to sponsor their dependants for residency; that is, his or her spouse, and children below the age of 18. A Hong Kong *permanent* resident is also permitted to sponsor his or her parents aged 60 or above. Whether you are coming together or joining later, for the first visa application you'll need passports and birth certificates (or copies) and a marriage certificate. The Immigration Department will require proof that the sponsor is able to support the dependants, and that the dependant has no criminal record. The relevant application form is available from the Immigration Department, and can also be downloaded from the website (www.immd.gov.hk). There was some good news in 2006, when the government announced that dependant spouses of those holding work visas would be allowed to find employment, whereas previously this was not allowed.

The Whole World's Your Home

Explorer Residents' Guides are going global with new titles for locations as far flung as Dublin and New Zealand in the pipeline. So if you fancy living abroad check out the complete list of current and upcoming Explorer guides on our website ***www.explorer publishing.com*** Remember life's a trip…all you need to do is pick a destination.

ID Card

The Immigration Department requires that all residents, aged 11 and above, register for a Hong Kong Identity Card. There are two types of card – one states that the holder has 'the right of permanent abode in the Hong Kong Special Administrative Region,' whereas the other does not. The website www.immd.gov.hk explains the process.

To register for a card you can make an appointment by phone on 2598 0888, via the website www.esd.gov.hk, or head down to one of the five 'Registration of Persons' offices (we advise you arrive for opening) and wait for as long as it takes. Be warned though, if you do this you run the risk of leaving empty handed, since the offices have a daily quota which they could reach before you are seen. The whole process takes a little over an hour at the most, and all you need to take is your passport with a valid visa. There is no fee (unless you're replacing a card that has been lost or damaged).

Once you've completed the forms, the photographing and the fingerprinting, you'll be given a temporary identity receipt, which serves as proof of having applied, and a date on which the card can be collected. If you can't go on the allotted day, someone with an identity card can collect it for you, as long as they have a letter of authorisation from you and the temporary ID receipt. The ID card is valid for as long as you are resident in Hong Kong, and you should carry it with you when you go out.

Some points to be aware of:
• If a card-holder dies overseas, Immigration must be notified so that the card can be cancelled.
• If you lose your card or it gets damaged, the replacement fee is $395.
• New cards are now being issued, called Smart Identity Cards. They have an embedded chip with the holder's information. These are swiped in machines at the airport or border crossing by train or ferries into China.

ID Card Offices
There are five 'Registration of Persons' offices. The website www.immd.gov.hk has location maps and opening hours. The Wan Chai office is on 8/F, Immigration Tower, 7 Gloucester Road – an address you may become quite familiar with during your first few weeks in Hong Kong! Office locations and numbers:
Wan Chai – 2824 6111
Sham Shui Po – 2150 7933
Kwun Tong – 2755 9545
Fo Tan – 2653 3116
Yuen Long – 2475 4114

Health Insurance

The Hong Kong government healthcare system is modern and fairly inexpensive, but expats are not expected to use it. In fact, it is a criterion for employers in Hong Kong to make sure their foreign employees are not a burden on the local healthcare system. You should therefore have private health coverage through your employer, and consult only private doctors on your own or as recommended by your company. There are many private hospitals, like the Adventist, Matilda and Canossa, that are used by expats, and healthcare clinics too. See p.131 for more details. Many insurance plans from your home country may also cover medical bills abroad, so be sure to ask ahead before you arrive in Hong Kong.

A standard health insurance plan through your company is more than likely to cover general consultation with a reimbursement of up to 80% of the fees. It differs from company to company on how they deal with coverage for pregnancy, accidents, emergencies, check-ups, alternative consultation and dental care. Be sure to ask so you're clear on what's what. If you have to get your own coverage, there are many health insurance packages to choose from. They differ in cost, so shop around. Talk to a few and compare the plans before choosing. Some of the plans do not cover dental or maternity; others are all-inclusive. If your company has group coverage you get discounts for a larger group. Coverage can be annual or monthly and can be anywhere from $30,000 to $200,000.

It is worth remembering that if you employ and sponsor a domestic helper, then it is your responsibility to provide them with health insurance. See the table of Health Insurance Companies on p.126.

Driving Licence

Other options **Transportation** p.156

Other options **Transportation** p.156

Government Approved Test Centres

Government approved driving test centres include Happy Valley Driving Test Centre (2574 5857), Chung Yee Street Driving Test Centre, Ho Man Tin (2711 7670) and the Hong Kong School of Motoring test centres in Sha Tin (2636 1721) and Yuen Long (2442 5622).

International Licence

For an international driving licence you need two photographs, $80 and to have filled out the relevant application form available from the Transport Department. An international licence is valid for one year and is not transferable.

Permanent Licence

As a foreigner, you can apply for a full driving licence without a test if you already hold a valid licence from approved countries (see the list on p.64) and are over 18 years of age. Your licence must be current and valid (or not have expired more than three years ago). You must hold a passport of the licence issuing country and have lived in that country after it was issued for no less than six months, and held the licence for five years or more. If your licence is not in English, you'll need to have it officially translated.

A form filled in with your personal details, the original and photocopies of your driving licence, identity card, passport and $900 cash or cheque made out to 'The Government of the Hong Kong Special Administrative Region' should be submitted to the Transport Department on the 3rd floor of United Centre in Admiralty. For those 60 years and above, the fee is $52 per year. It takes three weeks to process and is valid for 10 years, but must be renewed at least four months before it expires. If you leave and return, the licence is renewable unless it expired more than three years ago. If you lose your licence or change your address, you should report this to the Transport Department. Their website is www.td.gov.hk and the 24 hour hotline is 2804 2600.

Licence and Registration

The rules and laws of driving are strictly adhered to. While there are no spot checks, you can be stopped even for the most minor of violations. Always have your identity card and driving licence with you and be sure to have your car registration and insurance papers on hand.

Driving Schools

City Driving School	Wan Chai	2838 1133	www.citydrivingschool.com.hk
Henry Driving School	Causeway Bay	9091 1755	na
HK School of Motoring	Aberdeen	2555 8306	www.hksm.com.hk
International Driving	Kowloon City	2715 0972	www.i-learndrive.com.hk

Temporary licence

If your country is not on the approved list (see p.64), you can obtain a temporary licence that lasts for three months and allows you to drive while you arrange to take a driving test. If you do not pass the test, you will need to reapply for a new temporary licence and take the test again within the three months of validity.

Learner's Licence

A Learner's Licence is valid for 12 months from the date of issue, and only when driving in the company of a qualified driving instructor and in a specified vehicle.

Motorcycle Licence

Two compulsory courses for motorcycle training have to be passed through the HK School of Motoring, a government-recognised school. The first is a an oral course on understanding the skills of manoeuvring a motorcycle and the second is learning techniques to ride in a city. A learner's driving licence costs $548, plus another $260 for renting a motorcycle for a road test. The first year licence is probationary. Note that wearing a helmet is compulsory for all motorcyclists.

62

The WALKMAN® logo and symbol are registered trademarks of Sony Corporation.

I  beautiful music

Music now looks as beautiful as it sounds. The new W880i Walkman® phone with up to 900 songs, it's just as beautiful on the inside.

sonyericsson.com/walkman

Sony Ericsson

◄ **Automatic Licence Transfer**
List of approved countries: Australia, Austria, Belgium, Bangladesh, Canada, China, Denmark, Finland, France, Germany, India, Ireland, Israel, Italy, Japan, Korea, Luxembourg, Malaysia, Netherlands, New Zealand, Nigeria, Norway, Pakistan, Portugal, Singapore, Spain, Sweden, Switzerland, South Africa, United Kingdom, United States

Car Driving Test

For a driving test, an application form should be filled out and submitted to a licensing office. This is valid for 18 months and if you fail or miss the test you have to apply again, unless you give sufficient notice or have a health problem. (If you do miss your test, send a letter to the Commissioner of Transport and if accepted, a new date will be set). There are three parts to the driving test. The first part is written, the second is an exam on driving techniques on and off the road and finally there is the practical road test. The Hong Kong Driving Guide is available in bookshops for $88 and serves as a useful navigational tool for the streets of Hong Kong, so keep a copy in your car. If you are a new driver or are new to Hong Kong, get a copy of the Road User's Guide available at the Transport Department office in Admiralty for $100. This will help you with road signs and driving rules.

There are two types of car test: one for automatics and another for manual cars. If you pass the manual test you can also drive an automatic car, but not vice versa.

Licensing Offices	
Hong Kong Island	2804 2600
Kowloon	2150 7728
Kwun Tong	2775 6835
Sha Tin	2606 1468

Birth Certificate & Registration

Every district in Hong Kong has its own hospital, so the birth of your baby is recorded by the hospital and the details sent to the district registrar for the preparation of the birth certificate. Hong Kong local law requires that your child be registered locally in the district in which they were born within 42 days of birth (see www.immd.gov.hk/ehtml/bdmreg_1.htm).

The birth certificate takes at least two weeks to prepare and can be collected at the registrar office in your district by either parent. Be sure to bring your marriage certificate, your passport (both parents if possible, originals and copies) and Hong Kong identity cards.

District Registering Hospitals

On Hong Kong Island the District Registering Hospitals are Canossa Hospital, Matilda Hospital, Queen Mary Hospital, Adventist Hospital, Hong Kong Sanatorium & Hospital, St Paul's Hospital, Pamela Youde Nethersole Eastern Hospital. In the Kowloon and Tsuen Wan districts there is the St Teresa Hospital, Kwong Wah Hospital, Queen Elizabeth Hospital, United Christian Hospital, Baptist Hospital, Princess Margaret Hospital and the Tsuen Wan Adventist Hospital. In the Sha Tin, Tai Po, Fanling and Sheung Shui districts you'll find the Prince of Wales Hospital, Sha Tin International Medical Centre Union Hospital and the Alice Ho Miu Ling Nethersole Hospital. In the Tuen Mun and Yuen Long districts there's Tuen Mun Hospital. See the hospital listings starting on p.128 for contact details.

It is important to apply for your child's passport as early as possible. In the case of urgent, unexpected travel, your child will need a passport. And you may need to secure a visa for your child, which also requires a passport. As soon as you have the first set of paperwork complete, you'll need to notify your embassy. Parents from different countries have to decide which embassy to register with. It is common practice to go with the father's nationality, but this is not written in stone. Once one passport is done, most embassies will allow you to apply for dual-citizenship for your little one. It's best to do one at a time.

Procedures will differ from country to country so it's best to find out how your consulate deals with these things ahead of time. Be sure to enquire about the cost (it varies widely), and if the baby gets a separate passport or if he or she will go on the mothers passport up to a certain age (usually 12). You'll need your marriage certificate, passports and Hong Kong identity cards as well as the child's birth certificate when applying for a passport. Parents do not have to be married but there are certain formalities, so check with your consulate/embassy in advance (especially for paperwork requirements). You need to bring the mother's Hong Kong ID card and, at either the father's or mother's request, a court order confirming the child's father/mother or a written statement from the father/mother if either want to be on the certificate. For more information on the registrations of births, deaths and adoption, as well as certified copies, contact The Births & Death General Register Office in Queensway (2867 2785).

Dependant Visa ◀

The process is the same as for spouse visas and should be taken care of by the sponsor. If you decide to give birth abroad and are returning to Hong Kong, you should get your baby's passport while you are away as well as a dependant visa for Hong Kong, similar to your own.

Citizenship

Even if your child is born in Hong Kong, this does not grant automatic citizenship or residency. A person under 21 years born in Hong Kong to a parent who is a permanent resident of the HKSAR in category D, before or after the establishment of the HKSAR, has the right to citizenship if at the time of his/her birth (or at any later time before the age of 21 years), one of his/her parents earns the Right Of Abode in Hong Kong. This type of permanent residency will expire once they are 21 years of age, but he/she can then apply to the Director of Immigration for the status of a permanent resident under category D at any time.

Christenings

Whatever your faith, there are churches, mosques, synagogues and temples where your child can be initiated into your religious affiliation. Call to check about bookings, procedure and payment for these ceremonies. See the Places of Worship table on p.17.

Adoption

Expats wanting to adopt in Hong Kong must have spent at least 12 months or more in the country. The Social Welfare Department Adoption Unit (2852 3107) handles the process from A to Z. Once you've made your decision and are sure you want to go ahead, you can attend a briefing session where you'll fill in a short application form, followed by a lengthy 16 page application. A caseworker will contact you for home study and a final interview and you will have to pay a court fee of $2,840. If the child is adopted from abroad, the Social Welfare Department contacts the International Social Services who will prepare all the paperwork. Orphanages include Mother's Choice (2537 7633), Po Leung Kok (2277 8888), Christopher's Home (2520 1056) and Evangel Children's Home (2323 8224). Adoptive Families of Hong Kong (9100 8095) is a support group that meets a few times a year.

What's in a Name?

After marriage, many women keep their maiden names and avoid the hassle of changing passports, identity cards and bank accounts until they start a family or return home. If you decide to change yours, you'll need a new identity card. For this, you'll need the marriage certificate, proof that your husband can support you if you're not working, and your old identity card.

Registry Offices

Marriage Registration and Records Office, Queensway	2867 2787
City Hall, Central	2523 0725
Cotton Tree Drive, Central	2869 0725
Hong Kong Cultural Centre, Tsim Sha Tsui	2312 0929
Sha Tin Town Hall, Sha Tin	2604 6974
Tuen Mun Government Offices, Tuen Mun	2451 3005

The Cost of ◀
Getting Married

When you get married you'll have a few fees to pay. First you'll need to pay a filing and exhibition of notice fee of $305. An application for marriage will cost you $140 and a certificate of marriage registration costs $325.

Marriage Certificate & Registration

Getting Married

Whatever your faith, when you want to get married in Hong Kong you'll find the religious establishment of your affiliation. There are churches, mosques, temples, synagogues and the government registry, all located in main commercial and residential areas. See the Places of Worship table on p.17 for contact details.

Many expats go home to get married, others plan spiritual or dream weddings in many of the exotic resorts around South East Asia.

Getting married in Hong Kong is an expensive affair. As soon as the date is set, health check-ups and weight loss programmes become incredibly popular, and the spending begins. Clothes and accessories, whether you order a gown or hire one, are pricey. So too are invites, photographers, flowers, food and musicians. If you are pressed for time and have the cash, save yourself the headache and hire a wedding planner to do it all for you!

Living in Sin
There is no law against couples living together without being married. It's an open and free environment. Though local traditional values prevail, they do not apply to foreigners.

The Paperwork

The legal age for getting married is 16. While Muslims, Hindus, Buddhists and Jews have their religious ceremonies; churches in Hong Kong will only perform a religious ceremony once the civil ceremony has taken place. This can be arranged through the Marriage Registration and Records Office, as well as in the City Hall Marriage Registry or Cotton Tree Drive Marriage Registry (see p.65). You can get certificates for absence of marriage records and certified copies of marriage certificates here. You can book the registry online by visiting http://wedding.esdlife.com/home/eng/default.asp. This is a nifty way of doing things since the website will tell you immediately if your dates are available, and if not you can keep trying till you find a day that is. You'll receive a confirmation and that's your cue to go along to the registry to fix the time for the ceremony. Be warned, if you get no confirmation of this online booking, don't assume – call and check that it went through. You can book up to three months in advance. A notice of the marriage is then displayed in the registrar's office for three weeks.

You then have three months in which to get married. Otherwise you will have to register a second time and pay the fees again. A civil celebrant will perform the ceremony for a fee. You can find one through the registry or visit www.hklawsoc.org.hk.

Once all is done and you have your marriage certificate, you can proceed with a religious ceremony. Yet again, book well ahead of time, at least three, if not six months earlier. All arrangements like flowers, choir and organ player will be at your expense. There is no fixed cost for the ceremony but a donation is expected.

Muslims can arrange for a maulvis to perform the nikah but don't need to go to the mosque. Call the Islamic Union of Hong Kong (2575 2218) to find out about availability and cost.

Chinese Wedding Superstitions
Choosing a lucky date with a feng shui master is a norm if you are marrying a Chinese person. If you see a park with many brides, you'll know it's an auspicious day to get married. Clocks are a big faux pas as a gift and are considered extremely bad luck. Giving cash is the norm. Clean, crisp notes of $100 bills in a red envelope, available in local stationery shops, is the most common present. The number four should also be avoided as it sounds like the word for death in Chinese whilst the number eight is considered very lucky, so an amount like $800 or $208 would be perfect.

The Jewish wedding ceremony, Hatuna, takes place at the synagogue. It's recommended to book in advance. The best person to call is Rabbi David Kopstein (2117 2415 or 2523 2985). A donation equivalent to the United Jewish Club joining fee is expected if you or your partner are a not member of the congregation.

The Hindu mandir (2572 5284) and the Sikh gurdwara (2572 4459) have marriage halls where priests perform ceremonies, but the expense of food and entertainment is entirely yours. Book well ahead of time.

The registries in the table on p.65 are venues for marriage ceremonies and also provide marriage certificates.

Death Certificate & Registration

In The Event of a Death

The first thing you need to do is to call someone. Very few doctors make house visits but many clinics and hospital emergencies are open round the clock. When a person dies at home, you can call an ambulance on 999, or the St John Ambulance Service on 2576 6555 (Hong Kong), 2713 5555 (Kowloon), or 2639 2555 (New Territories). Queen Mary Hospital's Emergency Services are on 2855 3838.

Traffic Accidents

The Hong Kong Police are doing everything to minimise accidents through education and improved road signs and systems. Out in the New Territories where there are highways and flyovers, fatal accidents involving large trucks and cars are a reality, especially on flyovers without dividers, at sharp bends and uphill and downhill curves. See the statistics info on p.161.

Investigation & Autopsy

If death occurred suddenly, through violent or accidental circumstances, or suicide, the police will have to be involved and a full investigation will proceed, including a coroner's autopsy. An inquest will only be requested if the death took place under dubious or suspicious circumstances. The Hong Kong Police and judiciary system are efficient and tactful, offering legal advice and so on. You can contact the Coroner's Court in Wan Ho at 2886 6871.

If you are not satisfied with the investigation you can make a complaint through the Independent Police Complaints Council (IPCC) on 2866 7700. They provide a 24 hour service.

Registering A Death

Death from natural causes such as illness must be registered within 24 hours in the district's registry. This report is also sent to the coroner who investigates the cause of death and informs the registrar. The death is registered within a week and the deceased's relatives are informed of the cause by letter.

To register a death you must have the medical certificate of Cause of Death signed by the registered doctor, the Hong Kong identity card or travel document of the deceased and information on occupation, nationality, age and marital status. The person registering the death must also show their own Hong Kong identity card or a travel document. The Death Certificate costs $170 in Hong Kong and $275 if the application is made from overseas.

Returning The Deceased to their Country of Origin

You'll need to apply for a Permit of Removal of Dead Body from Hong Kong if the body is to be moved to another country. Fill in application form (SF/BDR/3) from the Immigration Department with information about when and where the body will be taken. Sometimes immigration will ask to see the permission for entry in that country before issuing the permit.

There is no fee for this permit. The coroner will issue a certificate that shows death did not occur through any communicable disease ten days after the post mortem report. This certificate can then be used to transport the body for burial. Urgent but normal death registration for all districts is available at the Births and Deaths General Register Office in Admiralty. See the table below for contact details.

Local Burial Services

The Hong Kong Funeral Home (2561 5227) arranges traditional western funerals. For Muslims, the Islamic Union (2575 2218) arranges burial services, or you can contact the Muslim Cemetery manager (2575 2967). Contact the HK Cemeteries and Crematoria Office (Hong Kong 2570 4318, Kowloon 2570 4318) for coffin burials. Temples, synagogues and churches also hold burial services. Contact your religious establishment to check on ceremony arrangements, booking and cost (normally in the form of a donation). See the Places of Worship table on p.17.

Cremation

An appointment can be made with The Food and Environmental Hygiene Department for cremation in an area of your choice and through registered undertakers. (Hong Kong 2570 4318, Kowloon 2365 5321, New Territories 2150 7502).

Organ Donation

The Chinese believe the body should be buried whole with no missing parts, so organ donation is not common and there is a long list of people waiting for donors. If you wish to become a donor, contact the Hong Kong Medical Association (2527 8285). A form will be scanned into the system and hospitals linked to this system can access the information.

Birth & Death Registration Services

The Births and Deaths General Register Office	Kowloon	2961 8841
The Births and Deaths General Register Office	Cheung Sha Wan	2368 4706
The Births and Deaths General Register Office	Admiralty	2867 2785

Keeping it in the Family ◀

There was a time when expats employed only expats because there were plenty of them around and no visa hassles, but many of these have long gone. With more Chinese companies on the market, employing Chinese nationals is the trend. Much sought after, they have the language skills and qualifications and can integrate into both worlds comfortably.

Working in Hong Kong

Hong Kong is an attractive relocation spot. It is home to many international companies, because of its sound legal and financial infrastructure, low tax, reasonably stable government and its geographic location. Foreigners and locals have worked side by side for close to two centuries, with few frustrations and big rewards.

The 1990s

The late 90s was a time marred with doubt, fear of change and the unknown, as Hong Kong was due to return to China. By 1997 localisation of jobs in the government sector had already begun and expats became an expensive and often futile commodity. But that was still no deterrent. Though opportunities were slim, they were still there for the picking.

China's economic birth had begun and fully operational Special Economic Zones began to spring up on the mainland. Hong Kong was flooded with multinational companies and opportunity seekers and backpackers continued to be drawn in.

Soon after the handover to China, the fear factor kicked in for real. Uncertain of what would happen under the Chinese government, people and companies began to move out. As quickly as it had sprung, it had plummeted. The Asian economy took a massive downturn and the stock market fell. The property market shifted and landlords were left holding properties that would never cost the same astronomical amount again. Recession hit and hundreds of expats were made redundant as companies downsized.

A Decade Later

Today, strong economic recovery is pushing up rents, construction is in full swing, stock markets are high and the good times are rolling. People remain cautious however and things have changed for expats. Previosly, foreign workers walked straight into jobs, often not requiring a visa to enter or work. Stories abound about backpackers who became managing directors.

It's a little different now. Immigration laws are strict and though citizens of some countries are allowed visa-free stays, many need sponsored visas. In order to work here you have to be a professional with good qualifications and proven experience. Ideally you'll be given a complete expat package so as not to be a burden to social security, but at the very least the Immigration Department will need to be convinced that you'll contribute to Hong Kong's economy. Immigration also needs to be satisfied that this position can't be filled locally before permitting an expat to be employed. Even volunteer work now requires approval from Immigration.

Language is another important requirement. Almost all jobs require either Cantonese or Mandarin, or both, as well as English. More doors open to you if you can speak a local language. Degrees are worshipped and the Ivy League colleges of the US are much revered. Companies are also positioned differently. Previously it was the norm for expats in Hong Kong to have every perk imaginable but now many get just a basic salary. Some companies, especially investment banks, offer cushy packages including medical, housing, paid annual holidays to the home country, and education for children. Others may include perks like expensive apartments, a car and driver, entertainment allowances, club membership and sometimes biannual paid home leave. Don't get too excited though – this type of deal is likely to be for a short assignment or for a senior position. You could be offered a local package, which may not include housing, medical and education or annual home leave. If you still want to move here, prioritise. Decide why Hong Kong, what you hope to gain out of your stay here and what you may be prepared to sacrifice for the opportunity.

Cross-Cultural Frustrations

Not knowing the local language very often leads to frustrations and misunderstanding. Work ethics are deeply embedded in the Asian values of hierarchy, where the divide is wide between management and personnel. This extends to behaviour, communication and management style. Seniors are not addressed by first name and are expected to be reserved and formal at all times. Some companies provide cross-cultural orientations that can be helpful in understanding and managing office staff and conducting meetings but most do not, and often the culture shock will leave you stumped for a while.

Making it on Your Own ◄

It is said that Hong Kong is a place where you can find opportunities and create openings. You can do anything here - from relocation companies to drama clubs. Businesses often become regional as expanding into neighbouring countries like Macau, Thailand and Singapore is the next obvious step once Hong Kong has been taken care of.

Competition in the Job Market

Competition has shifted into the Chinese scene. The talk is now about competition between local, mainland and overseas Chinese as the government now has a talent scheme to allow people from the mainland with specific experience and skills to work in Hong Kong if needed. Mainland Chinese who have lived abroad for more than a year are also allowed to come and work in Hong Kong if they have a much-needed qualification. Expats are not only competing with other expats but with the Chinese as well and tend to lose out because of the language skill. If companies can find someone locally with the same qualifications, they will, rather than recruit from abroad. Some multinationals continue to keep expats from the home country in certain positions, especially senior positions but they employ non-managerial and other staff locally.

Business Culture & Etiquette

- Business cards are an important part of the business culture. Have them printed in English on one side and Chinese on the other and present them with both hands. The Chinese write their family names first, then the given name that is either Chinese or Christian.
- Suits are worn in most offices, and most definitely for business meetings. For women, trouser or skirt suits and dark shoes would be appropriate.
- A Chinese banquet of eight to 10 courses is often the norm for overseas business visitors, so get your belly ready.

Full of Pros ◄

Often referred to as an employees' market, Hong Kong has plenty of qualified and experienced locals and foreigners. Employment agencies can give you an idea of the market scale of salaries for different jobs. Check the dailies like the South China Morning Post *on Saturdays and* Hong Kong Standard *on Fridays for job and salary listings.* Recruit *is available on Fridays in MTR stations.*

- Christmas office parties are celebrated in clubs or hotels with gift exchanges. Chinese New Year dinners are big events. You are expected to hand out 'lai see' (good luck money) – red packets with small amounts of bills to anyone junior to you and wish them 'Kung Hei Fat Choy'
- Chinese never open gifts in your presence; they will thank you but not talk about them.
- If you are handling business deals with Chinese be sure to get briefed about it. You must remember that even if the person is educated abroad and westernised, their thinking may not be the same as yours – don't assume anything.
- Saving face is very important and so admitting to being wrong or being confronted and made to lose face is not taken well and you will be looked upon negatively.
- Superstitious interpretations can be heard all the time but don't try to make sense of them, and attempt not to succumb to them.
- Don't be shocked if you are asked personal questions like how much money you earn and how much your accessories or clothes cost. It's perfectly normal here and isn't considered rude or prying.
- Be careful what you talk about, it may be a topic that shocks them. So listen first and follow your host's lead.
- Women are a strong working force here, holding senior positions in banks and government jobs. Several professional women's organizations are set up and for many women it's a forum for networking and support.

Unions

Workers' unions are few and not vocal or strong so you'll often hear stories of labour exploitation such as being overworked and underpaid with not enough holidays. The Labour Department does routine checks and employers are subject to fines if found to be out of line.

Setting-up A Business

Hong Kong is famous for being one of the freest economies in the world with the lowest tax rates of all Asian countries and one of the lowest in the world too. Income from business profits, salary and property in Hong Kong is taxed and the amount is assessed on the basis of the fiscal year starting on April 1st. Dividends to shareholders here or overseas, and overseas branch profits brought in to Hong Kong, as well as capital gains, are not taxed.

Immigration and Inland Revenue rules are simple and straightforward. There are no hefty fees to pay either. As long as you fulfil the entry criteria set out by the Immigration Department and get your paperwork done properly with the Inland Revenue Department, you'll be clear of any problems and obtain a company incorporation certificate. There are no long drawn-out glitches or bureaucratic run-arounds in getting a business registered and up and running.

The award winning government organisation Invest Hong Kong (www.investhk.gov.hk) was set up in 2000 to invite businesses to set up in Hong Kong and assist them through the process. They will help partnerships, sole proprietorships, joint venturess, private limited companies, and overseas branches or representative offices.

To start and register a new company in Hong Kong, you need a name, a memorandum of Articles of Association, to pay the required fee and get the Certificate of Incorporation. All in all this takes about six working days.

Business Registration

Companies Registry Office	2867 4570	www.cr.gov.hk
Business Registration Office and New Business Enquiry	187 8088	www.ird.gov.hk
Business Licence Information Centre	2398 5133	www.success.tid.gov.hk
Invest Hong Kong	3107 1000	www.investhk.gov.hk
Hong Kong Trade and Industry Department	2392 2922	www.tid.gov.hk
Hong Kong SAR Government Information Centre	2842 8847	www.info.gov.hk

Working Hours

Though official working hours are 09:00 to 18:00, it's perfectly normal to have never left the office on time, especially if you are in a managerial role, and many offices have Saturday as a half working day. Banks and government offices are open till noon. Government Office working hours are normally 08:30 to 17:30, bank hours are from 09:00 to 17:00 and office hours 08:30 to 18:00. Staggered hours are not common but it depends on the company. Retail shops are open until 18:30 in business districts and until 21:00 in other commercial areas. The night markets close at midnight.

It's also not unusual to be asked to entertain visiting clients. The novelty wears off quickly but if you want to make something of yourself here, then elbow grease and some brow sweating is par for the course. Many companies regularly hold staff training seminars and workshops. The Hong Kong government sets all annual religious and national holidays. These are called statutory holidays and all employers, including employers of domestic helpers, must adhere to these dates. See p.11 for the dates of holidays.

Business Councils & Groups

American Chamber of Commerce	2526 0165	www.amcham.org.hk
Australian Chamber of Commerce	2522 5054	www.austcham.com.hk
British Chamber of Commerce	2824 2211	www.britcham.com
Canadian Chamber of Commerce	2110 8700	www.cancham.org
Chamber of Hong Kong Listed Companies	2970 0886	www.chklc.org
Chinese General Chamber of Commerce	2525 6385	www.cgcc.org.hk
Financial Women's Association	2813 4754	www.fwahk.org
HK General Chamber of Commerce	2529 9229	www.chamber.org.hk
HK Trade Development Council	183 0668	www.tdctrade.com
HK Women Professionals & Entrepreneurs Association	2289 3350	www.hkwpea.org
Women Business Owners Club (WBOC)	2541 0446	www.hkwboc.org

Networking

Try and get to as many events and social lunches as possible. The Chamber of Commerce and the embassies host regular networking events. Print your business cards in English and Chinese and hand them out as you go. Mingle and ask around about companies worth contacting. The lively areas of Lan Kwai Fong and Wan Chai should definitely be on your list. If all else fails, start cold calling. Forget the nerves and consider it tenacity.

Finding Work

While the economy has picked up, there are immigration rules in place that make finding work here tricky. Depending on your skills and qualifications, you can land a job from overseas but getting here and looking for a job can be an uphill struggle. Not too many employers want to get into the sponsoring role as it's a hassle convincing Immigration the position cannot be filled locally. If you are highly qualified in finance and IT, you could get lucky and find work in a multinational or Chinese company.

When you find a job, you'll have to wait till your sponsor applies for the visa and hope that it gets approved. You can't work till the visa is granted which can take about three to six months, depending on the job and the company. The visa is non-transferable so if you leave or lose your job, you won't be able to use it for another one.

Going it Alone

Writing, desktop publishing, copywriting, editing, ghost writing, photography and tutoring are just some of the areas you can work in. Competition is pretty tough. Rates are difficult to assess because people short sell themselves to get work. Companies thrive on the low-ballers and will commission the lowest bidder. Once you have informed Immigration, you can set up as a business and register with the Business Registration (187 8088) in Wan Chai.

Finding Work Before You Come

If you are keen to work in Hong Kong then do as much homework as you can. Contact friends and contacts and let them know that you are planning to apply for jobs. Ask for any tips or leads they can give you about companies and recruitment websites. Check government websites for the latest on entry and work visas.

Most big companies have websites with a section for careers and jobs. It might be worthwhile to check out some of the big names. Be realistic and target companies that will make use of your experience and qualifications. You should also scour the job sections of the local daily newspapers on-line. See p.49 for details. Once you have the information you need, prepare your cover letter and CV and start applying. It is also worthwhile sending blind applications to companies you're interested in but that haven't posted jobs – you never know, you could be lucky.

Finding Work While You're Here

Make a list of names of any contacts, acquaintances and recruitment agencies. While agencies are on everyone's list, how effective they are depends entirely on what kind of agency it is and if they have any openings for what you are looking for. Newspapers have a job section but most demand proficiency in Cantonese or Mandarin. Check the *South China Morning Post* jobs section on Saturdays and the *Hong Kong Standard* jobs section on Fridays and *Recruit* after 17:00 on Fridays at all MTR stations and Chinese magazine outlets.

Recruitment Agencies

Keeping an updated list of recruitment agencies will be helpful. The work actually starts when you build a rapport with the agent looking after your file. You don't get filed in the database and forgotten. Some recruitment agencies will only handle niche sector placements, some only work with senior level jobs, and there are also those who specialise in jobs in China. Do your homework and save yourself some time, find out who does what and which agency will be in a better position to help with your case.

Recruitment Agencies

Barons & Company	2721 5000	www.barons-co.com
Bennet Associates	2810 7933	www.bennett-hk.com
Boyden Global Executive Search Limited	2868 3882	www.boyden.com
Charteron Human Resources	2519 6218	www.charteronhr.com.hk
Computer Recruitment Consultants	2861 3181	www.crcltd.com.hk
Drake International	2848 9288	www.drakeintl.com
Egon Zehnder International	2525 6340	www.egonzehnder.com
Korn Ferry International	2971 2700	www.kornferry.com
Norman Broadbent (HK) Limited	2810 0283	www.normanbroadbent.com
Sara Beattie Appointments	2507 9333	www.sarabeattie.com
Spencer Stuart & Associates	2521 8373	www.spencerstuart.com
Staff Service Company	2506 2676	www.staffservice.com
Taylor Abbott Associates Limited	2110 2980	www.taylorabbott.com
Templar International Consultants	2970 2722	www.templarsearch.com
Wall Street Associates	2111 7711	www.wasgroup.com

Voluntary & Charity Work

Charitable and community organisations need your time and skills but you'll need approval from Immigration. There are over 50 organisations that take on volunteers but some of them are entirely Chinese and if you don't speak Cantonese you'll be of little use.

Certain programmes are set up to help teach conversational English in poorer schools or to offer scholarships. Others are a little more hands on, but if you have the time and the goodwill, call up and find out what you can do to help.

Finding a Job Online
Some of the top websites
for finding work online are:
www.monster.com.hk
www.careertimes.com.hk
www.classifiedpost.com.hk
www.hkjobs.com
www.jobsdb.com.hk and
www.hudson.com.hk.

Volunteer Organisations in Hong Kong

Crossroads International in the Gold Coast (2984 9309) is a large charitable enterprise that takes donations of clothes, furniture, books, stationary, toys, computers, bedding and other relief goods. The group is often looking for volunteers with computer skills to help in their office, or someone to cook for other volunteers and to sort and label the donated goods.

Hong Kong Vocational Council in Sai Ying Pun (2813 4550, wwwhkvc.org.hk) was set up to help English-speaking adults with developmental disabilities to lead normal lives by facilitating everyday activities like shopping, cooking, using public transport and learning computer skills and other tasks. Volunteers are needed to help and are assisted by a manager.

Po Leung Kuk in Causeway Bay (2576 3386) was set up in 1878 to provide shelter for abducted women and children in Hong Kong. Today it is an orphanage where volunteers can assist with childcare from newborns to infants.

Hong Kong Society for the Blind in Sham Shui Po (2778 8332) provides an audio library for the blind.

Riding for the Disabled (2550 1359) is held at the Pok Fu Lam Riding School. Volunteers are needed to help a disabled rider by leading or walking with the horse, so some experience with horses is helpful, but not necessary.

Watchdog Early Learning & Development Centre in Mid-Levels (2521 7364, www.watchdog.org.hk) is a pre-school programme for Hong Kong's children who are slow developers due to Down's Syndrome and cerebral palsy, as well as other intellectual and physical problems.

Mother's Choice in Mid-Levels (2537 7633) is a home for unmarried mothers who are too young, sick or poor to care their baby. All these children eventually get adopted.

China Coast Community in Kowloon(2337 7266) is a home for the English-speaking elderly of Hong Kong. Many of these are long-term residents of Hong Kong who did not return to their home countries.

Helpers for Domestic Helpers on Garden Road (2523 4020) is a non-profit organisation set up to provide legal advice for employment issues and counselling for domestic helpers of all nationalities.

The Society for the Prevention of Cruelty to Animals (2802 0501, www.spca.org.hk) has shelters and care clinics in its many branches around Hong Kong.

Employment Contracts

Gratuity

Depending on your position and level in the company, a gratuity is part of the wage structure and must be paid on completion or termination of the employment contract. It can be withheld if you are fired for bad conduct or if you break your contract.

Multinational companies based in Hong Kong function on their own policies and procedures when it comes to contracts. They are still expected to follow the basic government guidelines and most probably will have adopted international corporate ethics and rules of conduct in order to attract qualified and skilled personnel from around the world.

So what happens when they want to hire you? Firstly you will receive a formal offer. Sometimes, this is done verbally but it's usually in the form of a letter of offer. The letter should include your title and salary, probationary period, an outline of benefits and a start date. If you agree to the details in the letter (you'll have already discussed this so there should be no surprises), you are expected to confirm your acceptance by letter (keep a copy for yourself). You will then receive the contract detailing everything again, with some additional bits covering medical insurance, annual leave, housing, education, tax assistance, salary increases and other employee entitlements. Contracts are mostly in English. It is perfectly normal and acceptable to negotiate salary and the terms, but be sure to do this before you sign. Probation periods vary; usually six months for senior executives and three months for junior staff. Resignation notices also vary; three months for senior level management and one month for others. Your contract will be either continuous or time-specific according to the job and terms. You are entitled to continuous contract terms if you have worked 18 hours a week for four weeks or more.

Changing Jobs

Maternity Leave

For details of how much maternity leave Hong Kong mums are entitled to, turn to the Maternity section on p.134.

Jumping ship is highly frowned upon by the Immigration Office. Your work visa is valid only with the sponsor who employed you and that visa is valid as long as your contract is. If you terminate your contract, you are only entitled to remain in Hong Kong for two weeks thereafter. Your visa is non-transferable, so a new employer will have to sponsor you and apply for a new visa for you to work. All the usual visa requirements must be met, including evidence that the employer was not able to fill the post locally. If you happen to be highly qualified and specifically skilled, you can be headhunted for other jobs or find openings on your own.

Company Closure

The labour laws require that an advance notice be given to employees before the company closes down. If for some reason the employer doesn't and compensation to employees is not paid, employees have the right to contest the situation by contacting the Labour Department's Labour Relations Division (2717 1771).

Employees are also free to contact the Immigration office and request the opportunity to seek another job. The office will consider the case and respond with a yes or a no. Do seek legal advice if you find yourself in a tight spot. Be sure to find a law firm that specialises in employment issues (see the table on p.77). Also, the Labour Department's Labour Relations Division (2717 1771, Citizen's Easy Link 1823) is helpful in all employment issues, as is the Labour Tribunal (2537 7652) and the Legal Aid Department (2530 4411, www.lad.gov.hk).

73

Bank Accounts

Happy Banking

Banks will not cash a cheque from abroad but may deposit it into an existing account. There is a charge for this service, normally around $60. Fees for a bank draft range from $30-$60. You'll have to pay a fee to change currency, and sometimes a commission. These fees vary from bank to bank so ask before opening an account if you expect to change money frequently as it can add up. Bank hours are from Monday to Friday, 09:00-17:00, Saturday, 09:00-12:00. Most banks offer online and phone services.

Hong Kong has over 250 banks from around 30 countries. This is after-all the world's ninth largest international banking centre so leading international and local banks, both investment and retail, have a presence here. Some have head offices in exclusive buildings, others will have a regional office, and all of them are in Central, the business district of Hong Kong.

The largest and most visible of the banks is HSBC (Hong Kong Shanghai Banking Corporation) with branches all over the city and its own Automated Teller Machines (ATMs) as well as a subsidiary, Hang Seng Bank. You will see many local banks but because of language differences, expats tend to use banks they are familiar with, the branches of which are conveniently located in big malls and main streets with ATMs and counter services.

Banks here offer savings, current or checking and multi-currency accounts. You will need an opening amount, usually $1,000, although this will differ from bank to bank and from account to account. You can also apply for a credit card.

All banks, (except HSBC), offer ATM service through the JETCO system; check the reverse of your bankcard. You cannot draw foreign currency from ATMs.

Aside from the varied accounts, banks offer a multitude of services (such as security boxes) and plans ranging from car, home and domestic help insurance, pay plans to financial planning and investment services.

To open any kind of account you need to have a valid Hong Kong identity card. If you are opening a joint bank account then both parties have to be present with identity cards. Different banks will require different documents to open an account. The usual requirements include a passport and sponsor's letter of employment. In some cases someone holding an account can introduce you. You'll be asked for proof of your Hong Kong address, such as a utility bill.

For Americans opening an account with an American bank, the social security number is an extra requirement in order to report income interest to the US Internal Revenue Service. For the contact details of the main banks, see p.45.

Financial Planning

Making a Will

Drawing up a Last Will & Testament in Hong Kong is easy and advised if you plan on staying here for a while. If you don't have one, the fate of your assets and children will be down to the Hong Kong court system. Most expats hold assets in other countries and without a will, the laws of those countries will prevail. If you are holding assets abroad then you'll need to contact financial advisors and trust companies. Several overseas trust companies are represented in Hong Kong to help you deal with your offshore investments.

Hong Kong is an attractive place to go to work, more so for the sometimes-excellent expat packages offered (including housing, maid, car and driver, free education for your offspring, health club membership, and many other benefits), than it's relatively low tax rate. Although you only pay 16% of your annual salary in tax, the high cost of living here often cancels that out. If you are looking for a financial planner, choose one that has offices overseas, as you want to be able to reach the company and enjoy the same access to advice, and of course to your investments, when you leave. It may be better to use an independent company or advisor who is not tied to a specific bank or savings company, and therefore will objectively offer you the full range of savings products on the market.

Many expats set up offshore accounts in tax havens such as the Isle of Man, Jersey and Guernsey, which allow easy access to your money and the option to choose the currency you want your investments in.

MPF (Mandatory Provident Fund Scheme)

Set up in 2000 by the Mandatory Provident Fund Authority, this scheme provides the city's workforce with security in retirement. Both the employer and employee contribute 5% of the salary but either party can voluntarily contribute more. The employee must be between 18 and 65 years and all earnings such as salary, wages, bonus, gratuity, leave pay, commissions, etc

Financial Advisors

Anson Investment Management Fund	2230 0722	www.eanson.com
Expat Planner	2525 2209	www.expatplanner.com
Henley Group	2824 1083	www.thehenleygroup.com.hk
JF Investment Centre	2265 1133	www.jffunds.com
Schroders Investment Management	2869 6968	www.schroders.com.hk
Templeton Asset Management Ltd	2820 2400	www.franklintempleton.com
TG Holborn Group	2111 2168	www.holborn-group.com

are added up for this contribution, except housing allowance and rent.

The employer has to start his contribution as soon as the employee begins work. The employee starts to contribute after the first 30 days. The employee will receive a slip showing the amount contributed by the employer each month.

There is tax deduction of a maximum of $12,000 on the mandatory amount for the employee and 15% of the employee's total amount for the employer.

This fund can be taken out when an employee is leaving Hong Kong, if retiring or ill and unable to contribute anymore. If the circumstances are a change of job within the same industry, the amount can be transferred but only if the new employer has the same scheme.

Some people are not included in this scheme such as domestic help, self-employed hawkers and their employees, and those covered by another scheme or pension fund like teachers or civil servants. People who come to work in Hong Kong for less than 13 months or who have retirement schemes abroad and those working in the European Union Office of the European Commission in Hong Kong are also not covered.

For more information call 2918 0102 or contact the Mandatory Provident Fund Authority (www.mpfahk.org).

The Dollar

The Hong Kong dollar has been pegged to the US dollar since 1983 at the official rate of HK$7.68-$7.82 for US$1 and is known to fluctuate a bit every now and again. There is no mint in Hong Kong so The Hong Kong Monetary Authority, HSBC, Standard Chartered Bank and Bank of China issue bank notes. The notes have different designs and colours and come in denominations of $1,000, $500, $100, $50, $20, $10 and coins of $10, 50c, 20c, 10c.

Taxation

Hong Kong has one of the lowest tax rates in Asia, and in the world. Only local salaries, business profits and property are taxed. Capital gains and profits from a company's branch or dividends brought in to Hong Kong, or dividends paid by Hong Kong companies to shareholders here or abroad, are not taxed. There is no sales tax. A stamp duty is paid on certain documents like share transfers, leases and the buying and selling of property. There is tax on betting and a duty for hotel guests. If you are donating money to approved charitable donations, you are eligible for a 25% rebate on the total amount of the donation. Property loan payments and self-education expenses are also not taxed.

People visiting Hong Kong for entertainment or other types of performances like sportsmen, singers, and actors, are liable to pay tax even though they are not residents. The maximum tax you would pay on your salary is 16% of your overall income, including all allowances and bonuses. Your employer does not deduct your salary tax; that is your responsibility.

The fiscal year for tax assessment is from April 1 to March 31. An Assessment Form will be sent to you to fill in details about your annual income – your salary if you are an employee or profit made if you have a business. You and your spouse can also apply for joint assessment which may work out more favourable than separate assessment. Employers are expected to notify the Inland Revenue of all payments to full-time or part-time employees, and for freelance work or projects.

TRC Scheme

An easy way to pay bills and save money is to use an electronic Tax Reserve Certificates (TRC) scheme. You can save and pay tax through autopay. You can get these certificates from banks and the Inland Revenue Department (it's free with the latter but banks will charge a fee). Check for details on www.ird.gov.hk.

75

Income or salary is taxed when in excess of $30,000 a month. The Assessment Form must be completed whether you anticipate earning that much or not and it's simple enough to fill in yourself. You will receive an assessment of what you have to pay in the autumn, after which you are taxed in two instalments, the first in January and the second in April.

Legal Issues

Jury Duty

All Hong Kong residents between the ages of 21 and 65 can be called in for jury duty. You must be able to speak English or Cantonese and must have a valid excuse to be exempt. A letter to the judge requesting exemption is either accepted or denied. Doctors, lawyers and students are automatically exempt. If you are selected, you will be paid per day.

There is a long established Judiciary that is independent of the executive and legislative branches of government. Rich or poor, everyone has a right to legal recourse for all civil and criminal cases. Both English and Cantonese are official languages and proceedings can take place in either. Information pamphlets are available online (www.doj.gov.hk) and in public libraries.

Hong Kong works on a tier system similar to the American Supreme Court. The top tier is taken by the Court of Final Appeal, which deals with appeals and proceedings of civil and criminal cases. Cases referred by the attorney general and secretary of justice are heard at the Court of Appeal High Court. The High Court hears adoption applications, trade union appeals, taxes and legal aid appeals. District Courts deal with civil action, criminal and equal opportunities cases, stamp duty appeal and tax claims. Divorce and child maintenance cases are heard in the Family Court. Landlord appeal, governmental renting and rates, construction and demolishing cases all go to The Land Tribunal. The Labour Tribunal advises and mediates on employment matters. The Small Claims Court hears cases for monetary claims for less than $50,000.

Divorce

It is possible to get legally divorced in Hong Kong. To apply for divorce here, a petition is sent to the Family Court Registry (M2, Wan Chai Law Courts, Wan Chai Tower, 12 Harbour Road, 2840 1218). Couples should be married for at least a year for the petition to go through. Once both parties agree to a divorce, an appropriate form is filled in and sent to the registry. Filing costs approx $630.

The judge will decide on custody matters for children under 18 years as well as financial maintenance for older children if they are still completing their education. The court also decides on the divvying up of assets and transfer of property. Applications for the Legal Aid Scheme from the Legal Aid Department (2537 7677) are accepted. If you can afford it, you are advised to hire a private solicitor. The Law Society of Hong Kong publishes a directory of Hong Kong Law Firms. Public Service Centres and the public libraries here have information about the laws and procedures if you want to read up on your own.

Crime

The crime rate is surprisingly low and Hong Kong is often considered a safe destination, especially for single women visiting or living on their own. This doesn't mean that crime is non-existent – pick-pockets and bag snatchers are the worst, so always keep an eye on your belongings and don't carelessly leave anything beside you or under your table or chair that can be swiped.

Dangerous Areas & Petty Crimes

Everywhere and anywhere can be subject to crime. Be smart and responsible about your home and belongings; don't give anyone the chance to take advantage. Petty crime is the biggest risk, although dangerous, more serious crimes are not unheard of and cases of rape and assault have been reported in large public housing estates.

Swervy Driving

Not too many people drink and drive as public transport is cheap and convenient. When the trains and buses do stop for the night, people usually take taxis. There's a zero-tolerance policy for drink driving, with an arrest first, question later policy.

Public Nuisance
Areas around Wan Chai on Hong Kong Island are known for brawls and drunken misbehaviour, more so when naval ships are docked and the servicemen get a bit carried away.

Stick to busy well-lit areas at night, like the night markets of Mong Kok in Kowloon. Shenzhen, across the border, has a bad reputation but is still visited for the night shopping. Going for hikes alone is not recommended with an increasing number of hold ups being reported. As with any city, be street-smart and confident and you'll avoid unwanted attention.

Drug Possession

Possessing drugs can get you deported or imprisoned. It will depend on the amount you have and the circumstances surrounding your case. You will probably go into a drug detention centre until your case is investigated. Depending on the results, you will be confined or asked to attend counselling. If you are caught trafficking, then it is a Customs and Excise police matter. A case will be made against you and you will go to court, a situation that could take months. Get yourself in this kind of mess and you can bet you'll need a good lawyer. Hong Kong does not appreciate any form of drug abuse and has a zero tolerance policy.

Call The Cops
Most people are very honest, especially taxi drivers, and generally the passengers that ride in after you, so if you happen to leave something in the back of a cab, there's a very good chance you'll see it again. Regardless and as a just-in-case precaution, as soon as you've discovered you've lost your bag or wallet with your identity card in it, file a report with the nearest police station and then cancel your credit cards. All public transport companies have lost and found hotlines.

You're Nicked

When expats get into trouble they often rely on their consulate officer-in-charge to come to the rescue, however police involvement is unavoidable if there is a murder or physical assault. Land in prison and you have a few rights to cling to. You can make calls or send faxes but these are at your own expense. You are also allowed visits from family, friends and welfare agents. Visits are by appointment during visiting hours: Monday to Wednesday, 09:00–17:00, and 09:00-13:00 on other days.

Depending on the crime, you can contact your consulate for assistance but if it involves murder or drug possession, you will need a lawyer and local law will apply. And just as back home, this will be on your record.

There are different institutions for different offences or crimes and each has a judge to hear cases. You can get free legal advice from the Duty Lawyer who can be contacted in this situation. If you are accused of a serious crime, you can apply for Legal Aid and a lawyer will be appointed to you. These arrangements are part of a government scheme for people in trouble with the law and cannot get help or who are visitors in Hong Kong. Prisons are spread out in different parts of Hong Kong and prisoners are divided by gender and age. There are a few maximum security prisons, some minimum security and the rest are correctional institutions, detention and rehabilitation centres, and halfway houses.

Hong Kong Police

Hong Kong policemen and policewomen are vigilant and efficient. They can be seen patrolling the streets wearing navy blue uniforms in winter and light khaki ones in summer. If you want to ask a policeman for directions, look for a red band under the shoulder badge, these are the English-speaking police.

You'll see police vans parked around Hong Kong, these are part of the Crime Prevention Bureau, with a mission to alert people about petty crimes. The main police station is located at 10/F, Arsenal House, No.1 Arsenal Street in Wan Chai (www.info.gov.hk/police). The emergency police number is 999. For complaints against the police, there's an English-speaking 24 hour hotline (2527 7177).

Law Firms

Allen Overy	2794 7000	www.allenovery.com
Arculli Fong & Ng	2848 4848	www.kingandwood.com.hk
Baker & Mackenzie	2846 1888	www.bakernet.com
Barlow, Lyde & Gilbert	2526 4202	www.blg.com.hk
Clifford Chance	2825 8888	www.cliffordchance.com
Coudert Brothers	2218 9100	www.coudert.com
Deacons	2825 9211	www.deaconslaw.com
Johnson Stokes and Master	2843 2211	www.jsm.com
SAR International	2803 0572	www.profwills.com

Housing

Housing in Hong Kong is extremely expensive, whether buying or renting. The hilly topography makes it difficult to build on Hong Kong Island and since there are no open spaces for houses and villas, the only solution is tall blocks stacked to the hilt with tightly packed apartments. And they're getting higher by the day, as the demand for good housing rises with the increase in population. And despite the shockingly high rents on Hong Kong Island, it's incredibly popular. If you don't mind the commute though, you're better off venturing further out to get more for your money.

Renting in Hong Kong

No Control

There is no rent control in Hong Kong and few laws to protect tenants. Landlords can charge any amount of safety deposit, though the standard is two to three months. If a landlord does not agree to a lease renewal and for disputes over rent adjustment or repairs, take your case to the Lands Tribunal, a government judiciary body that deals with such matters.

Rent is calculated on the square footage of the floor area, inclusive of the car park, foyer elevator area and stairwell, so check how much of this is actually your apartment. Quoted rents are per month.

Many expats have their rent paid by their company and thus tend to live in high rental homes. There are expat enclaves with luxurious apartments perched on top of steep hills with spectacular views, and often include facilities like a swimming pool, tennis courts, gym, children's play areas and shuttle service.

Changes within the apartment can be made with the permission of the landlord, even if they are structural, but landlords expect you to remove them when you leave and hand the place over as it was. If you don't then you may have to forfeit the deposit. Most high rental apartments have one parking space with the option of paying for a second. Apart from the rent, you'll pay a monthly management fee, which in some apartments includes air conditioning and covers the quarterly government rates determined by the Rating and Values Department based on the age, type and size of the building. When viewing properties, the rent will either be quoted as 'inclusive' meaning management and rates are included, or 'exclusive' meaning rates will be quoted separately.

Rent increases depend entirely on market conditions. If the market is down, you can negotiate a lower rent or expect no increase. If it's high, rent increase could be 30% and if you can't afford it or if the company refuses to pay the new rent, you may have to move out, which is actually a pretty regular occurrence here.

It is customary to negotiate. If the market is down, individual landlords may be willing but big property companies adjust according to the current market and don't tend to yield much. Depending on how hot the rental market is, landlords sometimes offer one or two weeks free rent, throw in some appliances and furnishings, or fix up parts of the house at your request, so learn the game and play it.

Housing Abbreviations

Meaning	Abbreviation
Air-conditioner	A/C
Amah's or maid's quarters	AQ/MQ
Balcony	BALC/BAL
Bathrooms	BTHRMS
Bedroom with attached bathroom	ENSUITE
Bedrooms	BRS/BDRS
Car park	CP
Club	CL
Covered car park	CCP
Decorated	DEC
Designer furnished	DF
Duplex	DUP
Exclusive	EXCL
Floor	FLR or FL.
Full Facilities	FFAC
Fully furnished	FF
Furniture	FURN
Garden	GDN
Green garden view	GV
Gymnasium	GYM
High floor	HF
High-rise/Low-rise	HR/LW
Inclusive	INCL
Kitchen	KIT
Living/Dining	L/D
Living/Dining	LIV/DIN
Location	LOC
Low floor	LF
Management/Security	Mgmt/Secu
Middle floor	MF
Million/Thousand	M/K
Mountain view	MV
Open car park	OCP
Open view	OV
Partial harbour view	PHV
Partial sea view	PSV
Partly furnished	PF
Playground	PG
Racecourse view	RV/RCV
Roof garden	RG
Sea view	SV
Square Foot	SF
Storage	STR
Swimming pool	SP
Tennis	T
Terrace	TER
Townhouse	TH
Unfurnished	UF

Finding a Home

Most people use a real estate agent when looking for a home. Set your priorities before searching and be prepared for trade offs. You may like an apartment but not the neighbourhood, or you may get a very small apartment for your budget with many facilities. You should take into consideration public transport or buying a car if you'll be commuting. Be sure about how high a floor you are comfortable living on, as an apartment on the 21st floor may have stunning views but what's the point if your legs turn to jelly every time you look down or step out on the balcony. Another important factor is the security and safety aspect. Look around to see how well the building is managed, and ask the agent as many questions as you can think of.

Other Options

You can try renting on your own but you won't get much variety and if you were to drive round checking for 'to let' signs, you wouldn't find too many. Besides, landlords don't want to deal with foreigners or be bothered by the hassles of negotiating and the other demands of leasing. However, with low budget accommodation like studio flats and flat shares, serviced apartments and short lease accommodation, they won't want to pay commission to an agent so they'll be more inclined to deal with tenants directly. You'll have to do all the negotiating and lease signing by yourself – a headache if the two parties speak different languages.

Leading dailies have a property supplement – the South China Morning Post comes out on Wednesdays and The Standard on Fridays. Square Foot is a new fortnightly property magazine in Hong Kong with interesting articles and property advertisements. Free publications including HK Magazine, BC, and Inside DB advertise serviced apartments, flat shares and rooms. You can advertise in these magazines for a small fee, especially if you are looking for a short-term lease or a flatmate. The internet is another good source of information – try www.geoexpat.com, www.asiaxpat.com and www.hongkong.alloexpat.com. You can also spread the word through people you know and through notice boards in supermarkets and buildings.

Real Estate Agents

Agents advertise online, in newspapers and magazines. You pay them half a month's rent as commission and they get the same from the landlord. They are all licensed and must display their certificate, which they've sat a government exam to gain. Most real estate agents speak English, and expat agents are employed by both local and expat companies. Some property companies have a car and driver, and the agent picks you up for property viewing. Agents from smaller companies will take you around in taxis. Agents prepare the offering letter for the landlord and are involved in all negotiations before lease signing.

Real Estate Agents

Asia Pacific Properties	2868 0966	www.asiapacificproperties.com
At Home	2819 8523	www.athomeinhongkong.com
Boutique Residential Leasing Specialists	2140 6553	www.hkrentals.com.hk
Centaline	2834 3298	www.centanet.com
Century 21 Property Agency Ltd	2850 6363	www.century21-hk.com
Chesterton Petty	2877 5511	www.chesterton.com.hk
Colliers	2822 0743	www.colliersresidential.com
Eastmount Property Agency	2791 0498	www.eastmount.com.hk
Habitat	2869 9069	www.habitat-property.com
Hong Kong Homes	2866 0130	www.hongkonghomes.com
House Hunters	2869 1001	www.househunters.com.hk
Iglu Property Consultants	2581 1710	www.iglu.com.hk
Jones Lang La Salle	2846 5000	www.joneslanglasalle.com.hk
Ka Man Properties (Discovery Bay area)	2987 7611	www.kaman.com.hk
Knight Frank	2810 8123	www.knightfrank.com
KPC Agency	2719 3399	www.karlson.com.hk
L.J. Hooker	2869 8822	www.ljhooker.com.hk
Landmark Asia Realty	3571 9122	www.landmarkasia.com.hk
Lifestyle Homes (Discovery Bay area)	2914 0888	www.lifestylehomes.com.hk
Midland Realty	2311 1200	www.midland.com.hk
Pacific Relocations and Pacific Properties	2521 2821	www.worthenpacific.com
Peninsula Properties	2813 7266	www.peninsulapropertieshk.com
Proway-Personalized Relocation	2866 1886	www.proway.com.hk
Ricacorp	2506 0060	www.ricacorp.com
Sallmanns Residential	2537 5338	www.sallmannsres.com
Santa Fe	2574 6204	www.santaferelo.com
Savills Hong Kong	2842 4400	www.savills.com.hk
Sino Group	2721 8388	www.sino-land.com
Treasureland, International Property Consultants	2866 8258	www.expathome.com.hk
Wheelock Properties	2118 8036	www.wheelockproperties.com.hk

The Lease

A rental lease is usually for two years, with a break clause after one year with two or three months' notice. Common terms in a lease may include tenant's responsibility for repairs, a ban on sub-letting and indemnity insurance. The lease is always in English and both you and the landlord will receive a signed copy. There is a standard government lease but some landlords may add in their own stipulations – always, always, always read before signing! Check for binding clauses or any liability such as structural repairs. If something seems off, have a chat with your agent, and don't be afraid to go straight for the jugular and consult a lawyer if necessary.

If the company is signing the lease, Human Resources will take care of it. Even so, ask to see it and stay in the loop.

If you're the one signing, you'll need a copy of your identity card and your company's letter of employment. Once signed by both parties, it will be filed by the government and a government stamp duty of 0.5% of the annual rent must be paid. This is shared between the landlord and tenant.

To renew the lease, the landlord will send you a notice enquiring about your intentions. Often the same lease continues but the rent will change depending on the property market. It's a good idea for you to check about rent increases three months before your lease expires in case you'll have to move out. That should give you enough time to find a new home.

Housing

Main Accommodation Options

Show Flats

When a new building comes on the market for sale or rent, one flat is decorated as a display unit to show buyers the layout and space. When all units are rented or sold this particular unit goes on the market. These are always popular even though the asking price is higher than the rest of the units. If you can, grab one – you will be living in a designer showroom. Prices may be $50,000 upwards, depending, among other things, on whether it's furnished or unfurnished.

Houses

Large and exclusive colonial mansions with sprawling gardens and long driveways are located on Hong Kong Island, and sometimes in Kowloon. Newer buildings are popping up in the New Territories. Normally owned by the people living in them, they are sometimes rented out to senior diplomatic officials or business people. For your rent you can expect 5,000 square feet, and a pool, separate servant housing and five or six bedrooms on two or three levels. These are obviously out of reach for most people since rents can start at $150,000.

Townhouses

Townhouses can be small or big with four or five levels, lots of stairs, a porch or small garden and parking space. Typically you would enter via a dining or living room and go up or down into the bedrooms. Anyone living in such housing is the envy of the garden-starved, because not many enjoy the privilege of having a garden or backyard. Rents start from $90,000.

Duplex or Penthouse

These apartments have two levels in a high-rise block. One level has a study, a guest bathroom, the living, dining, kitchen and utility area, and maid's quarters. Upstairs will be two or three bedrooms and bathrooms. A storeroom may be either upstairs or under the stairs. These make spacious homes and often have terrace gardens on the roof. But they can be expensive to heat and cool because of the depth of the apartment. Prices start at around $60,000.

Furnished Apartments

Furnished apartments are available but are not very common. Sometimes a landlord will offer to furnish the apartment at a cost, or your company might offer to rent the furniture and appliances for you. This last point is normally dependant on your length of stay.

Old Apartment Blocks

Apartments in old blocks tend to be large with huge balconies and can range from 1,800 to 3,000 square feet. The bigger places sometimes have two maids' rooms, a storage room, a guest bathroom and two ensuites but no facilities like pool, shuttle or clubhouses. The entrance is open and spacious and parking spaces might be uncovered. If you like homes with character, this type of housing is full of it. If the block is small, the management fee is higher and government rates can sometimes be high depending on the age of the building. Bidding starts at $25,000.

Government apartments come onto the market from time to time, and are often old but large and in good locations. There's no negotiating and the lease is for two years, unless they plan to redevelop soon in which case it's just a year at a time. These can be rented directly or through their appointed agents. All repairs and painting will be at your expense.

New Apartment Blocks

These are in great demand and are changing the look of Hong Kong. They have good quality bathrooms and kitchen fittings with fancy flooring and light fixtures. Every facility imaginable is provided: clubs with activities like yoga, gymnastics for kids, swimming, squash and tennis, hot and cold pools. Some have supermarkets, restaurants, schools or playgroups, ATMs, shuttle services, hairdressers, parking and play areas. A part of the complex will also have furnished apartments with maid service. Expect to pay high management fees here. Starting price $50,000.

Studio Flats

Basically, a studio is one big room, about 300-400 square feet, with living, sleeping, bathroom and kitchen facilities in the one space. The rent could be high if it is well decorated or furnished. You'll have to rent a parking space (about $2,000 per month). Rents are from $8,000 upwards.

About Those Fancy Housing Complexes...

The new apartment blocks are very posh and ornate with names like 'Regency Royale' and 'Legends.' Trimmed bushes, waterfalls, decorative lighting and fancy brickwork, lobbies furnished with ornate designer 'stuff', hi-tech elevators some with screens displaying schedules of what's happening in the building and news broadcasts, others with windows offering breathtaking views. In one building, 'The Summit,' tenants are served tea, coffee and Danish pastries in the lobby before departing for work or school each morning!

The management office of a residential building will have a manager in charge of everyday matters. Watchmen are on duty in shifts at the gates and they check your identity and note down any visitors to the building. Mostly, those who are Chinese speak no English, although they are starting to be replaced by Nepalese nationals who speak good English.

Flat Shares

This is a practical option if you cannot afford to rent an apartment and don't want to live in a hovel. It can be a big or small apartment. Utilities, rent, management fees and government rates can all be shared. Rent depends on size and location and how you arrange to split the expenses.

Serviced Apartments

Rising in popularity, the units are sometimes attached to hotels, located in upmarket complexes and in commercial and business districts. If you are coming on short assignments or waiting for your shipment to arrive, live in one of these. The rental period can be short or long term and prices range from $10,000 to $50,000.

Other Rental Costs

A month's rent is often required as a holding deposit while the lease is being signed. This is later used as the first month's rent or is refundable, but make sure you get this in writing. Management fees are also payable, to cover the maintenance of facilities, a cleaning and security service, and sometimes for maintenance and use of air-conditioning. A stamp duty fee, 3% of the monthly rental, is shared between you and the landlord. If a lawyer is consulted about the lease there will be legal fee to pay. If you share the lawyer with the landlord, then you share the fees too. Charges are based on the scales set by The Law Society of Hong Kong (2846 0500, www.hklawsoc.org.hk). Deposits for gas ($200-$700) and electric ($2,000-$4,500) and water ($100) connections will also be required. Sometimes landlords will let you continue the use of utilities and pay the monthly charges without having to go through the reconnection and deposit. Telephone and fax installation ($110), Internet installation ($138 with broadband high-speed internet, $196 for unlimited use for single user) and extra charges for extensions also have to be factored into the rental costs. Since most apartments do not come with light fixtures, buying and fixing them will also be part of your additional expenses.

Buying Property

Real Estate is a lucrative business in Hong Kong and almost all local companies have some involvement in it. Property companies make up more then 10% of the Hang Seng Index. The Hong Kong Government owns all the land and is said to be the biggest landowner in the world. Land is sold on tender with large developers trying to outbid each other.

Since 2005, luxury residential (over $29,000 per square metre) and commercial rents have risen almost steadily. Much of this is tied up with how much the mainland Chinese are spending in Hong Kong, trade and investments and, of course, the confidence of investors. Property in Hong Kong is far too expensive and volatile and small investors tend to be overly cautious, especially given the fact that the amount of money you put down and what you get for it is enough to make you go elsewhere. Long-term expats are also wary of the unpredictable highs and lows of the property market and many choose to rent, even for periods of 10 or 20 years. Some have bought and lost out while others are now millionaires.

Buying to rent or simply buying as an investment is not a priority or even a thought for most expats, since there is always an end to a contract and a desire to go home when that time comes. For those who do, they tread a minefield of factors such as investing in old or new buildings, what area to chose, legalities, mortgage plans, interest rates and other government formalities. Interest rates in Hong Kong are deregulated and banks take care of their own regulations based on US Federal Reserve trends.

Buying to Rent

Property tax is 16% on annual rent with a statutory deduction of 20% for repairs and other expenses. While you pay no capital gains tax if you own the property for a year, there will be a large tax payment at buying time, expenses for consultation, and if it's an old apartment or building, you will be paying for an evaluation of repairs and refurbishing.

The Process

To buy property in Hong Kong, you must be 18 years or and a Hong Kong resident, whether you intend to inhabit the place or are buying as an investment opportunity. When arranging for a mortgage, be sure to talk to several banks and compare interest rates and monthly payments. Many banks, including some government organisations like the Housing Authority (2712 2712) and Housing Society (2839 7888) offer attractive deals. The Hong Kong Mortgage Corporation (www.hkmc.com.hk) has a list of approved mortgage sellers that is worth a look through. Also, save yourself some hassle and hire a solicitor to handle your mortgage arrangement when you begin negotiations on a property deal.

Your property agent will prepare due diligence on the landlord, offer price comparison and then negotiate for you and set a date for the transaction. Once you are sure about buying the place and agree on the price with all terms and conditions understood and accepted, the agent prepares the offer letter and arranges for signing of the Provisional Sales and Purchase agreement. A deposit (5% of the sale price) is paid to the owner or owner's solicitor. You are now bound to this deal.

If you change your mind, you lose the deposit and still have to pay the agent's fee of 1% of the price.

Within 14 days, with the help of solicitors from both sides, the Formal Sales and Purchase Agreement is signed with another deposit of 5-10% making this deal legally binding and you will sign the Assignment Deed. By now the mortgage should be confirmed and the Mortgage Deed signed as well.

The process is complete within two to three months when the remaining amount is handed over to the owner's solicitor. During this time, you can check the premises again to make sure it is in the condition as agreed upon in the terms. The owner's solicitor will inform you about paying government rates and management fees. You will also have to pay stamp duty to the Inland Revenue Department.

Sometimes there is a pre-sale of apartments in a building under construction. These can be bought for your own use, to rent out or even to sell on and some people do this before they are even completed and still make a pretty profit. You must let the developer know when reselling as sometimes there are transfer charges and changes need to be made in the provisional title. To protect yourself in case the construction is never completed, you can ask for a guarantee from the developer's solicitor.

A small deposit is made at the time of signing the Memorandum for Sale and after that both buyer and developer sign the Sales and Purchase Agreement, confirming the buying price and date of delivery. The final part of the transaction is the Assignment Deed, signed by both parties. An Occupation Permit is issued and the buyer takes possession of the property. The Hong Kong Land Office has to be notified of all transactions.

Selling Property

When to sell is as important as when to buy. If you are moving out of Hong Kong or the market is hot, you may decide to sell. Typically, you will advertise through an agent to get wider publicity, to do your bidding and also take care of the paperwork. There will be expenses for fixing up your property to make it attractive and sellable before putting it on the market. Legal fees for a solicitor, stamp duty and the agent's commission of 1% of the sale price should be factored in. First you will get 5% of the sale price if the buyer is satisfied with your property and signs the Provisional Sales and Purchase Agreement. If all goes well at the next signing of the Sales and Purchase Agreement, you are paid another 5 to 10% till the deal goes through and you are paid the lot. Have your solicitor work with the buyer's solicitor on legal matters. There are numerous solicitors dealing with property and mortgages and you can either go on recommendation or choose a certified one on your own after carefully considering credentials and experience.

Property Developers		
Cheung Kong Infrastructure Holdings Limited	2122 3133	www.cki.com.hk
Chinachem	2739 8811	www.chinachemgroup.com
Hang Lung Development Limited	2879 0111	www.hanglung.com
Henderson Land Development Company	2908 8037	www.hld.com
Hong Kong Land	2842 8428	www.hkland.com
Hopewell Holdings	2528 4975	www.hopewellholdings.com
Hutchison Whampoa	2128 7500	www.hwpg.com
New World Development Company Limited	2523 1056	www.nwd.com.hk
Sino Group	2721 8388	www.sino-land.com
Sun Hung Kai Properteis	2827 8111	www.shkp.com.hk
Swire Properties	2844 3046	www.swireproperties.com

Useful Numbers
The Hong Kong
Mortgage Corporation
(www.hkmc.com.hk),
general line 2536 0000,
Mortgage Insurance
Programme Hotline
2536 0136

Property Developers

Like the game Monopoly, just about everything in Hong Kong is owned by a bunch of large property companies, from hotels, airlines, utilities, telecommunications, retailing and food companies. These well-known companies have developed properties in China, other parts of Asia and sometimes even expanded globally. They also tend to own a large share of, and manage, residential housing in the fancier areas of Hong Kong. These are well-maintained and good quality housing complexes where mainly expats choose to live, such as Chinachem's posh townhouses in Tai Tam, and Sun Hung Kai's apartments in Repulse Bay, which have floor to ceiling windows.

Mortgages

All banks are geared to offer mortgages and protection against rising interest rates. There are many plans to choose from so the best way to do this is talk to several banks and compare their plans and the terms and conditions. Most banks will cover around 90% of the cost of the property especially on a flexible loan scheme. Some waive valuation and handling fees and others will tailor a mortgage plan for you with long repayment facilities, mortgage insurance and approval within 24 hours.

Mortgage companies will have different mortgage criteria but age, your earnings and what monthly repayments you can afford will be a definite consideration.

Mortgage Providers

ABN – AMRO Bank	2176 8833	www.abnamro.com.hk
AIG Finance (Hong Kong) Limited	2917 2917	www.aigfinance.com.hk
American Express Hong Kong	2277 1468	www.americanexpress.com/hk
Bank of China	3669 3233	www.bochk.com
China Construction Bank (Asia)	2805 2383	www.asia.ccb.com
DBS (Hong Kong) Limited	2961 2288	www.dbs.com.hk
GE Capital (Hong Kong) Limited	2961 1688	www.gemoney.com.hk
Hang Seng Bank	2822 0228	www.hangseng.com
The Hong Kong Housing Authority	2712 2712	www.housingauthority.gov.hk
HSBC ▶ p.109	2748 8030	www.hsbc.com.hk
Inchroy Credit Corporation limited	2872 3456	www.inchroy.com
Lloyds TSB ▶ p.47	2847 3000	www.lloydstsb.com.hk
Pacific Finance (Hong Kong) Limited	2881 6189	www.pfhkl.com.hk
Standard Chartered Bank	2886 8855	www.standardchartered.com.hk

Other Purchasing Costs

After paying for the property, a commission of 1% of the purchase goes to the property agent. The seller pays the same. Buyers must also a pay stamp duty, calculated on the value of the property and usually between 0.75 and 3.75%. The Capital Gains tax is paid at this time and then after a year of owning your property.

Other expenses could include legal fees, renovation costs if necessary and if you have consulted engineers or architects to evaluate the property before you bought it. You will also be paying your solicitor for services during the transaction.

Real Estate Law

There are two Sales and Purchase Agreements signed during the stages of the transaction, one is provisional with a 5% deposit paid, binding the buyer to the purchase. The second is the Formal Sales and Purchase Agreement, with another 5-10% payment required. After this, you are well on your way to becoming a proud property owner.

When the paperwork begins, you will need a solicitor to handle the deeds, deposits and payments at the signing of the Sales and Purchase Agreements, and to work with the owner's solicitor to get the transaction completed smoothly. A solicitor will offer advice, alert you to any discrepancies and most of all, provide solid advice should you have any questions, fears or doubts. This might be good time to consider writing up a will too.

85

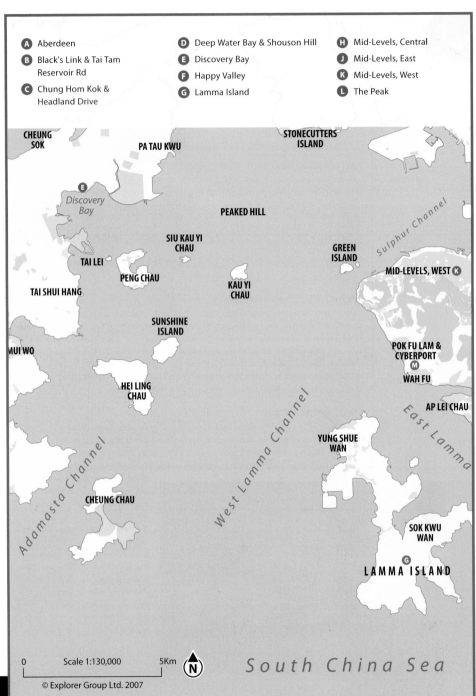

Ⓐ Aberdeen
Ⓑ Black's Link & Tai Tam Reservoir Rd
Ⓒ Chung Hom Kok & Headland Drive
Ⓓ Deep Water Bay & Shouson Hill
Ⓔ Discovery Bay
Ⓕ Happy Valley
Ⓖ Lamma Island
Ⓗ Mid-Levels, Central
Ⓙ Mid-Levels, East
Ⓚ Mid-Levels, West
Ⓛ The Peak

CHEUNG SOK

PA TAU KWU

STONECUTTERS ISLAND

Discovery Bay **Ⓔ**

PEAKED HILL

SIU KAU YI CHAU

Sulphur Channel

GREEN ISLAND

TAI LEI

PENG CHAU

KAU YI CHAU

MID-LEVELS, WEST **Ⓚ**

TAI SHUI HANG

SUNSHINE ISLAND

POK FU LAM & CYBERPORT **Ⓜ**

MUI WO

WAH FU

HEI LING CHAU

AP LEI CHAU

East Lamma

West Lamma Channel

YUNG SHUE WAN

Adamasta Channel

CHEUNG CHAU

SOK KWU WAN

LAMMA ISLAND **Ⓖ**

0   Scale 1:130,000   5Km   **N**

South China Sea

© Explorer Group Ltd. 2007

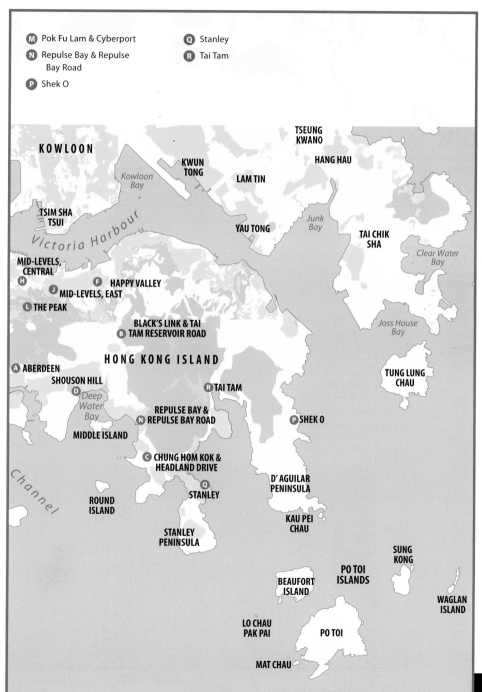

M Pok Fu Lam & Cyberport

N Repulse Bay & Repulse Bay Road

P Shek O

Q Stanley

R Tai Tam

KOWLOON

Kowloon Bay

KWUN TONG

LAM TIN

TSEUNG KWANO

HANG HAU

TSIM SHA TSUI

YAU TONG

Junk Bay

TAI CHIK SHA

Clear Water Bay

Victoria Harbour

MID-LEVELS, CENTRAL

H

J F HAPPY VALLEY
MID-LEVELS, EAST

L THE PEAK

BLACK'S LINK & TAI
B TAM RESERVOIR ROAD

HONG KONG ISLAND

Joss House Bay

A ABERDEEN

SHOUSON HILL

D Deep Water Bay

R TAI TAM

REPULSE BAY &
N REPULSE BAY ROAD

SHEK O P

TUNG LUNG CHAU

MIDDLE ISLAND

C CHUNG HOM KOK &
HEADLAND DRIVE

D'AGUILAR PENINSULA

Channel

ROUND ISLAND

Q STANLEY

KAU PEI CHAU

SUNG KONG

STANLEY PENINSULA

PO TOI ISLANDS

BEAUFORT ISLAND

WAGLAN ISLAND

LO CHAU PAK PAI

PO TOI

MAT CHAU

Traffic & Parking

Aberdeen is a large area with massive housing estates and some factories so parking is almost impossible. The Aberdeen Town Centre has a carpark for $15 per hour with a two-hour minimum requirement. Traffic is heavy all day as hundreds of buses and minibuses move around the housing estates.

Safety & Annoyances

Housing estates do report a fair amount of robberies and sometimes rapes and muggings. This is a busy, crowded and noisy area with people milling around, and noise from traffic that moves all day on the wide, open roads and flyovers.

Aberdeen

This was once a fishing village and the area where incense used to grow which is how Hong Kong (meaning 'fragrant harbour') got its name. That was a long time ago and though you may still see fishing junks, a wholesale fish market and a small fishing community that still live on houseboats, the majority have long since gone. This is an entirely Chinese area with huge housing estates. Behind the town centre on a high hill is a Chinese cemetery as well as the Aberdeen Country Park with nature trails and paths and the Aberdeen reservoir.

Over the bridge is the island of Ap Lei Chau, where expats live in South Horizons, a sprawling complex with about 20 blocks of apartments arranged around a shopping complex.

Accommodation

Housing here is basic and low budget. You can get an 800 square feet apartment in South Horizons with two bedrooms, kitchen, bathroom and a living area, furnished or unfurnished for about $7,000 to $12,000. Pok Fu Lam Terrace near Wah Fu Estates, has a smart but small two-bedroom apartment block complete with amenities going for $15,000 to $18,000. Serviced apartments are also available and with reasonable rents. Depending on the quality, size and amenities, these can cost anywhere between $12,000 and $20,000.

Shopping & Amenities

The Aberdeen Town Centre is a big shopping area with markets, supermarkets, restaurants, hardware stores, stationery shops, bakeries, hairdressers, framers, post offices and a bus terminus.

Entertainment & Leisure

The food here is mainly local except for an Indian and Thai restaurant and a McDonald's. You can catch a ferry from here to Lamma Island for a hike and a bite to eat at one of the many seafood restaurants.

Aberdeen Boat Club and Aberdeen Marina Club are in Shum Wan but are exclusive and open to members only.

Ocean Park (p.203) is a good venue for a family outing. It has a kids' world, cable cars to the other side of the mountain and the marine world, shark aquarium, rides and a revolving restaurant. Opening hours are from 09:00 to 18:00. Entry costs $185 for adults, and $93 for children between 3 and 11 years. An annual pass costs $295 and allows unlimited visits for a year. You can even have your wedding and birthday celebration inside the park.

Health

Located on the main Pok Fu Lam Road is Queen Mary hospital (p.129), a government hospital that has an outpatient department, although the wait for a consultation can sometimes take over an hour. It's known for its excellent 24 hour emergency service, pharmacy, and other specialist departments. Buses from all over Hong Kong stop in front of the hospital, and minibuses go right up to the main building. In Aberdeen, the Caritas Centre (2552 4215) is a medical and dental consultation clinic.

Education

The Canadian International School (p.149) has a campus on Nam Long Shan Road on the far side of the mountain and follows the Canadian educational curriculum. Close by is Singapore International School (2872 0266) which works in English, but Mandarin is compulsory.
Kellet School (p.151) is a non-profit school in Wah Fu Estates on Pok Fu Lam Road. South Island School (2555 9313) on Nam Fung Road is an ESF school.

Black's Link & Tai Tam Reservoir Road

Traffic & Parking

Close to the lower Tai Tam reservoir is a small public carpark, which will set you back some $10 per hour. No public transport comes this way but you can walk down to the main Wang Chuk Hang Road and catch buses to Aberdeen, Repulse Bay or Central.

These are expensive areas. Tai Tam Reservoir Road has tall luxurious apartments with multi dimensional views of Hong Kong. Black's Link is on a high hill and is quiet and private. There are low-rise apartments and townhouses with long uphill driveways and distant views of the sea and golf course. Most are privately owned .
Parkview, a popular expat complex in this area, is situated at the entrance of Tai Tam Country Park on Tai Tam Reservoir Road.

Accommodation

Black's Link is mostly townhouses. The apartments in this area mainly occupy Tai Tam Reservoir Road in Park Place, Celestial Court and 3 Repulse Bay Road, a new upmarket development. Rents range from $50,000 to $90,000.

Safety & Annoyances

During weekends and holidays the Country Park and reservoir attract a lot of people and it gets pretty crowded. However, because of the open space, the noise level does not disturb the residents. Clouds descending on the Parkview apartments block out the view and bring high humidity rates, a common complaint from residents.

Shopping & Amenities

Up in Parkview there is a ParknShop superstore which has everything you could possibly want, including a florist, fresh fish, a bakery and more. There is an ATM and a sports club with an indoor and outdoor pool and a gym. A shuttle bus runs to Central and Admiralty throughout the day.

Entertainment & Leisure

Restaurants in the Parkview Club are open to anyone. Behind this complex, the Tai Tam Country Park has barbecue pits, trails and paths to stroll and enjoy the open scenery. The lower Tai Tam Reservoir has a small recreation area with toilet facilities and paddleboats for hire by the hour. Central is 20 minutes away, as is Causeway Bay.

Healthcare

The Adventist Hospital (p.131) is the one that expats generally visit. It has outpatient consultation till late in the evening with child specialists, gynaecologists and general physicians. Emergency services are available 24 hours.

Education

Bradbury Junior School (2574 8249) and the French International Schools (p.150) are very close. Parkview International Pre-school (p.147) is conveniently located inside the Parkview complex.

Chung Hom Kok & Headland Drive

Traffic & Parking
Public transport is routed through here to Ma Hang estates and Stanley. There is no parking at all and the lanes leading to residences are private and deserted.

A five minute hop, skip and jump from Stanley, this neighbourhood used to be quiet and secluded but a few years ago a massive government housing estate, Ma Hang, was constructed on a stretch of wild land between Stanley and Chung Hom Kok. A main road, a thoroughfare for public buses and minibuses, now links the two neighbourhoods. Much construction is ongoing here as the aging apartments are being either demolished or renovated.

Headland Drive is a quiet, secluded place just as you come up the road from Chung Hom Kok on the way to Repulse Bay. It's a long drive down to the old and spacious apartments and townhouses with beautiful sea views. These are expensive. Some are privately owned and seldom come on the leasing market.

Accommodation

Safety & Annoyances
The south side fire station (2813 2496) is located here. This is now a thoroughfare with heavy traffic throughout the week. As is the norm here, apartment blocks have security and even the old apartments (which used to allow anyone to walk in) now have encoded entrances. If you are on the main road, you'll get noise from the traffic, and you may also hear construction somewhere nearby.

You have a choice between aging townhouses with high rents and small low-rise, old style apartments that are less expensive. Many are gradually being refurbished as the property market picks up. Roads and lanes lead in different directions where rows and rows of town houses and private homes are hidden away on the sides of steep hills. The houses can be up to five storeys with sea views. Rents range from $30,000 to $90,000 upwards.

Shopping & Amenities

Sunny Beauty Salon (2813 0299), Dolphin dry cleaners (2813 0618) and a Wellcome supermarket are located in a small building with free parking. A Chinese language centre, Beijing Mandarin (2865 1660), offers courses in Mandarin.

Entertainment & Leisure

The beaches along the coastline are secluded and rocky, and see no real crowds. Stanley is a few minutes away and buses run this route all day.

Healthcare

Nearby in Stanley and Repulse Bay, both approximately five minutes by car, are medical practitioners covering this neighbourhood. The Quality Healthcare Medical Centre (2812 2392) is in Stanley Plaza, and on Beach Road in Repulse Bay there's Medical Practice (2592 9000).

Education

Being close to Hong Kong International School (p.150) is one of the reasons people choose to live here, and there's a choice of playschools in nearby Tai Tam and Repulse Bay, taking 10 or 15 minutes to reach.

Deep Water Bay & Shouson Hill

Traffic & Parking
There are parking meters by the beach but it can be hard to nab a spot. Buses pass through here to Repulse Bay, Stanley and Aberdeen. Traffic flows in Deep Water Bay all day, but Shouson Hill only sees cars passing through and an occasional minibus.

Deep Water Bay is a main road starting at Black's Link, down through Shouson Hill and coming out by the Golf Club. It leads to Repulse Bay through Island Road, a quiet and exclusive place that's green and hilly, with narrow winding roads and townhouses by the sea and low-rise apartments overlooking from the slopes behind. Away from the main road, people choose to live here because of the lush surroundings, and the roomy old apartments and townhouses. For public transport, you have to walk down to the main road, though a mini bus going to Central runs through it. It takes 10 minutes to get to Happy Valley, Wan Chai and Causeway Bay – the main business and commercial areas of Hong Kong.

Safety & Annoyances ◀
All buses run on the main road so the noise and crowds don't affect the residential part unless of course you happen to live on the main road. Like the other Southside residential areas, this is also safe and quiet.

Accommodation

Privately owned, expensive town houses are scattered along the Seaview Promenade and a few old apartments can be seen on Deep Water Bay Road. Housing on this road and in Shouson Hill is low-rise and a mix of old and new. Large, new townhouses have been built here recently and renovations are ongoing in parts. Many secluded private homes are built on hills with views of the sea. Some even have helipads. Rents range from $35,000 to$100,000 upwards.

Shopping & Amenities

Supermarkets and other shopping facilities are available in Repulse Bay or nearby Aberdeen. A ParknShop supermarket is located on Shouson Hill Road.

Entertainment & Leisure

A nine-hole golf course in Deep Water Bay Golf and Country Club lies in a deep gully way below the Repulse Bay Road. Close by is Ocean Park (p.203) with exhibits and a water world. A closed cable car with breathtaking views (not for the fainthearted) gets you over the mountain to the other side of the park. Here you can see a shark museum, dolphin and whale shows, exhibits about the Middle Kingdom and then descend down on a giant escalator (the longest in the world, apparently) to public buses.

You can get a seasonal pass for the whole family that works out cheaper than paying for each visit. With Disneyland stealing the show, Ocean Park has its own plans to lure folk its way. The Hong Kong Country Club is also located here but is strictly members only.

The beach is small and crowds descend on it, meaning traffic gets choked up at all hours of the day. A small cafe by the beach serves cold beer and other soft drinks with light snacks.

Healthcare

Repulse Bay is the closest way to get to a doctor as opposed to Admiralty or Central, and will take you anywhere between 20 and 40 minutes depending on the time of day.

Education

The ESF South Island Secondary School (2555 9313) is located nearby on Nam Fung Road. Hong Kong International School (p.150) is not far off in Repulse Bay and Tai Tam.

Traffic & Parking ◀
For golf buggies there are places to park but because there are no private cars and heavy public transport, traffic is not an issue and you don't need parking.

Discovery Bay

This is a resort-like residential place where expats with families like to live, particularly since you get more space and a garden for your buck and you're that little bit further away from the big smoke. It's a self-sufficient community with its own 24 hour ferry service, a clubhouse for residents, a plaza where everyone hangs out, a marina, a golf course and lots of activities for residents.

There are no cars but people drive around in golf buggies that are limited in number. To get one, put your name on a waiting list as soon as you've decided you want to live here. With no major public transportation, there is less pollution and plenty of space for children to play and run around safely.

Small buses at the ferry terminal will take you to your home or other destinations. Pick up the free magazine *Inside DB* for information on services, products, events and entertainment happening in Discovery Bay. The website www.discoverybay.com.hk also has information.

91

Safety & Annoyances ◀

Discovery Bay is a safe place but people find they have to plan their life around the ferries. When they are on other islands, the ferry crossings dictate when they must leave and this dependence on the ferry can be annoying and restrictive.

Accommodation

Mainly low-rise and small apartments for medium range rents but the spacious houses on Headland Road and Seabee Lane come complete with gardens and pools. Siena, a new and fancy complex, has all the facilities and is a new look for Discovery Bay. Apartment blocks are set apart from each other so there's no overcrowding and the area is surrounded by wide-open spaces. Rents range from $30,000 to $90,000.

Shopping and Amenities

A branch of the Wing On department store, ParknShop supermarket, Mannings and Watson's chemists are all here. Hardware stores, florists, hairdressers, DVD rentals (Movieland, 2987 7111), property and travel agents, HSBC and financial services, vets and health products can be found in the main shopping area.

Residents still commute to Hong Kong Island to meet friends, shop in malls, visit the theatre or cinema and, of course, go to work.

A Catholic and Anglican Church, and International Community Church serve the residents. A post office, a fire and ambulance service (2987 7502) and a police post (2987 7502) are all located in the main areas.

There are sports and activities centres including a resident's club, a golf and marina club and a few bars, restaurants and cafes.

The DB Ferry pier is located near the plaza and the crossing times are displayed outside.

Education

Discovery Bay International School (p.149) often has a waiting list. Pre-schools and kindergartens include Sunshine House Kindergarten and Nursery (p.147), Discovery Mind Kindergarten (2897 8088) and Discovery Mind International Play Centre (2987 8028). There is also a children's art school, Treasure House (2987 4217) and the DMR School of Ballet (2987 4338).

Healthcare

Medical services are provided by the two medical clinics serving the island: Discovery Bay Medical Services (2525 6798, 24 hour emergency 9181 6540) and Island Health (2987 7575, emergency 9185 3271). There is also a Medical Services hotline (2525 6798) and a Health & Dental Care Clinic (2666 6183) and the Hung Shing Medicine Company (2987 4138) for Chinese medicine and physician.

Leisure & Entertainment

The Discovery Bay Resident's Club offers facilities such as a swimming pool, tennis courts, and social events for adults and children.

If you join the Discovery Bay Golf Club (p.244), you'll get the pleasure of playing a round on high hills with beautiful views. If you decide to sail or invest in a boat, there is a marina where - for a fee - you can keep your boat but you will have to join the Marina Club. Club Siena in the new housing, Siena One, also offers facilities and activities for members and residents.

Happy Valley

Happy Valley's claim to fame is the fact that it is situated around a horse racing track. It feels like a village – a factor that many seem to like. It is a short distance from Causeway Bay, Mid-Levels and Central, and all local amenities are within walking distance from the apartments. It's generally a clean place with no massive construction going on.

Plenty of buses, minibuses and trams go to all business and commercial districts. Inside the racecourse there are playing fields, a running track and a large park.

Residential Areas

Traffic & Parking
There are more parking meters around this area than anywhere else on the Island. You can park using an octopus card ($2 per 15 minutes). Traffic is heavy all day with buses, minibuses and a tram around the racecourse to Chai Wan in the east and Kennedy Town to the west of the island.

Accommodation

Many of the apartments are small, with no views, and often of not very good quality – perfect for meagre budgets! The layouts are old fashioned and often the kitchen and bathrooms are deal breakers. Entrances and lobbies have been spruced up and residents get a security code to enter the building. While this is a low-rise area, new towering apartment blocks like The Leighton Hill, keep popping up with ongoing redevelopment. There are serviced apartments like the Eaton House (3182 7000) and The Emperor Byron Hotel (2893 3693) on Wang Tak Street. Rents can go from $20,000 to $50,000.

Shopping & Amenities

There is a post office on Po Shun Street, Wellcome and ParknShop supermarkets, a local market for fresh meat and produce, a deli, banks, bakeries, florists, many dry cleaners, Movieland DVD rental (2836 3885), property agents, hardware stores and much more, all on the main roads, keeping this place buzzing all day. There are two petrol stations and leading off from the main road, car repair garages in narrow lanes.

Once you walk away from these village-like amenities towards Causeway Bay, you see ornate furniture shops, and shoe and bag shops where you can have any style copied for a small price. Keep walking for 15 minutes and you will reach Times Square (p.323), the big fancy shopping mall with 10 floors of shopping and lots of restaurants in the Food Forum.

Safety & Annoyances
A large police station is located here. When you park using the meters, don't stay a minute over or you'll get a ticket because traffic wardens are always on the prowl. On race nights, the flow of traffic is controlled and traffic backs up all around the track creating delays, noise and fumes. Roads can be blocked for hours on these nights.

Entertainment & Leisure

There are local restaurants and fast food outlets everywhere. Causeway Bay is almost walking distance with all the shopping and entertainment you could want. Races are held on Wednesday and Saturday nights and inside the track there are sports fields where teams from schools or associations practise and play matches. You can go inside and watch. Walk around the cemetery and check out the history of Hong Kong on the tombstones. Three clubs are located here but all are for members; The Hong Kong Jockey Club (p.269), the Hong Kong Football Club (p.269) and the Craigengower Cricket Club (p.268).

Healthcare

The Hong Kong Sanatorium and Hospital (p.132) on Shan Kwong Road, is a private hospital with the latest x-ray facilities, out patient and emergency services.

Education

The French International School (p.150) and the Japanese International School (2574 5479) are a few minutes away up in Jardine's Lookout, as is the Bradbury Junior School (2574 8249) on Upper Stubbs Road. Woodland Pre-School (2575 0042) for children aged 1 to 6 years, is located on Hawthorn Road.

Traffic & Parking
There are no cars or public transport on this island so it's either walking or cycling. Most people tend to walk since everything is close by. Goods are transported in little open buggies and of course the ferries and private boats and junks come to the island all day bringing visitors or hikers and residents.

Lamma Island

This is the closest island to Hong Kong with public ferries operated by New World First Ferry going from pier seven of the Outlying Islands Ferry Terminal across from IFC Tower 2 in Central. It takes about 25 minutes by fast ferry and 40 minutes by ordinary ferry. Private ferries from Aberdeen get you there in 20 minutes. There are two sides to this island. One side, Sok Kwa Wan, has fresh seafood restaurants and a few private homes. Yung Shue Wan on the other side is about 20 minutes walk away and home to many expats. When the property market was at an all time high in the 90s, expats who could not afford the rents elsewhere moved to Yung Shue Wan. It fast became known as the trendy place to live for entrepreneurial and arty expats.

Accommodation

Living in Yung Shue Wan you can have the luxury of a small courtyard or garden. It's a quaint little neighbourhood with narrow streets lined with small houses and shops. Rents range from $4,000 to $15,000.

Shopping & Amenities

Safety & Annoyances
Break-ins can happen but generally Lamma Island is a safe place. During weekends and other holidays, it can get crowded and noisy and the restaurants are packed. One big annoyance on Lamma is the China Light and Power (CLP) plant. While it is said to be an environmentally friendly plant, people are sceptical and continue to complain about it. Whatever stance you take, the plant is considered by many residents as an eyesore with its tall, smoky chimneys blocking the view.

You can get basic things like fresh vegetables, fruit, meat and fish from the grocery shops. Local mini supermarkets sell canned and frozen imported food, snacks and toiletries. Green Cottage, on the main street, is good for organic grains, fruit preserves, fresh bread, cheese and other foodstuffs. A small organic farm by the beach sells freshly picked herbs and lettuce.
Ferries to Central or Aberdeen leave every 30 to 40 minutes.

Leisure & Entertainment

Further into the island is Concerto Inn (2982 1668) a small hotel on the beach where you can have a meal or a cup of tea between blooming trees while looking out to sea. The famous pigeon restaurant Han Lok Yuen (2982 0680) also draws people to this side of the island regularly. You need to make reservations so that they can prepare in advance. A few Chinese seafood restaurants and bars and cafes serving western food can be found on the main street, but the Bookworm Café is the highlight of this island with its Mediterranean style vegetarian and organic dishes.
A quick walk down paved paths with open sea views will get you to Sok Kwa Wan and more Chinese seafood restaurants and a temple. Take the steps up and cross the island through thick foliage to get to that big beach at Mo Tat Wan.

Mid-Levels, Central

Traffic & Parking
It often seems impossible to find a space anywhere in Mid-Levels. We highly advise that you leave your car and take public transport as much as you can, or better still, walk! Parts of Mid-Levels, like Kennedy Road, Magazine Gap Road, May Road and Old Peak Road, are too narrow and winding for trucks or big buses and are served by minibuses and taxis only, so unlike some other areas, there is no heavy traffic.

Safety & Annoyances
Like all other parts of Hong Kong, this is a safe area but because apartments are close together, watch out for break-ins by cat burglars who could be working a few floors above or below you. Try and keep your windows closed, especially so if there's no one home.
Some sections like Bowen Road, MacDonnell Road, May Road and Old Peak Road are overbuilt with tall blocks. Older and smaller apartment blocks were torn down to make room for these, with construction ongoing for the last 10 years. For now it's quiet but being an expensive area and with climbing rents, building could start again.

This is the middle part of the island where winding roads run along the sides of steep hills facing the harbour. High apartment blocks are built up on the slopes offering incredible views of the harbour and also influencing the rent prices.

Mid-Levels is a dense and very prestigious residential part of Hong Kong. In some parts, rows of buildings are stacked tightly together and your only view is the apartment next door. If you're lucky enough to live higher up though, you'll enjoy a spectacular harbour view. Everyone wants to live here because it's just 10 minutes by taxi or minibus into Central and Admiralty, the main business and commercial areas, and a pleasant strolling distance from parks.

Most of the strictly expat enclaves are right here with large and expensive apartments and penthouses. Walking paths, steps and trails are everywhere, the most popular being Bowen Path that takes you all the way past Wan Chai to Stubbs Road. You can walk through the sprawling Zoological and Botanical Gardens, the first park built for expats back in the 1800s, and through Hong Kong Park all the way down to Central.

The most sought after areas are Upper Stubbs Road (that continues on as Peak Road), Coombe Road, Magazine Gap Road, May Road, Tregunther Path and Old Peak Road. Bowen Road, then MacDonnell Road and down to Kennedy Road are slightly lower rental areas but still close to Wan Chai, Central and Admiralty.

Accommodation

Much of Mid-Levels is considered upscale; the apartments here tend to be large and expensive with good views and many blocks have penthouses, often with a roof garden or terrace. This is an expat-concentrated area so you won't get much of the local culture on your doorstep. New blocks like Dynasty Court, Queen's Garden, Clovelly Court, Mayfair Aigburth and many others offer facilities such as a a swimming pool, tennis court, gym, clubhouse with activities and shuttle bus service. Old apartments still attract hefty rents even though the newer blocks are slowly creeping in. But it's the older buildings that provide a sense of character with excellent layout, space and large balconies. Rents range from $35,000 to $120,000.

Shopping & Amenities

Clovelly Court on May Road has a small Wellcome supermarket serving that area. On MacDonnell Road, Coda Plaza has a few floors of shopping, a ParknShop supermarket and a carpark. If you spend $200 at the supermarket you get one hour free parking. There's also been a flower shop here for as long as anyone can remember.

Pacific Place, Central and Wan Chai are close by and everything you could possibly want is there. Malls and markets, theatres and cinemas, hotels, bars and restaurants, are all within walking distance. Shuttles from various buildings go back and forth all day to Central and Admiralty taking their tenants to work, to the shops, and to bigger transport hubs.

Entertainment & Leisure

Up on Old Peak road is the Ladies Recreational Club (p.269). It used to be a women's club but now membership is open to couples and families. Typical club facilities and activities are offered to members, while restaurants and rooms can be hired for parties, weddings and seminars.

The YWCA English Speaking Members Department on MacDonnell Road (3476 1340), offers courses ranging from cooking, painting, yoga, mah-jong, hikes, historical tours and activities for children.

Most residential blocks have play areas for children but and the Zoological and Botanical Garden (p.208) with reptiles, monkeys and other animals is also nearby. Hong Kong Park (p.201) has a goldfish and turtle pond where cygnets gracefully float around, a tai chi court and aviary, and a planetarium with some interesting displays. The Museum of Teaware (p.196) is also located in the park. A children's park and public playgrounds with swings and slides can be found in Brewin Path and Coombe Road, with octopus card metered parking.

Close by, in the back streets of Central, are SoHo and Lan Kwai Fong, the trendy, but pricey, restaurant and bar area. Prepare yourself for happy hour, and by late evening the whole area turns into one big party.

Healthcare

Run by the nuns from the Canossian Order, is the Canossa Hospital (p.131) on Old Peak Road. Nearby, Hong Kong Adventist Hospital (p.131) and Hong Kong Heart Centre (2574 6211) is run by the Seventh Day Adventists and is located on Upper Stubbs Road. Both are private hospitals catering to expats, and provide full medical facilities including emergency services, outpatient consultation and well-woman clinics.

Education

The English Schools Foundation's head office (2574 2351/2818 6332) is located on Upper Stubbs Road, close to one of its schools, the Bradbury Junior School (2574 8249). The ESF Island Secondary School (2524 7135), Small World Christian Kindergarten (p.147) and Carmel (Jewish) School of Hong Kong (p.149) can be found on Borrett Road.

Traffic & Parking
Tai Hang Road is the main road with heavy traffic all day, easing up as you drive further into residential areas. There is no meter parking but carparks are located in the two shopping complexes.

Mid-Levels, East

This area includes Tai Hang Road and Jardine's Lookout, parts of town that overlook Happy Valley and just a short 15 minutes from Causeway Bay. Many expats live here but it is neither a complete expat enclave nor overly sought-after, unlike the Southside or Mid-Levels Central. This is a quieter area and feels like a suburb with wide roads, supermarkets and plenty of public transport. Here you'll find houses owned by consulates for their senior consular officers and many private houses.

Accommodation

You'll find a mix of high-rise and old, low-rise apartments with reasonably low rents depending on the building, size and quality of the apartment. Here and there, you'll see Chinese-style private homes and high-rise government apartments that are soon to be demolished. Apartments like Cavendish Heights have clubhouse facilities but other apartments may have only a pool and tennis courts. Rents from $25,000 to $60,000.

Safety & Annoyances

This is a quiet neighbourhood, mainly residential, with schools in cul-de-sacs so there's little clogging up of the main roads. Some people find this part of town a bit out of the way, the housing too old and some of it just downright ugly. To its advantage, this is an open and quiet neighbourhood, with plenty of amenities and it's conveniently close to Happy Valley and Causeway Bay, the busy commercial districts. You can get an old-style renovated apartment for a reasonable price.

Shopping & Amenities

There are two small shopping complexes here; one has a ParknShop supermarket, the other has a Wellcome supermarket, Mannings chemist, Clean Living dry cleaners (2334 0141), HSBC ATM, a post office and a gas station.

Entertainment & Leisure

A 20 minute taxi ride gets you to the heart of Causeway Bay, complete with shopping, cinema, restaurants and bars as well an MTR station to whisk you to other parts of Hong Kong.

Healthcare

The Adventist Hospital (p.131) is the nearest hospital with emergency services, out-patient consultation, travel immunisation advisory and a pharmacy.

Causeway Bay

Education

French International School (p.150) has two campuses located here. The FIS bases its curriculum on the British school system, and prepares students for the GCSEs from Cambridge University. The Japanese International School (2574 5479) is also in this area but mainly for Japanese expats. Starters School is for children aged 2 to 6 years. Its two schools are located at 3 Tai Hang Road (2527 8676) and 12-22, Queen Road East (2577 9328).

Traffic & Parking

Because of narrow and winding lanes, parking is difficult and there's no meter parking. People living here often don't own cars but those who do end up paying extra for parking privileges.

Mid-Levels, West

The residential part above Central is considered Mid-Levels West. This includes Glenealy, Robinson Road, Conduit Road, Poshang Road, Kotewall Road, Bonham Road and Caine Road. All these, and many other paths around them, are choc-a-bloc full of old apartments, jammed against each other, darkening the inside and blocking out the others' views.

Up until the end of the Second World War, this was the original Mid-Levels and when the other side of the mountain developed into the fashionable Mid-Levels of today, this was reduced to a 'has-been' with aging and dated-looking structures and poorly valued property. Some parts have been gutted and redeveloped but the smart new blocks contain tiny apartments that still attract high rents.

Ever since the Mid-Levels escalator was constructed in the 90s from Central to Caine Road and Robinson Road, the back streets over which it passes, have developed into trendy areas for wining and dining. Living around here means you are close to everything and public transport is efficient so commuting is not an issue. This area has good housing options for those on a budget.

Accommodation

Some people choose to live here because of the old-world atmosphere. While some parts are all concrete, other sides are overrun with old trees and rustic gardens. The bathrooms and kitchens of old apartments leave much to be desired. The layout is tight and because of the density of apartments, they tend to be dark inside which - for Chinese - is bad feng shui or unlucky. But foreigners will lease them for low rents, from $25,000 to $50,000.

97

Safety & Annoyances
*Some areas are quiet
and serenely secluded
and some parts are
noisy with traffic and a
heavy stream of
people. If you live close
to the Escalator and
Central and if you
happen to be living
above a bar or near a
restaurant, beware: the
revelry goes on all
night, and is especially
wild on weekends.
The rule for keeping
windows locked if you
are out and about
applies here too.
The density of
buildings lined along
narrow roads can be
visually stressful. Some
parts further along the
mountain are far
removed from most
amenities, though
public transport is
conveniently available.
Much construction is
going on as old
buildings are being
gutted and new ones
take their place.*

As you come onto the lower parts, like Caine Road and Bonham Road, studio and serviced apartments become more prolific. Normally apartments would be considered low budget but since it's close to Central, the cost is similar to apartments a short distance away in Sheung Wan or 30 minutes away in Happy Valley and Causeway Bay. Rents vary widely from $15,000 to $40,000.

Shopping & Amenities

If you are up on Conduit, Robinson, Kotewall and Poshang area, there are no amenities close by except for a few good walking trails. You're looking at walking to the Central Escalator or taking public transport to Caine Road or Bonham Road to buy your groceries, mail a letter, eat out or see a film.

On Caine Road and Bonham Road you'll find banks, convenience stores, fast food, hardware stores, bakeries, and Wellcome and ParknShop supermarkets. Since all supermarkets deliver, you can go to any that is convenient for you. Plenty of public buses, mini buses and taxis can be found in these parts. Steps and paths lead you down to Central and Admiralty, so people walk down but tend to take a taxi back rather than attempt the uphill trek. Alternatively, many ride the Central Escalator, which runs uphill after 10:00 when the office crowds have gone.

Entertainment & Leisure

Restaurants, bars, art galleries and trendy night life areas like SoHo and Lan Kwai Fong are all around the Central Escalator and Wan Chai bars and restaurants are a 20 minute taxi ride. The Fringe Club (2802 0088) and the Foreign Correspondents' Club (2521 1511) are on Ice House Street. The Fringe Club displays local artwork (p.189) and stages plays and talks by visiting and local groups. On the rooftop is a restaurant and bar (p.395) where people hold meetings or just drop by for drinks and snacks after work. The FCC is a well-known writers' and journalists' haunt. There was a time when you would see famous journalists or writers hanging around the wood-panelled bar. The membership is different now but the colonial atmosphere still lingers.

From Hatton Road, off Kotewall Road, a wooded path leads all the way up to Lugard Road on the Peak, where early morning walkers can be seen with their dogs.

Healthcare

There are private doctors and healthcare clinics in many of the office buildings in Central. Check the *Yellow Pages* or pick up *HK Magazine's Big Black Book* in bookstores.

The HK Central Hospital (p.132) is located on Lower Albert Road and Canossa Hospital (p.131) on Old Peak Road is a private hospital run by the Canossian nuns. It has maternity services, a travel advisory clinic, a nutritionist, dental clinic and general medical consultation.

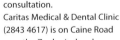

Caritas Medical & Dental Clinic (2843 4617) is on Caine Road near the Zoological and Botanical Gardens.

Education

The ESF Glenealy Junior School (2522 1918) is located on Hornsey Road, off Old Peak Road. Woodlands Mid-Levels Montessori Pre-School (2549 1259) is located on Caine Road.

Traffic & Parking ◀

Public parking is available under the Galleria and if you have shopped or eaten there you can get your parking ticket stamped for some free parking time. Octopus operated meter parking is also available on the main road. Traffic gets very bad during weekends and holidays and during Chinese festivals. Buses and mini buses are abundant and the ride up from Central is truly spectacular as the bus climbs upwards.

Safety & Annoyances ◀

The Peak tram area is a busy tourist area and all visitors to Hong Kong make a pilgrimage to the Peak to walk around and enjoy the views. The hustle and bustle makes this part of town a tad noisy and crowded on most days of the week but more so on weekends and holidays. If you live away from the Galleria and the Peak tram, you won't be disturbed as much but traffic quickly chokes up the main road. Rents are very high. Some apartments are far from the main road, which means walking some distance to the bus stop or alternatively catching a cab. You can call a radio taxi; keep a handy list by the phone. (Hong Kong Taxi Centre 2574 7311; Wai Fat Taxi 2861 1008; Wing Tai Radio Taxi 2865 7398)

The Peak

This area boasts some of the most expensive residential real estate in Hong Kong. It is 554 metres above sea level with panoramic views of the harbour and the islands. When humidity rises in the spring and during typhoon season, apartments get very damp which is off-putting for those looking to live here, but it's still an address that raises eyebrows.

The Peak starts at Guildford Road and Barker Road and continues up to Mount Austin Road with side roads like Plantation Road, Mt Kellett Road and Gough Road.

Good views can be seen from all around, some parts are quiet and private, and there's a choice of luxurious, good quality houses or old, low-rise apartments that are full of character without the sparkle of modernity.

Basic amenities like supermarkets, public transport and the Peak tram are available. There are hikes and walks to many parts of the island through the Aberdeen Country Park, including the Hong Kong Trail that ends up in Shek O.

Visitors and residents ride the famous Peak Tram (p.205) up from Central to enjoy the view, stroll around Lugard Road and walk the many lush trails leading down to different parts of the Island through country parks.

Accommodation

Houses and low-rise apartments, some from the 40s and 50s era, are perched on top of hills all around the Peak or tucked away down a quiet lane. To get to the markets or public transport you will need to walk or take a taxi to the main road but most people living here own cars.

Longstanding companies such as HSBC own apartments here for their employees. Smart new houses are sprawling and swallowing old architecture, and are a far cry from the colonial structures that they replace. Rents range from $50,000 to $200,000.

Shopping & Amenities

The famous Peak Tram takes you through deep ravines and past the high buildings of Mid-Levels into Central in seven minutes. It runs from 07:00 to midnight, leaving every 15 minutes.

You can take bus number 15 from Exchange Square in Central and then on weekends and holidays buses 515 from Shau Kei Wan and 15B from Tin Hau, every 10 to 15 minutes. The ride takes about 30 to 40 minutes depending on the traffic. Green minibus number 1 from City Hall leaves every 10 minutes.

Galleria, the big shopping mall in the area, sits right next to Peak Tram station and has three floors with all kinds of shops from clothes to books to shoes to paintings. There's a ParknShop supermarket on level two.

Dine at Café Deco (p.372) on the top floor with stunning views. Or just go up to the roof to get a free view.

Shooters 52 (2838 5252) on the ground floor is a good family restaurant serving American style food. Galleria also houses a Delifrance and a Haagen Daaz ice cream parlour. On the main road is a shopping complex with a florist, a Wellcome Supermarket and Mannings chemist with parking for customers only. A mobile post office is parked near the Galleria everyday.

Entertainment & Leisure

The Peak Tram station opposite Galleria is crowded with people all the time. Browse here for typical tourist stuff like postcards and souvenirs. The Galleria has a selection of shops, mainly catering to tourists.

The icon Peak Tower, which was recently renovated, also has shops as well as a Madame Tussauds wax museum, and a rooftop viewing terrace.

The Peak Lookout, (p.375) across from the Galleria serves fine food, with a mix of Asian and western dishes. There's an outdoor seating area with amazing views that's perfect in good weather. Reservations are recommended.

A stroll around Lugard Road takes about an hour along a lush and shaded path. The Governor's Walk is a set of steep steps and a winding path, bringing you to the wide-open and quiet Victoria Peak Garden (p.202) making it well worth the 30 minute climb. As you walk down Mount Austin road, you pass Mount Austin Park, the road that will take you back to Peak Tram and Galleria.

There are also nature trails leading off to Pok Fu Lam and Aberdeen country parks, and you can easily turn them into all day hikes that are best done in groups.

Education

The English Schools Foundation Peak School (2849 7211) is located on Plunkett Road. On level three of Galleria is the Sunshine Pre-School (2849 7123). Further down on Guildford Road is the German Swiss International School (p.150) with a British grammar school curriculum and preparation for GCSE, A/S and A-level examinations.

Highgate House School (p.146) is at 100 Peak Road and the Woodland Peak Pre-School (2849 8007) is on 81 Peak Road.

Healthcare

Matilda Hospital (p.142) on Mt. Kellett Road is where most expats tend to go. The hospital has undergone total renewal and now looks more like a four-star hotel.

The Matilda Child Development Centre (2849 6138) offers an early intervention program for the development of mentally handicapped children with assessment and counselling for all ages.

Pok Fu Lam & Cyberport

Traffic & Parking

Pok Fu Lam neighbourhood is on both sides of Pok Fu Lam Road, a straight road with no bends or curves like the rest of the Island. There are speed cameras along this stretch so one day you might find a speeding ticket in the mail. While this is indeed an open area, there is not much free parking around.

The main Pok Fu Lam Road and Victoria Road lead on to the Aberdeen Praya Road that continues on to the Southside and links up with roads going to Deep Water Bay, Repulse Bay and beyond to Stanley and Tai Tam. The Hong Kong University campus is spread along both sides of Pok Fu Lam Road. Mount Davis Road, Sassoon Road and Bisney Road are low-rise, small and old housing areas with no views. Living here means you get more space for your money if you have a lean budget. This is an open area with steep mountains, deep gullies, and wide sea views looking far over the South China Sea.

Down by the sea is Victoria Road, a big Christian Cemetery, Sandy Bay (where there is a home for the elderly) and the Sandy Bay Hospital for Handicapped Children.

Ten minutes away is the Cyberport, a new IT centre, with towering apartment blocks looking out towards the Lamma Channel. Cyberport is a neighbourhood unto itself, with housing, offices, a mall, a post office and a Meridien Hotel.

If you would like to volunteer for charitable causes, the Springboard Project for special needs children aged 5 to 18 years (p.72), Riding School for the Disabled, the Sandy Bay Hospital for Children, the Ebenezer School and the Home for the Visually Impaired are all located here and can always use an extra pair of hands.

Safety & Annoyances

This part of town is as safe as anywhere but be careful about leaving windows open. It is a long commute to the rest of the island because the route goes through some congested parts like Bonham Road and Caine Road or Des Voeux Road and Kennedy Town. This area is on the far side of the Hong Kong Island, away from the main business and commercial districts.

Accommodation

You can choose from several well-known housing complexes complete with facilities. Options range from the new Belchers, which is very small, ornate and expensive for this area, to the Baguio Villas and Scenic Villas which are old, large apartments with big balconies. Around Mount Davis Road and Bisney Road there is a mix of high and low rise, old and small apartments. On one end of Sassoon Road you'll find some exclusive town houses tucked away, and Victoria Road is home to large exclusive villas. Residence Bel Air in Cyberport has small but smart apartments and penthouses. The second phase of the complex is still under construction. Rents go from $20,000 to $60,000.

Shopping & Amenities

Wellcome supermarket is located in Scenic Villas and ParknShop supermarkets are in Baguio Villas and Cyberport. The Belchers shopping mall, Westwood, has a McDonald's, Panash bakery and cafe, a big Wellcome supermarket and retail outlets. Close by is Kennedy Town with its hardware stores, $10 stores, more supermarkets, fresh food local markets, bakeries, laundry and dry cleaners, furniture shops, photo developing, banks and restaurants serving mainly local fare. The post office in Kennedy Town is located on Hau Wo Street.

From here, plenty of buses and minibuses go to Central, Causeway Bay and across the harbour to Kowloon and the New Territories.

In the Cyberport mall, which is still new and undiscovered, you'll find banks, ATMs, wedding gown stores, toy and furniture shops and a food court. You get two hours free parking if you show a receipt from any restaurant, supermarket, cinema or shop. If you are going in for the late show, get your parking ticket stamped in the mall by the entrance before the movie starts.

Entertainment & Leisure

Broadway cinema, in the Cyberport mall, screens the latest Hollywood releases and on Tuesdays you can see a film for the discounted price of $40 instead of $60. Restaurants serving Japanese and Chinese fare are the only options of an evening. There is a food court but it's only open during the day and is mainly frequented by office workers. The Meridien Hotel has two restaurants. Other than that, if you want to have a proper night out you're looking at a bit of a trek to Central or Wan Chai.

The Pokfulam Riding School (p.248) is located near the entrance of the Pok Fu Lam Country Park. From the main Pok Fu Lam Road, before the Chi Fu Estates, you can enter the park and walk up to the Peak and onwards to Central or to Wan Chai and Aberdeen. This is a good hike on any given day with lots of wild trails, steps, a reservoir, paved paths and breathtaking views.

Healthcare

Queen Mary Hospital (p.129) is situated on Pok Fu Lam Road and is known for its efficient emergency and 24 hour pharmacy services. While you can use the hospital for emergencies, you need to be referred by a doctor for other consultations. Waiting time for consultation can be up to one hour even with an appointment made months in advance but if its urgent they'll arrange for a doctor to see you.

Education

West Island School (2819 1962) is located on Victoria Road and Kennedy Junior School (2855 0711) is on Sha Wan Drive in Sandy Bay. Both are ESF schools.
Sunshine House Pre-School and Kindergarten (2551 3213) is located in Chi fu Fa Yuen. Kellet School (p.151), an independent non-profit English school is located in Wah Fu Estates on Pok Fu Lam Road.

Traffic & Parking
Traffic is generally bad on weekdays, holidays and during rush hours. There is parking in The Repulse Bay, a small parking lot by the beach and in the Dairy Farm complex and plenty of octopus card parking meters by the beach. You can buy an octopus card or top up at the 7-Eleven on Beach Road.

Repulse Bay & Repulse Bay Road

This is one of the most popular residential neighbourhoods in Hong Kong, both with expats and Chinese. For expats, it's like living in a resort, as the apartments and townhouses are perched along the edge of the sea with stunning views and breathtaking sunrises and sunsets. For Chinese it has good feng shui with the sea in front signifying abundance and mountains behind providing protection.

Well-known for its beach and an old, upscale hotel facade with a shopping arcade known as The Repulse Bay, this area lies around the bay with a main road running through it, making it a very busy suburb during the day, and even more so at the weekends. Since everything is so close by you can walk to the market, the beaches and restaurants, the post office on South Bay Road and the shops in the arcade.

Repulse Bay Road starts near the Cricket Club and runs all the way into Repulse Bay. Expensive apartments, old and large, are situated along this road. There are no markets nearby so it means driving or hopping onto one of the buses into town or to Repulse Bay – a trip that affords spectacular views. You're recommended to take a ride down this road on the top deck of a bus (about $6) from Central to Stanley.

Safety & Annoyances
The main road that runs through the neighbourhood is a thoroughfare for buses and minibuses so there's no let up in traffic. South Bay and Beach Road can remain choc-a-bloc for hours when tourists arrive in droves to see the statues of deities on the beach. Buses line up to load or off-load people, with traffic backing up and long delays resulting in blaring horns and lots of loud cursing. When the beach is packed on weekends, the noise level is known to reach apartments on high floors.

Accommodation

Towering apartment blocks with open sea views are all along Repulse Bay Road. In the Repulse Bay area, well-maintained old (but expensive) apartments are always in demand. New townhouses along the sea on South Bay Road are noticeably smaller. Generally the housing here is not the best and apartments have a large turnover. Rents range from $40,000 to $90,000, but can be much higher.

Shopping & Amenities

An upmarket shopping arcade, previously the famous Repulse Bay Hotel but now known simply as The Repulse Bay, has a Wellcome supermarket, Pacific Coffee Company, Ellespa Beauty Spa (p.273), HSBC Premier Banking and ETC, Taipan dry cleaners (2812 6488) and many shops selling Asian artefacts and good quality home decorations. There are also doctors and dentists here.

Restaurants in the arcade are expensive but well worth it. Spices (p.356) serves Asian food and The Verandah (2292 2822) offers typically western cuisine. A Japanese restaurant, Y-By-The-Bay (2812 2120), has a great open terrace where food is served on garden tables. Victoria City Seafood restaurant (2803 1882) is an upscale Chinese restaurant. Reservations are recommended for them all.

The sprawling gardens of the old hotel are also used for marriages and parties.

Down by the beach, there is a Movieland video and DVD rental shop (2803 1980), Goodwins dry cleaners (2812 2400), a florist, Classica Beauty Corner (2812 0202), Medical Practice (2592 9000) and Veritas Medical Clinic (2812 2677). A Mannings pharmacy and a small Wellcome supermarket cater to beach goers. Pizza Hut (2812 2445) delivers and has a take out service. A 7-Eleven shop sells beach paraphernalia, drinks, frozen foods and barbecue items like coal, forks, marinated meat and sauces.

On South Bay Road, there's a petrol station and around the corner is the post office.

Entertainment & Leisure

This area has the pick of the beaches. The busiest is Repulse Bay Beach (p.199). It's one of the biggest in Hong Kong and probably the most popular. Further down on South Bay Road is Middle Bay Beach, and if you keep going you get to a dead end and South Bay Beach (p.200). Restaurants come and go by the beach, although a mall is under construction and is expected to improve the food scene but also bring in the tourists. As it stands, the only place to eat here is at Pizza Hut. From the beach road, a promenade leads off to Deep Water Bay. If you venture away from the beach and go up South Bay Close by the Hong Kong

International School, you will see steps leading through trees and shrubs. Follow these steps and you will be climbing up a dried streambed, emerging at a junction where the trail then leads down around the intermediate Tai Tam Reservoir into the country park. Put your leg muscles to the test and take on the1,000 step climb over the Twin Peaks to Stanley and you'll be rewarded with breathtaking views.

Healthcare
Byrne's Hickman & Partners Physiotherapy Centre (2812 7231) and Bayley & Jackson Dental Consultants (2812 2358) have branches in the arcade. Down by the beach is Family Medical Practice (2592 9000, emergency 6291 0902) and Veritas Medical Clinic (2812 2677). Appointments are recommended to avoid long waits.

Education
The Hong Kong International School (p.150) has its upper and lower primary campus at 23 South Bay Close. There's a choice of pre-schools from The Woodland Montessori School (2803 1885) and Pre-school (2812 0274) and the Southside Kindergarten (2592 7527).

Shek O

Situated at the southern tip of Hong Kong Island, this is a sleepy village complete with narrow lanes lined with random homes and the odd cat or dog roaming about. It's a 40 minute commute or more to the nearest anything. This village by the sea has fine private homes with lush gardens, hidden from view down long driveways. They are owned or rented by a mix of wealthy Chinese and expats.

Accommodation
Small houses are close to the sea and some expats like to live here for that cosy village atmosphere. There are a few apartment blocks but it's generally a small community. On the main road are the sprawling homes built a century ago, owned by either companies or wealthy individuals. You'll need a retinue of servants to run and maintain them. Rents range from $15,000 to $40,000 in the village, and $300,000 to $500,000 for private vintage houses.

Shopping & Amenities
A small neighbourhood supermarket serves this area, but for most of your shopping or other amenities you will be going to Stanley or Shau Kei Wan.

Entertainment & Leisure
A famous and fairly easy hike, Dragon's Back, runs along the ridge of a high mountain. As you hike along, you'll see hang gliders waiting to take off – they need a licence to do that by the way, just in case you are getting any ideas! Shek O Beach (p.199) is small, but about 10 minutes from the village is Big Wave Bay (p.198), the only beach around Hong Kong with big waves, especially during typhoon season when many brave the rough seas to swim and surf. Shops by the beach rent out equipment and sell drinks, ice cream and snacks. A few local style restaurants serve steaming bowls of noodles or stir-fried meat and vegetables. The beach gets crowded on holidays and weekends during the summer season.

Down in the village, local restaurants serve simple Chinese and Thai food and are visited by hikers who usually end up there for a cold beer and a hot meal. Black Sheep is a famous restaurant here and a recent addition is The Shining Stone, both serving western food. The exclusive Shek O Golf and Country Club (p.246) is sprawled along the main spread with the fairway extending all the way to the edge of the sea.

Traffic & Parking
You can catch a minibus or bus number 9 from Shau Kei Wan MTR station to Shek O village and back and also interchange buses at a roundabout for Tai Tam or Stanley. Extra services run on weekends and holidays but with different fares to the village and the beach. There are octopus card operated parking meters by the beach in the village and near Big Wave Bay.

Safety & Annoyances
On weekdays this is a quiet and calm place, but come weekends and holidays, hoards of people descend on the beach and the village. Cars are parked everywhere, and buses block the traffic as they stop to pick up and let off passengers. Because this area is wild and green, snakes are seen regularly.

Stanley

This is one of the most popular residential areas of Hong Kong and has been an expat enclave ever since anyone can remember, though it was a fishing village before the British chose Hong Kong as a stopover port when they were trading up the Pearl River Delta. People with young children like it here because of nearby Stanley Beach and the convenience of the famous Stanley market. St. Anne's Catholic Church, the Carmelite convent for nuns, Stanley Fort (now defunct and waiting to be redeveloped) and a war cemetery maintained by the International Commission for War Cemeteries, are all located here. Also in this area is a Chinese special needs schools, other Chinese schools of high repute, a prison and a youth rehabilitation centre.

Accommodation

Apartments and townhouse here tend to be old, small and low rise, but rents are expensive. There are some large houses at the edge of the sea. Many old blocks have been demolished to make way for new ones, giving Stanley an overall new and improved look but also losing some of its historical character. Unless your place is along the sea, there may be no view at all. Rents can range from $40,000 to $150,000. Inside the market, leading off from the narrow alleys are small apartments with low budget rents. There are no elevators in them, so sometimes that means walking up four or five flights of stairs. Rents here are from $12,000 to $18,000.

Shopping & Amenities

Stanley market opening hours are 10:00 to 18:00. The market is loaded with Chinese handicrafts, fabrics, and the best kitsch ever. There are framers, barbers, hardware shops, and fruit and flower shops. On the main road you'll find veterinarians and pet food stores, a Wellcome supermarket, the neighbourhood post office and a petrol station.
By the sea wall is Stanley Plaza, a big shopping mall with a bakery, wine shop, a ParknShop superstore, banks and ATMs, hairdressers, pharmacy, Po Fat dry cleaners (2813 2062), photo developing shops, home furnishing stores and a $10 store where you can buy anything for your home from hangers to a mattress.

Entertainment & Leisure

Along the sea wall are many restaurants and bars. During weekends, this area becomes pedestrian. Murray House is an old colonial building that was moved from Central and rebuilt here. It has restaurants and the Hong Kong Maritime Museum (p.196). The famous dragon boat races are held around June/July, a time when parking is virtually impossible.
Land reclamation has pushed the Tin Hau temple away from the edge of the sea where it used to be.

Healthcare

Quality Healthcare Medical Centre (2812 2392) is in Stanley Plaza and nearby on Beach Road in Repulse Bay is Medical Practice (2592 9000). Both centres have general physicians, paediatricians and counsellors. Call ahead to check who's on duty.

Education

St. Teresa's Kindergarten (2812 8567) is for children aged 2 to 5. Redhill Peninsula in Tai Tam has more playschools. The Sunshine House International Pre-School (p.147) takes

---

Traffic & Parking
Octopus card operated two hour or 30 minute ($2 per 15 minutes) parking meters can be found in streets around private residences and on Stanley Beach Road. Buses and minibuses from a hub opposite the market on Main Stanley Road will get you to Central, Causeway and Aberdeen in about 45 minutes via Repulse Bay and to Chaiwan via Tai Tam on the eastern part of the Island.

Safety & Annoyances
A police station (2813 1717) serving Tai Tam, Repulse Bay and Chung Hom Kok, is located here. Because of the beach and Stanley market, it gets very crowded on weekends and other holidays which can be annoyingly disturbing, be prepared to put up with noise and honking till late in the evening. All through the week too, busloads of tourists come to shop for local handicrafts and souvenirs. The hub for buses and minibuses keeps the area noisy and busy all day with roads that tend to get congested at any time of the day. Because of renovation of old apartments, there could be drilling and hammering all day for months.

children from 18 months to 6 years, Woodland's Tai Tam Montessori Pre-School (2525 1655) admits children from 12 months to 6 years, and Tutor Time (p.148) takes children from 6 months to 5 years. These are all located in Redhill Plaza and have bright, colourful rooms, qualified staff and are accredited by various international bodies.

Not far is the Hong Kong International School's lower and upper primary campus in Repulse Bay (2812 5000) and middle and senior school campus in Tai Tam (3149 7000).

Tai Tam

Traffic & Parking
Traffic can get heavy on weekends and rush hours. There are parking meters across the road from the American Club and bus stops along the main road.

Located on the south side of Hong Kong Island, Tai Tam has breathtaking open sea views and what seems like a never-ending range of rolling green hills. It's a quiet and much sought after location by expats even though it's a long haul from shopping, entertainment and working areas. It starts near Stanley and extends to Tai Tam Country Park and Reservoir and includes the Redhill Peninsula. Families who have children going to the Hong Kong International School tend to live here. Stanley is just a short taxi or bus ride away, or you could walk if you're close enough. Walking to Stanley from Redhill Peninsula is not a good idea though, because of the narrow road and the distance.

Accommodation

Safety & Annoyances
Safety and security are no problem in this very expat enclave. Security guards can be seen at the entrance of all buildings. They check identity cards and note visitor car numbers. All lobby entrances or street gates have a code that residents use to enter the premises.

The tall apartment blocks with penthouses, and small units with full amenities are in great demand. Rows of upmarket townhouses are dotted along the cliff edge and come complete with stunning sea views and gardens. Many complexes have security, clubhouses and all the amenities such as a swimming pool, tennis courts and a shuttle service to the nearest MTR station in Chai Wan, about 30 minutes away on the eastern side of the island. Some homes even have private pools. Apartments come in various sizes and are generally in good shape. Since the property market here is high, the aging properties continue to get facelifts. Rents range from $45,000 to $150,000.

Shopping & Amenities

Redhill Plaza is a small mall for the peninsula neighbourhood with a Wellcome supermarket, a bakery, pre-schools and real estate offices.

Entertainment & Leisure

The entrance to Tai Tam Country Park and Reservoir, rich in fish and turtles, has family picnic areas. Hiking trails and paths within lead to Quarry Bay, Repulse Bay and all the way to Parkview Apartments and Repulse Bay Road. Turtle Cove beach is a well-kept secret and doesn't get as crowded as the other beaches. It has a long and winding approach down to the waters edge. There's a scout camp for school excursions and a sea inlet where people keep their sailing boats.

The American Country Club (p.268) is also located nearby. Stanley is not too far away, and is home to many more restaurants, beaches and shopping areas. See p.104.

Healthcare

The closest consultation clinic is Quality Healthcare Medical Centre (2812 2392) in Stanley Plaza, with various specialists available.

Education

The Hong Kong International School middle and senior campuses (p.150) are located here, with on-campus apartments for teaching staff. Nearby is the Redhill Plaza with three pre-schools: Sunshine Playschool (2813 0713), Woodlands Playgroups (2525 1655) and Tutor Time (p.148).

Other Residential Areas

Cheung Chau (Map 13-B2)

This is a well-developed island, but was once just a fishing centre. It has a strong Chinese presence. Local stories still circulate about a pirate, Po Tsai, and his cave that many come to see. The Bun Festival (p.50) is held every year during April or May and ceremonies are

performed in front of the Pak Tai Temple. Floats and parades fill the streets and bun towers attract residents and visitors. When Hong Kong became a British colony, many companies had weekend homes here for their senior employees. R'nR retreats were opened for priests and missionaries going back and forth to China. The retreats are still here and used by groups and schools for excursions and seminars. On the waterfront there are seafood restaurants that get busy on weekends and of an evening. There are supermarkets, convenience stores, local fresh produce shops and a large beach by Hotel Warwick (2981 0081). You can also rent rooms and apartments at the weekend. The big attractions are the sights along the paved paths and the big Chinese graveyard. Only a few expats live here because of the long commute to Central and Kowloon, but many people visit on weekend excursions.

Clear Water Bay (Map 11-A4)

Clear Water Bay is wild with foliage and trees and has little residential concentration. Houses, townhouses and village houses (as they are called) with small terraces and gardens are located down lanes off the main road and often along the seafront. Most people own cars to get around, though there is public transport to main Chinese housing estates or working areas. The nearest town area is Sai Kung, a 20 minute drive away. The newly developed area of Heung Ha is closer for shopping and the MTR. The Clearwater Bay Golf and Country Club is located by the water's edge. The Clear Water Bay Country Park gets busy with picnickers and hikers and the main road gets blocked with parked cars and public transport during weekends and holidays.

The University of Science and Technology (p.153) is located here and there are a few schools, such as the Abacus International Kindergarten (2719 5712) in Mang Kung UK Village, and ESF Clearwater Bay School (2358 3221) on Clear Water Bay Road.

Harbour City (Map 15-C4)

Harbour City is a huge mall with hotels, shopping, restaurants and furnished and self-serviced apartments in Tsim Sha Tsui, the main business and commercial district of Kowloon. It's just a short ferry ride to Central, and is a popular choice for shopping lovers and those who have no families.

Ho Man Tin (Map 15-D2)

This area used to be a place where British government employees lived in large apartments which are now on the market for a reasonable rent of $20,000 to $40,000. It is also close to Nathan Road, the big shopping district of Tsim Sha Tsui.

Several schools are located nearby, serving the New Territories as well. They include the American International School (p.148), Australian International School (p.148), ESF schools, King George V School (2711 3029), Kowloon Junior School (2714 5279), Jockey Club Sarah Roe School (2761 9893), Delia School of Canada (2336 7331), pre-school Tutor Time (2337 0822) and YMCA International Kindergarten (2268 7766).

Hong Lok Yuen (Map 6-B1)

Just off the main Tai Po Road, this is a self-contained expat neighbourhood with independent garden houses, and a clubhouse with a pool, tennis courts, a gym and a supermarket. A few minutes drive on the freeway and you are either in Tai Po market or Sha Tin, depending on which way you aimed. Hong Lok Yuen International School (p.150) and Hong Lok Yuen Kindergarten (2657 0270) are located in this complex, and not far away in Sha Tin there's Sha Tin Junior School (2692 2721) and Sha Tin College (2699 1811). Close by in Tai Po are the Japanese International School (2834 3531), the Norwegian International School (2658 0341) and Valerie's Kindergarten (2665 2838).

Kadoorie Avenue (Map 15-D2)

This was once a very prestigious address in Hong Kong and in a way it still is because accommodation is mainly big, old houses with gardens. The avenue is named after a high-profile entrepreneurial expat family who moved from Shanghai during the communist revolution. They are still prominent in the hotels and property business. The place is now very developed with houses and apartments to rent all around here. Nathan Road, the big shopping area with malls, markets and everything else you can think of, is a few blocks away. Rents would be in six figures for the houses, and apartments are around $35,000 to $55,000.

Need Some Direction?

The *Explorer Mini Maps* pack a whole city into your pocket and once unfolded are excellent navigational tools for exploring. Not only are they handy in size, with detailed information on the sights and sounds of the city, but also their fabulously affordable price means they won't make a dent in your holiday fund. Wherever your travels take you, from the Middle East to Europe and beyond, grab a mini map and you'll never have to ask for directions again.

Lantau Island (Maps 8,9,12 & 13)

This is the largest island, even larger than Hong Kong, but not fully developed. After Hong Kong's international airport at Chek Lap Kok was completed in 1998, roads were built or widened throughout the island, and townhouses were built. In some places the island has begun to lose its natural flora and fauna. Discovery Bay, an expat residential enclave (see p.91), and Disneyland are on the east coast of the island. Public ferries will take you to Mui Wo where you can rent bicycles, hop onto a bus to Cheung Sha beach, up to Po Lin Monastery or around the island to the fishing village of Tai O, where people still live in stilt-houses and dry fish in the sun on the pavements. Worth noting is the fact that Tung Chung is developing into a sizeable community given its proximity to the airport.

North Point (Map 17-C1)

North Point is going through a thorough clean-up and new complexes with full amenities are constantly springing up. Being a commercial area, and just a few minutes from Causeway Bay and Central on the MTR, it does have its appeal. Cloudview Road and Braemar Hill are the low-budget, residential areas of this district and the Chinese International School (2510 7288) and Quarry Bay Junior School (2566 4242) are also located here. Plenty of buses and minibuses will take you down to North Point, Quarry Bay and Causeway Bay, the commercial areas where you can get everything you need. Rents can range from $25,000 to $45,000.

Sai Kung (Map 6-F4)

Sai Kung is very popular with expats, and many long term or permanent residents have bought homes here. You can find simple village houses, low-rise apartments and townhouses. People who choose to live out here like the feel of being out in the country. Homes tend to have more space and often a garden or backyard, for less than you'd pay near the city. And no one seems to mind the hour or so commute to the main parts of Hong Kong. Many expat amenities are available here. There is a small shopping centre with supermarkets, hardware stores, banks, beauty salons, some western style restaurants, many bars and lots of Chinese seafood restaurants along the waterfront

Sai Kung

There is a clubhouse with facilities for members and a marina where people moor their private boats. The sprawling Sai Kung Country Park has a campsite, nature trails and the MacLehose trail that begins around the large High Island reservoir. The Outward Bound school for outdoor recreation and physical training (p.265) is also located here. Sai Kung Pre-school (2791 7354) is in Che Keng Tuk village but for other schools it would be a commute to Kowloon or Sha Tin where there are many ESF schools.

Sheung Wan & Kennedy Town (Map 16)

This is an old part of Hong Kong, dense with ageing buildings and shops selling wholesale Chinese herbal ingredients and dried fish. This is, and always has been, a Chinese commercial and residential area. Tourists can be seen walking around on self-guided tours, checking out the colourful shops and taking in the fast fading local scene. Gradually, this is undergoing a change and expats who cannot afford rents in Central or Mid-Levels are moving into new apartments like The Belchers, a huge residential complex with full amenities such as pool, gym, park and access to Pok Fu Lam and Kennedy Town. On the street level where you exit to Kennedy Town is the Westwood mall with a Wellcome supermarket, fast food outlets, clothes and accessories. Everything else you might need is available in Kennedy Town. Rents here range from $35,000 to $50,000 even though appartments are small, but the amenities and quality of the building are the reasons for these high prices.

Tai Koo Shing (Map 17-E2)

In Tai Koo Shing there are many apartment blocks to choose from, but the accommodation can be small. The area is popular with the expat community because of its close proximity to the MTR and Cityplaza, a huge mall with just about anything you could ever want or need. See p.318 for details. Inside this complex is Delia School of Canada (2885 4786) and about 20 minutes away is the Chinese International and Quarry Bay Junior Schools. Rents can range from $20,000 to $40,000.

Tai Po (Map 6-B1)

This is a fast developing area in the New Territories with constant land reclamation. Science Park, a government research venture, and the Chinese University campus (p.151) are located here, with the surrounding housing area taken up by university staff. Close by is Sha Tin, just two stops away on the KCR. The Sha Tin Town Plaza (p.325) at the train station has restaurants, shops, and banks, and there is easy access to temples and museums nearby. Close to the station exit is a huge IKEA store. Buses and minibuses ply the highways and modern tunnels to all parts of Hong Kong. The KCR serves this widespread area and has recently added an extension, KCR West Rail, that goes all the way to Tuen Mun.

Tung Chung (Map 8-D4)

Not long ago this was a quiet village with an old abandoned fort and not much else. Because of its proximity to the new airport at Chek Lap Kok, it has developed into a small community with mostly high-rise apartments rented by expats who work at the airport or for the local airlines such as Cathay Pacific and Dragonair. Nearby is Citygate, a small mall with a ParknShop supermarket, cinema, restaurants and the MTR service that gets you to the airport in 20 minutes. There's also a ferry service to the airport and plenty of buses going to all parts of Lantau Island. ESF's Bauhinia School (2624 4110) serves Discovery Bay and there is Tinkerbell Nursery School (2109 3873) for the little ones.

International investment
OFFSHORE FUND & PRODUCT AWARDS
WINNER 2004
IN ASSOCIATION WITH STANDARD & POOR'S
Best Offshore Structured Product

International investment
OFFSHORE FUND & PRODUCT AWARDS
WINNER 2005
IN ASSOCIATION WITH STANDARD & POOR'S
Best Offshore Bank Product Range

investment
INTERNATIONAL FUND & PRODUCT AWARDS
WINNER 2006
Best Offshore Bank Product Range

However you view your expat experience in Hong Kong, we can find the right offshore solution designed with you in mind.

Although HSBC Bank International is based in Jersey, we also have a representative branch on level 6 within the HSBC Main Building here in Hong Kong.

We can provide a range of offshore banking and investment solutions to suit your individual needs and our professional team is on the ground ready to help you make the most of your money.

Call 2822 3225

Email jasonfurness@hsbc.com

Click www.offshore.hsbc.com/hongkong

HSBC

The world's local bank

Issued by HSBC Bank International Limited – Hong Kong Branch which is licensed by the Hong Kong Monetary Authority as an Authorised Institution in Hong Kong and licensed for type 1 "dealing in securities" as well as type 4 "advising on securities" under the Securities and Futures Ordinance. HSBC Bank International Limited's principal place of business is Jersey. Please remember that with investments the value of shares and the income from them may go down as well as up, is not guaranteed, and you may not get back the amount you invested. This could also happen as a result of changes in the rate of currency exchange, particularly where overseas securities are held. This advertisement does not constitute an invitation to buy or the solicitation of an offer to sell securities or make deposits in any jurisdiction to any person whom it is unlawful to make such an offer or solicitation in such jurisdiction. Please note, calls may be recorded and may be monitored for security and training purposes. ©HSBC Bank International Limited – Hong Kong Branch. 2006. All Rights Reserved.
MC6774REAWHK

Need Some Friends?
*Now you've set up
home, next you need
to fill it with dinner
parties for new
friends. There are
various social clubs
and organisations in
Hong Kong where
you can meet people
with similar interests
and backgrounds.
Turn to p.262 for
more information.*

Setting Up Home

Once you have signed the lease for your apartment or house, you will be moving in within a month or earlier depending on how much painting and repair work has to be done. The company's settling in allowance can be used to help make your house your home. Relocation consultants, often hired by companies, can help with the big and little things, from ordering curtains to familiarising you with the daily amenities in your neighbourhood. Of course, you can do just as well on your own, because Hong Kong is easy to navigate.

Sometimes, you are better off shipping very little because you can get everything here within different budgets. Much of your buying and ordering will depend on the size of your home and how long you will be living in Hong Kong.

Moving Services

Multinational companies often use relocation firms as a one-stop shop for new staff. A relocation package should include pre-arrival information, packing and moving, visa and other documents, school admissions, home search, unpacking and arrival orientation. They also take care of custom clearance of your home shipment so you don't have to worry about paperwork and inspections.

When moving from one apartment to another, removal companies check the size of the apartment, the amount of furniture, appliances and breakables before giving you a quote. You can always negotiate and reduce the expense by packing books and clothes yourself. You have to clarify whether you expect them to unpack at the other end.

Relocation Companies

GS Fourwinds Hong Kong	2885 9666	www.fourwinds.com.hk
Asia Pacific Properties	2868 0966	www.asiapacificproperties.com
At Home	2819 8523	www.athomeinhongkong.com
Habitat	2869 9069	www.habitat-property.com
Pacific Relocations and Pacific Properties	2521 2821	www.worthenpacific.com
Peninsula Properties	2813 7266	www.peninsulapropertieshk.com
Pricoa Relocation Hong Kong Limited	2804 6790	www.pricoarelocation.com
Proway-Personalized Relocation	2866 1886	www.proway.com.hk
Santa Fe	2574 6204	www.santaferelo.com

Furnishing Your Home

Unless you are renting a furnished or self-service place, there is absolutely no rule or norm about furnishings and fixtures when renting in Hong Kong. It all depends on the market, the landlord, the rent you are paying or how much you want done before you move in. To put it simply, everything is negotiable. Luxury apartments come with an oven and sometimes a fridge and microwave. If you're lucky you'll get a washing machine and dryer, but this is not a hard and fast rule. Sometimes light fixtures and closets are missing and unwanted furniture has to be removed.

Furnishing your home in Hong Kong will also depend entirely on the size and type of apartment or house. Furniture, carpets, curtains, paintings, curios, kitchenware and light fixtures can all be bought here in a huge variety and for a wide range of prices. Cheap outlets like IKEA and Pricerite are good for short-term furnishing and those with humble budgets. But if you would rather choose your own design and order, then go along to Queen's Road East in Wan Chai where you can order rosewood, rattan or wrought iron furniture as well as other types of woodwork. See Home Furnishings & Accessories on p.302.

Removal Companies

Allied Pickfords ▶ p.xvi		2736 6032	www.alliedpickfords.com
Asian Express International Movers		2893 1000	www.aemovers.com.hk
Chunkie International Removal Ltd.		2690 0188	www.chunkie.com.hk
Global Silverhawk		2878 9200	www.globalsilverhawk.com
Prudential International Moving Limited		2618 6888	www.prudentialmovers.com
Schenker (HK)		2585 9688	www.schenker.com.hk

Transient Treasures

You can find many essentials second-hand and still in good order and high quality. People are always moving and selling off their belongings. They could be moving out of Hong Kong and selling cars, plants, curtains, appliances and furniture. Sometimes people even give things away, simply because they need to clear out the apartment quickly. Check the supermarket notice boards – the best ones are in Repulse Bay, Stanley and Chung Hom Kok as these areas have a high concentration of expats and the turnover is constant.

Second-Hand Items

Free magazines like *Dollarsaver*, *HK Magazine* and *South China Morning Post*'s *Trading Post* (Sunday's classified section) are good places to check for second-hand items. Websites like www.asiaxpat.com and www.geoexpat.com also have a trading section and it's amazing what you can buy and sell online.

Two good dealers in second-hand goods are Kingsway Appliances (2814 8770) selling large, second-hand appliances with a six-month guarantee and Expressions (2975 9797, www.exfurniture.com) a second-hand furniture shop with a delivery service. They have a big warehouse filled with cabinets, tables, dining sets, shelves, beds and other pieces, all reasonably priced.

Tailors

A concentrated number of tailors and upholsterers can be found on Queen's Road East in Wan Chai. There's so much to choose from, in terms of imported fabrics and wonderful things you can do with it. Prices can range from $40 to $200 per yard. Browse through the fabric and furniture on display, ask about the prices, the delivery time, deposit and payment methods. Stores also accept cheques and credit cards. Curtain shops will send someone to your house to measure the windows and give you a quote based on the cost of labour, amount of fabric and whether you want it with or without lining. Some will give you a free quote, some will charge you about $200 or $300. Be sure to check before you book an appointment. Upholstering is also an option for your home furnishings, refresh an old sofa or armchair or make beanbags, stools and cushions to order. Roman and Venetian blinds can also be made in these stores.

Tailors

Bean Bag City	2975 9797
Bricks & Stones	2520 0577
Fabrics etc.	2810 7360
King's Home Furnishing Company	2885 4715
OPTIONS Home Furnishings Ltd.	2552 3500
Simply Sofas	2580 7436
Sofamark Ltd.	2959 2920
T.O.D Interiors	2520 6266
Wai Kee Decoration & Furniture Co.	2392 0211

If you are ordering furniture, ask to see the catalogues. Be sure to discuss the wood and the filling that will be used in the cushion seats. Feather filling will cost you more and a mix of feather and cotton helps to keep the shape and is more reasonably priced. Synthetics like foam leave a bad smell during days of high humidity unless you expect to have non-stop air-conditioning. Allow at least three to four weeks for delivery. Sometimes delivery is included in the price but check to avoid surprises. Stores normally ask for a deposit of around 50% of the total, and the rest you pay on delivery. If you order only cushions or beanbags you will most likely have to pick them up yourself. There are upholstery and curtain shops in Central on Wellington Street and Lyndhurst Terrace. Horizon Plaza in Ap Lei Chau near Aberdeen, with its many floors of shopping, is another favourite.

111

Household Insurance

Hong Kong is a safe place and break-ins are almost unheard of but if they do happen chances are they are random and on a small scale. Caretakers and watchmen check everyone's identity card and monitor the comings and goings of guests, gas and electric meter readers, and delivery and repairmen. If there is construction work going on in your area or building, that's the time to be wary. Comprehensive coverage for typhoons and storms, flooding and landslip is more practical than theft and fire. General insurance plans tend to be all inclusive. Insurance against flooding and typhoon damage is worth considering if you are living out in the New Territories, as Hong Kong gets its share of typhoons and rains during the summer season.

Some insurance companies insure on the value of your goods and each item will have to be appraised. Some companies insure by the size of your apartment. You can also go for a package that will offer certain coverage worth a certain amount. Be sure to check if your coverage increases in value annually and if there is a no-claims discount. Consider talking to your bank, as most will offer home insurance plans.

Household Insurance		
Cigna International Expatriate Benefits	2539 9222	www.cigna.com.hk
Expat Services	2893 3344	www.expathk.com
HSBC	2822 1111	www.hsbc.com.hk
Ing General Insurance International	2850 3030	www.ing.com.hk
Manulife Insurance	2510 5600	www.manulife.com.hk
Sun Life Financial	3183 3143	www.sunlife.com.hk
Zurich Insurance Group HK	2967 8393	www.zurich.com.hk

Laundry Services

Dry-Cleaning Prices
Men's two-piece suit $45-$80
Men's shirt $13-$40
Trousers $15-$29
Women's suit $45-$70
Trousers $18-&23
Blouses $22-$34
Skirts $21-$45
Darning and mending charges depend on how much time and labour is needed. Expect to pay $20-$80.

Most people have washing machines and dryers in their apartments. People living in small apartments normally have a washer-dryer as a single unit to save on space but if you are living in a low budget housing area, you can walk down to the neighbourhood launderette and have your laundry washed in a few hours. Price is according to weight and can range from $25-$29 for 6-12 lbs or $4-$8 per pound. Ironing is not included and some will give you damp clothes that you can take home and iron yourself. Those launderettes with an ironing service will charge you extra.

All drycleaners and laundry companies offer a variety of services ranging from laundering, darning, mending, stain removal and even dying clothes. Goodwins are the stain-removing specialists in town, known to successfully remove all stains, but for a price. Some will dryclean or treat seat covers, bedding, rugs, curtains and even stuffed toys and carpets. They also have facilities to store your expensive furs and coats. Free pick-up, delivery, urgent or one-day laundry and drycleaning are part of the service. Do compare prices though as many places offer occasional discounts.

Laundry Services	
7 Seas Laundry & Dry Cleaning	2571 9559
A & D Laundry Service	2549 8871
Clean Living	2334 0896
Creative Dry Cleaning and Laundry	2851 0168
Dolphin Dry Cleaners, Laundry & Mending.	2813 0618
Goodwins of London	2812 2400
Jeeves of Belgravia	2973 0101
The Maid Dry Cleaning & Laundry Service Company	2559 8168
Po Fat Dry Cleaning & Laundry	2813 2062
Sunshine Laundry Convenience Store Company	2572 2582
Taipan Dry Cleaners	2812 6488
Well Supreme Laundry	2987 5151

Part-time Domestic Help ◀

Part-time help is illegal and your domestic help should only work in your home and nowhere else or you may face prosecution and your help deported. That said, this is often overlooked and you can find part-time help for $55-$65 per hour. Helpers who are available for part-time work are sometimes allowed by their employers (who may be single, a couple or with grown up children) to work for a few hours a day or week with friends or anyone else who wants to hire them. People often share domestic help by having one person sponsor and sign the contract, but all share paying the salary and working hours. A few agencies like Merry Maids (2857 4038) offer a part-time service to help out at parties or for general cleaning. You can put up signs in your building or supermarket for part-time help, or look in Dollarsaver magazine for notices.

Domestic Help

Other options **Entry Visa** p.59

Many expats in Hong Kong have foreign domestic help, mostly full-time and live-in. It's an affordable luxury here and the convenience is hard to pass by. They'll cook, clean, shop for fresh groceries, run errands and also take care of your children. Many are also trained nurses, teachers and accountants. The trade-offs include compromising your privacy, a bit of a daily power struggle and being constantly in the role of employer.

Domestic helpers come from India, Sri Lanka, Thailand, and Indonesia, but the majority are Filipino. Almost all speak English.

The best way to get a maid is through word of mouth, through your friend's helper, notices at supermarkets, in your building and through *Dollarsaver*, a free classifieds magazine.

There are agencies to help you find the ideal person. They'll often have a maid's personal profile and video so you can choose someone in Hong Kong, trained and familiar with the local system, or hire in someone from abroad and train them from scratch. Agency fees range from $2,500 to $3,000.

When interviewing, it's important to have a list of questions ready so you don't leave anything out. More importantly, get a telephone reference from a recent employer and make sure that the contract with the previous employer was not broken. If the contract was broken, it will mean a long drawn out procedure with immigration and the helper may not even get a visa to work with you.

Sponsoring a Live-in Maid

Maids are sponsored from overseas on a full-time, live-in contract. Any other arrangement is illegal because they are here on a domestic visa and if you are the sponsor then they must live in your home. See Visas on p.21.

A simple government contract is signed between the employer and maid, before a witness. This contract covers all your responsibilities as an employer; the monthly salary, paid holidays, food allowances and details of board and lodging. The contract will be for two years and is renewable after that period. You will be required to provide a return air ticket for the maid. You must also provide her with health insurance, since neither you nor your employee are supposed to burden Hong Kong's public healthcare system.

Four copies of the contract are signed. One goes to her home consulate, one will be kept at the Immigration office and there's a copy each for you and your employee. Contract processing times vary depending on the consulate. The Hong Kong visa costs $135.

To end a contract before it expires, you must give a month's notice, a month's salary if you want her to leave without serving her notice, and her fare home. If she leaves without giving notice, she forfeits her salary. Immigration allows her two weeks to get another job after which her visa is

113

Domestic Help Agencies		
Amah Net	2869 9330	www.amahnet.com
Energetic Employment	2893 4422	http://eeagency.portfolio.anywhere.com.hk
Housework Express	2832 9626	na
Jem Employment and Trading	2850 5970	www.jememployment.com
Josie James Personnel	2377 1598	na
Merry Maids	2857 4038	www.merrymaids.com.hk
Ready Maid Personnel	3188 2826	www.readymaid.com.hk

cancelled and she must return home. If you don't have room for your domestic helper in your apartment and they have to live outside your home, you must notify Immigration, who will consider the case before giving permission. The onus is on you to pay her rent and money for daily transport.

Domestic helpers are paid a monthly sum of $3,320 – a sum fixed by the government. An additional $300 as food allowance is paid if the maid buys her own food. Rice is provided as part of the food allowance. As a sponsor you pay a levy of $400 per month to the government, either quarterly or annually. A helpful source to consult is 'Guidebook for the Employment of Domestic Helpers from Abroad' available free from the 2/F, Immigration Department Tower on Gloucester Road in Wan Chai.

Babysitting & Childcare

Many families have live-in domestic help so hiring a babysitter is pretty uncommon. People without domestic help will use one babysitter on a regular basis as and when needed.

If you have just arrived and haven't employed domestic help yet, you can get a babysitter for the going rate of around $60 per hour, from a posting in your building or supermarket, or better still through someone you know on recommendation. In expat enclaves, you're bound to know someone (or will easily find someone) with a teenager who'll babysit for around $50 an hour.

Babysitting & Childcare	
Annerly Midwife	2983 1558
Rent-a-Mum	2523 4868

Playgroups and educational programs are available for children as young as 6 months but most will ask that the mother or helper accompany the child.

Babysitting services are available but expensive because the nannies are officially trained and are professionals. All hotels provide babysitting services for their guests and if you do find one you like you can always get the babysitter's telephone number and continue to use her when at home. They may not often agree though, and will most likely be very expensive.

See also Nurseries in the Education section, p.146.

Domestic Services

Pest Control

Truly Care Environmental Pest Control Services (2458 8378) will take care of any rats, cockroaches, woodworm, ants, bugs and any other nasty creepy crawly that happens to take up residence alongside you.

Living in a housing complex means you are spared the headache of any major maintenance and repairs, all included in the management fee. The more they manage and maintain, the heftier the fee. Prestigious and posh buildings have elaborate maintenance programs carried out by specialist management companies. Some expats prefer to live in such housing and companies are usually happy to place employees in them if they are on a two or three year assignment. It's a win-win situation because you won't have to deal with annoying problems like leaks and faulty air-conditioning. There are plenty of handymen and maintenance companies if you do need to get things fixed on your own, but it can be expensive since the cost of labour is high in Hong Kong. Make sure you call a few and compare quotes. The best way to find a reliable handyman is in *Dollarsaver* magazine. You can also call the Community Advice Bureau (2815 5444) for recommendations.

Domestic Services

Name	Area	Phone	Type of Service
Allan Engineering	Various	2887 6638	Locksmith, electrical, plumbing, carpentry, air-conditioning
Biocycle Hong Kong Ltd	Kowloon Bay	2799 6206	Insect and pest control and termite prevention and control
Casey Workshop	Wong Chuk Hang	2552 1999	Electrical, carpentry , plumbing, glass and lock replacement, brick and tile work, sofa upholstery,
Eddy Chuek's Workshop	Taikoo Shing	2570 9772	Painting, electrical and plumbing, carpentry, metal work, air-conditioners, locks and glass replacement
Johnny Electrical & Decoration Co	Various	2729 1516	Electrical, plumbing, air-conditioning, carpentry, tiling, wall papering
Mr. Hammer	Kennedy Town	2816 6383	Painting, plumbing, carpentry, electrical, upholstery, glass and tile replacement, metal work
Truly Care	Tsuen Wan	2458 8378	Biodegradable products to kill ants, cockroaches, rodents, mosquitoes, fleas, termites
Winkle Design & Decoration Ltd	Wong Chuk Hang	2554 1269	Carpentry, interior design and decoration, locks and glass replacement, plumbing and electrical, upholstery

DVD & Video Rental

High rents and pirated or cheap copies of DVDs and VCDs have pushed movie rental chains to the brink. Across the border in Shenzhen, pirated new releases are sold for $5 to $10 depending on your bargaining skills. Beware: the copies are poor quality, but what can you expect for $5? You can be stopped at the border and searched; if caught carrying pirated products you'll have them confiscated and, depending on the amount of goods, you can be fined.

Movieland, a well-known chain, still has a few outlets in expat areas. It offers free membership and a good selection of films. On Tuesdays you can rent any new release for $10 a night and the older movies cost about $10 for two nights. The normal price is $25 a night for new releases and $20 for old DVDs and videos.

DVD & Video Rental

7 Star Enterprises	Central	2523 2252
Hollywood Video	SoHo	2524 3978
Movie Box	Mid-Levels	2868 3678
Movieland	Discovery Bay	2987 7111
Movieland	Happy Valley	2836 3885
Movieland	Lan Kwai Fong	2526 8549
Movieland	Repulse Bay	2803 1980
Moviexpress	Ap Lei Chau	2552 1381

Other rental places have Chinese movies, either local or from Taiwan and China.

Generally, some stores will ask for a deposit, returned when you bring the DVD back. Others offer membership for just a few dollars. New releases cost more and if you rent more than one or two together you might be able to swing a discount and perhaps even keep them for longer. Renting VCDs is cheaper than DVDs. If you damage them, be prepared to pay the sale price.

Most of these rental places are in commercial and densely populated residential areas like the Mid-Levels. You will also find random shops selling cheap VCDs everywhere, but the quality and the selection can be hit and miss.

Pets

In spite of the often cramped living conditions, lots of people still have a pet. Cats and dogs still top the list, but anything is possible, from rabbits to hamsters, mice to chinchillas. You can buy youngsters or fully-grown animals in pet shops located in commercial areas. Even better, you can buy pets from a reliable breeder or get them from an animal welfare agency like the Society for the Prevention of Cruelty to Animals (SPCA, 2802 0501) where abandoned animals are housed. The Agricultural and Fisheries Conservation Department (AFCD, 2150 6655) encourages people to get a pet from the SPCA since abandoned pets will be put down after a certain amount of time.

Abandon your pet at your own peril, since it is an offence and you can be tracked down through your animal's microchip and fined.

Since the outbreak of SARS the government has banned the keeping of dogs and certain other pets in public housing estates.

Cats & Dogs

Licensing, Microchips & Vaccination
Government Animal Management Centres that provide these services can be found across Hong Kong. Visit www.afcd.gov.hk for locations or call the interactive hotline: 2708 8885. Citizen's Easy Link 1823

Make sure your landlord or housing complex allows pets before you decide to bring them into the country. Being near a park, walking path or trail is good if you're getting a dog. By law, dogs are to be kept on a lead. For this privilege however your dog has to be tame, trained and pass a test set by AFCD. Signs are posted in residential areas where dogs are not allowed to foul and you are definitely expected to pick up after your furry friend. Failure to do so faces a hefty fine of about $1,500.

Your dog must be immunised against rabies at 5-8 weeks and get a booster shot after 12 weeks, plus an annual booster.

Make an appointment and take your pet to the government-run Animal Management Centre as soon as it's over 3 months for the rabies shot and for implanting a microchip. The chip carries a number, vaccination records and owner details. All this takes about 15 minutes and costs $80. You can also go to an authorised vet and pay for the same service. The price varies depending on the clinic. You must renew your pet's licence every three years.

Dogs on Show
The Hong Kong Kennel Club (2523 3944) is affiliated with the Kennel Clubs of Canada, Australia, and the US, and has been in Hong Kong for 60 years. They hold dog shows and issue pedigree certificates. Call to check for upcoming events.

Report lost pets to the police, SPCA (2802 0501), Animal Welfare Centres or the Animal Management Centre at Citizens' Link 1832. Your identity card number and the microchip number will be noted. If you fail to report a missing pet and the authorities find it, it will be handed over to the SPCA for adoption or worse, put down after four days.

You must notify AFCD within five days of any change of address or ownership. Failure to do so could land you in hot water and you'll be served with a $5,000 fine.

Neutering and spaying your pet is also recommended by AFCD and SPCA and the procedure can be done in any of the government Animal Management Centres. SPCA has a mobile neutering service in the New Territories.

Pet Rules
• Exotic animals are banned in Hong Kong
• A dog over 20kg will need permission to be brought in
• Owning fighting dogs will send you to jail for three months and earn you a $25,000 fine.

Fish & Birds

A single bird fluttering and singing in an ornate wooden cage is a common sight in Hong Kong and an age-old Chinese way of keeping pet birds. With the threat of bird flu however, this is not so much of a common sight, and even the famous Yuen Po Bird Market in Mong Kok is quiter than it once was.

A trip to the goldfish market in Mong Kok will get you everything you need to tend a pet fish. In wet markets around Hong Kong you'll spot little corner shops selling fish, tanks, accessories and fish food.

Pet Shops

All pet shops are licensed by the AFCD. When buying pets from these places, check the animals carefully and ask as many questions as you need. If your Cantonese is still a little rusty, we suggest you stick to English speaking stores, which you'll find mainly in commercial districts. They sell pet food and accessories, but even this can be bought in supermarkets and from companies who import the food and deliver to your doorstep. AFCD and pet care organisations encourage people to adopt animals from their

> **Lucky Fish**
> Large and elaborate tanks with beautiful fish, such as carp, goldfish and other varieties, are placed according to feng shui in banks, restaurants, offices and homes. The Chinese believe that fish bring luck and prosperity, so you'll see eight goldfish (a lucky number) and one black goldfish, believed to absorb the negative energy around the place. When a fish dies, all bad luck goes with it. Even the placement of the fish tank is important. A wrongly placed tank can bring money problems and even lawsuits. If this happens, call in the feng shui expert to shift it to a more lucrative spot!

Veterinary Clinics

Animal Medical Centre	Tai Po	2656 1168
	Mong Kok	2713 4155
	Mid-Levels	2140 6581
The Ark's Veterinary Hospital	Sai Ying Pun	2549 2330
The Cat Hospital	Aberdeen	2975 8228
Chris & Nicola's Animal Hospital	Tin Hau	2570 6048
Creature Comforts	Shau Kei Wan	2915 3999
Plover Cove Animal Hospital	Sha Tin	2653 9399
Sha Tin Animal Clinic	Sha Tin	2694 1452
Stanley Veterinary Clinic	Stanley	2813 2030
Valley Veterinary Centre	Happy Valley	2575 2389
Wan Chai Animal Clinic	Wan Chai	2572 5422

shelters rather than go out and buy from pet shops. There are many such organisations to contact for a pet that would welcome your love and care.

Vets & Kennels

Prices differ depending on location and if they are expat or local vets. Consultation cost depends on the examination and whatever medication is needed.

Kennels are usually located out in the New Territories where there is more space. Your pet will be picked up and delivered back to you (except on holidays). Make sure the place you choose is licensed, employs a team of qualified staff and that it's clean.

It's a Dog's Life
Areas are marked off where dogs are allowed. Some beaches and country parks, for example allow you to let your dogs run free, but some will not allow them at all. It has been known for poisoned food to be left out in certain areas to get rid of dogs. Police have no idea who does this, so when you take your dog out for a walk, be alert and don't let it eat anything off the ground.

Grooming & Training

Pamper your loved one for the day at any of the grooming centres in Hong Kong. It may set you back as much as $500 or $600 depending on the size of your dog or cat and the services you choose, ranging from a bath, haircut, nail clipping and ear cleaning. If your dog is not in regular air-conditioning then regular trims are recommended since Hong Kong gets hot and sticky. It takes about two hours and you need to make an appointment. Dogfather's Mobile Dog Groomer will come to your house. For dog training, you can also have someone come to your home, or else head down to one of the training centres. This can last for one week up to a month or even more depending on the age, type and temperament of the dog.

Importing & Exporting Your Pet

A new rule since September 1, 2005 requires that all dogs and cats that come to Hong Kong must be implanted with a microchip with complete identification details. The number of the microchip must be printed on the animal's health certificate for identification purposes.

For importing or exporting your pet, apply for a permit from the AFCD. You can download an application form (Form AF240) from its website (www.afcd.gov.hk), send it with the fees required (one animal is $432, then it's $102 for every additional animal) either as a crossed local cheque or via e-payment. If you are applying from abroad, fees should be paid by bank draft (made by a licensed bank in Hong Kong) in Hong Kong currency payable to 'The Government of the Hong Kong Special Administrative Region.' For any questions about payment, contact 2150 7062.

A permit is issued at counter 10, 5/F Agricultural and Fisheries Conservation Department, Cheung Sha Wan Government Offices, 303, Cheung Sha Wan, Kowloon. Allow five working days from the time you apply. You can have someone collect the permit for you if you can't go. For those applying from abroad, get pet movers to do it all and send you the certificate. This permit is valid for six months and is for one entry so be sure to get your pet in within that timeframe.

You must have your pet's health certificate and an up-to-date immunisation record. Rabies vaccinations should have been administered within one year, but no less than

Pets Grooming/Training

Dogfather's Mobile Groomer	Mid-Levels	9460 0389	Bathing, hair and nail cutting, brushing.
Forever Beauty Pet Grooming Centre	Mid-Levels	2525 4515	All grooming services for cats and dogs
SPCA	Kowloon City	2713 9104	Full professional grooming, flea baths, nail clipping
	Wan Chai	2802 0501	Full professional grooming, flea baths, nail clipping
Stanley Pet Station	Stanley	2813 7979	Haircutting bath nail clip cleaning

117

Pets Boarding/Sitting

DB Pet Shop	Sai Kung	2194 4885	Training at home and at their centre
Dogotel	Kowloon City	2711 0019	Training in a class of 3 dogs with or without owner
I-Kennel Club	Sha Tin	2471 6939	Training, lodging, pick up service
Kennel Van Dego	Sai Kung	2792 6889	Grooming & training, pick up or delivery service and
Lotus Kennel	Yuen Long	2488 8969	Boarding and obedience and behaviour training, grooming

30 days before leaving. If a country has a quarantine period, then immunisation rules may not be as strict. If your pet is coming from a country not on the list of exemptions, expect a four-month quarantine.

You can avoid the hassle of bringing your pet into Hong Kong and government bureaucracy and let professional pet movers take charge for you. They'll handle everything from A to Z, including the messy bits in the middle, such as

Pet Movers

Aeropet	2744 3330	www.aero-pet.com
Export-A-Pet	2358 1774	www.export-a-pet.com
Ferndale Kennels & Cattery	2792 4642	www.ferndalekennels.com
Pet Movers	3404 0061	www.petmovershk.com
Wish You Were Here	2899 0817	www.wishyouwerehere hk.com

immunisations, paperwork, air booking, lodging prior to departure and on arrival, and delivery to your doorstep. The cost will depend on many factors including the size and type of animal, the country it's going to or coming from, packing and airfare.

Animal Welfare Organisations

Animal welfare organisations are non-governmental and non-profit, and play a big role in educating people about owning, handling and caring for their pets. Their main goal is also to rescue abused or abandoned animals and care for them in shelters set up around Hong Kong. Such groups also run foster homes and take in pets when people cannot find a home for them. Through events and campaigns, these organisations raise funds and have extended community support. If you can't adopt, sponsorship is worth considering.

Advice and counselling is readily given with regards to caring for and handling pets. If you decide to adopt an animal from them, they'll expect you to spend time with the animal to bond with it,

Animal Welfare Organisations

Asian & Hong Kong Daschund Society	6173 5298	www.lapcheung.org
Companion Animal Federation	2146 4383	www.hkcaf.org
Dr Rabbit	9859 6259	doctor_rabbit@mail.hongkong.com
Hong Kong Alleycat Watch	9310 0744	www.hkalleycats.com
Hong Kong Dog Rescue	9448 1128	www.hongkongdogrescue.com
Lamma Animal Protection	2928 4018	www.lap.org.hk
Lamma Animal Welfare Centre	2982 0800	www.lammaanimals.org
Protection of Animals	2984 1626	www.pals.org.hk
Society for the Prevention of Cruelty to Animals	2802 0501	www.spca.org.hk
Society for Abandoned Animals	2150 6655	www.saa.org.hk

offer a donation and make sure you are ready for a pet in your home.

Organisations like SAA (Society for Abandoned Animals) arrange for blood donors and will check your dog before taking blood. HK Alleycat Watch give vet recommendations, and tell you how to adopt and foster, and CAF (Companion Animal Federation) offer health and nutrition counselling. Hong Kong Dog Rescue offer adoption advice, organise dog walkers and raise funds through regular auctions.

When the sad time comes to lay your pet to rest, call Goodbye Dear (2951 0819) or Wonderland Pets Cremation (2631 1092).

Babywear p.98
Bank Loans p.22

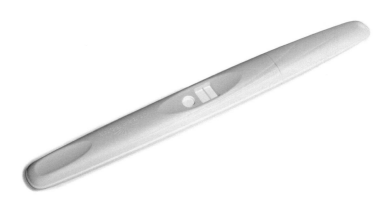

Written by residents, these unique guidebooks are packed with insider info, from arriving in a new destination to making it your home and everything in between.

Explorer Residents' Guides
We Know Where You Live

Abu Dhabi · Amsterdam · Bahrain · Barcelona · Dubai · Dublin · Geneva · Hong Kong · Kuwait
London · New York · New Zealand · Oman · Paris · Qatar · Shanghai · Singapore · Sydney

EXPLORER
www.explorerpublishing.com

Transformers & Adaptors

Electricity voltage is 200/220 and 50 hertz. For appliances from the US you'll need a transformer. This should be bought from a proper electrical shop like Paul Cheung Radio Company Limited (2528 0805). You'll find all kinds of transformers and adaptors here so explain what you need it for and they'll know what to give you. Since hertz cannot be transformed, appliances over 50 hertz should not be used.

Electricity

Two major private companies provide electricity in Hong Kong. Hong Kong Electric Company (HKEC) supplies Hong Kong Island and Lamma Island while China Light & Power (CLP) supplies Kowloon, New Territories and the outlying islands.

Electricity bills are high during summer, since air conditioners and dehumidifiers are on most of the day. This will be at your own expense – it's highly unlikely that your company will pick up the tab. Of course, the larger your apartment, the higher your electricity bill. Air conditioners also provide relief from mould and the unpleasant smells that come from humidity, so often people leave them on all day. If your building has central air conditioning, its consumption, repair and maintenance may already be included in the rent.

Before you move into your home, the leasing agent should have all the utilities connected. To do it yourself, you can go along to any consumer centre of the HKEC Pay-in Centre, C2 & C3, G/F, Worldwide House, Central and Customer Service Centre, 9/F Electric Centre, 28 Garden City Road, North Point. You can also call Customer Services at 2887 3411 during office hours or write to HEC, P.O. Box 915, General Post Office.

For CLP, you can go in person to 147 Argyle Street, Kowloon and 46-48, Granville Road, Tsim Sha Tsui or call 2678 2678. Fill in a form for Supply/Transfer and it should take two working days for a new connection and one day for transferring the account to your name. The deposit varies as it is calculated on the size of the apartment and possible consumption. Keep the receipt of this deposit if you want the deposit back when leaving. Be warned – no receipt means no return.

You can pay all your utility bills through post offices, by autopay system, at an ATM or by cheque to addresses given on the back of the bill. Forms for setting up autopay are available at banks and at consumer centres.

An agent of HKEC will come to your home to read your electric meter, which is normally in the kitchen or utility area. You must ask the meter reader for identification before letting him into the house. You'll be billed monthly and your bill may seem high at first when you have just moved in but it will be adjusted according to consumption and any overcharged amount will be credited to your account.

Hong Kong works on a three-pin-square plug system. However, many old apartments that have not been renovated still use the old-style two-pin round ones. Whatever the appliance, you can either change the plug or get a square plug adaptor. By law you are required to use a registered electrician for any electrical work around the house.

Water

There are 17 reservoirs around Hong Kong supplying drinking water, and the rest comes from China.

Drinking water in Hong Kong conforms to WHO (World Health Organization) standards but few expats drink straight from the tap, and instead spend hundreds of dollars buying distilled and mineral water. Boiling and filtering are perfectly safe ways to drink, without half of the expense of buying bottled water. You can buy a variety of well-known brands and good quality filters or filter jugs like Brita, from department stores.

Drinking water suppliers offer a wide range of bottled water, sparkling, still, distilled, mineral, imported and local varieties. Supermarket shelves are weighed down with choices.

When moving into your new home you don't need to worry about the water being disconnected. The account is simply transferred into your name and you will need to pay a deposit of $400. Bills are sent quarterly.

The Water Supplies Department Consumer Enquiry Centre can be contacted on 2824 5000.

Water Suppliers	
Aqua Pure Distilled Water Company Ltd.	2680 2680
Bonaqua TM	2210 3311
Canadian Glacier Water	2580 0006
Healthy Spring	2636 1997
Nanotechnology Limited	2723 0003
Oasis Pure Distilled Water	2264 6338
Rocky Canada	2580 0161
Vita Pure Distilled Water	2468 9898
Watson's Water	2660 6688

Water Tips

During the summer months the humidity climbs to 90-98%, so dehumidifiers are on all day, filling up their containers with water. Save this water and use it for watering your plants, or washing the kitchen and bathroom floors. Dehumidifiers are sold in department stores and large electrical shops like Fortress, a well-known chain in Hong Kong, and can cost anywhere from $2,000 to $5,000 depending on the brand and capacity.

When turning on the water in the morning, let it run for a few minutes before using it to drain off accumulated lead or impurities.

Because of old water pipes in some buildings and a perceived lack of maintenance in water storage tanks, people avoid drinking tap water at home or in restaurants.

Water heating geysers must be checked for leaks periodically in old apartments. Accidents from gas-leaking geysers used to happen frequently but with new and improved versions, it's now much safer. Precautions should be taken to open windows in case you smell gas or when the geyser has been on for a while.

Sewerage

Water and air pollution are worrying issues in Hong Kong. The Environmental Protection Department (EPD) manages waste disposal. Sewage from residential and commercial buildings is treated in government-run, environmentally friendly plants. Through the Harbour Area Treatment Scheme (HATS) harbour sewage is collected and treated at Stonecutter's Island. Studies show that red tides, that bring industrial pollution into Tolo Harbour, are down by 50% and waste pollution has reduced from 52% to 15% around the beaches. Beach waters are monitored constantly.

Gas

Hong Kong & China Gas Company is privately owned. It supplies a natural gas known as 'Towngas' to much of Hong Kong except some parts of the New Territories and some old apartments on Hong Kong Island. Towngas is used for heating water and cooking. Bottled LPG (Liquid Petroleum Gas) is used in areas where natural gas is unavailable, but there are a few providers who deliver on order.

If your apartment uses gas for both heating water and for cooking, the bill is going to be higher than if using electric water heaters and gas for cooking alone. You could be paying anything from $300 to $800 a month. Gas meters are read every two months.

To get your gas connected, send a cheque for $600 as a deposit along with an application form stating your telephone number, address and identity card number to Towngas, G.P.O. Box 134, Hong Kong or go in person to the centres in

Bottled Gas Suppliers	
Kong Lee	2543 2895
Shell Company	2560 7000
Tai Ying	2817 8828

Kowloon on G/F, New World Centre, Tsim Sha Tsui and on Hong Kong Island G/F, Riviera Mansion, 59-65, Patterson Street, Causeway Bay. Their Customer Service Hotline is 2880 6988.

Doing Their Bit

Government programmes and green groups send messages through television and in print to educate people about recycling. Campaigns and community walks are also held and programmes are organised in schools and housing estates, while corporations are being approached to help with environmental issues.

Rubbish Disposal & Recycling

With population numbers rapidly increasing in a short span of time, one obvious problem is a resulting increase in waste. Garbage is collected daily from the back doors of the apartments all over Hong Kong and carried away in big trucks to landfills. An even bigger issue is construction waste as buildings are being torn down and apartments are gutted and redecorated. Add to this the rubbish generated in parks and picnic areas during festival celebrations and holidays and you'll understand why Hong Kong is running out of landfill space. It's estimated that in six to 10 years' time there may be no space left for landfill and China is unlikely to allow Hong Kong to start using its territory. For now, the landfills are located in the distant parts of New Territories where, after reducing the gas and smells, they are covered with green areas such as golf clubs, playing fields and parks.

Large bins for separating glass, plastic and paper can be found in parks, housing estates and other public places. For a list of collectors of recyclable items and information on recycling and EPD activities, call EPD Recycling hotline: 2838 3111. EPD Recycling Centre (28/F, Hennessy Road, Wan Chai) 2835 1018. To check the air pollution index call 2594 6413.

121

Directory Enquiries ◀

*The telephone enquiry
service 1081 gives you
any number you want,
and for another $1
will connect you
directly to the number
and bill you in your
monthly account.*

Telephone

For home use, Pacific Century Cyber Works (PCCW) has the monopoly on residential landline phones and a huge share of the market for internet and mobile phone services. Hutchison Global Communications (HGC) is the second big player with a good share of office and residential landlines, broadband and dial up internet services.

Getting connected when you move into your new home is simple and quick. You can go to the retail shops in any shopping area, fill in a form, show your Hong Kong identity card, and you'll be dialling home within the week. You can also make an appointment with your desired company. The HGC customer service hotline is 1220, and PCCW is 1000. You can get the paperwork done while the installation process is being completed. There is a charge of about $200 for extra extensions.

Fax and internet lines are separate so there's no need to forfeit one whilst using the other. Ask about other services like voicemail, caller display, call blocking, conference calls and call waiting, as well as any other bells and whistles you fancy. Some of these are free and some are charged at about $10 to $16 per service. A telephone can be bought or rented from a PCCW shop, located in malls and on the main roads in commercial areas.

The monthly service charge for PCCW is $110 and installation costs $475. This is often waived if you join through some promotional plan, of which there are many.

HGC has a monthly basic plan for $83.80. Local calls are free. Bills are sent on a monthly basis, two weeks before the due date. If you haven't paid your bill, you'll receive messages reminding you to do so. If

Telephone Companies

City Telecom	2926 1234	www.ctihk.com
ecTelecom	2157 2157	www.ectelecom.com.hk
Hutchison Global Communications	2128 2828	www.hgc.com.hk
New World Telecom	2133 1133	www.newworldtel.com
One Tel	2907 6000	www.onetel.com.hk
Pacific Century Cyberworks	2888 0008	www.pccw.com.hk

you still don't pay, service will be cut off one week after the payment due date. You can check, make changes, send queries and pay your bills online using your credit card or bankcard through Easy Pay System (EPS).

There is no area code within Hong Kong.

Public telephones, with multilingual instructions, can be seen near bus stops, ferries, and hotels, as well as in the main shopping and business areas of the city. Local calls from public phones cost $1 for five minutes. You can use $1, $2, $5, $10 coins or a phone card that comes in values of $50 and $100, available in telephone shops and at convenience stores. Your nifty octopus card will also work in public phones.

To make overseas calls, you can subscribe to PCCW's International Direct Dial (IDD) service (0060 and 001). Other companies offering a similar service at competitive rates include Hutchison Global Communications (0080), New World Telephone (009), One Tel (1686) and ecTelecom (1507).

Mobile Service Providers

There is a citywide obsession with the ubiquitous mobile phone. According to the Office for the Telecommunications Authority (OFTA), 2005 figures showed that mobile penetration had reached 120%. That means for every 100 residents there are 120 phones registered. There are more mobile phones than landlines in offices and homes, which is not surprising because Hong Kong has amongst the cheapest subscriber fees in the world.

Mobile phones here work on a GSM 900 system (Global System for Mobile Telephones) or other networks like PCS 1800 and CDMA. There is a roaming agreement set up with most international networks. There are six mobile phone

122

service providers in Hong Kong running 11 networks (see table). They all have WAP (Wireless Application Protocol) Services. Choose from any of these, with each offering some

Mobile Service Providers

3 GSM (PCCW)	2888 2888	www.pccwmobile.com
CSL	2888 1010	www.hkcsl.com
New World Telecom	2131 3377	www.newworldtel.com
One2Free (CSL)	2972 2123	www.one2free.com
People's Phone	2945 8888	www.peoples.com.hk
Smartone-Vodaphone	2868 1768	www.smartone.com.hk
Sunday	2113 8000	www.sunday.com

promotional deal or a competitive plan on a service or handset. Their retail shops can be easily found in the main shopping malls and streets.

To register for a mobile phone, your Hong Kong identity card and proof of residential address is needed. You can pay cash or with a credit card, preferably a locally issued credit card.

For those who don't expect to be using the phone too much, or if at some point you want to discontinue a subscribed service, a SIM card ranging from $48 to $180 is all you need. You can top up every six months by re-registering so you can keep the same number.

If you are coming from abroad you can rent a mobile phone at the airport (2883 3938) or if you already have a handset, just pick up a SIM card to get you operational. Handset rentals start at about $35 per day with a refundable deposit of $500. If you lose your phone, report it immediately and have the account blocked.

Blogs

Here are some blogs about Hong Kong that you may enjoy reading:
www.ordinarygweilo.com
www.chattergarden.com
www.feer.com/tales
www.cloudless.net/blog
www.mdmechiang.
blogspot.com

Surf & Travel

If you are travelling a lot consider a roaming internet service offered by most companies with rates ranging from $0.06 to $1.50 per minute. Internet service plans can be for single or multiple users if there is more than one person at home using a computer. Companies offer additional MB bandwidth for a fee. Many companies also have 56K dial-up services for customers unable to utilise broadband.

Internet

Other options **Websites** p.49, **Internet Cafes** p.388

It's quick and easy to get internet connection in Hong Kong. Most people subscribe to Netvigator broadband service from Pacific Century Cyber Works (PCCW). The basic plan runs for $198 and offers unlimited hours online and one e-mail account. Most Hong Kong website addresses end in .com, .com.hk or .org.hk.

• Hutchison Global offers home users a 12 month plan of unlimited hours for $160 for a single user.
• Pacific One has a monthly service which costs $148 (1.5M/256K) for unlimited hours.
• Netfront Internet's monthly broadband fee is $288 (1.8 MBPS) with no installation fee and $4 per hour for 56K dial-up service.
• Vision on Line will do a personal web page for dial-up users and dial-up service is $6 per hour. There's an annual fee of $360 and monthly $132 plus $80 for setting up with an offer of free 5MB storage and an e-mail account.
• Pacific Supernet offers roaming service, and a broadband service at unlimited hours for $168 (15MB) monthly with no installation fee.
• Asia Pacific Net offers web design and development and broadband services.

See table of service providers and check their websites for details of the service plans and products.

Internet Service Providers

Asia Pacific CompuNet Ltd.	2976 9995	www.ap.net.hk
Hutchison Global Communications	2128 2828	www.hgc.com.hk
Netfront Internet Services	2517 1209	www.netfront.net
Pacific One Net	2119 0111	www.onebb.com
Pacific Supernet	2335 4388	www.pacific.net.hk
PCCW	1833 833	www.netvigator.com
Vision On Line	2311 8855	www.vol.net

123

Bill Payment

Telephone, mobile and internet connection bills are paid monthly. E-bills are becoming the norm now and if you want a hard copy there's a charge of about $10 to $20. You can now check your accounts, make enquiries and change or update billing information online. Mobile telephone and internet e-bills are sent by email monthly with a due date. If your mobile bill is overdue, a message will come up on your handset every time you use the service to warn you of a cut-off date.

You can also pay bills through ATMs, at the telephone company's shop or online.

Post & Courier Services

Hong Kong Post is a well organised and efficient government department with reliable mail delivery to homes and offices. They offer a mail redirecting service when you change address and a courier service called Speed Post that also offers insurance. They have 133 post offices, two mobile post offices that move through the different districts on different days, and 1,700 delivery offices and postmen's beats to take care of the region's postal needs. There is no postcode system. Instead, everything works on the district system.

Each district has a post office where you can buy stamps, and mail letters by ordinary, urgent, registered or Speed Post. Outside the post offices there are stamp vending machines, which are particularly useful during holidays when everything is shut. Mailboxes are located around the city for convenient mailing of standard letters, but for big packages, registration or Speed Post you have to go into a post office.

The general post office is located by the Star Ferry in Central and is open from Monday to Saturday, 08:00 to 18:00 and Sunday 09:00 to 12:00.

Mail Zones

Mailing is divided into two zones.

Zone 1 is all destinations in Asia and standard postage costs $2.70. Delivery time is three to five days. Zone 2 is Japan and all other destinations and standard postage costs $3.00. Delivery time is five to seven days.

Standard local postage is $1.40 for 30gm and $2.40 for 50gm. Local delivery time is within two working days. Mail is collected twice a day, at 10:00 and 14:00, and on holidays once at 14:00 only. For more information call 2921 2222 (Hong Kong office) or 2828 6247 (Kowloon office).

Courier Companies

Overseas courier service companies like UPS (United Parcel Service), DHL, Federal Express and others all have business in Hong Kong and there are several local ones too. Some of them have counters in malls and MTR stations where you can mail your packages. Call for locations close to you.

Internet Help
Most internet sites have a webmaster or customer service to e-mail or call for complaints and support. You'll find support for hardware and software online too. The Hong Kong Government's Office of the Telecommunications Authority is an organisation that keeps a check on all things IT. Whether it's spam, Internet or mobile phone company charges, or if you have questions about the range of telephones when hiking in far flung locations, check the website or call them on 2961 6333, www.ofta.gov.hk

Renting a Post Box
It costs $500 a year to rent a small box at the General or TST Post Offices, and $650 for a large box. Rates differ at other post offices depending on the sizes available. You can find a small box for $270 and $320 for the larger size, a little further out of commercial districts. Kowloon post office has only the small size available, for $320 a year.

Services

Other services include permit mailing and Speed Post freight, both for bulk mail. There is Postal Plus for logistics mailing and PayThruPost for paying utility bills, taxes, school fees, police penalties as well as licence and certificate fees. The Hong Kong Circular Postal Service will mail notices and promotions for services and products. To redirect your mail will cost $100 for three months and $300 for businesses. A full year will cost around $250.

For tracking lost parcels or a letter, you'll need to fill in a form at the post office within a year of mailing the item. Large packages sent by surface mail are not delivered. Instead you will receive a notice to come collect it. If it's not collected before the final date marked, you'll be charged storage fees.

Courier Companies		
DHL International	2400 3388	www.dhl.com.hk
Federal Express Corporation	2730 3333	www.fedex.com/hk
SpeedPost	2921 2288	www.hongkongpost.com
TNT Express	2331 2663	www.tnt.com
UPS	2735 3535	www.ups.com

Radio

There are 13 radio channels, seven of these are publicly funded and broadcast educational and informative programmes in Chinese.

For good English programmes, tune into Radio Television Hong Kong (RTHK) Radio 3 (567 AM, 1584 AM) and you can hear local and international news all day, both financial and political with music programmes interspersed, from pop to rock. There are fun phone-in talks like Back Chat to listen to and call in with your two cents worth.

RTHK Radio 4 (97.6 FM to 98.9FM) plays Western and Chinese classical music and focuses on art and culture. You can hear the BBC World Service 24 hours a day on RTHK Radio 6, broadcasting news, documentaries and music. Metro Plus (1044 AM) is bilingual with the focus more on the English and broadcasts regional news and lively discussions in between an assorted music mix.

Check the daily newspapers for waveband and frequencies of the stations. If you are driving, the reception is not always clear and can become unstable in the south side of Hong Kong Island.

Television

There are two domestic, free terrestrial television channels in English, ATV World (Asia Television) and TVB (Television Broadcast) Pearl, as well as two Chinese language channels, ATV Home and TVB Jade.

There is plenty to watch with a good selection of the latest and well-known television programmes. Local coverage includes local, regional and international news in Putonghua (a spoken version of Mandarin), financial reports, weather news, talk shows and interviews. Some sports programmes on Chinese channels can be picked up with English commentaries.

Satellite TV & Radio

Satellite receivers perched on top of buildings are now a common sight. A few companies provide programmes on subscription, but with high hills and concentrated high-rise buildings, not all areas can enjoy satellite viewing. Most of the programmes are in Mandarin and Cantonese and in other regional languages and there's not much in English. There are two English-language cable stations: Now TV and Cable Television, both of these are pay-as-you-watch. Between them you can pick up the Discovery channels, all the international news channels, documentaries like National Geographic, sports, movie channels like MGM, Cinemax, HBO, Turner Classic Movies, Hallmark, Star Movies and Star World and Cartoon Network.

When you watch PCCW's (Pacific Century Cyber Works) Now TV what you see are programmes received via satellite and delivered by cable through IPTV (Internet Protocol Television). You get a digital decoder, a small box that is linked by cables to your telephone line and to your television set. You can have more than one decoder in the house. The charges start with an $800 deposit for the decoder and $30 per month for rental. The line rental charge is around $118 and installation costs $530. But if you already subscribe to PCCW's broadband service, all this is free bar a $15 membership fee. Installation charges for iCable costs $600 for the first outlet installation, $154 for a converter and $308 for a basic monthly package. To check programme listings log on to www.now-tv.com or www.cabletv.com.hk. Look out for channel promotions.

Most hotels have cable TV and many of the bars like Smugglers in Stanley and Madison in Central entice huge crowds to their big screens on match days.

Satellite/Cable Providers		
Hong Kong Cable Television (Cable TV)	183 2888	www.cabletv.com.hk
Now TV ▶ p.viii	2888 0008	www.now-tv.com
TVB Pay Vision	3168 2888	www.tvbpayvision.com

125

Private in Public
You can go to the main
government hospitals
and ask for private
treatment. It will cost
almost as much as a
private hospital, but
you get what you pay
for. You'll be seeing a
different doctor, have
rooms in a different
area and better food. If
you are a visitor and
need hospital
treatment, the charges
are enormous even in a
public hospital,
because as a non-
resident you are not
actually eligible for
healthcare here.

General Medical Care

Healthcare in Hong Kong is considered to be excellent by international standards. Life expectancy is high and infant mortality is low. Many people tend to use both western treatment methods as well as Traditional Chinese Medicine (TCM) to heal and balance the body.

There are 56 hospitals in Hong Kong, all with A&E units and general practice. Of these, 12 are private hospitals and 44 are public hospitals that come under the Government Hospital Authority (2300 6555).

Private practising doctors have their own consulting clinics but use hospital facilities for surgeries and other treatments. Most of the doctors are local Chinese, with some foreign. Almost all of them have overseas qualifications. Some hospitals have specialisations, such as coronary care or oncology centres and some, like the Adventist Hospital, offer classes to combat stress, aid weight reduction and to quit smoking and alcohol.

There are three kinds of medical treatments in healthcare: primary (general practice, from coughs to immunisations), secondary, and tertiary (illnesses that require long term hospitalisation or rehabilitation).

Most private hospitals have primary and secondary medical services. The government-run healthcare centres cover all three types, and some hospitals only specialise in tertiary care for chronic conditions.

Government Healthcare

Many of the hospitals provide all kinds of subsidised services to government employees, both local and expats. Many of these hospitals are also attached to universities and double up as teaching hospitals, like Queen Mary in Pok Fu Lam and Prince Philip Dental Hospital in Sai Ying Pun.

Wealth Service
Of the 10,000 doctors
in Hong Kong, one third
work in government
hospitals and clinics,
and are said to be
among the highest
paid in the world.

Government hospitals and clinics are 95% subsidised for in-patient treatment and 87% for out-patient and are amazingly inexpensive.

If you have a Hong Kong identity card, you can go to any hospital and enjoy the subsidised rates but be prepared for communication problems, bad food and long waits for out-patient service and appointment times.

If you plan to visit a government clinic or hospital, the wait could be over an hour and there they take only cash. Consultation costs about $60 for a specialist and about $45 for general consultation, plus any follow up tests or medicines.

You will need to have a resident identity card and make an appointment. In some specialised hospitals, you are expected to come with a doctor's referral and sometimes doctors will refer you to a government hospital because of a special test or treatment available only in that hospital.

Health Insurance Companies

A.I.A	2881 3333	www.aia.com.hk
AXA China Region	2519 1770	www.axa-chinaregion.com
Blue Cross	3608 2888	www.bluecross.com.hk
Bupa	2517 5175	www.bupa.com.hk
Cigna International Expatriate Benefits	2539 9222	www.cigna.com.hk
Expat HK Medical Insurance	2893 3344	www.expathk.com
Global Health	2526 0505	www.globalhealthasia.com
Globalsurance	3113 1331	www.global-health-insurance.com
Manulife	2108 1313	www.manulife.com.hk
Prudential	2525 2367	www.prudential.com.hk
Standard Life Asia	2169 0300	www.standardlifeasia.com.hk
Sun Life Insurance	2103 8888	www.sunlife.com.hk
William Russel (Far East) Limited	3690 2145	www.william-russell.com

Private Healthcare

Private healthcare is very expensive and only those with private health insurance or who are covered by employing companies visit private doctors and hospitals. These hospitals, like Adventist, Matilda and Canossa, are located in expensive residential parts of Hong Kong where expats live. Doctors tend to use private hospitals for surgery or treatments. Some private hospitals and doctors are non-profit like the Adventist and Baptist hospitals (i.e. they don't pay the 28% corporate tax as do private hospitals and rely on donations to subsidise operations).

No matter where you go, private or public, you have to make an appointment and be prepared to wait for 30-40 minutes (sometimes longer in public hospitals) before you see the doctor, unless it's an emergency.

Emergency Services
Dial 999 or call a hospital directly. You can also call the St John Ambulance Service (Hong Kong 2576 6555, Kowloon 2713 5555, New Territories 2639 2555). Most emergency hotlines should be able to answer in English.

Health Insurance

If you have insurance from home, it may apply to your stay in Hong Kong, since many companies have branches or at least affiliates here. You may also have health coverage as part of your relocation package but dental, preventive or alternative treatments are often not included.

There are many health insurance companies in Hong Kong and some of the banks here offer health insurance packages.

See the table of Health Insurance Companies on p.126.

Pharmacies

Pharmacies are located in hospitals where, after consultation with a doctor, you hand over your prescription. Chains like Watsons and Mannings have pharmacies in some of their branches.

There aren't many medicines in Hong Kong that can be sold without prescription. The Department of Health requires all medicines and pharmacists to be registered. If you go into any chemists' you'll see very few over the counter medicines on the shelves but you will see local brands of Chinese herbal concoctions, which are usually milder forms of the real stuff.

Health Check-ups

Health check-ups are available in public and private hospitals and clinics. They are sometimes called an executive health package for men and include a heart and chest check up, prostrate test, cholesterol and blood sugar test. But you can choose a package for whatever type of tests you want to have.

There are Well-Woman clinics in all hospitals that provide mammograms, gynaecological checks, cholesterol and blood sugar tests. Your weight and blood pressure are always checked during these visits. If anything comes up in the tests you'll be referred to your doctor for further investigation.

Government health clinics and family planning (adult line 2572 2222, youth line 2572 2733) clinics provide health check-ups and are located in different districts. They offer counselling on contraception and advise young women on the importance of regular check-ups. They will only do routine checking and advise you to see your doctor if something comes up. Being a government clinic, the cost is very low.

Stop Smoking

There are several places you can contact if you want to join a 'stop smoking' programme. Some hospitals have group counselling programmes for smokers trying to quit. Check with Adventist Hospital about its community programmes. Melanie Bryan (2575 7107) uses hypnosis as does Dr. Katherine Meggyes (2121 1402) who will assess your situation and tell you how many sessions you'll need.

Call the Department of Health Smoking Cessation hotline (2961 8883) or the Smoking Cessation Service (2753 8115) at the Jockey Club's Education & Training Centre of Family Medicine. You will need to see a doctor for about eight weeks and will get nicotine withdrawal medication like a patch, chewing gum or an inhaler.

Donor Cards

Getting organ donation in Hong Kong is not easy since the Chinese believe the body should be buried whole with nothing missing or cut up. The trend is slowly changing with a new, younger and less traditional generation coming in

127

but there is still a long list of people awaiting donors.

For an organ donor card you can go to any government public library, get a card, fill it in and keep it in your wallet. Another way is to contact The Hong Kong Medical Association (2527 8285). You will need to get forms or download them from the website (www.hkma.com.hk), get your relatives to fill in the section required of them and mail it back to HKMA. A card is not necessary in this new system as the form is scanned into a donor's database and hospitals that are in this system can access the information through your Hong Kong identity card.

Queen Mary Hospital (p.129) on Hong Kong Island, Prince of Wales Hospital (p.129) in Sha Tin, and Queen Elizabeth Hospital (p.129) in Kowloon are all linked to the database for donated organs. See Certificates & Licences on p.62.

Giving Blood

Donating blood is organised mainly by the Hong Kong Red Cross Society (2710 1333, www.redcross.org.hk). They have mobile units, donor centres and four collection buses that can be seen parked in main shopping areas during their street campaigns. Blood donation advertisements are aired on TV with information on where to go and who to call if you want to donate blood, as well as campaigns to motivate people to donate regularly.

Main Government Hospitals

There are many government hospitals and rehabilitation centres around the territory. All of them come under the umbrella of the Hong Kong Hospital Authority. There are 15 public hospitals under the Hospital Authority that provide Accident & Emergency (A&E) Services. The Hospital Authority website (www.ha.org.hk) lists lots of useful hotlines for advice on various health issues. The Authority's 24 hour information line is 2882 4866. Most of the treatments are subsidised and meant for people who cannot afford good healthcare, are retired or too ill to earn an income. Expats who have used the hospitals for any treatments find the service and treatment excellent.

You must have a Hong Kong identity card to use government hospital services. If you prefer to use private services, the fees are different and if you do not have a local identity card or private health insurance it will cost you.

Because the healthcare system is providing much of the tertiary healthcare, hospitals support each other and private doctors refer patients from other hospitals. The cost for an emergency visit can be $100, and for the non-eligible about $560. Consultation costs are about $100 for the first visit and $80 for any follow-ups.

111 Wing Hong St
Sham Shui Po
🚇 *Sham Shui Po*
Map 15-C1

Caritas Medical Centre

3408 7911 | *www.ha.org.hk*

It provides 24 hour accident and emergency service, general outpatient service, and inpatient and outpatient specialist services. Caritas also has the largest Development Disabilities Centre (Project Sunshine).

25 Waterloo Rd
Yau Ma Tei
🚇 *Yau Ma Tei*
Map 15-A2

Kwong Wah Hospital

2332 2311 | *www.ha.org.hk*

The hospital operates a 24 hour accident and emergency service, and provides a full range of acute care services, mainly to the population of the West Kowloon and Wong Tai Sin areas. There is a maternity and a Well-Woman clinic, a Chinese medical clinic and a rehabilitation centre for physio and speech therapy. It also has a home care service for the elderly.

3 Lok Man Rd
Chai Wan
Map 10-E4

Pamela Youde Nethersole Eastern Hospital
2595 6111 | www.ha.org.hk
This is a large, recently expanded and renovated hospital situated in Chai Wan, the eastern-most part of Hong Kong Island. Aside from the general medical services, there is a Patient Resource Centre for community health projects, health education and information, self help groups and much more. Services also include clinical psychology, physiotherapy, pharmacy, occupational therapy, podiatry, dietetics and speech therapy. The hospital has a 24 hour accident and emergency service.

30-32 Ngan Shing
Sha Tin
Map 6-D3

Prince of Wales
2632 2211 | www.ha.org.hk
This has a 24 hour accident and emergency service and doubles up as a teaching hospital. Located in the city centre of Sha Tin, Prince of Wales can be reached by the KCR. Services offered range from family medicine, surgery, gynaecology to psychiatry and paediatrics among others.

2-10 Princess Margaret Hospital Rd
Ngau Tau Kok
Map 10-A1

Princess Margaret
2990 1111 | www.ha.org.hk
Being close to the airport, this hospital provides medical care for travellers and is equipped to handle emergency in air disasters as well as a 24 hour accident and emergency service. It serves Kowloon West, South of the New Territories and has a community resource centre for self help, information and counselling besides other medical services.

30 Gascoigne Rd
Jordan
🚇 *Jordan*
Map 15-D3

Queen Elizabeth Hospital
2958 8888 | www.ha.org.hk
There's a 24 hour accident and emergency service in this hospital and 13 clinical departments serving one third of all Hong Kong cancer patients. It has full medical services and specialist clinics in three different blocks. There's an electronic medical record system in the operation rooms. It's also a teaching and training centre for basic and post-graduate training of doctors and nurses.

102 Pok Fu Lam Rd
Pok Fu Lam
Map 16-B3

Queen Mary Hospital
2855 3838 | www.ha.org.hk
Located in the south-western part of Hong Kong Island, this is a teaching hospital for the University of Hong Kong's Faculty of Medicine. It has 24 hours accident and emergency services, and is one of the most well-known of the government hospitals. Services range from surgery, paediatrics, clinical oncology, radiology, and gynaecology to obstetrics, dental surgery, ear nose and throat treatment and many more, including a pharmacy that is open 24 hours. They have a private clinic where patients pay full charges for consultation, surgery and rooms – the rest is subsidised for government employees and the general identity-card-holding public.

266 Queens Rd East
Wan Chai
🚇 *Wan Chai*
Map 17-A2

Ruttonjee Hospital
2291 2000 | www.ha.org.hk
A general hospital that provides 24 hour emergency services with a special outpatient department, cardiac and intensive care unit, cosmetic surgery, pathology, respiratory medicine, pharmacy amongst others. A Health Resource Centre provides self-help groups, a library, health education and information.

129

St. John Hospital

Cheung Chau
Hospital Rd
Cheung Chau
Map 13-B3

2981 9941 | www.ha.org.hk
This hospital offers a 24 hour emergency centre, general outpatient consulting, family planning, and maternal and child health. Other services include physiotherapy, x-ray, occupational therapy, methadone detoxification and a dental clinic.

Dermatologists		
Dr. Ho Lai Yung Connia	Tsim Sha Tsui	2367 6274
Dr. Ip Wing Kin	Mong Kok	2393 3133
Dr. Ku Lap Shing Simon	Central	2525 2212
George Ng. Dermatology	Central	2523 5995
HK Dermatology Center	Central	2810 0680
Skincentral Dermatology Aesthetics and Lasers	Central	2901 1281

Tseung Kwan O Hospital

2 Po Ning Lane
Tseung Kwan O
Map 10-F2

2208 0111 | www.ha.org.hk
This hospital provides secondary medical care. Its services include a 24 hour accident and emergency service, a specialist outpatient service, intensive care unit, and a health resource centre.

Tung Wah Eastern Hospital

19 Eastern
Hospital Rd
Tai Hang
🚇 *Tin Hau*
Map 16-D1

2162 6888 | www.ha.org.hk
This is another part of the Tung Wah Group of hospitals. It has inpatient and outpatient speciality clinics for diabetes and a diabetes dental clinic, the first of its kind set up with the Faculty of Dentistry of HKU Medicine and the Prince Philip Dental Hospital. Some of the other speciality services include stroke and cardiac rehabilitation, geriatrics, ophthalmology, rehabilitation services and grammatology, ophthalmology, orthopaedics, medicine, and a resource centre.

Tung Wah Hospital

12 Po Yan St
Sheung Wan
🚇 *Sheung Wan*
Map 16-D1

589 8111 | www.ha.org.hk
One of the oldest hospitals and the original building of the Tung Wah Group of Hospitals, this was set up over a 100 years ago to provide Chinese style treatment for the Chinese who wanted to have nothing to do with western medicine. It provides care for patients from Queen Mary and for the community specialising in ear, nose and throat treatments, radiology, stroke rehabilitation and much more.

United Christian Hospital

130 Hip Wo St
Kwun Tong
Map 10-E2

3513 4000 | www.ha.org.hk
This is the main hospital in the eastern part of Kowloon providing a wide range of services including 24 hour accident and emergency. Other services include general surgery and intensive care, obstetrics and gynaecology, paediatrics, orthopaedics, psychiatry and counselling, ear, nose and throat treatment and a dental clinic. There's inpatient, day-patient and outpatient care.

Other Government Hospitals		
The Duchess of Kent Children's Hospital	Pok Fu Lam	2817 7111
The Hong Kong Buddhist Hospital	Kowloon City	2339 6111
The Hong Kong Eye Hospital	Kowloon City	2762 3007
The Kowloon Hospital	Kowloon City	3129 7111
North District Hospital	Sheung Shui	2683 8888
Our Lady of Maryknoll, Wong Tai Sin	Kowloon City	2320 2121
Pak Oi Hospital	Yuen Long	2478 2556
Tsan Yuk Hospital	Sai Ying Pun	2589 2100
Tuen Mun Hospital	Tuen Mun	2468 5111
Yan Chai	Tsuen Wan	2417 8383

Main Private Hospitals

There are about a dozen private hospitals in Hong Kong dealing mainly with primary health care. Some are located in Kowloon, some in New Territories but most of them on Hong Kong Island. The consultation fee does not include drugs, treatment, investigation, tests and procedures. You can pay by cheque, credit card or your health insurance card. All hospitals are easily accessible by public transport and some have shuttles going back and forth from ferry piers, train stations and the MTR stations. Remember to make an appointment well in advance because the hospitals get busy and unless it's an emergency, you can't walk in and expect service, unless you are prepared to wait.

40 Stubbs Rd
Happy Valley
🚇 *Causeway Bay*
Map 17-B3

Adventist Hospital
3651 8888 | *www.hkah.org.hk*

This is one of the most popular hospitals for expats and provides a great variety of medical services. It has a first rate International Travel Medicine service and is a good place to find out about vaccinations, prevention and treatment of diseases before and after travelling. With a customised physical examination package for families, individuals and companies, there's a Heart Centre and a women's and a men's health check programme. They have a dental clinic, ear, nose and throat specialists, maternity packages and paediatricians, sports and orthopaedic medicine and plastic surgery. Check with them about classes and seminars on healthy living and counselling on weight loss, smoking and drinking. Consultation costs about $400 but more if you see a specialist. Medicines and tests will be charged separately. There's also an Adventist Hospital in Kowloon.

1 Old Peak Rd
Mid-Levels
🚇 *Central*
Map 16-E2

Canossa Hospital
2522 2181 | *www.canossahospital.org.hk*

This hospital is run by the nuns of the Canossian order and is located in a very green part of the Mid-Levels near the Ladies Recreation Club and above the Botanical and Zoological Gardens. They have a dental clinic, gynaecology and maternity services, a dialysis unit, an orthopaedic ward, intensive care unit and outpatient services including a nutritionist and a child health centre. Consultation is around $190 before 17:00 and $240 after 17:00. Medicines and test costs are extra.

222 Argyle St
Kowloon City
Map 15-E1

Evangel Hospital
2711 5221 | *www.evangel.org.hk*

The Evangel Church of America and China set up this hospital in the 1960s. Dental, maternity and specialist clinics cover many services ranging from ENT, plastic and reconstructive surgery, cardiology, psychiatry as well as provision of vaccinations. Its charitable reach in the community involves cataract surgeries, health screening and a help team for people needing care at home. The outpatient consultation service hours are from 08:00 to 24:00. General consultation fees start at $155 without the cost of tests, medicines or injections.

222 Waterloo Rd
Kowloon Tong
Map 10-C1

Hong Kong Baptist Hospital
2339 8888 | *www.hkbh.org.hk*

Full medical services are available in this hospital that has been around for over 40 years. It has skin and laser centres, a cardiac clinic, an ENT department and a Chinese Medicine Clinic. You can have your health screenings done here, see a dietician or have physiotherapy. Baptist also has a web baby service to put your babies photo on the web for your friends and family to see. Consultations start at $170, holidays and evenings, $250

131

Hong Kong Central Hospital

1 Lower Albert Rd
Central
🚇 *Central*
Map 16-E2

2522 3141 | www.hkch.org

Located on Albert Road, this hospital is in the heart of Central close to the foreign Correspondents' Club on Ice House Street. It has a 24 hour outpatient service seven days a week with extended services including x-ray, CT Scan, operating theatre and dispensary service. Other services are cosmetic laser treatment, oncology, endoscope, dietician services, sleep apnea, health assessment, paediatrics and psychology. Outpatient consultation costs between $150 and $300 and waiting time is not more than 30 minutes. Cost of any tests and medicines are extra.

Hong Kong Sanatorium & Hospital

2-4 Village Rd
Happy Valley
🚇 *Causeway Bay*
Map 17-B3

2572 0211 | www.hksh.org.hk

This private hospital is over 80 years old and provides 24 hour general outpatient service. Check its service packages that sometimes include health screening and weight management as well as a Well Woman clinic. They also have pre-marriage and pre-pregnancy screening. Its diabetics centre provides counselling and advice for diabetics. The ophthalmology department has laser surgery, glaucoma screening, cataract surgery and optometrist examination. Consultation fees are around $160 for morning and holidays and $200 in the evening. Tests and medicines are extra.

Matilda International Hospital

41 Mount Kellett Rd
The Peak
Map 16-D4

2849 0111 | www.matilda.org

This is an old, historic hospital in the upscale area of Peak. It's popular amongst expats especially for its maternity ward. Recent refurbishing has upgraded it to look like a luxury hotel, a far cry from the 1940s bare, clinical place that it used to be. They have many facilities for medical, surgical and paediatric care, with health assessments by the latest imaging technology and an EBCT heart scan. There's also orthopaedic, cosmetic and reconstructive, and hernia surgery utilising the latest in minimal invasive techniques. Perched on top of a hill, the views all around and from the rooms are spectacular, but it is far from everything and the only way to get up there is to drive, take a taxi or take their complimentary shuttle bus from Queen's Pier in Central. Consultation fees are $500; tests and medicines are extra.

St. Paul's Hospital

2 Eastern Hospital Rd
Causeway Bay
🚇 *Causeway Bay*
Map 17-B2

2890 6008 | www.stpaul.org.hk

Services here include medical check ups, inpatient services including eye checks, cardiac investigation, x-ray centre, pharmacy, dental department, vaccination, ear, nose and throat unit, plastic surgery, dental and eye clinic, laser surgery, breast clinic, Well-Man clinic, and chiropody. It also has a Chinese medicine clinic where you can have acupuncture and be prescribed Chinese herbal medicines. The practitioners are registered with the Chinese Medical Council of Hong Kong. Consultation fees start at $120 from 09:00-19:00, $180 from 19:00 to 24:00, and $280 between 24:00 and 08:00.

Government Health Centres/Clinics		
Caritas	Wan Chai	2843 4617
Central Kowloon Health Centre	Mong Kok	2762 1456
Chai Wan Health Centre	Chai Wan	2556 0261
Fanling Family Medicine Centre	Fanling	2639 4601
Hung Hom Clinic	Hung Hom	2356 9281
Mona Fong	Sai Kung	2792 2601
North Lamma Clinic	Lamma Island	2983 1110
Sha Tin Clinic	Sha Tin	2691 1618
Tuen Mun Clinic	Tuen Mun	2452 9111
Tung Chung Health Centre	Lantau Island	2109 6830
Violet Peel Health Centre	Wan Chai	2835 1767
Yau Ma Tei Jockey Club Clinic	Yau Ma Tei	2272 2400

St Teresa's Hospital

327 Prince Edward Rd
Kowloon City
🚇 Kowloon
Map 15-E1

2711 9111 | *www.sth.org.hk*

St Teresa's is commonly known to locals as the 'French Hospital.' The Sisters of St Paul de Chartres started it in 1940 and over the years it has established itself as a main caregiver for the community. There is a 24 hour outpatient service, 22 consultation rooms and a treatment

Diagnostics

Angel Health Medical Centre	Central	8207 7331
Ausmed Immuno Diagnostic Service	Central	2522 1537
Complex Lab	Wan Chai	2511 1460
Diagnostix Medical Centre	Central	2877 9329
Mobile Medical Diagnostic Centre	Tsim Sha Tsui	2369 0071
Premier Medicare Service	Causeway Bay	8102 3818

room for general and special outpatient services. It also provides services for dental, plastic surgery, neurology, geriatrics, cardio-thoracic surgery, delivery packages, an intensive care unit, a physiotherapy department and other services. Expect to pay between $120 and $280 for an outpatient consultation

Tsuen Wan Adventist Hospital

199 Tsuen King Circuit
Tsuen Wan
🚇 Tsuen Wan
Map 5-F4

2276 7676 | *www.twah.org.hk*

When this hospital first opened in 1964 it was surrounded by squatters but that has all since changed. Check-ups are available for men, women, children, students and domestic helpers. These can be standard check ups or pre-employment ones. Specialties include a dental department, nutritional counselling and dietician service, hospital chaplaincy, circumcision and plastic surgery. Consultation fees start at $160, not including medicines and tests.

Union Hospital

18, Fu Kin St
Tai Wai
Sha Tin
Map 6-B4

2608 3388 | *www.union.org*

Located in Sha Tin, this hospital has polyclinics in Tseung Kwan O (2721 0100), Ma On Shan (2631 5208) and Tsim Sha Tsui (2375 3323). It has 10 new operation theatres available for 24 hour emergencies. In its Minimally Invasive Centre, doctor's use the keyhole method of surgerywhich avoids extensive scarring or recovery. They also have general surgery, in and outpatient services, diagnostic services, health screening for domestic helpers, pre-marital and pre-employment check-ups. There's also a Well-Woman and Man's screening programme. Consultation fee ranges from $150 to $240, not including any tests or medicines. Free shuttle buses run between Union Hospital and Tai Wai KCR Station.

Private Health Centres/Clinics

Central Medical Practice	Central	2521 2567
Dr. Vio & Partners	Tsim Sha Tsui	2369 3329
Family Medical Practice	Repulse Bay	2592 9000
Foster & Stevenson Medical Practice	Central	2881 8131
Lam Tin Clinic	Lam Tin	2717 3777
Lucy Lord & Associates	Wan Chai	2824 0822
Ngau Tau Kok Clinic	Ngau Tau Kok	2757 6922
Owen Trodd & Partners	Wan Chai	2824 9112
	Central	2521 3181
	Clear Water Bay	2719 6366
	Repulse Bay	2813 1978
Quality Health Care Medical Centre	Sheung Wan	2523 8166
Raffles Medical Centre	Central	2525 1730
Sha Tin Clinic	Sha Tin	2699 1113
Susan Jamieson & Associates	Central	2523 8044
Veritas Medical Clinic	Repulse Bay	2812 2677

133

Maternity

Other options **Maternity Items** p.307

You can either have your baby in a private hospital like the Matilda (p.132), Adventist (p.135) or Canossa (p.131), or in a public hospital like Queen Mary (p.129), Pamela Youde Nethersole (p.129) or Queen Elizabeth (p.129). Some people prefer home delivery with the help of a midwife.

Ask your gynaecologist or obstetrician where the delivery will be. The main reason being the location of the hospital and the chances of difficult birth, since some hospitals are better than others to take cake of complications and emergencies. Your gynaecologist will be able to help you should the need arise.

If you already have a preference of where you want to deliver your baby, start to find out about the costs early on. If you are covered by health insurance then you have little to worry about. Keep all your bills and complete the paperwork after the delivery. You can file your claim for reimbursement as soon as you are fit and ready. While some hospitals will allow your husband or partner to be in the delivery room, others will not. Make sure you discuss this with your doctor as well as any other birth plans you may have. Many government hospitals are now changing their policies and some have introduced a 'husband accompanying programme.' Check before choosing a hospital.

You can ask for an epidural, which can cost from $3,000 to $5,000 in a private hospital. Most hospitals will keep you in for four or five days, and during that time will help you to nurse your baby.

Once your baby is born you'll need to start the process of acquiring a birth certificate so that you can get a passport and then a visa for the baby.

See Birth Certificate and Registration on p.64 for more information.

Government Hospitals

Government hospitals provide good service and are fully subsidised so you would be paying only for the bed (about $80 a night) and admittance, which is also a small amount. You can ask for private care, which is personalised and a little more expensive, in fact almost as much as a private hospital.

The downside here is that you don't necessarily see the same doctor every time you visit, so you don't get a chance to build a rapport over the nine months of check ups. In fact, a doctor you may not have seen before may well deliver your baby.

Queen Mary Hospital (p.129) has up-to-date equipment so many people prefer to go there and pay the private rates. Others prefer Pamela Youde Nethersole (p.129) where, throughout pregnancy and postnatal, the nurses train you how to bathe and massage your baby and give lots of details on baby care. They give you full antenatal care that include regular check-ups, scans and AIDS tests from the minute you find out you are pregnant right up to birthing. Prince of Wales (p.129) is said to have the best neonatal care unit in Hong Kong and women have been pleased with its services.

Day Care Centres in hospitals organise prenatal and antenatal talks and courses that can be helpful if you are a first time mother and husbands are also welcome. Some government hospitals share the maternity care with Maternity Health Clinics and Centres where you would go for monthly check ups and then move to the hospital in the later part of the pregnancy or in case of complications that may arise.

You can opt for a Caesarean birth, but you'll need a better reason than vanity. If you have personal plans for how you'd like the birthing process to go, be sure to have discussed the details with the nurse or doctor months in advance to avoid any disappointments on your big day.

Baby Groups

For details of groups in Hong Kong that offer activities for babies and young children, see Mother and Toddler Activities on p.253

Valuables

When you're checking into a hospital, remember to leave your jewellery and other valuables at home. You should find everything for your ready-to-go bag at the Wing On Department store on Des Voeux Road, and other stores like Watson's and Mannings.

Labour rooms in government hospitals are clean and modern with the best equipment, and the nurses are fully trained and the epitome of professionalism.

Vaccinations are part of the whole package till your little one reaches five years. Once you are in the system you can go to any hospital for any treatment. They also monitor you for postnatal depression with continuing check-ups. Most hospitals and centres will have support groups and classes that are open for you to attend.

Some of these hospitals are teaching hospitals so you could end up with students watching the check-ups and practicing on you but they will ask for your permission beforehand and you have the right to refuse.

Private Hospitals

Private hospitals offer complete maternity packages that can seem a little expensive. Matilda Hospital (p.142) on The Peak is by far the most visited hospital for births by expat women. The rooms are like five star hotel rooms, the views from the balcony are breathtaking and husbands are allowed to stay overnight. The labour wards here are clean and have the latest equipment, trained nurses and support staff. There is also a 'mom and baby' club that offers activities as a means of continuing support. It's a good hospital for routine delivery, but the obstetrician, paediatrician, and anaesthesiologist all have very high fees.

Other private hospitals also have good locations, top-quality antenatal care, well presented rooms but with a hefty price tag. With so much competition, it's worth checking the different maternity packages on offer and what they include.

Going Home to Have the Baby

Sometimes expat women go home to have a baby to be with their family and in familiar surroundings with a family doctor. Should you decide to head home, be sure to get a record from your doctor that will have a chart of your weight, blood pressure and other details for monitoring your pregnancy. Also check before you leave what you would need for the baby to re-enter Hong Kong. While you are home, you'll need to arrange for the birth certificate and passport. Remember to bring the birth certificate back with you. Airlines restrict travel during pregnancy so ask your travel agent to check for you or call the airline and check their policy for pregnancy travel. Singapore Airlines for example, allows you to travel up to 35 weeks of pregnancy, and United Airlines will let you travel till 40 weeks but if you are beyond that then you need a doctor's certificate, which should be issued within 72 hours of travel and will need to say that you are fit for the journey. Lufthansa wants you to be less than 36 weeks into your pregnancy before you board. Since airlines seem to vary in policies, it's best to call the one you are planning to travel with and check before booking.

Maternity Hospitals & Clinics

Adventist Hospital	Tsuen Wan	2402 1328	Private
	Happy Valley	2574 6211	Private
Annerly Midwife	No City	2983 1558	Private
Canossa Hospital	Mid-Levels	2522 2181	Private
Caritas Medical Centre	Sham Shui Po	2746 7911	Government
Dawn Midwives	Wan Chai	2705 9322	Private
Hong Kong Baptist Hospital	Kowloon Tong	2339 8888	Private
Kwong Wah Hospital	Kowloon City	2385 2276	Government
Pamela Youde Nethersole	Chai Wan	2595 6205	Government
Prince of Wales	Sha Tin	2632 2810	Government
Princess Margaret Hospital	Kowloon City	2419 2662	Government
Queen Elizabeth Hospital	Kowloon City	2958 6049	Government
Queen Mary	Pok Fu Lam	2855 3400	Government
St. Teresa's Hospital	Kowloon City	2711 9111	Private
Tuen Mun Hospital	Tuen Mun	2468 5405	Government
Union Hospital	Tai Wai	2608 3388	Private
United Christian Hospital	Kwun Tong	3513 4000	Government

Antenatal Care

There's good antenatal care in both government and private hospitals. If you are using private service then you'll be seeing a doctor in a clinic on a monthly basis and then at the time of labour and delivery you will go to the hospital of your choice. You can consult a doctor in a hospital too. Obstetricians deliver babies, but you can opt for a midwife to be present or even conduct the birth.

Antenatal support classes are provided in all hospitals, some of which are in the evenings and some will allow your partner to join. In government hospitals, there are support groups and courses about breast feeding, parenting, health and childcare.

Government hospitals have tests and check ups either on site or in a sub-clinic of which there are many around Hong Kong. If you are over 35 and having your first child, you might have to endure extra tests and regular scans. If you are in good health, have given birth before and are having a normal pregnancy, there shouldn't be any need for extra monitoring.

Double Trouble!

If you have twins or triplets, then double or triple congratulations are in order, as is a good support group, because your hands will be well and truly full. Call Mothers of Multiples (MOMS) on 2987 2096 or 9191 2424. It will cost you $350 for membership and you can download the application form from its website (www.moms-hongkong.com). The group holds special lunches with guest speakers, playgroups for under 3s, coffee mornings and social events at Halloween and Christmas.

Postnatal Care

Home visits are not part of postnatal care because generally people here have maids to help take care of the baby and housework. Alternatively, you can arrange for a midwife to come two or three times a week at first if you don't have a maid, or just need professional support and advice. You'll be expected back in the hospital four to six weeks after giving birth for a follow-up consultation. Your baby will be weighed and measured by a nurse followed by a full check up by a paediatrician. Some hospitals like Adventist (p.131) provide 24 hour telephone advice with a paediatrician and unlimited consultation with nurses for the first two weeks after birth.

If you are experiencing problems with breast feeding and the hospital just isn't doing it for you, there are other forms of help. Contact the La Leche League for a start (2257 6757, www.lllhk.org) and attend their courses.

An excellent follow up postnatal system in both government and private hospitals can keep postnatal depression at bay but sometimes this isn't enough. Postnatal depression is serious but easily worked through. Talk to your doctor or seek out a good counsellor. Whatever you do, this is beyond pride so don't be embarrassed to get help. Contact ReSource the Counselling Centre (2523 8979) or St. John's Cathedral Counselling (2525 7207).

Losing a child is devastating and grief stricken parents need all the support and attention they can get. Bereaved Parents Support Group (Colin Wall, 2813 2884) is an organisation that is set up to help anyone that needs it. Alternatively, call the Samaritans (2896 0000).

If you are expecting your domestic help to take care of your baby and are planning to go back to work, contact The Family Zone (2530 1905, 9887 3235). Set up by Yvonne Heavyside, they train helpers in small groups in child care and CPR for $1,600 for 11 hours, and one-on-one for $2,900 for five hours. A certificate is given after passing an examination. Once your helper is trained to take care of your newborn and manage your home, you'll feel comfortable about returning to work knowing your baby is in good hands.

Maternity Leave

Women get a mandatory 10 weeks paid maternity leave in Hong Kong (if on a continuous contract and having worked for 40 weeks). You will need to get a Certificate of Pregnancy from a doctor, stating the expected due date. Be warned, days taken for check-ups are counted as sick leave. Sometimes an additional two to four weeks leave can be agreed, but this is at the discretion of the employer. Pay is at a rate of 4/5th of the usual wage. Pregnant employees cannot be made to work in hazardous areas or with heavy equipment. Any mishaps or failure to pay the salary and the employer will be fined $50,000, and/or expected to pay the medical bills. Pregnant employees cannot be dismissed without good reason. An employer will be fined $100,000 for the unfair dismissal of a pregnant employee, as well as being liable for one month's wages and 10 weeks' paid maternity leave.

Gynaecology & Obstetrics

If you are going to a private hospital you will be checked by a gynaecologist. If you would prefer a woman doctor, be sure to specify – no one will be offended, this is a personal choice and you need to feel comfortable. Be sure to also specify that you want to see the same doctor every time, unless of course you don't. In a public hospital you won't be seeing one doctor regularly and you cannot request to see one because it depends who's on duty. Being in a new place also means that things are done differently and doctors are different in their practices so if you have met people who have had babies you can ask for their opinion and experience on doctors, hospitals and birthing choices.

The Family Planning Clinics located around Hong Kong (Hong Kong 2919 7777, Kowloon 2711 9211, Mobile Clinic 2711 9656) offer contraception counselling for both men and women.

Gynaecology & Obstetrics		
Dr. Alexander Doo	2523 3007	www.thewomensclinic.com.hk
Dr Arabinda Ghosh	2812 2677	www.veritas-medical.com
Dr. Joseph Depasquale	2525 1730	www.rafflesmedical.com
HK Adventist Hospital	2835 0566	www.hkah.org.hk
Quality Health Care Medical Centre	2523 8166	www.qhms.com
Dr. Sally Ferguson	2824 9112	www.otandp.com

Paediatrics

You can find a paediatrician either in a hospital or in private practice. If a paediatrician at a government hospital sees your baby but you are not happy, you need not worry because it won't be the same one again next time, and the same applies to private hospitals. Whoever is on duty sees your baby but in a private hospital you have the choice to request to see a particular paediatrician. The best way to find one you are happy with is to ask people for referrals. Ask the hospital, your friends or your company to make a recommendation.

At birth, vaccinations are given free at government hospitals but there is a fee in private hospitals. You'll have to check the price list since costs differ between hospitals and between paediatricians. Canossa Hospital offers the five in one vaccination, which includes Diphtheria, Pertussis, Tetanus, Polio and Hepatitis B in just one shot. Until they are older, babies will not get any of the other shots. Babies are not given flu shots but toddlers will pick up sniffles and runny noses no matter what you do, especially when you start taking them to a playgroup and when they start pre-school.

Special Needs

Hong Kong has many support groups, schools and associations that are charitable and government subsidised for children with special needs. To find a school or medical assistance, contact the Social Welfare Department (2343 2255, www.swd.gov.hk) or the Community Advice Bureau (2815 5444) to put you in touch with relevant groups and educational resources. Another useful contact is the Matilda Hospital (2849 6138) where they have a resource library and support groups that can provide useful information and advice. See also Special Needs in the Education Section p.153.

Paediatrics			
Name	Area	Phone	Hospital/Clinic
Dr Yvonne Ou	Wan Chai	2824 0822	Dr. Lucy Lord & Associates
Dr. Alfred Tam	Central	2526 6332	Children at 818
Dr. Chris Howard	Wan Chai	2824 9112	Dr. Owen Trodd & Partners
Dr. Ken Chan	Central	2877 6068	Dr. Lauren Bramley Partners
Dr. Kenneth Lau	Mid-Levels	2835 0566	Adventist Hospital
Dr. Leo Chan	Central	2525 5755	na
Dr. Rulin Fuong	Wan Chai	2824 0822	Dr. Lucy Lord & Associates
Dr. Susannah Cho	Central	2526 6332	Children at 818
Dr. Tanpa Thondup	Wan Chai	2877 3118	The Veritas Medical Practice

Dentists/Orthodontists

There are dental clinics in all private hospitals and in most government hospitals. Dentists and orthodontists are well qualified and provide all dental services.

Dentist visits are generally expensive and a simple cleaning can cost around $90 to $600. Appointments are necessary.

Orthodontist treatment is lengthy and costly, yet popular. Initial consultation fees range between $400 and $500.

Dentists/Orthodontists		
Bayley & Jackson	Repulse Bay	2812 2358
Canossa Hospital	Mid-Levels	2522 2181
Dr. Eric Carter	Central	2525 4285
Dr. James Costello	Central	2877 9622
Dr. Richard Tinlin & Associates	Tsim Sha Tsui	2869 8198
HK Adventist Dental Practice	Mid-Levels	2835 0500

Opticians & Opthamologists

There's a wide variety of shops with a good selection of frames to choose from, regular or designer, and to suit any budget and style.

Opticians tend to be located in malls and in the main shopping areas. Most of these shops will also have the equipment to test your eyesight and prescribe lenses as you need them.

Opticians & Opthamologists		
Hong Kong Eye Centre	Mid-Levels	2522 2181
The Optical Shop	Various locations	2523 8365
PMG Optik	Central	3526 0641
Senses Optik	Central	2869 5111

Once you've chosen a frame, it can take about a week to have your glasses prepared for you. Some shops may ask for half of the price to be paid as a deposit and the rest upon delivery. Contact lenses are also sold here, and qualified opticians will be on hand to answer any questions you may have.

If you need a more thorough eye test, decide whether you'd prefer to visit a private optometrist or make an appointment to see an ophthalmologist in a hospital. All private and government hospitals have an ophthalmology department. The hospital will probably be better equipped for corrective surgery, but a private doctor will provide any necessary referrals.

Pale Face

The most popular trend among Hong Kong women is skin whitening. The lighter the skin the better, so whitening products weigh down the shelves in many a cosmetic store and pharmacy. All the brand names in facial care have whitening creams and solutions. Beauty salons promise lightening miracles and the cost can easily climb into the thousands.

Cosmetic Treatment & Surgery

The most common cosmetic treatments carried out in Hong Kong are breast enhancements, eyelid surgery and liposuction. Breast enhancing can cost more than $35,000 and double eyelid surgery costs around $18,000, excluding consultation fees and hospital costs.

Botox is gaining popularity, with several places offering you a firmer visage. The Face Magic Haven in Central (2524 6882) offers Botox and speciality facials for $3,800, but that tag includes a free top-up two weeks after the initial procedure. They also have the IPL (Initial Program Load) treatment, which uses bright flashing lights to penetrate deeply into the skin and stimulate the collagen that reduces spots and freckles. There are several IPL centres offering this non-surgical treatment including the Hong Kong IPL & Laser Institute (2191 6730) that also offers Botox.

Cosmetic Treatment & Surgery		
Dr Otto Y.T. Au	Central	2522 9365
Dr. Daniel T.C. Lee	Central	2526 6681
Dr. Francis Ho	Kowloon City	2309 2888
Dr. Franklin W.P. Li	Central	2522 3441
Dr. Gordon Ma	Central	2525 5355
Dr. Kenneth Hui	Central	2523 7690
Dr. Ng Lung-Kwan	Central	2543 3633
Dr. Philip Hsieh	Central	2521 8292
HK Society For Plastic and Reconstructive Surgery	Pok Fu Lam	2855 4990
Hong Kong Plastic and Cosmetic Surgery Center	Kowloon City	2396 5566

smartbaby
Preserving New-Born Stem Cells

"They gave Jesse a 0% chance of survival. But we had his cord blood and he's still alive."

Lisa Farquharson, Sunday Times

Please call 2868 5046 to register for our next talk on stem cells.

Protecting your baby's health – long into the future

Smart Cells International Ltd are the UK's leading provider in new-born stem cell preservation.

Once collected and stored these stem cells are ready to protect your child from debilitating and life-threatening illnesses for at least the next 25 years – without any risk of rejection.

Thousands of parents have realised that this life-saving procedure is a golden opportunity not to be missed.

For details on how to preserve your baby's stem cells, telephone our Careline on 2868 5046 or visit us online at www.smartcells.com

SMART CELLS

SMART CELLS INTERNATIONAL LTD

OFFICES IN: LONDON · HONG KONG · DUBAI · NETHERLANDS · PORTUGAL · SOUTH AFRICA

Alternative Therapies

Alternative Therapies	
Balance Asia	2530 3315
Integrated Medicine Institute	2523 7121
Optimum Health Centre	8108 7850
Vitality Centre	2537 1118
Zama International	2850 6400

Alternative therapies are common among locals and expats and all kinds of remedies are available. They may seem costly, but keep in mind it's probably because you'll need a course of treatments and not just one visit.

Most of the practitioners are certified in Australia and the U.K. Some places offer courses and train people in different remedies. The New Age Shop (2810 8694) is a resourceful place for books, meditation tapes, scented candles, homeopathic remedies, organic teas, beauty products and vitamins. They also have in-house healers, hypnotherapists, psychics, and offer workshops and seminars about keeping mind and body balanced. Heartbeat (www.heartbeat.com.hk) is an excellent directory for locating alternative remedy services and just about everyone who is in the business of promoting natural living. It also includes a list of organic meat and vegetables distributors.

There are many health centres that offer these remedies and most are located in Central.

Acupressure/Acupuncture

Acupressure/Acupuncture		
Dr. Cecilia	Central	2537 1118
Encore Herbal Store	Tsim Sha Tsui	2147 1368
Guo Health Center	Central	2581 3803
Health Home Acupressure & Massage Centre	Causeway Bay	2838 6438
Hong Ling Health Care	Wan Chai	2311 1000
Quality Chinese Medical Center	Wan Chai	2881 8177
Steve Paine	Central	2523 8360
Virtue International	Tin Hau	2850 6400

Acupressure involves the systematic placement of pressure with the fingertips on established meridian points on the body. It is not that expensive and classes are also offered for those who wish to learn how to do it. Acupuncture is an ancient Chinese technique that uses needles to access the body's meridian points, and is commonly used to treat ailments such as asthma, rheumatism and other serious diseases.

Aromatherapy

This is one of the most promoted therapies to add balance to your health using essential oils derived from plants and flowers. You can buy aromatherapy oils and candles in many Hong Kong shops. Aromatherapy massage is available at the Vitality Centre (2537 1118) and the Love & Care Centre (2914 0350). Many beauty salons and spas also use aromatherapy oils for massage. See Spas on p.272.

If you want to learn the use of aromatherapy and massage and maybe even set up on your own, call Asia-Pacific Aromatherapy (2882 2444) or DH Aromatherapy (2771 1284) to gain a fully-fledged diploma.

Healing Meditation

Healing Meditation		
Hong Kong Vipassana Meditation Center	Sheung Shui	2671 7031
Ishayas' Ascension Hong Kong	North Point	2887 1498
Raja Yoga Meditation Center	Tin Hau	2806 3008
Siddha Yoga Meditation Center	Central	2522 6802
Simply Seeing Ltd.	Central	2544 8803
Vajradhara Buddhist Center	Wan Chai	2507 2237

Meditation can offer inner peace as well as a disease-free mind and body. Meditation groups meet in certain yoga centres but Reiki masters lead healing meditation groups and holistic healers like Jenny Lethbridge (2523 8360) and Marie Rasborn (2987 7812). Meditation retreats are held in quiet areas on outlying islands.

Homeopathy

Homeopathy strengthens the body's defence system using natural ingredients. Certified homeopaths were practising in Hong Kong long before other remedies arrived. Established practitioners like Alexander Yuan at Optimum Health Centre and Graeme Stuart Bradshaw of Integrated Medicine Institute have health food and a dispensary selling homeopathic medicines and special vitamins in their centres.

Homeopathy

Arden Wong Natural Medicine Center	Sheung Wan	2815 9900
Dr. Josiah Auyeung	Central	2521 2111
Graeme Stuart-Bradshaw	Central	2523 7121
Healing Plants	Central	2851 1988
Integrated Medicine Institute	Central	2523 7121
Jennifer Walker	Central	2850 6400
Ling Goh	Sheung Wan	9518 5564
Optimum Health Centre	Causeway Bay	2577 3798
Pat Kane	Central	2537 1118

Other Alternative Therapies

The Alexander Technique is a posture correcting method, used by trained practitioners and available at Alexander Technique HK (2715 4577) and BalanceAsia (2530 3315).

Ayurveda remedy is available through Ayur Yoga International (2771 1405) who will arrange a personalised programme upon request.

The Buteyko Method is about learning to breathe differently to help with rhinitis, asthma, allergies and sleep problems. Jac Vidgen (9378 5185) offers private consultations, lectures and workshops four times a year when he visits Hong Kong from Bangkok.

Colon Hydrotherapy – yes we all know what it is but have we tried it? If you have symptoms such as bad breath, headaches, back ache or indigestion, try HydroHealth (2530 9999 & 2882 5533).

CranioSacral Therapy is a balancing therapy available at BalanceAsia (2530 3315) and The Body Group (2167 7305).

Ear Candling not only removes wax and toxin build up in the ears, but also clears the sinuses, eases earache, headaches, hay fever and insomnia. The treatment is available at Body Conscious (2424 6171), DK Aromatherapy (2771 2847), Semtimento (2122 9266), The Retreat at the Firm (2525 6696) and Ziz (2111 2767).

Reflexology/Massage Therapy

Bua Hom Essential Thai Massage	Central	2234 9322
CA Center of Acupressure and Massage of the Blind	Tsim Sha Tsui	2721 5989
Francis Lo	Central	2877 8218
Ines De Beer	Wan Chai	2824 9112
Les McClure	Central	2523 8360
Shelagh Ho	Central	2537 1118

Kinesiology is a method of testing muscles to trace illness to its root and then helping the body to heal itself. You can have this treatment at the Holistic Healthcare Centre (2523 8360).

Life Coaching is aimed at allowing people to free themselves from stress and emotional issues, and to achieve their full potential. Barbara Clegg (2791 7281 or 9867 1544) and Monika Parker (9127 4340) are both experienced Life Coaches.

Qigong exercises are healing techniques using yin and yang to treat serious conditions like cancer. Lawrence Tse (2618 0744), a Qigong consultant, provides free consultation.

Rolfing is a technique where muscles and tissues are kneaded to ease chronic pain and stress. Rolfing is available at Indigo Rolfing (2530 3315) and the New Age Shop (2810 8694).

Also see p.275 for details of where to find classes in Pilates, yoga and tai chi.

Rehabilitation & Physiotherapy

For sports injuries there are clinical and other types of massage available at Balance Asia (2530 3315) and Byrne, Hickman & Partners (2526 7533). Hospitals have physiotherapy centres for rehabilitation and therapies. Public hospitals like Pamela Youde Nethersole, Ruttonjee, St John, Queen Mary and private ones like Adventist, Matilda and Canossa, offer orthopaedic, surgical, paediatric and sports related physiotherapies, with some for pregnant women also. See p.128 for contact details.

Back Treatment

You can find chiropractors and osteopaths through the natural life directory (www.heartbeat.com.hk). Most of them are located in Central, either practising on their

141

own or in health centres along with practitioners of other remedies. The Cosman Health Group (2975 4114) has a mix of practitioners ranging from chiropractors, osteopaths and physiotherapists. At The Chiropractic Centre (2973 0353) an x-ray is taken to see how much degeneration or misalignment is there. Once these are complete, a decision is made about the length of time needed for complete or near-complete correction. A plan is drawn up and this could be for about 12 months with each visit costing up to $430 per session. The price will of course depend on your age and condition.

Aside from chiropractors and osteopaths, you can consult practitioners who use different remedies and therapies for back pain like deep tissue message, kinesiology, shiatsu or traditional Thai message.

Rehabilitation & Physiotherapy		
BalanceAsia	Central	2530 3315
Byrne, Hickman & Partners	Central	2526 7533
Central Physiotherapy	Central	2545 7222
Matilda Hospital	The Peak	2849 0760
Petra Rauszen	Central	2523 8360
Physiocentral	Central	2801 4801
Sports and Spinal Physiotherapy Ctr	Central	2530 0073
Stretch	Central	2167 8686

Chinese Medicine

Somewhat part of the alternative remedies is Chinese medicine, with century-old methods and natural, herbal concoctions. Herbalists are mostly Chinese speaking and the shops can be seen (and smelt) in most parts of Hong Kong. These remedies can be made from parts of trees, flowers, weeds, and assorted teas along with other weird and wonderful fruits of nature. Other methods include acupuncture, acupressure, bone setting and massage with herbs. These and other remedies are available at HK Baptist University Chinese Medicine Clinic (2794 1483), Quality Healthcare (2529 8668) and Healthwise Chinese Consultancy (2526 79080).

Nutritionists & Slimming

Hospitals will have their own dieticians or nutritionists that will make out a weight-reducing plan for you and chart your eating pattern through weekly visits. There's also Weight Watchers (2818 6602) with weekly meetings in different areas.

Slimming clinics and spas offer a combination of treatments and diet plans, depending on how overweight you are. These can range from slimming massages to detoxification with mud or seaweed body wraps, ultrasound for cellulite to lymphatic drainage, thermal fat burner and sauna to steam baths. Expect to pay anywhere from $600 to $1200 per hour for such treatments.

At LS Healthtech Slimming Institute in Central (2869 6878), treatments include special vitamins, use of machines and a personal slimming plan. The 4D Well Being (3188 2221) is a male slimming centre that uses lymphatic drainage, isometric muscle contraction and infrared muscle stimulation. If you have stubborn areas of fat, Elemis Day Spa (2521 6660) uses aroma clay and algae to try and shift the bits you can't. You can hire a personal exercise trainer for private sessions at your home for approximately $600 to $650 per hour. Some trainers will only offer their services as part of a complete package (say, 10 sessions), a double edged sword since it is costly but it means that once paid you'll feel obliged and have no excuse to be lazy.

Back Treatment		
CDr Russell Williams	Central	2854 1234
The Chiropractic Centre	Central	2973 0353
Cosman Health Group	Central	2975 4114
Dr. Alex Ling	Central	2234 9898
Dr. Claudia Ng	Central	2111 9911
Dr. Heidi Patrick	Central	2234 9898
NetworkCARE	Central	2868 9792

Counselling & Therapy

Counselling is available through most public and private hospitals, churches and community counselling centres and from support groups. You can contact St. John's Cathedral Counselling (2525 7207), which has professionally qualified counsellors with a sliding cost, which allows you pay what you can afford. ReSource The Counselling Centre (2523 8979) also has a sliding fee arrangement. Therapy Associates (2869 1962) has support groups, meditation workshops and offer different types of therapies, vocational and psychological advice and counselling. Alternative remedy counselling often includes NLP (Neuro Linguistic Programming) hypnotherapy and holistic therapies like Bach Flower essences and

Nutritionists & Slimming		
Beauty Trim International Ltd	Tsim Sha Tsui	2739 3930
Body SOS Co	Wan Chai	3105 1968
Evergreen Beauty & Fitness Center Ltd.	Happy Valley	2892 2702
La Bon Skin And Body	Central	3102 1966
LS Healthtech Slimming Institute	Central	2869 6878
MSL Nutritional Diet Centre	Central	2526 0888
Quality Healthcare	Sheung Wan	2598 9133
Slim Magic Co Ltd	Causeway Bay	2836 9000
Slimtech Beauty Institute	Causeway Bay	2893 8828

142

Chakra therapy with meditation.

You can contact private specialists like Cathy Tsang- Feign (2122 9386) and Lesley Lewis (2872 2578) who can deal with family counselling cases of culture shock and relocation issues. For serious psychiatric counselling, it is best to contact a hospital or private doctor. Schools also have their own psychologists who deal with student and educational counselling.

Counsellors/Psychologists

Cathy Tsang-Feign Psychotherapist	Central	2122 9386
Dorcas Allen PhD. Counseling Psychologist	Central	2869 1962
Dr. Jadis Blurton	Central	2869 1962
Hong Kong Psychological Services	Central	2810 1993
Levy Lynette	Central	2869 1962
Marriage & Personal Counselling Service	Central	2523 8979
Richard Gee (for men)	Causeway Bay	2836 7658

Psychiatrists

In addition to those listed in the table, all major hospitals in Hong Kong will have psychiatrists on their staff. See p.128 for contact details of the hospitals.

Support Groups

Expats have set up many support and help groups, and associations that provide ways to meet people in similar situations to yourself, whether newly relocated or suffering from home-sickness. Some organisations offer programmes for newcomers to help them get to know Hong Kong and find their way around. YWCA's English Speaking Members' Department has a course 'At Home in Hong Kong' led by expats that involves an orientation session and regular networking excursions. The American Women's Association offers Foon Ying ('welcome' in Chinese) for new members with orientations and excursions, and a mother's group that arranges activities for children. See Social Groups on p.262 for details.

Psychiatrists

Dr David Ying Kit Lau	Causeway Bay	3586 9881
Dr. Chee-hung Chan	Central	2815 5111
Dr. Irene Kwok	Central	2526 9933
Dr. Singer Karam	Central	2525 7518
Dr. Sylvia Chia-lu Chen	Mong Kok	2770 3808
Dr. Wai ling Chan Yeung	Central	2522 5544
Dr. William Green	The Peak	2849 6309

There are also plenty of support groups dedicated to women. For women writers there's a Women in Publishing Society (www.hkwips.org), and for business and professional women, the Women Business Owners Club (2541 0446, www.hkwboc.org), the Hong Kong Association of Business and Professional Women (6342 2755, www.hkabpw.org) and Women's Forum (2504 5149, www.womensforum.com.hk).

The following support groups help people with various needs and issues. Call the Community Advice Bureau (2815 5444) for a full list of all support groups.

Adoptive Families of Hong Kong (9100 8095) provide support for families who have adopted a child.

Adult Children of Alcoholics (2855 0924) meet at Union Church on Kennedy Road, Mid-Levels.

Alcoholic Anonymous (25222 5665) meets daily.

Circle of Friends (2240 9888) is a support group for people with cancer.

Kely (Kids Everywhere Like You) Support Group (2521 6853) helps teenagers help themselves work through peer pressure, relationship problems and drugs.

Mother's Choice (2868 2022) is a support organisation for pregnant young women, especially teenagers.

Overeaters Anonymous (2548 5800) offers support for those with eating disorders.

Samaritans (2896 0000) is a suicide prevention hotline, but is also on hand just to listen and help with any problems.

Soultalk (2525 6644) is a specialist support group for women in crisis, with a sanctuary in the New Territories called Loving Home. It's for women of all nationalities during difficult times.

Education

Hong Kong has high literacy rate and a big share of the government budget goes towards education. School here is free and compulsory, but children of expats almost always go to fee-paying international schools that follow the curriculum and graduation requirements of their home country.

International schools tend to be larger than regular schools and many have impressive facilities. The English Schools Foundation (ESF) has 10 primary and five secondary schools situated in different districts of Hong Kong. This school system dates back to the colonial days when British children went to school in their 'catchments' as they called it, meaning the area where they live. This process of placement still applies, but if there are vacancies in another 'catchments' the child could apply for admission there.

Community Service

Community service is part of the curriculum in some schools, and is either an elective or extra-curricular activity in others.

Most international schools have a debenture system so companies buy debentures for their employees to ensure a place in the school. This could be an amount between $25,000 and $80,000, which is refunded when the child leaves. School books and supplies, bus services and field trip costs are not included in the fees, which are charged either monthly or quarterly.

The ESF schools entrance fee is $10,000 for primary and $16,000 for secondary school, balanced later by the school fees. Smaller schools charge an entrance fee.

The school year for all schools in Hong Kong starts from August or September and runs through to June or July.

Typically there are up to 100 children in a class, they are then randomly split into four classrooms. Staff are recruited from abroad or locally from other international schools if they have the credentials.

School days are from Monday to Friday with varying hours. They close for Christmas for about two to three weeks, a week for the Chinese New Year, a week for Easter and then for about two months in the summer. Some schools work on a semester system while others divide the teaching year into terms.

Before you move to Hong Kong, you'll have to contact the school you are choosing for your children and enquire about placement and what they need for admission. There are a series of forms to fill in, as well as providing the necessary paperwork including, but not exclusively: transfer certificates, grades or report cards, health certificates and sometimes a letter from the head master (this depends on the school). The same process, or similar, will apply if and when you move back home, or depart for a new country. You'll need to get all the paperwork done while you are here so as to avoid lengthy and painful bureaucracy.

If your child has special needs, check ahead of time whether the school you choose is adequately adept. Don't assume that all schools are prepared for the needs of your child, and don't sell your child short by forcing them to stay in an education system that isn't working from them.

HK Institute of Languages

22 Years in Hong Kong

ENGLISH, FRENCH, GERMAN, SPANISH, MANDARIN, CANTONESE & JAPANESE

Courses for adults

○ **GENERAL LANGUAGE COURSES**
All levels taught from beginner to advanced, including preparation for examinations (TCF, DELF, IELTS, HSK...)

○ **BUSINESS COURSES**
100% personalised to your specific needs and objectives.

Courses approved by the Continuing Education Fund
French for General & Social Purposes - Elementary Level
English for General & Social Purposes - Intermediate Level

For the Ultimate Language Experience Join our Overseas Study Programmes!

Courses for children and teens

○ **GENERAL LANGUAGE COURSES FOR CHILDREN & TEENS – All levels taught**

○ **EXAM REVISION COURSES**

○ **SPECIAL YOUNG LEARNER PROGRAMMES FOR CHILDREN 3-6**

WHY CHOOSE HK INSTITUTE OF LANGUAGES?
○ Proven 22-year track record
○ Qualified, experienced native-language teachers
○ Comfortable, spacious, and well-equipped language centre
○ Lessons also available at your home or office

 HKFPE 香港私立教育機構聯會 The Hong Kong Federation of Private Educators

 Commitment · Quality · protection 優質保證 HKFPE

 **TRINITY** REGISTERED EXAMINATION CENTRE

 持續進修基金 Continuing Education Fund

 職業英語運動 WORKPLACE ENGLISH CAMPAIGN

Hong Kong Institute of Languages, 3/F, 5/F & 6/F, Wellington Plaza, 56-58 Wellington Street, Central, Hong Kong
Tel: (852) 2877 6160 - Fax: (852) 2877 5970 - Email: info@hklanguages.com - Website: www.hklanguages.com

Nurseries & Pre-Schools

Lack of Space
Nurseries and pre-schools are usually in apartments and are small establishments. This may be a turn off, but do remember this city is tight for space. Rest assured, they are checked by the Education and Social Welfare Departments for hygiene and safety and the teachers have certified qualifications for the programmes being offered.

There is such a demand for all sorts of pre-schools and nurseries that new ones get good business on opening and the established ones continue to expand with branches in many locations. They all have to be licensed by the Education Department. Some are mere playgroups where mother and a 3 or 4 year-old child go together. Some are for babies as young as 6 weeks up to 6 months to help their development and growth, like PEKiP (Prague Parent-Infant Program) where either a helper or mother has to take the child. But a pre-school like Woodlands or Sunshine accept children from 3 1/2 years to 6 years and there are also certified Montessori schools like the Woodland Montessori School that take them from 3 years. The recently opened Rumpus Room has become so successful that the owner is planning to open another branch. Pre-schools offer a less rigid form of learning and education and is a good way to get your child socially and mentally prepared for school. Fees can range from $5,000 to $8,000 and the established ones have a debenture system whereby there is an admission fee, which is refundable, as well as a monthly school fee. To this you can add costs like the school bus that all children in Hong Kong use, even the little ones, and though some are driven to school in chauffeur driven cars this is not a 'mums driving kids to school' culture.

When deciding on a pre-school for your child, you can make an appointment and they will show you around, or you can sign up for orientation sessions.

When applying for admission, schools need health certificates, photos and the application form to be filled in by the parents.

Most schools offer a casual and fun summer programme in July and August, which any child from any school can join, keeping both the children and the parents happy.

In addition to the nurseries and pre-schools below, many of the international primary and secondary schools listed on p.148 also offer kindergarten places.

> **The PPA**
> The Pre-School Playgroups Association (PPA) runs a chain of seven playgroups that are not structured like the standard pre-schools, and children are accompanied by a parent. Tea and coffee are provided for parents, and courses and meetings are organised. Contact them on 2523 2599 or visit www.hkppa.org for details of their locations.

Highgate House School

100 Peak Rd
The Peak
Map 16-E3

2849 6336 | *www.highgatehouse.edu.hk*
Teaching here is based on the philosophies of Rudolph Steiner: that a child is to be nurtured and developed without pressure or pushing. Located on The Peak, the school has 8,000 square feet with an outdoor playground, and enjoys great views over Pok Fu Lam Country Park. They have sessions for parent/carer and child from 1 year, the nursery group for 2 to 3 years and kindergarten for 3 to 6 years.

Hong Kong Academy

Chung On Hall
15 Stubbs Rd
Happy Valley
Map 17-B3

2575 8282 | *www.hkacademy.edu.hk*
An international pre-school with an international and national curriculum that includes Mandarin, technology, maths and sports. Admission age is from 3 to 6 years. A rooftop, community rooms and indoor areas provide space for 180 students. Extracurricular activities include rollerblading, hiking, funk dancing, cooking and drama.

Montessori for Children

House A, Phoenix
Garden
Stanley
Map 14-D2

2813 9589 | *www.montessori.edu.sg*
This is a certified Montessori school complete with Montessori environment, material and methods for children from 2 years and up. It serves the southside areas of Stanley, Repulse Bay, Tai Tam and Chung Hom Kok. The students are international and the

curriculum prepares children for schools in Hong Kong and abroad. Everything is taught in English, while lessons in Mandarin are also on offer. There are half-day sessions from 08:30 to 11:30 and 12:30 to 14:30, plus extended sessions from 08:30 to 14:30.

Parkview International Pre-School (PIPS)

88 Tai Tam
Reservoir Rd
Hong Kong Island
Map 17-C4

2812 6023 | *www.pips.edu.hk*

This school's philosophy is learning through informal play to build confidence. Mandarin is also on the curriculum. Students are mainly from the expat community living in the Parkview complex where the school is located, but some are from a little further afield. With over 150 students, 20 staff and an outdoor play area with slides and a sandpit, the facilities were recently bought up-to-date with a computer room, music rooms, library and brightly coloured classrooms.

PeKip

Various locations

2573 6623 | *www.pekip.com.hk*

PeKip (Prague Parent-Infant Program) takes care of babies from 6 weeks to 10 months. There is a distinct effort made to focus on body movements and coordination. The group boasts over 100 activities and games for visual motor co-ordination. Babies are without clothes and the room temperature is a comfortable 26 to 27 degrees C all the time. Locations: Discovery Bay, Mid-Levels, and Pok Fu Lam.

Rumpus Rooms

Jade Ctr, 98-102
Wellington St
Central
🚇 *Central*
Map 16-E2

2543 5488 | *www.therumpusrooms.com*

This is a new concept in Hong Kong and is doing very well. For mother and baby or toddler, just drop in for play and for song time circle. Each visit costs $75 and the place is also available for birthday parties (on Saturdays only). Rooms with fun and educational toys provide a social and playful time for both child and parent.

Small World Christian Kindergarten

10 Borrett Rd
Mid-Levels
🚇 *Admiralty*
Map 16-F3

2525 0922 | *www.swck.edu.hk*

Six morning classes and three afternoon sessions are offered according to age. Limited places are available for special needs children who are put into mainstream classes but parents must provide an updated assessment in order to accommodate the child. The emphasis here is on learning about everyday life based on Christian principles. Children learn about creation and science, music and dancing, physical education, art and creativity. Admissions start in April and September. It's located in an old Victorian building, surrounded by greenery with plenty of outdoor space.

Starters School

12-22 Queens Rd East
Wan Chai
🚇 *Admiralty*
Map 16-F2

2527 8676 | *www.starters.edu.hk*

This is one of the oldest pre-schools in Hong Kong where children are prepared for ESF schools. The curriculum is based on thematic learning with a friendly atmosphere to make your child feel secure and motivated. School buses are provided with a supervisor. Admission age is from 2 to 6 years. It has a morning session from 09:00 to 12:00 and an afternoon session from 13:00 to16:00. A session for Primary One runs from 09:00 to 14:00.

Sunshine House International Pre-School

Discovery Bay Plaza
Discovery Bay
Map 9-B3

2987 8143 | *www.sunshinehouse.com.hk*

True to its name, the premises are bright, colourful and spacious, an important facet for a stable and comfortable learning environment. Sunshine House has branches all over Hong Kong, and each has highly qualified teachers and over 200 children. Admission

147

age starts at 18 months and goes up to 6 years. There is a clear focus on each child and the main goal of Sunshine House is to provide stimulation for growth and a love for learning. The other locations are in Tai Tam, Tung Chung, The Peak, Pok Fu Lam, and Chi Fu. See the website for contact details.

Universal Trade Ctr
3-5A Arbuthnot Rd
Central
🚇 *Central*
Map 16-F2

Toddler Kindy GymbaRoo

2457 1510 | *www.gymbaroo.com.au*

For children from 6 weeks to 5 years and older, this school uses research-based programmes for early development using GymbaROO trained teachers. Each session lasts 45 minutes and the philosophy behind this is to help children with any learning difficulties as early as possible. All material used is developed by the programme.

Red Hill Plaza
3 Red Hill Rd
Tai Tam
Map 14-F1

Tutor Time International Nursery & Kindergarten

2529 1188 | *www.tutortime.com.hk*

This nursery was awarded 'The Centre of Excellence Award' in 2004 for programme, curriculum, management and vision. Aside from the main learning topics, it includes character building into its curriculum, with a belief that this should start as early as possible. Admission age is from 6 weeks to 5 years and children can start any time of the year. Another branch is located in Kowloon Tong (2337 0822).

Various locations

The Woodland Group of Schools

2559 4855 | *www.woodlandschools.com*

With a presence in Hong Kong for over 25 years, its Montessori and Pre-schools are located all over the city. Admission starts at 12 months, and goes to 6 years. Some of its schools are certified Montessori, while others are playgroups and playschools – so check at the branch you are applying to. There are morning and afternoon sessions and the schools provide transport, with a supervisor on hand.

Primary & Secondary Schools

Hong Kong has hundreds of primary and secondary schools. Those listed below are the international schools that are most popular among the expat community. Facilities and standards are generally first class. The high tuition fees will often be covered by the parents' employers.

125 Waterloo Rd
Kowloon Tong
Map 10-C2

American International School

2336 3812 | *www.ais.edu.hk*

This is a WASC (Western Association of Schools and Colleges) accredited school and a member of EARCOS (East Asia Regional Council of Overseas Schools). Located in Kowloon Tong, it has a program called Early Childhood Development for 3 to 5 year olds and elementary, middle and high schools. High school graduation requirement is 4 years with a minimum of Carnegie Credit Units for a diploma and at least 60 hours of community service.

3A Norfolk Rd
Kowloon Tong
Map 10-C2

Australian International School

2304 6078 | *www.aishk.edu.hk*

With 1,020 students from many nationalities, AIS has a multicultural environment with an emphasis on promoting Asian culture. The curriculum follows the Board of Studies New South Wales, so children can relocate to the Australian system. Graduation requirement for Higher School Certificate requires 11 to 12 curriculum years and for School Certificate, 7 to 10 years. The school campus has won architectural awards for good use of open space to encourage student mixing and interacting.

Canadian International School

2525 7088 | www.cdnis.edu.hk

The Ontario Ministry of Education inspects the high school annually and authorises them to grant credits for the Ontario Secondary School Diploma (OSSD), recognised by universities around the world for higher education admission. For an OSSD, a student must earn a minimum of 30 credits, of which 18 are compulsory credits and 12 optional credits. Students must also complete a minimum of 40 hours of community service and must pass the Ontario Secondary School Literacy Test (OSSLT). The school offers the Advanced Placement (AP) programme, which gives credits equivalent to a first year in college. Since 2006, the IB programme has also been offered as part of the curriculum. For reception classes, children should be between the ages of 3 and 5 by December 31 of the year they are applying. Admission to other classes depends on age and academic level.

36 Nam Long Shan Rd
Aberdeen
Map 14-B1

Carmel School

2964 1600 | www.carmel.edu.hk

Founded in 1991 as a pre-school, it has grown to encompass a primary and middle school with over 200 students and also has a Child Care Centre with structured activities for 1 to 3 year olds. It is accredited by Western Association of Schools and Colleges (WASC) and follows a US style curriculum that's been adjusted to suit students living in a multi-cultural environment. While there is emphasis on Jewish traditions and religious learning, Carmel has students from other secular backgrounds too. Admissions are based on academic record, level of English language proficiency and performance during an interview.

10 Borret Rd
Mid-Levels
Admiralty
Map 16-F3

Chinese International School

2510 7288 | www.cis.edu.hk

This school has a bi-lingual programme where students are taught in Mandarin and English. It is accredited by the European Council of International Schools, New England Association of Schools and Colleges and the International Baccalaureate Organisation (for the IB Diploma and MYP programmes). It also conforms to Hong Kong Department of Education regulations for international schools in Hong Kong. The school year goes from September through to June. Admissions for reception open in January. Children have to be 4 years in June to be admitted to the reception class. Admission to other classes depends on space, language skills and reports from previous school. Older children are given placement tests.

1 Hau Yuen Path
Braemar Hill
Map 17-D1

Discovery Bay International School

2987 7331 | www.dbis.edu.hk

A UK National Testing (SATS) at P2 and P6 levels and optional tests in P4 and P5 are used. The curriculum is based on that of England and Wales and all the teaching is in English. Nursery admissions are at 3 years and primary education starts at 5 years in

Discovery Bay
Lantau Island
Map 9-B3

English Schools Foundation

These schools were set up during the colonial times for the children of British expats in government service, and now cater to both the international and local communities. Conveniently located in different residential areas, you can go to the one in your 'catchment' if they have a place, or to the next nearest 'catchment' until there's space available closer to home. The schools still follow the British curriculum with GCSEs and A-Levels offered. Admission age starts from 4 years in the primary schools. The schools are large with comprehensive facilities, and offer plenty of after-school activities and field trips. For more information on the ESF, and for locations of their schools, visit www.esf.edu.hk or call 2574 2531. They also have a 24 hour hotline with recorded information (2818 6332).

---

the September of the year they turn 5. There are two years of Kindergarten (Nursery and Reception) and six years of Primary school, from years one to six.

French International School

165 Blue Pool Rd
Happy Valley
Map 17-C4

2577 6217 | *www.fis.edu.hk*

FIS has two streams of education, the French and then the International, which offers the International Baccalaureate Program and follows the British curriculum. There are 400 students enrolled in the international stream. It's not possible to move from one stream to the other halfway through. Admissions are based on testing and this can also be done if the child is abroad at a cost of $100 for reception and primary and $200 for secondary. Priority is given to children who have siblings already enrolled and those who hold a debenture. Admission age for reception classes is 3 to 4 years. The reception and primary campus is located in Jardine's Lookout, and the secondary school is nearby on Blue Pool Road.

German Swiss International School

11 Guilford Rd
The Peak
Map 16-E3

2849 6216 | *www.gsis.edu.hk*

The German Swiss International School also has an international stream besides the German Swiss stream. For international kindergarten, children must have turned 3 and for primary they must have turned 5 by September 1 when starting school. Admission priority is given to those whose admission form is received by a specified time, hold a debenture, have a sibling or parent teaching at the school and are German, Swiss or Austrian nationals. Kindergarten admission depends on an interview, while primary school children are given a test in April or May. Secondary school children will have to sit an entrance examination in January or February. Changing streams is not encouraged so parents have to decide and stick to their final choice. From the age of 7 to 9 (Forms 1 to 3), GSIS has developed its own curriculum but for secondary school they follow a traditional British Grammar school curriculum to prepare students for GCSE, A/S and A-Level examinations.

Hong Kong International School

Various locations

2812 5000 | *www.hkis.edu.hk*

One of the oldest established international schools in Hong Kong, HKIS has four campuses, the upper and lower primary in Repulse Bay (2812 5000) and middle and high school in Tai Tam (3149 7000). From a few hundred students it has grown and now teaches over 2,000 students with a solid professional teaching, administrative and support staff, and is accredited by the Western Association Of Schools and Colleges (WASC). Admission priority is given to students holding debentures, students coming from American school systems and other students who meet the criteria of language and level of placement for a grade. A pre-entry test is given and sometimes an interview is held with parents and students. Students also have to take a language assessment test for English. Students are waitlisted till space is available. It offers an American curriculum and prepares students for American universities.

Hong Lok Yuen International School

Twentieth St
Hong Lok Yuen
Tai Po
Map 3-B4

2658 6935 | *www.hlyis.edu.hk*

HLYIS is accredited by the Council of International Schools (CIS) and is located in Tai Po in the New Territories, serving the expat community in that area. It has an international student population of 380 with a class size of between 24 and 27. School curriculum is based on the UK Literacy and Numeracy Strategy and the National Curriculum of England. Admission priority is given to students from Hong Lok Yuen, siblings of students, children of school staff and children who will stay for their full primary education in the school. Children are tested for their level of English language proficiency and if there is space in the EAL intensive language programme, those who are not fluent will be admitted to improve their language skills.

2 Wah Lok Path
Wah Fu
Pok Fu Lam
Map 16-C4

Kellett School

2551 8234 | *www.kellettschool.com*

Kellett School uses English National Curriculum adjusted to suit local needs. The entry age for reception is 4 years and the curriculum centres on personal development, literacy and numeracy skills with information communication technology and music forming an important part of the programme. Class size is about 24 with one teacher for every 12 children.

University & Higher Education

There are seven universities in Hong Kong, the oldest of which is Hong Kong University, but at over 30 years old Chinese University is a close contender. Some institutions have recently been given university status like City University, Baptist and Lingnan University. These were previously colleges, polytechnics or Open Universities. The University of Science and Technology is also a young university having been established by the government in 1991. All these universities have expanded, and developed programmes and courses to serve the growing and sophisticated needs of the community. Funded by the government and supported by high profile businesses and other community leaders, scholarships are available as are funds for research.

All the colleges have openings for international students either to study programmes or courses through summer school, student exchanges for language and culture or research programmes.

All foreign students have to get a student visa and universities have their own criteria for accepting a student. If you are a foreigner and living in Hong Kong with a permanent or dependent visa, you are considered local and local terms apply. Colleges accept an International Baccalaureate Diploma (IB) or a year completed in a recognised college, where the rest of the three years will be completed. In the case of a visiting or exchange student, GCSEs from a recognised local or overseas school will be accepted. Space is always a big factor, and the competitive environment means only the best and the brightest get into the university of their choice.

Universities

Sha Tin
Map 6-D2

Chinese University of Hong Kong

2609 6000 | *www.cuhk.edu.hk*

This is considered to be a leading research university in Hong Kong, bringing together the best minds of the east and west for research and development in science and technology, in a multicultural environment. Graduate and undergraduate programmes are offered in 10 faculties. There were 27 postgraduate diploma programmes offered in 2005 and 2006.

83 Tat Chee Ave
Kowloon Tong
🚇 *Kowloon Tong*
Map 10-B1

City University

2788 7654 | *www.cityu.edu.hk*

City University has grown in its 20 years from a small university with 1,000 students and nine academic programmes to an average of 1,200 undergraduates and 3,000 postgraduates studying in the Faculty of Humanities and Social Sciences, Sciences and Engineering and in the School of Creative Media, Law and Graduate Studies. Its School of Law is the first in Hong Kong to offer a J.D (Juris Doctor) programme that enables admission to the bar.

Various locations
HKU SPACE
2559 9771 | www.hkuspace.hku.hk
SPACE (the School of Professional And Continuing Education) is part of the University of Hong Kong. They are very active in offering professional courses in many disciplines, to degree, diploma and certificate qualification level. Short courses are offered regularly throughout the academic year at various locations throughout Hong Kong. Many courses are conducted in the evenings. Check the website for new courses and enrollment dates.

224 Waterloo Rd
Kowloon Tong
🚇 *Kowloon Tong*
Map 10-C1
Hong Kong Baptist University
2339 7400 | www.hkbu.edu.hk
Situated in Kowloon close to the MTR and KCR, it has the longest established business programme in Hong Kong and an international faculty holding doctoral degrees. The School of Business is the first to offer BBAs and MBAs with a focus on China business and also in human resource management and corporate governance. Classes are small to make interaction easy. Teaching and research are equally emphasised.

Yuk Choi Rd
Hung Hom
Map 15-D3
Hong Kong Polytechnic University
2766 5111 | www.polyu.edu.hk
The university has 71 programmes funded by the University Grants Committee and 83 that are self-financed. It has 11,500 full-time students and 5,000 part-time students enrolled in various programmes. Offering research programmes in PhD/MPhil in many academic disciplines, it also has a student exchange programme and summer school for international students, with Chinese language and culture classes available. The most significant part of the university is the consultancy service provided to business and industry in Hong Kong on technical information, construction and use of land, textiles, engineering, health and social sciences and business management.

Tuen Mun
Map 4-F2
Lingnan University
2616 8888 | www.ln.edu.hk
This is the only Liberal Arts University in Hong Kong offering honour programmes in Bachelor of Arts, Bachelor of Social Sciences, Bachelor of Business Administration at masters and doctoral level. An exchange programme for undergraduate international students offers scholarship and assistance to deserving students. To apply for this programme, students must have completed a year of their 4 years of college in a recognised school or have an International Baccalaureate (IB) Diploma but places are also subject to availability.

30 Good Shepherd Rd
Ho Man Tin
Map 15-D2
Open University of Hong Kong
2711 2100 | www.ouhk.edu.hk
This institution was first set up by the government as an open learning centre in 1989 and after many successes it was given university status. It is now financially independent and offers more than 100 postgraduate degrees, associate and sub-degree programmes. Working on a credit system, it allows students to collect credits for courses that lead to diplomas, degrees and final certificates. Tailored courses and programmes are offered to students with disabilities, and to students through distance and online learning. The schools for Arts and Sciences, Business and Administration, Education and Languages, Science and Technology offer programmes and courses.

Pok Fu Lam Rd
Pok Fu Lam
Map 16-C2
University of Hong Kong
2859 2111 | www.hku.edu.hk
This is the oldest university in Hong Kong and one of the top 50 universities in the world. It has been ranked by Asiaweek as the third best of the Asia Pacific and Australian universities. The student population is about 20,000, which includes undergraduates,

postgraduates and about 1,000 international students. There are 10 faculties and the departments provide teaching and research supervision for MPhil and PhD students. International students can come on a visiting student status for a year or a semester but only those who will benefit from the programme are considered, given the shortage of space. Some of the disciplines offered under this programme include Business and Economics, Humanities and Science Studies and Asian Heritage. International student exchange programmes are arranged through universities in 15 countries. Visiting scholars and delegations come all year round and 45% of the staff is international.

University Rd
Clear Water Bay
Map 10-F2

University of Science and Technology
2358 6000 | *www.ust.edu.hk*

In 1991 the government set up this university in Clear Water Bay for the country's general development and to help its economic growth through research and technology. Even though it's a young university, it's already ranked 20th amongst the world's top 100 engineering and IT universities. It has four schools that include Humanities and Social Sciences, Sciences, Engineering and Business Management offering postgraduate programmes including PhD and general education for undergraduates. The faculty is international and the overall emphasis is on research. Short-term overseas students are able to take courses without being fully enrolled in a particular programme. Under such circumstances they can stay for a minimum of one semester and a maximum of two. An enrichment centre in the School of Humanities provides language courses in Japanese, Cantonese, Putonghua, Arabic and German.

Special Needs Advice
The Social Welfare
Department (2343 2255,
www.swd.gov.hk) and
the Community Advice
Bureau (2815 5444) will
help put you in touch
with relevant groups
and educational
resources. The Matilda
Hospital (2849 6138) has
a resource library and
support groups.

Special Needs Education

Most international schools do not have the resources for special needs students but a few of them (Bradbury and Island Schools) take in children as long as they can be in the classroom with other students and their disabilities allow them to still function in a regular classroom. Admission is on case-by-case basis.

Several organisations have been set up for children and adults in Hong Kong with varied special needs. These are mostly expat ventures, set up by parents who found there was nowhere for them to find support and education for their own children with special needs. Most of these organisations are supported and funded by the Social Welfare Department and through fund raising in the community. The expense of paying for therapists and the special tools and equipment needed for specialised teaching makes the cost of running these projects high, so community donations are always encouraged and fund raising is organised to make people aware of the needs of these projects and schools. Walks and marathons, theme banquets and the sale of Christmas cards and donations from foundations and trusts provide the much-needed funds for the running of these programmes.

Volunteers are always needed to help with outings, administrative duties, to organise fund raising campaigns, as well as in the classrooms. If you can spare the time, call and offer your skills.

2B Tin Kwong Rd
Ho Man Tin
Map 15-E2

Jockey Club Sarah Roe School
2761 9893 | *www.jcsrs.edu.hk*

The Jockey Club Sarah Roe School is part of the English Schools Foundation in Hong Kong. The school was formed in 1991 and is located on the premises of King George V School and near the Kowloon Junior School, both ESF schools. The school can accommodate 60 students aged 5 to 19 who have severe learning difficulties. The emphasis is placed on identifying the children's strengths and creating an atmosphere of encouragement. The school's curriculum, EQUALS (Entitlement and Quality Education for Pupils with Severe Learning Difficulties) is used in many other schools. Through physiotherapy, hydrotherapy and occupational therapy, children learn to be independent and social.

153

Matilda Child Development Centre

41 Mount Kellett Rd
The Peak
Map 16-D4

2849 6138 | www.cdchk.org

This centre provides an early intervention programme for children from birth to 6 years with special needs. Partially subsidised by the Social Welfare Department, services funded by the government include a pre-school programme, individual education services and a baby clinic. The centre provides a parent and toddler programme, individual private therapy, parent support group and family counselling. All nationalities are accepted and teaching is in English.

Nesbitt Centre (Hong Kong Vocational Centre)

Sai Ying Pun
Community Complex,
2 High St
Mid-Levels
Map 16-D2

2813 4536 | www.hkvc.org.hk

This vocational centre is funded by the Social Welfare Department and provides facilities for adults with special needs and disabilities. All the resources and facilities help them to develop skills so that they can live independently and responsibly. Volunteers and supervisors run the centre. Employment is arranged in restaurants, in associations and at charitable organisations like Crossroads where they help pack things sent as donations around the world. A residential programme opened in Discovery Bay allows those attending the centre to experience home life, including carrying out domestic chores like shopping, cooking, cleaning and learning to share and work together under the support staff's supervision.

Rainbow Project

Hong Kong Academy
15 Stubbs Rd
Mid-Levels
⊜ Wan Chai
Map 17-B3

2573 0996 | www.rainbowproject.org

The aim of this project is to provide facilities for children with autism and similar disorders. The project needs volunteers for fundraising, general help and to get donations from the community. They work out of the Hong Kong Academy premises but the waiting list is long so the intention is to find separate premises to accommodate more children.

Springboard Project

122 Pok Fu Lam Rd
Pok Fu Lam
Map 16-C3

2813 4508 | www.growingtogether.org.hk

This project provides special education for children between 5 and 18 years with mild to moderate learning disabilities. It is funded and supported by the Social Welfare Department and the Education Department who provide rooms in the community centre in Pok Fu Lam for classes. Parents pay fees and make donations but the project is dependent on community donations and fundraising to cover the cost of specialised teachers and equipment. Volunteers help in the classroom and with administrative work.

Watchdog Early Learning & Development Centre

12 Borrett Rd
Mid-Levels
⊜ Admiralty
Map 16-F3

2521 7364 | www.watchdog.org.hk

The Watchdog programme was based on the Australian Macquarie Programme for Developmentally Disabled children when it was first started and many methods are still used in the programme. The centre can accommodate 65 children under 6 years who are developmentally challenged. Programmes are in Chinese and English. Professionally trained people such as speech and occupational therapists, psychologists, child-care and social workers are employed at the centre. Children who have cerebral palsy, hyperactivity, autism, Down's syndrome and other learning difficulties and behaviour problems can join the programme. Classes are divided by age and various therapies are used. Parents are offered training and are asked to observe in order to continue work with their children at home.

Learning Chinese

Other options **Language Schools** p.250

Cantonese is the local language, not Mandarin. With seven tones, it has a reputation for being hard to learn but some expats learn enough to use it daily and others have even mastered it completely.

Mandarin, however, is much in demand both by foreigners and locals who either work in China or have dealings there. To improve job prospects, people want to learn Mandarin or Putonghua, which is the spoken, less formal form of Mandarin. Whatever you decide to learn, it makes a big difference in understanding the culture and relating to it. Even knowing basic Cantonese will be helpful, even if it's to score brownie points with the locals and get some approving nods. See also Language Schools on p.250.

Learning Chinese		
Beijing Mandarin	2865 1660	www.beijingmandarin.com
Berlitz	2826 9223	www.berlitz.com.hk
Essential Chinese Language Centre	2545 8315	www.eclc.com.hk
Executive Mandarin	2537 0837	www.execmandarin.com
Happy Jellyfish Language Bureau	2984 2772	www.happyjellyfish.com
HKPCC Mandarin & Cantonese	2832 2062	www.hkpcc.com.hk
Hong Kong Institute of Languages ▶ p.145	2877 6160	www.hklanguages.com
MSL Learning Center	2854 3039	www.msllearningcenter.com
Pacific Language Centre	2287 5115	www.pacificlanguage.com
Talking Mandarin	2139 3226	www.talkingmandarin.com
YWCA ESMD	3476 1340	www.esmd.ywca.org.hk

Part Time Courses

If you wish to further your professional skills or simply want to keep a sharp mind, almost all the universities (such as Hong Kong Baptist (p.152), Chinese University (p.151) and the Open University (p.152) offer continuing diploma and degree programmes in many disciplines. You can often follow these at your own pace and convenience, through online activities and evening classes.

Look for advertisements and announcements from associations, clubs, institutes and universities for seminars, courses and talks. They'll appear in newspapers, emails, association newsletters and other places and cover a variety of topics. You can also go to the universities' learning centres in

Part Time Courses		
Asian Gemmological Institute	2723 0429	www.agil.com.hk
British Council	2913 5100	www.britishcouncil.org.hk
Frederique Academy	2522 2526	www.frederique.com.hk
Gemmology Institute of America	2303 0075	www.giahongkong.com
YWCA	3476 1340	www.esmd.ywca.org.hk

town and pick up their term prospectus to check their courses.

Some institutions you may wish to consider include:

Asian Gemmological Institute & Laboratory – this institute specialises in diploma courses in jade identification, and other gemmology and jewellery designing.

British Council – they offer an English Language Teaching (ELT) programme for people interested in teaching English.

Frederique Academy for Holistic Health and Beauty Courses – one of Hong Kong's most famous beauty salons and spas now offers over 100 courses including spa management, media, theatre and bridal make up.

Gemmology Institute of America (GIA) – this internationally recognised institute offers accredited professional and graduate diplomas in precious stones, pearls and diamonds.

YWCA – a very popular destination for expats, offering a huge range of courses including languages, photography and computing.

155

Transportation

Other options **Car** p.40, **Getting Around** p.38

A choice of buses, minibuses, trams, ferries, the subway/underground (MTR or Mass Transit Railway), trains and taxis make up the efficient network of public transport in Hong Kong. Everyone uses it even if they own cars and have their own drivers. Buses are the most popular because they cover all areas of Hong Kong, closely followed by taxis, which are easy to hail and not at all expensive. Besides, it's just convenient to use public transport to get to the busy parts of Hong Kong like Central, Admiralty, Causeway Bay and Tsim Sha Tsui where parking is limited and expensive. For more information see Getting Around on p.38.

You can also car pool to work, or arrange with a particular taxi driver to regularly drive you around, paying on a monthly basis. This can be convenient if three or four people live in the same building and work in the same area. Some offices have parking for their employees and some provide drivers, but you can also buy a monthly parking pass from car parks which can cost anywhere between $2,000 and $5,000 depending on the location.

Driving in Hong Kong

Commuting

If you are living in southside areas like Repulse Bay or Stanley, the commute to Central, Admiralty or Causeway Bay by bus or car could take more than an hour in the morning and evenings rush hours. At other times of day that same commute can be done in 40 minutes or less.

Hong Kong traffic is seen as crazy and disorganised by some, whereas others say it's disciplined and well-regulated – it all depends on where you are coming from. In general, traffic is well controlled and traffic police are vigilant. In the busy downtown areas, traffic moves bumper-to-bumper most of the day, with buses, minibuses and taxis hogging the narrow roads. Expect small scratches and dents now and then, especially in tight carparks when people park their huge cars in small spaces.

Driving is on the left side of the road with right hand drive cars, mainly automatic. All road signs are in English and Chinese.

To ease congestion, many streets and lanes in the busier parts of town are one way. In areas like Sheung Wan, Central, Causeway Bay and other parts along the harbour, there are underpasses and flyovers. Highways and freeways are mainly in the New Territories. The outlying islands have no cars except on Lantau Island, but even there it's limited and you need a special permit to drive.

There are pedestrians everywhere. They will dart across main roads and streets even when it's not a pedestrian right of way. In busy areas like Central and Admiralty, overhead bridges connect buildings and you can walk through several buildings and avoid the suffocating emissions and street crowds. There are underpasses for pedestrians in some areas like Happy Valley and Tsim Sha Tsui.

For information on Driving Licences see p.62.

Traffic Rules & Regulations

Keep Calm in the Car

With limited space and not many areas to speed and overtake, people in Hong Kong don't often suffer the tantrums of road rage. Occasionally someone may get in a tizzy over a slow driver, but there's nothing that can be done when you are on narrow roads or mountainsides with nowhere to go, so save your honking and keep a cool head.

The speed limit is set between 50 and 70kmph in most parts of Hong Kong. Some highways go up to 80 or 100kmph and in the more congested or residential areas the limit is 30kmph. Be mindful of speed limit notices along main roads, tunnel entrances and on highways. The fine for speeding is $320. If you are caught during spot-checking you get a ticket there and then. You have to mail the ticket stub along with a cheque to the Transport Department before the due date or face a greater fine. Everything you need to know will be on the ticket, including information about where and when to send it. If you forget, a reminder will follow so there's no excuse.

In some parts of Hong Kong where the roads are open and people tend to speed, hidden cameras register your speed and you can get a ticket by mail informing you of the day, time and place where you were speeding – there is nowhere to hide. You can protest the fine by writing a letter to the address on the ticket and you'll be

summoned on a date to plead your case. The ticket is always mailed to the person in whose name the car is registered. Hong Kong works on a points system when it comes to traffic violations; 15 points within two years will earn you a ban, so drive responsibly.

Parking

Limited space means that there is absolutely no such thing as free parking anywhere in Hong Kong, and what you do find will be expensive. It's incredibly difficult to find parking in busy areas like Central, Causeway Bay and Tsim Sha Tsui.

All parking meters in Hong Kong are now operated by an Octopus card. These prepaid cards are widely available, and can be easily recharged with additional credit. Parking is paid for in 15 minute blocks. It costs $2 for 15 minutes and if you are late even by a few minutes you may be unlucky enough to find a ticket on your windscreen.

Stanley market area, Beach Road in Repulse Bay, and streets in Happy Valley have metered parking, and most parks, gardens, playgrounds, beaches and schools also have metered carparks nearby. Parking meters operate from 08:00 to 24:00, Monday to Saturday, and 10:00 to 22:00 on Sundays and public holidays. Parking in office buildings and malls can cost from $20 to $40 per hour with a minimum of two hours.

Government owned multi-storey car parks, like Murray car park in Admiralty, City Hall near the Star Ferry, Middle Road behind the Sheraton Hotel and many more, are conveniently located in busy areas. Newer buildings tend to have carparks in the basement.

Some government offices allow public parking during the evening, and this is normally a cheaper option if you can find it. The rates per hour will be clearly signposted at the entrance to the carpark. You can often use your Octopus card in these car parks too. Many residential buildings don't have guest parking. Those that do charge by the hour.

Petrol (Gas) Stations

Petrol stations are mainly located in residential areas and you'd have a hard time finding one in places like Central or Admiralty. You will see a lot more in the south side of the Island. Service stations operated by the likes of Caltex, Shell, Mobil and Sinopec also provide general servicing, a carwash and some repairs if they have a mechanic on hand. For any major repairs or overhauling, you will have to take your car to a garage or your dealer.

Attendants at petrol stations will fill your car, clean your windows if you want and check the water, oil and tyre pressures.

Petrol is considered expensive in Hong Kong and it's all unleaded. Super unleaded petrol costs about $14.28 per litre and regular unleaded costs about $13.48 per litre. These go by brand names in different petrol stations. You can get diesel for about $8.86 per litre and also Liquid Petroleum Gas (LPG) for about $3.29 (now used by all taxis because it's environmentally friendly). All petrol stations accept cash or credit cards and sometimes offer deals with certain credit cards.

Company Cars

Company cars are either bought for employees or leased if it's a short-term contract. Some companies don't want the bother of buying, selling and maintaining cars so leasing is a good option because that takes care of everything. Some expats, depending on their position in a company, get a car and driver. Others get a car allowance so they can buy or lease their own.

Vehicle Leasing

With public transport being so easily available and given the compact layout of Hong Kong, renting a car is rare. Rental cars, with or without drivers, are more likely to be used by companies than by individuals and more so for special occasions than daily

Vehicle Leasing Agents		
Avis	2890 6988	www.avis.com.hk
Car Fans Club Motor Plaza	2730 8033	na
Galaxy Travel	2702 7088	na
Hawk Rent a Car	2516 9822	na
Hertz Rent A Car	2525 1313	www.hertz.com
Rent A Car Hong Kong	2550 3333	na
Toyota Rent-a-Car	2511 9430	na
Wing Hing Hire Car Co Ltd.	2838 2733	na

use. There are many local and foreign car rental companies in Hong Kong providing limousine service for airport pick-ups, tours and sightseeing, and weddings. Hotels also have cars for leasing but advance booking is recommended. Whether it's for a day or for longer, hiring terms differ between companies and the price will depend on the length of time you want the car as well as the type of car you choose. Be sure to check about discounted rates or special deals.

To lease a car, you have to be over 25 years old and must have had your driving licence for at least two years. You will need to give copies of your passport, driver's licence and a copy of a credit card.

Buying a Vehicle

To buy a car, you need to be a resident as you'll need to have a Hong Kong identity card, a local driving licence, and an address when registering, or transferring it to your name if it's a used car. Insurance companies will ask for the same information. New cars are expensive in Hong Kong but even used cars can cost a lot when you add up the costs of the vehicle licence fee, insurance, repairs and general maintenance. You'll find just about any model in Hong Kong. Luxury cars like Rolls Royce, Bentley, Jaguar, Mercedes Benz, BMW and other European brands are status symbols and are in great demand. Even fast cars like Ferrari, Porsche and Lamborghinis are seen racing around the mountainous roads of Hong Kong.

A good-condition, second-hand European luxury car can be bought for about $150,000 and a Japanese car can be bought for about $80,000 depending on the model and age. You can buy older European models for much less but it will cost you to maintain them as parts and servicing for older European cars are expensive. They also don't seem to do too well in the heat and humidity. Japanese cars like Lexus, Honda and Toyota are often favoured because of the high resale value and low maintenance costs.

All brands have their own showrooms, mainly in Wan Chai along Gloucester Road and some in Causeway Bay and Happy Valley. New cars are also displayed in malls like Pacific Place and car shows are held in the Convention Centre.

Used cars can be bought through dealers like Expat Motors and Fookie Motors or from individuals as a private sale. Private car sales are a great way to find a good deal, especially if an expat is leaving and needs to sell up quickly.

Generally, cars in Hong Kong don't have too much mileage because of the limited driving opportunities, so what you buy should be reliable, unless it's very old and has changed hands many times. You'll find advertisements in newspapers, free magazines like *Dollarsaver*, on websites like www.asiaxpat.com and on supermarket notice boards in expat areas like Repulse Bay, Stanley and Mid-Levels.

Importing a Vehicle

If you want to import a vehicle you will need to notify the Customs and Excise Department, the Environmental Protection Department and the Transport Department through the Tradelink's import hotline (2599 1700). There is no custom tax but you'll have to pay a registration tax based on the taxable value of the car. Within 14 days of importing you must get the car inspected by the Environmental Protection Department before it can be registered and licensed at the Transport Department and have the registration tax calculated. Left hand drive cars cannot be imported, unless it is a consular car.

New Car Dealers

Name	Phone	Web	Brands
AutoFrance	3118 1828	www.peugeot.com.hk	Peugeot
Car City Auto Service Co	2983 6126	www.carcity.com.hk	Various
Crown Motors	2866 1020	www.crown-motors.com	Toyota, Daihatsu
Dah Chong Hong Ltd	2768 3388	www.dch.com.hk	Various
European Motors Ltd	2641 8098	www.europeanmotors.com.hk	Various
Exclusive Cars Ltd	2578 6221	www.exclusivecars.com.hk	Various
Harmony Motors Ltd	2882 8938	www.vwasia.com	Volkswagen
Honda Motors	2827 8622	www.honda.com.hk	Honda
Kingsway Motor Co	2834 7822	www.kingswaycars.com.hk	Luxury cars
Mercedes-Benz	2895 7288	www.mercedes-benz.com.hk	Mercedes-Benz
Motor Image Enterprises	2511 2727	www.motorimage.net/hk	Subaru
Porsche Centre Hong Kong	2926 2911	www.porsche.com.hk	Porche
Universal Cars Ltd	2414 0231	www.mitsubishi-motors.com.hk	Mitsubishi
WALD	2838 8410	www.wald.com.hk	German/Japanese

When buying from a dealer, negotiating is expected but the age, model, condition and mileage will of course influence the price. You should drive the car and have a garage check it out.

Used Car Dealers

Auto Stream (Asia) Limited	Wan Chai	2525 2109	www.at1000.com
The AutoMall	Wan Chai	3113 2111	www.auto22.com
AutoMart Co Ltd	Kowloon City	8109 1421	www.automart.com.hk
DCH Quality Used Car	Kowloon Bay	2262 1118	www.dch-usedcar.com
Expat Motor Services Ltd	Sai Kung	9674 7454	www.expatmotors.com
Fookie Motors	Shau Kwei Wan	2565 6166	na
Great Hero	Various	2383 9042	www.ghmotors.com.hk
Hill Top Motors Ltd	North Point	2979 0001	na

Vehicle Insurance

By law you are required to have third party insurance for your car. After that it's up to you as to whether or not to sign yourself up for a more comprehensive insurance that will include theft, fire, accident, personal or any other complication. Insurance will depend on the age and size of the car and coverage is for 12 months at a time. In the event of an accident, some insurance companies do not cover the cost of repairs if it's less than a certain amount. You will need to check with the company you are using exactly what you get for your money.

Insurance companies like Asia Insurance, Allianz Insurance, Prudential and Royal & Sun Alliance offer comprehensive coverage for private car insurance.

Prudential offers an additional $100,000 benefit for personal accident and death and Allianz's comprehensive policy has a no claim protector as long as no claim over $60,000, or 15% of the car's value, has been made. Asia Insurance gives compensation in a hit and run case besides paying for personal injury. Royal & Sun Alliance has a comprehensive insurance package called MotorGuard, offering a 24 hour hotline for roadside emergencies and

Vehicle Finance

Asia Commercial Bank	2541 9221	www.asia-commercial.com
DBS Bank (Hong Kong)	2500 6028	www.hk.dbs.com
Hang Seng Bank	2198 2735	www.hangseng.com
HSBC	2288 8688	www.hsbc.com.hk
Orix Asia Ltd	2862 9268	www.orix.com.hk
Standard Chartered Bank	2282 3175	www.standardchartered.com.hk

Vehicle Insurance

Allianz Insurance	2521 6651	www.allianz.com
Asia Insurance Co Ltd.	2867 7988	www.asiainsurance.com
Bank of China	3669 3003	www.bochk.com
China Ping An Insurance (HK) Co. Ltd.	2827 1883	www.cpaihk.com
Kwiksure	8202 7001	www.kwiksure.com
Prudential	2525 2367	www.prudential.com.hk
Royal & Sun Alliance	2968 1636	www.royalsunalliance.com.hk

Penalty Points
*A points system for
traffic violations adds
up your offences over a
two-year period. If you
have between eight and
the maximum 15 you
can expect a stern
warning. Cross the 15
point mark and there'll
be no driving for you for
three months.*

a free towing service. You can even qualify for a home mortgage as part of the deal with some companies. The costs of any coverage will depend on the type of car, your age and if you have had previous claims.

Registering a Vehicle

All cars are registered at the Transport Department licensing offices with branches in different parts of Hong Kong. The main office on the Island is on the 3rd floor in United Centre, Admiralty. You and the person you are buying from must go to this office, get a registration form and fill it in and pay the $1,000 processing fee. If you are buying from a car dealer you can negotiate this into the price and if you are buying a new car, the showroom will take care of it. Before the transfer, the department will check if there are any outstanding fines on the car and driver.

All cars in Hong Kong over six years old must have a roadworthiness check-up before you can apply for the annual vehicle licence. The licence fee is paid according to the cylinder capacity of the car. It can be paid quarterly or annually at a Transport Department office. Certain garages have been appointed by the government to conduct these check-ups. The cost of the check up is $530. If the car fails, all repairs must be completed within 14 days. The retest costs $165. Delay it beyond 14 days and you'll find yourself coughing up another $530. The Transport Department website is www.td.gov.hk.

Hands Free
*If you are driving and
talking on your mobile
phone, you can be fined
$2,000. Use a headset or
a car kit to avoid the
hefty bill.*

Traffic Fines & Offences

Most of the fines in Hong Kong are given for speeding, parking in the wrong areas or forgetting to top up the meter. You will also be fined for talking on a mobile phone while driving, making a wrong turn, running a red light, and crossing double white lines. Fines here work on a sliding system, with the more major incursions like driving under the influence costing far more than not having your seat belt on. Speed cameras are in place in parts of Hong Kong. Tickets are often issued on the spot, but your payment should be sent by post to the relevant government office.

Breakdowns

If your car breaks down on a highway or in a busy part of town, put on your hazard lights. If there is too much traffic to get out, keep your seat belt on and stay in the car. If you have children with you, try and get onto the hard shoulder and get them out of the car. Assuming that you have a mobile phone, or if there's an emergency roadside phone, call 999 and tell them as much about your location as you can. You can be sure the traffic police will get there in a hurry to keep the traffic moving.

It's a good idea to sign up for membership with a service such as the Hong Kong Automobile Association (2739 5273, www.hkaa.com.hk). For an annual fee of $660 they provide 24 hour towing services and on the spot repairs, as well as any other assistance you may need. There are other recovery services out there too, so it may pay to shop around.

Recovery Services/Towing (24 hour)	
Brother Transport Service Co	2346 7601
Challenger	2570 8110
Dah Chong Hong Motor Service Centre	2216 8138
EasyTowing Service	2145 0833
Hong Kong Automobile Association	2739 5273
Hong Kong Motor Car Association	2780 2870

Towing charges range from $200 to $400 depending on where you are and how far the car has to be towed. Whoever you decide to call, make sure to stay with your car. If they see no one by the car, they'll just leave. If for some reason you need to leave your car, put some newspaper in the boot with a section flapping outside so the police know the car broke down and you went for help. This will also keep any tickets at bay.

If you break down inside one of the many cross-harbour or mountain tunnels, the tunnel patrol will be there to move you so that the flow of traffic is not interrupted.

Accident Statistics

In 2005, according to the Transport Department's accident record there were 139 fatal accidents, 2,504 serious accidents and 15,062 slight accidents. The number of deaths totalled 151 and serious injuries 2,688.

Traffic Accidents

If you find yourself in the unfortunate position of being involved in an accident, call 999 and then don't move or touch anything till the police arrive. If there is an injury call an ambulance immediately.

Remember to always keep your insurance and vehicle registration papers in your car, as well as recovery companies and ambulance numbers. Always carry your Hong Kong identity card and driving licence with you every time you drive.

In a minor accident with little damage, both parties exchange information and settle repair costs between them. Take note of the car number, the driver's identity card number and then wait for the police to arrive. Also, it's best not to move the car(s) until the police get to the scene. If it's a serious accident, a report and an investigation will follow to determine any external factors like drug or alcohol abuse. In such cases maximum fines and severe penalties may apply. Depending on the presence of witnesses, the case may go to court for investigation. In some cases appeals are made on television for eyewitnesses to give information.

Vehicle Repairs

If you take your car for repairs after an accident and claim insurance then you'll need to collect the police report and an estimate of the cost of repairs from your garage before approaching your insurance company for coverage. Sometimes insurance companies have their own garages to provide repair estimates and some will agree to your choice of a garage, but it depends on the company and you should discuss this before taking out insurance.

Depending on the cost of the repair, your premium may go up and some insurance companies don't pay anything if the cost of repairs is low. So it's usually up to the driver to cover slight scratches and the odd dent.

People generally tend to use the dealership garage for repairs and replacement of parts. Although this service is expensive, the brand agents tend to have the necessary parts and information to deal with problems faster and more efficiently.

The most common problems suffered by cars here are as a result of the heat and humidity, which can cause the failure of electronic control panels and air-conditioning systems.

Repairs (Vehicle)		
Art Motor Sport	Sai Ying Pun	2803 7211
Auto 1 Service Station	Tsuen Wan	2363 6117
Autowrx	Sai Kung	6505 8605
Challenger	North Point	2341 1868
Cheung Wah Kee Motor Services	Causeway Bay	2807 3208
Dah Chong Hong Motor Service Center	Various locations	2216 8138
Hong Kong Automobile Association	Kowloon City	2739 5273
Hong Kong Vehicle Repair Mechants Association	North Point	2399 7977
HP Cars	Sai Kung	2791 4145
Onbase	Yuen Long	2488 1823
Shine Ho Motor Co	Sheung Wan	2549 7187
Sing's Auto Service	Sai Kung	2792 9797
Single Engineering Co	Hung Hom	2764 4668

161

Raw power, refined.

The new Chevrolet Tahoe refines the raw power of a 355 horsepower Vortec V8 engine and couples it with smooth handling and a quiet ride. Examine Tahoe's luxuriously appointed interior and you'll find refinement in every detail.

CHEVROLET

Tahoe 2007

Exploring

Explore This Site
The website of the
Leisure and Cultural
Services Department
(LCSD) is a good
resource for people
wishing to explore
Hong Kong. The site
features information
on the SAR's parks,
beaches and other
leisure facilities, plus
details of museums
and heritage
attractions. You can
even take a look at the
register of 'old and
valuable trees.' See
www.lcsd.gov.hk.

Exploring

If you are an explorer at heart – then Hong Kong will provide plenty for you to search out and discover. It's surprisingly rich in cultural and scenic gems. With a city so dense, a territory so mountainous and a coastline so indented, a modest 1000 sq km can provide an incredible number of attractions.

A number of stock labels are regularly applied to Hong Kong – Pearl of the Orient, City of Life, Asia's World City – but these do little to describe the great diversity which exists within this unique region on the coast of China. Hong Kong is a meeting point of cultures from all over Asia and beyond. Its heritage draws on influences from the imperial Chinese, the colonial British, and traders and adventurers of a hundred nationalities; and it is home to communities from all corners of the world. Food, architecture, religion, government and language all bear the imprints of a century and more of international exchange.

The glittering harbour is the centrepiece of a loud, crowded, sometimes overwhelming city, but it is compact, and escape to the mountains or islands is quick and easy. Hong Kong's public transport is cheap, frequent and goes almost everywhere. The areas not covered by MTR or KCR are generally saturated by bus routes, and you'll find that even the smallest village is served by a green minibus. Where minibuses fail, then there is always the taxi, also relatively cheap and in good supply. Regular ferry services are supplemented by sampans and 'kaido' village ferries. An Octopus card is a useful tool for public transport, but as yet it is not accepted in taxis or red minibuses.

Besides transport, sightseeing is also very affordable. If no admission fee is mentioned for the following entries, you can assume there is none. Some municipal museums charge a token fee for entry, usually as little as $10 for adults, but even that is often waived on one day per week.

If time is short, then there is a range of guided tours aimed at people who want to see a lot in a few hours. If you need a change of pace, surroundings or culture, then it's easy to visit the border cities of China, or the former Portuguese enclave of Macau. And many of Asia's most popular attractions are within a three-hour radius by air. This section covers these too.

Each of Hong Kong's areas has its own character, sights and environment, whether rural or urban. Each area is described in detail, allowing you to plan a day trip. Use this chapter in conjunction with the maps starting on p.409.

As Hong Kong people say, jau la – let's go!

Tsim Sha Tsui's Avenue of Stars

See the Big Buddha p.193
Lantau Island's major cultural attraction sits atop a hill beside the Po Lin Monastery. Thanks to the new Skyrail cable car, it's now even easier to reach the heights of enlightenment. Visit the exhibition gallery underneath the Buddha and round off with a vegetarian lunch at the monastery.

Eat Seafood by the Water p.168
Sai Kung, Lamma Island, Cheung Chau, Lei Yue Mun – these outlying districts all possess seafood restaurants on their waterfronts. Chilli prawns, squid, clams and steamed fish all taste better when eaten alfresco to the sound of swishing waves. A cold beer is the standard accompaniment.

Visit the Peak at Night p.185
Hong Kong is at its most spectacular when seen from above on a clear night. Take the Peak Tram to the top station, walk to one of the vantage points and marvel at the glittering panorama of city and harbour. Several restaurants at The Peak have picture windows so you can eat while enjoying the view.

Cheer on a Dragon Boat Team p.204
The dragon boat races take place in bays and harbours all over Hong Kong, usually in June. Fiercely competitive teams train up for months ahead of the event. Admire the elaborately carved and dressed dragon boats, enjoy the drum-thumping excitement of the final push to the finishing line, or get in on the action by joining a team.

Take a Tram Through Town p.205
See the city from the top deck of a rattling, clanking old 'ding ding' (as Hongkongers call them). The ride is an unequalled bargain at just $2. Trams run frequently, so if the first one is too crowded, just wait for the next to ensure you get that all-important front seat upstairs.

Go to the Races p.204
Horse racing runs in the blood of Hong Kong people. Prior to the handover, Deng Xiaoping found it necessary to reassure Hongkongers that the races would continue after 1997. You can visit the racecourses at Happy Valley or Sha Tin. Have a flutter while watching from the terraces, or get close to the track to see hooves pounding the turf.

Enjoy the Symphony of Lights p.206
The waterfront at Tsim Sha Tsui has a panoramic view of Hong Kong Island and Victoria Harbour, and it's the best spot to enjoy the multimedia light show which takes place nightly at 20:00. Over 30 buildings on both sides of the harbour are lit by laser beams during the spectacle. While you're there, check out the Avenue of Stars, a stretch of promenade devoted to the leading lights of Hong Kong film.

Street Markets p.333
Air-conditioned shopping malls spring up like weeds but the street markets still survive. Whether you're on the lookout for souvenirs, jade, flowers, clothing, collectibles, electronics or art, you'll find a vendor who has it. Don't accept the first price quoted, keep cool and enjoy the bargaining.

Take a Hike p.247
Close to 40% of Hong Kong's territory is protected by country parks, and a good proportion of the rest is rural and undeveloped. Discover some of the SAR's natural treasures by taking a walk over the mountains or along beach-fringed shorelines. It's the best way to see the other side of Hong Kong. Trails are well signposted.

Sample Some Dim Sum p.358
Going for dim sum – whether for breakfast or lunch – is a Hong Kong institution. These little snacks, both savoury and sweet, arrive at your table in steaming bamboo baskets. Try rice-flour rolls, steamed pork dumplings, fried taro cakes, lotus paste buns or any of the numerous other choices on offer, and wash it all down with Chinese tea.

Explore a Seaside Village p.179
Hong Kong's history has been defined by the sea, and its waterfront settlements are some of the oldest. A visit to Tai O, Tap Mun, Shek O, Cheung Chau or any such seaside town gives you an insight into how people have lived on the south China coast for generations. The devoted upkeep of Tin Hau temples demonstrates an enduring connection to the ocean.

Attend a Chinese Festival p.50
Ching Ming, the Bun Festival, Tin Hau's Birthday, the Hungry Ghost Festival, Chinese New Year, the Mid-Autumn Festival: the calendar is chock-a-block with age-old events. It seems there's always some excuse to thank the gods, ask them for favours, or simply get together with family. Whichever one it is, you can guarantee there will be noise, colour and food involved.

Visit Ocean Park p.203
Taking the cable car over the headland is just one highlight of a day at Ocean Park, Hong Kong's marine-themed amusement park. You can see pandas and dolphins, sharks and sea lions, and take some wild rides on roller coasters and motion simulators. It's both entertaining and educational for the kids.

Become a Junk Trip Junkie p.212
Get some mates together and hire a pleasure boat for the day. Your choice of seaside destination is limited only to your understanding of the map – and the captain will be able to make suggestions. Head for an outlying island, a sheltered cove or simply enjoy the sunshine on the water as you sail away from the city.

Step Inside a Chinese Temple p.190

Chinese religion is a complicated affair: Buddhism, Taoism, Confucianism, animism and ancestor worship all play a jade-bangled hand in it. Find out what goes on by paying a visit to one of Hong Kong's many places of worship. Wherever you are, city street or village harbour, there will be a temple near you.

Spend a Day at the Beach p.198

You're never far from the sea in Hong Kong, and beaches are easy to reach. Some are close to the city, others are located on offshore islands or in remote parts of the New Territories. Choose between busy beaches backed by hotels and restaurants and deserted sweeps of sand, miles from the nearest road.

Go to Macau p.217

Hong Kong's sister SAR has a character all of its own. Settled by the Portuguese over 400 years ago, it boasts fine colonial architecture, great food and a slower, more relaxed atmosphere. It's now in the process of reinventing itself as Asia's Las Vegas with new hotels and casinos opening at a fast pace.

Rise Above It All p.214

It's a splurge, but one you won't forget. Hong Kong really has to be appreciated in three dimensions, and the manoeuvrability of a helicopter gives you the chance to see the city and the New Territories from every angle possible. Sightseeing tours depart from the rooftop helipad of the Peninsula Hotel.

Bone Up on History and Culture p.194

The city's museums are varied, focusing on history, railways, medicine, traditional heritage, coastal defence, science and art, among other subjects. They make a good fallback option in case of rainy weather, but are well worth visiting in their own right to give greater depth to your Hong Kong experience.

Have a Big Night Out p.390

Nightlife is part and parcel of Hong Kong's identity. Lan Kwai Fong, SoHo and Wan Chai are preferred watering holes for the expat crowd; locals go for karaoke in Tsim Sha Tsui and Causeway Bay. Happy hours run round the clock and there are no restrictions on closing times, so you can happily party until the sun comes up.

Cross the Harbour p.211

The Star Ferry has been making the trip across Victoria Harbour for over 100 years and the magic of the crossing is still there. It's best at dusk, when the cityscape starts to light up with neon on both sides of the water. As an alternative, take a harbour tour. The extended routes give you different perspectives of Hong Kong's greatest natural asset.

A Central, Western & Mid-Levels
B Eastern District
C Lantau Island
D Mong Kok & Yau Ma Tei
E North and East Kowloon
F North New Territories

G Outlying Islands
H Pok Fu Lam and Aberdeen
J Sai Kung
K Sha Tin
L Southside
M The Peak

N Tsim Sha Tsui
P Wan Chai, Happy Valley & Causeway Bay
Q West New Territories

LAU FAU SHAN
TIN SHUI WAI
NGAU TAM MEI
F NORTH NEW TERRITORIES
PING SHAN
KAM TIN
HA TSUEN
YUEN LONG
SHEK KONG
Q WEST NEW TERRITORIES
TUEN MUN
LUNG KWU CHAU
HONG KONG GOLD COAST
SO KWUN WAT
TAI LAM CHUNG
SHAM TSENG
TSUE WAN
PEARL ISLAND
TSING LUNG TAU
SHA CHAU
MA WAN
TANG LUNG CHAU
TSING YI
SIU MO TO
SUNNY BAY
TAI MO TO
CHEUNG SOK
PA TAU KWU
STONECUTTERS ISLAND
CHEK LAP KOK
Discovery Bay
PEAKED HILL
SIU KAU YI CHAU
TAI LEI **G**
TUNG CHUNG
TAI SHUI HANG
PENG CHAU
KAU YI CHAU
GREEN ISLAND
C LANTAU ISLAND
MUI WO
SUNSHINE ISLAND
TAI O
HEI LING CHAU
West Lamma Channel
CHEUNG SHA
YUNG SHU WAN
SHEK PIK
Adamasta Channel
CHA KWO CHAU
Lantau Channel
SHEK KWU CHAU
CHEUNG CHAU **G**
SIU A CHAU
CHEUNG MUK TAU
YUEN CHAU MA CHAU
SOKO ISLANDS
South China Sea
TAI A CHAU
YUEN KONG CHAU
TAU LO CHAU

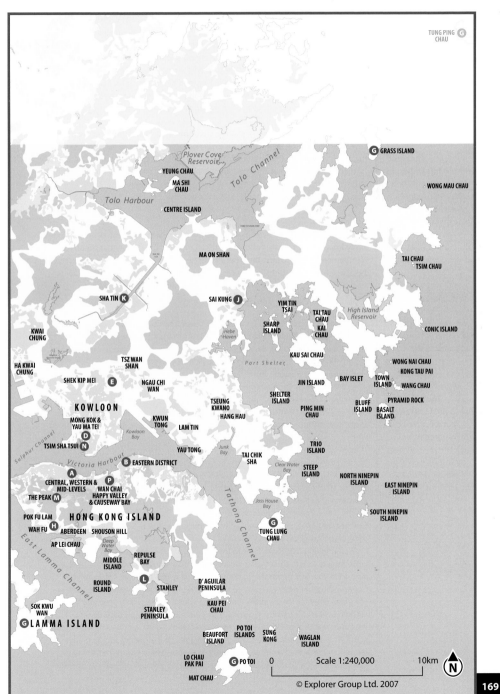

TUNG PING **G** CHAU

G GRASS ISLAND

WONG MAU CHAU

Plover Cove Reservoir

YEUNG CHAU

MA SHI CHAU

Tolo Channel

Tolo Harbour

CENTRE ISLAND

TAI CHAU
TSIM CHAU

MA ON SHAN

SHA TIN **K**

SAI KUNG **J**

YIM TIN TSAI

TAI TAU CHAU

High Island Reservoir

KWAI CHUNG

SHARP ISLAND

KAI CHAU

CONIC ISLAND

Hebe Haven

KAU SAI CHAU

HA KWAI CHUNG

TSZ WAN SHAN

Port Shelter

WONG NAI CHAU
KONG TAU PAI

SHEK KIP MEI **E**

NGAU CHI WAN

JIN ISLAND

BAY ISLET

TOWN ISLAND

WANG CHAU

PYRAMID ROCK

KOWLOON

SHELTER ISLAND

MONG KOK & YAU MA TEI **D**

KWUN TONG

TSEUNG KWANO

HANG HAU

PING MIN CHAU

BLUFF ISLAND

BASALT ISLAND

Kowloon Bay

LAM TIN

TSIM SHA TSUI **N**

YAU TONG

Junk Bay

TAI CHIK SHA

TRIO ISLAND

Sulphur Channel

B EASTERN DISTRICT

Victoria Harbour

A

Clear Water Bay

STEEP ISLAND

NORTH NINEPIN ISLAND

CENTRAL, WESTERN & MID-LEVELS **P**

WAN CHAI

EAST NINEPIN ISLAND

THE PEAK **M**

HAPPY VALLEY & CAUSEWAY BAY

Joss House Bay

POK FU LAM

HONG KONG ISLAND

SOUTH NINEPIN ISLAND

WAH FU **H**

ABERDEEN

SHOUSON HILL

G TUNG LUNG CHAU

AP LEI CHAU

Deep Water Bay

East Lamma Channel

MIDDLE ISLAND

REPULSE BAY

ROUND ISLAND

L

STANLEY

D'AGUILAR PENINSULA

SOK KWU WAN

STANLEY PENINSULA

KAU PEI CHAU

G LAMMA ISLAND

PO TOI ISLANDS

SUNG KONG

BEAUFORT ISLAND

WAGLAN ISLAND

LO CHAU PAK PAI

G PO TOI

0   Scale 1:240,000   10km

N

MAT CHAU

© Explorer Group Ltd. 2007

169

Map 16 ◀

Central, Western & Mid-Levels

Officially known as Victoria until the name went out of fashion, the financial and administrative centre of Hong Kong now goes by the more prosaic name of Central District. It's still the headquarters of government and big business, with local and international banks and hongs (trading houses) represented by ever-higher and shinier office towers. Central has been linked to Kowloon by the Star Ferry for over a hundred years, and its piers also service Macau and Hong Kong's outlying islands.

Land has been reclaimed here ever since Hong Kong was first settled and, to the dismay of harbour activists, it's an ongoing process. Queen's Road Central roughly follows the route of the original shoreline. Stepped streets and the handy outdoor Mid-Levels Escalator lead uphill from here to the district's oldest areas. Among these, SoHo has blossomed into a bohemian neighbourhood of small bars and boutiques. Rising further up the foothills of The Peak, Mid-Levels is almost entirely residential. Western District, which encompasses everything from Sheung Wan to Kennedy Town, is an old part of town in which many traditional trades survive.

Residential

The location of the Mid-Levels, high above the office district of Central, makes it one of Hong Kong's most popular residential areas for expats. As a result, it's expensive. Further down the Escalator, the older part of Central known as SoHo has lower rents, but these have risen as the area becomes more hip. Western is much more down at heel and good deals can be found for those who value location over luxury.

Retail

The commercial landlords of Central never tire of letting us know that the district is full to bursting with outlets of the world's top luxury brands. If you're looking for Prada, Tiffany, Burberry and their ilk, you'll find them and countless others in malls like The Landmark, Chater House, Pacific Place and ifc mall (see p.321).

Hollywood Road is famous for its art and antique traders. At its western end, the shops and stalls extend onto the former thieves' bazaar of Upper Lascar Row, more commonly known as Cat Street (see p.334).

Sheung Wan is the centre of Hong Kong's traditional (and pungent) dried seafood trade. Your nose will guide you to Des Voeux Road West and its neighbouring streets.

Places of Interest

The Star Ferry was once the only way to reach the mainland from Hong Kong Island. Its route is now duplicated by road and rail tunnels, but it remains the best way to cross Victoria Harbour, and it is a steal at just $2.20 for the crossing to Tsim Sha Tsui. The pier is located near the General Post Office. A few of Hong Kong's last remaining rickshaw pullers hang around for photo opportunities.

Reached by underpass from the Star Ferry concourse, Statue Square is the nearest thing Hong Kong has to an official city centre. It's worth standing here to take in some of the landmarks. With your back to the harbour, you face the striking headquarters of HSBC and, to its left, the angular Bank of China. Clanking trams cross your field of vision. On your left stands the colonnaded building which houses the Legislative Council. On other sides you can see the Hong Kong Club, the Cenotaph and the Mandarin Oriental. On Sundays, surrounding streets are pedestrianised and the square is taken over by thousands of domestic helpers vocally enjoying their day off.

Pass underneath the HSBC Building to reach Queen's Road Central and take a flight of stone steps up the other side to reach Battery Path. The attractive building up on the left was formerly the French Mission and now houses Hong Kong's Court of Final Appeal. Beyond it, St. John's Cathedral stands on Hong Kong's only plot of freehold

---

Lowdown ◀

The place of work for Hong Kong's business and government elites, plus interesting historical neighbourhoods.

The Good

Central bears witness to much of Hong Kong's history. A cosmopolitan mix of residents and visitors ensures a good variety of shops, restaurants and cultural venues.

The Bad

Rush hours and office workers' lunch breaks see huge numbers of people mill out onto the area's narrow streets. As a result, they're best avoided.

The Must Dos

Take a tram to Western Market; browse for kitschy bargains on Cat Street; cross the harbour by Star Ferry; enjoy a night out in Lan Kwai Fong or brunch in SoHo.

land (all the rest is held by the government). The other ends of this quiet, leafy compound lead to Hong Kong Park (p.201) and the Peak Tram (p.205).

If you return to Queen's Road, walking straight ahead brings you to the busiest part of the district, jammed solid with human traffic. A left turn up D'Aguilar Street puts you on course for Lan Kwai Fong, Central's after-work bar zone. Popular with expats and Westernised locals, drink prices are generally top-end. Above Lan Kwai Fong, Wyndham Street flows into Hollywood Road, which is then crossed by the Mid-Levels Escalator. The older streets around here are packed with activity and are worth a wander.

Map 17 ◀

Eastern District

The northern shore of Hong Kong Island is one solid conurbation from one end to the other. Eastern District refers to all areas east of Causeway Bay: from Tin Hau through North Point and Quarry Bay to Chai Wan. It's all accessible by MTR and tram.

Much of the district was originally shipyards. Now it's primarily residential and working-class, although one developer is trying to rebrand the district 'Island East' to promote the high-tech office zone at Quarry Bay.

The Lowdown
A high-density residential area with harbour views and a smattering of cultural attractions.

Residential

Much of Eastern District consists of older private buildings or public housing. Higher-end developments with good harbour views can be found at Braemar Hill and in a few places along the waterfront.

The Good
This down-to-earth district shows how everyday people live.

Retail

In true Hong Kong style, every street and alley is lined with shops providing local goods and services. There are also shopping centres – Cityplaza (p.318) at Taikoo Shing is the largest, with an ice rink, a Japanese department store and a cinema.

The Bad
It can take some time to get from one end to the other, especially at busy hours. If you take the MTR, you miss all the street life.

Places of Interest

The best way to see this district is by tram. Take a seat on the top deck and watch crowded neighbourhoods pass leisurely by. The line ends at Shau Kei Wan, a firmly working-class district which used to be a fishing port and still has a typhoon shelter full of boats. You can follow Shau Kei Wan Main Street East to reach the Tam Kung Temple on the waterfront. This was built in 1905 and is

The Must Dos
Learn about Hong Kong's maritime history at the Museum of Coastal Defence; see typical urban life from the top deck of a tram.

Museum of Coastal Defence

the largest in Hong Kong dedicated to this god. The Museum of Coastal Defence (p.197) is just a little further along on your right.

The hills above Chai Wan are terraced with tightly-packed cemeteries (a grave overlooking the sea is considered good feng shui). Among them, the Sai Wan War Cemetery is a tranquil place which remembers the Commonwealth soldiers lost to the fighting in Hong Kong.

From King's Road in Quarry Bay, Mount Parker Road leads uphill into Tai Tam Country Park, passing Woodside, a red-brick colonial mansion. A side trail leads off to an area of hillside cooking stoves, built before World War Two to feed the population in the event of siege, but never used.

There is a small street market at Marble Road in North Point. For an alternative harbour crossing experience, ferries sail from the North Point piers to Hung Hom, Kowloon City and Kwun Tong.

Maps 8, 9, 12 & 13

Lantau Island

Lantau Island is the first part of Hong Kong that most new arrivals see as they touch down on the runway at Chek Lap Kok – but they are whisked straight into the city over the spectacular Tsing Ma Bridge, and some never return to see the island's attractions, which are many.

Much larger than Hong Kong Island but with a fraction of the population, Lantau has historically been a place of retreat. Its valleys hide dozens of monasteries and nunneries. The geography is dramatic, with hills rising steeply from shallow bays to high plateaux and sharp peaks. Lantau's Chinese name of Tai Yue Shan – Big Island Mountain – is a good description. The island has two sides: North Lantau is being developed, with the airport, a new town, theme park and more in the pipeline; while South Lantau is partly protected by Country Parks and retains more of its original character.

The Lowdown
Hong Kong's largest island is the antidote to urban Hong Kong. It is a popular residential and weekend retreat.

The Good
Hidden monasteries, striking mountain scenery, sandy beaches.

The Bad
Partly due to the airport, Tung Chung experiences the worst air pollution in Hong Kong. Pearl River silt means the seawater at beaches is murky.

The Must Dos
Pay your respects to the Big Buddha; visit the stilt village of Tai O; enjoy drinks on the beach.

Residential

South Lantau remains rural, with mostly village homes. These are popular with expats who enjoy more space and a greener environment than that offered by city life. Discovery Bay is a self-contained modern development. Opposite the airport, Tung Chung is a typical new town.

Retail

Lantau Island is not a shopping destination. There are souvenir stalls at the tourist attractions and a normal range of shops at Tung Chung, Mui Wo and Discovery Bay.

Places of Interest

Ferries from Central dock at Mui Wo (also called Silvermine Bay for the abandoned mines which can still be found at the head of the valley). There are waterfalls further uphill. Following the South Lantau Road, the next stop is Pui O, which has a wide sandy beach. A herd of wild water buffalo live in the estuary here.

The road carries on past Cheung Sha, across the dam of the giant Shek Pik Reservoir, and then forks at a pass: uphill to Po Lin and the Big Buddha (p.193), and downhill to Tai O (p.194). The valley descending to Tai O is dotted with numerous Buddhist monasteries. For hikers, the Lantau Trail makes a 70km circuit of the island. It crosses the airy summits of Lantau Peak and Sunset Peak, Hong Kong's second and third highest mountains, and takes in much of the island's southern coastline. On a lonely part of the trail south of Tai O, Fan Lau village has two deserted beaches on opposite sides of a tombolo. Kau Ling Chung nearby is a romantically secluded beach backed by a small lagoon. There are many other walking routes to follow. A stone trail leads downhill from Po Lin to Tung Chung, passing a cluster of bamboo-hidden monasteries at Tei Tong Tsai. Another popular hiking route, between Discovery Bay and Mui Wo, passes by the Trappist Monastery.

A figure at the Big Buddha

Tai O

Map 15

Mong Kok & Yau Ma Tei

When a district is often heard described as 'the most densely populated area in the world', you expect crowds. But when those crowds are joined by honking taxis, pollution-belching minibuses and the heavy humidity of a Hong Kong summer, you begin to realise just what an ordeal a visit can be. The population density is only increased by the general lack of open space.

This doesn't mean you shouldn't visit the area. In many ways it is a distillation of everything business-minded in Hong Kong, and thrives on commerce. Nathan Road is the main north-south artery through the two districts, and the MTR runs underneath it all the way. Outdoor markets run parallel to it on either side. Every teeming street, lane and alley – and there are many packed into the area's tight layout – is lined end to end with shop fronts or street stalls. No space is wasted in the effort to make a dollar.

It's hard not to notice the red-light aspect of the district, particularly to the north of Temple Street. As with the rest of Hong Kong however, the area is rarely intimidating.

The Lowdown
Mong Kok and Yau Ma Tei are busy, hot and crowded, but offer some interesting shopping opportunities. The neon-lit streets represent many tourists' mental image of Hong Kong.

The Good
Raucous markets and street life at its busiest. Some streets have been pedestrianised in an effort to accommodate the crowds.

The Bad
People, people, and more people, crammed into narrow streets with angry traffic – avoid if you are in any way claustrophobic.

The Must Dos
Shop at the night markets, listen to Cantonese opera at Temple Street or birdsong at the Bird Garden.

Residential

High-rise tenements of a certain vintage, the 'real Hong Kong' in a sense, but not one that most expats choose as home.

Retail

Yau Ma Tei and Mong Kok are old-style Hong Kong, and most shopping is still done at street level. Not all the street markets are aimed at tourists – some sell jade, clothing and birdkeeping paraphernalia to a mainly local clientele. There are also a few air-conditioned malls, notably the plush new Langham Place.

Places of Interest

The somewhat over-promoted Temple Street night market, selling clothes, CDs and electronic gadgets until 23:00 every night, commences its lengthy passage just north of Jordan Road, and is broken halfway by the public square outside the Tin Hau temple (p.192). Here, fortune tellers sit at lamp-lit tables, employing a number of different means to divine the future, and Cantonese opera groups sometimes come to practise their music in public. The Mido Café, a teahouse which has changed little since the 1960s, overlooks the square.

Two other attractions close by are the Jade Market (10:00-16:00), where all kinds of jade carvings, pendants and bangles are on sale; and the Broadway Cinematheque, Hong Kong's largest arthouse cinema.

Mong Kok's Ladies' Market (actually called Tung Choi Street) starts further north and on the other side of Nathan Road. The open-air market sells mostly women's clothing and accessories and stretches even further than Temple Street. It buzzes until around 22:00. See p.333. Further up the same street you'll find many shops supplying exotic fish for home and office aquariums.

The Flower Market (p.334) is located beside Mong Kok Stadium, venue of league football matches. Here you'll find fragrant flowers and indoor plants galore. It's busiest in the mornings – opening at 07:00 – but carries on until 19:30.

Maps 9 & 10

North and East Kowloon

When you look across the harbour from Hong Kong Island, you can see that the flat peninsula of Kowloon is enclosed by a steep ring of mountains. Urban Kowloon had been spreading north for many years, but the foothills of these mountains were settled en masse by refugees from China following the end of the Chinese civil war in 1949. After a fire in 1953 destroyed over 2,000 ramshackle squatter huts, the government embarked on a massive plan of public housing, the results of which can still be seen across the outskirts of Kowloon today. In fact, the scale of the projects made the Hong Kong Government the world's biggest landlord.

This area extends from Kwai Chung in the west to Yau Tong in the east. A handful of cultural treasures is hidden between the high-rise estates and industrial warehouses.

The Lowdown

A land of gargantuan housing estates and crowded urban temples demonstrates how ordinary Hong Kong people live their lives.

The Good

Vibrant, traditional temple culture; some good shopping bargains.

The Bad

Poor urban planning in recent years translates into a surfeit of flyovers, heavy traffic and dusty air.

The Must Dos

Wander the temple grounds at Wong Tai Sin; enjoy seafood on the harbour at Lei Yue Mun.

Residential

Housing in the districts of north and east Kowloon is characterised by the giant resettlement estates built to house hordes of new migrants from the 1950s onwards. They have been redeveloped in stages, and there are now also private estates. Kowloon Tong stands apart as a high-class garden suburb with pricey two-storey villas.

Retail

In Cheung Sha Wan, factory outlets sell clothing at reduced prices. Apliu Street in Sham Shui Po is good for cheap electronic and audio-video goods. The Golden Arcade nearby is Hong Kong's mecca for computer hardware and software. Large shopping mall Festival Walk (p.320) is notable for its ice rink; there is another in the Dragon Centre (p.324).

Places of Interest

Kwai Chung is the site of Hong Kong's vast container port. While not practical to visit, the view of the yards from the hills behind Kowloon is impressive, especially at night. When the brick tomb at Lei Cheng Uk was discovered in 1955, it gave the first indication that Hong Kong had been settled by the Chinese as far back as the Eastern Han dynasty (AD25-220). Bronze and ceramic relics were found inside, and were put on display in a small museum on the site.

From Wong Tai Sin, Sha Tin Pass Road leads uphill, passing a 150 year-old Kwun Yam temple on its way to Lion Rock. From this high vantage point, all of Kowloon is laid out at your feet. Also near Wong Tai Sin, the Buddhist Chi Lin Nunnery is new, but it is built in a very attractive Tang dynasty style. The grounds include a lotus garden.

Hong Kong's airport was formerly located at Kai Tak, its runway pointing far out into the harbour. It was closed in 1998. Reclamation and a new town are planned for the derelict site, but little has happened so far. The area adjoining the old airport, known as Kowloon City, is famous for its Thai restaurants. After the airport closed, the old 16 storey height limit for buildings in Kowloon was removed, and higher structures have started to appear, changing the face of this old-fashioned district.

Kowloon City has historical connections. At some point after 1279, a rock was inscribed with the characters 'Sung Wong Toi' to commemmorate the fact that two Sung emperors stayed in the area. The rock was blown up by the Japanese in the 1940s but the part with the inscription survived intact. After the war, it was placed in the small garden where it sits today.

Nga Tsin Wai is Kowloon's only remaining walled village, possibly dating back to 1352. It is being bought up by a property developer and will not exist much longer. From Kowloon Bay through Kwun Tong the cityscape is mainly industrial, but at the far southeastern tip of the urban sprawl, the straggling village of Lei Yue Mun sits at the narrowest point of Victoria Harbour. It's known for its seafood restaurants, and you can walk along the shore to a Tin Hau temple. There is another village temple to Tin Hau in nearby Cha Kwo Ling.

Maps 2, 3, 5 & 6

North New Territories

The northern part of the New Territories butts onto the border with China which, since it was opened in 1979, has become one of the world's busiest crossing points. The three old market settlements of the area – Tai Po, Fanling and Sheung Shui – have been developed into large satellite towns, and each is a stop on the KCR which runs between Kowloon and Lo Wu. You'll pass through them if you make a shopping trip to Shenzhen.

The Lowdown
The northerly edge of the SAR has a mostly rural feel, but sees plenty of traffic to and from the border.

The area has been settled for centuries and there are many historic villages. In most cases, the new towns have been built around them, leaving their layout intact. Further away from the main towns, the scenery is largely rural, and there are beautiful hiking routes over the mountains and along the coastlines.

There are crossings into China at Lok Ma Chau, Man Kam To, Sha Tau Kok and Lo Wu. Most travellers will use the latter. All these points are in the Frontier Closed Area, a buffer zone closed to the public since the 1950s. As a result, it is mostly undeveloped, and provides a curious contrast to the megacity of Shenzhen across the river.

The Good
Lots of open space and some historic villages.

Residential

The new towns contain high-rise housing but the villages offer life on a more human scale, even if their surroundings are not necessarily rural. Hong Lok Yuen is a low-rise 'expat enclave' which could be a slice of suburbia anywhere in the western world.

The Bad
Commuting from the north's New Territories usually means taking the KCR, and that means competing for seats and enduring the noisy television screens in carriages.

Retail

Shops in the northern New Territories have suffered in recent years as many Hongkongers prefer to take their retail therapy over the border in Shenzhen.

The Must Dos
Take the kids to the railway museum; visit a walled village; hike the ridge of Pat Sin Leng.

Places of Interest

The wooded hill above Tai Po Market KCR station is crowned by some of the town's surviving colonial-era buildings. Near the Railway Museum (p.197), an attractive Man Mo temple is jammed between shops on Fu Shin Street. Island House stands on what was originally an islet in the Lam Tsuen River's estuary. Built in 1905, it served for many years as the residence of the District Officer and is now a conservation study centre run by WWF Hong Kong. Cycle paths run southeast and northeast from here, along the shores of Tolo Harbour.

Sheung Wun Yiu village outside Tai Po has a Fan Sin Kung temple which was built in 1790. Uniquely for Hong Kong, it is dedicated to the patron god of potters; the village was once noted for the porcelain produced there. Several old kilns remain. The nature reserve at Tai Po Kau is the oldest in the territory. It has mature trees and several nature trails. You may even catch a glimpse of a wild macaque.

The Lam Tsuen Valley is also famous for trees – namely, its two stately Wishing Trees near the Tin Hau temple in Fong Ma Po. Traditionally, paper wishes have been thrown up into the branches tied to oranges. If they lodged there, your wish was likely to be granted. However after one of its boughs came crashing down under the weight of oranges, the larger tree has been fenced off for safety. The temple dates from the Qing dynasty.

East of Fanling, Lung Yeuk Tau is a grouping of 11 villages founded during the Yuan dynasty by the long-established Tang clan. Five of the villages are walled. The gatehouse and corner towers of Kun Lung Wai in particular are still intact. The Tang Chung Ling ancestral hall, possibly dating from the 16th century, is one of the largest such structures in Hong Kong. You can follow the Lung Yeuk Tau heritage trail, which marks out 12 points of interest. Another celebrated ancestral hall is the Liu Man Shek Tong on the northern edge of Sheung Shui. Built in 1751, it belongs to the Liu clan and has attractive wood carvings.

East towards the sea, the Pat Sin Leng mountain range is a challenging but spectacular hike. Below it, beside the dam of the Plover Cove Reservoir, Tai Mei Tuk is a favourite place for barbecues. The beauty spot of Bride's Pool is a little further up the road. Villages past here are accessible only on foot; the trek out to Lai Chi Wo is long but recommended.

The Lowdown

Hong Kong's offshore islands come in all shapes and sizes, and many are easily accessible by public ferry services. They offer coastal exploring, great food and a taste of traditional rural life away from the city.

The Good

Quick ferry crossings, al fresco dining, fresh air, beaches, seaside villages.

The Bad

If you get too engrossed in eating or sightseeing, you can miss your return ferry!

The Must Dos

Enjoy fresh seafood for lunch or dinner; watch the processions at the Bun Festival, or cheer on a dragon boat team; take a junk trip and go swimming in a remote bay.

Outlying Islands

Hong Kong Island is just one of many mountainous isles included in the SAR. All told, there are more than 230 of them. Many have been inhabited for centuries by fishing or farming communities and their traditions live on to the present day. If you visit at the right time, you may happen upon a temple festival, a fishermen's dragon boat race or a Cantonese opera performance in a bamboo theatre.

Many visitors come not for culture but for sun and seafood, and the islands have plenty of both. Harbourside restaurants do a roaring trade catering to ferry passengers and weekend sailors. Although there are several beaches manned by lifeguards, a junk allows you to sail anywhere you please, and there are scores of deserted bays for you to drop anchor.

Another positive aspect is the absence of motor traffic. The air is clearer on the islands and you can let animals and young children run freely.

Several different ferry companies run services and fares are low. Journeys typically take between 20 minutes and an hour, apart from the route to Tung Ping Chau. Links to timetables can be found below. Holiday apartments are available for rent on Lamma Island and Cheung Chau, so your visit need not end with the last ferry.

For Lantau, by far the biggest of all the outlying islands, see p.177.

Residential

Housing is all village style, i.e. modern three-storey villas. Lamma Island, Cheung Chau and Peng Chau have become popular residential areas for expats who appreciate cleaner air, a quieter environment and a more laid-back way of life.

Retail

Shopping opportunities generally come in the form of handicrafts. The main street of Yung Shue Wan on Lamma Island is particularly good for these.

Places of Interest

With a variety of islands in all shapes and sizes there is plenty to explore; from secret beaches, challenging walks, raves and great seafood, the choice is yours. Also worth a mention are the Soko Islands, an uninhabited archipelago off the south coast of Lantau Island. They are a popular destination for junk trips, and Siu A Chau has a nice beach.

Cheung Chau (map 13-B2)

Cheung Chau is the most populous outlying island, thanks to its long-established fishing industry. More than 20,000 people are somehow crammed into the tiny town. On arrival, the ferry passes rows and rows of deep-sea boats anchored in the island's harbour. Their harvest is put to good use: dozens of alfresco seafood restaurants line the town's waterfront.

In the north, the Pak Tai temple is Cheung Chau's most famous, and was built in 1783. It is the site of the annual Bun Festival (p.50) which usually takes place in May. Towers of steamed buns are erected in the forecourt, and competitors climb them to see who can get the highest bun.

South of the pier, the Hung Shing temple is a well-kept building hidden amidst a jumble of old-world streets. Uphill from here, the Kwan Kung Pavilion, a shrine devoted to the god of justice, is set in pleasant gardens.

The southwest corner of the island holds what is said to be the treasure cave of Cheung Po-tsai, the notorious pirate, but it is only a clammy fissure in the rock. Nevertheless, a nice trail leads along the southern coast. Start it by taking a sampan from near the main pier to Sai Wan, and then follow the signs along Peak Road back to the main town.

Access by ferry from Central, TST or Mui Wo.

Timetables: 2131 8181 or www.nwff.com.hk

Lamma Island (map 13-F3)

Lamma is the closest to Hong Kong Island and the most popular with expat residents. The main settlement, Yung Shue Wan, has a relaxed holiday atmosphere, with a good range of dining options. A cross-island trail leads south to Sok Kwu Wan, the other main village, which is well known for its seafood. Both places have ferry services and both have Tin Hau temples.

A power station behind Yung Shue Wan provides electricity to the whole of Hong Kong Island, and the ungazetted Tai Wan To beach beside it is popular with dog owners and volleyball players. It's also a venue for occasional rave parties.

A circular hike can be made from Sok Kwu Wan which includes the old villages of Mo Tat and Tung O, a couple of sandy beaches and a climb up to a pass with great views. The bay of Sham Wan to the south is the only beach in Hong Kong which turtles still visit to lay eggs.

Access by ferry from Central or Aberdeen. For timetable information ring 2815 6063 or visit www.hkkf.com.hk. For the Aberdeen to Sok Kwu Wan route try 2375 7883 or www.ferry.com.hk.

Peng Chau (map 9-C4)

Nestling close to the eastern coast of Lantau, Peng Chau is a tiny island with a large commuter population. Reached by ferry from Central or Mui Wo, it boasts a few temples and old market streets. Its appeal has been damaged in recent years by the construction of needlessly high sea walls, but the easy climb up Finger Hill still gives good views of the Western Harbour and its islands, and of the Tsing Ma Bridge.The Green Peng Chau Association has published a beautiful hand-drawn map of the island's attractions.

A 'kaido' (village ferry) service covers the short distances between Peng Chau, Discovery Bay and a pier near the Trappist Monastery on Lantau Island. Timetables: 2131 8181 or www.nwff.com.hk

Poi Toi (map 14-F4)

Po Toi is found to the south of Stanley. The steep, round island has a small village with beachside seafood restaurants, and some rock formations to the south which are popular with Chinese tourists. The bay is often full of pleasure boats.

Access by ferry from Stanley (Sundays only) or Aberdeen (Tuesdays, Thursdays, Saturdays and Sundays).

Departures are not that frequent so check the schedule first at www.ferry.com.hk or by calling 2375 7883.

Tap Mun (map 1-F1)

Tap Mun, also known as Grass Island, is a very old-world place at the entrance to Tolo Harbour. Its fishing villages are pleasingly free of modern buildings. A simple circuit of the island can be made, taking in its Tin Hau temple and the grassy eastern coast, and finishing at the island's seafood restaurant near the pier. There are no night-time ferries so make an early start for this expedition.

Access by ferry from Ma Liu Shui, near University KCR station, or from Wong Shek Pier in Sai Kung. Call 2272 2022 for schedules or go to www.traway.com.hk.

Tung Lung Island (map 1-F4)

Tung Lung Island guards the eastern approaches to Victoria Harbour, and so it is no surprise that remains of a Qing dynasty fort were found there. It has become a popular place for rock climbers (see p.234). The island has no permanent population but a few noodle cafes are operated on weekends.

Access by ferry from Sai Wan Ho (Hong Kong Island) or Sam Ka Tsuen (Kowloon). Call 2131 8181 for schedule details.

Tung Ping Chau (map 1-F1)

Tung Ping Chau (also known as Ping Chau) is the furthest-flung of all Hong Kong's outlying islands, way out in the northeast corner of Mirs Bay. It is very close to the coast of China. Being distant from the rest of Hong Kong, it has a different geology: sedimentary rock is revealed in layers which glitter when wet, and erosion has created rock towers on wave-cut platforms.

The island and its waters are protected as country and marine parks. On land you'll find ghostly abandoned villages, while underwater there are coral reefs. On weekends, villagers return to run noodle shops. Some beds can be rented.

Access by ferry from Ma Liu Shui, near University KCR station. There are just two departures on Saturdays and one on Sundays so check www.traway.com.hk or call 2272 2022 before setting off.

Need Some Direction?

The *Explorer Mini Maps* pack a whole city into your pocket and once unfolded are excellent navigational tools for exploring. Not only are they handy in size, with detailed information on the sights and sounds of the city, but also their fabulously affordable price means they won't make a dent in your holiday fund. Wherever your travels take you, from the Middle East to Europe and beyond, grab a mini map and you'll never have to ask for directions again.

Maps 14 & 16 ◄

Pok Fu Lam and Aberdeen

The southwest corner of Hong Kong Island has a long maritime heritage: incense was being exported from Aberdeen harbour long before the British arrived on the scene. Indeed Aberdeen's Chinese name – Heung Gong Tsai – is what British sailors heard when they asked the name of the island they were visiting. From this came the name 'Hong Kong'.

Aberdeen harbour is still active today, with a large fleet of ocean-faring fishing boats and sampans to service them. Ocean Park (p.203), one of the largest theme parks in Southeast Asia, occupies a hill beside the harbour.

Pok Fu Lam was undeveloped until the late 19th century. Dairy farms were then established there to provide Hong Kong's European community with fresh milk, and the French Mission moved in to open a printing press. Nowadays the area has scattered upmarket housing which enjoys expansive sea views to the west.

The Lowdown ◄
A tale of two cities – Pok Fu Lam is a leafy, upscale residential area, while Aberdeen is a down-and-dirty fishing port.

The Good
Great sea views and a bustling harbour.

The Bad
Aberdeen is cut off from the sea by a six-lane highway.

The Must Dos
Take a sampan trip across Aberdeen harbour; treat the kids to a day at Ocean Park.

Residential

Upmarket housing in Pok Fu Lam and in South Horizons on Ap Lei Chau generally comes with elevated sea views. Prices are lower than on the Southside and the city is easily accessible.

Retail

Pok Fu Lam is mostly residential, with few shops – the nearest large shopping centres are at Chi Fu and Kennedy Town, although Baguio Villa and Cyberport offer some facilities. Aberdeen, on the other hand, has all the shops you might expect to find in an urban area. Horizon Plaza on Ap Lei Chau (p.331) is a popular shopping destination; expats flock there to buy carpets, upholstery, barbecues and outdoor furniture.

Places of Interest

Starting from the north, Mount Davis is topped by wartime gun emplacements which can be explored. A youth hostel up here is a world away from the madding crowd below. The new Cyberport development on the coast was touted as an IT hub, but take-up of its high-tech office space has been slow. Its shopping arcade has Pok Fu Lam's only cinema. University Hall and Bethanie, two attractive colonial buildings, survive on Pok Fu Lam Road near the original Pok Fu Lam Village, which is now an untidy sprawl of ramshackle homes. Two nearby octagonal cowsheds dating from the 19th century were recently converted into the Wellcome Theatre.

Passing Wah Fu, a big public housing estate, the road descends to Aberdeen. The town has a waterfront fish market which starts early. Ferries run from the harbour to Lamma Island (p.178) and Po Toi (p.179).

Aberdeen Harbour also has two giant floating restaurants, the Jumbo and the Tai Pak, serving Cantonese cuisine. Free sampans run from the waterfront. A western restaurant has recently opened on the top level of the Jumbo. On the same stretch of water, marina clubs have moorings for pleasure boats.

Ap Lei Chau is connected to Aberdeen by bridge but also by sampan, which is a more interesting journey. There is a Hung Shing temple close to the sampan landing steps at Ap Lei Chau.

Aberdeen

Maps 6, 7 & 11

Sai Kung

With more than their fair share of natural beauty, the Sai Kung and Clear Water Bay peninsulas are known as Hong Kong's 'back garden'. The landscape is spectacular, the coastline green and the water often crystal clear. A heavily indented shoreline hides many bays which are popular destinations for junk trips and diving parties, while the hill trails are a big draw for hikers. Most of the land, and some of the water, is protected by the country parks system. The Country and Marine Parks Authority manages trails, provides shelters and barbecue areas, and runs visitor centres, making life easy for the explorer.

As well as being the gateway to the country parks and over 70 offshore islands, Sai Kung town is also a great place for eating out. Alfresco seafood restaurants line the waterfront where you can choose your dinner from one of the big glass tanks.

The Lowdown
Hong Kong's eastern fringes are a place of leisure; where hikers stretch their legs, sailors weigh anchor and diners eat their fill.

The Good
Mountains, beaches and islands to explore.

The Bad
Sampan ladies can overcharge you if you don't speak Cantonese.

The Must Dos
Make the trek out to Tai Long Wan; take a sampan trip to offshore islands; enjoy seafood on the waterfront at Sai Kung town.

Residential
Sai Kung and Clear Water Bay are popular with expats who like a green environment but don't want to be subjected to ferry schedules. Housing is mostly village type, with a few upscale townhouse developments such as Marina Cove and Portofino.

Retail
Only Sai Kung town has a full range of shops. Several shops here specialise in art and handicrafts. It's also a good place to buy fishing gear.

Places of Interest
If you approach Sai Kung from Kowloon via the Clear Water Bay Road, you're given a wonderful bird's eye view of the whole district from the pass at Razor Hill. The road then forks, left to Sai Kung and right to Clear Water Bay. Going north up Hiram's Highway, Hebe Haven is a picturesque bay full of yachts and junks. There is a small but busy Kwun Yam temple. Sampans run from the pier to various points offshore.

Sai Kung town is also served by sampans – the wizened operators will accost you on the waterfront. Popular destinations are Hap Mun Bay (p.199) and Yim Tin Tsai, but they will go further if you ask (and bargain). Kau Sai Chau, the largest offshore island, is home to a public golf course (p.245) and Hung Shing temple, which won a UNESCO award for its restoration.

The far-flung group of villages known as Leung Shuen Wan is located on High Island, which has been joined to the mainland since the construction of the giant High Island Reservoir. Sha Kiu Tau has seafood restaurants and a Tin Hau temple, while Pak Lap Wan is a quiet pine-backed beach with rooms for rent. You can access these places by sampan, as well as by hiking.

Moving on from Sai Kung town, the road stays close to the verdant shore of Port Shelter, passes a monument to wartime guerrillas and soon enters the protected Country Park area. Private vehicles are not permitted to pass Pak Tam Chung. The MacLehose Trail starts here, taking in some fabulous sea and mountain scenery.

The line of beaches at Tai Long Wan (p.200) is rated by many as Hong Kong's most spectacular vista. The bus route ends at Wong Shek Pier; speedboats run from here to Chek Keng, from where you can walk over the pass to Tai Long Wan. Boats also run from the pier to nearby Tap Mun Island (p.179).

Going south, the barbecue area at Tai Hang Tun overlooks the ocean and is a hotspot for kite-flying. The beaches at Clear Water Bay are followed by Po Toi O, a small fishing village with seafood restaurants. At the furthest end of the peninsula lies the Clearwater Bay Golf & Country Club (p.268) and the isolated Joss House Bay.

Map 6-C4

Sha Tin

Sha Tin lies in a wide, flat valley south of Tolo Harbour, and in ancient times was famed for the quality of its rice. Villagers dug for shellfish along the sandy shore. Development began when the Kowloon-Canton Railway arrived in 1910, and accelerated in the 1960s and 70s when the Hong Kong Government chose the area as the site for one of the first new towns. Today it's a sprawling city of half a million people, sitting roughly midway between Hong Kong Island and the Chinese border. The Hong Kong Civil Engineering and Development Department's website has a brief history of the city's growth, plus some interesting 'before and after' photographs. Visit www.cedd.gov.hk, then click About Us and navigate to Achievements & New Developments, Regional Development Services, and then Sha Tin New Town.

Sha Tin is surrounded by green hills on three sides, and is separated from Kowloon by a line of mountains known as Unicorn Ridge. The city is split in two by the Shing Mun River, which flows north-east along a straight-edged, man-made channel towards Tolo Harbour. Amah Rock, a stone formation resembling a woman carrying a baby on her back, looks down on the city from the south.

The Lowdown
This enormous New Territories city sits astride the north-south KCR line.

The Good
Remnants of culture can be found hidden throughout the new town. There are good transport connections to all parts of Hong Kong and the New Territories.

The Bad
The scale of Sha Tin can sometimes seem a bit daunting.

The Must Dos
Hike uphill to the Ten Thousand Buddhas Monastery; absorb local culture at the Heritage Museum.

Residential

Sha Tin is made up of many private developments among a forest of public housing estates. Housing is mainly high-rise, but there are some low-rise villages on the outskirts.

Retail

Gigantic shopping centres have the full range of international brands and Hong Kong chain stores. New Town Plaza (p.325), near to the KCR station, is particularly popular. It is actually two malls connected by a walkway. As well as numerous shops, it has a cinema, amusement arcade and a Snoopy-themed playground. Just north of the railway line is Grand Central Plaza, which is home to an Ikea store.

Places of Interest

Tai Wai is the KCR's first stop after exiting the tunnel from Kowloon. Here, the railway meets the Shing Mun River, which has some nice promenades that are good for cycling and strolling.

On the north bank of the river you'll find the Hong Kong Heritage Museum (p.196), with a wealth of displays and exhibits. Past the museum, Sha Tin Park leads towards the town centre, where there's a theatre, hotel, library, cinema and the huge New Town Plaza system of shopping malls (p.325). The Ten Thousand Buddhas Monastery (p.192) is a short walk from the town. The name is fast becoming out of date, as at the last tally the number was approaching 13,000.

Travelling further north-east from the town centre takes you past the Hong Kong Sports Institute and on to Sha Tin Racecourse (p.204). It has a capacity of 80,000 spectators, and is a hive of activity on race nights.

South of the river, the popular Che Kung Temple (p.191) is served by its own KCR station, and Tsang Tai Uk (p.194), a walled village built by the Tsang clan in the 1840s, is nearby.

The east bank of the Shing Mun River has a 'floating' restaurant which is in fact made out of stone. Wong Uk, on the same side, is an old house which has been preserved. North of Sha Tin, the Chinese University of Hong Kong is spread over a headland overlooking Tolo Harbour. The pier below it has ferry services to Tap Mun and Tung Ping Chau (p.197).

The separate new town at Ma On Shan has a beach where pedalos may be hired. Nearby, the former Vietnamese detention camp at Whitehead is now a golf driving range (p.246).

Map 14 ◀

Southside

Unlike the northern side of Hong Kong Island, the Southside has generally retained its natural coastline intact – and what a coastline it is. Glittering shores incorporate headlands and beaches, bays and offshore islets. Its natural beauty and close proximity to the city make it a prestigious place to live.

When the British arrived in 1841, the fishing village at Stanley was the largest settlement on the island. Barracks and a police station were built there to deter pirates. A road around the coast was completed only in the 1920s, and it was followed soon after by the construction of the famous Repulse Bay Hotel. The Southside has been popular as a place of rest and recreation ever since.

The Lowdown ◀

The south coast of Hong Kong Island is both a weekend getaway for city people and home to the wealthy.

Residential

Residences on the Southside come at a premium but that doesn't seem to harm their popularity. Once characterised by standalone villas, the area now has many high-rise developments, particularly in Repulse Bay and Tai Tam. Redhill is a self-contained development of townhouses overlooking Tai Tam Harbour. If you're looking to escape the high-rises completely, go beyond the Dragon's Back, everything between Shek O and Big Wave Bay is either villa or village.

The Good

Many beaches with full facilities, plenty of dining options, inland hiking routes, wonderful sea views.

Retail

The Southside caters well to expats, with shopping centres like The Repulse Bay and Stanley Plaza accommodating western-oriented supermarkets. The crowded maze of Stanley Market is good for buying souvenirs.

The Bad

Hairpin roads to Stanley are narrow and easily congested. Beaches are as busy as MTR platforms on summer weekends.

Places of Interest

There are several routes from the city to the Southside, but the best is via Wong Nai Chung Gap Road; it crosses the central heights of Hong Kong Island by way of a high pass, and your descent to Repulse Bay is marked by stunning views of land and sea. Perched above the water, The Repulse Bay is a dining and shopping complex which is a faithful recreation of an old colonial hotel. From the beach, a coastal footpath leads north to Deep Water Bay – it is well used by joggers and gives nice views of the Middle Island yacht moorings.

The Must Dos

Take a hike through Tai Tam Country Park or over the Dragon's Back; relax over dinner at Stanley or Shek O.

Stanley Market

Travelling south, the narrow road twists and turns towards Stanley. This relaxed town is sandwiched between a beach on one side and a waterfront on the other. After getting jostled in the lanes of Stanley Market, you can wind down with dinner or drinks at one of the waterfront restaurants.

In the days of pirates, it was said that Cheung Po-tsai, king of vagabonds, used the town's Tin Hau temple as a lookout post. Built in the 1760s, it stood until recently amidst a valley of squatter huts, but is now surrounded by an open plaza. An incense-blackened tiger skin hangs on the wall inside – the unlucky creature was shot by a policeman in 1942.

183

The old Stanley police station, built in 1859, is Hong Kong's oldest surviving police post. The building is on Stanley Village Road, close to the bus station. At the end of the peninsula, Stanley Fort is now occupied by the People's Liberation Army and it only opens its gates for occasional events such as charity rugby matches.

Moving north, the road passes the premises of the American Club (p.268) before reaching the stone dam of the Tai Tam Tuk Reservoir, an elegant construction completed in 1918. The road runs along the top of it, but it's very narrow and buses need the full width to themselves. Hiking routes lead inland from here to cross a huge area of protected hill country. Tai Tam Harbour below is a broad, sheltered inlet often used for sailing.

The Dragon's Back is a mountain ridge popular with hikers. On the far side of it, the laid-back villages of Shek O (p.199)and Big Wave Bay (p.198) enjoy splendid geographic isolation. The art-deco bus station at Shek O hints at how time can move more slowly in these far-off parts. Be sure to explore Shek O village and headland, and feed yourself at one of the busy Chinese-Thai restaurants. The village is bordered by the genteel Shek O Golf & Country Club (p.246), which has changed little since it was laid out in the 1920s.

Stanley

Map 16-E3 ◀

The Peak

Victoria Peak rises 550m above Central and commands views of everything from Kowloon to the hills of the New Territories. Once a restricted residential area for the self-appointed cream of colonial society, governors used to live up here until the mists and access problems got to them. Now it's a de rigeur stop on all tour itineraries.

The time-tested manner to reach The Peak is aboard the Peak Tram, but the alternative bus journey (no. 15) is also recommended, as it takes a different route and offers great views of Wan Chai, Happy Valley and Aberdeen.

The Lowdown ◀

The Peak is Hong Kong's most popular tourist attraction. Surveying the city from these heights gives you a good understanding of how Hong Kong is laid out.

Residential

The Peak was traditionally the preserve of taipans and top government figures. Today it's still an impressive high-class address, but not as popular as it once was. Prices are top-end.

The Good

This incomparable vantage point – overlooking a spectacular city around a gleaming harbour – should not be missed.

Retail

Two shopping centres – the Peak Tower and Peak Galleria – are aimed squarely at the tourist trade. Both have decent viewing platforms.

Places of Interest

The terminus of the Peak Tram (p.205) is on the ground floor of the Peak Tower. Emerging onto the street outside you'll see the Peak Galleria's cybernetic fountain, which is fun for kids. Opposite, the Peak Lookout is hidden behind a hedge. This restaurant was built in 1901 as a rest pavilion for exhausted sedan chair bearers. Turn right and take the rightmost track leading around the hillside. This is Lugard Road and you can follow it to make an easy circuit of The Peak. Halfway around, it meets a playground area where another track leads southwards to climb High West, a steep hill with dramatic views. Lugard Road runs into Harlech Road, which ends at the Peak Lookout.

The road which leads directly uphill from the Peak Tower ends at Victoria Peak Garden (p.202). The very top of the mountain cannot be reached, as it is occupied by radio masts. To the south, Mount Kellett is crowned by the Matilda International Hospital. When it opened in 1907, sedan chairs were the only means of transport to reach it. That heritage is the basis for the annual Sedan Chair Race, which takes place there every November and raises money for charities.

You can walk down from The Peak via leafy pedestrian paths: Hatton Road and Old Peak Road lead down to Mid-Levels, while Pok Fu Lam Reservoir Road ends by the riding school at Pok Fu Lam (p.248).

The Bad

Worsening air pollution, and little action to combat it, make clear views rare and unpredictable.

The Must Dos

Ride uphill on the Peak Tram, make a circuit of The Peak via Lugard Road to see the city below.

Map 15-C4

Tsim Sha Tsui

The epitome of urban, close-quarters Hong Kong, Tsim Sha Tsui is loud, crowded, and very much a 24 hour kind of place. It's also one of Hong Kong's most cosmopolitan areas and many large hotels are found here. The district occupies the southern tip of the Kowloon peninsula and enjoys unrivalled views across the harbour. Ferry routes run to Central, Wan Chai and Cheung Chau, and from the China Ferry Pier, to faraway destinations in the Pearl River Delta. In everyday conversation, Tsim Sha Tsui is usually referred to as 'TST'.

The Lowdown

This bustling downtown area with fabulous harbour views is a major hotel district.

Residential

As a noisy area at all times of the day and night, TST is a place people usually prefer to visit rather than inhabit. Housing stock is mostly old.

The Good

TST never stops, and the buzz is contagious – ideal for night owls.

Retail

As well as street-level shops and large shopping centres, TST also has hotel arcades selling luxury items. Harbour City (p.320) is one of Hong Kong's largest malls, stretching the entire length of Canton Road, with around 700 shops under its roof. A warning is in order if buying consumer electronics anywhere in TST: avoid those shops which do not display prices.

The Bad

Tailor-shop touts and fake Rolex salesmen on every street corner won't take no for an answer.

Places of Interest

Nathan Road is the main commercial artery of TST. It runs from Kowloon Park down towards the venerable Peninsula Hotel, from where Salisbury Road leads to the Star Ferry pier. Canton Road runs from here up to the China Ferry Terminal, lined on both sides with hotels, cinemas and shopping centres. The smaller streets branching off these main roads are packed solid with restaurants, shops and bars.

Mody Road leads to TST East, which is a reclaimed area full of hotels. Beyond these you'll find the Hong Kong Coliseum, an indoor stadium used most often for marathon runs of Canto-pop concerts, but which also sees the occasional international act.

The Must Dos

Marvel at the night-time harbour panorama; learn about the story of Hong Kong at the Museum of History; take high tea at The Peninsula.

Map 17 ◀

Wan Chai, Happy Valley & Causeway Bay

OK, so its reputation precedes it, but Wan Chai is more than just a girlie-bar zone. The district has historical neighbourhoods, street markets, hotels and government office complexes. Causeway Bay is one of Hong Kong's prime shopping districts, while Happy Valley is centred on its racecourse.

The area's geography was radically different when the British arrived. Happy Valley was a malarial swamp until it was drained in the mid-1800s. Modern Wan Chai and Causeway Bay are built almost entirely on reclaimed land – the tram line traces the original shoreline to some extent.

The district had a close association with the Royal Navy for many years: the open-air Tamar Site, now often used for concerts and fairs while stakeholders debate whether to build a new government headquarters there, was formerly the naval dockyard. Today, the nearby Fleet Arcade on Fenwick Pier welcomes sailors from visiting ships.

Residential

Wan Chai and Causeway Bay are dense districts with older high-rise buildings. Noise and air quality are a problem. Happy Valley is quieter and more upmarket, and has its own self-contained 'village' feel.

Retail

Furniture shops cluster along Queen's Road East and in Happy Valley. Causeway Bay boasts upmarket clothing boutiques, department stores such as Sogo (p.328) and large shopping malls like Times Square (p.323). Wan Chai has a good line in computers and related equipment, and the open-air market which occupies Cross Street and Tai Yuen Street is worth a wander.

Places of Interest

The Hung Shing temple on Queen's Road East is built around a boulder which stood on the original shoreline. Place names around here – Ship Street, Schooner Street – attest to the fact that the sea was once much nearer.

Further up the road, the Hopewell Centre was Hong Kong's tallest building when it was built; the external glass lift to the top-floor revolving restaurant still gives a thrill. The tiny Environmental Resource Centre nearby, at the corner of Wan Chai Gap Road, is housed in the oldest surviving post office building in Hong Kong.

Wan Chai's bar district is centred at the intersection of Lockhart and Luard Roads. You're well advised to avoid any bar which employs girls to beckon you inside; these establishments make their money from fleecing sailors and other men too drunk to notice. Other bars and restaurants are run on a normal basis, and there are some good choices here. See Going Out, starting on p.349.

Among the commercial buildings of Wan Chai North you'll find Immigration Tower and Revenue Tower, both home to government departments which you are likely to have dealings with. The Hong Kong Academy for Performing Arts, a venue for plays and concerts, has its compound opposite the Arts Centre (p.189).

Elevated walkways snake across to the Convention & Exhibition Centre (p.205) and to the Star Ferry pier, which has services to Tsim Sha Tsui and Hung Hom.

Moving along the coast to Causeway Bay, the Royal Hong Kong Yacht Club (p.259) has its clubhouse on Kellett Island – once an offshore isle but now firmly joined to the city by reclamation. Its marina borders the Causeway Bay Typhoon Shelter which is full of boats. On the waterfront here sits the Noonday Gun, an old naval cannon which is ritually fired every day at twelve noon. It was mentioned in the Noel Coward song 'Mad Dogs and Englishmen'. Thanks to the wisdom of having a twelve-lane highway on the harbourfront, you need to reach it by taking an underground tunnel from beside the Excelsior Hotel.

The Lowdown ◀

Shopping, gambling and nightlife: three vices catered for in three neighbouring districts.

The Good

Lots of options for dining and entertainment, and plenty of street life to observe.

The Bad

Street-level pollution is severe. The cross-harbour tunnel entrance is often backed up with traffic at rush hour.

The Must Dos

Have a flutter on the races; enjoy a night out in Wan Chai

Central Library (p.252), Hong Kong's largest, overlooks Victoria Park from the south. Inland from there, in an older district known as Tai Hang, the Lin Fa Kung temple sits in a small garden. It was built in 1864 in an unusual style. The streets nearby are the location of the annual Fire Dragon Festival, a celebration which coincides with the Mid-Autumn Festival.

On the west side of Happy Valley, opposite the entrance to the racecourse, colonial cemeteries represent most denominations of Hong Kong's early settlers.

The pedestrian-only Bowen Road runs along the hillside above Wan Chai and Happy Valley, and is a regular route for joggers. Halfway along, a path leads up to Lover's Rock, a phallic monolith visited by women in search of husbands.

Maps 2, 4 & 5 ◀

West New Territories

The geography of the western New Territories makes it starkly different to the rest of Hong Kong. Instead of being mountainous, it is largely flat: a wide plain rich with alluvial silt. This made it good land for farming, and many of Hong Kong's earliest-established clans migrated here from the north, from the 12th century onwards. Many of their heritage structures – temples, study halls, walled villages – still stand.

The Lowdown ◀

Hong Kong's northwest is a fast-changing area of farms, villages and gigantic new towns.

In more recent years, the government has built enormous new towns in the western New Territories. These are connected by the LRT light rail system, and are linked to the city by the new KCR West Rail. A bridge over Deep Bay is under construction to link the area even more closely to Shenzhen in China.

The Good

If you look beyond the surface, you'll find evidence of centuries of heritage.

Residential

Outside the new towns of Tuen Mun, Yuen Long and Tin Shui Wai, there are several upmarket residential enclaves with their own clubs and leisure facilities. Of these, Gold Coast and Fairview Park are the best known; Gold Coast's location opposite the airport makes it popular with air crew. Other housing is mostly village-style.

The Bad

Some parts of the new towns can be downright dystopian in scale and design. Traffic jams are the rule on the Tuen Mun Highway. Disruptive infrastructure projects seem to be never ending.

Retail

The new towns have large shopping centres, with a local Chinese focus.

Places of Interest

From the MTR terminus at Tsuen Wan, Castle Peak Road runs westwards past the Gold Coast to Tuen Mun, perhaps Hong Kong's most intimidating new town. Ferries run from here over to northern Lantau Island. Hung Lau, an old house on Tuen Mun's outskirts, was used by Sun Yat-sen, the founder of modern China. Castle Peak Monastery is said to have been the home of Pui To, a legendary Buddhist monk, and it is the starting point for a hike up the dramatically steep Castle Peak.

The Must Dos

Make an expedition to at least one of the area's historical relics; sit with the birdwatchers at Mai Po or the Wetland Park.

Ping Shan is an ancient group of villages founded by the Tang clan, who still live there. A short heritage trail has been laid out, encompassing ten antiquities including Hong Kong's only pagoda (p.194).

On the coast of Deep Bay, which is in fact very shallow, Lau Fau Shan is a fishing town famous for its oysters. Inland, Kam Tin is known for its walled villages – fortified grid structures with towers on each corner. Among them, Kat Hing Wai is the easiest to find and has attractive iron gates. You may be charged a few dollars to enter.

North of Yuen Long and past the turning to Mai Po, San Tin is another huddle of old villages with a couple of heritage sites. Close by, the manically busy Lok Ma Chau border crossing is also the location of the Lok Ma Chau lookout point. This was popular when the border was closed and people wanted a sneak peek into China. It's not needed now, but the view from it is a fascinating contrast of urban Shenzhen and Hong Kong's undeveloped Frontier Closed Area.

Museums, Heritage & Culture

Hong Kong has had a doubly rich history. Existing for thousands of years on the fringes of the Chinese world, and then becoming an outpost of British colonialism, its architecture, fortifications and religious sites draw on both eastern and western heritage. Unfortunately other factors have also been at work over the past 150 years. The small size of the territory, together with its consistent lure for new migrants, means that land has always been in short supply. When this is further combined with a commercial mindset on the part of both government and people, then you begin to understand why so much heritage has been razed and redeveloped. What remains, however, is well worth visiting, and traditional culture seems to thrive nonetheless.

Archaeological Sites

The earliest sites of human habitation in Hong Kong are found on sand bars above beaches. Archaeological digs on Lamma Island, Lantau Island and Ma Wan have uncovered relics dating back to Neolithic times (approximately 6,000 years ago). The largest recent excavation was in Sai Kung in 2002, where many Bronze Age artefacts were unearthed.

No archaeological sites are available for viewing, but ancient carvings are still visible on rock faces at Cheung Chau, Wong Chuk Hang, Po Toi, Shek Pik and Tung Lung. They are generally swirling geometric patterns and are thought to date from the Bronze Age.

Art Galleries

Other options **Art** p.285 **Art & Craft Supplies** p.285

Central, and in particular SoHo, is the place to go for browsing art. The streets around Hollywood Road and beside the Escalator have a liberal sprinkling of commercial art galleries, often focusing on contemporary Asian art. Each year many of these galleries throw their doors open for the ArtWalk fundraising event, a night of wine, mingling and art appreciation. See www.hongkongartwalk.com for details. Listed below is a roundup of non-commercial galleries. See also the Hong Kong Museum of Art on p.195.

63 Ma Tau Kok Rd ◀
To Kwa Wan
Map 15-E2

Cattle Depot Artists' Village

This colonial-era slaughterhouse has been converted into an alternative cultural venue, housing progressive artists instead of cattle. Various independent arts groups have their offices in the red-brick buildings, and exhibitions, book fairs and performances are staged here. It's located in one of Kowloon's oldest neighbourhoods.

2 Lower Albert Rd ◀
Central
🚇 *Central*
Map 16-E2

Fringe Club

2521 7251 | *www.hkfringeclub.com*
It's amazing how much art and culture can be crammed into one small space when necessity calls for it. The diminutive Fringe Club houses two theatres, three exhibition galleries, a pottery workshop, rehearsal rooms, two cafe bars and a fine dining restaurant. As well as hosting events year-round, many of which are free, the Fringe Club also runs the annual City Fringe Festival which involves international performances. The building was originally an ice house and dates from 1913.

2 Harbour Rd ◀
Wan Chai
🚇 *Wan Chai*
Map 16-F2

Hong Kong Arts Centre

2582 0200 | *www.hkac.org.hk*
Established in 1977, the Arts Centre is tasked with developing local contemporary arts and promoting cultural exchanges between east and west. The facility has exhibition galleries, art shops, a cafe and three small theatres. It's worth checking in occasionally to see what's on.

189

4 Po Yan St ◀
Sheung Wan
🚇 *Sheung Wan*
Map 16-D1

Para/Site Art Space

2517 4620 | *www.para-site.org.hk*

This non-profit contemporary art gallery is hidden down a side street off Hollywood Road. Putting on ten exhibitions a year, the organization aims to assist the development of visual arts in Hong Kong and to promote local artists. Open from 12:00 to 19:00, Wednesday to Sunday.

404 Shanghai St ◀
Yau Ma Tei
🚇 *Yau Ma Tei*
Map 15-C2

Shanghai Street Artspace

2770 2157 | *www.ssa06.org*

This small centre holds events on photography, books, cinema and other multimedia arts. Taking its inner-city location as a cue, its aim is to bring art closer to the man on the street. The Artspace promotes cultural exchange by presenting 'meet-the-artist' forums, outreach workshops for schools and small-scale performances. Open from 11:00-20:00, closed Mondays.

Forts

Early forts in the Hong Kong area were built to protect trade routes. Pearls from Tolo Harbour were among these precious shipments. These Chinese forts were abandoned at the British takeover, and Britain built its own fortifications to protect the new city from naval attack. In addition to the forts listed below, the restored fort in Kowloon Walled City Park (p.201) and the Lei Yue Mun site at the Museum of Coastal Defence (p.197) are both worth a look. It's also common to come across remains of wartime defence works when hiking in the hills around Kowloon and on Hong Kong Island.

5km SW of Shek Pik ◀
Lantau Island
Map 12-A3

Fan Lau Fort

Qing dynasty soldiers once watched over the Pearl River estuary from this point on the southwestern tip of Lantau Island. It was abandoned when Britain took over the island in 1898. Now in ruins, it's a short detour from Section 7 of the Lantau Trail. An ancient stone circle and a remote Tin Hau temple can also be found nearby.

Sheung Ling Pei Village ◀
Tung Chung
🚇 *Tung Chung*
Map 8-E4

Tung Chung Fort

Until recently the cannons of this 19th-century fort pointed out to sea but its views are now blocked by towers of the new town. Nevertheless, it's worth a passing visit as a reminder of the days when Tung Chung was a remote agricultural community which needed to protect itself from pirates. Open 10:00-17:00 every day except Tuesdays.

Temples

Temple tasters are in for a treat in Hong Kong. Every neighbourhood has shrines and temples both large and small, and the panoply of gods is wide. Tin Hau, protector goddess of fishermen, is perhaps the most widely worshipped – not surprising in a city which is associated so closely with the sea. Other popular deities include Hung Shing, Kwun Yam and Hau Wong.

Temples tend to have a standard symmetrical layout – a main hall with a statue of the god at the back, flanked by minor deities and accoutrements such as drums and ceremonial martial arts weapons. A table for offerings stands in front and the hall is accessed through a central doorway with a raised threshold. A second doorway follows immediately afterwards, designed to foil evil spirits who can travel only in straight lines. Rooms on either side are used to worship other gods or as quarters for temple keepers. Many temples have bells; the casting date of these often gives some clues as to the building's age.

The temples below are some of the most colourful, authentic or accessible.

Che Kung Temple

Che Kung Miu Rd
Sha Tin
Map 6-C4

2603 4049

This large and very popular temple is dedicated to General Che, a historical figure of the Sung dynasty who suppressed an uprising in southern China. A giant statue of the general stands in the main hall, and worshippers come to make offerings and spin windmills for good fortune. There is also a row of fortune tellers. Chinese New Year is the temple's busiest time, when many people, traditionally including Hong Kong's Secretary for Home Affairs, come to seek good luck for the year ahead. The modern temple, which has a definite Japanese style to it, was built only in 1993; the original, which is 300 years old, is much smaller and is hidden away behind the main hall. Open daily 07:00-18:00. Access: KCR Che Kung Temple Station.

Ching Chung Koon

Tsing Chung Koon Rd
Tuen Mun
Map 4-F2

This Taoist temple is well known for its collection of bonsai trees, which have been nurtured over the course of many years. The complex sits amidst gardens, pavilions and fishponds designed in traditional Chinese style. It was originally a remote rural hideaway, predating the new town which now surrounds it, but still manages to feel like a haven away from the city. Open 07:00-18:00. Access via Ching Chung LRT station.

Wong Tai Sin Temple

Hau Wong Temple

Nr Yat Tung Estate
Tung Chung
Tung Chung
Map 8-E4

Tung Chung has a place in the imperial Chinese history book – the bay was the site of a 13th-century naval battle which saw the deaths of the two boy emperors who were the last of the Sung dynasty. Local villagers began to venerate Marquis Yeung, the boys' loyal protector, and this temple to him was built on the coast at Tung Chung in 1765. The grassy area in front of the temple is used as a site for Cantonese opera and other seasonal activities. This is also the starting point for a coastal hike which passes through several old villages on the way to Tai O. Access via Yat Tung Estate.

Man Mo Temple

Hollywood Rd
Central
Sheung Wan
Map 16-D1

Dedicated to the gods of literature and war, the Man Mo Temple is one of the oldest on Hong Kong Island, harking back to the earliest days of British rule. The temple is well known for its gigantic incense coils which hang from the ceiling, filling the interior with thick, fragrant smoke. It is popular with tour groups so try to pay a visit when there are no coaches parked outside, but be warned it closes at 18:00.

Ten Thousand Buddhas Monastery

Nr Grand
Central Plaza
Sha Tin
Map 6-C3

2691 1067

Above the older part of Sha Tin, figures of golden monks line the approach route to a hillside monastery famous for its gaudy Buddhist statuary. The walls of the main hall are bedecked with more than 10,000 Buddha figurines, all slightly different. The body of the founding abbot is also gilded and on display – a rather gruesome exhibit. There is a canteen which serves cheap Chinese vegetarian food. Open 09:00-17:00 daily; allow 20 minutes or so for the walk up to it. Access: KCR Sha Tin Station.

Tin Hau Temple (Joss House Bay)

Nr Clearwater Bay
Golf & Country Club
Clear Water Bay
Map 11-A4

This remote inlet south of Clear Water Bay comes to life just once a year, on the occasion of Tin Hau's birthday. At that time, flotillas of fishing boats and ferries bring thousands of visitors to worship at the temple, which may be Hong Kong's oldest – a Sung dynasty rock inscription on the hillside above dates back to the year 1274. The large, imposing temple looks out across the channel to Tung Lung Island (see p.179). Access: via footpath beside the entrance gate of the Clearwater Bay Golf & Country Club.

Tin Hau Temple (Tin Hau)

10 Tin Hau Temple Rd
Tin Hau
🚇 *Tin Hau*
Map 17-C2

Tin Hau, the goddess and protector of fishermen, is Hong Kong's most worshipped deity. Temples devoted to her can be found in most coastal areas. This particular one is so popular that it has given its name to the surrounding district. Built in the early 18th century, it's a good example of traditional temple architecture. Open 07:00-17:00.

Tin Hau Temple (Yau Ma Tei)

Public Square St
Yau Ma Tei
🚇 *Yau Ma Tei*
Map 15-C3

2332 9240

When it was built by seafaring worshippers, this temple was close to the shore. Many years of reclamation have pushed it far inland, and it is now the backdrop to the nightly circus of humanity which is the Temple Street market. Besides Tin Hau, four other deities are worshipped at the temple. Its tree-shaded forecourt is full of people at all times.

Wong Tai Sin Temple

Wong Tai Sin Rd
Wong Tai Sin
🚇 *Wong Tai Sin*
Map 10-C1

Wong Tai Sin, a shepherd boy of legend, is one of the most popular gods in Hong Kong, and this temple is the busiest. It has extensive grounds with gardens, pavilions and water features. A wall of nine dragons echoes a similar sculpture from Beijing's Imperial Palace. Soothsayers are on hand to tell fortunes and there is a Chinese medicine clinic for the poor. The temple combines the teachings of Taoism, Confucianism and Buddhism and, with an area of 18,000 square metres, it is large and varied enough to occupy visitors for a good few hours.

Heritage Sites – City

Other options **Temples** p.190, **Museums – City** p.194, **Art** p.284

In many cases, memorial plaques are all that remain of former historic buildings but a scattering of old structures has been preserved. These give an insight into how people lived and worked in old Hong Kong. They range from colonial police stations and market buildings to Qing-dynasty Chinese mansions and walled villages. Some are in use as museums (see section below).

Five heritage trails have been marked out by the government's Antiquities and Monuments Office; two in the New Territories at Ping Shan and Lung Yeuk Tau, and three on Hong Kong Island covering Central, Western and The Peak. Visit www.amo.gov.hk for details.

10 Hollywood Rd
Central
🚇 *Central*
Map 16-E2

Former Central Police Station

Also incorporating the former Magistracy and Victoria Prison, and occupying an entire city block, this collection of imposing colonial buildings is unique in Hong Kong – other heritage sites are much more fragmented, thanks to the wrecker's ball. Recently vacated, the Victorian structures and courtyards now stand empty, awaiting a decision on future use. Not yet open to the public.

Upper Albert Rd
Central
🚇 *Central*
Map 16-E2

Government House

2530 2003

The longtime residence of British governors was rejected as accommodation by Tung Chee-hwa, Hong Kong's first post-handover leader, but current chief executive Donald Tsang saw no problem in moving in. The building dates from the 1850s, although its Japanese-style tower was added during the war years. It is open to the public only on special occasions.

323 Des Voeux Rd
Central
Sheung Wan
🚇 *Sheung Wan*
Map 16-D1

Western Market

Once a working wet market, this handsome Edwardian building was converted in 1991 into a gentrified retail centre. Inside you'll find silk merchants, collectible boutiques, a Chinese dessert house, an art gallery and a smart dim sum restaurant which also serves as a dance hall. It is open daily until 19:00. The 'Sheung Wan Fong' piazza nearby has compass tiles which point out local centres of the dried seafood trade.

Heritage Sites – Out of City

Other options **Museums – Out of City** p.196, **Tours & Sightseeing** p.209

Ngong Ping
Lantau Island
Map 12-C1

The Big Buddha

2985 5248 | *www.plm.org.hk/blcs/en*

Po Lin Monastery was built in the 1920s as a quiet mountain retreat for Buddhist monks. How things have changed! Since the bronze Buddha statue was unveiled in 1993, it's become one of Hong Kong's major tourist draws. It's located high on the Ngong Ping plateau but the new Ngong Ping Skyrail gets you up there easily, providing panoramic views along the way. There is also now a theatre, retail and dining outlets on the site, in addition to the 'Walking With Buddha' experience, which is an educational tour offering visitors a helping hand on the path to enlightenment. Visit www.np360.com.hk for maps, times and prices.

You need to climb a long flight of steps to reach the serene-looking Buddha's outdoor platform. He is surrounded by elegant bodhisattva figures carved in stone and there are three exhibition halls underneath the pedestal. The Buddha is open 10:00-18:00.

You should take a look around the Po Lin Monastery while you are here. East from the monastery lies Hong Kong's only tea farm. A little further uphill you'll find the Wisdom Path – a small garden in which 38 wooden obelisks stand, each inscribed with a calligraphic verse from the Heart Sutra, an important Buddhist text.

To access the site take buses 2 or 23 from Mui Wo or catch the Ngong Ping Skyrail from the terminal near Tung Chung MTR.

Wing Ping Tsuen
San Tin
Map 2-D3

Tai Fu Tai

This elegant mansion, built in 1865, belonged to a mandarin from the Man clan. Its architectural features have been carefully restored and the house gives a good idea of how Qing dynasty notables lived. An ornamental board inscribed with not only Chinese characters but also Manchu script, the native language of the Qing court, is the only example of this script in Hong Kong. Opening times: 09:00-13:00 and 14:00-17:00 daily, except Tuesdays.

193

20km from Mui Wo
Lantau Island
Map 12-B1

Tai O

Once the largest settlement on Lantau Island, Tai O has a long history as a centre of salt production. The main export now is shrimp paste, which you will see drying on flat rattan baskets. Tai O is famous for its waterways and its old stilt houses – tin shacks standing on wooden piles in the creek. They are inhabited mainly by the Tanka people. Among other attractions are the Yeung Hau Temple (one of Hong Kong's most picturesque), the Tai O Culture Workshop, a small museum run by a local fisherwoman, quick dolphin-spotting boat trips, and the Hong Kong Shaolin Wushu Culture Centre. To reach the town, take buses 1 or 11 from Mui Wo.

Sha Tin Rd
Sha Tin
Map 6-C4

Tsang Tai Uk

This walled village has a unique style and is unusually well preserved in its original state, despite being still inhabited. It was built by the Tsang clan in the 1840s. Because the Tsangs were Hakkas who came from the northeastern part of Guangdong, the village looks different to others in the New Territories. Three archways lead into interior courtyards with wells. The four grey-brick corner towers are topped by iron tridents, probably to deflect bad feng shui. You are free to wander around and see the ancestral hall in the centre of the village but some areas are out of bounds. Access: KCR Sha Tin Wai station.

**Nr Tin Shui Wai
Station**
Tin Shui Wai
Map 2-A4

Tsui Shing Lau Pagoda

Possibly dating back 600 years, Tsui Shing Lau is Hong Kong's only ancient pagoda. It's a miracle it has survived so long; surrounded for years by scrapyards and now on the edge of a new town, it was made a protected monument only in 2001. The three-storey tower was built by the Tang clan of Ping Shan to improve feng shui. Open 09:00-13:00 and 14:00-17:00 every day except Tuesdays. Access: Tin Shui Wai Station, KCR West Rail.

Museums – City

Other options **Heritage Sites – City** p.192, **Art** p.284, **Temples** p.190

Most museums in Hong Kong are run by the government's Leisure and Cultural Services Department. A few are operated by private groups or other government departments. Displays are all bilingual in Chinese and English. LCSD museums are usually closed on one weekday per week – check each listing for details.

50 Lei King Rd
Sai Wan Ho
🚇 **Sai Wan Ho**
Map 17-F1

Hong Kong Film Archive

2739 2139 | *www.filmarchive.gov.hk*

Want to see a kung fu epic or a technicolour costume drama? Hong Kong has been producing Chinese-language movies for nearly 100 years. The Film Archive was set up to preserve film prints and other materials from the golden ages of Hong Kong cinema. As well as putting on retrospective programmes, the centre shows regular exhibitions on different aspects of film. Open daily except Thursdays, 10:00-20:00.

Kowloon Park
Tsim Sha Tsui
🚇 **Tsim Sha Tsui**
Map 15-C4

Hong Kong Heritage Discovery Centre

2208 4400 | *www.amo.gov.hk*

The Discovery Centre is housed in two old military buildings in the middle of Kowloon Park. It aims to educate the public about Hong Kong's archaeological and architectural heritage. To achieve this, thematic exhibitions are on display. It is open from 10:00 to 18:00, except on Sundays when it stays open until 19:00. Closed Thursdays.

10 Salisbury Rd
Tsim Sha Tsui
🚇 **Tsim Sha Tsui**
Map 15-D4

Hong Kong Museum of Art
2721 0116 | www.lcsd.gov.hk
Established in 1962, this museum aims to conserve the cultural heritage of China and promote local art. There are more than 14,000 items in its collection, including Chinese calligraphy and paintings. Open 10:00-18:00 daily except Thursdays. Admission $10.

100 Chatham Rd
South
Tsim Sha Tsui
🚇 **Tsim Sha Tsui**
Map 15-D3

Hong Kong Museum of History
2724 9042 | www.lcsd.gov.hk
Originally located in Kowloon Park, this museum now has its own purpose-built premises in which to tell the story of Hong Kong's development. The main exhibition includes over 4,000 items and uses multimedia displays and dioramas to vividly illustrate history. Other thematic exhibitions focus on particular aspects of Hong Kong's heritage. Set aside at least two hours to do it justice.
Adult admission is $10. Opening hours 10:00-18:00, except for Sundays when it stays open until 19:00. Closed on Tuesdays.

Hong Kong Museum of History

2 Caine Lane
Mid-Levels
🚇 **Sheung Wan**
Map 16-D2

Hong Kong Museum of Medical Sciences
2549 5123 | www.hkmms.org.hk
This privately-run museum is housed in the Old Pathological Institute which was built in 1906. Galleries in each room of the beautiful old building track the advances made in health in Hong Kong, including in times of plague. The grounds of the museum are planted with herbs often used in Chinese medicine. Opening hours: 10:00-17:00 Tuesdays to Saturdays, 13:00-17:00 Sundays, closed Mondays. Adult admission is $10.

Wong Nai Chung Rd
Happy Valley
🚇 **Causeway Bay**
Map 17-A2

Hong Kong Racing Museum
2966 8065 | www.hkjc.com
This museum overlooking the racecourse looks at the long history of horse racing in Hong Kong and the charitable activities carried out by the Jockey Club. One exhibit – the skeleton of the three-time champion horse 'Silver Lining' – lets you study the anatomy of a racehorse. The museum is open 10:00-17:00, except on racing days when it closes early at 12:30. Closed Mondays.

2 Science Museum Rd
Tsim Sha Tsui
🚇 **Tsim Sha Tsui**
Map 15-D4

Hong Kong Science Museum
2732 3232 | http://hk.science.museum
This four-storey facility covers a wide range of science subjects, from robots and communications to food science and meteorology. Two thirds of the exhibits require participation, so kids can learn through experience. It's open on weekdays 13:00-21:00 and on weekends 10:00-21:00. Closed Thursdays. Admission for adults is $25.

10 Salisbury Rd
Tsim Sha Tsui
🚇 **Tsim Sha Tsui**
Map 15-D4

Hong Kong Space Museum
2721 0226 | http://hk.space.museum
This planetarium was the first to bring the Omnimax film projector to Asia. As well as film shows, the dome-shaped museum has two exhibition halls focusing on astronomy and science. Admission is $10; Omnimax show $24. Open 13:00-21:00 weekdays and 10:00-21:00 on weekends. Closed Tuesdays.

195

10 Cotton Tree Drive
Central
🚇 **Admiralty**
Map 16-F2

Museum of Tea Ware

2869 0690 | www.lcsd.gov.hk
This branch of the Museum of Art occupies Flagstaff House in Hong Kong Park, which for many years was home to the Commander of British Forces. It is in fact the oldest colonial building still standing in Hong Kong. The collection includes exhibitions on Chinese ceramics and the art of drinking tea. A teahouse next door in the K. S. Lo Gallery wing serves tea and holds regular teamaking demonstrations. Opening hours: 10:00-17:00 daily, closed Tuesdays. The Teahouse is open 10:00-22:00 daily. Free admission.

27 Coombe Rd
The Peak
Map 16-F3

Police Museum

2849 7019 | www.info.gov.hk/police/hkp-home/english/museum
Located behind a public garden at the junction of Coombe Road and Stubbs Road, the Police Museum tells the story of the Hong Kong Police Force from Victorian times to today. There is a permanent display on the rituals and paraphernalia associated with triad societies. It's open on Wednesdays to Sundays 09:00-17:00, Tuesdays 14:00-17:00, and is closed on Mondays and public holidays. If you're feeling fit, you can walk up to the museum from beside the old post office on Queen's Road East.

Museums – Out of City

Other options **Tours & Sightseeing** p.209, **Heritage Sites – Out of City** p.193

45 Tung Tau Wan Rd
Stanley
Map 14-D2

Hong Kong Correctional Services Museum

2147 3199 | www.csd.gov.hk
Outside the forbidding walls of Stanley Prison you'll find the entrance to the Correctional Services Department's collection of artefacts relating to law and order. You won't be committing any crimes once you've seen some of the punishments meted out to former prisoners. One gallery focuses on the story of the Vietnamese boat people who were held in camps in Hong Kong for many years while awaiting settlement elsewhere. Open Tuesdays to Sundays 10:00-17:00.

1 Man Lam Rd
Sha Tin
Map 6-C4

Hong Kong Heritage Museum

2180 8188 | www.heritagemuseum.gov.hk
Opened in 2000, the Heritage Museum is modelled on the structure of a typical Chinese courtyard home, but on a much greater scale. The exhibitions; on subjects like Cantonese opera, Chinese art and New Territories heritage; are designed to be interactive. A special Children's Discovery Gallery introduces archaeology, history and the Hong Kong toy industry to the under 10s. This is the largest museum in Hong Kong and getting round to see all twelve exhibition galleries takes a long time. Opening hours are 10:00-18:00, except on Sundays when it stays open until 19:00. Closed Tuesdays. Adult admission is $10.

Murray House
Stanley Plaza
Stanley
Map 14-D2

Hong Kong Maritime Museum

2813 2322 | www.hkmaritimemuseum.org
Murray House used to be located in Central but the colonial edifice was taken apart stone by stone and rebuilt on the waterfront at Stanley. Its ground floor now hosts the new Maritime Museum which looks at South China's connection with the sea from prehistoric times up to the present day. Among other exhibits, a hands-on interactive game challenges you to pilot a huge modern ship through Victoria Harbour. Open 10:00-18:00 except Mondays. Adult admission is $20.

Hong Kong Railway Museum

13 Shung Tak St
Tai Po
Map 6-B1

2653 3455 | www.heritagemuseum.gov.hk
Steam trains used to make the journey from Tsim Sha Tsui to the border. Learn all about the early days of the Kowloon-Canton Railway at this small but charming museum. The old Tai Po station building acts as the exhibition hall, and is an exhibit itself, being the only station on the line built in Chinese style. Half a dozen coaches and locomotives are kept in sidings outside. Vendors used to wander through the high-ceilinged carriages selling beer – very different to the sterile commuter experience of today. Open 09:00-17:00 every day except Tuesdays.

Law Uk Folk Museum

14 Kut Shing St
Chai Wan
🚇 *Chai Wan*
Map 10-E4

2896 7006 | www.lcsd.gov.hk
Chai Wan nowadays is a roaring industrial suburb. But until fairly recently, it was a quiet rural bay inhabited by Hakka farmers. Only one village house – Law Uk – survives from that time, and it has been converted into a small museum. Farming implements, furniture and old photos make up an exhibition of rural life and local history. If you're wondering, 'Law Uk' simply means 'house of the Law clan'. Opening hours: weekdays 10:00-18:00, Sundays 13:00-18:00. Closed Thursdays.

Museum of Coastal Defence

175 Tung Hei Rd
Shau Kei Wan
🚇 *Shau Kei Wan*
Map 10-E4

2569 1500 | www.lcsd.gov.hk
Although one of Hong Kong's more recently opened attractions, this museum occupies part of the 19th-century Lei Yue Mun Fort. This cape overlooks the eastern approaches to Victoria Harbour, and as such it was a natural place to build coastal fortifications. The top-secret Brennan Torpedo was also installed at the water's edge to head off feared French and Russian attacks. Today, the central redoubt of the fort serves as a series of absorbing exhibition galleries, and a historical trail takes in some of the hillside batteries and other military relics. Open 10:00-17:00 every day except Thursdays. Adult admission is $10.

Sam Tung Uk Folk Museum

Kwu Uk Lane
Tsuen Wan
🚇 *Tsuen Wan*
Map 5-F4

2411 2001 | www.heritagemuseum.gov.hk
This Hakka walled village dating from 1786 was evacuated in the 1970s as Tsuen Wan new town sprang up around it. It has a classic symmetrical layout, with the clan's ancestral hall in the centre. Now restored, it's run as a small museum with a permanent display of village life and local history. Open 09:00-17:00 except Tuesdays.

Sheung Yiu Folk Museum

Pak Tam Chung
Nature Trail
Sai Kung
Map 7-B3

2792 6365 | www.heritagemuseum.gov.hk
Sometime in the 1800s, a Hakka clan built a small fortified village overlooking the kilns where they made lime. As this rural industry declined, the inhabitants moved out. Now, Sheung Yiu is a small folk museum holding an exhibition of rural life. It enjoys a beautiful location beside the mangroves of the Pak Tam Chung stream, close to the starting point of the MacLehose Trail. Open 09:00-16:00 except Tuesdays. Access: 15 minutes walk from Pak Tam Chung bus terminus.

Hong Kong Museum of History

197

Parks & Beaches

In a city as packed to the gills as Hong Kong, some kind of pressure valve is needed. Luckily the SAR has plenty of open space both in and outside the city. In urban areas there are large and small parks with good facilities. Above and around the city, much of the territory's green highlands and islands are protected by a system of 23 country parks which are easily accessible by public transport. If a sea breeze is more your thing, then you're spoiled for choice with dozens of beaches.

Beaches

Other options **Swimming** p.264, **Parks** p.201

The SAR's deeply indented coastline is blessed with a multitude of sandy shores. Water quality varies and is always better in the eastern waters, i.e. around Sai Kung and Clear Water Bay, because it is further from the Pearl River's silty estuary.

All beaches are open to the public at no charge. Some are run by the Leisure and Cultural Services Department (LCSD). These 41 gazetted beaches have lifeguards, showers, changing rooms and other facilities. Water temperature and quality is posted daily, and there is a flag system to indicate whether swimming is safe: a red flag means you should not enter the water. However, lifeguards are on duty only from April 1 to October 31 at most beaches. See www.lcsd.gov.hk/beach for details. Ungazetted beaches have few or no amenities, and no lifeguards. Remember to always take care when swimming: don't swim at night or alone, don't swim immediately after eating and watch out for strong tides.

How to Avoid Shark Attacks
Sharks visit Hong Kong waters only when the temperature rises above a certain point, and this rarely happens. Nevertheless shark prevention nets have been installed at most gazetted beaches. To stay safe, observe the following guidelines:
- Swim within the net area (marked by the red boomlines).
- Do not swim alone or in poor light.
- Do not swim if you are bleeding or if you have an open wound.
- Do not swim if the blue-and-white shark warning flag is hoisted.
- Always follow lifeguards' instructions.

Hak Pai Rd
Cheung Chau
Map 13-C3

Afternoon (Kwun Yam) Beach
2981 8472 | www.lcsd.gov.hk/beach

This is a regular meeting place for windsurfing devotees, and equipment can be rented here. It's where Lee Lai-shan, Hong Kong's only Olympic gold medallist, learnt her craft. As well as lifeguards, showers and changing rooms, there are cafes at either end of the beach. A small temple to Kwun Yam can be found up some steps at the southern end.

Big Wave Bay Rd
Shek O
Map 14-E1

Big Wave Bay Beach
2809 4558 | www.lcsd.gov.hk/beach

As its name suggests, this village beach is frequented by surfers, although Hong Kong waves are never very big, except during typhoons. You can rent boards and enjoy a barbecue at this beach, which also has showers and changing rooms. The village marks the end of the Hong Kong Trail.

South Lantau Rd
Lantau Island
Map 12-E2

Cheung Sha Beach
2980 2114 | www.lcsd.gov.hk/beach

There are two beaches here, Upper and Lower. Both have lifeguards and showers. Upper is Hong Kong's longest: 3km of powdery sand. Lower Beach on the other hand has more facilities, including two pleasant beachside restaurants and a small village. Plonk yourself down at a table here to enjoy sundowners while watching beach activities. The above number is for the Upper Beach. For the Lower Beach ring 2980 2674.

Parks & Beaches

Tai Au Mun Rd
Clear Water Bay
Map 11-A3

Clear Water Bay Beaches
2719 0351 | www.lcsd.gov.hk/beach
Connected to the MTR system by bus, this pair of beaches is the closest seaside escape for residents of Kowloon, and can be packed on weekends. The bay is scenic, surrounded by hills, and is often full of pleasure boats. Facilities include refreshment kiosks, lifeguards and changing rooms.

Island Rd
Shouson Hill
Map 14-C1

Deep Water Bay Beach
2812 0228 | www.lcsd.gov.hk/beach
Victoria Recreation Club and the Hong Kong Golf Club look out onto this narrow beach. Facilities include a Mediterranean cafe, showers, changing rooms and a barbecue area. The beach is especially popular with elderly morning swimmers and is the only one on Hong Kong Island with a year-round lifeguard. Its one drawback may be its close proximity to the road.

Sharp Island
Sai Kung
Map 11-A1

Hap Mun Bay
2796 6788 | www.lcsd.gov.hk/beach
This pretty beach is located on the southern tip of Sharp Island and is accessible by sampan from Sai Kung town. It has a lifeguard, changing rooms, campsite and barbecue area. It's busy on summer weekends.

Nr Yung Shue Wan
Lamma Island
Map 13-F2

Hung Shing Yeh Beach
2982 0352 | www.lcsd.gov.hk/beach
This beach is busiest at weekends when it is invaded by city dwellers, but its proximity to Yung Shue Wan means it is well used during the week too. It has lifeguards and full facilities, and a small hotel at the back of the beach serves food and drinks. The southern end features an organic herb garden with rabbits, chickens and an outdoor teahouse.

Nr Sok Kwu Wan
Lamma Island
Map 13-F3

Lo So Shing Beach
2982 8252 | www.lcsd.gov.hk/beach
One of Hong Kong's quietest gazetted beaches, this horseshoe bay is a little gem. Backed by trees, it has lifeguards and showers, and a barbecue spot on a rocky outcrop with lovely sea views. It's 15 minutes walk from Sok Kwu Wan ferry pier.

Beach Rd
Repulse Bay
Map 14-C1

Repulse Bay Beach
2812 2483 | www.lcsd.gov.hk/beach
Perhaps the most bustling of the city beaches, it sometimes seems as if everyone has decided to come to Repulse Bay on the same day. There are plenty of dining options to feed the hungry masses and, besides the usual showers and changing rooms, there is also a volleyball court. A kitschy statue garden can be found at the southern end.

Nr Shek O Village
Shek O
Map 14-F2

Shek O Beach
2809 4557 | www.lcsd.gov.hk/beach
The hill road to Shek O is so winding, and the village so ramshackle, it's easy to forget you're on the same island as Central and Wan Chai. It's a charming seaside spot with a large beach. Full beach facilities include a crazy golf course and plenty of parking.

Mui Wo
Lantau Island
Map 9-A4

Silvermine Bay Beach
2984 8229 | www.lcsd.gov.hk/beach
One of the most accessible beaches on Lantau Island is just a short walk from the ferry pier at Mui Wo. It has lifeguards, showers and changing rooms. There is a hotel behind the beach as well as small cafes and barbecue areas. At low tide, many people come to collect shellfish.

South Bay Rd
Repulse Bay
Map 14-C2

South Bay Beach
2812 2468 | www.lcsd.gov.hk/beach
Much quieter than Repulse Bay, this strand faces west and enjoys nice sunsets. The descent through the trees passes old bathing sheds. The beach has showers, changing rooms and a snack shop.

Wong Ma Kok Path
Stanley
Map 14-D2

St. Stephen's Beach
2813 1872 | www.lcsd.gov.hk/beach
A watersports centre is the focus of this small neighbourhood beach close to the Stanley military cemetery. As well as the usual facilities, there is a pier which has a Sunday ferry service to Po Toi.

Stanley Beach Rd
Stanley
Map 14-D2

Stanley Main Beach
2813 0217 | www.lcsd.gov.hk/beach
The venue for the annual Stanley dragonboat races is one of Southside's busiest beaches. It's just a short walk from the bus terminus and has changing rooms, showers and a fast food kiosk, but not much shade. The Hong Kong Sea School has its jetty at one end of the beach.

Sai Kung East
Country Park
Sai Kung
Map 7-E3

Tai Long Wan
This large bay has four ungazetted beaches: Sai Wan, Ham Tin Wan, Tai Wan and Tung Wan. Tai Wan is the longest; Sai Wan and Ham Tin Wan have tiny villages offering refreshments and limited lodgings. Facing southeast, with the tall spire of Sharp Peak watching over it, the bay receives a decent swell and is a popular hangout for Hong Kong's small surfing community. Access via Stage 2 of the MacLehose Trail.

Nr Hebe Haven
Sai Kung
Map 10-F1

Trio Beach
2792 3672 | www.lcsd.gov.hk/beach
This small beach is a popular stop-off point for junk trips. It has a lifeguard and shower facilities, and can be reached by sampan from Hebe Haven or by hiking from Hiram's Highway.

Cheung Chau
Beach Rd
Cheung Chau
Map 13-B2

Tung Wan Beach
2981 8389 | www.lcsd.gov.hk/beach
A short walk through the town from the ferry pier, this beach is popular but a bit stark, there is precious little shade to be had. It has lifeguards, showers and changing rooms, and there are snack shops nearby. There's an interesting view of Hong Kong Island from the beach.

Parks

Other options **Beaches** p.198

Absolute necessities in built-up areas, Hong Kong's urban parks are well used by the general population. Besides greenery, they contain facilities such as cafes, jogging tracks, sports pitches, swimming pools and play areas for children. There are no entry charges and below you'll find some of the most popular and attractive green spaces in the city. For more information visit www.lcsd.gov.hk, navigate your way to the English site, then click on the Parks link.

If you head out of the downtown area you'll find some challenging walks and breathtaking vistas. Hong Kong's highlands were originally saved from development by the need to safeguard water catchments. By the time Hong Kong started importing water from China, the public had come to realise the value of these untouched mountain areas, and a system of country parks was set up which now covers roughly 40% of the territory. Some of Hong Kong's most spectacular landscapes are found within the parks, all of which are crossed by hiking trails of varying difficulty. Country Parks Visitor Centres at popular entry points provide background information on geography, ecology and local culture, and trails have designated campsites and barbecue areas. See www.afcd.gov.hk for more information.

Access from Cotton Tree Drive
Central
🚇 *Admiralty*
Map 16-F2

Hong Kong Park

2521 5041 | *www.lcsd.gov.hk*
Formerly the site of Victoria Barracks, a British Army garrison, this park was opened in 1991 as a welcome green lung linking Central and Admiralty. A partly outdoor restaurant is surrounded by water features. Other attractions include an aviary, a tropical plant house and the Museum of Tea Ware (p.196). Several former military buildings can be found in the park. One is in high demand as a marriage registry; another houses the Visual Arts Centre, an exhibition and studio facility for artists. The park is open daily until 23:00, while the aviary closes at 17:00.

Kowloon Park Drive
Tsim Sha Tsui
🚇 *Tsim Sha Tsui*
Map 15-C4

Kowloon Park

2724 3344 | *www.lcsd.gov.hk*
Like Hong Kong Park, this green haven in the centre of crowded TST was originally a British army barracks. Its facilities are well used. There are several water features, a maze, a sculpture garden, sports halls and an outdoor swimming pool. As for wildlife, there is a flamingo pond and an aviary with 38 species of exotic birds. Martial arts displays take place every Sunday afternoon at the Sculpture Walk, and an arts and crafts fair is also held on Sundays at the Loggia from 13:00 to 19:00. Opening hours of the park are 06:00-24:00.

Kowloon Park

Carpenter Rd
Kowloon City
Map 15-E1

Kowloon Walled City Park

2716 9962 | *www.lcsd.gov.hk*
As its name suggests, this park stands on the site of a former walled city. The story behind it is intriguing. A fort was first built here in 1810, and was expanded following the British takeover of Hong Kong Island in 1841. By 1898, there were 500 troops stationed in the Walled City, which had become an important link in the chain of China's defences. In that year, the British moved in to take control of the New Territories, which included the Walled City. However, Qing officials continued to occupy the site and the British allowed them to stay. They were eventually expelled, but a legal

vacuum ensued, with neither Britain nor China exercising sovereignty over the City. By the 1960s, the City had evolved from a Qing fort into a sunless, high-rise slum full of opium dens, brothels and unlicensed dentists. It became a hideout for all kinds of criminals; the Hong Kong police were unwilling to bring prosecutions to Hong Kong courts for fear of causing a constitutional crisis with China. Finally, an agreement was reached in 1987 to demolish the City and build a park in its place.

During demolition, remains of the original Yamen (the fort's headquarters) were found, and the building has been restored. Some historical items are displayed inside and part of it is used as a teahouse. The park is laid out in the style of the early Qing dynasty, and includes several other relics which were salvaged – flagstones, cannons, lintels and the remains of the South Gate. The park is open 06:30-23:00.

Access via Taikoo Shing Estate
Taikoo Shing
🚇 **Tai Koo**
Map 17-E1

Quarry Bay Park
2513 8499 | www.lcsd.gov.hk

It's bisected by entry ramps to the Island Eastern Corridor, but this park deserves a mention since it has one of the few accessible harbour promenades. Hong Kong's first locally-built firefighting boat, the 500 tonne Alexander Grantham, was recently retired after 49 years of service and placed here as a public exhibit. The park is open 06:00-23:00.

Victoria Park Rd
Causeway Bay
🚇 **Tin Hau**
Map 17-B2

Victoria Park
2570 6186 | www.lcsd.gov.hk

A large green space between the typhoon shelter and the tram line, Victoria Park was laid out in 1957 and is the biggest park on Hong Kong Island. Facilities include tennis courts, lawns, a swimming pool, a roller-skating rink and a pool for model boats. It's open 24 hours and is especially busy on Sundays. The park is the venue for one of Hong Kong's biggest Chinese New Year fairs, when thousands of people come to buy flowers.

Mount Austin Rd
The Peak
Map 16-D2

Victoria Peak Garden
www.lcsd.gov.hk

This open space is built upon the granite foundations of Mountain Lodge, a former governor's summer residence which fell into ruin and was demolished after the war. As you ascend Mount Austin Road you pass the former gatehouse on your left. Built around 1902, it is being refurbished and will serve as a historical exhibition gallery. The garden enjoys exceptional views out towards Lamma Island, particularly from the lookout point. There is a refreshment kiosk.

A footpath called 'The Governor's Walk' is an alternative route back down to Harlech Road.

Access via Wah Fu Estate
Pok Fu Lam
Map 14-A1

Waterfall Bay Park
2551 0100

Before the founding of Hong Kong, British sailors en route to Canton or Macau used to call near the present-day Wah Fu to stock up on water. The cascade has been reduced to a trickle by upstream catchments and reservoirs, but the spot is now a narrow waterside park with barbecue areas, and it's worth a quick look as a rare example of a waterfall which falls directly into the sea.

Yuen Po St
Mong Kok
🚇 **Prince Edward**
Map 15-D1

Yuen Po Street Bird Garden
www.lcsd.gov.hk

At the end of Flower Market Road you'll find the entrance to the Bird Garden, a place where old men gather to show off their warbling feathered treasures. Shops sell birdfeed (including live crickets and grasshoppers), water bowls and beautifully made birdcages. Avian flu hysteria has given the garden a knock but as long as you don't handle the birds, you'll be fine. It's open 07:00-20:00.

Amusement Parks

Ocean Park, Hong Kong's long-established marine amusement park, now has competition in the form of Disney. Both vie for business from tour groups from mainland China as well as from locals and western tourists. Disneyland has two hotels on site, but Ocean Park isn't taking the challenge lying down – it has ongoing plans to build a trio of hotels beside the park's entrance.

Next to MTR Station
Lantau Island
🚇 *Disneyland Resort*
Map 9-C2

Hong Kong Disneyland

183 0830 | *http://park.hongkongdisneyland.com*

The economy was suffering back in 1999, and someone in the government had the bright idea of boosting tourism by spending public money to entice Disney to Hong Kong. The 126 hectare park, standing on reclaimed land at Penny's Bay, finally opened in 2005. It's similar in design to other Disney parks – there are themed areas such as Main Street USA, amusement rides, a fireworks show every evening, a nightly parade of Disney characters and, of course a Sleeping Beauty Castle. The park is smaller than other Disney parks, but is also cheaper, and more attractions are expected to open in due course.

The park has had trouble managing demand, and has attracted considerable criticism for it, so it is best avoided on public holidays and at other busy times. Admission is $295-350 for adults and $210-250 for children up to the age of 11. Opening hours are normally 10:00-20:00 but these vary.

Ocean Park Rd
Aberdeen
Map 14-B1

Ocean Park

2552 0291 | *www.oceanpark.com.hk*

Opened in 1977 and recently enjoying increased popularity, Ocean Park is an educational theme park occupying two sides of a coastal mountain. The headland and lowland areas are linked by a cable car which offers spectacular views of the land and sea below. Attractions include the Ocean Theatre, with dolphins and sea lions; a walk-through shark aquarium; a Giant Panda Habitat with two pandas; and plenty of adventure rides, including the Abyss Turbo Drop – a heart-stopping freefall experience. It's well worth at least half a day. The park is open daily 10:00-18:00, and ticket prices are $185 for adults and $93 for children.

In addition, the park has a separate conservation foundation which aims to help preserve the habitats of Asia's wildlife.

Ocean Park

203

Dragon Boat Races

Among the fastest growing team water sports, dragon boat races are traditionally held to commemorate the death of Qu Yuan, the patriotic Chinese poet, and it's the only sport to be celebrated as a National Holiday. The Hong Kong Tourist Board have worked hard to promote it worldwide, even donating boats to other countries. The sport is recognised internationally with governing bodies, and a range of racing distances from 200m sprints to 100km epics like the Three Gorges Dam Rally through the Hubei province of China.

When in Hong Kong, seeing these decorative vessels carve through the water is a must. During the festival you'll catch local races off Aberdeen and Stanley, and international events a week later off the coast of Sha Tin. There are several organisations and clubs where you can join the action (see p.239), but if you're happy to stay on dry land, watching is a big rush too and you'll fast become a fan.

Horse Racing

Other options **Horse Riding** p.247

With the exception of licensed mahjong dens, all gambling in Hong Kong is strictly monopolised and controlled by the Hong Kong Jockey Club. (Nobody bothers about those grannies playing cards in the park!). As well as horseracing, the Club controls football betting and the twice-weekly Mark Six lottery.

A night at the races can be a real thrill. Bets start off cheaply at $10, and the terraces offer clear views of the course. Meets take place on Wednesdays and Saturdays during the racing season, which runs from September to June. See p.209 for details of the Come Horse Racing tour. As well as the two racecourses, the Jockey Club operates off-course betting shops in every urban district. They are easily identified by the crowds of pencil-toting men surrounding them.

Wong Nai Chung Rd
Happy Valley
🚇 *Causeway Bay*
Map 17-B3

Happy Valley Racecourse

1817 | www.hkjc.com

Happy Valley has been echoing with the thud of hooves upon turf since the 1840s. Regular punters arrive in droves but you don't need to be an expert on racing form to enjoy yourself. Bets are cheap starting at $10, the terraces offer a great view of the track and there's food and drink available. Alternatively you can have it all organized for you by joining a horseracing tour (see p.209). Races take place once a week, usually on Wednesday evenings.

Tai Po Rd
Sha Tin
Map 6-D3

Sha Tin Racecourse

1817 | www.hkjc.com

Hongkongers love their horses. Opened in 1978 to reduce the pressure on Happy Valley, the Sha Tin Racecourse can accommodate more than 80,000 prospective punters. It has its own KCR station, which opens only on race days – Wednesdays and weekends during the racing season. Enclosed by the racecourse you'll find Penfold Park, a public garden open 09:00-17:00, except Mondays.
Access: KCR Racecourse Station, Sha Tin.

Landmarks

5 Edinburgh Place
Central
🚇 **Central**
Map 16-E2

City Hall
2921 2840 | www.lcsd.gov.hk

Hong Kong's first purpose-built performing arts venue played an important role in the development of local arts groups. Now in its 45th year, City Hall continues to host regular performances of all sorts. As well as a theatre, concert hall and exhibition galleries, the two-block complex has a well-regarded Chinese restaurant and a public library. It opens from 09:00 to 23:00.

1 Expo Drive
Wan Chai
🚇 **Wan Chai**
Map 17-A2

Hong Kong Convention & Exhibition Centre (HKCEC)
2582 8888 | www.hkcec.com

The HKCEC is Asia's largest convention venue outside Japan, with five exhibition halls, two ballroom-sized convention halls, two theatres and 52 meeting rooms. It also has six restaurants for delegates and visitors. It's continually busy with events year-round. The distinctive new wing, which extends over the harbour, was completed in time for the Handover ceremony which was held there in 1997. A tacky Golden Bauhinia statue on the promenade outside commemorates this event.

10 Salisbury Rd
Tsim Sha Tsui
🚇 **Tsim Sha Tsui**
Map 15-C4

Hong Kong Cultural Centre
2734 2009 | www.lcsd.gov.hk

Occupying a prime site on the TST waterfront, but curiously having no windows, the Cultural Centre is one of Hong Kong's largest performance venues. In addition to regular shows, free performances are often held in the foyer or on the outdoor piazza which faces the harbour. The centre is open from 09:00-23:00. The clock tower, which stands between the Cultural Centre and the Star Ferry, dates from 1915 and is the only surviving part of the former railway terminus.

55 Eastern Hospital Rd
Causeway Bay
🚇 **Causeway Bay**
Map 17-B3

Hong Kong Stadium
2895 7895 | www.lcsd.gov.hk

Built in 1994, this venue can accomodate 40,000 spectators. Music events are hampered by noise regulations, so it focuses on sports events such as football matches – Real Madrid and Liverpool are among the teams to have played here. In March each year, the Stadium hosts the Hong Kong International Rugby Sevens, the biggest fixture on the SAR's sporting calendar.

Garden Rd
Central
🚇 **Central**
Map 16-E2

Peak Tram
2849 7654 | www.thepeak.com.hk

This funicular railway was built in 1888 and has been carrying residents and visitors up The Peak's steep incline ever since. The scheme was initiated by a canny hotelier who found that sedan chairs were bringing insufficient numbers of guests to his establishment. It's an exciting but brief journey – you are high above the harbour before you have time to get comfy in your seat. There are four intermediate stations along the route but few people use them.

The tram operates from 07:00 to 24:00, with departures every 10 to 15 minutes. Adult fare is $20. The lower terminus is on Garden Road, Central, and a shuttle bus runs there from the Star Ferry Pier.

Tsim Sha Tsui
Promenade
🚇 *Tsim Sha Tsui*
Map 15-D4

Symphony of Lights & Avenue of Stars

3118 3000 | www.avenueofstars.com.hk

The sparkling jewel in TST's otherwise somewhat grimy crown is its harbour promenade, or at least the view from it. It's a 180° panorama of the Hong Kong Island waterfront, backed by a mountain ridgeline, and is most spectacular at night when neon lights are reflected in the harbour. A synchronised sound and light show – the Symphony of Lights – takes place every evening at 20:00, and this is the best place to appreciate it. Outside the New World Centre, a stretch of the promenade has been transformed into the Avenue of Stars, a Hollywood-style place paying homage to the celebrities of Hong Kong cinema. There's also a long-awaited bronze statue of Bruce Lee, probably Hong Kong's most famous icon.

Avenue of Stars

Natural Attractions

Wong Nai Chung Gap
Hong Kong Island
Map 17-C4

Wong Nai Chung Reservoir Park

Just downhill from Parkview, you can rent a pedal boat and join terrapins and ducks out on the water. There is a cafe beside the stone dam. The little reservoir was built in 1899 to supply the growing city far below.

You can set off from here for hikes into Tai Tam Country Park.

Aquariums & Marine Centres

Hoi Ha Village
Sai Kung
Map 1-F1

Hoi Ha Marine Life Centre

2328 2211 | www.wwf.org.hk

Located in the only marine park in Hong Kong which is accessible by road, the Marine Life Centre stands on stilts over the waters of Hoi Ha Wan. It is run by the WWF with the aim of increasing awareness about our endangered marine environment. The bay is home to more than 50 types of coral, which attract over 100 species of reef fish, and it has been protected since 1996. The centre's glass-bottomed boat allows clear viewing of this underwater world.

The centre is currently open only to students and teachers, and visits must be arranged in advance.

Alternatively, the Country & Marine Parks Authority runs free guided ecotours around Hoi Ha each Sunday and on public holidays. Tours start at 10:30 and 14:15 from the marine park warden post, are limited to 25 people each and are on a first-come-first-served basis.

Nature Reserves

In spite of its small size, Hong Kong is remarkably rich in biodiversity – it is home to one third of all the bird species in China, and over 230 types of butterfly. In addition to the very extensive country parks system, certain areas of forest, shoreline and wetland have been singled out for exceptional ecological value. These are managed by government bodies or wildlife organisations. Some have international significance – Mai Po, for instance, is listed as a globally-important Ramsar site for migratory birds. Most of these reserves can be visited.

Serving a different but complementary purpose, several wildlife education centres exist to bring nature closer to city people. Most country parks visitor centres have some display of local ecology.

Is getting lost your usual excuse?

Whether you're a map person or not, this pocket-sized marvel will help you get to know the city like the back of your hand... so you won't feel the back of someone else's.

Singapore Mini Map
Putting the city in your pocket

Abu Dhabi • Amsterdam • Bahrain • Barcelona • Dubai • Dublin • Geneva • Hong Kong • Kuwait
London • New York • New Zealand • Oman • Paris • Qatar • Shanghai • Singapore • Sydney

EXPLORER
www.explorerpublishing.com

Hong Kong Park

Nr Wetland Park LRT Station
Tin Shui Wai
Map 2-A4

Hong Kong Wetland Park

3152 2668 | www.wetlandpark.com

The development of Tin Shui Wai entailed the loss of many fishpond areas, and the Wetland Park was planned as part of environmental mitigation measures. It's intended to educate the public about the value of wetlands, and also to be an ecotourism destination in its own right. It borders the Mai Po marshes which are an important migratory site for birds. Open 10:00-17:00, closed Tuesdays. Admission is $30 for adults and $15 for kids.

Pak Ngau Shek, Lam Kam Rd
Tai Po
Map 5-F2

Kadoorie Farm and Botanic Garden

2488 1317 | www.kfbg.org.hk

This sprawling farm on the slopes of Kwun Yam Shan was established in the 1950s to develop agricultural improvements for poor farmers. Today, with agriculture in decline, its role has evolved towards the conservation of flora and fauna in Hong Kong and southern China. The farm operates a Wild Animal Rescue Centre with a veterinary hospital and takes in endangered species seized by customs officers. Certain areas of the farm are open to the public – you can visit an Amphibian and Reptile House, a Deer Haven, and a Raptor Sanctuary which houses birds of prey. There is also a Wildlife Pond, a Butterfly Garden, a Waterfowl Enclosure and an Insect House. On Sundays, the farm's own organic produce is on sale in the reception area. Opening hours are 09:30-17:00 daily, and there is an entry fee of $10 for adults.

1km N of Hebe Haven
Sai Kung
Map 6-F4

Lions Nature Education Centre

2792 2234

Once a government farm, this open-air centre just past Hebe Haven is designed to give city children a better understanding of nature. Outdoor displays include a fruit tree orchard, rock garden, herb garden, arboretum and dragonfly pond. Indoors there is an exhibition of traditional means of local agriculture. Other facilities include a cafe run by people with hearing disabilities. Open 09:30-17:00, closed Tuesdays. Access via Hiram's Highway.

Nort West New Territories
Map 2-C3

Mai Po Nature Reserve

2526 4473 | www.wwf.org.hk

Originally an area of seasonally-drained shrimp ponds at the Deep Bay mouth of the Shenzhen River, Mai Po is recognised as a bird migratory site of international importance and is managed by the World Wide Fund for Nature (WWF). Up to 68,000 birds spend the winter here before returning to their breeding grounds further north, and many are endangered species. The number of visitors is restricted and you need to apply in advance – call the hotline or download the application form from the WWF website.

Zoos & Wildlife Parks

Albany Rd
Central
🚇 Central
Map 16-E2

Zoological & Botanical Gardens

2530 0154 | www.lcsd.gov.hk

Lemurs, jaguars and orangutans share space with birds and reptiles in these gardens which were laid out in the 1860s. A very pleasant fountain terrace is popular with joggers and there is an aviary, greenhouse, bamboo garden and refreshment kiosk. Historical features include a statue of King George V and a memorial arch to Chinese soldiers. Most parts of the gardens close at 19:00, but the fountain area stays open until 22:00.

Tours & Sightseeing

Other options **Weekend Break Hotels** p.222, **Out of Hong Kong** p.217, **Activity Tours** p.210

You don't need to be a clueless group traveller to take a tour. If you have limited time, then they can be just what you need, delivering an array of worthwhile sights in a set number of hours. Tours in Hong Kong cover the gamut from shopping in the city to discovering heritage in the New Territories, and you can travel by bus, boat, limousine or even helicopter, depending on your preference and budget.

It's a good idea to update yourself with the latest packages before you make any reservations through travel agents or via hotel counters, and the information below will allow you to do this. Remember to look for licensed agents who are members of the regulatory Travel Industry Council of Hong Kong (TIC). The TIC guarantees a 100% refund within 14 days if you are not satisfied with the service given. See p.215 for details of Tour Operators.

The Hong Kong Tourism Board operates the Quality Tourism Services scheme; shops and restaurants signed up to the programme have been audited and found to provide clear pricing and genuine products.

If you have any concerns, you can seek assistance from the above two organisations (TIC 2807 0707; HKTB 2508 1234) or the Consumer Council (2929 2222). For more consumer information, please see www.tar.gov.hk/eng/tips/inbound.html.

Sightseeing & Shopping Tours

Hong Kong Island Tour

This tour gives you a view of the famous Victoria Harbour from The Peak, then takes you to the Aberdeen typhoon shelter, where you can watch the fishing community at work. On the way to Stanley Market, you can enjoy stop-offs at Repulse Bay and Deep Water Bay. This is recommended for first-time visitors to Hong Kong. Operated by Able & Promotion.

Come Horseracing Tour

Along with investing in IPOs, horseracing is one of the most popular Hong Kong pastimes. You can show up at the racecourse on your own, but a tour makes sure you're in the right places for views and excitement. Choose to place your bets at either the Sha Tin or Happy Valley racecourses. Morning and evening packages are operated by Splendid Tours & Travel on Wednesdays, Saturdays or Sundays during the racing season, which runs from September to June.

'The Land Between' Tour

Between urban Hong Kong and mainland China lies the fertile New Territories. This Gray Line tour showcases the enduring traditions of Hong Kong's rural hinterland. You'll get to see the Yuen Yuen temple complex, Tai Mo Shan, Luk Keng, a walled village at Fanling and the fishing village at Sam Mun Tsai, accompanied along the way by some great sea-and-mountain landscapes.

Kowloon Discovery Tour

Starting with a drive along Kadoorie Avenue, named after one of the city's wealthiest and most prominent families, you're then taken to the Tang-style splendour of Chi Lin Nunnery. After a visit to the Lung Cheung Road Lookout Point to view a panorama of Kowloon, you can stop by Shek Kip Mei Housing Estate and Apliu Street Market in Sham Shui Po for a taste of local street life. Operated by C&A Tours.

Little Wonder

Expats may feel they can't live without The *Hong Kong Explorer*, but it's a bit of a beast to hoist about while sightseeing. Fear not - despite the exhaustive amount of tourist information packed into its little pages, the *Mini Hong Kong Explorer* fits into even the teeniest back pocket. It's ideal to give to visitors, who may soon end up knowing more about Hong Kong than you do.

Sea & Land Tour

In the morning, jump on board a Chinese pleasure junk to see Hong Kong's beautiful skyline from the water, and watch the firing of the Noon Day Gun in Causeway Bay's typhoon shelter. After a lunch of dim sum, you can choose to go on a Hong Kong Island Orientation Tour or a Kowloon and New Territories Tour. Both are operated by Splendid Tours.

Hong Kong Back Garden Tour (Sai Kung)

This Jubilee International tour is a vivid meeting of old and new, as well as east and west. It starts off with a visit to the Che Kung Temple in Ho Chung, followed by a cruise to a local fishing village and then to the Hung Shing Temple on offshore Kau Sai Chau. Shopping and alfresco dining are waiting for you when the boat pulls up at the waterfront in Sai Kung town.

Kowloon & New Territories Tour

Specialist markets exist all over Kowloon, selling everything from clothes and jade to goldfish and flowers. Tell your guide what you want to buy and you should find fulfilment. This Splendid Tours trip then goes over the hills of Kowloon to the peace of the country parks. You'll see the Kam Tin walled villages, Lok Ma Chau and the Wishing Tree.

Helicopter Tours

An extravagance maybe, but a once-in-a-lifetime experience which you should try if you have the chance. With its vertiginous skyline, steep mountain ridges and hundreds of offshore islands, Hong Kong is a city which truly deserves to be seen from the air. Heliservices offers a range of sightseeing tours which fly over Hong Kong, the New Territories and Lantau Island; ranging in length from 15 minutes to an hour. Tours pick up from the rooftop helipad of The Peninsula in TST. See p.214 for more details.

Outdoor Adventure
In addition to the tour companies listed here, the firms featured in Team Building in the Activities section offer a range of tours and courses aimed at those who love the great outdoors. See p.280 for details.

Activity Tours

Other options **Tours & Sightseeing** p.209

Tai Long Wan

Tai Long Wan in Sai Kung is one of Hong Kong's finest beaches. Surfers flood in during the summer, but you should not miss out on what the area has to offer hikers. A full day of hiking, with unparalleled vistas over sparkling water and striking mountains, ought to top up your feel-good factor. And you can go for a swim afterwards. Operator: Natural Excursion Ideals.

Po Lin Monastery / South Lantau

After a ferry ride to Lantau, the largest island in Hong Kong, a bus journey takes you up to the dizzy heights of Po Lin Monastery, where you can pay your respects to the Big Buddha. After lunch, choose between a challenging trek around mountain peaks or a gentle walk downhill; both options end at Tai O, where local fishing people still live in stilt houses over the water. Operated by Walk Hong Kong.

Amah Rock / Che Kung Temple

A legend explains the landmark of Amah Rock. A fisherman's wife carried her baby daily to this spot to wait in vain for her drowned husband to come home. Finally, she was turned to stone. Hike this romantic trail above Kowloon and Sha Tin, which culminates in the towering outcrop of Lion Rock. This Walk Hong Kong tour offers fabulous views of not only beautiful natural scenery but also of the city far below, and also takes in one of Hong Kong's most popular temples.

Boat & Yacht Charters

Other options **Junk Trips** p.212, **Dinner Cruises** p.362

Tung Fong Bld, 151-155
Johnston Rd
Wan Chai
🚇 *Wan Chai*
Map 17-A2

Dragon Marine

9755 2146 | www.dragonmarine.com

Charter a yacht for your private or corporate party. Dragon Marine will organise the whole event and sail you away in luxurious surroundings to outlying islands or just out to sea. They can also supply speedboats, water-skiing or a live band to make your party rock.

Aberdeen Marina Club
Aberdeen
Map 14-B1

Simpson Marine Ltd

2555 8377 | www.simpsonmarine.com

Charter a yacht through this company and experience the same luxury as a five-star hotel. Cordon Bleu meals fit for a king are served on the aft deck; qualified watersports instructors are available to teach diving, waterskiing, jetskiing, sailing or windsurfing. Boats can be chartered in Asia, the Caribbean, the South Pacific or the Mediterranean.

Boat Tours

Pearl of the Orient Dinner Cruise

See Victoria Harbour from the Bauhinia, on which you can enjoy a buffet dinner, followed by an evening of music and dance, with a live band. The glittering city and harbour is a perfect backdrop. Nightly departures at 19:30 (from North Point ferry pier, Hong Kong) and 20:00 (from Hunghom ferry pier, Kowloon).

Symphony of Lights Cruise

The Guinness Book of World Records has declared the nightly Symphony of Lights to be the world's largest permanent sound and light show. The energy of colours and lights are accompanied by music and narration. Take a two-hour cruise aboard a traditional Star Ferry, and enjoy this spectacular multimedia show while catching the sea breeze.

Pearl By Night

Enjoy a western-style buffet dinner on a boat sailing around Victoria Harbour, followed by a trip up to the Mid-Levels to see the spectacular panorama of the city at night. This Able & Promotion tour ends at the Temple Street night market in Kowloon, where you can shop for gifts and souvenirs. Daily departures from selected hotel lobbies at 19:30-20:00.

Outlying Islands Escapade (Lamma Island and Cheung Chau)

The offshore islands provide a real change of pace to the city. This five-hour HKKF tour takes you away from the hustle and bustle to Cheung Chau, known for its bun festival and alfresco seafood restaurants. The itinerary includes the island's famous Pak Tai temple. A charter boat then delivers you to Lamma Island, where you can walk from Sok Kwu Wan to Yung Shue Wan, admiring great sea views along the way. Daily departure at 09:15 from Outlying Islands Ferry Pier No. 4, Central.

Cheung Chau Island Tour

This tiny dumbbell-shaped island is rich in local culture and traditions, and seeing its historical sites gives you an insight into Hong Kong's old way of life. You will visit the Pak Tai and Tin Hau temples, walk along Tung Wan Beach, examine ancient rock carvings and finally take a ride on a sampan – altogether, a great day out in the open air. Operator: Tiptop Tours.

Island-Hopping Pass

For convenience, you can buy a special pass which allows unlimited travel on New World First Ferry routes to the outlying islands. You can hop between Cheung Chau, Peng Chau and two points on Lantau Island, enjoying a day of sightseeing and alfresco dining, before heading back to the city. It's flexible – you can travel on any sailing you like. The pass comes with a free guidebook to help you get the most out of your island tour.

DIY Junk Trip

Several boat operators are willing to hire you a pleasure junk for the day, and it's up to you where you take it. A captain and skeleton crew are provided, and you're the navigator. There are dozens of islands, beaches and bays where you may weigh anchor, or you could simply make a circuit of Hong Kong Island, enjoying the breeze and views from the sun deck. A junk generally holds up to 30 people; get all your friends to bring food and drink for a great day out. Just make sure they are good friends, because you won't be able to leave halfway through the day. See below for more details.

Junk Trips

Other options **Dinner Cruises** p.362, **Boat & Yacht Charters** p.211

If at all possible, you must go on a junk trip while you're in Hong Kong. They are an extremely enjoyable and popular way to spend an afternoon. Junks, traditional style wooden boats, are hired for the day and make the perfect venue for a party, good food and a brief escape away from big city life. A skipper comes with the junk, so there are no marine skills to master. All you have to do is board and party. Some boats are more basic and you have to bring your own drink, while others are upmarket and cater for your every need. Sometimes, it is possible to drop anchor and swim to a remote beach and other trips will take you to restaurants on outlying islands.

Neich Tower
128 Gloucester Rd
Wan Chai
🚇 *Wan Chai*
Map 17-A2

Duk Ling Cruises

2573 5282 | *www.dukling.com.hk*
Used as the symbol of the Hong Kong Tourist Board, a trip on the Duk Ling ('clever duck' in Cantonese) is the ultimate in Hong Kong luxury. Chilled champagne cocktails, cold beer and cute canapés are all served on board for you to enjoy as you sail to Lamma Island, Lei Yu Mun or Po Toi for a seafood meal. Choose from Sunset Harbour Cruise on Thursdays, Sunset and Firework cruises on Fridays, and Outlying Islands Cruises on Saturday afternoons. The boat can also be personally or professionally chartered. Unsurprisingly, it all comes at a rather steep cost.

Hong Kong Explorer 1st Edition

Jaspas Party Junk

28 Staunton St
Central
Ⓜ *Central*
Map 16-E2

2869 0733 | www.jaspasjunk.com

Jaspas fusion restaurants in Central and Sai Kung (13 Sha Tsui Path) are well known in Hong Kong for their friendly service and great food. They also run junk parties (2792 6001 for bookings) with fully-equipped kitchens and wine and beer fridges. Each charter comes fully staffed with chef and waiters. You can start your party from Causeway Bay, Noon Day Gun, Sai Kung or Pak Sha Wan Pier. Their junks will hold up to 40 people, with a minimum booking for 14. As well as great food it is also possible to do waterskiing, wakeboarding and have a banana boat ride.

Mes Amis

83 Lockhart Rd
Wan Chai
Ⓜ *Wan Chai*
Map 16-F2

2527 6680 | www.mesamis.com.hk

Mes Amis has three very popular bars and also has its own party vessel. Their 44ft pleasure junk can accommodate up to 32 people and has a fully-equipped kitchen and stocked bar. Onboard staff will take care of partiers. To book, simply download the form from the website. A cost of $350 for each person includes food and drink.

Pana Oceans

Kai Tak Commercial
Bld, Des Vouex Rd
Central
Ⓜ *Central*
Map 16-E1

2815 8235 | www.panaoceans.com

They have a range of cruisers including a wooden junk which seats up to 33 people. It has the advantages of air conditioning and a karaoke machine. Catering can be provided and there is an extensive range of party buffet menus to select from.

Saffron Cruises

Yu Yuet Lai Bld
43-55 Wyndham St
Central
Ⓜ *Central*
Map 16-E2

2857 1311 | www.saffron-cruises.com

They have a range of vessels to choose from, including a traditional wooden junk with sails. The preferred catering on board is done by Gingers – a wonderful restaurant which serves high quality food. Each party can be tailored to suit your needs. They offer a buffet, barbecue, dinner or cocktail party. An alternative phone number is 9754 2928.

Sai Square Junks

Sai Square, Waterfront
Park
Sai Kung
Map 7-A4

2488 0611 | www.saisquare.com/junks

Based in Sai Kung, they offer junk packages to suit your requirements, with a variety of junks to choose from. You can have your party catered with an extensive menu. Their 'special' junk is 'Tanka' which can hold 18 people and comes with a high class chef. This is a five-star dining experience on the water. They are part of Sai Restaurant in Sai Kung and can arrange transport from Central to Sai Kung, if necessary. Fully-qualified boatman and waiting staff will be on board. Reservations can be made online.

Dolphin Watching

Hong Kong Dolphinwatch

Various locations

2984 1414 | www.hkdolphinwatch.com

Want to see the Chinese white dolphins up close? You'll find they actually appear pink, possibly due to blood rushing to their skin as they chase after fish. Join a Hong Kong Dolphinwatch excursion, which brings you to these endangered cetaceans' natural habitat around Sha Chau and Lung Kwu Chau islands. Dolphins are seen on over 97% of outings but, if there is no sighting, then you can join another trip free of charge. Tours operate every Wednesday, Friday and Sunday with a coach pick up at 08:30 from the main entrance to City Hall (facing Queen's Pier) or 09:00 at Kowloon Hotel Lobby in Tsim Sha Tsui. Bookings in advance are essential and payment must be made by cash or cheque at least one day before the trip at the Tsim Sha Tsim office. Please note there is no tour desk at the pick-up locations. The coach will take you to board a cruiser at 09:30 at Tung Chung New Pier, North Lantau and each tour lasts around two and a half to three hours. After the trip you will be taken back by coach to your original pick up point. Adults $320, children under 12 $160.

Helicopter Tours

Other options **Flying** p.243

The Peninsula
Tsim Sha Tsui
🚇 *Tsim Sha Tsui*
Map 15-D4

Heliservices Hong Kong Limited

2802 0200 | *www.heliservices.com.hk*

Heliservices operate from the rooftop helipad of The Peninsula Hotel, Tsim Sha Tsui, Kowloon and offer various tours, including a 15 minute journey around Hong Kong Island, 30 minute tours of Hong Kong Island, Kowloon and the Big Buddha, 45 minutes over Hong Kong Island and New Territories, and an hour around Hong Kong Island, New Territories, Lantau Island, including the Big Buddha and the Airport. Each helicopter takes up to five passengers and prices are for the charter of the helicopter regardless of the numbers. There are also special services such a Fly-and-Dine package, which includes a 15 minute sightseeing tour over Hong Kong, followed by dinner in one of The Peninsula's swish restaurants. The Heli/Seafood Tour takes you from The Peninsula out to Sai Kung Country Park for lunch at a traditional seafood restaurant. Personalised tours can also be arranged on request, and Helisevices will try to accommodate different pick up points when possible. Prices start from $4,250.

Heritage Tours

Hong Kong Traditional Lifestyles Tour

Try early morning tai chi as the antidote to hectic city life, then move onto feng shui appreciation at the Lantau Link Viewpoint. After a tea demonstration and practice at a local teahouse, you will have a new perspective on traditional Chinese culture. Every Monday, Wednesday and Friday at 07:30 (at The Excelsior, Causeway Bay) and 07:45 (at the YMCA, TST). Operated by Sky Bird.

Feng Shui Tour

'Feng shui' literally means 'wind and water' – it's an ancient system designed for man to live in harmony with nature. On this Sky Bird Tour, you will learn how its principles influence the local community, and how it has helped Hong Kong become a major financial centre. Examples will be drawn from the Tsing Ma Bridge, the Nine Dragons Wall and the architecture of Central. Tours depart on Tuesdays, Thursdays and Saturdays at 08:45 (from The Excelsior, Causeway Bay) and 09:15 (from the YMCA, TST).

Cantonese Opera (Behind the Masks) Tour

Cantonese Opera is more than just traditional music. It is a style of dance which employs graceful, stylised body movements and expressions. The Cultural Link Centre offers two tours that offer foreign language speakers the chance to appreciate the beauty and value of this very Cantonese art form.
In the first – 'Painting a face the Chinese Operatic Way' – you will be dressed in full costume and taught to pose by a professional photographer. In the second – 'Appreciation of Cantonese Opera' – you will be introduced to the music, face painting and acting techniques.

214

Tours Outside Hong Kong

Shenzhen City Tour and Lo Wu Shopping Mall Tour

The special economic zone of Shenzhen is separated from Hong Kong by just a river, but it really is another world. These tours give you a chance to experience life in modern, commercial China. At the Lo Wu Shopping Mall, you can put your bargaining powers to the test, but be warned the shopkeepers are far more practised than you are. You can also opt to include theme parks like Splendid China, the China Folk Culture Villages and Window of the World. Tours are operated by Gray Line and China Travel Service.

Macau Tour

In 2005, the historic centre of Macau was successfully listed as a World Heritage Site, making it the 31st site in China to be granted this status by UNESCO. Get a taste of the city's mixed Portuguese and Chinese legacy on a China Travel Service tour. You'll see the A-ma Temple, the ruins of St. Pauls, the Macau Tower and other unique attractions.

Main Tour Operators

Southgate Commercial Ctr
Tsim Sha Tsui
 Tsim Sha Tsui
Map 15-D4

Able & Promotion Tours

2544 5656 | www.able-tours.com

Able focuses on serving frequent individual travellers, employing the services of veteran tour guides. If you enjoy adventure and excitement, they can book you onto helicopter or speedboat tours.

Koon Fook Ctr
9 Knutsford Terr
Tsim Sha Tsui
Tsim Sha Tsui
Map 15-D3

C&A Tours

2369 1866 | www.cnatours.com

C&A offers French and German speaking tours as well as tours in English. Experienced tour guides pledge to provide the best experience possible; compensation is offered to any customers not satisfied with the standard of service.

CTS House, 78-83
Connaught Rd
Central
Sheung Wan
Map 16-F1

China Travel Service (Hong Kong)

2853 3533 | www.chinatravel1.com

Founded in 1928, CTS was the first Chinese-run travel agency. It's now one of the largest in the territory, with branches in Macau and Guangzhou. It specialises in tour arrangements for local residents, as well as overseas tourists, and can also assist in visa processing.

Cheong Hing Bld
72 Nathan Rd
Tsim Sha Tsui
Tsim Sha Tsui
Map 15-D4

Gray Line Tours

2723 1808 | www.grayline.com.hk

Gray Line has been in the travel industry since 1959. In that time it has built up a worldwide network covering 150 destinations, serving over 25 million travellers per year on six continents. Locally, it offers airport-hotel transfers and sightseeing tours in Hong Kong, Macau and China.

Far East Consortium
Bld, 121 Des Voeux Rd
Central
Central
Map 16-E1

Jubilee International Tour Centre

2530 0501 | www.jubilee.com.hk

With years of experience in providing recreational tours and boat trips, Jubilee's services also include cocktails, barbecue and buffet catering. The company has its own cruise vessels and coaches, and customers automatically receive safety insurance.

215

Hon Kwok TST Ctr, 5-9
Observatory Court
Tsim Sha Tsui
🚇 *Tsim Sha Tsui*
Map 15-D3

Sky Bird Travel Agency

2369 9628 | www.skybird.com.hk

Specialising since 1995 in services such as tours, travel arrangements and events management, Sky Bird places the emphasis on tailor-made tours that exactly match customers' needs.

Oterprise Square, 26
Nathan Rd
Tsim Sha Tsui
🚇 *Tsim Sha Tsui*
Map 15-D4

Splendid Tours & Travel

2316 2151 | www.splendid.hk

Splendid aims at providing foreign visitors with a wide range of local tour products in terms of sightseeing and cultural visits, as well as services in ticketing, hotel bookings and short trips to Macau and China. They are supported by a team of knowledgeable, friendly staff.

Star House
3 Salisbury Rd
Tsim Sha Tsui
🚇 *Tsim Sha Tsui*
Map 15-C4

Watertours of Hong Kong

2926 3868 | www.watertours.com.hk

Established in 1959, Watertours organises sightseeing cruises in the harbour or to the outlying islands on motorised, Chinese-style vessels which can carry up to 250 people. They are fully air-conditioned, guaranteeing a comfortable environment for tourists.

Other Tour Operators		
Cultural Link Centre	2541 0078	na
Harbour Cruise – Bauhinia	2802 2886	www.cruise.com.hk
Heliservices Hong Kong Limited	2802 0200	www.heliservices.com.hk
HKKF Travel	2815 6034	www.hkkf.com.hk
Hong Kong Dolphinwatch	2984 1414	www.hkdolphinwatch.com
Natural Excursion Ideals	2486 2112	www.kayak-and-hike.com
New World First Ferry Services	2131 8181	www.nwff.com.hk
Pana Oceans	2815 8235	www.panaoceans.com
Standard Boat Agency	2570 1792	www.standardboat.com.hk
Star Ferry	2118 6228	www.starferry.com.hk
Tiptop Tours & Travel	2366 7070	na
Viking's Charters	2814 9899	www.vikingscharters.biz.com.hk
Walk Hong Kong	9359 9071	www.walkhongkong.com

Out of Hong Kong

Other options **Weekend Break Hotels** p.222

Geographically, Hong Kong sits on the eastern edge of the Pearl River Delta, a fast-developing part of Guangdong Province. Its neighbouring cities are close and easy to get to, with an overlapping network of transport options. Just an hour away by train, ferry or bus; they are popular choices for a day trip or weekend break. Go during the week to avoid the crowds and to get better deals on hotels.

Ferry Good
The TurboJet ferry service between Hong Kong and Macau runs 24 hours a day, and the journey takes less than an hour. For details on fares and timings, visit www.turbojet.com.hk.

Macau

Hong Kong's sister SAR returned to Chinese control in 1999, two years after Hong Kong did. It's much smaller than Hong Kong but has a longer history of foreign influence. The Portuguese established themselves here from the 16th century onwards.

The city's economy is based almost entirely on tourism of one kind or another. Some tourists come for the roll of the dice; as the only casino city on Chinese territory, it has over a billion willing baccarat gamblers on its doorstep. Some come to make use of the city's hotels as an escape from the working week in Hong Kong. Others visit for the cuisine and to admire Macau's many historic buildings.

One man had a monopoly on Macau's casinos for much of the last half-century. That restriction has now been removed, and glitzy new gambling palaces are springing up all over the enclave. To add to the pizzazz, a Fisherman's Wharf entertainment complex has opened beside the ferry pier. The Macau Tower is another modern attraction worth a look – its glass-floored observation deck gives a giddying perspective of Macau and its surroundings. Cybernetic fountains in the Nam Van Lakes far below put on sound and light shows on weekend evenings.

Make a Copy
Travellers are officially required to carry their passport at all times in China, but losing it will cause serious trouble. Instead, just make a photocopy of the pages carrying your details and your visa, and carry that with you. Leave your passport in the hotel safe.

In noticeable contrast to Hong Kong, Macau has done well to balance modern development with heritage preservation. The streets are lined with Portuguese mansions, Chinese shophouses, churches and temples. The city centres on the Leal Senado, a Mediterranean-style cobbled square surrounded by elegant colonial buildings. Following narrow pedestrianised streets from here takes you to the ruins of St. Paul's, the surviving façade of a burnt cathedral which is one of Macau's best-known sights. Above it, the raised Monte Fort provides a cannon's-eye view over the city. The fort now houses the Macau Museum, which tells the story of the city's history and coexisting cultures in a very visual way – a visit here is recommended.

At the Maritime Museum to the west you can explore Macau's seafaring heritage. This is located near the A-Ma Temple at Barra Point, itself a living remnant of the local people's connection with the sea. Elsewhere in the central part of town, Guia Hill is topped by the oldest lighthouse on the China coast.

South of the city, two outlying islands are reached by means of bridges and causeways. Taipa, the nearest, is undergoing rapid development, but the original village remains untouched. It's popular for its restaurants. The Macanese House Museum here, located in a restored seafront villa, recalls the lifestyle of 1920s Macau.

Don't Go Changing

The Macau pataca is almost at parity with the Hong Kong dollar, and merchants in Macau will accept Hong Kong currency at equal face value, saving you the bother of changing money.

Coloane, the further island, retains more of a rural character than Taipa and has several beaches easily accessible by bus. The peaceful Coloane Village is a very attractive place to stroll around; attractions here include a Tam Kung temple, the chapel of St. Francis Xavier and boatyards which still build wooden junks.

Hong Kong expats rave about the food in Macau. It may be no better or worse than that available in Hong Kong, but the more relaxed ambience of Macau adds extra pleasure to the act of dining. All kinds of restaurants can be found but the city's unique cuisine is Macanese – a blend of Portuguese, Cantonese and African influences, which sprang from attempts by cooks imported from Portugal's African colonies to recreate traditional Portuguese dishes using locally available ingredients.

High-speed hydrofoil ferries run from Hong Kong to Macau 24 hours a day, mainly from the Macau Ferry Terminal at Sheung Wan but also from the China Ferry Terminal in TST. No visa is required for most nationalities; in most cases, you will be given 30 days upon arrival.

Fly Bye

It's much cheaper to fly to cities in China from Shenzhen than from Hong Kong, so some Hong Kong travellers cross the border to fly from Shenzhen's airport at Baoan.

Shenzhen

Twenty-five years ago, Shenzhen was a collection of small villages on a flood plain bordering the New Territories. Then, the Chinese government decided to designate it as one of the country's first special economic zones. Today's huge modern conurbation is China's richest city. It also hosts China's busiest border crossing. A city made up mostly of young migrants from all parts of the country, it's the only place in Guangdong where you'll hear Mandarin spoken more widely than Cantonese.

Most people travelling north from Hong Kong do so for the shopping. It's cheap, partly because many of the goods are knock-offs of famous brands but also because labour costs are low. Many people come to Shenzhen to be measured up for suits or dresses, or to have curtains made at a fraction of Hong Kong prices. Shenzhen merchants have wised up to this trade; many will now deliver to Hong Kong, saving you the hassle of a return visit.

It's not all shopping. Others visit for the golf – a series of courses north of the city extend over a vast area. Other attractions include theme parks such as Window of the World, a place where the world's most famous landmarks are recreated in miniature form; Splendid China, which does the same for China's heritage sites; and the China Folk Culture Villages, which showcases the architecture and cultures of the PRC's 55 ethnic minorities. There's a safari park – and a waterland resort spread over an area of lakes and fishponds. If you have a taste for the bizarre, you can visit Minsk World – a military-style theme park centred around a former Soviet aircraft carrier, which caused jitters when it was towed around the world to Shenzhen.

The city does have a reputation for petty crime, particularly around the downtown border area of Lo Wu; you ought to be on your guard at all times.

The simplest way to get to Shenzhen is by KCR; trains leave from TST in Kowloon. There are also bus services which use a different border crossing point, and there is a ferry service to Shekou district in the west. To enter Shenzhen you will need a Chinese visa. Prices vary depending on your passport. Certain nationalities can obtain a visa at the border but for others it is necessary to apply in advance.

Zhuhai

As Shenzhen is to Hong Kong, Zhuhai is to Macau – a special economic zone on the Chinese side of the border which has grown from nothing into a modern city since the 1980s. One difference is that urban Macau extends right to the border, so you can simply walk across into China. Hong Kong also has direct links to Zhuhai by ferry, from both the Macau Ferry Terminal in Sheung Wan and the China Ferry Terminal in TST. You'll need a Chinese visa to enter.

Zhuhai promotes itself as a garden city, with park areas and waterfront boulevards. Shijingshan Park has a cable car which climbs up to a vantage point overlooking the city and sea. The statue of the fisherman's daughter, offshore of Haibin Park, is often used as a symbol of the city.

The New Yuan Ming Palace is a full-scale replica of Beijing's ruined Old Summer Palace, set in extensive grounds. Folk performances are staged there daily. The Tang dynasty-style Chinese Medicine Valley offers bathing and traditional herbal medicine treatments. Sport attractions include several golf courses, plus the Zhuhai International Circuit, China's first permanent motor racing track which hosts both Formula 1 and Motorcycle Grand Prix races.

Zhuhai is also promoted as the 'city of a hundred islands' – this refers to the archipelago of small isles which extends far to the southeast and comes within Zhuhai's borders. These can in fact be seen from Hong Kong Island on a clear day. Some of the islands are inhabited, and you can make use of their ferry services to visit some beautiful sandy beaches.

The city is spread out, with the three main areas of Gongbei, Jida and Xiangzhou well separated from each other by hills. You'll need buses or taxis to get around.

To the west, hot springs have been developed into resort areas which are justifiably popular with visitors. Outdoor bathing pools are infused with essences of flowers, fruit and even wine. Further north of Zhuhai, Zhongshan is a riverside city with a well-preserved town centre reminiscent of old Macau. It's known throughout the country as the birthplace of Sun Yat-sen, the founder of modern China.

Macau

Weekend Breaks

Macau, Shenzhen and Zhuhai each have enough attractions to merit more than just a day trip. If you want to stay longer or if you simply need a pampering break from Hong Kong, then these hotels and resorts are worth checking out.

Weekend Break Hotels

Other options **Tours & Sightseeing** p.209, **Holidays from Hong Kong** p.224, **Hotels** p.31

1085 Heping Rd
Lo Wu District
Shenzhen

Best Western Shenzhen Felicity Hotel

+86 755 2558 6333 | *www.bestwestern.com*

On the banks of the Shenzhen River, opposite Hong Kong, the Best Western is a short stroll from Lo Wu KCR station. The 28-floor hotel offers over 500 guest rooms and suites, and can cater for up to 1,000 people at a time for exhibitions, seminars or banquets. The Orient Station Night Club and Fairy Land Club are at hand for entertainment, and there are private karaoke rooms, each of which is decorated in a unique style. The Best Western is a member of InterContinental Hotels and Resorts.

Shuiwan Rd, Gongbei
Zhuhai

Grand Bay View Hotel

+86 756 887 7998 | *www.gbvh.com*

Just a few steps away from the Jiuzhou ferry terminal, and in view of the Macau skyline, the modern Grand Bay View is easy to reach from either Macau or Hong Kong. It's close to the Gongbei border crossing, and 45 minutes drive away from Zhuhai International Airport. All rooms have safes and security locks and in-room broadband is available. Restaurants serve a cosmopolitan selection of cuisines and there is a full range of leisure facilities, including a swimming pool, fitness centre, massage parlour and sauna.

2-4 Avenida de Lisboa
Macau

Hotel Lisboa

+853 577 666 | *www.hotelisboa.com*

The distinctive Lisboa, long a landmark of Macau, has transformed itself into a city within a city aimed at catering to the needs of visiting travellers. It is not only a hotel but also the largest casino in the enclave, with the widest choice of round-the-clock games and slot machines. Apart from shopping for jewellery in the arcade, you can go for a workout at the fitness centre, have a makeover in the beauty salon or enjoy the nightly Crazy Paris Show.

Estrada Almirante
Marques Esparteiro,
Taipa Island
Macau

Hyatt Regency Macau

+853 831 234 | *www.macau.hyatt.com*

This Taipa Island resort offers a wide range of recreational activities in three acres of luxuriant greenery, including a large orchid-shaped swimming pool. To revive yourself after a good swim, choose from Macanese, Chinese and Portuguese cuisine. Afternoon tea in the Greenhouse is a pleasant way to relax close to nature. There is a fully supervised childcare centre where your children are looked after while you enjoy yourself.

Doumen Town
Zhuhai

Imperial Hot Spring Resort

+86 756 579 7128 | *www.imperial-hot-spring.com*

This popular resort to the west of Zhuhai, near Doumen, features over 20 open-air hot pools infused with various health-benefitting substances. The 70 degree waters come from two natural springs, and are rich in important minerals like manganese and zinc which help to improve the skin and relax the muscles. Firm-handed masseurs are on call to make sure all stress is dispelled from your body. Accommodation at the resort offers you the chance to indulge in Chinese dining or enjoy nightclub entertainment.

Jingdi Hotel

Yanmei Rd, Dameisha
Yantian District
Shenzhen

+86 755 2525 8888 | www.jingdihotel.com

If a spectacular sea view is on your shopping list, you'll find it at the Jingdi. The hotel is located close to Dameisha, a beach to the east of town with a reputation for pure sands and inviting sea. On-site restaurants serve European, Asian and Chinese cuisine, and you can enjoy drinks around the illuminated swimming pool at night. The hotel has full modern amenities, including a business centre, and is suitable for conventions.

Mandarin Oriental

956-1110 Avenida
Amizade
Macau
Map 16-E2

+853 567 888 | www.mandarinoriental.com

Located close to the jetfoil pier, the Mandarin has easy access to shopping, entertainment and transport. The spa centre is a haven of relaxation, set amidst tropical gardens with a landscaped outdoor heated pool and waterfall. Good sports and recreation facilities include a 20 metre swimming pool, an extensive sun deck, air-conditioned squash and tennis courts and a gym. The Mezzaluna and Dynasty restaurants specialise in Mediterranean and Chinese cuisine, while the hotel's main bar is a popular late-night hangout with live music.

Mission Hills Resort

1 Mission Hills Rd
Guanlan Town
Shenzhen

+86 755 2802 0888 | www.missionhillsgroup.com/en

The only five-star golf resort in China, Mission Hills is located in Guanlan, to the north of the city. It has 228 guest rooms and suites with private balconies overlooking the golf course. It's a good choice for family holidays, as well as a popular hangout for local celebrity golfers. Fine-dining Asian cuisine can be enjoyed at Imperial Court and Sasaki, while the Piano Bar and the member's lounge serve a range of beverages and snacks.

Nan Hai Hotel

1 Gong Ye 1st Rd
Nanhai Blvd, Shekou
District
Shenzhen

+86 755 2669 2888 | www.nanhai-hotel.com

With an open sea view, the Nan Hai has one up on other hotels in the Shekou district. Access to other parts of Shenzhen is easy with an efficient traffic network, and the ferry pier to Hong Kong is within walking distance. The Penthouse Grill, Hai Xu Restaurant and the lobby coffee shop provide a mix of eastern and western dishes, while evening entertainment can be found at Club Tropicana. Splendid China and other famous tourist spots are close by.

Paradise Hill Hotel

193 Shi Ching Shan Rd
Zhuhai

+86 756 333 7388 | www.paradisehillhotel.com

The Paradise Hill is located in the financial district of Zhuhai, with scenic views of both the sea and the Nantian mountains. There are over 200 rooms and suites of various types, including villa-style. Bars and restaurants serve European and Japanese dishes, or you can choose between Chinese regional cuisine such as Cantonese, Chiuchow and Sichuanese. There is an Executive Floor Lounge where you can make use of business facilities if necessary.

Pousada de Sao Tiago

Fortaleza de Sao Tiago
da Barra, Avenida da
Republica
Macau

+853 378 111 | www.saotiago.com.mo

Situated in the historic area at the tip of the Macau Peninsula, along the Praia Grande Bay, the Pousada occupies part of the 17th-century Barra Fort. The rooms are furnished in the traditional Portuguese style. Two restaurants, the Os Gatos and the Terrace, serve specialities from Portugal, Spain, Italy and Greece. The function rooms are available for conventions and western banquets. Complimentary services like pier transfer, currency exchange, secretarial services and tour arrangements are laid on to make your stay more relaxing.

1918 Estrada de
Hac Sa, Coloane
Island
Macau

Westin Resort

+853 871 111 | *www.westin.com*

The Westin is hidden away on the peaceful island of Coloane, surrounded by forested hills, overlooking the long expanse of Hac Sa Beach and benefiting from the South China Sea breeze. Elegantly designed rooms with spacious private terraces add to the sense of romance, making it a great getaway for couples. Café Panorama and Porto Bar provide fine Portuguese wines and cuisine. The adjacent Macau Golf and Country Club has an 18 hole golf course.

Yuehai Rd East
Gongbei
Zhuhai

Yindo Hotel

+86 756 888 3388 | *www.yindo-ohm.com*

The Yindo is the only five-star hotel in Gongbei, the hustle-and-bustle zone next to the border with Macau. It has around 300 deluxe rooms and suites of international standards. Seven restaurants, such as the continental Huntress Grill, serve innovative menus. Recreational facilities such as mini golf, bowling and sauna ought to help you unwind, and the night flea market just around the corner is highly recommended for street snacks and handicraft souvenirs.

Weekend Break Hotels

Name	City	Phone	Web
Best Western Shenzhen Felicity Htl	Shenzhen	+86 755 25586333	www.bestwestern.com
Grand Bay View Hotel	Zhuhai	+86 756 8877998	www.gbvh.com
Hotel Lisboa	Macau	+853 577 666	www.hotelisboa.com65
Hyatt Regency Macau	Macau	+853 831 234	www.macau.hyatt.com
Imperial Hot Spring Resort	Zhuhai	+86 756 5797128	www.imperial-hot-spring.com
Jingdi Hotel	Shenzhen	+86 755 25258888	www.jingdihotel.com/eng/index.html
Mandarin Oriental	Macau	+853 567 888	www.mandarinoriental.com
Mission Hills Resort	Shenzhen	+86 755 28020888	www.missionhillsgroup.com/en
Nan Hai Hotel	Shenzhen	+86 755 26692888	www.nanhai-hotel.com
Paradise Hill Hotel	Zhuhai	+86 756 3337388	www.paradisehillhotel.com
Pousada de Sao Tiago	Macau	+853 378 111	www.saotiago.com.mo
Westin Resort	Macau	+853 871 111	www.westin.com
Yindo Hotel	Zhuhai	+86 756 8883388	www.yindo-ohm.com

Hong Kong's busy streets

"It's that Volkswagen feeling!"

It Gets Me.

I can't quite say why I'm so madly attracted to my Volkswagen. It's like we share an uncommon passion. Sure, it feels so safe and sound on the road, while also looking sleek and styled on the outside. It also feels nice and comfortable on the inside, too!
But it's really more than all that. It's another dimension. A real connection – it's like a soul mate. I guess I can say it's the ONE for me. So why do I always go for a Volkswagen? Because it simply gets me.

For the love of automobiles

Holidays from Hong Kong

Hong Kong is a big air transport hub and its people make good use of those connections to fly frequently. The following destinations are all within a few hours' flight of Hong Kong, and if you're staying here for any length of time you should check a few of them out. Short-haul flights are often inexpensive. Even cheaper deals may sometimes be found with the budget airlines flying out of Macau, but remember to add on the cost of return jetfoil tickets.

Flight time: 3.5 hours
Time difference:
1 hour ahead
Best time to visit:
Oct – Apr

South Korea

A rash of popular films and TV series have brought Korean culture to the fore in Hong Kong, and more people are travelling north to enjoy the Confucian heritage and peppery food of the hermit kingdom. Besides the bustle of modern Seoul, it's also an outdoor adventure destination, with established mountain trails and winter ski slopes.

Flight time: 2 hours
Time difference:
none
Best time to visit:
Sep – Dec

Shanghai

The most commercial-minded city in China is expanding at breakneck pace, with a full complement of futuristic towers facing the historic facades of the Bund, and the world's first Maglev train in operation between the city and the airport. Stroll down the busy shopping artery of Nanjing Lu, take a sightseeing cruise along the Huangpu River or enjoy trendy restaurants and bars in the restored old quarter of Xintiandi.

Flight time: 3.5 hours
Time difference:
none
Best time to visit:
June – Sep

Beijing

China's capital is gearing up for the 2008 Olympics in a big way, with new stadiums and performance venues replacing the age-old hutong districts of courtyard houses. Ancient attractions like the Great Wall, the Temple of Heaven and the Forbidden City remain big tourist draws and you shouldn't really leave China without seeing them. Don't forget to try the Peking duck.

Flight time: 4.5 hours
Time difference:
1 hour ahead
Best time to visit:
Feb – Apr; Oct – Nov

Japan

A perennial favourite among Hong Kong travellers, Japan is visited for its ski slopes and its irresistible pop culture. Stretching from the snow-bound hills of Hokkaido to the sun-soaked isles of Okinawa, it offers all kinds of holiday options. Tokyo is one of the most striking, and expensive, cities on the planet, but as well as an excess of shopping and dining choices it has ancient temples and exquisitely designed gardens.

Flight time: 3 hours
Time difference:
1 hour behind
Best time to visit:
Sep – Feb

Thailand

Spa addicts flock to Thailand to make use of luxurious beachside facilities, but a trip to the Land of Smiles could equally involve trekking among hill tribes in the north or simply enjoying the steaming buzz of urban Bangkok. Easygoing people, stunning scenery and truly wonderful food make this a must-do destination. Direct flights go to Phuket as well as Bangkok.

Flight time: 2 hours
Time difference:
1 hour behind
Best time to visit:
north Sep – Apr; south Dec – Mar

Vietnam

Vietnam had a late start as a tourist destination but its charm has put it on the fast track to popularity. An ancient culture is tempered with traces of French colonial architecture and food, and fertile, green deltas give way to boisterous market towns and cities. It's a long, narrow country with beaches on one side and forest-clad mountains on the other. Major destinations are Hanoi in the north and Ho Chi Minh City (formerly Saigon) in the south.

Flight time: *3 hours*
Time difference:
1 hour behind
Best time to visit:
Nov – Feb

Cambodia

The forgotten jungle temples of Angkor Wat have long been a major draw for tourists and, as Cambodia rebuilds after decades of conflict, the country is starting to appear on travellers' to-do lists. Phnom Penh, the charmingly sleepy capital, should not be overlooked; there are waterways to explore in the interior and beaches along the coast.

Flight time: *2 hours*
Time difference:
none
Best time to visit:
Sep – Nov

Taiwan

Largely an unknown quantity to most outsiders, Taiwan has mountain resorts, beach towns, friendly people and a scenic east coast. Taipei, the dynamic capital, is the site of the National Palace Museum, by far the world's greatest collection of Chinese cultural treasures. It's a good place to brush up your Mandarin.

Flight time:
3 hours
Time difference:
none
Best time to visit:
Sep – Apr

Philippines

Seven thousand tropical islands make a wealth of choices for a beach holiday, but most Hong Kong travellers head for a tried-and-tested handful of palm-fringed isles; these include Boracay, Cebu and Palawan. Diving and watersports are popular pastimes, and English is widely spoken. Flights go direct to some resort destinations; for others, you'll need to pass through the chaotic capital of Manila.

Flight time:
4 hours
Time difference:
none
Best time to visit:
Year-round

Singapore

Hong Kong has a love-hate relationship with its competitor city-state to the south. While the two try to outdo each other in business derring-do, Hong Kong citizens are frequent visitors to the tiny Lion City. Singapore is clean, well organised, and everybody speaks English among a multitude of other tongues, so it's an easy introduction to Asia. The city looks after its heritage well, and it's deservedly famous for its food, which is easily accessible in hawker centres.

Travel Agencies

Any Tour Enterprises	2369 7251	www.anytour.com.hk
China Travel Services (HK)	2853 3533	www.chinatravel1.com
Gray Line Tours	2723 1808	www.grayline.com.hk
Hong Thai	2534 0500	www.hongthai.com
Oriental Travel	2865 2618	www.orientaltravel.com
Splendid Tours & Travel	2316 2151	www.splendid.hk
Wing On Travel Services	2852 6868	www.wingontravel.com

Flight time:
5 hours
Time difference:
none
Best time to visit:
Year-round

Indonesia

This vast archipelago stretches along the equator for what seems like forever; from the southern tip of Thailand to the northern edges of Australia. Its islands range from heavily populated Java to barely explored Papua; from giant Borneo to tiny Bintan. While mostly Muslim, it has a Hindu heritage which is most clearly seen in Bali, a beach destination rich in art and culture. Flights go direct from Hong Kong.

Singapore

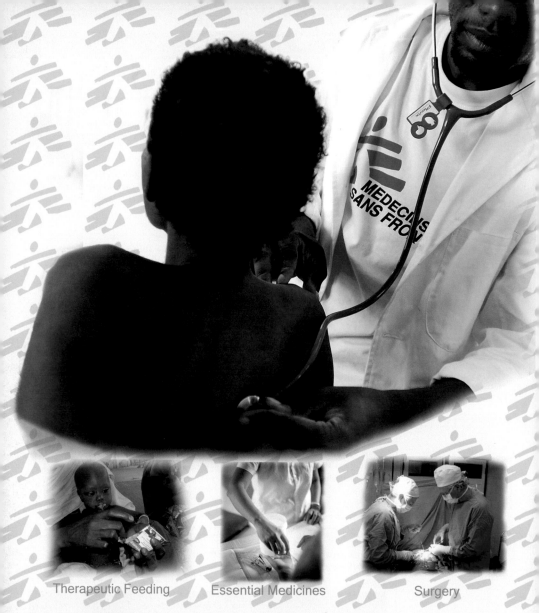

Therapeutic Feeding   Essential Medicines   Surgery

MEDECINS SANS FRONTIERES

أطـبّـاء بـلا حـدود

Providing emergency medical
relief in over 70 countries.

help us help the helpless

Activities

Activities

Sports & Activities

Although Hong Kong is known as a shopper's paradise, there are plenty of other ways to spend your time. The city is very built up and heavily populated, but Hong Kong does have many green areas for outdoor activities such as hiking and biking, as well as

world-class golf courses and sports facilities for everyone. The government has invested heavily into tennis courts, basketball courts, swimming pools and many open spaces to encourage people to follow a fit and healthy lifestyle, in what can often be a stressful place to live. There are some fantastic private clubs that offer wonderful food and stunning sports facilities, rather like a five-star hotel. Surrounded by water, Hong Kong has clean and safe public beaches open throughout the year and many people enjoy watersports such as sailing, windsurfing, or just taking a junk trip to soak up the scenery and fine food.

There are official sports leagues and clubs for almost every sport you can imagine. Most have a website which gives up-to-date information on meetings, venues and fixtures for each season. The website of the Sports Federation and Olympic Committee of Hong Kong has a page giving details of NSAs (National Sports Associations), with details and links to websites of official HK sporting bodies and associations. Visit www.hkolympic.org, find your way to the English site and then click the 'NSAs Directory' link.

Activity Finder

Aerobics & Fitness Classes	229	Golf	243	Singing	260
Archery	229	Hashing	246	Skateboarding	261
Art Classes	230	Hiking	247	Skiing & Snowboarding	262
Basketball	232	Hockey	247	Social Groups	262
Bird Watching	232	Horse Riding	247	Softball	264
Bowling	233	Ice Hockey	248	Surfing	264
Camping	233	Ice Skating	249	Swimming	264
Chess	233	Kids' Activities	249	Team Building	265
Climbing	234	Kitesurfing	250	Tennis	266
Cookery Classes	235	Language Schools	250	Triathlon	266
Cricket	235	Libraries	252	Wakeboarding	266
Cycling	236	Martial Arts	252	Water Polo	267
Dance Classes	236	Mother & Toddler	253	Windsurfing	267
Diving	238	Mountain Biking	256	**Sport & Leisure Facilities**	
Dragon Boat Racing	239	Music Lessons	256	Sports & Country Clubs	268
Drama Groups	240	Netball	257	**Well-Being**	
Fencing	241	Paintballing	257	Beauty Salons	270
Fishing	241	Rollerblading/Skating	257	Hairdressers	270
Flower Arranging	242	Rugby	258	Health Spas	272
Flying	243	Running	258	Pilates	275
Football	243	Sailing	258	Stress Management	276
Frisbee	243	Salsa Dancing	260	Yoga	276

Hong Kong Explorer 1st Edition

Aerobics & Fitness Classes

Other options **Pilates** p.275, **Yoga** p.276

Aerobics and fitness classes are available all over Hong Kong. In some cases the classes are run by the sports and country clubs and membership is necessary, although not always. It is a good idea to contact the clubs to check their regular schedules and membership rules (see p.268). As with a lot of things in Hong Kong, they love their rules.

Another option is to try the hotels. Again though, the gym and fitness facilities (many of which are superb) are likely to be reserved for guests staying at the hotel, or those that have paid to join the hotel's health club.

If joining an expensive club is beyond your budget, there are independent fitness centres and gyms all over the place. Most require a commitment to join for one year, and then a payment for each class is required as and when you take advantage of it, but there are those that have drop in classes available. Some of the gyms also offer deals just after Christmas when everyone is full of turkey and resolutions.

Talk To Us...

In preparing this first edition of the Hong Kong Explorer we scoured the SAR in an effort to bring you all the activity info you could possibly need. However, if your club or organisation isn't listed and you'd like a mention next time around, just drop us a line and we'll give you a shout in the second edition. Visit www.explorerpublishing.com and click on Reader Response to share your thoughts, ideas, and unbridled praise. And while you're on the website, why not check out the rest of our product range. From visitors' guides and maps to photography books and restaurant guides, Explorer has a cracking collection of products just waiting for you to buy!

Archery

Koon Fook Ctr
9 Knutsford Terrace
Tsim Sha Tsui
🚇 *Tsim Sha Tsui*
Map 15-D3

Hong Kong Archery Centre

2739 8969 | *www.hk-archerycentre.com*

The Archery Centre is actually a shop that has a short range where you can test and tune your archery equipment. There is extensive stock on offer, together with seasoned professionals to offer advice. There is also an archery clinic where you can get tips on how to improve your aim, set up your equipment accurately and ensure your shot is straight.

Kei Lung Wan Service
Reservoir
Pok Fu Lam
Map 14-A1

Hong Kong Island Archery Club

9801 0830 | *www.archery.com.hk*

This friendly, yet competitive, members club has an open lawn range with eight to ten lanes and a maximum practice distance of 70m. Opening hours are 15:00 to 18:00 on Saturday and public holidays; and 09:00 to 13:00 on Sunday. Unfortunately, there are no parking or washroom facilities at the range. Membership needs to be approved, although you don't always have to join to participate in training courses at elementary level. Most courses are conducted in Cantonese, although there are some bilingual coaches.

Lung Mun Rd
Tuen Mun
Map 4-F3

Tuen Mun Recreation and Sports Centre

2466 2600

Tuen Mun Recreation and Sports Centre is a public sports centre with a 70m archery range for group or individual use. However, it is important to note when booking that qualified supervision of the range is required. The Centre regularly organises training courses and archery competitions.

Art Classes

Other options **Art Galleries** p.189,
Art & Craft Supplies p.285

Various locations

Anastassia's Art House
2719 5533

Anastassia runs workshops for children and adults at Clearwater Bay Country Club, Clearwater Bay Primary School and Hong University of Science and Technology (HKUST). Anyone can enroll on the courses and access into the venues is then arranged. There are two adult classes, one on Monday mornings (10:00-12:00) in oil painting at HKUST, and the other on Tuesdays (11:00-13:00) in watercolour painting at Clearwater Bay Country Club.

123 Wellington St
Central
Central
Map 16-E2

Art Jam
2541 8816 | www.artjamming.com

What is an art jam? It's nothing to do with strawberries or blackcurrants, it's an opportunity to get together with a group of people and painting materials, not forgetting the music and optional food and drink, and create a painting. You can art jam with your friends by reserving a time for your own personal art jam party, or you can turn up and art jam during their regular sessions from Tuesday to Friday 14:00 to 21:00, or Saturday from 14:00 to 02:00 or Sunday from 13:00 to 18:00. Art Jam also offers portable art jamming parties for private events or launch parties.

Portwealth Ctr
83 Queen's Rd East
Wan Chai
Wan Chai
Map 17-A2

Chameleon Workshop
2527 2251 | www.chameleonworkshop.com

Eleanor McColl (mobile number 9048 1592) is an artist who runs courses for children and adults. The courses are in blocks which need to be paid for in advance. The children's courses are to give them experience in all aspects of art, and hopefully nurture a life-long love of art. Some of the courses for adults include oil painting, sculpture, life drawing, acrylic painting, collage and printing, as well as sketch tours once a month and paint parties for a minimum of eight and maximum of 12 people.

Goldfield Ind Ctr
1 Sui Wo Rd
Sha Tin
Map 6-C4

Ji-Kiln Studio
2787 5544 | www.i-kiln.org.hk

Ceramics courses are offered and conducted in English or Cantonese depending upon requirements. The teachers are experienced artists from local or overseas universities. Beginners in ceramics can take an eight-week course covering basic hand-building techniques and glaze application. More advanced courses in throwing and raku firing are available for the more experienced.

24 Hollywood Rd
Sheung Wan
Sheung Wan
Map 16-D1

Klei Pottery Studio
2526 8567

Pottery lessons in eight-week sessions take place throughout the week: on Wednesdays and Fridays they're from 14:00 to 17:00, on Tuesdays and Fridays from 18:00 to 21:00, Saturdays 10:00 to 13:00, and Sundays 14:30 to 17:30. Classes include throwing, handbuilding and glazing techniques.

Walk For Your Art

If you like art, then you'll love the annual Hong Kong ArtWalk. The concept is quite simple – you buy a ticket, and then on the night you start at any of the participating art galleries (50 galleries took part in 2007). After viewing the art on display, and enjoying a glass of wine and some light bites, you move onto the next gallery, taking whichever route you choose. Tickets can be bought from the participating galleries, and you're advised to get them early because the ArtWalk is always a sell-out. The event usually takes place in March, and all money raised goes to a designated charity. See www.hongkongartwalk.com.

Small but indispensable…

Perfectly proportioned to fit in your pocket, these marvellous mini guidebooks make sure you don't just get the holiday you paid for, but rather the one that you dreamed of.

Explorer Mini Visitors' Guides
Maximising your holiday, minimising your hand luggage

Abu Dhabi · Amsterdam · Bahrain · Barcelona · Dubai · Dublin · Geneva · Hong Kong · Kuwait
London · New York · New Zealand · Oman · Paris · Qatar · Shanghai · Singapore · Sydney

EXPLORER
www.explorerpublishing.com

Fringe Club
Central
Central
Map 16-E2

Pottery Workshop

2525 7949 | www.ceramics.com.hk

The Pottery Workshop is a studio offering space for local and overseas ceramics artists to exhibit their work. They also offer regular courses in ceramics for different levels and students and children of varying backgrounds. Occasionally, overseas artists are invited to give talks and demonstrations.

Basketball

Basketball is extremely popular. The sport takes up a relatively small space and just about every public housing estate or small town has at least one basketball court. They are busy places, and usually become social, as well as sports areas. Serious games take place in organised leagues.

Winway Bld
50 Wellington St
Central
Central
Map 16-E2

Asia Basketball Academy

2975 4104 | www.eteamz.active.com

Asia Basketball Academy works with the Hong Kong National Team and also organises basketball development coaching sessions to teach basic skills and drills beyond the level of street basketball. Tim Darling, coach, is available during school holidays for one-on-one and team basketball classes. Darling has worked with the Hong Kong National Team since 1998 and his CV can be found on the Asia Basketball Academy site.

Shek Tong Tsui
Municipal Bld, 470
Queen's Rd West
Sai Ying Pun
Map 16-C1

South China Basketball League

9639 0397 | www.scbleague.com

This is a well organised league with more than 25 teams who play at indoor courts located near Central. Their games are year-round, usually once a week for each team. There is a newly established mixed division and there will soon be a kids' division. Most players come from an international background and most divisions have a height restriction of 6' 2". For further information call David on the above mobile number.

Birdwatching

Hong Kong Park
Central
Admiralty
Map 16-F2

Early Morning Birdwatchers

2853 2566 | www.lcsd.gov.hk/parks

This is a free service organised by the Leisure and Cultural Services Department in conjunction with the HKBWS for those interested in bird watching. Sessions take place between 08:00 and 10:00 every Wednesday morning. The meeting point is Hong Kong Park Conservatory. Contact on the above number or 2521 5059.

Various locations

Hong Kong Bird Watching Society

www.hkbws.org.hk

For a very modest fee you can join this society and get really involved in birdwatching. Hong Kong is famous for large numbers of Easter Palearctic waders and the Territory regularly attracts species that are rare in Britain or North America. They organise regular interesting activity trips for members around Hong Kong throughout the year which are led by experienced locals. The trips will sometimes be to China or other areas in the region. They even offer discounts on new ornithological book titles. This Society is very much into conservation and has been responsible for setting up the HKBWS China Conservation Fund with an aim to raise money for this purpose. They have a 'Birdline' in both English and Cantonese for the latest bird news: 2667 4537 (English speaking) and 2465 6690 (Cantonese speaking).

Bowling

There are numerous ten pin bowling alleys around the territory, some are public and some are attached to private clubs such as the Hong Kong Club and the Kowloon Cricket Club. Go along for fun or join a league if you are serious, it is an Olympic sport after all.

Bowling Alleys

Name	Address	Area	Telephone	Number of Lanes
Belair Bowling Centre	Belair Garden Shopping Arcade	Sha Tin	2649 9022	18
Dragon Bowling	Amoy Plaza	Ngau Tau Kok	2116 1536	18
	Yan Oi Tong Centre	Tuen Mun	2452 2119	30
Mei Foo Super Fun Bowl	95C Broadway	Lai Chi Kok	2742 5911	24
Olympian Super Fun Bowl	18 Hoi Ting Rd	Yau Ma Tei	2273 4773	22

Camping

Other options **Outdoor Goods** p.310

It is possible to camp in Hong Kong as there are small designated sites in most of the country parks offering 'basic facilities', such as a toilet and a barbeque pit. During public holidays, particularly Lantern Festival in September, people want to get away from the city and enjoy the stars, so many of the beaches and islands become crowded with tents and campers. Some more hardy types, especially those on long hikes, camp away from the designated areas off the main trails on higher areas of land. Whenever or wherever you decide to go you will have to carry everything on your back – there are no campsites where you can park a car and then set up next to it. Chalet-style accommodation can be found in one or two of the holiday camps and the country parks. These, again, are basic, with a shared kitchen area. They are often used by school parties and can be booked by groups or individuals at a reasonable cost.

What to Take

You should consider taking the following equipment:

- Tent
- Lightweight sleeping bag
- Thin mattress (or air bed)
- Torches and spare batteries
- Coolbox
- Water (always take too much)
- Camping stove, or BBQ and charcoal
- Firewood and matches
- Insect repellent and antihistamine cream
- First aid kit (including personal medication)
- Sun protection (hats, sunglasses, sunscreen)
- Jumper/warm clothing
- Spade
- Toilet rolls
- Rubbish bags (ensure you leave nothing behind)
- Navigation equipment (maps, compass, GPS device)
- Mobile phone (fully-charged)

Chess

1102 Wilson Hse
19-27 Wyndham St
Central
 Central
Map 16-E2

Chess School

2899 9240 | www.chessschool.com

Classes in chess are held from Monday to Sunday on a flexible basis at Wyndham Street, or there are other organisations around Hong Kong who have chess teachers registered with Chess School, such as YMCA, Clearwater Bay School and The American Club. They have courses for people of all levels, which include a 30 minute lesson, and 30 minutes of playing time. The usual ratio is six to one, and places are limited. Classes are allocated according to age and level.

233

Climbing

Rock climbing in Hong Kong is unique – there is something to satisfy any rock climber's wish, be it long multi-pitch routes on Lion Rock and Kowloon Peak, or seaside bouldering on Chung Hom Kok and the hills of Tsuen Wan. The high ratio of beautiful urban landscapes within such close proximity to each other is hard to match anywhere else in the world.

The main areas for climbing in Hong Kong are Lion Rock (15 routes or so, 250ft high and can be done in two to five pitches) and Kowloon Peak (a couple of hundred routes scattered over the mountain), while Beacon Hill, Tung Lung Chau, Central Crag and Braemar Hill are great for bolted single pitch climbing (120ft maximum). There are also plenty of undeveloped crags to be explored, and a fair bit of climbing on Sai Kung Peninsula. Furthermore, since Hong Kong is the 'Heart of Asia,' there is plenty of opportunity to climb in both established and untouched regions of South East Asia, such as Yangshuo in Guangxi, China or Krabi, Thailand. For those who want to sharpen and strengthen their skills for when they get on a real rock face there are some artificial climbing walls of various levels.

With such a variety of climbing, Hong Kong has a strong climbing community, and finding partners is no problem whatsoever. The website www.hongkongclimbing.com is a simple and effective way to do it, with links to numerous climbing gear and guide suppliers as well. Accessibility to climbing and bouldering areas is easy; most are just a five to 40 minute walk from civilisation, and all areas can be reached by public transport: taxi, bus or ferry. Climbing during weekdays is normally quiet while weekends can get quite busy, particularly in areas like Tung Lung and Beacon Hill. Most importantly of all – climbers must make sure they pick up their rubbish!

Jct of Texaco Rd &
Sha Tsui Rd
Tsuen Wan
Map 5-F4

Boulderland

perry_tong@hotmail.com

A high quality, private gym with good facilities and bargain rates. For serious, disciplined climbers who have had previous training. Non-members can accompany members on Monday, Tuesday and Thursday evenings (except public holidays). Contact via email.

22-28 Kennedy St
Wan Chai
🚇 *Wan Chai*
Map 17-A2

Climberland

2893 6479

A superb wall with many boards, which are mainly horizontal. There is also a system and a campus board. The facility is particularly suited to those with a little more climbing experience. Open between 14:00 and 23:00, Monday to Saturday. The cost is $30 each visit or $300 for 12 visits.

Radio City
505 Hennessy Rd
Causeway Bay
🚇 *Causeway Bay*
Map 17-B2

Hong Kong Sport Climbing Union

6019 8344 | www.hkscu.org

This is an official club for those interested in sport climbing. They offer advice on climbing on crags around Hong Kong as well as the various climbing walls available. They also offer some basic courses for those who have no experience in rock climbing but would like to start.

30 Luck Hop St
San Po Kong
Map 10-C1

Kai Tak East Sports Centre

2326 9940

A small indoor facility with a 7m high wall, open from 07:00 until 23:00. To climb here you need to already have the Hong Kong climbing qualification, as they don't provide instructors. The fee is $47 for one hour.

234

290 Nam Cheong St
Sham Shui Po
Map 10-B2

Shek Kip Mei Park Sports Centre
2784 7424 | www.lcsd.gov.hk

The second highest artificial outdoor wall in Hong Kong (15m high, 16m wide), with eight lanes, this is cccasionally the venue for youth climbing competitions. Elementary climbing training courses are run four times a year by the Hong Kong Mountaineering Union (2504 8124, www.hkmuorg.hk), priced $180.

Shun Lee Tsuen Rd
Kwun Tong
Map 10-D2

Shun Lee Tsuen Sports Centre
2951 4136

This venue is an outdoor wall with a glass roof, reaching 12m high with ceiling. Level two training courses are run here by the Hong Kong Mountaineering Union (2504 8124, www.hkmu.org.hk) four times a year, for a fee of $350.

Salisbury Ctr
Salisbury Rd
Tsim Sha Tsui
🚇 **Tsim Sha Tsui**
Map 15-C4

YMCA
2260 7000 | www.ymcahk.org.hk

They have an indoor climbing wall open to people of all ages once they have successfully passed a basic climbing assessment task. If you are a complete beginner there are courses offered regularly to help you pass the assessment. After that you can use the wall at any time.

22 Gascoigne Rd
Jordan
🚇 **Jordan**
Map 15-D3

YMCA King's Park Centenary Centre
2782 6682 | www.kpcc.ymcahk.org.hk

At 18m high and 16m wide, and providing over 300 sq m of terrain, the climbing wall here is the largest in Hong Kong. There are approximately 15 routes up the wall, and 30 climbers can use it at the same time. Just as with the indoor wall at the YMCA in TST, new climbers must complete a simple assessment prior to use. Cost is $80 per session.

Cookery Classes

1 MacDonnell Rd
Mid-Levels
🚇 **Admiralty**
Map 16-E2

YWCA ESMD
3476 1340 | www.esmd.ywca.org.hk

Cooking classes to learn how to cook dishes such as Thai, Peruvian, Indian, Japanese and Vietnamese are offered at the YWCA regularly. They are held during the afternoons and evenings, so you should find a time to suit you. The sessions are two hours long. Prices vary from approximately $200 to $500, depending on the ingredients you need.

Cricket

Cricket is played seriously and regularly throughout the season (September to April) in Hong Kong and there is an organised league and numerous clubs. The grass wickets available are at Hong Kong Cricket Club and Kowloon Cricket Club and there are other artificial surfaces where games are played. The Hong Kong Cricket Association is the governing board and it is necessary to register with them if you want to play in the league. Most international schools from primary to secondary have teams and there are women's teams too.

Olympic House
1 Stadium Path
So Kon Po
🚇 **Causeway Bay**
Map 17-B3

Hong Kong Cricket Association
2504 8102 | www.hkca.cricket.org

If you are interested in playing cricket at league level you must register with this association. This is simple to do, just download the membership application form from their website. There is an annual subscription or you can opt to pay a lifetime membership fee. League matches are played at weekends. Saturday League consists of 17 teams who play each other once per season. They compete in the Saturday Cup. The Sunday League is made up of seven teams and is more serious, following ICC International rules. There are also regular coaching and training sessions organised for umpires. Visit their website to find out about all cricket clubs in Hong Kong.

Cycling

Other options **Sporting Goods** p.315, **Mountain Biking** p.256, **Cycling** p.236

Olympic House
1 Stadium Path
So Kon Po
 Causeway Bay
Map 17-B3

Hong Kong Cycling Association

2504 8176 | www.cycling.org.hk

This is the official cycling association of Hong Kong and they are responsible for organising major events throughout the year including road races, indoor cycling and track races. They also have connections with BMX and mountain biking. Hong Kong itself hosts a stage of the annual Tour of South China Sea race. The races are efficiently organised and there are categories for men, women and juniors of various age groups.

Dance Classes

Other options **Salsa Dancing** p.260, **Music Lessons** p.256

The Helena May
Central
Central
Map 16-E2

Carol Bateman School of Dancing

2525 3751 | www.cbsdhk.com

This is Hong Kong's oldest ballet school. Many students of this school have gone on to participate in the Hong Kong Ballet or teach in some of Hong Kong's leading dance schools. All teachers are qualified in the Royal Academy of Dance method. There are classes for children from age 3 upwards and graded examinations are taken. Adult ballet classes are also offered as well as Pilates to improve flexibility. The two other locations are 1/F 204 Prince Edward Rd West in Kowloon (2397 4769), and the Music Room at Sha Tin Town Hall (2397 4769).

69 Jervois St
Sheung Wan
Sheung Wan
Map 16-E1

Dansinn Dance Studios

2581 1551 | www.dansinn.com

Group or private lessons in all the ballroom dance styles are available in this spacious studio. Group lessons are scheduled in 12 week courses, but you can take them to fit around your own schedule. So, if you need to learn to dance before your wedding, Dansinn is the place!

V.Heun Bld
138 Queen's Rd
Central
Central
Map 16-E2

Feather Motion Dance Club

2815 4555 | www.arthurmurrayhongkong.com

Feather Motion is an Arthur Murray franchise, opened in March 2006. They offer classes in traditional ballroom dancing such as the fox trot, waltz and quickstep as well as more upbeat rhythmic dances like the cha cha, rumba, jive and salsa. Your first class is free so you can have a taste of what's to come. If you want to dance at your wedding they have a class for that too.

60 Blue Pool Rd
Happy Valley
Map 17-B3

Hong Kong Ballet School

2573 7398 | www.hkballet.com

Hong Kong Ballet School has an education department which runs courses and exhibitions for schools and individuals who have an interest in dance. The courses will suit different ages and levels of experience and are updated regularly.

236

Hong Kong Highlanders Reel Club

Hong Kong Cricket Club
Happy Valley
Map 17-C4

2574 6266 | *http://personal.cityu.edu.hk/~eljyoung/reelclub.htm*

For beginners to advanced dancers there is a regular Monday night meet from 19:00 to 22.00. The first hour is for easy dances, followed by more challenging stuff for advanced levels. It's not compulsory to be Scottish but you do need soft-soled shoes, dance shoes or sports shoes. The meetings are held at Hong Kong Cricket Club and members get special rates. For further details call Joseph Schembri (2761 6884) or Jean Young (2788 9991).

Jean M Wong School of Ballet

Various locations

2886 3992 | *www.jmwballet.org*

This is a prestigious ballet school which offers courses in classical ballet linked to the Royal Academy of Dance syllabus. They have classes for experienced dancers of all ages and also for adults and teenagers with no previous training. Venues are in North Point (2886 3992), Happy Valley (2577 2112), Caine Road (2869 6288), Kowloon (2754 2277), Kowloon Bay (2756 8226), Tsuen Wan (2498 2345), and Sha Tin (2697 0188).

Lead and Follow

Various locations

8203 3313 | *www.leadandfollow.com*

Lead and Follow offers classes in tango for all levels, taught in English and Cantonese. Their teachers run courses at different dance studios around Hong Kong. No previous experience or partner is necessary. Check the website for the latest schedule and for information about where each course takes place.

Oasis Dance Centre

Anton Bld, 1 Anton St
Wan Chai
🚇 *Admiralty*
Map 16-F2

2522 6698 | *www.oasis-dance-centre.com*

The signature dance at Oasis is belly dancing. They have classes and a 'Bellyjam' every day and specialise in Middle Eastern and Indian Bollywood moves. As well as dancing it's a great workout. Wear comfortable clothes and bring a scarf for the hips.

Ones to Watch Dance Company

2 Austin Ave
Tsim Sha Tsui
🚇 *Jordan*
Map 15-D3

2376 2133 | *www.onestowatch.com.hk*

This dance studio is really friendly and offers modern dance classes with young talented instructors throughout the week. Classes on week days start around 17:30, while on weekends they are earlier. They run eight-week courses for beginners to advanced level, or just drop in to the open classes to suit your own schedule. Hip hop, jazz funk, pop jazz, popping & locking, house, breaking, street jazz – they've got it all.

Southern School of Dance

Various locations

2555 6917 | *www.southernschoolofdance.com.hk*

This school operates in locations around Hong Kong and the New Territories, including Wong Chuk Hang, Kowloon and Hong Kong Cricket Club. They offer classes for children in pre-primary ballet, primary classical ballet, grade 1 to 8 classical ballet, jazz dance and tap dance. The dance studios are spacious and modern. Courses run throughout the school term and there's also a summer school which is very popular, so it's best to register early. Contact Managing Director Marion Knight on the number above, or Sadhdb McKarrick on 2555 6917.

The Helena May
Central
🚇 **Central**
Map 16-E2

Tango Tang

8209 0520 | www.tangotang.com

This is the Hong Kong Tango Club, an organisation which promotes and practises tango in Hong Kong. There are weekly practices on most days. They have regular dance workshops by experts from Hong Kong and overseas that are open to all members.

1 MacDonnell Rd
Mid-Levels
🚇 **Admiralty**
Map 16-E2

YWCA ESMD

3476 1340 | www.esmd.ywca.org.hk

The English Speaking Member's Department (ESMD) of the YWCA offer several dance classes, such as Latin, basic social dancing for couples, clogging and jazzercise. Check the schedule at the ESMD website to find out dates and times of courses offered throughout the year.

Diving

Despite the polluted harbour, reclamation works and busy shipping lanes, Hong Kong has many beautiful areas to go diving. There are lots of marine parks and even some coral reefs in Hong Kong's New Territories, where you can spot anemonefish, angelfish, barracuda, crab, coral trout, cuttlefish, lionfish, octopus, scorpionfish, yellowtail jacks, moray eels, trumpetfish, pufferfish, grouper and a variety of nudibranchs. On rare occasions you may see rays, barracuda, cuttlefish and lobster on the same dive.

Various locations

Asiatic Marine

2104 2297 | www.asiaticmarine.com

If you are big, rough and tough, plus a qualified diver, this company arranges shark diving expeditions for divers interested in studying and working with sharks for conservation, filming or research purposes. Chain mail Neptunic suits are provided (phew!) and all safety procedures and risks assessed. Underwater filming tuition and assistance in underwater photography techniques are given. Contact Managing Director Charles Frew MSc on the above number, or his mobile 9831 5410.

30 - 32 Robinson Rd
Mid-Levels
🚇 **Central**
Map 16-D2

French Divers

2523 5268 | www.frenchdivers.com

This company offers diving courses at all levels starting with children aged 8, right up to adult instructor level. Courses can be tailored to suit individuals or groups and their aim is to have a 100% exam pass rate. Courses can be carried out in your own pool before progressing to open water. For further information contact the above number, or 9501 0748. And no, you don't have to be French.

Various locations

Hong Kong Underwater Club

www.hkuc.org.hk

This is Hong Kong's oldest diving club, catering specifically for qualified divers who are fit to dive and have qualified with officially recognised training agencies. New members are welcome to go on their regular dives and social events. Dive trips leave from a variety of places around Hong Kong including Aberdeen Boat Club, Wong Chuk Hang in Aberdeen and in the New Territories from Tso Wo Hang, near Sai Kung and Tai Mei Tuk, Tolo Harbour near the western side of Plover Cove. The club can be contacted via email – info@hkuc.org.hk.

Various locations

Marine Divers

2656 9399 | www.marinedivers.com

This club organises both diving and training trips. Most introduction courses are in the USRS pool in Kowloon. They are a branch of the BSAC diver training agency, so all courses are well-run and safe. You will get your certification/qualification immediately. It is possible to hire equipment so you don't have to commit to buying all the gear until you become an expert. Experienced divers meet for ocean dives in Hong Kong as well as overseas trips. For more information call the number above or 9194 0221.

Various locations

South China Diving Club
www.scdc.org.hk

This non-profit diving club is part of the British Sub Aqua Diving Club, and welcomes new members, whether they are qualified as a BSAC diver or not. They emphasise continuous self-improvement and offer many skill development courses. Training is held at the Stanley Ho Sports Centre, Sha Wan Drive, Pok Fu Lam between May and October from 19:30 to 20:30. They have dives most weekends around Hong Kong waters which are sometimes family-friendly and include time on a beach. Every Thursday, they meet at 20:00 at the Aberdeen Boat Club for a drink and a chat, and they also organise other regular social events.

Hong Kong Marina
Sai Kung
Map 6-F4

Splash Hong Kong
2792 4495 | *www.splashhk.com*

Dive courses run by English speaking, qualified PADI Instructors and Dive Masters with years of experience under their weight belts. You can learn to dive and receive certification in small groups of no more than five. Courses start with PADI Open Water Course and go through to Rescue Diver. All equipment is included in the price of the course. Contact Damon Rose, Master Diving Instructor/Commercial Diver on the above number or mobile 9047 9603.

Dragon Boat Racing

Dragon boat racing in Hong Kong is part of a traditional festival dating back centuries and commemorates the death of Qu Yuan, a minister from 340 to 278BC. It takes place in May and June, and training starts one or two months before the big day, depending on how serious the teams are. Almost every organisation has a team. Bus drivers, schools, software companies, doctors, you name it. On race day the events are over quite quickly with prizes such as whole roast pigs to tempt the teams to the finish lines. It is a really colourful cultural event as the boats are brightly decorated to represent dragons. The boats are long and have paddlers sitting side by side while a drummer at one end keeps the rhythm.

Some say it is the training that can be the most rewarding. The unity achieved as 16 to 22 people hone their skills and strength while paddling around the beautiful outlying islands dotted around the South China Sea is definitely an experience worth trying. However, don't be fooled into thinking this is a romantic way to explore the sea, it is serious business. If you are ready to commit to a team there are many willing to train you up to the required standard. Most have an official coach who will not be taking things lightly, so be prepared to sweat.

Olympic House
1 Stadium Path
So Kon Po
 Causeway Bay
Map 17-B3

Hong Kong Dragon Boat Association

2504 8 332 | www.hkdba.com.hk

This is the controlling body for all dragon boating in Hong Kong. All clubs and teams are part of the association, as are other individuals who simply love the sport. The association's aim is to preserve the traditions of dragon boat racing while promoting the present-day practise of the sport. It organises and trains a top-level team to send to overseas competitions, including the World Dragon Boat Championships. They also train umpires and coaches. The website has a calendar of races and events, plus details of how to get involved.

Victoria Recreation
Club
Deep Water Bay
Map 14-C1

Hong Kong Island Paddle Club

www.hkipc.com

HKIPC was established 12 years ago and is one of Hong Kong's most successful dragon boat clubs. It has won the Stanley Residents Association dragon boat race several times. Unlike many other clubs, their paddling season never ends. From January to June they train and race dragon boats in international competitions held in places such as Penang and Macau, as well as in numerous local fisherman and dragon boat races. From July to December they paddle and use outrigger canoes (a seagoing canoe) to take part in distance races in local waters, Hawaii and Micronesia – plus an expedition to Macau. HKIPC also organises its own annual Deep Water Bay dragon boat race, held in May. The club welcomes new members.

96 Stanley Main St
Stanley
Map 14-D3

Stanley Residents Association

2813 0564 | www.dragonboat.org.hk

The Stanley Residents Association was originally created to develop the community spirit of the fishing village of Stanley through recreational and sporting events. The annual dragon boat race then became such a popular event, they decided to set up the Stanley Dragon Boat Association and focus on promoting the sport in Hong Kong and across the world, with regular workshops for dragon boat officials. To get involved contact Connie Cheng on the above number.

Drama Groups

1 Gloucester Rd
Wan Chai
 Wan Chai
Map 16-F2

Academy for Performing Arts

2584 8500 | www.hkapa.edu

The Academy runs dance and drama classes on a part-time basis, evenings and school holidays (as well as full-time courses for enrolled students). It's quite serious and auditions have to be passed for entry onto some courses, depending on the level.

Aberdeen Marina
Tower, 8 Sun Wan Rd
Aberdeen
Map 14-B1

Colour My World Youth Theatre

2580 5028 | www.colour-my-world.com

This theatre group involves children and adults and offers a great variety of drama and art workshops. No previous experience is necessary, but you will be required to take an audition in a friendly, non-intimidating atmosphere before you are accepted for a production.

Various locations

Faust International Youth Theatre

2547 9114 | www.faustworld.com

This drama group for all ages is run by Faust World (which also offers creative writing courses, French and Spanish lessons and even maths lessons). It is very popular among expats. The ability to speak English is essential to register. They put on at least two productions a year and run auditions, after which rehearsal schedules can be quite demanding – though always fun. Payment and commitment is required for one term at a time.

Hong Kong Players

On Cheong Factory Bld
19 Tai Yip St
Ngau Tau Kok
Kowloon Bay
Map 10-D2

2331 2005 | www.hongkongplayers.com

This community theatre group takes its work seriously and many regular talented amateur actors are involved. New members are encouraged to join and apart from producing shows, Hong Kong Players is a busy social organisation as well. The Social Secretary (social@hongkongplayers.com) arranges various functions throughout the year and invites all members to participate. It's a great way to meet like-minded people. They have regular auditions and the best way to get to know about them is to register on their site. You will then be automatically notified of planned productions and audition dates. The Hong Kong Players hold theatre workshops to help improve acting and improvisation techniques. Get in touch with the Chairman, Stephen Bolton, on the number above.

Hong Kong Singers

Hong Kong Academy
for Performing Arts
1 Gloucester Rd
Wan Chai
Admiralty
Map 16-F2

2537 4180 | www.hksingers.com

Present in Hong Kong since 1931, this company has put on shows such as The Boyfriend, Annie, Kiss Me Kate and My Fair Lady. The Singers obviously don't just sing; you can go along if you are interested in directing, producing, choreographing, and acting as well.

Hong Kong Youth Arts Festival

Westland Ctr
20 Westlands Rd
Quarry Bay
Quarry Bay
Map 17-E1

2877 2625 | www.hkyaf.com

Schools, colleges, youth organisations, individual young artists, young people of all cultures and backgrounds are all welcome to join this arts-dedicated festival if they are between 5 and 25 years old. The recent production of 'Fame' was very well-received. The basic qualification is enthusiasm.

Fencing

Hong Kong Fencing Association

Olympic House
1 Stadium Path
So Kon Po
Causeway Bay
Map 17-B3

2504 8106 | www.hkfa.org.hk

This association handles membership and organises regular tournaments for various age groups and categories throughout the year. Courses and coaching sessions are also offered at locations throughout the Territory, and fencing is taught in some of the local schools.

Fishing

Other options **Boat & Yacht Charters** p.211

Hong Kong is surrounded by water so there are obviously plenty of opportunities to fish. It's a common sight to see people fishing off piers and rocks and having success. The waters around Hong Kong are polluted so it's your choice whether you eat it or throw it back. There are lots of fishing tackle shops as well as boats to charter to go further out to sea and deepwater fish, for which there are very few restrictions. However, be aware that there are limits on the quantity and size of fish you can catch from Hong Kong's 17 freshwater lakes. You will also need a licence, available from the Water Supplies Department (2824 5000) for $24 and valid for three years. Alternatively, the Tai Mei Tuk Fish Farm (2662 6351) is a large artificial pond by the harbour, filled with freshwater fish. Rods cost $10 to rent, and you can pay either by the hour or for a full day visit.

Asiatic Marine

Various locations

2104 2297 | *www.asiaticmarine.com*

Contact Mr. Charles Frew who will organise full boat fishing charters which include all fishing gear, tuition, drinks and snacks. There are a variety of locations around local waters and the target fish are Chinese mackerel, tuna mackerel, Chinese seer fish and barracuda among others. All trips are weather dependent so be flexible when making arrangements. Charles' mobile number is 9831 5410.

Easy Fishing Hong Kong

Marina House
68 Hing Man St
Shau Kei Wan
Shau Kei Wan
Map 17-F2

3580 0008 | *www.hkeasyfishing.com*

Board the air-conditioned boat at Sai Wan Ho Public Pier or Lei Yue Mun and within 25 minutes you will be fishing off the coast of Tung Lung Chau – far from busy city life. The company provides fishing equipment, as well as refreshments to sustain you as you fish. They also do round-island and family-friendly trips. Contact via the above number, or try the hotline on 9733 3128.

Mandarin Sports Fishing Club

6 Hillier St
Sheung Wan
Sheung Wan
Map 16-E1

www.msfc.com.hk

This fishing club has over 80 members and has been going for 30 years. They have regular meets, socials and overseas trips. They also have family and junior members. They arrange local tournaments and help to host the Asian Game Fishing tournament in Hong Kong. The contact person is Virgil Lau, Club Treasurer.

Flower Arranging

Other options **Gardens** p.300, **Flowers** p.297

Views of stunning floral arrangements as they are ferried to some lucky person are a common sight in Hong Kong, especially around the Prince Edward area in Kowloon, where the Flower Market (see p.334) is found. The flowers are, as you would expect, exotic, while the displays are stunning and artistic.

Hong Kong Academy of Flower Arrangement

Li Dong Bld, 9 Li Yuen
St East
Central
Central
Map 16-D1

2882 1832 | *www.hkafa.com.hk*

Hong Kong Academy of Flower Arrangement offers classes for beginners and experts, and every level in between, from how to arrange flowers for weddings and parties, to training for globally-recognised professional certificates and diplomas. The classes are international and conducted in English for most levels. Class times are spread throughout the day to suit different work schedules, and most courses last from two to four months. The course fees vary according to the level. The materials required to do the practical part of each class must be bought through the Academy. Their second location is found at 17/F Commerce & Business Bld, 761 Nathan Road, Mong Kok, but the number above is a hotline, valid for both locations.

YWCA ESMD

1 MacDonnell Rd
Mid-Levels
Admiralty
Map 16-E2

3476 1340 | *www.esmd.ywca.org.hk*

Flower arranging courses are often available – those interested just need to check the website. Recent classes have included an introduction to contemporary flower arranging using tropical and Asian flowers. The classes are sometimes based around celebrations or festivals. For example, during Chinese New Year or Easter the arrangements will be appropriate to the season. Members pay $200, while the non-member's fee is $250.

Flying

Other options **Helicopter Tours** p.214

31 Sung Wong Toi Rd
To Kwa Wan
Map 10-C2

Hong Kong Aviation Club

2713 5171 | www.hkaviationclub.com.hk

It is possible to learn to fly and obtain your Private Pilots' Licence with this club. Hourly lessons are available which include practical and theory components of the course. They also offer aerobatics and are currently running a young eagles program to allow young people the opportunity to experience flying. The club owns a number of light aircraft and helicopters, with all flying activities taking place at Shek Kong. There are club house facilities as part of the Aviation Club and they have a restaurant and bar.

Football

Various locations

Brazilian Soccer School

2385 9677 | www.icfds.com/hongkong

The catchphrase of this soccer school is 'learn to play the Brazilian way'. It is a well-organised school which teaches as well as competes in leagues around Hong Kong (and outside). This style of football uses a weighted size two ball with little bounce and the emphasis is on fun, as well as rapidly increasing players' ball skills. Children from 5 to 14 are welcome. There are regular games and training, as well as special school holiday courses. Check the website for details.

Various locations

Yau Yee League

2904 9491 | www.yauyeeleague.com

Yau Yee League officially runs Hong Kong's premier amateur football league. There are lots of clubs organised into four divisions and they use stadiums in Happy Valley, Pok Fu Lam, Aberdeen and Causeway Bay for their matches. They have a very comprehensive website with team pages and links to the participating teams' websites where possible. It also includes fixture lists, results, and even details of every goal and card. Contact the league on the number above, or email thetreasurer@yauyeeleague.com.

Frisbee

Various locations

Hong Kong Ultimate Players Association

2570 6020 | www.hkupa.com

Hong Kong Ultimate Players Association is the official body that plays and promotes Ultimate Frisbee in Hong Kong and the China region. They run two 12 week leagues during the year as well as beach tournaments, and participate in events throughout Asia. Being a member of this group gives you access to fields to play on. It's difficult to find areas in Hong Kong big enough for Ultimate Frisbee, so the club pays for places with its membership fees. Have a go: first-timers get a free game. They use different fields around Hong Kong depending upon availability, so it's best to check the website for up-to-date information on training and planned events.

Golf

There are some rather lovely golf courses in Hong Kong, as well as some driving ranges. All but one of the courses is privately-owned, and most require membership, which can come at a premium. There is one public golf course, in Sai Kung, operated by the Hong Kong Jockey Club on behalf of the government.

243

Asia Golf

688 Lai Chi Kok Rd
Cheung Sha Wan
🚇 *Cheung Sha Wan*
Map 10-A1

2361 3972 | www.asiagolf.hk

Asia Golf has the longest range in the city (220 yards) with turf imported from Australia. Each bay is 5m wide so there's plenty of swing room. This club provides short game practice and an area to develop skills. It's also home to J and J Golf Academy, which offers a top-class professional teaching service. Non-members are welcome although membership is relatively inexpensive and offers cheaper hourly rates. To contact J and J Golf Academy for lessons, call 2361 8080.

City Golf Club

8 Wui Cheung Rd
Jordan
🚇 *Jordan*
Map 15-C3

2992 3333 | www.citygolfclub.com

This is a club situated in the very busy area of Kowloon near the harbour front in Tsim Sha Tsui. It is not a golf course but a facility offering a 200 bay driving range over a 200 yard distance, together with a putting green, sand bunker and private golf practice rooms. It is possible to become a member and use the facilities, which include two restaurants and professional club making. Thai Mary, their restaurant, has a very good reputation. Non-members can also pay to use the bays at a slightly higher rate.

Clearwater Bay Golf & Country Club

139 Tai Au Mun Rd
Clear Water Bay
Map 11-B4

2335 3888 | www.cwbgolf.org

This has a stunning 18 hole course set on Clear Water Bay Peninsula which is a green, mountainous and very beautiful area of the New Territories. The club has hosted numerous local and international tournaments. It is possible to join the Golf Club independently of the Country Club and there is a separate clubhouse. Membership gives access to the facilities of the Country Club. Non-members can enjoy a round on week days and corporate packages can be arranged. Weekends and public holidays are reserved for members.

Discovery Bay Golf Club

Valley Rd, Discovery
Bay
Lantau Island
Map 9-B3

2987 7273 | www.hkri.com

Discovery Bay is situated on the east coast of Lantau Island. To get to the golf course you need to take a ferry from Hong Kong island (to 'DB', as its known in these parts), then take a taxi or bus. No private cars are allowed on Discovery Bay. It has a 27 hole golf course (3 x 9 holes) set among green and mountainous terrain with wonderful views of Hong Kong and Kowloon. Non-members can make bookings for the 18 hole course on Monday, Tuesday and Friday from 07.30 to13:00.

Garden Farm Golf Centre

8C Tseng Tau Village
Shap Sze Heung
Sai Kung
Map 6-E2

2791 9098 | www.gardenfarmgolf.com

This driving range is out in the countryside so you can enjoy the green hills of the New Territories while using the driving bays (Course A has 63 and Course B has 30). There is also a short game area, putting area, sand bunkers and pitching area. Parking is free, plus there is a snack bar and barbeque area. It is open every day including Sundays and public holidays. It is possible to rent clubs if necessary. Families welcome.

Ho Chung Golf Driving Range Centre

88 Ho Chung Rd
Sai Kung
Map 10-F1

2243 0909

A very pleasant, although small, driving range set in the country surroundings of Sai Kung. It's open from 09:00 to 24:00 Monday to Friday, and from 07:00 to 22:00 during weekends and on public holidays. Professional coaching is available and you can also hire clubs.

Hong Kong Golf Club

Deep Water Bay Beach
Shouson Hill
Map 14-C1

2812 7070 | *www.hkgolfclub.org*

This is home to the Hong Kong Open and the club has a history dating back to 1889. It is a world-class course and attracts big names each year. The facilities at Deep Water Bay include a nine-hole Par 3 golf course, a swimming pool, a gym and two restaurants – one Chinese and the other with a European menu. The second location, Fanling, is at Sheung Shui (2670 1211, map 2-F3). Facilities here include three 18 hole courses (Old Course, New Course and Eden Course), a 34 bay driving range, four tennis courts, a swimming pool, two billiard tables, teaching professionals, caddies and a dining room. There are also 40 twin-bed rooms at Fanling, available for members and reciprocal guests only. Visitors can book rounds at either venue on weekdays between 09.00 and 14.00 if they have a handicap certificate.

Island Golf Club

8 Oi Tak St
Sai Wan Ho
Sai Wan Ho
Map 17-F2

2886 8980 | *www.islandgolf.com*

With a fantastic view of Victoria Harbour, this driving range has a lot to offer enthusiasts. Its facilities are top class, plus it's conveniently located just a short stroll from Sai Wan Ho MTR Station. It has 112 bays on four levels with a 22 yard distance range, night lighting, and real turf putting green. Golf professionals, with very impressive credentials, are available, for lessons and coaching. There is a comfortable shower and changing room area, as well as first-class Thai cuisine in Island Thai Restaurant. Non-members are welcome, with prices slightly higher per half hour than for members. Parking is available. The booking hotline is 2513 9888, and restaurant reservations are on 2886 0166.

Jockey Club Kau Sai Chau Public Golf Course

Kau Sai Chau
Sai Kung
Map 7-B4

2791 3388 | *www.kscgolf.com*

This is the only public golf course in Hong Kong, set in idyllic Sai Kung. Kau Sai Chau is actually an outlying island and to get to the course the club provides a regular ferry service from Sai Kung pier which takes around 20 minutes. It is a non-profit-making organisation, so there is therefore no membership or subscription fee and no admission fee is payable. They have a 36 hole course designed by Gary Player, plus a 60 bay driving range, chipping and bunker areas together with a putting green. The club house has a restaurant which serves Chinese food and an international buffet. It has beautiful views across the South China Sea and is often described as the best public course in Asia – a reputation it lives up to with no trouble at all.

Oriental Golf City

Kai Tak Runway
Kai Fuk Rd
Kowloon Bay
Kowloon Bay
Map 10-D3

2522 2111 | *www.ogcgolfcity.com*

This driving range is on Hong Kong's old airport runway, so it's in the heart of Kowloon with stunning views over the harbour to the island. It has 145 bays and 30 yards of range, as well as a super nine-hole executive golf course. It is open from 07:00 to 24:00, Monday to Friday and public holidays, and 07:00 to 18:00 on Sundays. Prices vary according to the time you use it. Members' prices are lower than non-members. Members can use the regular complimentary shuttle bus service from Telford Plaza. The range also has a golf training centre and professionals available for lessons if required.

SCAA Golf Driving Centre

Caroline Hill Rd
Causeway Bay
Causeway Bay
Map 17-B3

2577 4437 | *www.scaa.org.hk*

South China Athletics Association has its own driving range which has 51 bays and two bunkers, together with video facilities for analysis of your golf swing. The facilities are available to members only.

245

5 Shek O Rd
Shek O
Map 14-F1

Shek O Golf and Country Club

2809 4458

This exclusive 18 hole golf course is set on the south side of Hong Kong island and is strictly for members or guests of the club only. It has a 10 bay driving range and caddies (no carts), as well as a function room and coffee shop.

Lung Mun Rd
Tuen Mun
Map 4-F4

Tuen Mun Golf Centre

2466 2600 | *www.esd.gov.hk*

This is a driving range opened by the HK government in 1995. It is very reasonably priced and is accessible to anyone wanting to practise their swing or interested in learning. It has a 91 bay driving range, a practice green plus a club house and cafe. There are often courses offered for beginners and advanced learners.

Olympian City One
11 Hoi Fai Rd
Sham Shui Po
🚇 *Mong Kok*
Map 15-B2

Waterfall Golf Driving Range & Gym

2875 5380

This club has a 52 bay driving range that is open from 07:00 to 23:00. Members pay $40 per hour, while for non-members the cost is $60 per hour. It is possible to arrange coaching and there is a putting surface and sand bunkers. There's also a bar and coffee shop.

Whitehead
Ma On Shan
Map 6-E2

Whitehead Club

2631 9900 | *www.whiteheadclub.com*

This is a new driving range in Ma On Shan which is a beautiful, picturesque area in the New Territories overlooking Plover Cove Reservoir. It has 160 real grass chipping bays and a four-hole green field. There are also changing rooms, a VIP room, conference room and snooker room. Lessons suitable for beginners and advanced golfers are offered, with tuition from professional trainers. As well as golf, the club has a large barbeque area by the shoreline. Food can be bought at the club and the staff will even help with the lighting of the stoves. Ride a bike or walk along the seashore path and generally enjoy this peaceful spot. From Monday to Friday it is $50 per hour and $70 per hour at weekends. Use of the four-hole field is $80 an hour Monday to Friday and $100 at weekends.

Hashing

Other options **Bars & Pubs** p.390, **Running** p.258

If you are new to expat life this could all seem bizarre and silly. In fact, if you are a seasoned expat it still seems bizarre and silly. But it is, so there you go! It is all about running (on and on), having a laugh and not really caring who wins (or do they?). Go on, give it a go, you might like it. There are quite a few groups in Hong Kong – check out the websites below for membership details (the 'Hash Kash' are usually in charge of the money) and routes for regular weekly runs. Look out for the chalk marks.

Hashing	
Hong Kong Hash	www.hkhash.com
Kowloon Hash House Harriers	http://home.netvigator.com/~hasher/kh3news
Ladies Hash	www.hkladieshash.com
Little Sai Wan Hash	www.datadesignfactory.com/lsw
Northern New Territories Hash	www.n2th3.com
South Side Hash	www.rs2h3.com
Wan Chai Hash	www.wanchaih3.com

Hiking

Other options **Outdoor Goods** p.310

There are many hiking trails in Hong Kong. It is a very mountainous territory and 40% of it is country park. For such a highly populated area it has many open spaces which remain protected even under such high demand for building land. The hiking trails, usually concrete paths, are well sign-posted and of various difficulties, and most include at least one hard climb. There are guidebooks and maps available with information on routes such as the Dragon's Back across Shek O Country Park on the south side of the Island, and the MacLehose Trail, which is a huge 100km walk in ten stages across the New Territories. On Sundays and public holidays some of the hikes get very crowded. The website www.lcsd.gov.hk/healthy/hiking is a link to the HK Government's Hiking Scheme and gives basic details of 40 routes, as well as safety tips for hikers. Further recommended reading includes The Hiker's Guide to Hong Kong published by FormAsia, and Hong Kong Pathfinder published by Asia 2000.

Various locations

Hong Kong Trampers
8209 0517 | www.hktrampers.com
Walks are planned one week in advance, and usually take place on Sundays. Check the website for details. If there is no itinerary posted that means no one has proposed one as yet. As they do not keep a mailing list, it's best to post questions on their website message board. Everyone is welcome.

Various locations

Roz's Hiking Pages
www.hkcrystal.com/hiking
Although the founder no longer lives in Hong Kong, the group that bears her name still organises regular walks. Details of forthcoming walks, including start times, duration, and meeting points, are posted on the website. If you want to go along on a walk, just call or email the hike leader in advance.

Hockey

Other options **Ice Hockey** p.248

King's Park Hockey Ground, 6 Wylie Rd
Mong Kok
🚇 *Yau Ma Tei*
Map 15-D2

Hong Kong Hockey Association
2782 4932 | www.hockey.org.hk
Hockey is quite popular in Hong Kong and this association is responsible for running the league as well as promoting the sport. They have courses and training sessions for all age groups to teach hockey as well as coaching and umpire courses. Men and women's teams play regularly, from beginners to veterans.

Horse Riding

Beas River Country Club
Sheung Shui
Map 3-A2

Beas River Riding School
2966 1990 | www.hkjc.com
Beas River Riding School is part of the Hong Kong Jockey Club and is open to members of the club and their guests only. They have top-class facilities for horses and riders including all-weather areas, open paddocks, covered paddocks and cross-country courses. Riding instruction is available. Hong Kong Jockey Club also runs three other schools – Lei Yue Mun, Pok Fu Lam, and Tuen Mun – that are open to non-members. See below.

247

45 Lung Mun Rd
Tuen Mun
Map 4-F4

Hong Kong Pony Club
2461 3830 | www.hongkongponyclub.com
This is affiliated to the UK Pony Club and Hong Kong Equestrian Federation and promotes riding and caring for ponies and horses among young children in Hong Kong. They run many courses in riding and stable management at Pok Fu Lam or Tuen Mun Riding Schools throughout the year.

75 Chai Wan Rd
Lei Yue Mun
🚇 *Shau Kei Wan*
Map 10-E4

Lei Yue Mun Public Riding School
2568 9776 | www.hkjcridingschools.com
Situated behind Lei Yue Man Park Holiday Village, this is very close to Central and therefore offers a quick, convenient getaway for a peaceful ride. Professional training up to British Horse Society (BHS) Stage III Riding and Care is available, as well as riding lessons, mostly for groups of six. There's a long waiting list for beginner riders, and the best way to get to the top of it is to join a summer course or take private lessons during non-peak hours. Once you can ride off the lead rein, it is easier to get into a regular class. Competition training for jumping and dressage is also regularly available. The school primarily caters for Cantonese speakers with limited lessons in English.

Ho Sheung Heung
Sheung Shui
Map 2-F2

Lo Wu Saddle Club
2673 0066 | www.lowusaddleclub.org
This club is the oldest and largest in Hong Kong. It has over 40 horses, most of them ex-racehorses. They have regular courses in showjumping and flatwork for riders of all abilities and ages. Their courses also place importance on the care of the horses.

75 Pok Fu Lam
Reservoir Rd
Pok Fu Lam
Map 16-C3

Pokfulam Public Riding School
2550 1359 | www.hkjcridingschools.com
Located at the foot of Pok Fu Lam Reservoir Road right in the country park, this is a beautiful setting in which to ride. It is a popular riding school and very family-orientated. The school is also home of the Riding for the Disabled Association.

Lot No. 45 Lung
Mun Rd
Tuen Mun
Map 4-F4

Tuen Mun Public Riding School
2461 3338 | www.hkjcridingschools.com
This riding school is managed by the Hong Kong Jockey Club which has lessons and competitions for all levels of riders throughout the year. It is a large area (34,000 square metres) in the west of the New Territories. There are other facilities such as archery, a golf driving range, and a climbing wall. The school can accommodate up to 60 horses.

Ice Hockey
Other options **Ice Skating** p.249

Hung Kei Bld
58 Queen Victoria St
Central
🚇 *Central*
Map 16-E1

Ice Hockey League
2521 9922 | www.hockeynightinasia.com
This league is really well organised into four divisions. At the time of writing, all games were played at The Sky Rink in The Dragon Centre, Sham Shui Po, but there are plans to also use a new ice rink being built in Kowloon Bay. All training will also be done there. Both rinks have lockers and bag storage to rent. The league is for adults and children.

Dragon Centre
Sham Shui Po
🚇 *Sham Shui Po*
Map 10-B2

Women's Ice Hockey Organisation
9313 6018 | www.icehockey.com.hk
This organisation is very friendly and welcoming to new female skaters, whether you're a beginner or a more experienced skater. They are also very keen on safety – you won't be allowed on the ice without a helmet, and shoulders pads are available. All equipment, including skates, can be borrowed.

Ice Skating

Other options **Ice Hockey** p.248

There are three public ice rinks which are each quite small compared to European or American ones. They are all inside huge shopping malls (The Dragon Centre, Festival Walk and City Plaza), and are usually very busy with people of all ages using the ice for exercise – with some even trying a few nifty spins and turns. If anything, it makes a great spectator sport inbetween shopping. There are organised lessons for children depending on their ability and age, as well as an Ice Hockey League at The Dragon Centre with teams of all ages and both sexes. It is very popular among the Canadian and American community, who enjoy a little taste of home.

Festival Walk
Kowloon Tong
🚇 **Kowloon Tong**
Map 10-B1

Glacier

2265 8888 | *www.glacier.com.hk*

Open from Monday to Thursday, you pay one fee for an unlimited time on the ice. Morning sessions are $40 and run from 10:30 to 12:00, while the afternoon to evening session is $50 and runs from 12:00 to 22:00. During school holidays all sessions are $60: morning sessions are from 08:00 until 15:00, afternoon sessions are from 15:30 to 17:30, and evening sessions are 18:00 to 22:00. Glacier also hosts a Sunday Minor Hockey Leage (October to March), Skate for Love evenings and Asian Novice Figure Skating Championships.

Cityplaza
Taikoo Shing
🚇 **Tai Koo**
Map 17-E1

Ice Palace

2844 8688 | *www.icepalace.com.hk*

This ice rink is open from 09:30 until 22:00 from Monday to Thursday and offers unlimited skating for $45. On Fridays, the day is split in two by a 30 minute break at 12:00, with a slightly higher $50 fee for the afternoon and evening session. Lessons are also available on Fridays. Regular themed events are held here, such as 'Romance on Ice' evenings, when couples can skate together to romantic songs, and the Chinese New Year celebrations. Their 'Vision on Ice' scheme aims to raise the local ice skating standard to Olympian level by nurturing talented young skaters.

Dragon Centre
Sham Shui Po
🚇 **Sham Shui Po**
Map 10-B2

Sky Rink

2307 9264 | *www.dragoncentre.com.hk*

Sky Rink has a 17,000 sq ft rink which simulates snow falls. Special discounts are available for adults on weekdays – check the website for details. The skating school (2307 9604) also offers lessons. The rink is open from Monday to Friday, 09:00 to 13:00, then 13:00 to 22:00. An unlimted skate is $40 in the mornings, and $45 in the afternoons. During weekends, public holidays and school holidays, opening times are 09:00 to 22:00, and an unlimited skate costs $55.

Kids' Activities

Sun House, 181 Des
Voeux Rd
Sheung Wan
🚇 **Sheung Wan**
Map 16-E1

ESF Educational Services

2711 1280 | *www.esf.org.hk*

ESF Educational Services is part of the English Schools Foundation, which operates international secondary, primary and kindergarten schools in Hong Kong. The Educational Services section runs after-school and holiday sports programmes for all school-aged children, whether they are an ESF student or not. The range of sport on offer is immense and the standard of coaching is top class. The sports on offer include Tennis, Swimming, Gymnastics, Football (Soccer), Basketball, Inline Skating, Inline Hockey, and Martial Arts (Taekwondo, Kung Fu and Judo).

249

The activities are held at the various ESF school sites around Hong Kong, so depending upon the facilities the sports on offer may vary from site to site. As well as sports coaching and clinics, there are sports memberships available which means that a family can join and make use of the sports facilities at their nearest school. That could mean a swimming pool, courts, shower facilities, and even parking, which is always a bonus to have.

The website has good information on the sports offered and the locations of the schools.

Kitesurfing

Other options **Beaches** p.198, **Windsurfing** p.267

It is possible to kitesurf (or kiteboard) off some beaches in Hong Kong if you are experienced and have your own gear. Lung Kwu Tan in the west of the New Territories, Pak Sha Chau, Sai Kung in the east of the New Territories, and the islands of Cheung Chau and South Lantau all make great spots. At the moment, the scene is still flourishing, and there are only about 50 kitesurfers in Hong Kong. Be warned – these are quite small areas and there are not strong or steady enough winds every day. Also, please note that you are not allowed to kitesurf in areas designated for swimming. The website, www.kite2high.com is useful, listing information on kitesurfing events in Hong Kong, as well as where to go to catch the best winds and other advice.

Language Schools

Other options **Learning Chinese** p.155

Sadly most of the expat population in Hong Kong does not learn Cantonese, although many arrive with every intention of learning the local dialect. There are occasions when you'll find yourself in a situation where no one speaks English, so it is very useful to learn at least a few choice phrases. There are a couple of important facts every student should know before enrolling on a course: Cantonese is not a written language but a dialect, and Mandarin, or, using its more politically-correct name, Putonghua (pronounced poo tong wa), is a written language that everyone reads, but rarely uses. However, it is becoming more widespread as a spoken language now that more people want to speak the language of their mother country, China. Language courses in Putonghua are therefore very useful if you have business connections in mainland China. There are also many other world languages on offer.

123 Hennessy Rd
Wan Chai
 Wan Chai
Map 17-A2

Alliance Francaise

2527 7825 | www.alliancefrancaise.com.hk

Alliance Francaise is a non-profit organisation supported by the French Government, specialising in French language courses that also educate students about the cultural aspects of France. Most of the teachers are native French speakers and their courses run throughout the year following three terms, as well as a summer school. There are regular cultural activities and events and it is also possible to enroll on online courses. The lessons are also held at G/F-3F 52 Jordan Road, Jordan (2730 3257).

Various locations

Amy Leung Language Services

9623 0312 | www.amyleunglanguage.com

Amy Leung has published books on the subject of learning Cantonese which are light-hearted and fun, such as 'No Sweat Cantonese' and 'No Sweat Canto-Love.' She makes her courses interactive and uses real-life situations and role play to ensure the learning part is fun. Amy will customise a syllabus to suit your level, be it complete beginner or intermediate, in a group or individually, depending upon your requirements.

Berlitz

Pacific Place
Admiralty
🚇 *Admiralty*
Map 16-F2

2826 9223 | www.berlitz.com.hk

Berlitz offers courses in many different languages in very interesting ways. They specialise in total immersion in a language, as they argue this method has been scientifically proven to build up language proficiency within a shorter time. Not all of their courses offer this approach, so you can select less intensive courses as well. Berlitz can arrange study in centres outside Hong Kong for academic, business or cultural purposes.

British Council English Language Centre

3 Supreme Court Rd
Admiralty
🚇 *Admiralty*
Map 16-F2

2913 5100 | www.britishcouncil.org.hk

The British Council in Hong Kong has very well-established links with local Hong Kong schools, businesses and students of all ages, and runs a variety of courses in English throughout the year. It is also a link to educational institutions in the UK, and offers advice about studying overseas.

Catherine Cheung

Various locations

6771 8359

Catherine is a native Cantonese and Mandarin speaker and teaches both languages. Her courses take place according to the student's preference so it can be in your home or your office. One-to-one or one-to-two teaching for more focused progress costs approximately $250 to $300 per hour with all teaching material included. It takes an estimated three to four months to go from absolute beginner to using simple sentences in Cantonese, and a little longer for Mandarin. Once students reach a certain level, situational role plays can be incorporated into the lessons, such as going shopping or ordering food in a restaurant.

Chinese Language Professional

Dah Sing Life Bld
99-105 Des Voeux Rd
Central
🚇 *Central*
Map 16-D1

2287 5039 | www.clprof.com

CLP specialises in teaching Mandarin as a business tool to assist professionals in their work in China. The classes therefore help you with the business side of the language as well as the social, which is essential when establishing new clients. Because they appreciate that not all students learn in the same way or have the same requirements, their courses are flexible and can be made as individual as possible to suit your learning style. The contact details above are for the company headquarters. The training centre is located at 16/F, Cheung Kong Centre, 2 Queen's Road, Central. The same telephone number applies to each.

EDC Languages

Room 701
28 Queen's Rd
Admiralty
🚇 *Admiralty*
Map 16-F2

2528 5200 | www.hkedc.com

This language centre offers tuition in Mandarin, Cantonese and English. They offer courses for adults and children using interactive methods and modern role play situations. The classes can be individual or in groups, but the price is lower if you go for the group option. They focus on getting you to speak as much as possible and have associations with many well-known international organisations. There is a free demonstration lesson for people interested in learning.

Executive Mandarin Learning Centre

Wilson House, 19-27
Wyndham St
Central
🚇 *Central*
Map 16-E2

2537 0835 | www.execmandarin.com

This centre offers courses for expats in Mandarin so that you can develop proper pronunciation, tone and intonation – essential for this language. Their methods encourage students to speak, understand, practise and apply what has been learnt to real life daily situations. They also offer courses for children. You can join a course at the centre itself, or arrange to be taught in your own home or office.

56-58 Wellington St
Central
Central
Map 16-E2

Hong Kong Institute of Languages

2877 6160 | www.hklanguages.com

If you want to learn Cantonese, Mandarin, French, English, German, Spanish or Japanese there are a variety of courses suitable for you. Depending upon age, level or the time you have available, the Institute can accommodate your needs. They have a lot of courses and teachers available and offer one-to-one private tuition right up to groups of 16, for adults, teenagers and younger children. They are also experienced in corporate teaching and will tailor courses for staff. There is a free assessment to find out your level before you begin a structured course or you can join a trail class as a taster.

Fortune House
61 Connaught Rd
Central
Central
Map 16-E2

MSL Learning Center

2854 3039 | www.msllearningcenter.com

MSL offers small group teaching in written and spoken Mandarin with experienced bi-lingual and native speaking teachers, for beginners upwards. There are various courses on offer such as a three-month intensive class, intended to teach Mandarin quickly but effectively. They use their own textbooks, and offer listening activities through podcasts, CDs and real life experiences.

Libraries

Other options **Second-Hand Items** p.313, **Books** p.288

There are 64 libraries in total of various sizes, as well as mobile libraries for some areas. The main website www.hkpl.gov.hk will give you details and telephone numbers of a library near to your residential area. Most have a section of books in English, but it depends upon the demographic population of the area as to the size of the selection.

66 Causeway Rd
Causeway Bay
Tin Hau
Map 17-B2

Hong Kong Central Library

3150 1234 | www.hkpl.gov.hk

The Hong Kong Central Library is a 12 storey building which opened in 2001. It is modern, airy and spacious, and has a well-stocked section of English language books in all categories including art, literature, children's and educational resources. It is free to join upon production of a Hong Kong ID card and it is possible for overseas visitors to join for three months. All libraries are connected, so membership is valid for any library in Hong Kong.

Martial Arts

Morrison Plaza
9 Morrison Hill Rd
Wan Chai
Wan Chai
Map 17-A2

Heng Yue Yen Long Kwon Association

2511 8787 | www.hyylkmartialarts.com

Heng Yue Yen Long Kwon is a modern Chinese martial art, founded in 1981. This association holds classes at various locations, as well as at their headquarters in Wan Chai. Their classes are often within schools or clubs, and they also offer private lessons. Classes are for children as young as 3 right up to adults. There are also ladies' self-defence classes and family classes.

Various locations

Hong Kong Aikido Association

2427 3540 | www.aikido.com.hk

Founded in 1971 and affiliated to the World Headquarters in Tokyo, this non-aggressive martial art is a system of self-control and self-defence. It is actually used by the Hong Kong Police. Regular training and competition takes place at dojos in Tsim Sha Tsui, North

Point and Bowring Street, while Kowloon training is available seven days a week. Contact via the above number, or email membership@aikido.com.hk.

Various locations

Hong Kong Mixed Martial Arts Association
www.hkmma.com

This organisation is responsible for martial arts fights of all weights as well as many different types of martial art, including sports for women. Classes take place in various locations, including Impakt Gym in Central (contact Karim Arditi on 9135 4724 or karimhongkong@yahoo.com), Brazilian Jiu Jitsu in Yau Ma Tei (contact Thomas Fan on 9833 1407), and the Wah Fat Ind Building in Kwai Chung (contact Donald on 9206 9690, or hk_budo_kan@yahoo.com).

Asia Standard Tower
59-65 Queen's Rd
Central
🚇 **Central**
Map 16-E2

THE ONE Martial Gym
2526 6648 | *www.fightinfit.com.hk*

This gym has classes in personal training, self-defence, kickboxing, karate, muay Thai, kidz karate and tae kwon do, to name just a few. It is also possible to have acupuncture treatment by appointment. A second location is found in the World Trust Tower in Central (2522 2248).

1 MacDonnell Rd
Mid-Levels
🚇 **Admiralty**
Map 16-E2

YWCA ESMD
3476 1340 | *www.esmd.ywca.org.hk*

There are a variety of martial arts courses at the YWCA and the schedule changes throughout the term. They offer specialist tai chi courses for beginners and experienced practitioners, as well as Tian Yan Nei Gong classes, which is the oldest form of Taoist energy work. The exercise promotes health, prolongs life and develops the spirit by collecting energy in the energy centres and circulating it through the human body. It builds inner calmness, physical strength and flexibility, as well as an increased sense of well-being.

Mother & Toddler Activities

Throughout Hong Kong there are play places for young babies and pre-school children. Most require a termly commitment paid for in advance, although some are more casual and offer drop-in soft play areas. There are a lot of play areas, such as swings and slides in parks and squares, and most have soft landing surfaces to cushion the inevitable falls. Taking your child to a regular playgroup is a great way to chat to other mums, although don't be surprised if the structure of the sessions doesn't allow time for this, and also be aware that many young children of working parents will be accompanied by their domestic helper.

Park View Ctr
7 Lau Li St
Tin Hau
🚇 **Tin Hau**
Map 17-C1

Baby Buddies
2881 8717 | *www.letter-land.com*

Baby Buddies have classes in English for Tiny Tots (from 6 to 18 months old), Baby Buddies (1 to 2 year olds), as well as Step 2s (2 to 3 year olds). They have a webcam facility, so even if you are in the office you can log on and watch your child at play. As well as free play, this play group offers more formal classes, introducing reading, shapes, colours and counting, depending on the age of your child. The schedule is structured termly, and fees and deposits are required in advance. A written report is given at the end of each term.

Early Adventures

13G Greenmont Court
Discovery Bay
Map 9-B3

2987 9644 | www.earlyadventures.net

This playgroup caters for 10 children at each session from 09:00 to 11:30 each day during term-time. Children from 18 months to 3 years are welcome to apply for a place. Sessions are payable one month in advance and are split up between those for older and younger children during the week. Early Adventures has a home and book corner, offers messy play, music and creative activities, as well as construction toys.

Gymboree

St. John's Bld
33 Garden Rd
Central
🚇 *Central*
Map 16-E2

2899 2210 | www.gymboree.com.hk

This is a very well known and popular play franchise, found not only in Hong Kong but all over the world. It has structured sessions catering for very young babies, from newborns up to 5 year olds. They offer baby gym, art, music and even sign language classes for babies and their parents. Some classes are very popular, so it is necessary to commit and pay in advance. They also do birthday party packages for 90 minutes with an instructor provided. It is located just above the Peak Tram Station, or a 10 minute walk away from Central station, from Exit J2.

Hong Kong Central Library

66 Causeway Rd
Causeway Bay
🚇 *Tin Hau*
Map 17-B2

3150 1234 | www.hkpl.gov.hk

This is Hong Kong's main library and it is vast. It has a very attractive children's area where there are often free activities in English for children to take part in, such as family story time and travel story-telling. Parents are required to accompany children for all activities.

Kindermusik

Suite 1005A
60 Wyndham St
Central
🚇 *Central*
Map 16-E2

2518 4840 | www.kateskids.com

Kindermusik offers fun music and movement classes aimed at young children and their parents: Kinder Village for newborns to 18 month olds, Our Time for 18 months to 3 year olds, Imagine That for 3 to 5 year olds, Adventures for 1 to 7 year olds, The Young Child for 5 to 7 year olds and Sing-Along for 2 to 5 year olds. There are also Storytime sessions with 3D books and puppets. The fees are payable in advance and are usually for semesters or courses, such as a 15 week semester or five week course. Kindermusik provides home materials with every course, with the aim that parents will continue the teaching at home with CDs, story books and musical instruments. Kindermusik Studio is based in Central, although they do run classes in other venues around Hong Kong, such as at the Kid's Gallery in Kowloon, Aberdeen Marina Club and the Royal Hong Kong Yacht Club.

The Little Gym

New World Ctr
18-24 Salisbury Rd
Tsim Sha Tsui
🚇 *Tsim Sha Tsui*
Map 15-D4

2368 8777 | www.thelittlegym.com.hk

The Little Gym is a franchised organisation offering programmes to help children develop physically as well as to boost their confidence. There are gymnastics courses for kids of all ages in a non-competitive environment. Sports skills and karate are also available. Birthday parties can be catered for and they even have a Parents Survival Night. They have a second location in Sha Tin, New Territories.

My Gym

The Centrium
60 Wyndham St
Central
🚇 *Central*
Map 16-E2

2577 3322 | www.mygymhk.com

This gym offers pre-gymnastic structured classes with music and dance. If your child is between 6 months and 3.5 years, then the parent participation classes are for you. These have shared physical activities on their custom-designed apparatus. From 3.5 to

5 years independent classes are offered. All have specialist instructors. Most classes are one hour and must be paid for in advance in 10 week sessions. My Gym can also organise children's birthday parties for up to 20 kids including a teacher-led activity for one hour and 45 minutes. They will provide decorations and refreshments and prepare games to suit whichever age group you bring along.

Lippo Centre, Tower 1
89 Queensway
Central
📍 *Admiralty*
Map 15-F2

Panda Junction

2855 0906 | *www.pandajunction.com*

This playgroup has scheduled classes depending upon the age or developmental progress of your child. It is very clean and friendly and the focus is on active learning and physical development. Each age group has a different time slot which lasts for one hour. It is necessary to book and pay in advance for one term. There is an extensive schedule throughout the day.

Maximall, City Garden
233 Electric Rd
North Point
📍 *North Point*
Map 17-B1

QQ Club

2234 6677 | *www.qqclub.com.hk*

This club offers a variety of courses in art, music, dance, sport, science and languages for children from 18 months to 12 years old. Not all courses are in English so check the website for details. Courses must be booked and paid for in advance and are usually in blocks of 10.

Jade Ctr, 98-102
Wellington St
Central
📍 *Central*
Map 16-E2

Rumpus Rooms

2543 5488 | *www.therumpusrooms.com*

The Rumpus Rooms is a soft play space for mums and babies which is informal and friendly. Mums and toddlers can drop-in and play for as long as they want and mums can chat. The sessions that you can book are slightly more structured, with songs and music. The rooms are divided up, so the crawlers are safe from the more active walkers. The reserved sessions take place every day from Monday to Friday, from 10:00 to 11:30 and 14:30 to 16:00. The pure drop-in and play sessions (when you can stay as long as you wish) take place Mondays to Fridays, from 11:30 to 14:00, and on Saturdays from 10:00 to 13:00.

Various locations

Soft Play Rooms

2414 5555 | *www.lcsd.gov.hk*

There are government-operated sports centres all around Hong Kong, and many have play areas and facilities for children. They are often free to use. To find one near you, from the homepage of the Leisure and Cultural Services Department website, hover over Leisure, then Other Leisure Facilities, then click on Children's Play Rooms.

St John's Cathedral
Central
📍 *Central*
Map 16-E2

St John's Playgroup

2523 4157 | *www.stjohnscathedral.org.hk*

This friendly group of volunteers which welcomes newcomers to Hong Kong. Their informal playgroup meets on Tuesdays in the Fanny Li Hall next to the cathedral, from 14:30 to 16:30. The cost of each session is a very reasonable $30 or $50 for two. Children from birth to four years old are all welcome. There is a range of toys and open space in which to play with other children. At the end of each session there is a story and a singsong. Parents must accompany their children and be responsible for their safety. They are also expected to lend a hand with activities and tidying up. This group has a parent's-only meeting on Thursdays from 14:30 to 16:30, to give parents a chance to socialise and swap notes.

255

Murray House
Stanley
Map 14-D2

Wildfire (Stanley)

2813 6161 | www.igors.com

This is a coffee shop with a great play place for small children supervised by a member of staff so that parents can relax. There are activities such as balloon twisting, creative painting and magic classes at the weekends and on public holidays. They also cater for children's parties on request. Murray House in Stanley has many popular themed restaurants operated by the King Parrot group. Every Sunday children can join in with the cooking at their Children's Cooking Class. The customer service hotline is 3162 3535.

Mountain Biking

Other options **Cycling** p.42

There is some politics surrounding the use of mountain bikes on the Country Park trails in Hong Kong. Although the parks have some marvellous routes for walkers, the authorities have a bit of an aversion to mountain bikes. However, there are currently 10 approved trails upon which mountain bikes are allowed, and more are in the process of being approved. The prerequisite to ride is to submit an application form to the Agricultural, Fisheries & Conservation Department for a permit to use the trails. Without the permit you could be stopped and turned back, and there is a threat of a fine. Also, please note that bikes are not allowed on the MTR. To find more information about trails and people to ride with, contact the Hong Kong Mountain Bike Association (www.hkmba.org or jackharriman@yahoo.com).

Yam Tze Commerical
Bld, 23 Thomson Rd
Wan Chai
🚇 *Wan Chai*
Map 17-A2

Asia Pacific Adventure

2792 7146 | www.asiapacificadventure.com

Asia Pacific organise outdoor skills courses in sports such as climbing, adventure racing, kayaking and also mountain biking. You can join a set course or they can run a course for a small group if you have enough people. For more information call the number above, or try Ryan S. Blair on his mobile, 9178 2140.

Music Lessons

Other options **Music, DVDs & Videos** p.309, **Dance Classes** p.236

There are hundreds of musical instrument teachers in Hong Kong, and the Chinese take their tuition very seriously. Many children of surprisingly young ages have already whizzed through their graded music examinations, especially in piano and violin. There are private teachers available who will come to your house, small music schools with practice rooms located all around Hong Kong, and music teachers from local and international schools who offer lessons during lunch times, after school or on Saturday mornings. There are also quite a number of excellent music shops (for example Tom Lee Music, and Parsons Music) that have a good stock of instruments and music. See p.309.

Drum Jam

Fringe Club
Central
🚇 *Central*
Map 16-E2

2982 1846 | *www.drum-jam.com*

Drum Jam is held every month at The Fringe Club. Kumi, an expert drummer, organsies these sessions, starting at 20:00. Make sure you get there early as it gets pretty packed. Another advantage about getting there early is that you get a seat and can take your pick of the drums available. You are also welcome to bring your own drum or any percussion instrument. As the name suggests, everyone jams along to the beat and a great time is had by all. Call Kumi on the above number, or on 9750 4212. Drum Jam and Live Drum Performance with Kumi can be hired for special events. There is also a Kidz Jam for any age group which can be booked for children's parties or for educational fun events in schools.

Tom Lee Music Foundation

6 Cameron Rd
Tsim Sha Tsui
🚇 *Tsim Sha Tsui*
Map 15-D4

2739 1389 | *www.tomlee.com*

Tom Lee Music Foundation offers lessons in a vast array of instruments and singing styles. They have centres all around Hong Kong, the New Territories and Kowloon. Some of the courses on offer include piano, band ensemble, pop singing, electric guitar and saxophone. You will need to check whether they offer the course you're after in English.

Netball

Netball is played by approximately 1,200 people at various levels in Hong Kong in many of the sports clubs and schools. There are women's teams as well as mixed teams. The Hong Kong Netball League runs from October to April every year, with three divisions. There is also a Netball Development Tournament and Festival of Sports Netball Tournament, in which a lot of local Chinese players participate. Hong Kong Netball will also take part in international and regional events, such as the World and Asian Netball Championship, which runs every four years. For more information, call the Hong Kong Netball Association on 2504 8208, email hkna@hkolympic.org, or check the website www.netball.org.hk.

Paintballing

Paintball Headquarters

Po Lung Ctr, 11 Wang
Chiu Rd
Kowloon Bay
🚇 *Kowloon Bay*
Map 10-D2

3106 0220 | *www.paintballhq.com.hk*

With a 10,000 sq ft indoor area, this company promises paintballing fun for all ages and levels. All the gear is provided, and you get 100 pellets for the price ($250 adult, $185 for students). Don't worry if you're a bit trigger-happy though – you can buy more if you run out. For maximum enjoyment, go as a group or reserve the whole place for a party.

Rollerblading & Rollerskating

Other options **Beaches** p.198, **Parks** p.201

YWCA ESMD

1 MacDonnell Rd
Mid-Levels
🚇 *Admiralty*
Map 16-E2

3476 1340 | *www.esmd.ywca.org.hk*

Rollerblading (aka inline skating) courses are run regularly here. A course of six sessions is around $900 for a non-member, while the member's fee is slightly lower. The tutor has professional inline skate qualifications and can teach skills such as a backward swizzle, spin stop, brake turn, crossover turn, stride two and many more. After the skills have been mastered, games are played so you can put what you have learnt into action. All protective gear is mandatory.
ESF Educational Services also offer inline skating courses and games, see p.149.

257

Rugby

Rugby is actively played by people of all ages in Hong Kong, and there are more women's teams starting up too. The many clubs are often run by people with a passion for rugby and rely on the goodwill of parents and players for coaching and support. The table below lists some of the clubs. On Sunday mornings, Kings Park in Kowloon sees an influx of rugby players from minis to biggies – and of course many mums and dads running up and down the touchlines with encouraging words of support for their offspring. Hong Kong Rugby (www.hkrugby.com, 2504 8311) has details of all clubs and leagues. Many of the international schools have their own league, but it's not played in the local schools. It is essential to mention the annual Hong Kong Rugby 7s here. The island is inundated with Rugby 7s fans from all over the world for three days every year, usually in March or April. This is primarily an expat pastime and seems to go unnoticed by the locals. For many, going to the 7s has very little to do with the rugby – being there is more important than following the games. Fancy dress is optional – but encouraged. The rugby is actually top-class, with international teams competing for the title.

Rugby Clubs	
Aberdeen	www.aberdeenrfc.com
Causeway Bay	www.cwbrugby.com
DEA Tigers	www.deatigersrfc.com
Discovery Bay Pirates	www.dbpirates.com
Flying Kukris	www.flyingkukris.com
Hong Kong Football Club	www.hkfcrugby.com
Tanner De Witt Nomads	www.hknomads.com
Valley Fort	www.stanleyfort.com

Running

Other options **Hashing** p.246

In Hong Kong, the air is never as fresh as you'd like but people still persist in running, either by themselves for general fitness or as part of a club. The Standard Chartered Marathon (www.hkmarathon.com) takes place every year, and attracts thousands of entrants. The Oxfam Trailwalker is another popular event. It's a 100km charity walk (or run) that runs the length of the MacLehose Trail. To find out more, visit www.oxfamtrailwalker.org.hk.

Olympic House
1 Stadium Path
So Kon Po
 Causeway Bay
Map 17-B3

Hong Kong Amateur Athletics Association

2504 8215 | *www.hkaaa.com*

There are around 17 running clubs affiliated to the HKAAA around Hong Kong, and many events as well as training workshops and physiotherapy information are offered throughout the year. Competitions run for all ages, ranging from junior to veteran. They are also responsible for the Hong Kong Athletics Team.

Hennessy Rd
Wan Chai
Wan Chai
Map 16-F2

Hong Kong Ladies Road Runners Club

9284 2314 | *www.hklrrc.org*

This is an active club that takes part in lots of races throughout the year, and also hosts three races themselves. There is a nominal annual membership fee and membership is open to students, individuals and families. Regular weekly track training takes place on Wednesday evenings at Sha Tin Sports Ground on Yuen Wo Road. All levels are welcome to join in. Meet at 18:30 to start at 19:00.

Sailing

Other options **Boat & Yacht Charters** p.211

20 Shum Wan Rd
Aberdeen
Map 14-B1

Aberdeen Boat Club

2555 6216 | *www.abclubhk.com*

A small sailing club established in 1967 by a group of friends who bonded through their passion for boats, Aberdeen Boat Club has moorings, sail training, dinghy and kayak hire, boat storage facilities and a large barbecue area. There's also a clubhouse, small pool and a gym. In addition, the club runs a sailing and recreation centre on Middle Island, with a regular ferry service from the main clubhouse to the island.

8 Shum Wan Rd
Aberdeen
Map 14-B1

Aberdeen Marina Club
2555 8321 | www.aberdeenmarinaclub.com

This club is quite stunning. Managed by the Shangri-La International Group, the Aberdeen Marina Club offers first-class service to members. As well as providing facilities to boat owners, the clubhouse has high class catering, a pool and a children's play area. They even have their own ice rink. Boating events take place throughout the year as well as social dos.

Hiram's Highway
Sai Kung
Map 7-A4

Hebe Haven Yacht Club
2719 8300 | www.hhyc.org.hk

Hebe Haven is a sociable sailing club. It is very popular with expats living in the Sai Kung area and, as well as facilities for mooring boats, it has a small relaxed bar and restaurant area. Racing is popular and races are held most weekends. It is the base for the annual 24 hour Charity Dinghy Race held every autumn, which many other clubs participate in.

To Tei Wan Bay
D'Aguilar Peninsula
Map 14-E2

Hong Kong Hobie Club
2813 5003 | www.hobie.com.hk

This is an enthusiastic sailing club with organised racing every two weeks from September to May. All members are either associated with or own a Hobie (for the uninitiated, a Hobie is a small catamaran). They have space for 70 Hobies so membership is at a premium, but they will endeavour to help individuals who are interested in the 'Hobie lifestyle'. Contact Club Secretary Chris Howard on the above number or email hobie@hobie.com.hk.

Discovery Bay
Lantau Island
Map 9-B3

Lantau Boat Club
9365 1018 | www.lantauboatclub.com

This is a friendly, family-orientated club catering for non-powered water-based activities. They have space for catamarans, dinghies, canoes and windsurfers. Their location makes it ideal for enjoying the warm waters of Hong Kong. There are three different levels of membership: full boat membership, canoe membership and social membership. They have regular events on the water as well as social gatherings.

Kellett Island
Causeway Bay
🚇 **Causeway Bay**
Map 17-B1

Royal Hong Kong Yacht Club
28320 2817 | www.rhkyc.org.hk

This very prestigious club dates back over 150 years. Its main base is in the beautiful setting of Kellett Island in Causeway Bay. It was even featured in one of the James Bond films. It also has two small branches in Shelter Cove, Sai Kung and Middle Island, Repulse Bay. If you have a lovely yacht and need to moor it, this is the place for you. Sailing is the main activity, however rowing is also big. Excellent facilities include a swimming pool, squash courts, a gym and a children's play area for members' use.

259

Royal Hong Kong
Yacht Club
Causeway Bay
🚇 **Causeway Bay**
Map 17-B1

Yachting Ventures

2566 4617 | www.yachtingventures.com

Yachting Ventures is attached to the Royal Hong Kong Yacht Club and offers various courses in sailing. Of the three courses on offer, the first is aimed at total beginners, the next level is for competent crew with intermediate experience and the last one is a skipper course. All courses are conducted in English on a 45 foot yacht moored at Royal Hong Kong.

Salsa Dancing

Other options **Dance Classes** p.236

Tung Yiu Commercial
Bld, 31A Wyndham St
Central
🚇 **Central**
Map 16-E2

Latin Dance

9490 3563 | www.latindancehk.com

There are regular group classes and over a few lessons, students will learn salsa dances, such as the merengue, bachata, lambada, rueda international latin, cha cha cha, samba, rumba, jive and paso doble, and ballroom dances, including the waltz, tango, foxtrot, quickstep and Viennese waltz. The emphasis is on having fun while dancing to the music and incidentally learning the moves. For further details contact Jason Gauci on 9490 3563 or email him on latindancehk@hotmail.com. The other two locations are Amico, 2F 167-169 Hennessy Road, in Wan Chai, and the Brasil Dance Studio, 4F Wing Fat Building, 3 Jervois Street, Central.

Happy Dancing Studio
161 Lockhart Rd
Wan Chai
🚇 **Wan Chai**
Map 17-A2

Quick Step Limited

2203 0413 | www.hkmambo.com

Salsa classes are on Tuesdays and Saturdays and there are various courses starting throughout the year for beginners, improvers, intermediates and advanced dancers. Payment in advance is required for a course of six lessons. Private or special group lessons can be catered for. Another location is the Eric Hotung Studio, 2 Harbour Road, Wan Chai (2922 2822).

Various locations

Salsaman

9410 8652

Franky Wong is Salsaman. He gives classes at various locations for beginners, improvers and advanced salsa dancing. You do not need a partner. On Tuesdays you can find him at the Hong Kong Cultural Centre, Tsim Sha Tsui, with lessons for improvers from 19:00 to 20:00, and for intermediate from 20:00 to 21:00. Thursdays he'll be at the Fringe Club, 2 Lower Albert Road, Central, with advanced lessons from 19:00 until 20:00, intermediate lessons from 20:00 until 21:00, and beginners/improvers lessons from 21:00 until 22:00.

Convention Plaza
Harbour Rd
Wan Chai
🚇 **Wan Chai**
Map 17-A2

Tribeca

2836 3690

Salmambo vs Latango is held every Sunday from 20:00 for beginners, improvers and intermediate salsa dancers. At 21:00 you can practise your salsa, cha cha and meringue. Admission is $90, which includes the class itself, as well as one drink and some tapas.

Singing

Other options **Drama Groups** p.240

St John's Cathedral
Central
🚇 **Central**
Map 16-E2

Hong Kong Welsh Male Voice Choir

9644 5842 | www.hkwmvc.com

Although its founders were Welsh, the Hong Kong Welsh Male Voice Choir of today is representative of Hong Kong's 'world city' status – its members hail from 12 different nations, including some from China. It is therefore not compulsory to be Welsh – but it is essential to be male and to be able to sing. One member describes the choir as 'the best gentlemen's club in town.' They meet at St. John's Cathedral on Garden Road, Central, every Tuesday evening at 19:30, and can be found frequenting the Old China Hand pub in Wan Chai post-practice. A talented, sociable bunch, they raise a lot of money for charity by singing at regular concerts in Hong Kong and abroad every year.

Arion Commercial Ctr, 2-12 Queen's Rd West
Sheung Wan
Sheung Wan
Map 16-D1

Katterwall

2575 3931 | www.katterwall.com

Katterwall is the umbrella-name for a variety of choirs and choruses. It provides high quality, enjoyable vocal experiences ranging from one-on-one singing lessons and one-off workshops, to year-round choirs including Kassia Women's Choir, Kassia Men's Chorus and Kassia Youth Choir for 13 to 18 year old girls. Anyone with a passion for singing is welcome to audition (the ability to read music is not a prerequisite and auditions are very simple). Musical styles include: pop, gospel, broadway, soul, world and country. Kassia choirs have appeared in many of Hong Kong's most prestigious venues including the Cultural Centre, City Hall and the Arts Centre.

Garden Rd
Central
Central
Map 16-E2

St John's Cathedral

25234 157 | www.stjohnscathedral.org.hk

The Cathedral Choir performs at the Eucharist every Sunday, at choral matins once a month, and also for special occasions, such as Christmas and Easter or weddings and memorial services. It mainly uses the standard cathedral repertoire. There is also an Evensong Choir who sing at 18:30 on the second Sunday of each month, from September to June. They start practising at 17:00 in the Cathedral and then go on to sing at the service, which lasts for approximately one hour. It helps if you are a good sight-reader, though all who can sing in tune are welcome. You just need to get to the Cathedral 10 minutes before the beginning of the practice.

Skateboarding

At the moment there are three public skate parks around Hong Kong all built by the government, with talk of more opening soon. When it comes to skateboarding, Hong Kong is very particular about safety – all rules have to be strictly adhered to. You will not be allowed on a park without a helmet and wrist guards. Although it is possible to ride in some street areas, it is not tolerated for long, and groups of lads are often moved on quickly if they try to grind on the metal railings or attempt a few eyebrow-raising tricks on steps.

There are parks in Mei Foo, Chia Wan and Moorse Park, as well as one opening soon in Sai Kung. These are public parks and anyone can use them. The park in Mei Foo has skate tips and hints from 14:00 every Sunday by skaters who just want to share their skills.

22 Gascoigne Rd
Jordan
Jordan
Map 10-B3

YMCA King's Park Centenary Centre

2782 6682 | www.kpcc.ymcahk.org.hk

The park has two opposing quarter pipes, separated by a fun-box with a grind bar running its length. There is also another grind bar and a drop-in ramp over to the side of one of the quarter pipes. The park is suitable for beginners as well as advanced skaters and costs $15 per session. It has three sessions everyday: 08:00-12:00, 12:00-16:00 and 16:00-22:00. Membership is required but free. You will need to show a HK ID Card to join (everyone over 11 has one, if you haven't got yours yet you can take your passport). Skaters under 18 must have parental consent before using the park. Knee pads, elbow pads and helmets are compulsory.

261

Skiing & Snowboarding

148 Electric Rd
North Point
North Point
Map 17-C1

Slope Infinity

2107 4567 | www.slopeinfinity.com

It's really true: you can ski in Hong Kong. Slope Infinity is in a high rise building (but don't worry, you are not expected to negotiate your way down the side!). It's an indoor revolving carpet which is similar to a brush artificial ski slope. It's quite good for building up your skill level after a break from real snow and it would give you a bit of a head start if you had never been skiing or snowboarding before and planned to go on a ski holiday. Instructors are available by appointment for adults and kids and it's possible to rent all the gear.

Social Groups

Other options **Support Groups** p.262

There are plenty of social organisations and groups among the thriving expat community of Hong Kong. Unsurprisingly for such a busy hub of economic activity, many of the clubs' members are well-connected within the business or diplomatic communities. However, a lot of the groups are not as exclusive, and welcome anyone just looking to make new friends, rather than useful business acquaintances.

C-7, Monticello
48 Kennedy Rd
Wan Chai
Wan Chai
Map 16-F2

American Women's Association

2527 2961 | www.awa.org.hk

The American Women's Association of Hong Kong is a voluntary organisation of international women, supporting Hong Kong charities and schools through community service and monetary grants, while also providing educational and social activities for members. They hold a CHAT (Come Have A Talk) every Thursday in the JW Marriot in Pacific Place. The AWA is open to women who are either US citizens, legal residents or spouses of US citizens.

Tesbury Centre
28 Queen's Rd East
Wan Chai
Admiralty
Map 16-F2

Australian Association

2530 4461 | www.ozhongkong.com

The Australian Association holds Chatterbox coffee mornings every Friday at Eden Coffee in Melbourne Plaza, Central. They also organise a monthly get-together for newcomers to Hong Kong, plus all manner of other social events.

2 Lower Albert Rd
Central
Central
Map 16-E2

Foreign Correspondents Club

2521 1511 | www.fcchk.org

The Foreign Correspondents Club in Hong Kong is an exclusive private club for members of the media, business and diplomatic community. It is in a beautiful old building in the heart of Central. Its facilities include a bar, restaurant, health club, sauna, library, media room and snooker room. It also has a popular jazz night in the bar.

Just Arrived?

The English Speaking Members Department of the YWCA offers a course of four sessions specially designed for newly arrived expat women in Hong Kong. It is described as their 'signature' course and has been running regularly for thirty years. The sessions are run at various intervals throughout the year, so cater for people arriving all the time. It is a basic introduction to Hong Kong designed to orientate newcomers into the territory in a sociable and friendly way, while at the same time giving the group members a chance to ask questions and, of course, make new friends. The last session includes lunch, and there is also an evening junk trip to Lamma Island for Chinese seafood, when spouses are invited. Contact the YWCA ESMD on 3476 1340 for details, or visit www.esmd.ywca.org.hk.

The Helena May

35 Garden Rd
Central
🚇 **Central**
Map 16-E2

2522 6766 | *www.helenamay.com*

This is a long-established club in Hong Kong, originally started up by Lady Helena May in 1916, to cater for the needs of unaccompanied women and girls arriving in Hong Kong. It is now a private members club where both men and women can enjoy tea and cucumber sandwiches, relax with a coffee and a magazine, meet up with friends for a drink, or simply escape the bustle of the Hong Kong streets. It is set in the peaceful, elegant surroundings of a heritage building that also offers accommodation facilities.

Hong Kong Club

1 Jackson Rd
Central
🚇 **Central**
Map 16-E2

2525 8251

This is a rather exclusive club in the middle of Central, located next to Statue Square. Founded in 1846, the club has a restaurant, library, squash court and even bowling facilities. A revered society, it is full of Hong Kong's expat movers and shakers.

Hong Kong Gaelic Athletic Association

Various locations

www.gaa.hk

This club is a sporting focus for the Irish community in Hong Kong. They have football teams for men and women who train and play regular matches, as well as go on tours to play or watch sporting events around Asia. Training locations are in Kowloon, Aberdeen, Happy Valley and King's Park. The website is very comprehensive with information about leagues, awards and links to other football-related sites.

Ladies Circle Hong Kong

L3 Scenic Villas
Scenic Villa Drive
Kennedy Town
Map 16-B3

www.ladiescirclehk.com

This is the women's section of the Round Table. They are a registered charity and usually meet on the first Thursday of the month for a dinner meeting and to promote friendship and fund raising, especially for local charities. Meetings are held at the Aberdeen Boat Club, but call or email to confirm.

Royal Asiatic Society

Various locations

2813 7500 | *www.royalasiaticsociety.org.hk*

The Royal Asiatic Society has been around in Asia for over 100 years and is still going strong. They have an interesting monthly journal that you get when you become a member. There are activities and trips led by veterans of Hong Kong to places you'd never know existed, and informative talks and overseas tours led by specialists of the area or the topic.

Royal Geographical Society

Various locations

2583 9700 | *www.rgshk.org.hk*

The Royal Geographical Society invites explorers, writers and adventurers. They have monthly meets or whenever they can bring in a speaker. Talks are usually held at Olympic House near the Hong Kong Stadium in Causeway Bay, but if it's a special guest the event will be held in Jardine's House.

Women's Corona Society Hong Kong

Mariner's Club
Middle Rd
Tsim Sha Tsui
🚇 **Tsim Sha Tsui**
Map 15-C4

2547 7100 | *www.coronahk.org*

This is a relaxed social group for English-speaking expat women in Hong Kong, of all ages and nationalities. Its current Patron is Elizabeth Bradley, wife of the British Consul-General in Hong Kong. Founded in 1952, the Hong Kong branch of the Society meets every Monday, from 10:00 at the Mariner's Club. A welcome table provides information

263

on volunteer work, local charities and events around the city, while a different guest speaker talks about a topic each week. There are monthly organised outings – cultural, culinary or sightseeing. There are weekly activities, such as walking, badminton, book or film clubs and mahjong. During the summer months there are coffee mornings in members' homes, as most of the club go back to their home countries. There are also annual formal lunches during spring and at Christmas to raise funds for the year's chosen charity.

Softball

Hong Kong Slo-Pitch Softball Association

King's Park
Yau Ma Tei
Yau Ma Tei
Map 10-B2

www.hongkongsoftball.com

The Hong Kong Slo-Pitch Softball Association (HKSPSA) currently plays every Saturday at King's Park in Kowloon. There are eight teams in the league and up to five games are played from 10:00 to 18:00. King's Park has parking and club house facilities, so family and friends can come along for a nice day out, even if they are not playing. The club does not have a telephone number, so any contact has to be via the website, or by email – info@hongkongsoftball.com.

Surfing

Other options **Beaches** p.198, **Kitesurfing** p.250, **Windsurfing** p.267

There are a few beaches in Hong Kong where it is possible to surf – but don't expect Waikiki. Big Wave Bay (2809 4558) is on the south side of the Island and is a fairly small area of sand, with lifeguards, small cafes and quite a few rental shops where you can hire boards of various sizes, as well as deck chairs, and even sun shades. There are also public toilets and changing rooms with outside showers. The beach is usually clean and on sunny days it gets very crowded. There are good days and bad days for the surf, as well as for the water quality, and on bad days you may find the odd plastic bag floating around. But don't be put off – the good days with hot weather and slightly smaller crowds are really pleasant. The beach is accessible by car or mini bus, but you should get there early if you want a parking place near the beach.

Another surfing beach is also called big wave bay, but in Chinese, so it's known as Dai Lang Wan. Situated in Sai Kung Country Park, it is not so accessible by car: you have to walk or go by boat and swim to it. It is pristinely clean, but very basic and remote, with just two small cafes and some basic toilets. This was where the Quicksilver Surf Championships of Hong Kong took place. It is quite a long and strenuous walk to reach it, but well worth the effort. Serious surf dudes should check out www.wannasurf.com for more information.

Picture Perfect

They say a picture can speak a thousand words so if you can't sum up the sights and sounds of a city in a sentence then grab a copy of one of Explorer's stunning *Mini Photography Books*. Showcasing a unique view of the city, make sure the next time you go on holiday you take home more than just your memories.

Swimming

Other options **Sports & Country Clubs** p.268, **Beaches** p.198

Hong Kong has 37 great outdoor pools run by the government's Leisure and Cultural Services Department. To find exact locations and advice about safety, as well as opening times and prices, go to www.lcsd.gov.hk. The pools are extremely clean with lifeguards on duty at all times. The outdoor swimming pool season runs from April to October, as the rest of the time the water is too cold (honestly!). Some pools have play pools with fun toys and fountains for the kids, while some even have slides with a splash pool. It is possible to swim serious laps too, and often there will be lanes cordoned off for speedy people.

Of course, you can swim in the sea as well, and there are lots of public beaches which are kept clean and monitored by lifeguards (see p.198). The duty times vary throughout the year. The LCSD website has details of good swimming locations. Be warned – some 32 beaches have shark nets, and lots of rules about keeping safe both in the water and on the beach. Also, the sea quality varies from day to day, as with most of the Hong Kong water. All the public beaches have toilets and showers as well as cafes and small shops to sustain you.

Harry Wright International

Various locations

2892 0224 | www.hwiswim.com

This company has been coaching and teaching swimming in Hong Kong for over 30 years. They operate lessons in various locations including West Island School, Pok Fu Lam, Causeway Bay, Aberdeen Marina Club, Ladies Recreation Club and Hong Kong Country Club. They provide tuition for babies right up to international competitive standard. Call Rob or Bev Wright on the number above, or Jayne Wright on 2552 1101.

Team Building

Dragonfly

Chekiang First Bank
Ctr, 1 Duddell St
Central
🚇 *Central*
Map 16-E2

2916 8230 | www.dragonfly.com.hk

This company specialises in leadership, team-building and environment and community programmes. Activities can include a mixture of hiking, climbing, canoeing, cycling and snorkelling, as well as courses to enhance environmental awareness and team building or leadership skills. Some of their courses or events are based in Hong Kong and the outlying islands, while others are further afield in China, Japan, Bali, Nepal and Canada. International schools in the region have used their services, and they have youth programmes in school holidays. Groups must have a minimum of three people.

Kayak and Hike

Nr Public Ferry Pier
Sai Kung
Map 7-A4

9300 5197 | www.kayak-and-hike.com

Paul Etherington, a very experienced outdoor sportsman, will personally guide small groups out into Sai Kung Country Park for outdoor adventure excursions. The trips can incorporate snorkelling, kayaking, hiking or mountain biking to suit the level or interest of the group. Lunch is included in the price. Transport can be arranged from the city into the Country Park if necessary, or you can be utterly indulgent and go for the Heli-Hike option, which includes a helicopter ride back to the city after a day snorkelling or hiking in the Country Park (see Helicopter Flights p.214). Call Paul for more details.

Outward Bound

Tai Mong Tsai
Sai Kung
Map 7-B3

2792 4333 | www.outwardbound.org.hk

Go on an Outward Bound Hong Kong course and you will find yourself out in the Sai Kung Country Park right next to the South China Sea. Courses range from five to 15 days and cater for individuals or schools, as well as adults and corporate leadership training. There is a huge choice of courses available depending on age and experience, and some of the activities include sailing, team-building exercises, hiking, camping, open-top kayaking, abseiling, rock climbing, rope courses, orienteering and raft-building. Some courses are also run overseas in China, Japan and the Philippines. Course fees include accommodation and food, but not airfares. Contact Jon D'Almeida, the Executive Director, on the above number for more information.

Tennis

Other options **Sports & Country Clubs** p.268

Various locations

Hong Kong Ladies Tennis League

9861 7538 | www.hkladiestennis.com

There are currently 700 ladies from private and public clubs and groups of independent teams from all over Hong Kong in this league. There are 77 teams in eight divisions with an age range from 16 to 70 and above with a wide cross section of nationalities who enjoy competitive tennis. There are two seasons: the first from September to December and the second from January to May, with registrations and schedules before the commencement of each season. Matches are played on weekday mornings from 09:00 to approximately 13:00. Lunch is usually provided by the hosting team. Check the website or email hkladiestennis@yahoo.com to find a game near you.

1 MacDonnell Rd
Mid-Levels
Admiralty
Map 16-E2

YWCA ESMD

3476 1340 | www.esmd.ywca.org.hk

Tennis is a popular class at the YWCA, and is taught by freelance professionals in a fun and enjoyable way. Choose a level to suit you (beginners/improvers or intermediate/advanced). Each course lasts around six weeks and will cost approximately $1,500. The classes actually take place at the tennis centre along Wong Nai Chung Gap Road which is between the French International School and the Hong Kong Cricket Club.

Triathlon

Olympic House
1 Stadium Path
So Kon Po
Causeway Bay
Map 17-B3

Hong Kong Triathlon Association

2504 8282 | www.triathlon.com.hk

This association is the governing board for triathlon, duathlon and aquathon events, which are regularly held in Hong Kong. There are the National and Regional Squads, and Age Groupers for younger athletes. As well as competitions, the association runs training sessions and introductory sessions in swimming, biking and running and there are a number of affiliated teams throughout Hong Kong.

Wakeboarding

Tai Mong Tsai Rd
Sai Kung
Map 7-A4

Sai Sha Water Sports Centre

2792 8307

If you want to learn how to wakeboard or you are an expert already, you can do it in beautiful Sai Kung with Sai Sha Water Sports. They will supply all the equipment and can fit five people in their speedboat. There are showers and parking facilities provided, and the instructors speak good English and are very helpful. They also offer other activities like banana boating and tubing. Its all good fun on very calm water.

Sun Hey Mansion
68-76 Hennessy Rd
Wan Chai
Wan Chai
Map 17-A2

SeaDynamics

2604 4747 | www.seadynamics.com

You can arrange a boat for wakeboarding through this company and they will provide all the gear you need, as well as instruction and a pick up from Sai Kung. Wakeboard clinics are also organised throughout the year, where you can get advice from some of Hong Kong's top wakeboarders and waterskiers. But don't be intimidated – the emphasis is still on having fun while learning new tricks.

Water Polo

Wan Chai Swimming
Pool, Harbour Rd
Wan Chai
Wan Chai
Map 17-A2

Hong Kong Water Polo

9020 9405 | www.hongkongwaterpolo.com

Hong Kong Water Polo has two main training locations: the Wan Chai Swimming Pool and Kowloon Park Swimming Pool. Evening training takes place six days a week – Tuesdays, Thursdays and Saturdays are held at Wan Chai, which includes a gym session before pool time. The other training days are at Kowloon Park. There is a junior and senior squad for men and women who compete seriously in international events as well as local events for schools. They have some members of the national team who train with them. All players are welcome and all abilities are represented. They are particularly interested in developing a female squad. The cost is $80 to register for a year and an additional $240 each trimester. This very reasonable fee allows participation in all training sessions.

Windsurfing

Other options **Kitesurfing** p.250

There are quite a few areas in Hong Kong where windsurfing is possible, with wind speeds varying from zero to typhoon strength. Some of the bays are sheltered so there are no waves, which are ideal for beginners, while on those windy days the more advanced surfers can get their kicks. Some beaches (the ones with no shark nets) have windsurfing equipment for hire, with a range of boards to rent on an hourly or daily basis. Some places will offer instruction if you want it.

Windsurfing Centres	
Cheung Chau	2981 8316
Chong Hing, Sai Kung	2792 6810
Lung Kwu	8101 2200
Sha Ha, Sai Kung	2792 5605
Stanley Main Beach	2813 9117
Tai Mei Tuk	2665 3591

Olympic House
1 Stadium Path
So Kon Po
Causeway Bay
Map 17-B3

Hong Kong Windsurfing Association

2504 8255 | www.windsurfing.org.hk

This association organises race competitions for various age groups at locations around Hong Kong. A nominal membership fee gives you race entry access. They also have coaching sessions for all ages and the website has useful information about weather and wind conditions so you can get your board out at the right time.

Wakeboarding
in Sai Kung

Sports & Country Clubs

Many people stump up the big money to join a club and take advantage of its sports facilities, teams, restaurants and bars, children's play areas and spas. Some clubs are very exclusive and expensive. There are various ways of becoming a member. Even if they say they have a waiting list, it may still be possible to join as a sports member if you are truly committed to a particular sport or have coaching experience.

Floors 48-49
Exchange Square Two
Central
🚇 *Central*
Map 16-E2

American Club

2842 7400 | www.americanclubhk.com

The American Club has two clubhouses, one known as the town, and the other as the country club (28 Tai Tam Road, Tai Tam, 2813 3200). Each venue has wonderful catering and sports facilities. The country club offers the largest selection, while the smaller town club offers a gym and sauna room in Central. The country club has a pool, a teen room, a spa and a golf driving range. It is a private members club, and some membership categories allow non-US citizens.

139 Tai Au Mun Rd
Clear Water Bay
Map 11-B4

Clearwater Bay Golf & Country Club

2719 1595 | www.cwbgolf.org

This is a stunning club with top-class golfing facilities, and a marina in which to moor your yacht (lucky you). The Clear Water Bay peninsula has breathtaking views out to the South China Sea. The easiest way to get to the club is to drive, although there is a shuttle-bus service for members from Hang Hau MTR Station. The restaurant and swimming pool area are beautiful; it's just like being in a five-star resort. A guided tour can be arranged if you are interested in joining. For golf membership contact Jerry Mo on 2335 3707, for country club or marina membership contact Shirley Wong on 2335 3746, and for the Membership Relations Office call Fanita Tam on 2335 3788.

188 Wong Nai
Chung Rd
Happy Valley
🚇 *Causeway Bay*
Map 17-A3

Craigengower Cricket Club

2577 8331 | www.ccc1894.com

Originally founded in 1894 as a cricket club, these days it provides many sports facilities for its members, and the whole site has been upgraded. It has golf driving bays, badminton courts, and an outdoor swimming pool. It also has lawn bowls, tennis and squash courts, as well as popular restaurants and bars.

Gold Coast
Tuen Mun
Map 5-A4

Gold Coast Yacht and Country Club

2404 2222 | www.goldcoastclub.com.hk

This is a splendid yacht and country club in the Gold Coast, Tuen Mun area of the New Territories. It has a marina for convenient parking for your yacht (there's space for 200 of them), as well as spa facilities to help you relax and be pampered after a hard day spent sailing and generally enjoying yourself. It has a wide range of sports facilities and also caters for children, with play areas and a computer games room. The design is old and colonial and you feel as though you are in California or Spain instead of Asia once inside.

137 Wong Nai Chung
Gap Rd
Happy Valley
Map 17-C4

Hong Kong Cricket Club

3511 8668 | www.hkcc.org

A friendly club which welcomes members and non-members (the latter only for a selected number of sports), there are also gorgeous views from the pool area and facilities of a high standard. It caters for families and often has fun days for children. They also have a very popular restaurant called DotCod, which is in The Prince's Building, Central.

Hong Kong Football Club

3 Sports Rd
Happy Valley
Causeway Bay
Map 17-B3

2830 9500 | *www.hkfc.com.hk*

This club was founded in 1886, and historically both Association and Rugby Football were played – hence the name. Today, the club is huge and renowned for its facilities and sports teams. They have teams, leagues and coaching, not just for football (both types), but for many other sports too. The club is right next to Happy Valley Race Course so it's possible to watch the horse racing on race days. Membership is currently closed, although it is possible to become a Sports Member if you meet the requirements of the club. To contact the Membership Services Manager directly, email kerry_ogle@hkfc.com, or call 2830 9502.

Hong Kong Jockey Club

Happy Valley
Clubhouse
Happy Valley
Causeway Bay
Map 17-A2

2966 1333 | *www.hkjc.com*

It is possible to become a member of the Hong Kong Jockey Club and enjoy the magnificent facilities at all three of their clubhouses, which have restaurants, swimming pools, tennis and squash courts, gyms and spas, and a riding centre (at the Beas River Country Club, 2966 1981). You can either become a racing member, full member or corporate member. The Sha Tin Clubhouse contact number is 2966 6500.

Kowloon Cricket Club

10 Cox's Rd
Jordan
Jordan
Map 15-D3

2367 4141 | *www.kcc.org.hk*

This is a very popular sports club in a very busy and built-up area. However, once you walk through the gate it is quite amazing to believe that you are still in the city. KCC takes its sport seriously and has many teams who play to a high standard. It has a lovely green cricket field, a beautiful pool with waited service, sports facilities and lots of restaurants and bars. The food itself is famous. Membership is sought-after – at the moment it is frozen and has been for the last three years. Contact the club directly for details of possible sports membership or corporate membership.

Ladies Recreational Club

10 Old Peak Rd
The Peak
Map 16-D3

3199 3500 | *www.lrc.com.hk*

This is an exclusive club for members only. Its facilities include indoor and outdoor pools, tennis and squash courts, a fitness centre and a spa. Founded in 1883, originally for lady expats to socialise and play sport, these days men are welcome too. Membership is around $2,500 at the moment. The Peak is 'the address to have' in Hong Kong, situated, as you would expect, on a hill with marvelous views and surrounded by green trees.

Repulse Bay Club

109 Repulse Bay Rd
Repulse Bay
Map 14-D2

2292 2900 | *www.therepulsebay.com*

This club is attached to a high-class housing development, although non-residents are welcome to join and enjoy the extensive facilities. These include a health spa, sauna, steam room, Jacuzzi, golf driving bay, indoor swimming pool, and tennis and squash courts. It also has a number of restaurants and cafes. The club organises a large variety of classes, such as aerobics, kick-boxing, yoga and ballet. The classes are for both adults and children.

United Services Recreation Club

1 Gascoigne Rd
King's Park
Jordan
Jordan
Map 15-D3

2367 0672 | *www.usrc.org.hk*

Situated in Kowloon, this club is tucked away from the busy city. It offers its members and guests park-like greenery and a peaceful shaded space to relax or make use of the sports facilities and pool. You can either play sport yourself or take advantage of their classes and coaching. The club house was built in 1911 and reflects the colonial era.

269

Well-Being

Whether it's a pampering session at a health spa, managing your stress, or bending your limbs into all manner of positions, whatever your definition of well-being there's a good chance that somebody, somewhere in Hong Kong will have the necessary skills and facilities to have you looking and feeling better in no time.

Beauty Salons

Other options **Perfumes & Cosmetics** p.311, **Health Spas** p.272

There is no shortage of beauty salons in Hong Kong. All budgets are catered for, from a basic hairdressers where you just queue up for a chair and a quick cut, to centres that offer decadent treatments where you can be pampered to your heart's delight. International names, such as Toni and Guy and Esprit Salon are available, and some places specialise in European hair styles with stylists from all over the world. Depending on your pocket and preference you can have whatever you wish for. Some of the smaller salons do not have a very good grasp of English, so explaining exactly what you want can be difficult – photographs and magazines will always help.

Hairdressers

Hong Kong has plenty of hairdressers, with a wild variety of taste, style and price. Salons are located in the main shopping areas, the more upscale fashionable places are housed inside buildings and hotels. Most, if not all of them, accept walk-ins. A haircut and blow dry can cost anything from $90 to $120 for men and $160 to $200 for women. Prices are normally displayed outside or in the window and magazines are full of advertisements for deals and special cuts and treatments. Many salons now incorporate a beauty section for complete pampering, offering services like manicures, pedicures, dying and tinting your hair, a hot oil treatment, waxing and eyebrow threading. Unless it's a barber shop where you pay about $60 for haircut, salons are unisex. You might read or hear of a hairdresser who will make house calls from time to time but because people come and go in Hong Kong, they might not be around for long.

Children's Hairdressers		
The Colour Bar	Central	2525 4228
The Firm	Central	2537 9132
Hair Studio	Stanley	2813 7808
Magic Mirror	Causeway Bay	2882 2122
Tala's	Sai Kung	2335 1694
Toni & Guy	Central	2801 7870

Many expats are in this beauty business and can do well once wealthy Chinese women discover them. These modern salons are for the most part located in Central and stock imported products that are also on sale. A haircut here can set you back a hefty $1,000 and if it's the top stylist you can add on a bit more.

Haircuts can be traumatic for children so when you go for yours, take them along so that they can see what happens and when their turn comes they might be more willing to sit still. See a list of hairdressers in the table above.

Prices range from $75 to $400. These salons have toys, videos and children's furniture. Magic Mirror offers a 15% discount on Fridays and Toni & Guy offer a 50% discount from Monday to Thursday. In Tala's, kids can watch a video while getting their hair cut.

Hairdressers		
Beyond the Fringe	Causeway Bay	2519 6988
Charmes de France	Wan Chai	2861 2288
Classica	Repulse Bay	2812 0202
The Colour Bar	Central	2525 4228
Emmanuel F	Central	2167 8280
The Firm	Central	2537 9132
Hair Studio	Stanley	2813 7808
The Hairdresser	Central	2973 0512
Hipp.Fish	Central	2281 5363
La Coup	Central	2868 2266
Paul Gerrard	Central	2869 4408
Philip George Salon	Central	2524 3143
QB (Quick Barber)	Wan Chai	2359 3300
Rever Beauty Salon	Tsim Sha Tsui	2366 7298
Taliana	Central	2523 6465
Toni & Guy	Central	2801 7870

Not big, but very clever…

Perfectly proportioned to fit in your pocket,
this marvellous mini guidebook makes sure
you don't just get the holiday you paid for
but rather the one that you dreamed of.

Singapore Mini Visitors' Guide
Maximising your holiday, minimising your hand luggage

Abu Dhabi · Amsterdam · Bahrain · Barcelona · Dubai · Dublin · Geneva · Hong Kong · Kuwait
London · New York · New Zealand · Oman · Paris · Qatar · Shanghai · Singapore · Sydney

EXPLORER
www.explorerpublishing.com

Health Spas

Other options **Sports & Country Clubs** p.268

Visiting a spa is an escape from Hong Kong's stressful pace of life. The range of treatments and general pampering available is extensive. Some are within five-star hotels while others are hidden away in a high rise but are surprisingly spacious once you get inside. Once you emerge, you will feel like a completely new person.

CNAC Group Bld
10 Queen's Rd
Central
Central
Map 16-E2

AsoSpa

2525 2578 | www.asospa.com

AsoSpa is Hong Kong's Japanese-style spa. Treatments include facials, body scrubs and wraps, massages, slimming treatments and a hydrotherapy bath. Their signature treatment is the Hot Sand Bath which is a traditional Japanese technique dating back 300 years for relaxation, discharging toxins and oxygenating the body – it is especially good for rheumatism or arthritis.

The Centrium
60 Wyndham St
Central
Central
Map 16-E2

Body Conscious Clinical Spa

2524 6171 | www.bodyconscioushk.com

The difference with this spa is that they use a diagnostic-based approach to each therapy treatment and encourage clients to be aware of their health and well-being. They advocate the idea that with the proper maintenance, the body will continue to work well into old age. Body Conscious treatments and massages include Shiatsu, Cranio-sacral therapy, Thai massage, reflexology, aromatic Swedish massage, aromatherapy massage, deep-tissue massage, lymphatic drainage, consciousness head massage and pregnancy massage.

18-20 Sing Woo Rd
Happy Valley
Causeway Bay
Map 17-B3

BodyWize

2838 5808 | www.bodywize.com.hk

This is a small boutique-style spa offering personalised service to each client. The small team are professionally trained and the atmosphere is very relaxing. BodyWize has experienced beauticians and uses well known spa products, such as Elemis, La Therapie and Dermalogica. Treatments include facial therapy, body therapy, hand and foot treatments and special packages each month.

Langham Place Hotel
Mong Kok
Mong Kok
Map 15-C2

Chuan Spa

3552 3510 | www.langhamhotels.com

The decor is Chinese-themed and the five elements of traditional Chinese herbal medicine are applied in the treatments. Its 41st floor-location at the Langham Place Hotel has magnificent views, and they offer a vast range of treatments. For a minimum fee of $750, (an hour's massage), you can make use of the spa's facilities for the rest of the day, including a rooftop pool, fitness rooms, relaxation rooms and a sauna.

Baskerville House
13 Duddell St
Central
Central
Map 16-E2

Decleor Spa

2890 2038 | www.decleor.com

This spa and beauty treatment salon offers a wide range of body and facial treatments using 100% natural Decleor skin care products. Decleor is an international range with spas all over the world. At the Central salon there are nine treatment rooms and changing rooms. The staff speak English and offer treatments for face and body including massage and waxing. For more information, try the above number or Phyllis Wong from Decleor Institut de Beaute on 2865 6811.

Elemis Day Spa

Century Square
1 D'Aguilar St
Central
Central
Map 16-E2

2521 6660 | www.elemisdayspa.com.hk

Elemis is popular with expats and offers an escape from hectic Hong Kong life. The tranquil environment promotes relaxation and 'a world of complete sensory heaven'. There are lockers and private changing rooms for every visitor. They offer a range of treatments including packages for men, slimming, tanning, facials, self-tanning, detoxing, floats and scrubs, and manicures and pedicures.

Ellespa

109 Repulse Bay Rd
Repulse Bay
Map 14-C1

2537 7736 | www.ellespa.com

Elle Spa has all the qualities you would expect from of a top spa: great staff, excellent products and a stylish design. It offers treatments for men and women and has special packages during pregnancy. However it has something that most HK spas lack – setting. It is located at Repulse Bay in a quiet section of the shopping complex. It faces the sea and you can catch glimpses of water and lots of sky. It allows to feel you have been transported somewhere else and this makes the experience even more relaxing and calming.

EQ Spa

59 Connaught Rd
Central
Sheung Wan
Map 16-D1

2787 7338 | www.eqspa.com.hk

They provide top quality spa services for both men and women. Treatments include Royal Thai spa, body massage, body slimming and facial treatment, as well as slightly more obscure ones such as Mini Cyclone Tatoo Craser Eye Brow, Eye Lash Perming, Aroma Ear Candling and Ginger Brown Sugar Baths. The professional beauty and massage therapists use both traditional and advanced technology to promote relaxation.

Chuan Spa relaxation room

Infinity spa pools at the InterContinental Hong Kong

Oriental Spa at the Landmark Mandarin Oriental

19-27 Wyndham St
Wilson House
Central
🚇 *Central*
Map 16-E2

Frederique Spa

2522 3054 | www.paua.com.hk

This is a tranquil environment with friendly staff. Each treatment room is private and the more pricey ones have their own shower facilities. The treatments on offer include Swedish body massage, Indian head massage, reflexology, St. Tropez air brush tanning, waxing, manicure, facial therapies, slimming and detox wraps, pre and post-natal packages, as well as extra special packages such as 'Pure Indulgence' (lime and ginger salt glow, exotic frangipani body nourish cocoon and well-being massage) They use Elemis products.

InterContinental
Hong Kong
Tsim Sha Tsui
🚇 *Tsim Sha Tsui*
Map 15-D4

I-Spa

2721 1211 | www.hongkong-ic.intercontinental.com

This is Hong Kong's only 'Feng Shui-Friendly' spa. It has luxuriously spacious spa suites, each with its own sauna, steam shower, Jacuzzi and massage facilities. Select from a range of treatments including 'Oriental Healing' and 'Jet Lag Relief'. The staff here are very friendly and the utmost privacy is afforded to every client. After treatments you will be left to enjoy the surroundings and relax for half an hour – but you still won't want to leave.

Soundwill Plaza
38 Russell St
Causeway Bay
🚇 *Causeway Bay*
Map 14-B2

Leonard Drake

3156 1181 | www.leonarddrake.com.hk

This international company has two locations in Hong Kong. The second is at Hotel Miramar, 118-130 Nathan Road, Tsim Sha Tsui, Kowloon (2735 6368). Their signature treatment is facial skin care using high quality products. Leonard Drake offers a face mapping service, where the skin on the face is carefully analysed which can be an indication of problems elsewhere in the body, such as the digestive system. Once this procedure is carried out they can then offer treatments to rectify any problems. They are affiliated to The International Dermal Institute in Los Angeles. For first-time customers the treatments are half price.

The Landmark
Mandarin Oriental
Central
🚇 *Central*
Map 16-E2

The Oriental Spa

2132 0188 | www.mandarinoriental.com/landmark

This spa takes up the entire 5th and 6th floors of this fabulous hotel. The schedule for customers is limited to keep the atmosphere calm and quiet. Each treatment or massage room is private and the decor is themed with natural products like bamboo and stone. The staff speak excellent English and will offer you tea before and after each session. Soft, fluffy robes are also supplied. Bliss.

The Peninsula
Tsim Sha Tsui
🚇 *Tsim Sha Tsui*
Map 15-D4

The Peninsula Spa by ESPA

2315 3322 | www.hongkong.peninsula.com

This is a very new spa situated on the Peninsula's seventh floor. Their treatments and rituals include Ayurvedic massage, distress packages, post- and pre- natal and bride-to-be treatments. The surroundings are as sumptuous as you would expect from Hong Kong's most famous hotel. You can book a whole day or half a day experience. If you book these spa packages the hotel encourages clients to arrive 60 minutes before the appointment time to make use of their facilities, such as the Asian Tea Lounge, thermal suite and crystal steam room. It is also possible to book a private spa suite for one or two, and prices for packages include a healthy lunch.

Two Intl Finance Ctr
8 Finance St
Central
Central
Map 16-E2

Pure Spa

8129 8883 | www.pure-spa.com

Pure Spa offers an extensive range of spa, beauty treatments and body therapies to relieve the stresses of day to day life. This is part of the 'Pure' organisation; they also have Pure Yoga and Pure Fitness. It is possible to become a member and buy treatments upfront. They use professional products such as Elemis and La Therapie. Their second location is in the Kinwick Centre, 32 Hollywood Road, Central (2970 3366).

10D Po Tung Rd
Sai Kung
Map 7-A4

Sabai

2791 2259

If you are looking for some pampering in Sai Kung out in the New Territories, Sabai offers you all you could possibly need. Although small, it is cosy and discrete, offering a professional service with a wide variety of treatments including facials and massages. The staff speak excellent English and the spa is very popular with the local expat clientele. Look out for Honeymoon Desert as a landmark – it's just above it.

60 Wyndham St
Central
Central
Map 16-E2

SE Spa and Salon

2530 3898 | www.se-spa.com

This spa, run by Swedish sisters, specialises in European treatments using organic products. The decor is contemporary using natural colours, wood and stone. They have five beautiful treatment rooms with names like 'aqua', 'relax', 'rejuvenate', 'regenerate' and 'refresh' where you will receive professional service by experienced spa therapists. Their treatments include therapeutic massage, a jet-lag recovery package, hand and feet indulgences as well as spa party packages or tailor-made packages. SE Spa also has a hair salon section offering the latest fashion in hair as well as specialising in hair treatment. Each customer receives a hair consultation followed by intensive hair treatment, including Swedish head massage techniques.

83A Hollywood Rd
Central
Central
Map 16-E2

Sense of Touch

2517 0939 | www.senseoftouch.com.hk

Sense of Touch has two locations; one on Hollywood Rd and a second at The Ovolo, 2 Arbuthnot Rd, Central, (2869 0939). It was voted the best small spa in Asia in 2005. As well as basic facials, massage, detox and nail care, there are many other packages available, offering a plethora of pampering. Decor is a mixture of modern and ethnic design. Their signature treatment is a Brazilian wax: they use special wax brought to Hong Kong from the US. Sense of Touch will even organise a spa party for a minimum of three or maximum of eight to make a great girl's day out. These can be at your own home or in the spa itself and are very popular with their expat clientele.

Pilates

Other options **Yoga** p.276

California Tower
30-32 D'Aguilar St
Central
Central
Map 15-E2

Iso Fit

2869 8630 | www.isofit.com.hk

This studio is equipped with a full range of Pilates equipment which is used in group or private individual supervised sessions. It is possible to purchase session packages of five, 10, 15 or 20 sessions as well as attend single drop-in classes. Each class lasts 60 minutes. New clients will be personally assessed so that each individual works at their own pace. Iso Fit has pre-natal Pilates and post-natal Pilates classes with a maximum of eight per class as well as 'Better Golf with Pilates' to improve your swing.

28 Man Nin St
Sai Kung
Map 7-A4

The Studio

2791 9705 | www.thestudiosaikung.com

The Studio is a small fitness centre in Sai Kung which offers a range of exercise classes throughout the week. Their specialism is Pilates, with classes available for complete beginners, through to advanced level. Antenatal Pilates classes are also offered.

1 MacDonnell Rd
Mid-Levels
🚇 *Admiralty*
Map 16-E2

YWCA ESMD

3476 1340 | www.esmd.ywca.org.hk

Pilates is a very popular class at the YWCA, especially the Pilates for pregnant ladies classes which promise to improve body control and stamina in time for childbirth. Lessons are open for members and non-members at various times throughout the morning and afternoon. The schedule of classes changes throughout the year. Check the website for details.

Stress Management

Other options **Support Groups** p.143

1 MacDonnell Rd
Mid-Levels
🚇 *Admiralty*
Map 16-E2

YWCA ESMD

3476 1340 | www.esmd.ywca.org.hk

The YWCA has a number of courses for people who need to reduce the stress in their lives – a common problem in Hong Kong. One such course is Mindfulness-Based Stress Reduction. This is free and open to people from all professions and walks of life. The initial session is an orientation to help you decide if it's the right course for you. Other courses include anti-aging, holistic skincare, acupressure, and improving eating behaviour.

Yoga

Other options **Pilates** p.275

This city is currently gripped by yoga frenzy, and there are many centres popping up all over the place. They tend to range from splendid small classes with excellent teachers, to large, sometimes impersonal studios. However, generally the instruction is top standard in all venues, despite some pressure to join as yearly members. Drop-in rates are available but these tend to be prohibitively expensive to encourage you to sign up. For the committed, annual packages do offer great value for money.

Sands Bld
17 Hankow Rd
Tsim Sha Tsui
🚇 *Tsim Sha Tsui*
Map 15-C4

Bikram Yoga

3165 8080 | www.bikramyoga.com.hk

Get ready to sweat, because the classes here are conducted in a hot studio (40ºC) which boosts flexibility and vitality. Groups are quite large, although there are lots of classes throughout each day, which seem to appeal to the younger end of the yoga market. The club has a spacious studio and pleasant changing facilities. There is some pressure to sign up for membership with offers of free classes and free gifts. They are linked to Planet Yoga.

Woodleigh House
80 Stanley Village Rd
Stanley
Map 14-D2

Flex HK

2813 2212 | www.flexhk.com

Located in Stanley, Flex HK is a dedicated Pilates and yoga studio. It offers private and semi-private Pilates instruction with a complete set of Pilates apparatus. Pilates and yoga classes are offered daily, including mat and allegro Pilates, pre/post-natal Pilates and yoga, Iyengar and Hatha Vinyasa flow yoga, as well as children's yoga.

International Yoga Institute

Valiant Commercial
Bld, 22-24 Prat Ave
Tsim Sha Tsui
Tsim Sha Tsui
Map 15-D4

2369 6696 | www.yoga-iyi.com

At the IYI, group classes take place in the afternoons and evenings. Lessons can be paid for individually, or you can sign up for a course of five or ten. People signing up for 10 sessions are allowed 12 weeks to finish them, thus allowing a little flexibility in your schedule. Private one-on-one sessions can also be arranged.

Planet Yoga

Silver Fortune Plaza
1 Wellington St
Central
Central
Map 15-E2

2525 8288 | www.planetyoga.com.hk

A huge yoga centre conveniently situated in Central with a floor space of 20,000 sq ft. There are four large studios in this space and the centre offers up to 200 classes each week. The shower and changing facilities are beautiful. There is also a steam room plus a lounge for meditation. They are linked to Bikram Yoga, and you can become a joint member of both Bikram Yoga and Planet Yoga allowing access to both centres.

Pure Yoga

Soundwill Plaza
38 Russell St
Causeway Bay
Causeway Bay
Map 17-B2

2970 2299 | www.pure-yoga.com

Probably the best of the yoga big boys, with literally hundreds of classes on offer throughout the week. The teachers are excellent and as they have three centres it means you are never far from a class. Absolute beginners to experienced yogis are all welcome. If you are interested in pursuing your hobby to a higher level, they offer regular training events and workshops to teach yoga. Other locations include 16/F The Centrium in Central (2971 0055) and 14/F The Peninsula Office Tower in Kowloon (8129 8800).

Yoga Central

13 Wyndham St
Central
Central
Map 16-E2

2982 4308 | www.yogacentral.com.hk

Unusually, this yoga studio requires no membership. You can pay per class or buy a few classes to be used within a certain time, which works out cheaper. The classes run throughout the day and evening with a maximum of 16 people in each class. All equipment is supplied, and Pilates classes are also available.

Yoga Limbs

69 Jervois St
Sheung Wan
Sheung Wan
Map 16-D1

2525 7415 | www.yogalimbs.com

This is a first-class studio with growing popularity, especially after opening their second Yoga Limbs in Clear Water Bay (2803 7101). It is a small family-run business offering Hatha, Ashtanga and an excellent teacher training programme – one of the best around. Their classes run throughout the day to suit office workers' lunch breaks and mums on the school run. Evening sessions are also available.

Yoga Plus

LKF Tower
33 Wyndham St
Central
Central
Map 16-E2

2901 2901 | www.yogaplus.com.hk

Classes in yoga, Indian dance and Pilates run every day in their three well equipped studios. The classes are in many different styles of yoga including Ashtanga, Hatha and Iyengar. The studios and changing areas are beautiful and there is also a spa offering pampering treatments. For a perk before you rejoin the Hong Kong throng you can treat yourself to a freshly squeezed health drink at the juice bar.

YWCA ESMD

1 MacDonnell Rd
Mid-Levels
Admiralty
Map 16-E2

3476 1340 | www.esmd.ywca.org.hk

There is an extensive range of exercise and fitness classes available at the YWCA. Yoga and Pilates are very popular. No membership is required to join the classes, which cost around $175 each.

The world has much to offer.
It's just knowing where to find it.

If you're an American Express® Cardmember, simply visit
americanexpress.com/selects or visit your local homepage, and click on
'offers'. You'll find great offers wherever you are today, all in one place.

selects

THE WORLD OFFERS. WE SELECT. YOU ENJOY.

Shopping

Shopping

Shopping in Hong Kong is not so much a chore or a necessity as an obsession. In a city so crowded that most residential or office developments are vertigo-inducing skyscrapers, it seems room can always be made for another capacious mall or upmarket shopping district – and there is never any shortage of customers eager to fill them. Most of Hong Kong Island's flashiest retail jewels are located in Central, Admiralty or Causeway Bay – home to a clutch of high-end designer stores and western-style malls – while an altogether more Asian shopping experience can be found amid the bright lights and sprawling markets of Kowloon.

Multitasking Malls
Most malls include a great deal more than just shops, with many sporting cinemas, ice rinks, foodcourts and upmarket restaurants. The Dragon Centre in Sham Shui Po even has a mini rollercoaster. See Places to Shop starting on p.318.

Prices for clothing, accessories, shoes and homewares are comparable with Europe, the United States and Australia, and both ends of the price spectrum are well represented. Cameras, computers and electronic equipment are slightly cheaper than in many countries but Hong Kong's reputation as a Mecca for such goods at bargain prices is beginning to wane. That said, the choice of electronic items on offer, from MP3 players and mobile phones, to flat-screen televisions and digital cameras, is jaw-dropping, and discounts can be obtained at some smaller retailers if you are prepared to haggle, although this is becoming less common.

There is no sales tax in Hong Kong, so there are no nasty surprises when you get to the till. Sales assistants at the large chain stores can be a little over-attentive, which can be irritating when you just want to be left alone to shop. Be polite but firm, however, and they will reluctantly leave you to your own devices. English is widely spoken and there is usually at least one person in each store who is fluent, so complicated gestures and explanatory actions are generally not necessary.

One thing to watch out for is that shops tend to open and close, or move premises, at a faster rate than in most other cities, so it's worth phoning first if the store you seek is out of your way.

There are a growing number of second-hand shopping options in this eternally image-conscious city. Websites such as www.geoexpat.com and www.hongkong.asiaxpat.com – where people leaving this transient metropolis, or merely upgrading their television, offload their unwanted furniture, electronic items and more at a fraction of the retail price – are perennial favourites. A shopping festival promoting the city's retail prowess, and featuring an array of special offers, events and discounts, takes place each year from the last week in June until the end of August, while there are sales periods between Christmas and Chinese New Year (early to mid-February) and around the end of July. Of particular note is the fact most shops start their sales halfway through December, meaning you can save a pretty penny if you don't mind leaving your Christmas shopping till the last minute.

Online Shopping

Although Hong Kong offers an unrivalled 'real world' shopping experience, online shopping is becoming increasingly popular, particularly for items that are not available locally. Unlike mainland China, there are no restrictions on what internet sites can be visited from Hong Kong computers, and credit cards from Hong Kong banks are accepted around the world. Customs officials are no more zealous than those in the United States and Europe, so unless your package is suspicious, there should be no problems in receiving your goods intact and on time. All the usual suspects, such as Amazon (www.amazon.com), As Seen On TV (www.asseenontv.com) and eBay (www.ebay.com), deliver to Hong Kong, as do the vast majority of sites that offer international shipping. Shipping fees from outside Asia typically cost from about $150 for a small to medium package, such as a hardback book, small gift or item of clothing, while larger purchases can cost substantially more. Locally, an impressive choice of books can be ordered from Paddyfield (www.paddyfield.com), where you should pay no more than the cover price, and who will deliver orders of more than $150 free of charge. Orders under $150 incur an $8 postage fee. HMV (www.hmv.com.hk) has a large selection of music and movies, and shipping rates start at $16. AsiaXPAT (www.hongkong.asiaxpat.com) and Geoexpat (www.geoexpat.com), meanwhile, offer a huge range of second-hand goods at negotiable prices. Other useful local shopping sites include Shop In HK (www.shopinhk.com) for books, DVDs and toys, the self-explanatory Luxury Gift Company (www.theluxurygiftcompany.com) and useful price-comparison service My Choice (www.mychoice.com.hk).

Refunds and Exchanges

Exchange policies vary from store to store, but in general refunds are rare unless goods are faulty – and even then you may have to make do with an exchange. It is imperative you keep your receipt as your chances of obtaining a refund or exchange without one are greatly reduced, although credit card bills can be a useful back-up as proof of purchase. Most international brands will allow an exchange of products returned in their original condition with accompanying receipt within an allotted period (usually seven or 14 days). Items bought on sale, however, usually cannot be returned or exchanged for any reason, so make sure it is what you want and in good working order before you part with your cash. Marks & Spencer are the notable exception to this rule (see Places to Shop on p.318).

Consumer Rights

Consumer rights have improved considerably in recent years, thanks mainly to the Hong Kong Tourism Board (HKTB) and the Consumer Council. The latter's website (www.consumer.org.hk) contains a wealth of information on what to do if you have a complaint, your legal rights and general consumer information such as product recalls and safety alerts. It also lists the Consumer Advice Centres around the territory. You can contact them by phone on 2929 2222. Buying from stores that display the Quality Tourism Services (QTS) logo gives added peace of mind. For more general shopping advice, the Community Advice Bureau (2815 5444; 09:30 to 16:30 daily, www.cab.org.hk) is an invaluable source of information. In the event of a serious dispute that requires immediate attention, the HKTB recommends calling the police on 999.

Shipping

As the former busiest port in the world (an honour recently taken by Singapore) and the gateway between west and east, there is no shortage of local and international shipping couriers ready and willing to whisk your package off around the world – or merely deliver it safely and in double-quick time across town. The government-run Hongkong Post (www.hongkongpost.com) is relatively cheap, safe and reliable, while their exhaustive website offers a useful postage calculator which will tell you the cost of sending an item to anywhere in the world. Packages of 2kg or less can be sent via their normal overseas postage service (surface or air), which is probably the cheapest option, although not the fastest. Hongkong Post's Speedpost is much faster, but pricier, while a bulk mailing service is also available. If you need something shipped fast, the usual worldwide shipping companies are well represented in Hong Kong, such as UPS (www.ups.com), DHL (www.dhl.com.hk) and FedEx (www.fedex.com) and rates are comparable to those in Europe and the United States. When buying furniture or other large items, many stores may offer to ship it for you. Prices and reliability vary, so it may be worth getting quotes from the aforementioned companies before you decide.

Quality Tourism Services

When shopping at smaller stores, look out for the Quality Tourism Services (QTS) logo, which indicates the shop is regulated by the Hong Kong Tourism Board. This is no guarantee the shop will exchange or refund goods for you, but it does mean, in the event of a dispute, you have a designated channel through which to appeal. A list of shops participating in the scheme can be found at the Hong Kong Tourism Board's website, www.discoverhong kong.com.

How to Pay

Like any major city, there are a number of payment methods open to the Hong Kong shopper. Visa, Mastercard and American Express are accepted at the vast majority of stores. Holders of Diners Club cards, however, will find the range of outlets in which they can flash their plastic somewhat reduced. Anyone with a local bank account (such as those at HSBC or Hang Seng banks) can pay by EPS, which debits the money straight from your account. This requires you to enter your PIN number into a handset attached to the till rather than signing a receipt. When bargaining in independent electronics or camera stores, paying in cash may secure you a better discount if you haggle. Cash is usually the only acceptable method of payment in markets. Currencies other than Hong Kong dollars are not generally accepted, although an increasing number of malls, international brands and department stores have begun to accept the Chinese reminbi and even US dollars. The exchange rate, however, is likely to be less generous than in banks.

Bargaining

Other options **Markets** p.333

Depending on where you shop, bargaining can be an acceptable and useful practice in Hong Kong, although this is becoming less prevalent. Attempting to haggle in the vast majority of stores will earn you nothing more than looks of puzzlement and scorn from the sales staff, but in the many electronics, camera and mobile phone shops of Tsim Sha Tsui and other areas it can lead to significant discounts or 'bonus' items, such as a free memory card or carry case. Retailers in such establishments seem more willing to lower their prices if you are purchasing more than one item, so, if possible, team up with a friend who is also looking to make a similar purchase. Another tip is to go around 10:30 or 11:00, when the shops are just opening. Superstitious shopkeepers are often keen to make their auspicious first sale of the day as early as possible and so may be more open to haggling. Bear in mind though that some, but not all, such retailers are telling the truth when they say their prices are fixed. If in doubt, walk away; anyone willing to bargain will soon chase after you. In the markets, feel free to bargain like crazy. As before, if the stall-holder lets you walk away you know you have the best deal – and a sense of humour and a smile is far likelier to reap a discount than a hard-nosed insistence that they give you their 'best price'. Even a little knowledge of Cantonese will go a long way to proving you are not a dumb tourist ripe for the fleecing.

What & Where to Buy – Quick Reference

Alcohol

Other options **Bars & Pubs** p.390

Passion for Pinot?
For wine connoisseurs,
Oliver's has a small
but well-chosen
vintage selection.

There is certainly no shortage of places to enjoy a tipple in Hong Kong, with enough licensed bars, clubs and restaurants to satisfy even the most avid of thirsts. The legal drinking age is 18, and although some bars and clubs have an over 21s door policy, this is rarely enforced. For those wishing to indulge at home, there are a large number of options, which vary greatly in terms of range and price. In general, a bottle of wine costs from about $50 upwards, beers cost about $10 a bottle or can, and spirits about $120 a bottle and up, although downmarket brands (such as the ubiquitous King Robert whiskey, gin and vodka) cost less. An extensive selection of vintages from every notable wine-producing country in the world can be found at Watson's Wine Cellar, priced from under $100 to several thousand

Alcohol		
Bordeaux Fine Wines	Admiralty	2312 0885
Castello del Vino	Various	See p.339
City'super	Various	See p.339
Delicatessan Corner	Tsim Sha Tsui	2315 1020
Eurotreat	SoHo	2537 0210
Fentons Gourmet	Happy Valley	3422 3411
Force 8 Cellars	SoHo	2527 6217
Gallerie du Vin	Various	See p.341
Gourmet	Lee Gardens	3693 4101
Great	Pacific Place	2526 2832
Il Bel Paese	Various	See p.341
In Senses	SoHo	2525 7075
Marks & Spencer	Various	See p.343
Maxi Wines	Central	2869 6805
Oliver's	Prince's Building	2810 7710
ParknShop	Various	See p.344
Ponti Food & Wine Cellar	Alexandra House/Chater House	2810 1000
SoHo Wines & Spirits	Various	See p.345
Taste	Festival Walk	2265 8698
UNY	Cityplaza	2885 0331
Viva Italia	The Peak	2849 2030
Watson's Wine Cellar	Various	See p.346
Wellcome	Various	See p.346

dollars a bottle. SoHo Wines & Spirits meanwhile offers an impressive range of beers, wines and spirits at its three locations, while you can also order online (www.sohowines.hk) and let them deliver to your door. An exhaustive selection of Italian wines can be found at Castello Del Vino in Central, while Bordeaux Fine Wines in Admiralty specialises in French varieties. For general alcohol purchases, supermarkets are usually the cheapest and most convenient options, as even the smallest stores generally have a fair-sized alcohol section. Wellcome and ParknShop can be found all over the city, while their flasher cousins, such as Great, City'super and Oliver's offer a huge choice of imported wines, beers, spirits and liqueurs. Last, but by no means least, is 7-Eleven, which can be found on almost every street corner and is open 24 hours. These sell beer, spirits and often wine around the clock… not to mention headache tablets for the morning after.

Antiques

Hong Kong has a colourful and varied array of arts, crafts and antiques for serious and not-so-serious collectors. Be careful though, as there are also expert forgeries and reproductions.

Most of the really good pieces are in private collections and are sold through Sotheby's or Christie's, who have a stunning selection of pieces up for auction. Both

283

houses have regular sales of ceramics, jewellery, jade, stamps, snuff bottles, calligraphy, and traditional and modern artworks. For more on art in Hong Kong, see p.284. If your budget doesn't stretch into the millions of dollars, head to the Central/SoHo area; it's a treasure trove for antique collectors. You can pick up anything from ten dollar bronze hair pins to Han dynasty pottery horses worth tens of thousands of dollars. Hollywood Road is lined with both pricey shops and small, family-run businesses selling bowls of old Chinese 'lucky' coins, a jumble of Chinese screens and furniture, Tibetan rugs, religious statues, traditional landscape paintings and Cultural Revolution bric-a-brac. The shops along the western end of Hollywood Road tend to be less expensive but more dubious. By all means try to haggle the price down, especially in the stalls selling cheaper items.

Antiques		
Altfield Gallery	Prince's Building	2537 6370
Arch Angel Antiques	SoHo	2851 6828
Art Treasures Gallery	SoHo	2543 0430
Artemis	SoHo	2530 2208
C. Y. Tse Antiques & Collectibles	Prince's Building	2525 6557
Classical Arts & Antique Company	Tsim Sha Tsui	2735 0936
Dragon Culture	SoHo	2915 1309
Honeychurch Antiques	SoHo	2543 2433
Nugget	Prince's Building	2523 5281
Picture This	Central	2525 2820
Teresa Coleman Fine Arts	SoHo	2526 2450
Zitan	SoHo	2523 7584

Reputable shops should display tags on all their items, listing the price, age of the item and any restoration work that has been done. Always ask the vendor for a certificate of authenticity for more expensive items. Zitan on Graham Street restores Chinese antiques in their workshop a few streets away, so they are able to keep a close eye on all restoration work being done on each piece. They also 'custom restore' so if you prefer a piece to keep its weathered look, they will only do structural repair work.

A gallery that's worth the detour off the antique-hunting map is Picture This on the sixth floor of Office Tower, 9 Queen's Road, Central. It's not the easiest place to find as the numbers aren't clear so bear in mind that number 9 is on the section of Queen's Road that's close to the HSBC building. This gem of a gallery stocks a range of old and affordable Hong Kong maps, photos and fun 1920s Shanghai retro posters.

Hong Kong's markets are another source of antiques – brand new ones. You can find countless reproductions of Buddhas, pillow boxes and Mao's little red book for a fraction of the price of the real thing.

Street Market

Art
Other options **Art & Craft Supplies** p.285, **Art Galleries** p.189, **Art Classes** p.230

Hong Kong is a hassle-free and generally trustworthy place to buy fine art from the region, particularly from mainland China and Vietnam, but also by local artists. There's a common misconception that nothing much happens in the art world here, and although it's far from mature, there is a buzzing scene if you look for it.

The Central/SoHo region is the hub of upmarket art galleries with a plethora of small, and a few large, galleries selling traditional and contemporary art of all styles. Hollywood Road is the main artery of art and antique shops, with numerous side streets, such as Staunton Street, Lyndhurst Terrace,

Art		
10 Chancery Lane Gallery	SoHo	2810 0065
Alisan Fine Arts	Prince's Building	2526 1091
Arch Angel Art	SoHo	2851 6882
Art Beatus	Exchange Square	2522 1138
Art Statements	SoHo	9502 3847
Connoisseur Art Gallery	SoHo	2868 5358
Fringe Club	Central	2521 7251
Gaffer Studio Glass	Aberdeen	2543 4088
hkfineart.com	The Centrium	2537 7322
Hong Kong Arts Centre	Wan Chai	2582 0200
Korkos Gallery	Mid-Levels	2987 1187
Opera Gallery Hong Kong	Central	2810 1208
Para/Site Art Space	4 Po Yan Street	2517 4620
Picture This	Central	2525 2820
Plum Blossoms Gallery	SoHo	2521 2189
Schoeni Art Gallery	SoHo	2869 8802
Sin Sin Fine Art	Mid-Levels	2858 5072
State-Of-The-Arts Gallery	Central	2526 1133
White Tube	Hong Kong Arts Centre	2824 5391

and, higher up the escalator link, Prince's Terrace, also lined with galleries.

The international craze for contemporary mainland art is ever growing and Hong Kong is the perfect place to pick up a young masterpiece. Some galleries such as the Schoeni Galleries on Hollywood Road and Old Bailey Street specialise in mainland art and sell top names like Wang Yidong and Liu Dahong, although for a price. Oil-painted scenes of Vietnamese beauties remain popular and a few galleries such as hkfineart.com in The Centrium on Wyndham Street concentrate on Vietnamese art. Opera Gallery sells a wide selection of well-known international artists – Dalis, Picassos, and Legers, to name a few, have passed through their slim gallery space – as well as big names in Chinese art like Chu Teh Chun.

Art Statements on Mee Lun Street and Para/Site Art Space on Po Wan Street in Sheung Wan are good places to head to if you like avant-garde art, including video works, installations and photographs.

If you are looking to decorate a flat rather than make an investment, head to Stanley Market. There are plenty of stalls offering original paintings, prints and copies for anything from $50 to $5,000. You can buy pictures without frames, or pay a little extra for them to fit one for you in an hour or so.

Art & Craft Supplies
Other options **Art Classes** p.230, **Art Galleries** p.189, **Art** p.284

This isn't the easiest town to find professional art supplies if you don't know where to look. But there are a few shops that stock a comprehensive range of paint, paper, easels, brushes and other specialist tools.

A good place to start is Artsman Company on Tin Lok Lane in Wan Chai. It's a fairly small shop but it's packed from floor to ceiling with top-brand imported art supplies.

If you're thinking of taking Chinese painting classes but don't know where to find the gear, look no further than Man Luen Choon in Central – it stocks black and coloured ink, rice paper, brushes and books on Chinese painting, as well as offering a mounting and framing service for your exotic masterpiece.

Art & Craft Supplies		
Artland	Wan Chai	2511 4845
Artsman Company	Wan Chai	2573 8159
Brush Strokes Workshop	Central	2521 3621
Brushstrokes	Central	2167 8100
Hong Kong Art Supplies	Mong Kok	2390 0228
International Art Supplies	North Point	2887 7202
Man Luen Choon	Central	2543 0515
Paper Art	Central	2545 8985

Many stationery shops sell coloured paper, cutting knives, glue and a limited range of paints and brushes.

285

Shopping for Kids?
For a general look round for children's toys, clothes and baby goods, Windsor House, the top shopping floor of Times Square, and Grand Century Plaza in Mong Kok are good places to start.

Baby Items

Other options **Maternity Items** p.307, **Kids' Clothes** p.305, **Kids' Toys** p.306

Hong Kong is a great place for kids – it's safe, there's plenty to keep them busy and the level of education is high. The summer months can be tough on pregnant mums though as the heat and humidity is high. If you can't imagine leaving the comfort of your air conditioner to go shopping for baby items, don't fret, o/3 Collection has an online shop (www.o3baby.com.hk) from which you can order a range of goods, from baby-friendly body lotion to car seats. If you spend over a thousand dollars, delivery is free. They also have three branches – in Tsim Sha Tsui, Tseun Wan and Tseung Kwan O.

Baby Items		
Ah Chi Co	Sai Ying Pun	2559 6730
Bumps to Babes	Various	See p.339
Eugene Group	Various	See p.340
Mon Bebe	Various	See p.343
Mothercare	Various	See p.343
o/3 Collection	Various	See p.343
ParknShop	Various	See p.344
Toys 'R' Us	Causeway Bay	2991 6222
Wellcome	Various	See p.346

But ask any expat parents for their favourite baby shop, and they will invariably say Bumps to Babes in Central, just above Shanghai Tang. They sell products from Early Learning Centre, Maxi-Cosi, Maclaren, Luice, Oscar and many more. They also stock the Organix range of organic baby food. Check out their stock online at www.bumpstobabes.com. Regular supermarkets like ParknShop and Wellcome stock different ranges of baby food as well as organic – Organix and Earth's Best respectively – but the organic range is better at Bump to Babes as they go right up to toddler level.

Nappies are no problem either – most supermarkets, pharmacies and the ubiquitous 7-Eleven stores stock a range.

Also stocking everything you could possibly need are the Eugene Group shops, with branches in the New Territories, Mong Kok and Causeway Bay. This chain is the Hong Kong equivalent of Mothercare, which also has branches here. You can join Eugene Group's VIP club for $150 and get 10% discount off everything you buy. Other baby shops also run similar reward schemes.

If you're on a budget, the tiny, pokey shop called Ah Chi Co on 38 Eastern Street in Sai Ying Pun is a gem. They have catalogues and stock everything you need, although some of it may not suit western tastes. It's great for basics like baths and nappy bins. Their products are good for small flats, too, as the changing tables and cots are Hong Kong size.

Nappy Valley
Mums here love Huggies in the red pack and Pampers Baby Dry, which are made in China but do a great job. Both are found in ParknShop.

Midwives Online
Want a midwife? Check out www.amidwife.com or call 2983 1558 for a team of English-speaking baby experts.

Beachwear

Other options **Clothes** p.291, **Sporting Goods** p.315

Beachwear		
Billabong	Times Square	2506 3118
Evelyn B	Central	2523 9506
Jilian Lingerie	Central	2826 9295
Lane Crawford	Various	See p.342
Marks & Spencer	Various	See p.343
Ozzie Cozzie	Central	2810 1356
Ripcurl	Causeway Bay	2808 4554
Roxy and Quicksilver	Tsim Sha Tsui	2263 3928
Running Bare	Central	2526 0620
Rush	Harbour City	3188 9956
Sabina Swims	Central	2115 9975
Seibu	Various	See p.344
Sogo	Various	See p.345
Vilebrequin	Various	See p.346
Wolford	Various	See p.347
XGame	Various	See p.347

Most clothing and department stores that sell swimsuits only have stock in spring, summer and autumn, but a few of the sports, surfing and swimwear specialist shops sell them all year round.

Jilian Lingerie stocks glamorous swimsuits for women, sized XS to XXL. You can buy tops and bottoms separately at the popular

Hong Kong's Largest

Mother & Baby Superstores

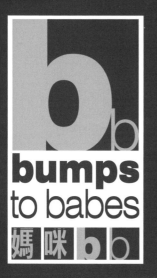

bumps
to babes
媽咪 b b

Horizon Plaza Store
Units 14-18, 21/F Horizon Plaza,
2 Lee Wing Street, Ap Lei Chau, Hong Kong
T (852) 2552 5000   **F** (852) 2552 5522
E sales@bumpstobabes.com
www.bumpstobabes.com
Monday to Saturday (10am-6pm)
Sunday & Public Holidays (11:30am-6pm)

Pedder Building Store
5/F Pedder Building, 12 Pedder Street,
Central, Hong Kong
T (852) 2522 7112   **F** (852) 2522 7311
E peddersales@bumpstobabes.com
Monday to Saturday (10am-7pm)
Sunday & Public Holidays (11am-6pm)

Sabina Swims on Wellington Street in Central. They have a good range of swimsuits available all year round.

Good places to head for hip bikinis and board shorts are the surfing brand shops, like Ripcurl, Billabong and Quicksilver. XGame stocks hip swimwear and water sports paraphernalia such as snorkel gear, wetsuits, surf boards and trendy surfer and skateboarder clothing, caps and flip flops. Vilebrequin in Pacific Place and The Landmark specialises in brightly patterned swim shorts for men. Sun protective suits for babies, children and adults can be found at Ozzie Cozzie on Lan Kwai Fong.

Bicycles

One look at the streets of Central or any of the surrounding built-up areas on Hong Kong Island should be enough to convince all but the most fanatical of cyclists that biking in the city is a bad idea. Apart from the problems posed by bumper-to-bumper traffic, tram tracks and aggressive drivers, the high level of air pollution on major roads makes cycling in these areas a genuinely dangerous pursuit. Away from the skyscrapers and flyovers, however, Hong Kong offers cyclists a range of tracks and trails to explore. Lamma Island is a favourite of mountain-bikers while Lantau Island, the New Territories and the south of Hong Kong Island (such as Shek O) are popular with road-bikers. A number of small independent retailers supply Hong Kong's biking needs, including Bicycle World in Wan Chai and The

Bicycles		
Bicycle World	Wan Chai	2892 2299
Chat Kee Bicycle Co	Wan Chai	2573 2620
Chung Yung Cycle	Sheung Shui	2670 3639
Flying Ball Bicycle Company	Cheung Sha Wan	2381 3661
Mong Kok Pro Bicycle Shop	Mong Kok	2380 9868
Tung Tat Bicycle Company	Causeway Bay	2576 1720

Flying Ball Bicycle Company in Cheung Sha Wan. Both of these stores cater to the casual cyclist and serious pedal-heads alike, and the latter is held in particularly high esteem by those in the know. An invaluable website for biking enthusiasts is http://mtb-post.interhk.net. Here you will find a huge range of new and used bicycles, bike parts, protective gear and accessories, including hard-to-find imports. For something a little more portable, Chung Yung Cycle in Sheung Shui has a range of Dahon folding bikes among its more conventional stock. Prices range from $1,000 to $16,000.

Books

Other options **Second-Hand Items** p.313, **Libraries** p.252

Bookworms and those looking for a riveting read for their commute to work are well catered for in Hong Kong. The largest chain of bookstores is Dymocks, which has nine branches – eight on Hong Kong Island and one in Discovery Bay – where you will find a fine range of fiction and non-fiction, travel guides, international magazines, children's titles and cookery books. Prices are close to the recommended retail price and the chain operates an ordering service for books that are out of stock or unavailable. Bookazine is another chain that offers a similar, though less extensive, range. Page One's four stores have probably the most impressive selection in town, particularly when it comes to art, design and architecture titles, travel guides and music or cinema books that are just aching to adorn your coffee table. HMV, meanwhile, is an

Books		
Bookazine	Various	See p.338
Cosmos Books	Various	See p.339
Dymocks	Various	See p.340
Flow	Various	See p.340
HMV	Various	See p.341
Hong Kong Book Centre	Various	See p.341
Jumbo Grade	Various	See p.342
Kelly & Walsh	Various	See p.342
Naxos	Wan Chai	2511 3611
Page One	Various	See p.343
Parentheses	Central	2526 9215
Pollux	Horizon Plaza	2873 6962
Relay	Hong Kong Int'l Airport	2116 8864
St John's Cathedral Bookstore	Central	2868 2848
Swindon Book Co	Various	See p.345

excellent place to shop for international magazines in English, particularly music magazines, while second-hand bookshop Flow, above Café Siam on Lyndhurst Terrace, is a treasure trove of pre-owned books of every description. You may not find what you're looking for there, but you are almost guaranteed to find something you like. There is also a branch in Sai Kung and both outlets accept trade-ins. Francophiles, meanwhile, should head to Parentheses on Wellington Street, Central, which is dedicated to French-language titles. Online, local bookseller www.paddyfield.com has a broad selection of titles from every category you could care to think of, including many Hong Kong-specific titles, and if you still can't find what you're looking for, there is always www.amazon.com, although expect to pay upwards of $150 for postage.

Camera Equipment

Other options **Electronics & Home Appliances** p.294

Whether you're after the simplest point-and-shoot or the most complicated professional-standard camera, you will not have to look far in Hong Kong. This is a city obsessed with cameras, and smaller, high definition models seem to be released every other week. As with the rest of the developed world, most cameras on sale are of the digital variety, with the likes of Canon, Sony and Nikon dominating most store displays. The best places to start your search for a new camera is at one of the two main electronics chains, Fortress or Broadway. Both have several branches throughout the territory and offer a large selection of digital cameras and camcorders by all the well-known manufacturers, as well as some traditional film-loading models by brands such as Minolta and Pentax. Prices are slightly less than you might expect to pay in Europe, and about the same as the United States. Both retailers are reliable and will exchange unsatisfactory products if they are returned in their original condition within 10 days, with a receipt. Hong Kong's reputation as a hotspot for bargain electronics has dimmed somewhat in the last few years, but those in search of a bargain may want to head to Tsim Sha Tsui. The area close to the Tsim Sha Tsui MTR stop on Nathan Road is choc-full of small independent electronics stores, most of which specialise in digital cameras. Depending on your bargaining skills and how successful a day the shop is having, you may be able to talk the sales assistants into a discount of up to 20 per cent or, more likely, some free accessories, such as memory cards or a carry case. Always check prices in Fortress or Broadway before you go, however, as there have been well-documented cases of unscrupulous retailers charging over the odds to unsuspecting tourists. It is also worth choosing shops with the QTS logo as these are regulated by the tourist board, although you will probably find that such outlets are unwilling to haggle over prices. For those with a more developed interest in photography (particularly non-digital), Stanley Street in Central should be your destination of choice. This thoroughfare features a slew of shops, such as the highly recommended Kinefoto, Photo Scientific and Chung Pui Photo Supplies, dedicated to cameras and their many accessories. Nearby, Hing Lee Camera on Lyndhurst Terrace is a popular option for serious snappers. Mong Kok also has many camera stores if you are willing to do a bit of exploring. At the other end of the spectrum, meanwhile, the Fotomax chain has a large selection of disposable cameras, and processes film and digital photos cheaply.

Lomo Lovers

If you're a fan of the cool and quirky world of Lomo photography, then you'd better point and shoot towards The Lomography Shop Hong Kong (G/F, 2 Po Yan Street, Sheung Wan, 2915 2205). Serving also as the headquarters of the Lomographic Society Asia, the shop sells a range of Lomographic cameras and accessories, and provides space for enthusiasts to get together and exhibit their work. See www.lomographyasia.com for more details.

Camera Equipment

Broadway	Various	See p.338
The Camera Shop	Harbour City	2730 9227
Chung Pui Photo Supplies	Central	2868 4135
Fortress	Various	See p.340
Fotomax	Various	See p.340
Hing Lee Camera	Central	2544 7593
Kinefoto	Central	2523 2087
Mirama Camera & Hi-Fi Co	Central	2501 0927
Photo Scientific	Central	2525 0550
Sogo	Various	See p.345

289

Car Parts & Accessories

Although it appears that the majority of Hong Kong's road users buy their vehicles brand new and require little or no modifications to be made, parts and accessories with which to soup up or repair your pride and joy are available from a number of garages and body shops. Many of the company showrooms can supply spare parts for newer cars. Otherwise, most businesses specialise in certain makes of vehicle, such as Ewig Auto Parts Company in North Point, where you will find original parts for chiefly Audi, Volkswagen, Opel and Peugeot models. Those in the know, meanwhile, swear by HP Cars and James Lien Motor Spare Parts, particularly for classic car parts. You will save yourself a great deal of time by calling first to ensure parts for the relevant brand are stocked. For accessories, with a little effort you should be able to unearth almost anything you require to enhance your wagon, from state-of-the-art body kits and stereos to neon lighting and seat covers. Best Product Enterprises in To Kwa Wan, for example, specialises in car covers and sunshades, while TEA in Happy Valley are dedicated to boosting the block-rocking capacity of your car stereo.

Car Parts & Accessories		
Best Product Enterprises	To Kwa Wan	2555 7782
Ewig Auto Parts	North Point	2802 6152
HP Cars	Various	See p.341
James Lien Motor Spare Parts	To Kwa Wan	2333 8763
TEA	Happy Valley	2834 0032

Cards & Gift Wrapping

Other options **Books** p.288, **Art & Craft Supplies** p.285

Send Cards, Save Children
Order packs of cards online from www.unicef.com. Packs range from $52 to $66 and proceeds go to helping needy children around the world.

English greeting cards are far from prolific in Hong Kong, especially ones without absurdly worded messages. Around Christmas time, the markets and small stationery shops have box loads of cards sporting cute Santas and long-lashed reindeers, but they are generally the type that should only be sent to friends with a cheesy sense of humour. If you want less tacky cards, head to bookshops or some of the larger department stores and supermarkets like Muji in Causeway Bay and City'super. Loft on level one of Seibu in Pacific Place has a good and reasonably priced selection. Hallmark Cards has outlets in Hong Kong which stock cards for all occasions imported from Europe, the US and Japan. If you're after something more sophisticated or artistic (and pricey), some stationers specialise in writing paper, invitations, gift wrapping and gifts for the more discerning customer. Head to the Prince's

Cards & Gift Wrapping		
City'super	Various	See p.339
H2 Cards	Central	2542 2880
Hallmark Cards	Various	See p.341
Impressions	Prince's Building	2851 9079
Loft	Pacific Place	2971 3837
Muji	Various	See p.343
Paper Art	Central	2545 8985
Paper n Things	Harbour City	3106 0226
Papyrus	Various	See p.343
Prints	Various	See p.344
Unicef	Happy Valley	2833 6139

Building for three such shops – Prints, Papyrus and Impressions. Many department stores offer a free gift wrapping service at Christmas and for the Chinese New Year. H2 cards on Lyndhurst Terrace have cards in stock and can custom-make top quality quirky cards, invitations and stationery. Their design style is contemporary Chinese meets urban cool.

Cars

Other options **Buying a Vehicle** p.158

Driving in Hong Kong can be an expensive business, with carparks around town not known for their reasonable pricing and parking spaces in prime locations often changing hands for exorbitant rates – up to $1,000,000 in some cases. Considering the city is home to a disproportionate number of luxury vehicles (it is often said that Hong Kong has more Rolls-Royces per capita than anywhere else in the world), there is rarely a shortage of drivers willing to pay to ensure a safe and convenient spot for their pride and joy. In the New Territories or south of Hong Kong Island, car ownership is a much more appealing and financially viable prospect, and for those who simply cannot do without their own set of wheels, there are a large number of showrooms to choose from. Most are located on or around Gloucester Road in Wan Chai, such as those operated by Ford, Lexus, Alfa Romeo, Audi and Lamborghini, to name just a few.

Classified Cars
Check the classified section of the South China Morning Post on Sundays for the latest used car ads.

Expect to pay slightly more than you would in Europe and significantly more than the United States. If money is no object, however, head to the Maybach showroom in Repulse Bay, where you can have the world's most luxurious car custom-made to your exact specifications, including gold and diamond-encrusted trims. Prices start at about $7 million. There is a thriving second-hand market in Hong Kong and there are bargains galore to be found as many drivers upgrade to a new model regularly. A three- or four-year-old hatchback in good condition, for example, might cost as little as $25,000 from one of the three main second-hand car markets – Automall (3113 2111), in the parking building beside the Grand Hyatt in Wan Chai, at the Hong Kong International Trade and Exhibition Centre in Kowloon Bay and at the space that was once occupied by Kai Tak Airport in Kwun Tong.

Clothes

Other options **Beachwear** p.286, **Lingerie** p.306, **Tailoring** p.316, **Sporting Goods** p.315, **Shoes** p.313, **Kids'Toys** p.306

Hongkongers have a passion for fashion, a fact reflected in the never-ending assortment of clothing shops that range from the budget to the outrageously expensive. At the pocket-friendly end of the scale, Baleno, Bossini and Giordano sell good-quality casual and sportswear at fantastically cheap prices. They are particularly useful places to stock up on underwear, T-shirts and socks. Also unlikely to tax your finances are the clothes on sale in the city's markets, such as the Ladies' Market in Mong Kok or Li Yuen Street East and West, where you will find everything from designer knock-offs to factory seconds and locally designed ranges.

At the other end of the scale, Hong Kong is awash with every designer label worth its thread, usually in stores that virtually redefine swish. Emporio Armani, Gucci, Louis Vuitton and Prada all have flagship boutiques in Central, as do the likes of Dolce & Gabbana, Paul Smith, Chanel and Christian Dior. Many of these outlets are located in The Landmark (p.321), probably Hong

Stanley Market

Clothes

A Bathing Ape	Central	2868 9448
Armani Exchange	Various	See p.338
Baleno	Various	See p.338
Blanc De Chine	Pedder Building	2524 7875
Bossini	Various	See p.338
Burberry	Various	See p.339
Chanel	Various	See p.339
Chevignon	Various	See p.339
Christian Dior	Various	See p.339
D&G	Various	See p.340
D-Mop	Various	See p.340
Dolce & Gabbana	Alexandra House/Chater House	2877 5558
Emporio Armani	Various	See p.340
Esprit	Various	See p.340
Evergreen	Causeway Bay	2581 9763
French Connection	Various	See p.340
Giordano	Various	See p.341
Gucci	Various	See p.341
Hugo Boss	Various	See p.341
I.T	Various	See p.341
Joyce	Various	See p.342
Juice	Causeway Bay	2881 0173
Lanvin	Various	See p.342
Louis Vuitton	Various	See p.342
Mango	Various	See p.342
Marc Jacobs	Various	See p.343
Marks & Spencer	Various	See p.343
Mr Yu Tailor	SoHo	2398 7273
New Exhibition Top Cashmere	Pedder Building	2526 8379
Once Upon A Time	Pedder Building	2186 7773
Paul Smith	The Landmark	2523 5868
Prada	Various	See p.344
Shanghai Tang	Various	See p.344
The Swank	Various	See p.345
Tuxe Top	Wan Chai	2529 2179
Vivienne Tam	Various	See p.346
Warwick Meyer Tailor	Central	2522 0896
Wing On	Various	See p.347
Yuen's Tailor	Central	2815 5388
Yves Saint Laurent	Various	See p.347
Zara	Various	See p.347

Kong's best luxury shopping mall. The city's only Harvey Nichols (p.326) can also be found here, while the local equivalent, Joyce, is across the street. Many designers mentioned here (and countless others cut from a similarly luxury cloth) can be found in Harbour City in Tsim Sha Tsui or in and around Lee Gardens in Causeway Bay, as well as in the shopping arcades attached to the city's swankiest hotels. Prices are much the same as you would pay elsewhere in the world. Many other designer labels can be found in the larger malls, such as Pacific Place or IFC Mall, while department stores Lane Crawford (p.327), Seibu (p.328) and Sogo (p.328) also stock a comprehensive range of designer wear at typically astronomical prices. Lane Crawford is particularly good for cutting-edge labels (as well as more established names), as are local boutiques D-Mop and I.T. (and its teen-oriented sister store i.t.). This is where dedicated followers of fashion regularly whip their credit cards into red-hot frenzies. Causeway Bay's trendy Paterson Street is awash with hip international and local labels, including Vivienne Tam, the New York-based designer who learned her trade in Hong Kong.

Between the high and low end of the clothing price spectrum you will find an abundance of mid-priced labels, such as Zara, French Connection, Mango and Esprit, as well as a number of local outlets carving their own particular niche. Evergreen Skateboards in Causeway Bay, for example, specialises in imported American streetwear by the likes of LRG and Lithium. For something with more of an eastern flavour, Shanghai Tang in Central is the last word in Chinoise chic. Indeed, Shanghai Tang has become something of an institution in Hong Kong and, even if you don't want to splash out on one of its signature Mandarin collar suits or lushly tailored cheongsams, it's worth stopping by for a tour and a taste of 1920s Shanghai style.

Formal Hire

Hong Kong's society calendar features a large number of charity balls and other black tie events. If you are likely to be attending these regularly, it might be worth having a tuxedo made (see Tailoring on p.316), but otherwise there are a small number of hire shops that can have you looking like James Bond in no time. Tuxe Top in Wan Chai

Explorer Online

No doubt now that you own an Explorer book you will want to check out the rest of our product range. From maps and vistors' guides to restaurant guides and photography books, Explorer has a spectacular collection of products just waitiing for you to buy, you genius! Check out our website for more info. *www.explorer publishing.com*

specialises in tuxedo rental (from $450 a night), and also has a selection of accessories, such as cummerbunds, bow ties and top hats for sale or rent. Mr Yu on the corner of Elgin Street and Caine Road in SoHo also has an excellent range of tuxedos for sale or rent, while Warwick Meyer Tailor in Central offers a hire service that is worth the extra dollars. Scottish formalwear, meanwhile, can be hired at Yuen's Tailor in the escalator shopping arcade.

Computers

Other options **Electronics & Home Appliances** p.294

Those in the market for a personal computer or laptop are spoiled for choice in Hong Kong as the range of products on offer – both new and second-hand – is overwhelming. As with most electronic equipment, good places to start are the two main chains, Fortress and Broadway. Both have broad ranges of laptops for sale by the likes of IBM, Sony, Compaq and Hewlett-Packard, with prices starting at around $8,000. If you're in the market for an Apple Mac, however, try one of the branches of Ultimate PC & Mac Gallery, a reliable store with informed staff. Floors 11 and 12 of Windsor House in Causeway Bay are dedicated to computers and offer a range of PC and Mac retailers selling new and used machines, as well as a huge selection of accessories, cables, software and upgrades. Mong Kok also has a proliferation of computer

Computers		
2C Computer	Various	See p.338
Broadway	Various	See p.338
Eastern Force Computer	Admiralty	2907 0088
Elite Multi Media	Central	2123 1432
Fortress	Various	See p.340
Impact Computer	Admiralty	2110 0798
Sogo	Various	See p.345
Tech Easy Computer Pro Shop	Various	See p.345
Ultimate PC & Mac Gallery	Various	See p.346

shops, including those located in the Mong Kok Computer Centre on Nelson Street, but for an unrivalled selection of computers and related products, Wan Chai is the easiest and best option. Two large multi-level shopping centres dedicated to computers sit across the road from each other beside the Hennessey Road exit of Wan Chai MTR station. Wan Chai Computer Centre and 298 Computer Zone have literally thousands of new and used laptops, computers and games consoles for sale as well as everything you could possibly need to accompany, repair, upgrade or modify one. This is where all the serious computer geeks flock for their electronic necessities and the staff at most shops are very knowledgeable, often to the point of confusion for those not fully versed in tech-lingo. New items here usually have a fixed price, although prices are generally as cheap as you will find elsewhere, and second-hand computer prices are often negotiable. It makes sense to do at least one circuit of each centre to compare prices, however, before making a purchase. Also, inquire about the extent of any warranty: many will only cover Hong Kong and not international repairs.

Costumes

Whether it's Halloween, themed parties, charity balls or the carnival of costumed conviviality that is the Hong Kong Rugby Sevens, the city's social calendar offers more excuses to dress up in silly attire than pretty much anywhere else in the world. Consequently, there are a small but reliable set of outlets dedicated to meeting your costume needs. The first stop for most revellers is Pottinger Street in Central; the area between Stanley Street and Wellington Street is a veritable dressing up box of party options, where you will find everything from Superman suits, Afro wigs and an astounding selection of false facial hair to masks, Viking helmets and sets of giant fake breasts considered de rigueur on rugby tours and stag nights. For something a bit more upmarket, try the Costume Depot Rental in Kowloon Tong, which has a selection of costumes and accessories for sale, such as nurses outfits, soldier uniforms and vampire attire fit for Dracula himself. If you really

Costumes		
Costume Depot Rental	Kowloon Tong	2342 3493
George & Me	Central	2975 0077
Hobby Horse	Prince's Building	2523 3814
House of Siren	SoHo	2526 2877
Partyland	Central	2147 9283

want to push the boat out, however, look no further than the lavish House of Sirens, where the only limits to what you can have made are your imagination and the size of your budget. Think extravagant French Revolution era dresses a la Dangerous Liaisons, British Brigadier outfits and luxurious capes for a midnight masquerade ball. They also offer a hire service.

Electronics & Home Appliances
Other options **Computers** p.293, **Camera Equipment** p.289

DVD Beware
Most DVD players sold in Hong Kong are set up to be multi-region. Check before you buy, however, as many DVDs on sale or in DVD rental stores are from regions other than Hong Kong's (region 3).

Walk past any electronics store in Hong Kong and the number and size of flat-screen and plasma televisions on offer is likely to be the first thing to grab your attention. From screens made to look like photo frames to 62 inch behemoths, the range of televisions on offer here is probably only bettered by Japan. Stereos, DVD players, MP3 players and every other gadget you can think of are also well represented, and generally a little cheaper than you would pay in Europe or the United States.
The usual suspects, Fortress and Broadway, are as good as any for providing a wide range of products to suit a variety of budgets. Both stores also stock home appliances such as microwaves, fridges and washing machines. Towngas boasts a large selection of cookers, dishwashers and washing machines, while Pricerite has a limited range of televisions and home appliances at easy-on-the-pocket prices, as does Wing On department store.
For high-end stereo equipment, it's hard to look past Bang & Olufsen and Bose, who offer the last word in aural pleasure, while A&A Audio & Video Centre and Universal Audio & Video Centre in Pacific Place have a wide range of speakers and stereos guaranteed to annoy your neighbours. Precision Audio in Central is the place to go for Linn appliances, while for a vintage stereo, check out the nearby Reference Audio. There is also a proliferation of small electronics stores in Mong Kok and Tsim Sha Tsui, although price and quality vary. If you don't mind buying second-hand, however, one of the best places to look is websites such as www.hongkong.asiaxpat.com and www.geoexpat.com, where a huge range of home appliances, televisions and other large electronic equipment is available from private sellers at knockdown prices. Most people that advertise here are either leaving Hong Kong or upgrading to a newer model, so prices are often generous, particularly if you can pick it up immediately.

Cooking Equipment
There are few things Hongkongers enjoy more than eating, as evidenced by the countless restaurants, bakeries and street stalls (dai pai dongs) that line the city's streets. From this dazzling assortment of eateries you might assume that no one cooks at home in this town, but a thriving cooking equipment industry reveals otherwise.
As with almost every other major city in the world, there are few basic cooking items you are likely to need that are not supplied by IKEA (various, see p.341). From cutlery and utensils to pots and pans, the Swedish home superstore is the place to go if you want to kit out your kitchen inexpensively in one fell swoop. Similarly economical is Pricerite, which has a fine selection of kitchen necessities, as well as cheap microwaves, kettles, toasters and other electronic labour-savers.

HOMELESS
the lifestyle store

www.homelessconcept.com
info@homelessconcept.com

Central flagship:
g/f, 29&31 gough st, central, hk.
tel: 2581 1880
Central accessories store:
g/f, 7 gough st, central, hk.
tel: 2581 1110

Causeway Bay store:
1/f, 17 yun ping rd, causeway bay, hk
tel: 2890 8789

Tsim Sha Tsui store:
g/f, 9 hau fook st, tsimshatsui, kln.
tel: 2780 1363

HOME L ESS

Electronics & Home Appliances

A&A Audio & Video Centre	Pacific Place	2845 3633
Bang & Olufsen	Various	See p.338
Bose	Various	See p.338
Broadway	Various	See p.338
Crown Digital World	Central	2524 5039
Fortress	Various	See p.340
Gome	Admiralty	2177 7188
Precision Audio	Central	2905 1919
Pricerite	Various	See p.344
Reference Audio	Central	2523 5787
Sogo	Various	See p.345
Towngas	Various	See p.346
Union Laservision & Video Centre	Prince's Building	2521 6266
Universal Audio & Video Centre	Various	See p.346
UNY	Cityplaza	2885 0331
Wing On	Various	See p.347

Department stores are also a good place to source cooking equipment, with Wing On offering a particularly extensive selection of reasonably priced utensils and electronic gadgets. Those with deeper pockets might want to investigate Sogo which features an impressive range of imported Japanese cookware. Specialty stores PanHandler in the Prince's Building (2523 1672) and Pantry Magic in the Pedder Building (2501 0988) are both Aladdin's caves of quality kitchen equipment, sporting rows of gleaming pots, pans, knives, utensils and everything else a budding chef might require. Meanwhile, the keen baker should head to Mini Store in Quarry Bay (2561 0814) for hard-to-find specialty products. Another option, and one for those who prefer a more local shopping experience, are the mainly Chinese cookwear shops on Shanghai Street, close to Exit C of Yau Ma Tei MTR station, where, with a little digging you can find a wide range of reasonably priced kitchen items, including specialised cooking tools. Supermarkets, such as the ubiquitous Wellcome and ParknShop, usually have a small selection of very cheap utensils, as does Japan Home Store, while more stylish (and correspondingly more expensive) versions can be found at City'super, G.O.D., and Great in Pacific Place (2526 2832). See Directory on p.338.

Eyewear
Other options **Sporting Goods** p.315, **Opticians & Opthalmologists** p.138

Finding spectacles and sunglasses in Hong Kong shouldn't be a problem. There is a range of styles to suit every taste and budget. Prescription lenses are offered at international prices and the standard of service is high. Chain shops like Hong Kong Optical tend to offer the lowest prices. If you want to browse, Queen's Road in Central has a range of opticians to choose from. Turn right onto Queen's Road from Central MTR station and you'll come across many eyewear shops. For hip specs and shades, head to the Alain Mikli boutique on Wellington Street, also in

Eyewear

Alain Mikli	Central	2523 0103
Hong Kong Optical	Various	See p.341
Lane Crawford	Various	See p.342
LensCrafters	Various	See p.342
Mandarin Optical	Central	2522 7944
Optical 88	Various	See p.343
Puyi Optical	Various	See p.344
Seibu	Various	See p.344
Sogo	Various	See p.345
United Optical Company	Various	See p.346
World Vision	Central MTR Station	2522 2025
XGame	Various	See p.347

Central, which is known for its range of Philippe Starcke frames. If you want a first-class eyewear shopping experience, head to one of the quiet, plush branches of Puyi Optical. They stock all the top names including Chanel, Armani and Versace.

Large clothing shops and boutiques often stock their own brand of sunglasses, amongst others, as do department stores and sports shops.

Flower Market ◀

Try buying flowers from the trucks parked along the side of the road at the Flower Market. They have no overheads so offer incredibly low prices.

Flowers

Other options **Gardens** p.300

Hong Kong city may be a concrete jungle, but there are pockets of nature, even if it's of the cut flower and potted plant variety. The best place by far to buy flowers is the Mong Kok Flower Market, just off Prince Edward Street West. There's a wide range of shops selling wholesale blooms from the ordinary to the exquisite, all at a fraction of the price you pay in most western countries. The flowers are mainly flown in from Kunming – the flower capital of China. Early mornings at the market can be busy as it supplies the hotel and restaurant business, so either wake up at dawn and choose the freshest bunches or take a later stroll down the colourful street and admire the hanging carnivorous plants, bright flowers and curving canes of bamboo. The market closes at 19:00 every day.

Flowers		
Anglo-Chinese	Central	2845 4212
Armani Fiori	Alexandra House/Chater House	2532 7766
Blooms & Blossoms	Tsim Sha Tsui	2721 4851
Empress Garden	Central	2140 6933
Flora 38	SoHo	2524 8601
Green Fingers	Central	2872 8280
Green Villa Floral Collection	Cityplaza	2886 4703
Lee Wing Kee	Central	2525 9719
Scent Flowers	Mid-Levels	2549 9180
Tiffany Flowers	Mid-Levels	2526 3606

The other end of the spectrum is Armani Fiori in Chater House in Central. Part of the Armani Emporium, this shop is the haute couture of flower arrangements with stunning floral designs at impossible prices. There are also plenty of smaller shops around town. Green Fingers and Anglo-Chinese in Central, Flora 38 on Staunton Street, and Blooms & Blossoms in Tsim Sha Tsui, sell flowers and make lush arrangements for special events. Central's Empress Garden and Lee Wing Kee (opposite the US Consulate General on Garden Road) and Scent Flowers on Caine Road in Mid-Levels are more reasonably priced, as is Green Villa Floral Collection in Cityplaza.

There are countless stalls in many of the fresh markets all over the city, too. Often, the seller's knowledge of English isn't good, but pointing and showing how many of each flower you want with raised fingers should suffice.

Food

Other options **Health Food** p.302

One of the main reasons expats find settling in Hong Kong such a smooth transition is the extensive selection of imported foodstuffs available. Expats are well catered for by Hong Kong's supermarkets, while there are a number of specialty bakeries, deli's and niche foodstuffs stores. Maxim's Cakes, for example, are located in almost every MTR station, among other locations, and sell a wide-range of baked treats – although

297

Food

The Bagel Factory	SoHo	2951 0755
Bon Bon Bon	Central	2523 6565
Castello del Vino	Various	See p.339
City'super	Various	See p.339
Delicatessan Corner	Tsim Sha Tsui	2315 1020
Eurotreat	SoHo	2537 0210
Fentons Gourmet	Happy Valley	3422 3411
Gateway	Central	2545 0338
Gourmet	Lee Gardens	3693 4101
Great	Pacific Place	2526 2832
Il Bel Paese	Various	See p.341
La Gouter Bernardaud	IFC Mall	2028 2029
Mini Store	Quarry Bay	2561 0814
Oliver's	Prince's Building	2810 7710
ParknShop	Various	See p.344
Ponti Food & Wine Cellar	Alexandra House/Chater House	2810 1000
Sogo	Various	See p.345
Taste	Festival Walk	2265 8698
UNY	Cityplaza	2885 0331
Viva Italia	The Peak	2849 2030
Wellcome	Various	See p.346

Oliver's, Great and City'super are among the best places to shop for western-style bread. The Bagel Factory in SoHo is also highly recommended. Il Bel Paese have three delis selling imported Italian cured meats, cheeses, wines and anti pasto, as well as freshly baked bread, while small importers such as Eurotreat on Staunton Street and Gateway on Des Voeux Road, offer a selection of imported sweets, snacks, biscuits and canned drinks. The former sells European chocolate, canned goods and more, while the latter is a haven for American's missing their favourite snacks. Baking enthusiasts should take a trip to Mini Store in Quarry Bay which specialises in hard-to find baking products, pans and equipment. For a more local shopping experience, however, there are several wet markets around the city, where many Chinese buy their meat, poultry, fish, fruit and vegetables. One of the best examples is around Peel Street in Central, although almost every district has its own version. Bon Bon Bon in Central, meanwhile, stocks a more upmarket range of mainly dried or packaged Chinese cookery ingredients.

Quirky Chinese Ingredients
If you're interested in Chinese food, take a walk down Queen's Road West or Des Voeux Road West – both these streets are lined with fascinating old shops packed with shark fins, desiccated sea cucumbers, roots and hundreds of unidentifiable dried goods, mainly for the restaurant trade. If you head to 88 Ko Shing Street, Sheung Wan early in the morning (around 09:30), you may get to see a shark's fin auction.

Wellcome

The most inexpensive of Hong Kong's supermarkets, you will find outlets of varying size wherever you venture in the territory; about 250, in fact, at last count. This is a good place to buy cheap meat, chicken, fruit and vegetables, as well as all manner of canned goods, biscuits and dairy products. Wellcome maintains quite a local flavour so don't be alarmed to see chicken feet, pig intestines or even live toads on sale, particularly away from Hong Kong island. The range of expat goods, though generally quite extensive, varies considerably depending on the location of the store. Don't expect to see a great variety of cheese, for example, in a store located in a mainly Chinese area. Most stores also deliver. See www.wellcomehk.com for a full list of locations.

ParknShop

Marginally more upmarket than Wellcome, ParknShop is equally ubiquitous and you will never be far from one of this chain's stores while you are in Hong Kong. Outlets vary from small mini-marts to sprawling superstores, and the latter sort often boast their own bakery, sushi counter and tanks full of live fish for you to choose from. Depending on store size and location, you will also find a fine range of imported goods that should put a smile on the faces of those missing a taste of home, wherever that may be. Taste, in Festival Walk, Kowloon Tong, is the first in a series of 'concept' stores the company plans to open and is comparable to Great, City'super and Oliver's. See www.parknshop.com for a full list of stores, most of which will also deliver.

Great

This supermarket in the basement of Pacific Place specialises in high-end imported products from a variety of countries. Expect to find imported 25 year-old Italian

balsamic vinegar, British jam and sausages, French cheeses and fine cuts of Australian and American meats on its shelves. It also sports a tempting ice-cream counter and a fresh juice bar. The increase in choice is, unfortunately, reflected in the prices.

City'super

Probably Hong Kong's number one food-shopping destination for affluent expats, City'super has restocking your larder down to a fine art. Its four stores offer a selection of imported products that will have you salivating like Pavlov's dogs long before you make it to the checkout. Their delicatessen counter, for example, offers an unrivalled selection of cold-cuts, cured meats and cheeses, while their meat and fish areas feature the finest cuts and catches in town. City'super is also the best place to shop for spices and hard-to-find cooking ingredients, as well as American snacks and candy.

Oliver's

Not on the same scale as City'super or Great, Oliver's ploughs a similar furrow, offering a range of imported foodstuffs from its smallish Prince's Building store. Where this store excels, however, are in its selection of wine and beers, its range of organic and imported fruit and vegetables, and its hot food counters. Carnivores should try their lauded roast chicken or specialty sausages. Oliver's also has a small bakery featuring western-style breads, bagels and rolls.

UNY

The food hall in the basement of this Japanese department store in Cityplaza specialises in – surprise, surprise – imported Japanese food and drink. As well as a weird and wonderful assortment of Japanese packaged snacks, soft drinks and sakes, UNY has one of the best sushi selections in town as well as fish straight from the tank and freshly made hot snacks, such as tempura prawns and deep-fried squid tentacles, all at surprisingly reasonable prices. It is also notable for the number of try-before-you-buy counters so you can happily nibble your way around the store.

299

Gardens

Other options **Hardware & DIY** p.301, **Flowers** p.297

Horizon Plaza
Horizon Plaza is a big shopping centre on Ap Lei Chau (see Streets/Areas to shop on p.331) with some great discount furniture and clothing factory outlets.

Ask city-dwelling residents where to get garden supplies, and most would be left scratching their heads. While many a flat balcony or window ledge in the residential areas of the city is covered with gorgeous potted plants, small trees and heavy-duty garden gear like spades and large bags of fertiliser aren't easy to come by. This is fairly surprising considering that only around 14 per cent of Hong Kong's land area is built on. If you are lucky enough to have a garden or a rooftop big enough for large plants or a potted herb garden, Chan Man Hop and Wong Yuen Shing, both on Connaught Road West, stock seeds, fertiliser and various garden supplies. Heading out of the city – physically and ethically – Green Earth Society in Sai Kung supplies environmentally friendly products.

If you're after garden furniture, Horizon Plaza on Ap Lei Chau (near Aberdeen) is the place to head. There's an extensive range of shops selling cast iron furniture, barbecues, umbrellas and swimming pool accessories.

Wing On department store, IKEA and G.O.D. also stock outdoor furniture.

Gardens		
Aloha Outdoor Furniture	Horizon Plaza	2552 0036
Chan Man Hop	Central	2544 1862
Everything Under The Sun	Horizon Plaza	2554 9088
G.O.D.	Various	See p.341
Garden Gallery	Horizon Plaza	2553 3251
Green Earth Society	Sai Kung	2792 0106
House & Garden	Horizon Plaza	2555 8433
IKEA	Various	See p.341
Resource Asia	Horizon Plaza	2554 9088
Wing On	Various	See p.347
Wong Yuen Shing	Central	2543 1896

Gifts

Tick Tock
Never give a Chinese person a clock as a gift – the word for clock rhymes with the word for end, so giving a clock suggests their time is running out.

It's unlikely you could ever run out of gift ideas in Hong Kong. From Chinese tat to priceless antiques, a Hello Kitty handbag to a Dunhill hip flask – you can find it all. If you need inspiration, head to Elgin, Peel and Staunton Streets in SoHo as there are many independent shops with great things for gifts. Stanley Market is a good place to buy gifts for overseas family and friends and makes for a pleasant outing, although it can get busy, so head out early. For gifts with a distinctly Hong Kong design flavour, check out the Trade and Development Council Design Gallery on level one of the Hong Kong Convention and Exhibition Centre. The gallery offers a quirky mix of local designs, from clocks to handbags, photo frames and dolls that double as hands-free phone speakers.

Gift Crisis?
If all else fails, concierge service Quintessentially promise to hunt down whatever your heart desires. You have to become a member, however, and membership fees cost anything from $30,000 to $300,000 per year. Check them out at www.quint essentially.com

For opulent Chinese designer clothing (for adults and a gorgeous range for kids), homeware, books, handbags, wallets and accessories, head to Shanghai Tang. For upmarket gifts in international styles, start with The Landmark in Central as it holds a variety of shops that cater to men and women with expensive taste.

Gifts		
Artshop Bijoux	Lee Gardens	2808 2866
Avante Garde Designs	Various	See p.338
Azahra	The Peak	2147 9741
Chinese Arts & Crafts	Various	See p.339
Dunhill	Various	See p.340
Harvey Nichols	The Landmark	3695 3388
Homeless	Various	See p.341
Lane Crawford	Various	See p.342
Maymaking	SoHo	2445 5655
Mont Blanc	IFC Mall	2234 7225
Morn Creations	SoHo	2869 7021
Seibu	Various	See p.344
Shanghai Tang	Various	See p.344
Sogo	Various	See p.345
TDC Design Gallery	HKCEC	2584 4146

Stuck finding a gift for the man who has everything? Check out Azahra's showroom on The Peak (by appointment only). This locally based company has handcrafted Spanish leather hip flasks, cigar holders, photo albums and briefcases.

Handbags

Hong Kong is all about labels. With every second person you see clutching a Louis Vuitton bag, if you want to be in with the locals, start parading some designer names on your clothing and accessories. The main shopping areas of Central, Causeway Bay and Tsim Sha Tsui have handbag shops to satisfy every taste and budget. Department stores like Lane Crawford and Seibu have a good range of upmarket bags. For designer bags at reduced prices, head to a Milan Station. This chain of shops sells 'slightly' used handbags, but despite the discount, they still aren't cheap. Lianca in Central (2139 2989) sells handbags and wallets designed in Hong Kong but made with top quality imported leather. For more affordable bags, Japanese store Log-On is a good bet as they stock functional as well as funky bags for men and women. Any of the markets around town sell cheap bags and designer rip-offs. See p.333 for contact details.

Hardware & DIY

Other options **Outdoor Goods** p.310

Interior Delights

There are a number of contractors and interior designers in Hong Kong that will be only too happy to help you achieve your vision of domestic bliss. Some of the most lauded ones are Jason Caroline Design (2893 4061), Ip Interiors (2399 0508), Fame (2642 0996) and Tsui's Contracting Company (2891 7796).

Whether you're intent on doing some home improvement or merely getting round to fixing that leaky tap that's been on your to-do-list since you arrived, there are several options open to you in Hong Kong. The ever-reliable IKEA is as good a starting point as any if you're looking for basic tools, fittings and brackets. Japan Home Store is another useful outlet for sourcing cheap tools, hooks, washers, bathroom sealants and the like; their range is fairly limited, but their products are inexpensive and they have stores all over the territory. A wider range of DIY goods can be found at one of the many family-run hardware stores you will see around town. One of the best of these is Housewares & Handicrafts on Caine Road, where you will find a large selection of inexpensive tools, hardware, paint and metal fittings, as well as electric drills for rent and a key-cutting service.

Hardware & DIY		
Cheung Kee Electric & Water Works	Mid-Levels	2523 7828
Housewares & Handicrafts	Mid-Levels	2522 2870
IKEA	Various	See p.341
Japan Home Store	Various	See p.342
Yuen Tung Lighting Co	SoHo	2851 6811

Nearby, Cheung Kee Electric & Water Works supplies all manner of plumbing and electrical equipment. It also operates a key-cutting service. If you are planning more than a few simple repairs, however, you may want to investigate the market area close to Sham Shui Po MTR station, where there are several shops selling wood, metal fittings, tools and fiddly essentials such as nails and washers. For a similar, but more plumbing-centred, experience, the area around Hennessey Road in Wan Chai should meet your needs.

Hats

Hats aren't as easy to come across. Winter hats and baseball caps can be found at The Tie Rack; this chain has small, well-stocked shops near MTR stations and in shopping malls. See the Directory (p.338) for numbers. Or there's Lids (3188 5116) at 59 Russell Street which stocks a wide range of caps. Evergreen (2581 9763), also in Causeway Bay, sells only the hippest caps and beanies to pair with baggy jeans and oversized T-shirts. For more formal ladies hats, try Evelyn B (2523 9506) on the seventh and eighth floors of the Grand Progress Building on Lan Kwai Fong. The shop keeps wide-brimmed hats for weddings and the beach all year round, as well as hats purely meant as a fashion statement.

301

A great find is Practical Hat (2854 1142) in the Lucinda Industrial Building in Tsuen Wan. The designer, Flora Chung, makes attractive straw hats with ribbons or other accessories. Call first to make an appointment.

Health Food
Other options **Food** p.297

Many people in Hong Kong eat out a great deal, and while there are many restaurants offering fairly healthy menus, there are also those that use a lot of oil, MSG and few vegetables. If you're finding you need to get back to basics, there are a good few places to find health food, like organic produce, vitamins and supplements, and foods for people with allergies and dietary concerns.

A health food institution on Lamma Island is The Bookworm in Yung Shue Wan. It's a vegan restaurant with a library and articles on the vegetarian revolution tucked under the glass table tops. Its sister restaurant is Life Café along the Mid-Levels escalator link. Besides healthy salads, gluten and sugar-free cakes, carob brownies, vegetarian lasagne, and delicious dahl, Life sells bottles of organic wines, lentils and quinoa by the kilogram, as well as Yogi teas, and Hong Kong's first organic draught beer at $50 a pint.

Health Food		
Ali Oli	Sai Kung	2792 2655
All Things Healthy	Central	2525 1778
American Nutrition	Various	See p.338
The Bookworm	Lamma Island	2982 4838
GNC	Central	2521 6136
Green Concepts	Various	See p.341
Green Earth Society	Sai Kung	2792 0106
Healthgate	Sheung Wan	2545 2286
Life Café	10 Shelly St	2810 9777
Mannings	Various	See p.343
Nature's Village	Various	See p.343
Oliver's	Prince's Building	2810 7710
Organic Produce Express	Central	2698 4866
Simply Organic	Causeway Bay	2488 0138

For fruits and vegetables, head to Simply Organic in Causeway Bay. They have also partnered with an online organic farm: www.organic-farm.com. Their novel approach is to deliver to your home a 3kg bag of fruit and vegetables on the same day every week. You don't get to select what's in the bag as it depends on what is freshest and in season that week.

Upmarket supermarkets like Oliver's in the Prince's Building also stock organic foods, but sometimes at ridiculous prices (an iceberg lettuce has been known to cost $70!).

Two chain stores that specialise in dietary and muscle-gain supplements have branches close to each other on Lyndhurst Terrace in Central – American Nutrition and Nature's Village – and your local branch of Mannings also stocks a wide range of vitamins, Chinese remedies and health supplements.

Home Furnishings & Accessories
Other options **Hardware & DIY** p.301, **Furnishing Your Home** p.110

Horizon Plaza

Horizon Plaza is a big shopping centre on Ap Lei Chau (see Streets/Areas to shop on p.331) with some great discount furniture stores.

There are three main areas dedicated to furnishing your home in Hong Kong. The first is Horizon Plaza in Ap Lei Chau, a small island connected by bridge to the southwest of Hong Kong Island, near Aberdeen Harbour. Here you will find a huge range of furniture to satisfy all preferences and budgets, from unique antique pieces to factory seconds. Tequila Kola is one of the best-regarded outlets in Horizon Plaza, featuring chic, modern furniture to suit eastern and western tastes, while the cavernous Carpet Buyer should meet all your flooring needs with its sizeable selection of quality carpets, rugs and runners.

The second area to explore when you are kitting out your new place (or sprucing up the old one) is situated around Hollywood Road in Central. Hollywood itself boasts a not inconsiderable number of furniture stores, many of them featuring antique pieces. For

Home Furnishing & Accessories

Altfield Home	Prince's Building	2524 3066
Aluminium	Various	See p.338
Andante	Ruttonjee Centre	2537 9688
Artemide	Ruttonjee Centre	2523 0333
Bfelix	SoHo	2367 1735
Carpet Buyer	Horizon Plaza	2850 5508
Chenmiji	SoHo	2975 9266
Desideri	Central	2950 4026
Flea + Cents	Wan Chai	2528 0808
Homeless	Various	See p.341
Ichi Ni San Shop	SoHo	2525 6649
IKEA	Various	See p.341
Inside	Various	See p.342
Lane Crawford	Various	See p.342
Le Cadre	Ruttonjee Centre	2526 1068
Louvre Gallery	Ruttonjee Centre	2762 2393
Lumino	SoHo	2736 2338
Magazzini	Various	See p.342
Mir Oriental Carpets	Central	2521 5641
Mobalpa Kitchens	Wan Chai	2988 1949
Old Shanghai	Horizon Plaza	3527 3135
OVO	Wan Chai	2526 7226
Persian Carpets Gallery	Central	2521 6677
Pricerite	Various	See p.344
Rare Carpets	Horizon Plaza	2537 6379
Rimba Rhyme	Horizon Plaza	8330 8100
Sogo	Various	See p.345
Space	Central	2851 6360
Tequila Kola	Horizon Plaza	2877 3295
Ulferts	Various	See p.346
UNY	Cityplaza	2885 0331
Wing On	Various	See p.347
X quisit	Central	2526 1660

more contemporary fare, nearby Lyndhurst Terrace and, to a lesser extent, Wyndham and Wellington streets are your best bets. Aluminium has a great selection of quirky furniture and lighting designs by such modern luminaries as Phillipe Starck, while Lumino boasts a sparkling range of modern light fittings and chandeliers. Wyndham Street, meanwhile, is better known for its carpet showrooms, such as the Persian Carpets Gallery. Smaller niche stores inhabit the many side streets around these three main arteries, including Chenmiji on Peel Street, which features a selection of Bauhaus-inspired pieces. For chic and expensive Italian furniture by the likes of Studio Minotti, head to the Ruttonjee Centre on Duddell Street. Lastly, but by no means least, is Wan Chai. Depending which room you are in the process of refurbishing, you will either want to head to Queen's Road East, between the Hopewell Centre and Admiralty, or the area around Hennessey, Lockhart and Johnston roads. The former features a number of classy furniture stores and smaller independent retailers, while the latter is a Mecca for anyone redecorating their kitchen or bathroom. Need a particular style of tile or a sunken Jacuzzi that will fit four people in comfort? This is the place.
There are also a few furniture chains that offer varying degrees of quality for similarly diverse budgets. Pricerite has a fair range of inexpensive furniture items, particularly sofas, chairs and tables, while IKEA offers every basic item you could possibly need at affordable prices. Fellow Swedish furniture chain Ulferts offers a slightly higher calibre of furniture product. A step above is G.O.D., a stylish emporium of hip furniture and accessories sure to have the interior-minded cooing with pleasure. Websites www.hongkong.asiaxpat.com and www.geoexpat.com are great places to pick up some second-hand bargains. See also Second-Hand Items on p.313.

Jewellery, Watches & Gold
Other options **Markets** p.333

Hong Kong is famous for its watches and jewellery, and justifiably so. There's every style, price range and material you could ever imagine. It's a good place to buy pearl and jade jewellery – pearls because of the wow factor you'll get from friends back home, and jade because it's an important, spiritual stone for the Chinese.

Many locals wear jade pendants to complement their star sign and bring them luck. An interesting place to head for jade jewellery and pearls is the Jade Market in Yau Ma Tei (open 10:00-17:00). You won't find high quality stones here, but it's a fascinating local experience and it's a great place to buy gifts. Bargaining is expected; drop to half of what they offer straight away. If you affect nonchalance, sellers have been known to agree to a final price of only 10 per cent of what they initially asked. Beware of fakes though and if at all possible, take a Cantonese-speaking friend with you.

Jade Booty
The quality of jade is judged by its translucency, consistency in colour and coldness to the touch. The most expensive jade looks like emerald.

If you're looking for a more reliable place to shop for jade, and other jewellery, Saturn Essentials is a lovely little shop off the cobbled steps of Pottinger Street in Central. You can find everything from cheap and cheerful bead earrings, to chunky necklaces of imported crystal, to silver rings and striking orange and green jade pendants. Another reasonably priced shop selling silver jewellery for men and women is simply called Silver Ware at 537 Jaffe Road in Causeway Bay.

For top of the line, exquisite pearls, head to Mikimoto in IFC Mall and Harbour City, Cartier in the Prince's Building, or Chow Tai Fook on Queen's Road Central.

If you want a watch or piece of jewellery but don't have anything particular in mind, Queen's Road in Central and the area's big malls – IFC Mall, The Landmark, Prince's Building – as well as Pacific Place and Nathan Road in Mong Kok have a mind-boggling range of jewellers and watch shops. Take exit C1 when coming out of Mong Kok MTR station and peruse the shops either side of Argyle Road. All of the famous local designers have shops here as this is where locals and mainland tourists come to shop for gold, diamonds and jade. Also on Kowloon side, but in Hung Hom, is 3-D Gold Store. Not only a giant gold and jewellery shop catering to busloads of mainland tourists, it also houses the world's most expensive toilets. Two solid gold toilets rest in a bathroom of gold – gold sinks, toilet brushes, toilet paper holders, tiles, doors and chandeliers. The bathroom ceiling is even studded with 6,200 rubies, diamonds sapphires and pearls.

Jewellery, Watches & Gold		
3-D Gold Store	Hung Hom	2766 3332
4 degrees C	Sogo	2122 9278
Bijoux Bijoux	Causeway Bay	3126 3907
Bulgari	Alexandra House/Chater House	2805 0010
Carnet	Alexandra House/Chater House	2805 0113
Cartier	Prince's Building	2522 2963
Chen	Prince's Building	2521 0263
Chinese Arts & Crafts	Various	See p.339
Chocolate Rain	G/F, 34B Staunton St	2975 8318
Chow Sang Sang	Various	See p.339
City Chain	Various	See p.339
Elegant Watch & Jewellery	Various	See p.340
Emphasis	Various	See p.340
Georg Jensen	Prince's Building	2868 0707
Hourglass	Tsim Sha Tsui	2369 9122
J's	Queensway Plaza	2265 8801
King's Watch Co	Central	2522 3469
Lane Crawford	Various	See p.342
Larry Jewellery	Central	2523 3883
Links of London	Various	See p.342
Masterpiece, King Fook	The Landmark	2526 6733
Mauboussin	IFC Mall	2234 7618
Mont Blanc	IFC Mall	2234 7225
Power Jewellery	Tsim Sha Tsui	2376 1782
Prince Jewellery & Watch	Various	See p.344
Saturn Essentials	Central	2537 9335
Silver Ware	Causeway Bay	2882 9433
Sum Yee Gem	Jade Market	9251 7289
Swarovski	Various	See p.345
Swatch Watches	Various	See p.345
Tayma Fine Jewellery	Prince's Building	2525 5280
Tic Tac Time	Festival Walk	2522 5777
Tiffany's	The Landmark	2845 9853
TimeZone	Various	See p.345
Van Cleef & Arpels	Prince's Building	2522 9677
Yue Hwa	Various	See p.347

If you're looking for something more sensible but still big and shiny, Central, Admiralty, Causeway Bay and Tsim Sha Tsui have the top international names in jewellery and watches – Tiffany's, Van Cleef & Arpels, Cartier and so on. Swarovski is particularly popular here for jewellery and cut crystal ornaments from the sublime to the ridiculous. Department stores also carry a range of designer and funky costume jewellery. For good prices on a range of watches, take a look at any one of the numerous City Chain, Elegant or Prince shops. They are reputable stores and sometimes offer attractive discounts. For fake watches and cheap costume jewellery, Hong Kong's markets offer an amazing selection.

Kids' Clothes

There are a few shopping centres that have whole floors dedicated to children's clothes. Prince's Building and Lee Gardens are great for designer gear. Abebi in Lee Gardens and other malls has a selection of top end brands in one shop. Windsor House, Harbour City and Times Square have a range of more reasonably priced shops. Zara has a kids' clothing section with cute styles, but they generally cost as much as adults' clothes.

Mothercare and Bumps to Babes also stock good quality baby and children's clothes.

Stanley Market sells end of line clothing at massive discounts. You can pick up outfits from Next, Osh Kosh, Tommy Hilfiger and so on for less than $100.

For shoes, head to Footstop on Pottinger Street – the shop

Kids' Clothes		
Abebi	Various	See p.338
Bumps to Babes ▶ p.287	Various	See p.339
Footstop	Central	2869 7922
Mothercare	Various	See p.343
Paul's Ballet Supplies Centre	Queensway	2527 2867
Pop Kid	Cityplaza	2567 3908
Seibu	Various	See p.344
Shoe Box	Various	See p.345
The Smock Shop	Star Ferry Pier	2524 8708
Sogo	Various	See p.345
Wing On	Various	See p.347
Zara	Various	See p.347

specialises in children's shoes, including half sizes and a choice of six widths. Seibu, Wing On and the sixth floor of Sogo in Causeway Bay also have a great selection, as does Shoe Box.

For party costumes, the stalls on Pottinger Street are packed with cheap and fun wigs, fake moustaches, masks, velveteen cloaks and plastic swords. Ballet outfits and accessories are at Paul's Ballet Supplies Centre, and cute, flowery dresses can be found at The Smock Shop at the Star Ferry Pier, Hong Kong side. Pop Kid in Cityplaza sells off-the-rack formal clothes for children.

Kids' Toys

Other options **Clothes** p.291

With a huge proportion of the world's toys being manufactured in China, it comes as no surprise that Hong Kong is well catered for in that department. The territory's many markets generally feature a range of cheap plastic playthings that should keep junior quiet for five minutes but which may not pass the stringent safety tests of western countries. For a better, more quality-controlled class of toy, the always reliable Toys 'R' Us is well represented here, selling everything from items aimed at infants to more adult-oriented board games. Bumps To Babes has a large selection of toys for kids of all ages, while Toys Club offers a range of toys and children's books with the emphasis on education. Wise Kids is in a similar vein and will also help you organise a party for your little darling.

Kids' Toys		
Bumps to Babes ▶ p.287	Various	See p.339
Party & Toys	Pedder Building	2813 2380
Sogo	Various	See p.345
Toy Museum	Prince's Building	2869 9138
Toys 'R' Us	Causeway Bay	2991 6222
Toys Club	Various	See p.346
UNY	Cityplaza	2885 0331
Wise Kids	Various	See p.347

Lingerie

Other options **Clothes** p.291

Many Hong Kong ladies dress more conservatively than westerners. This extends to their underwear, where cream cotton knickers are the norm, along with padded bras (as much for the extra cup size as covering unwanted protrusions in the over-air-conditioned buildings). So if you're after something a little more daring, head to lingerie specialists.

Jilian on Wyndham Street stocks glamorous, high-end underwear, swimwear, corsetry and sleepwear. They also stock a sexy maternity range. Their sizes range from XS to XXL, A to F+ cup.

Private Shop in The Landmark and Harbour City also stock an extensive range, as does Sogo department store. Wolford in the Prince's Building or IFC Mall is the place for tights, stockings and snug-fitting clothing.

There's also all the usual international brands of bras, knickers and nighties like Calvin Klein and Triumph, which have their own shops and are stocked within other stores. Their prices are generally comparable to overseas, but sometimes don't stock bigger than a C cup. Triumph has factory outlets in Kwun Tong and on Hennessy Road. The faithful Marks & Spencers stock an affordable range of plain and lacy bras, sleepwear, panties and thongs from small to extra large. A few of their lines of bras are specially designed for Asian sizes, so these tend to be smaller in the bust. They also stock sports bras. Bonluxe, near Times Square in Causeway Bay, offers custom-fitted bras from Japan from size AA to I. Make an appointment for a professional fitting. Prices are upwards of $1,000 per bra.

Lingerie		
Bonluxe	Causeway Bay	2573 1218
Calvin Klein Underwear	Various	See p.339
Glamrose	Causeway Bay	2572 2831
Jilian	Central	2826 9295
Kam Doo Ltd	Wong Tai Sin	2320 0616
Lane Crawford	Various	See p.342
Lingerie Philiosophy	Various	See p.342
Marguerite Lee	The Landmark	2367 2968
Marks & Spencer	Various	See p.343
Shanghai Tang	Various	See p.344
Sogo	Various	See p.345
Triumph	Various	See p.346
Wolford	Various	See p.347

Delicious Dubai

If you're lucky enough to visit Dubai then make sure you pick up a copy of the fabulous eating and drinking guide *Posh Nosh, Cheap Eats and Star Bars*. Not only is this coffee table style book full of stunning images of some of Dubai's most splendid establishments but it is also packed with over 350 impartially written reviews, detailed maps and fun directories.

Luggage & Leather

Other options **Shipping** p.281

As with all personal accessories, Hong Kong has an extensive range of luggage, purses, belts and briefcases, from the designer to the purely practical. For fashion conscious travellers where only a name will do, Louis Vuitton in the Prince's Building should be your first port of call. If you want the same level of quality but prefer stylishly plain, check out locally based Azahra – the shop stocks beautifully crafted leather products for men and women, all made from Spanish leather. They also have a line of corporate gifts, which can be stamped with a company logo. Their showroom is open by appointment only, but you can also order online at www.azahra.com.

For more casual luggage, the popular Mandarina Duck can be found in The Landmark. Sphere at 496 Lockhart Road, Causeway Bay, sells reasonably priced luggage. A lot of the shops that sell leather handbags stock purses, wallets and other leather goods too, as do the usual department stores like Lane Crawford, Sogo, Seibu and Wing On. For cheap knock-offs, head to any one of the city's markets.

For leather sofas, try the numerous furniture shops in Horizon Plaza on Ap Lei Chau or hip Asian-styled home furnishing store G.O.D.

Luggage & Leather		
Azahra	The Peak	2147 9741
G.O.D.	Various	See p.341
Goyard	Harvey Nichols	3695 3388
Lane Crawford	Various	See p.342
Louis Vuitton	Various	See p.342
Mandarina Duck	Various	See p.342
Rimowa	Central	2525 2780
Samsonite	Various	See p.344
Seibu	Various	See p.344
Sogo	Various	See p.345
Sphere	Causeway Bay	2572 7218
Sun Sun	Stanley	2813 0922
Wing On	Various	See p.347

Maternity Items

The local look for maternity wear tends to be voluminous grey pinafores, which you can pick up at Wing On department stores and Eugene Group shops at reasonable prices. If you're after something a little more fashionable, head to Mothercare (similar to UK branches) or Bumps to Babes in Central. The latter tends to be pricey, but many expectant mums and dads say it's worth it. They do issue VIP cards that entitle you to a small discount. For style queens, Linea Negra on the 20th floor of 1 Lan Kwai Fong, and Formes, also in Central, stock high-end clothing. Linea Negra and Jurlique sell skincare products for mums and tots.

Gennie in Causeway Bay sells bras (up to H cup size) and girdles for pregnant women.

Maternity Items		
Bumps to Babes ▶ p.287	Various	See p.339
Eugene Group	Various	See p.340
Formes	Central	2905 1200
Frankie Maternity	Causeway Bay	2834 4122
Gennie	Causeway Bay	2314 2675
Jilian	Central	2826 9295
Jurlique	Central	2259 5066
Linea Negra	Central	2522 7966
Mother Court	Central	2522 8934
Mothercare	Various	See p.343

Medicine

Other options **General Medical Care** p.126

Most of the over-the-counter medicines you can buy in western countries are available in Hong Kong. You can pick up painkillers, cold and flu remedies and other medicines for minor complaints in pharmacies, supermarkets and 7-Eleven stores. There's nothing too surprising in the list of prescription-only substances, except perhaps strong Ibuprofen pills which you can only access via a pharmacist. Luckily, bigger branches of the two main chains of pharmacy – Mannings and Watsons – often have pharmacists on duty. There are hundreds of branches of these shops in MTR stations, malls, and on

Medicine		
Fanda Perfume Co	Central	2545 2490
Healthquest Pharmacy	Central	2521 0933
Integrated Medicine Institute	Central	2868 2118
Mannings	Various	See p.343
ParknShop	Various	See p.344
Watsons	Various	See p.346
Wellcome	Various	See p.346
Yue Hwa Chinese Medicine Store	Various	See p.347

main roads. The pharmacists generally speak English and are helpful. The pharmacies usually stay open until 20:00, and the biggest branches until 23:00. The Mannings on D'Aguilar Street just up the hill from Central MTR station has a pharmacist on duty from Monday to Friday, 10:15 to 20:00 with lunch from 14:30 to 15:30, and on Saturday from 10:00 to 14:00.

Random Remedies

If you're interested in Chinese medicine, take a walk down Queen's Road Central from Sing Street to Bonham Strand. There are plenty of shops selling all manner of animal parts, herbs and swallow's nests. Most of the shopkeepers don't speak English, but it's still fascinating to have a look.

There are few major pharmacies that aren't part of the Mannings or Watsons chains. Fanda Perfumes Co at 19 Des Voeux Road, Central, offers some medicines not on offer at other pharmacies. They close earlier at around 19:00 daily.

Seeing a doctor is straightforward, with or without a Hong Kong Identity Card. Consultation fees for a GP are usually around $150-$200. For a list of surgeries, check the website for Quality HealthCare, one of Hong Kong's largest healthcare groups: www.qhms.com. They also have information on Chinese medicine and listings for traditional practitioners. Yue Hwa, a Chinese department store, has branches specialising in Chinese medicine, but they sell a limited range of western medicines too.

Mobile Telephones

Other options **Telephone** p.122

There's no two ways about it – Hongkongers are obsessed with mobile phones. And denizens searching for the newest, smallest, flashiest or most feature-packed model rarely have to stray far to indulge their passion. As with all things electrical in the city, the Fortress and Broadway chains are a good place to start looking and to gauge prices before scouring the smaller, independent retailers for bargains. The legion of electronics stores in Tsim Sha Tsui are filled with mobile phones, from the latest designs by the likes of Motorola, Nokia and Samsung to older models on sale at knockdown prices. Haggling here might reap discounts or free add-ons, such as car chargers or protective cases, although you will have a better chance of landing a bargain if you go for last year's editions, which most stores will be only too eager to shift at a pocket-friendly price. Similar independent mobile phone shops abound in every major shopping area, including Central, Causeway Bay and Mong Kok (especially Langham Place), and almost all stock countless phone accessories. Few will offer guarantees, so make sure the phone is in good working order before you leave the shop and look out for the QTS logo for extra piece of mind. BlackBerries and PDAs are also widely available at most

Mobile Telephones		
Broadway	Various	See p.338
CSL	Various	See p.340
Fortress	Various	See p.340
Lane Crawford	Various	See p.342
Mobile Phone Direct Selling	Central	2523 3329
One2Free	Various	See p.343
PCCW	Various	See p.344
SmarTone-Vodafone	Various	See p.345
Sunday	Various	See p.345
Three	Various	See p.345
Topview AV Center	Tsim Sha Tsui	2301 3289

mobile phone retailers. Hong Kong's main phone companies (such as Sunday, PCCW, SmarTone-Vodafone, One2Free and Three) all stock a range of the latest models in their stores, while tariff plans start from as little as $50 a month. Pay-as-you-go SIM cards are also available, but given that calls to landlines and other mobiles on your network are generally free with a tariff plan and contracts can be cancelled at a month's notice, they generally work out more expensive for all but the most occasional users. For a phone that will stand out from the crowd, it's hard to look past Vertu, available from Lane Crawford stores. Their luxurious designs are a favourite with the city's glitterati. The only drawback: prices start at about $37,000.

Music, DVDs & Videos

Jardine's Joy
The area around
Jardine's Crescent and
Jardine's Bazaar in
Causeway Bay has lots
of small shops selling
bargain DVDs and CDs.
You may have to trawl
through racks of titles
you've never heard of,
but it'll be worth it
when you find that cut-
price classic you've
always wanted.

At first glance, Hong Kong's music and DVD-buying options may seem quite limited and anchored in the mainstream. Dig a little deeper however and you will be rewarded with a surprisingly eclectic blend of stores dedicated to audio-visual entertainment. The first stop for most westerners is HMV. Its four stores stock an impressive selection of CDs, DVDs and VCDs, including some imports. DVDs start from as little as $20, while CDs are generally cheaper than in Europe or the United States, although expect to pay upwards of $200 for imported titles. Hong Kong Records offers similar fare, but is a good deal more mainstream and limited in its selections. That said, however, it can be a good place to hunt for Hong Kong martial arts movies, such as Shaw Brothers titles. Metal heads should head to Trinity Records in Mong Kok, while those with eclectic taste should find a satisfying selection of CDs at Records Rendezvous in Tsim Sha Tsui, Monitor Records in Jordan and White Noise Records in Causeway Bay, as well as a small selection of vinyl. Sam The Record Man in IFC Mall, meanwhile, specialises in Japanese

Music, DVDs & Videos		
Broadway Cinematheque	Yau Ma Tei	2388 0002
Flow	Various	See p.340
HMV	Various	See p.341
Hong Kong Records	Various	See p.341
Monitor Records	Jordan	2782 3562
Records Rendezvous	Tsim Sha Tsui	2716 9333
Sam The Record Man	IFC Mall	2892 1681
Trinity Records	Mong Kok	2383 2801
Walls Of Sound	Central	2805 1584
White Noise Records	Causeway Bay	2591 0499

first editions, which offer a far greater sound quality than regular CDs, while Walls Of Sound in Central has possibly the best selection of vinyl in the territory, along with DVDs and CDs.

In the unlikely event that you are a Canto-pop aficionado, Causeway Bay and Tsim Sha Tsui are teeming with shops selling CDs by the likes of Andy Lau and Twins as well as DVDs and VCDs of local and international titles. You will usually hear these stores before you see them. A fine assortment of world cinema, particularly Korean and Japanese titles, can be found in the shop attached to Broadway Cinematheque in Yau Ma Tei, while a mixed bag of second-hand CDs, DVDs and even VHS tapes can be found at Flow.

Musical Instruments

Other options **Music Lessons** p.256, **Music, DVDs & Videos** p.309

If you play an instrument, it will be music to your ears to hear that your art is well-catered for in Hong Kong. There are two main chains. Tom Lee Music has 18 branches around the territory and sells a wide range of musical instruments, including pianos, guitars, violins, brass and woodwind instruments, and almost everything else you might need to kit out a private orchestra. They also stock a large selection of sheet music and instructional manuals in both Cantonese and English, as well as various musical accoutrements, from guitar strings to saxophone reeds. An equally, if not more, extensive selection can be found at Parsons Music, which has 20 branches in Hong Kong. Particularly impressive is the flagship store in Whampoa Garden, Hung Hom, which, in addition to a jaw-dropping selection of guitars, pianos and other instruments, features access to a 100-seat auditorium and 40 classrooms for various instruments. There are several smaller independent stores, many located in Central or Mid-Levels, that specialise in one type of musical instrument. Continental pianos, for

Musical Instruments		
Continental Piano Co.	SoHo	2548 8138
Do Re Mi Studio	Mid-Levels	2522 7081
Great Music Centre	Mid-Levels	2973 6818
Parsons Music	Central	2858 9011
Piano One Two Company	Horizon Plaza	2552 8223
Tom Lee Music	Various	See p.346
Tsing Mui Piano Company	The Peak Galleria	3173 8810

example, has a wide range, including grand pianos. Do Re Mi Studio, meanwhile, has a range of mainly children's violins for sale, and also offers classes in several musical disciplines. For something with more of a local flavour, try Tsing Mui Piano Company in the Peak Galleria, where you will find traditional Chinese instruments such as the liuqin (a kind of lute) and the xiao (a bamboo flute).

Outdoor Goods

Other options **Camping** p.233, **Hardware & DIY** p.301, **Sporting Goods** p.315

Camping isn't a popular pastime in Hong Kong, so there aren't many dedicated stores selling all the necessary, and unnecessary, gadgets. But there are plenty of shops selling outdoor clothing, hiking boots, backpacks, and a limited range of sleeping bags. Check out the sixth floor of Times Square shopping centre in Causeway Bay for a range of outdoor brand stores including Patagonia, The North Face, and Columbia. These international brands sell at prices comparable to overseas.

Outdoor Goods		
Chamonix Alpine Equipment	Mong Kok	2388 3626
Columbia	Various	See p.339
Hong Kong Mountain Training Centre	Mong Kok	2770 6607
The North Face	Times Square	2953 2274
Ocean Diving	Tsim Sha Tsui	2366 3738
Ocean Sports Company	Mong Kok	2771 6286
The Outdoor Shop	Tsim Sha Tsui	2730 9009
Patagonia	Various	See p.344
Protrek	Various	See p.344
RC Outfitters	Mong Kok	2390 0020
Triton Fishing Equipment	Various	See p.346
Well Garden Camping Shop	Stanley Market	2813 9066
XGame	Various	See p.347

Various shops on Fa Yuen Street (better known as Trainers Street) in Mong Kok stock outdoor clothing and camping gear at reduced prices but the range can be limited and they don't have all the sizes. Your first stop should be RC Outfitters at 1/F, 134-136 Sai Yeung Choi Street South. For fishing supplies, head to one of the Triton Fishing Equipment shops. They are the biggest local company selling fishing gear.

Party Accessories

Other options **Parties at Home** p.404

If you're organising a party or a junk trip, or attending one of the rooftop barbecues so popular in summer, you won't have to stray too far to find the necessary odds and ends. Dedicated stores are few and far between, but most supermarkets, such as Wellcome and ParknShop, stock a good selection of paper plates, napkins and plastic cups, as well as balloons, glow sticks, party poppers, charcoal and barbecue forks. This can be extra-convenient as you can stock up on party snacks such as crisps and nuts, as well as booze and soft drinks while you are there. If plastic cups aren't flash enough for your bash, SoHo Wines & Spirits (www.sohowines.hk) operates a free glass hire service for functions and will also deliver to your home (orders over $500 are delivered free). At the other end of the scale, Yan Yan on Caine Road is packed with all manner of party favours and can compile loot bags for children's parties on request. Pottinger Street below Wellington Street offers similar

Party Accessories

Complete Deelite	Central	3167 7022
Cova	Various	See p.339
Hobby Horse	Prince's Building	2523 3814
Japan Home Store	Various	See p.342
ParknShop	Various	See p.344
Party & Toys	Pedder Building	2813 2380
SoHo Wines & Spirits	Various	See p.345
Wellcome	Various	See p.346
Wise Kids	Various	See p.347
Yan Yan	Mid-Levels	2810 1862

fare, as well as costumes, feather boas and masks. If the occasion demands a cake, the ubiquitous Maxim's cakes do ready-made versions, as does the Italian patisserie chain Cova. Although the latter is a good deal more expensive, one mouthful and you'll know where your extra dollars went. For something more original, www.icakeshop.com sells a variety of novelty designs and will deliver free to most areas if you spend $350 or more. Complete Deelite in Lan Kwai Fong is another fine cake option.

If you're organising a children's birthday party, Wise Kids can help you find everything you need to make it go with a bang, including face painting artists and clowns. Party & Toys in the Pedder Building, Central, is another great kids' party store. At Christmas time, decorations are available from a huge number of places, including the ever-reliable Wellcome and ParknShop, and many of the markets.

Perfumes & Cosmetics
Other options **Markets** p.333

Hong Kong being tax free on all but alcohol makes it the perfect place to buy perfume and cosmetics. Sasa stocks well-known perfumes, make-up, skincare and hair products. Department Stores, such as Lane Crawford and Sogo, have all the usual counters – Clarins, Estee Lauder, Aveda, Clinique and Christian Dior, to name a few. Some of these brands also have their own dedicated shops – the IFC Mall is a good place to start as they stock a good variety.

Pharmacies, such as Watsons and Mannings, have everyday men's and women's ranges like Neutrogena and Nivea, and some of the bigger branches have counters for more expensive brands, Borghese being a favourite. Supermarkets also stock a range of skin care products, body washes, shampoos and other toiletries.

For less mainstream high-end brands, head to local fashion emporium Joyce or recently opened UK department store Harvey Nichols. They have Chantecaille make-up, L'Artisan perfumes, and so on. Fairly new to Hong Kong is Australian skincare concept Aesop. At their signature shop on Lyndhurst Terrace, they can mix up just the right product with a variety of aromatherapy oils and plant extracts. Indulgence spa on Lyndhurst Terrace, a large, white space with a curving staircase up to the treatment rooms, has friendly staff that will do everything from massages to paraffin hand treatments and eyelash tinting. They can also order the hard-to-come-by MD Formulations and Dermalogica products.

Brits will be pleased to note there are hundreds of Body Shop branches all over the city.

Manicures and pedicures are reasonably priced in Hong Kong, and many salons like C'est la Vie in Central

Perfumes & Cosmetics

Aesop	Central	2544 4489
Aveda Spa & Salon	Various	See p.338
Body Shop	Various	See p.338
C'est la Vie	Central	2840 0333
Essential Spa	Various	See p.340
The Hairdresser	Central	2973 0512
Harvey Nichols	Central	2695 3388
Indulgence spa	Central	2815 6600
Joyce	Various	See p.342
L'Occitane	Various	See p.342
Lancome	Various	See p.342
Lane Crawford	Various	See p.342
Mannings	Various	See p.343
Sasa	Various	See p.344
Seibu	Various	See p.344
Shu Uemura	Various	See p.345
Sogo	Various	See p.345
Toni & Guy	Various	See p.346
Watsons	Various	See p.346

311

and Essential Spa stock nail colour favourites OPI and Essie.
For haircare products, supermarkets and pharmacies sell the basics, and for imported makes, visit your local hairdresser. A salon simply called The Hairdresser in Central sells the popular Fudge styling aids. Toni & Guy on Wyndham Street is a popular salon with expats, and stocks Tigi, Wella and Catwalk products.

Pets

Other options **Pets** p.115

Pet-minders

Going away and don't want to leave your pet in at a kennel or cattery? British couple Mark and Lyndsay run a pet-minding business called Wish You Were Here (www.wishyou wereherehk.com). They will come to your flat and spend an hour feeding, grooming, and playing with your animal. They'll even visit pets that have newly arrived in Hong Kong and are still in quarantine. Call them on 9755 1060.

Despite the tiny flats, keeping pets is a growing trend in Hong Kong. If you are after a scaled friend, Tung Choi Street in Mong Kok, known as the Goldfish Market, is lined with shops selling anything you could need for a salt or freshwater aquarium, as well as snakes, frogs, terrapins, lizards and scorpions. While buying pet fish from the market is fine, many vets recommend buying puppies from the SPCA (general hotline 2802 2502) rather than a pet shop, as many shops don't vaccinate and canine distemper is common. You can also get bunnies, cats and hamsters at the SPCA.
Supermarkets like ParknShop and Wellcome have a good range of cat and dog food. For pampered pets, Mid-Levels Pet Services on Mosque Street is the perfect place to head for special diet foods, cuddly beds and blankets and toys. They also offer a grooming and boarding service.

Pets		
Dog Paradise	Happy Valley	2792 6999
Dogs & the City	Mid-Levels	2121 1353
Kam Lun Aquarium	Goldfish Market	2393 4889
Mid-Levels Pet Services	Mid-Levels	2140 6112
ParknShop	Various	See p.344
Rex	Causeway Bay	2893 5660
Wellcome	Various	See p.346

If you're worried about keeping your canine friend amused, scamper down to Dog Paradise, where you can kit your dog out in anything from a pink jumper with matching hair clip to some tough denim workwear. You can then have him or her photographed against a backdrop – a wood-panelled study, chintz lounge or Mount Fuji... You can also take your dog out for coffee. Rex has a cosy pet section with enough space for dogs to laze around. There's a wide selection of pet accessories for sale, ranging from treats to collars and leashes.

Portrait Photographers & Artists

Hongkongers generally love photographs, and a look at a local's wedding album proves that there's no stigma against staged shots. You're bound to see brides and grooms posing in strange places around town, like boarding a tram or on the steps of the Hong Kong Cultural Centre. There are many photographers that can be hired to capture your special day, or in Hong Kong, the special day that is reserved for taking photos months before your actual wedding.
For basic shots for identity or passport photos, many MTR stations (Central station being one) have handy booths with instructions in English. You can choose the size and how many prints, as well as the best photo of yourself before they are printed. Make sure you have a charged Octopus card or a stack of coins (around $40-$50 depending on what you need) before starting though. Some photo developing shops can also take reasonably priced ID photographs.

Portrait in Prose

Want to record the life of a loved one for posterity? Biographer Tina Purvis will interview, collate and write an account of your life, add photos and custom design a striking volume. Prices depend on the scale of the project. Call 2882 4242 or 6191 0057.

For shots for the family album, head to a professional studio. There's one on Caine Road called Helen Studio. Photographer Rosa Tseng comes highly recommended by her peers and charges around $1,800 for a one-hour sitting for groups of four people or under. Lisa B charges a minimum fee of $10,000 but there's no time limit. For portraits of babies, children, graduation and mums-to-be, Baby Dreamland Portraits Studio is a good choice. Some photographers will come to your home, while some work from a studio only.

Portrait Photographers & Artists

Ant Yeung Photography	Causeway Bay	8101 2005
Baby Dreamland Portraits Studio	Chai Wan	2838 8544
Helen Studio Co.	Mid-Levels	2523 2870
Lisa B Photography	Central	2869 9732
Lover's Promise	Causeway Bay	9663 6348
Pretty Woman	Tsim Sha Tsui	2312 2302
Rose Tseng	Central	2294 0481
SDB Photo	Central	9277 1810

Second-Hand Items

Other options **Books** p.288, **Cars** p.290, **Furnishing Your Home** p.110

There isn't a huge second-hand shopping scene in image-obsessed Hong Kong, but what outlets there are tend to be of a high standard. The first place you should look in your quest for a bargain is www.hongkong.asiaxpat.com and www.geoexpat.com. Here you will find a huge range of items, from golf clubs to prams, although the websites are particularly useful if you're in the market for furniture, electronic goods or homeware items. It is free to buy or sell on the sites and most prices are extremely reasonable and negotiable. Pre-owned books, DVDs and CDs can be found at Flow, which is located above Café Siam on Lyndhurst Terrace and in Sai Kung. The owners buy, sell and trade books at pocket-friendly prices (some titles cost as little as $1), and the selection changes constantly. Nearby Walls Of Sound offers similar fare, including vinyl. Beyond this, there are a few second-hand furniture and clothing outlets, as well as charity shops such as Oxfam, the Used Clothes Programme and the Salvation Army Thrift Store. The latter two also accept donated items and Used Clothes Programme will also collect from your home. For second-hand designer wear, the Pedder Building has several stores selling once loved pieces.

Second-Hand Items

The 3rd Avenue	Pedder Building	2537 9168
Aroma Office Furniture	Cheung Sha Wan	2566 0898
Beatniks	Causeway Bay	2881 7153
Expressions Furniture	Aberdeen	2975 9797
Flow	Various	See p.340
George & Me	Central	2975 0077
The Low Price Shop	Sheung Wan	2805 1317
Oxfam	Central	2522 1762
Retrostone Used Clothes	Mong Kok	2332 8090
Salvation Army Thrift Store	Tin Hau	2887 5577
Second Hand Shop	Tsim Sha Tsui	2368 7990
Ty Treasures	Pedder Building	2810 1612
Used Clothes Programme	Kwun Tong	2716 8778

Shoes

Other options **Sporting Goods** p.315, **Beachwear** p.286, **Clothes** p.291

Shopping for men's shoes in Hong Kong can be an arduous process if you have feet sized UK 11 or above. Many stores simply do not stock shoes in these sizes, so it's worth asking the sales assistant if they have shoes in your size before you start browsing. You should also be wary that it is relatively common practice to bring you the largest available size (even if it is not the size you are looking for) without letting you know. Always double-check the size printed inside the shoe or on the box. One way around this problem is to purchase from Finnish shoemakers The Left Foot Company (www.leftfootcompany.com) in Tsim Sha Tsui. Using a specially developed machine, they can take a 3D reading of your foot, from which they will then create shoes to match your exact specifications. They cater only to men, shoes take about four weeks to make and prices start at $2,000 a pair. If you need your footwear a little quicker than

313

Shoes

Benland Shoes	Various	See p.338
Dr Martens	Various	See p.340
Ecco	Various	See p.340
Evergreen	Causeway Bay	2581 9763
GigaSports	Various	See p.341
Harvey Nichols	The Landmark	3695 3388
Jimmy Choo	The Landmark	2525 6068
JJ Partners	Happy Valley	2577 2383
Joy & Peace	Time Square	2506 2872
Kow Hoo Shoe Company	Prince's Building	2523 0489
Lane Crawford	Various	See p.342
The Left Foot Company	Houston Centre	2367 6007
Log-On	Various	See p.342
Manolo Blahnik	Various	See p.343
Marathon Sports	Various	See p.343
Marks & Spencer	Various	See p.343
Mirabell	Various	See p.343
Nine West	Various	See p.343
On Pedder	Central	2118 3489
Pedder Red	Various	See p.344
Rockport	Various	See p.344
Royal Sporting House	Various	See p.344
Seibu	Various	See p.344
Sergio Rossi	Central	2118 3489
Shoe Mart	Central	2869 7077
Sogo	Various	See p.345
Staccato	Various	See p.345
The Tie Rack	Various	See p.345
Timberland	Various	See p.345
UNY	Cityplaza	2885 0331
Wing On	Various	See p.347
Zara	Various	See p.347

that, there is no shortage of stores to hot-foot it to. Timberland, Rockport, Ecco, Mirabell and Dr Martens are just a few of the shops with branches across town, while department stores are also a fertile hunting ground for footwear of all descriptions. Lane Crawford, for example, has an excellent selection of upmarket brands in both casual and more formal styles. It is worth visiting the Pacific Place branch in particular to view its revolving shoe wall. UNY has a good selection of smart leather shoes at reasonable prices, while the budget-conscious may find a bargain or two at Wing On. GigaSports and Marathon Sports have decent selections of sports and hiking shoes, although the area of Fa Yuen Street known as 'Trainers Street' is a far better bet, both in terms of price and variety. Fans of skate brands might find skate shops a little hard to come by in Hong Kong, but Evergreen in Causeway Bay should fit the bill with trainers by the likes of Etnies, DC Shoe Co and DVS, often at discounted rates.

Ladies' Shoes

Hong Kong has an amazing selection of shoes from drop-dead $7,000 Jimmy Choo stilettos to cute $200 purple suede flats. On Pedder, which is located unsurprisingly on Pedder Street, and Sergio Rossi next door are a treasure chest of luxury shoes. Department stores Lane Crawford, Seibu and Sogo also have a wide range of upmarket shoes, and because many are imported from Europe, they have at least some styles in sizes up to a UK eight. The Landmark is a good mall to head to for designer shoe shops

Middle of the range shops stocking shoes include Nine West, Zara, Marks & Spencer, Joy & Peace, and On Pedder's 'younger sister', Pedder Red. The Tie Rack is good for beaded and bejewelled flip flops. Very cheap shoes of varying quality can be found in Hong Kong's markets. Unfortunately, Asian-made shoes, which tend to come with a lower price tag, usually only go up to size 38 or sometimes 39 (UK size five or six), so for tall ladies with large feet, finding shoes can be frustrating. Besides going designer, the reasonably priced Staccato branches sometimes stock larger sizes, or you could have a pair made. JJ Partners in Happy Valley is a gem. Their small shop is lined with hundreds of decent quality shoes and pretty strappy leather sandals. If you can't find any to fit or you would prefer the style in another colour, the friendly staff will measure your feet and make you a pair within three weeks. The best thing about this shop is the price – making a pair costs the same as buying one off the rack and price tags go as low as $400 for kitten-heeled sandals. The Kow Hoo Shoe Co in the Prince's Building is Hong Kong's oldest custom shoemaker; you're looking at $2,000 per pair at least but the shoes are of impeccable quality.

Souvenirs

Hong Kong is a great place to pick up souvenirs. There's a plethora of options – from fun $50 Mao watches and plastic models of the HSBC building to beautiful Chinese calligraphy scrolls and lacquerware. Cheap souvenirs can be snapped up at markets – Temple Street Night Market and Li Yuen Streets in Central are good places to start – and in the small, messy shops along Hollywood Road. You can pick up anything from a

Souvenirs

Chinese Arts & Crafts	Various	See p.339
Madame Tussauds	The Peak Galleria	2849 6966
Maymaking	SoHo	2445 5655
Shanghai Tang	Various	See p.344
Tsing Mui Piano Company	The Peak Galleria	3173 8810

pair of pretty embroidered Chinese ladies slippers for $20, adorable childrens' outfits for $50 and statues of Hong Kong's favourite goddess, the goddess of mercy called Kwun Yam, for a range of prices depending on quality and authenticity. Stanley Market has a variety of stalls selling souvenirs, and also art shops selling works by local and regional artists ranging from the reasonably priced to the expensive. Some of the shops also have calligraphers on hand to paint your (or a family member's) name in Chinese for a small fee – these make fun gifts.

The chain of Chinese Arts and Crafts shops have a fantastic range of Chinese goods – jewellery, carvings, silk clothing, cushion covers, tablewear and tea sets. Shanghai Tang also has lovely souvenirs and gifts with a designer touch – silver chopsticks, plush photo albums, handbags, baby booties embroidered with the Chinese characters for left and right, and their signature air spray that scents the shop in sweet frangipani hues.

Tourist sites, such as Madame Tussauds on The Peak, Ocean Park and Disneyland, all have dedicated shops selling souvenirs.

Sporting Goods

Other options **Outdoor Goods** p.310

There is virtually no sport you can't indulge in somewhere in Hong Kong, from football, basketball and ultimate Frisbee to wakeboarding, surfing and scuba diving. The range of outlets dedicated to kitting you out for these activities is similarly wide-ranging, and includes everything from general sports shops to highly specific speciality stores. If you're looking for basic sportswear, trainers and equipment, there are three main chains that will serve your needs. Gigasports, Royal Sporting House and Marathon Sports can be found all over the city and one or more of them appear in almost all of the larger shopping malls. They stock a good selection of trainers and clothing for various sports, and, in the larger outlets, a range of equipment, such as racquets and balls. For trainers, however, there is nowhere better than the section of Fa Yuen Street in Mong Kok between Argyle and Dundas streets, popularly known as 'Trainers Street'. As this moniker suggests, you will find just about every brand of sports footwear here, for just about every sport. Unlike most other sports shops in Hong Kong, even the largest of western feet should find their sole mate in one of the myriad shops in this area. Despite the name, the street offers a good deal more than just footwear, and is a treasure trove of sporting equipment, from studs for boots, shinguards and hockey sticks to golf, fishing and camping paraphernalia. Those who get their kicks sub-aqua, however, should splosh along to Bunns Diving Equipment in Mong Kok or Causeway Bay, which has an outstanding selection of professional scuba gear, while surfers might find the board of their dreams at the Quicksilver Boardriders Club on Leighton Road in Causeway Bay. The brand has several other outlets in Hong Kong, but this is by far the best-stocked. Golf stores abound in Hong Kong, with Metro Golf in Central being one of the largest. The somewhat less well-represented sport of ice-hockey is catered for by Asiasports on Lyndhurst Terrace.

Sporting Goods

ABC Golf Outlet	Admiralty	2861 2311
Asiasports	Central	2307 9264
Bunns Diving Equipment	Various	See p.339
GigaSports	Various	See p.341
Golf House	Various	See p.341
Golf Style	Admiralty	3428 8110
Marathon Sports	Various	See p.343
Metro Golf	Central	2537 6217
New Balance	Various	See p.343
Nike	Various	See p.343
Queensway Golf International	Admiralty	2866 0306
Quicksilver Boardriders Club	Various	See p.344
Royal Sporting House	Various	See p.344
Sogo	Various	See p.345

Stationery

There are hundreds of small stationery shops in residential and shopping areas selling all the usual office and home stationery. Supermarkets also sell basics like pens and glue. If only the best pen will do, the Pens Museum has an extensive range of pens costing up to $2,000 for Mont Blanc and Cartier. Department stores like Sogo in Causeway Bay also have a stationery section selling everyday and pricey ranges.

Stationery		
Bookazine	Various	See p.338
Capitol Stationers	Central	2521 3621
Hong Kong Book Centre	Various	See p.341
Jumbo Grade	Various	See p.342
ParknShop	Various	See p.344
Pens Museum	Various	See p.344
Sam & Company	Central	2521 0338
Sogo	Various	See p.345
Wellcome	Various	See p.346

Tailoring

Other options **Clothes** p.297, **Textiles** p.317, **Souvenirs** p.314

There are several things that Hong Kong excels in, and tailoring must be close to the top of that list. Tsim Sha Tsui contains probably the highest density of tailors in the territory. Take a stroll from the Star Ferry pier towards Nathan Road and you will quickly find yourself bombarded by representatives of the area's many Indian tailors offering to make you a suit, shirt, overcoat and anything else that might take your fancy. Price and quality vary greatly, but one solid option is Raja Fashions, a family business that has been suiting Hong Kong men and women for almost 50 years. Sam's Tailor is another well-regarded institution.

For a more refined tailoring experience, head to Central. Warwick Meyer Tailor is a long-established and much-respected choice for suits and Ascot Chang is the last word in deluxe shirt-making. For a touch of Chinois glamour, Shanghai Tang offers a bespoke tailoring service for men and women in sumptuous fabrics, while nearby New King's Fabric Company in Lan Kwai Fong specialises in making cheongsams. For Thai-style creations, try Siroporn, near the bottom of the escalator. There are a number of high-class tailors in Prince's Building and the nearby Galleria, while Melbourne Plaza on Queen's Road Central features a slew of inexpensive tailors and alterations experts.

Tailoring		
A-Man Hing Cheong Co	Prince's Building	2522 3336
Ascot Chang	Various	See p.338
Baron Kay's Tailor	Various	See p.338
British Textile Co	Central	2524 3894
Chinese Custom Tailor	Tsim Sha Tsui	2314 7064
Collars & Cuffs	Central	2868 0488
David's Shirts Ltd	Various	See p.340
Express Custom Tailors	Tsim Sha Tsui	2199 7965
Ideal Tailor	Prince's Building	2522 4861
Jim's Tailor Workshop	Tsim Sha Tsui	2721 9062
Mr Yu Tailor	SoHo	2398 7273
New King's Fabric Company	Central	3118 7672
Noble House	Tsim Sha Tsui	2302 4444
Raja Fashions	Tsim Sha Tsui	2366 7624
Sam's Tailor	Tsim Sha Tsui	2367 9423
Shanghai Tang	Various	See p.344
Siroporn	Central	2866 6668
Takly Custom Shirtmakers	Central	2523 5548
Warwick Meyer Tailor	Central	2522 0896
Yuen's Tailor	Central	2815 5388

Many of the large international brands can also perform alterations when you are making a purchase and some, such as Dunhill, offer limited bespoke tailoring.

Less glamorous, but wholly dependable, are local tailors Mr Yu Tailor, on the corner of Caine Road and Elgin Street, and Yuen's Tailor, in the escalator shopping arcade. Both make and supply suits and tuxedos as well as all the related accoutrements. Yuen's Tailor is one of the few places in Hong Kong where it is possible to have a kilt and accompanying Scottish formalwear made. Many Hongkongers, however, don't have their tailoring done in the territory at all. Take the KCR train to Lo Wu and skip across the border to Shenzhen and you will find innumerable tailors willing and able to knock up any and every item of clothing you might want for a fraction of Hong Kong prices.

Textiles

Other options **Souvenirs** p.314, **Tailoring** p.316

Two of the best areas in Hong Kong for purchasing textiles are the Western Market in Sheung Wan and Nam Cheong, Ki Lung and Yen Chow streets in Sham Shui Po. The former – an attractively restored old-style wet market building – houses around 20 stalls selling hundreds of rolls of fabric, from simple white cotton to richly adorned silk, and prices vary greatly depending on what exactly you want. The fabric markets in Sham Shui Po are a good deal cheaper, although a little chaotic, and in addition to rolls of fabric, you will also find every possible button, zip and buckle you could ever need. Also useful for sourcing material are Li Yuen streets East and West, between Queen's and Des Voeux roads in Central, where several shop and stalls have rolls of fabric for sale. Feel free to haggle at all of these locations. Shanghai Tang and many of the other stores listed in the tailoring section also sell luxurious rolls of material, while G.O.D. is a popular choice for stylish cushion fabric. If you're after a real bargain, however, take a day trip across the border to Shenzhen, where textiles are considerably cheaper, China being a massive textile manufacturing hub.

Textiles		
Fashion Fabrics Co	Western Market	2815 3713
Fu Lee	Central	2869 4199
G.O.D.	Various	See p.341
Shanghai Tang	Various	See p.344
Siroporn	Central	2866 6668
Universal Fabrics	Central	2526 2925

Wedding Items

Splash the Cash
If you're invited to a Chinese wedding banquet, guests are traditionally expected to give money rather than a gift. An average of $500 per guest is the norm.

No one should struggle to arrange or attend a wedding in this city. There are plenty of wedding planners, caterers, tailors, photographers and wedding outfit shops, never mind places to find the perfect gift. Any of the big department stores offer a wedding list service, and most have formal clothing suitable for attending weddings.

Bliss Creations wedding planners (2982 0192) will help you plan anything from a small and personal affair to a large and glamorous overseas excursion. They will help you design a dress or suit, send out invitations, find a photographer (see p.313 for a list of photographers) and choose complementary flowers.

If you prefer to do things your own way, Kimberley Road in Tsim Sha Tsui is lined with bridal shops, or there are countless tailors to suit every budget. The Prince's Building has many upmarket tailors. (see p.316 for more tailors and p.292 for formal wear hire).

Shanghai Tang has beautiful cheongsams as well as a tailoring service for Chinese-style men and women's smart outfits. For childrens' formal wear, Pop Kids in Cityplaza has off-the-rack frilly frocks and teeny tuxedos.

If you'd prefer to spend your savings on a glorious honeymoon than on a frock you will (hopefully) only wear once, head to Lover's Promise studio on Gloucester Road. Photographer Justin Yeung offers two wedding photo packages that come with a free wedding dress. He'll accompany you to scenic places like Tai Tam for the shoot and you can head home without changing.

Red's Best

Red is the colour of good fortune, which is why so many cards and decorations for Chinese weddings are red. White is traditionally the colour of mourning, although modern brides often choose a white dress as one of their outfits at a wedding banquet.

Wedding Items		
August Tailor	IFC Mall	2368 3037
Brides and Gowns	Central	2873 5558
Brides To Be	Central	2530 2345
Brooks Brothers	Central	2523 3366
Harmony	Cyberport	2989 6228
Matador Couture	Central	2896 2181
Merry & Marry Co.	Central	2543 2593
Pop Kid	Cityplaza	2567 3908
Pretty Woman	Tsim Sha Tsui	2312 2302
Tai Pan Row	IFC Mall	2147 2828
Tuxe Top	Wan Chai	2529 2179

317

Places to Shop

The following section includes Hong Kong's main shopping malls, as well as a selection of the hundreds of smaller malls found all over the territory. It also covers the main shopping streets and areas and the best markets.

Shopping Malls

Ask most locals how they spend their weekends and you will find "Eat, sleep and shop" is a popular answer. Shopping is considered as much an activity as having a barbecue with friends or playing sport. Unsurprising then, that Hong Kong has a fabulous range of malls from the sleek, white spaces of IFC Mall, Pacific Place, and Lee Gardens, to the busy, multi-levelled hive that is Times Square. There are also hundreds of small, jumbled malls tucked away in the basements of buildings, or on allocated floors of office towers. All malls are air-conditioned – over air-conditioned some would say – and the bigger ones have food courts, coffee shops, often a cinema, and a variety of surprisingly classy restaurants. Few have dedicated facilities for kids, although the big malls often have spectacular nativity, Easter and Chinese New Year scenes and activities for children. Hong Kong's malls are easy to reach using public transport. The few that aren't on top of an MTR station generally have covered walkways leading from the station into the mall. Parking in the busier shopping areas can be a problem.

Most malls stay open late for the restaurants within, but shops generally close around 20:00 in the upmarket malls, while those in the smaller malls may stay open until 22:00 or 23:00.

Shopping Malls – Main

18 Taikoo Shing Rd
Taikoo Shing
🚇 *Taikoo*
Map 17-E1

Cityplaza

2568 8665 | www.cityplaza.com.hk

This mall makes for a pleasant shopping experience for families, not least of all for its indoor ice rink, Ice Palace (see p.249). It is also known for its spectacular Christmas, Easter and Chinese New Year displays, as well as the art exhibitions held in nearby Devon House. There is a good range of affordable shops for adults' and children's clothing, jewellery, home furnishings, music, computers and gadgets. It has a less western feel than the malls of Central and Admiralty, and many of the shops are local or Asian chains. There's a good selection of Chinese and Japanese restaurants, and a food court called Food Republic with many stalls offering cheap and tasty Asian food. There are also western food outlets, like Pizza Hut, Mix, two branches of Pacific Coffee and American diner-style Ruby Tuesday. Within the mall are two department stores – Japanese UNY and local store Wing On – as well as Log-On, which could be classified as a department store given its range of goods that includes clothes, funky handbags, kitchen utensils, jewellery and skin care products. Cityplaza has a reasonable size Marks & Spencers, selling men's and ladies' clothing, shoes, and packaged food such as crisps, chocolate and wine. Most of the clothing shops are the usual stores like Esprit, Giordano, United Colours of Benetton and Mango, but there are some upmarket brands like DKNY, Armani Exchange and Tommy Hilfiger, as well as some good sports shops. One of the mall's speciality shops is The Best Tea House which sells tea and teaware. There's a large branch of Toys 'R' Us as well as a puzzle shop. Kids can play on small slides and rides in Jumpin Gym, which can also be hired for birthday parties.

A UA cinema shows reasonably priced movies, and it also has a VIP theatre with massage chairs and a waitress service.

Getting to the mall is simple – take the MTR to Taikoo, or buses to Quarry Bay. Parking is available and traffic in the area tends to move quite freely, even in peak hours. The mall is open from 10:00 to 21:30.

Great things can come in small packages…

Perfectly proportioned to fit in your pocket, these marvellous mini guidebooks make sure you don't just get the holiday you paid for, but rather the one that you dreamed of.

Explorer Mini Visitors' Guides
Maximising your holiday, minimising your hand luggage

Abu Dhabi · Amsterdam · Bahrain · Barcelona · Dubai · Dublin · Geneva · Hong Kong · Kuwait
London · New York · New Zealand · Oman · Paris · Qatar · Shanghai · Singapore · Sydney

EXPLORER
www.explorerpublishing.com

80 Tat Chee Ave
Kowloon Tong
Kowloon Tong
Map 10-B1

Festival Walk

2844 2200 | www.festivalwalk.com.hk

Located above the Kowloon Tong MTR and KCR stations, the elegant Festival Walk is a godsend for expats living or working in the New Territories or northern Kowloon. Its seven floors feature a well-thought-out blend of stores, ranging from designer labels, cosmetics boutiques and hi-tech electronics outlets to polished eateries and family attractions. Entering the mall from the MTR station (exit C), you will first encounter Taste, a large supermarket with an impressive range of imported products, a western-style bakery, an extensive sushi counter and an alluring selection of seafood fresh from the tank. Above the MTR level, the mall becomes airy, spacious and filled with natural light courtesy of a central atrium that stretches to the top. Before starting your shopping spree, take a minute to get your bearings. It is worth noting that Festival Walk is positioned on a slope and thus you can walk outside onto 'ground level' on more than one floor. Indeed, four floors are considered 'ground' floors (LG2, LG1, G and UG). If you're confused, head to one of the information desks to ask directions or pick up a mall guide. Follow the escalators skywards, you will find large branches of the likes of Marks & Spencer, Page One and Toys 'R' Us alongside about 200 smaller outlets by a cornucopia of respected brands. There is also a large branch of Log-On lifestyle store on the UG floor. Those in the mood for a bite will find several options on each level, from stylish restaurants and luxury chocolates to fast food, while entertainment of a different kind comes in the form of Hong Kong's largest ice rink and an 11 screen cinema, both on the UG floor. There is parking for 850 cars in the basement levels.

Canton Rd
Tsim Sha Tsui
Tsim Sha Tsui
Map 15-C4

Harbour City

2118 8666 | www.harbourcity.com.hk

Less a shopping centre than a metropolis devoted to retail therapy, Harbour City in Tsim Sha Tsui is by some margin Hong Kong's largest mall, with more than 700 stores, over 50 food and beverage outlets, three hotels and two cinemas across its four levels. Mercifully, for those without advanced degrees in orienteering, the mall has been divided into four connected shopping areas. Ocean Terminal should be your destination of choice if you're looking for children's wear and toys (ground floor), sportswear and cosmetics (level one) or young and fashionable casual wear (level two). Anyone who says size doesn't matter, meanwhile, obviously hasn't been to the Marco Polo Hongkong Hotel Arcade, which features an enormous Lane Crawford department store, a large branch of chic homeware purveyor G.O.D. and Grand Ocean, one of the city's largest cinemas. Ocean Centre is the place to go if you seek designer labels such as Burberry or Louis Vuitton, electronics stores or jewellery and watch outlets, while Gateway Arcade houses more designer boutiques, including D&G and Prada, plus another cinema and an impressive selection of international restaurants. As you might expect from a complex of

this size, there are numerous entry points, mostly dotted along Canton Road, a thoroughfare that Harbour City dominates. There is also a grand entranceway near the Star Ferry pier, and Tsim Sha Tsui MTR station and a bus terminus are close by. There are 2,000 parking spaces serving Harbour City, spread across three carparks (at Ocean Terminal, Gateway Arcade and Pier No. 3), with prices ranging from $16 to $24 an hour.

8 Finance St
Central
🚇 **Central**
Map 16-E1

IFC Mall

2295 3308 | *www.ifc.com.hk*

The IFC Mall is one of the city's newest and most easy to find malls thanks to its prime location right next door to Hong Kong's highest office building, the towering 88 floors of Two IFC. It's accessible via underground walkways from Central MTR station and the Airport Express train line. It's also handy for Lamma Island, Discovery Bay and other island residents as it's a short walk from the ferry piers. The mall houses over 200 shops and what is probably the city's most comfortable cinema. Plenty of leg room, wide red leather chairs, great sound – even the 1950s films they screen in one of the smaller theatres have never looked so good. It's also famed for its large City'super supermarket, and for being home to Hong Kong's first branch of Spanish fashion franchise Zara. Along with Mango, Evisu and Calvin Klein Jeans, this is as casual as it gets at IFC. After that it's designer all the way, especially on the upper levels. Lane Crawford department store on level three is a magnet for the hip, well-heeled shopper. White, sleek and cool, it's a world of cold, curving shapes and labyrinthine pockets of designer goods, jewellery, cosmetics and clothing. There is also a range of beauty and cosmetics shops on the ground floor, including Estee Lauder, Prada, Clarins, L'Occitane and Nina Ricci. Brits may also be pleased to hear that the mall houses the world's first Boots concept store with all the usual UK products on sale, as well as a one-on-one beauty consultation service.

It has a few well-known restaurants, Lumiere and Isola being two of them that enjoy great harbour views. For a quick bite and a coffee, you have sandwich-makers Pret, Costa Coffee, McDonalds and Mix for healthy wraps and juices. Musicians sometimes perform in the mall at weekends and there are usually impressive decorations and fun for kids around the Chinese New Year and Christmas. It's a popular mall, but it doesn't get so busy it's overwhelming. Shops are open daily, generally from 10:00 and close sometime between 19:00 and 22:30.

Pedder St
Central
🚇 **Central**
Map 16-E2

The Landmark

2921 2199 | *www.centralhk.com*

Pound for pound, dollar for dollar, The Landmark is probably Hong Kong's most exclusive shopping destination, a reputation that was sealed in 2005 by the addition of Harvey Nichols department store and the opening of the adjacent Landmark Mandarin Oriental, one of the city's finest hotels. Located on top of Central MTR station, The Landmark features five levels of high-end boutiques, principally fashion and cosmetics. These are organised around a large, square central atrium that lets in a great deal of natural light – a particularly pleasant feature if you stop for a coffee or a bite to eat at the airy Landmark Café located on its own 'island' in the centre of the

321

atrium on level 1. An arty water fountain completes the complex's look and adds to the relaxed and sophisticated atmosphere. As you might have guessed, The Landmark is not the place for those on a budget and many of the stores fall into the 'if you need to ask the price, you probably can't afford it' category. Here you will find attractive boutiques belonging to the likes of Louis Vuitton, Lanvin, Loewe, Paul Smith, Dior and Tod's, with the latter pair noted for their extravagant window displays. The Landmark is also a Mecca for shoe queens, with Sex and the City favourites Manolo Blahnik and Jimmy Choo having stores here.

Argyle Rd & Portland St ◀

Mong Kok

 Mong Kok

Map 15-C2

Langham Place

2148 2160 | www.langhamplace.com.hk

Langham Place is a 15 storey mall, 59 level office tower (the tallest in Kowloon and Mong Kok at 255 metres) and 665 room, five-star hotel complex, and its design is as impressive as its size. It has Hong Kong's only immense rooftop screen that shows psychedelic patterns and rolling clouds, as well as two of the territory's longest escalators within a mall, called the Xpresscalators, which together measure 83 metres. The light-filled atrium criss-crossed with metal supports and swirling installation art is a hot spot for people to gather for the New Year's Eve countdown and art and music shows. Every mid-priced brand known to the city can be found at Langham Place – anything from clothing, sports, shoes, and personal care to audiovisual and mobile phones. There's a Seibu department store, as well as a branch of local interiors shop, G.O.D., and Japanese psuedo-department store Lo-On. It's also a good place to head for affordable jewellery and watches. The Spiral is a corkscrew collection of shops on four floors that are buzzing with alternative fashion for hip teenagers. On Levels 12 and 13 there are a range of restaurants, bars and cafes that stay open till late and are perfect for hanging out and the mall also has a six-screen UA cinema.
Take the Mong Kok MTR Exit 3 to enter the mall via an air-conditioned walkway. Most shops open at 11:00 and close at 22:30 or 23:00.

88 Queensway ◀

Admiralty

 Admiralty

Map 16-F2

Pacific Place

2844 8900 | www.pacificplace.com.hk

The mall exists as part of the Pacific Place complex, which includes office towers, five-star serviced apartments, The Atrium and Parkside, and a conference centre. It's one of the most glamorous malls in Hong Kong. It has three top class department stores – Lane Crawford, Seibu and Sogo. Lane Crawford's interior design is impressive, particularly the men's fashion department on the ground floor. Trainers are suspended on a rotating shelf and a life-sized, Manga type figurine stands guard among the sleek, dark furnishings.
There are plenty of designer shops on the upper floors of the mall, including Prada, Burberry, Gucci, Dior and Aquascutum, and casual fashion outlets like Esprit, Mango and FCUK. If you're looking for jewellery or watches, there's Tiffany's, Cartier and Bulgari, to name a few, or for more affordable watches, try City Chain.
Among the specialist shops, there's audio-visual experts Bang & Olufsen, music shop Hong Kong Records, Liu Li Gong Fang for contemporary Chinese glass art and a contemporary painting gallery, Galerie du Monde. King & Country sells metal, hand-painted military and civilian figurines and polyresin models of buildings, aircraft and vehicles. They also design and manufacture corporate gifts for large businesses.
The mall has a good quality food court with Korean, Japanese, Thai and Chinese dishes on offer. It also has some good restaurants, including Thai Basil and Peking Garden. Many cinema-goers head to Dan Ryan's Chicago Grill for a burger or steak after a movie in the UA Cinema, situated on the ground level.

Pacific Place has direct, air-conditioned access to Admiralty MTR underground station. Smaller malls Queensway and the Admiralty Centre are also linked by walkways to Pacific Place. If you prefer to travel by taxi, avoid heading home between 17:30 and 19:30 on weekdays as taxi queues can be arduous. Shops open daily from around 10:00 till 20:00.

Hennessy Rd ◄
Causeway Bay
Causeway Bay
Map 17-B2

Times Square

2118 8900 | *www.timessquare.com.hk*

With its towering outdoor television screen, Times Square is a Hong Kong landmark and meeting point. It's also the heart of Causeway Bay's shopping district. Hundreds of

shops line the streets in the area, and the mega-mall that is Times Square shopping centre has more than 230 shops and a multi-cinema complex. The mall is designed so that all the shops form circles, one on top of another, with balconies looking down onto the central plaza below. Anything above the sixth floor can be unnerving for anyone suffering from vertigo, but keep away from the edge, and you should be fine. Shops are conveniently arranged so that similar stores are on the same floor. For example, most of the sports and outdoor gear shops are on the sixth floor. Floors 10 to 13 are all restaurants, offering a variety of Asian cuisines, and a few western. Times Square has a branch of Lane Crawford department store, as well as a

City'super. It has an extensive range of shops from children's clothes to fashionable trainer shops, to shops selling gadgets and audio-visual equipment, and Belgian chocolate. The Times Square carpark has 700 places and is open 24 hours, seven days a week. Traffic in the area can be congested however. It's not advisable to take a taxi home on Saturday afternoons, or try to get to or from Times Square on Wednesday nights as it's race night at the nearby Happy Valley race course. The mall is easily reached by bus or MTR – Causeway Bay MTR station has an air-conditioned walkway that leads directly into the mall. The shops generally stay open till 21:00 every night.

Shopping Malls – Other

Chater Rd ◄
Central
Central
Map 16-E2

Alexandra House/Chater House

2921 2497 | *www.centralhk.com*

Technically two separate shopping centres, Alexandra House and Chater House are joined by a covered walkway over Chater Road. They offer similar access to The Landmark and Prince's Building, meaning you can do most of your luxury shopping in Central without ever having to abandon the air-conditioning. Chater House is largely devoted to Giorgio Armani, including chocolate, flowers, accessories, homeware, cosmetics and of course, fashion boutiques from the Italian maestro. There is also a large Bulgari outlet here. Alexandra House, meanwhile, has flagship boutiques by the likes of Burberry, Ermenegildo Zegna and Yves Saint Laurent.
Other outlets include: Carnet, Dolce & Gabbana, Paule Ka, Ponti Food & Wine Cellar, Prada, Starbucks, The Swank, TSE.

323

Above the
MTR station
Kwun Tong
🚇 *Kwun Tong*
Map 10-E2

apm

2267 0500 | www.apm-millenniumcity.com

apm in Kwun Tong offers eight floors of shopping, dining and entertainment. Located on top of Kwun Tong MTR station, the mall is also served by about 50 bus and 20 minibus routes, making it a popular choice for people living in Kowloon or the New Territories. The clientele is mainly local and this mall is particularly popular with families and teenagers. As such, the decor is bright and playful, with several parents' rooms for baby changing, and multicoloured seating areas on several floors providing a pleasant place to wait or have a rest – a rarity in Hong Kong malls. As well as the usual mix of high-street stores, from trendy fashion outlets such as D-Mop and agnes b, cosmetics from the likes of Jurlique and L'Occitane and a clutch of stores selling the latest advances in electronics and audiovisual entertainment. There are also around 30 food and beverage outlets, including a City'super delicatessen, while entertainment attractions include a Palace cinema on level six and a Green Box karaoke lounge, a few floors up on level 11. Most stores are open until midnight, with restaurants and entertainment venues open later still. What really sets this mall apart from similar venues, however, is an outdoor garden area on level two, where you can have a break from the relentless shopping when the weather permits.
Other outlets include: Adidas, Bauhaus, Broadway, Chevignon, City Chain, ETE, Fortress, Jusco, New Balance, Quicksilver Boardriders Club, Stage Of Playlord, Starbucks, Swatch, The Body Shop.

Yen Chow St
Sham Shui Po
🚇 *Sham Shui Po*
Map 10-B2

Dragon Centre

2360 0982 | www.dragoncentre.com.hk

Located in Sham Shui Po, the Dragon Centre has more of a local flavour than most malls you will encounter. As such, you are probably unlikely to visit it unless you live or work nearby or are shopping in Sham Shui Po market. Its 10 floors don't have any stores you can't find all over Hong Kong and label-lovers are likely to be disappointed by the modest brands on offer. Although the Dragon Centre may lack class and sophistication, it has the honour of being the only mall in Hong Kong to have it's own mini rollercoaster. Perched on the top level, from which vertigo-inducing level the floor is some nine floors below, it offers a thrilling ride for kids, when you can find it open that is. There is also an ice rink, an amusement arcade and a basement carpark with 7,000 spaces.
Other outlets include: Baleno, Bossini, City Chain, Giordano, Ice Fire, Jumpin Gym USA, Mirabell, Okashi Land, Pricerite, Puzzle City, Sincere, Veeko, Wellcome.

1 Great George St
Causeway Bay
🚇 *Causeway Bay*
Map 17-B2

Island Beverly

This multi-floored mall is a great spot for checking out the work of Hong Kong's young fashion designers. There are hundreds of shops no bigger than a bus shelter selling funky independent clothing designs, brooches and badges, hair accessories and cute shoes. While most shops are catering for young women, there are clothes for grown-ups. Narcisse, on the first floor, number 179, sells evening gowns which they will custom-fit for you for a very reasonable price. A word of warning however, only head to this mall if you are in the best of spirits and have a lot of time as the walkways are cramped and it's very busy, especially at the weekends. Also, ladies above a UK size 12 may struggle to find clothes to fit as their 'one size only' tends to be small and shoes generally only go up to size 38 (UK size five). The shops open around 13:00 and close at 22:00.

Hysan Ave &
Yun Ping Rd
Causeway Bay
Causeway Bay
Map 17-B2

Lee Gardens

2830 5639 | www.lee gardens.com.hk

If you're after a serene shopping experience, Lee Gardens and Lee Gardens Two are the places to head. Even on weekends the malls are quiet, and the service in the shops and at the concierge desks is impeccable. Be prepared to spend however as the shops are almost all designer, or comparable to top international brand name prices. Even the kids' clothing, toys and shoe shops on the second floor of Lee Gardens Two are designer. The mall has a branch of Berry Bros. & Rudd, the world's oldest independent wine merchant that caters to the British royal family and international celebrities. It also has Hong Kong's only free-standing Y's Yohji Yamamoto shop.

The two Lee Gardens malls are part of a large complex of business and shopping blocks in Causeway Bay including Lee Theatre Plaza, Leighton Centre, Hennessey Centre and 111 Leighton Road. But Lee Gardens is the premier shopping site in the complex. Inside the buildings may be blissful, but outside is generally hot and crowded, as the complex is in the heart of the Causeway Bay shopping district. Streets are busy and there can be traffic jams. Testifying to the shortage of parking space, Lee Gardens offers free parking to shoppers, but you have to spend over $2,000 to qualify.

The complex is a five to ten minute walk from the Times Square exit of Causeway Bay MTR station. Most shops are open from 11:00 to 21:00 every day.

Beside Sha Tin KCR
East Rail Station
Sha Tin
Map 6-C4

New Town Plaza

2684 9175 | www.newtownplaza.com.hk

The sprawling New Town Plaza is the New Territories' most popular shopping destination, featuring several hundred stores, a liberal smattering of eateries and several family attractions. In reality, it is two malls (Phase I and Phase III) connected by a covered walkway. Phase I features an array of shops and restaurants across nine labyrinthine floors. Phase III is smaller and easier to navigate, with its stores grouped around an airy oval atrium. Phase III is also slightly more upmarket than its Phase I counterpart, boasting an impressive selection of children-centric shops as well as Japanese and western fashion and cosmetic outlets such as Seiyu, Muji, Anna Sui and Philosophy. Most shops here are of the high-street variety, so prices are fairly reasonable, and almost every base is covered, from sportswear, music and DVDs to electronics, homeware and furniture. You will also find a section devoted to travel agents here, should you be looking to book a holiday after all your shopping exertions. The mall's other attractions include a 10 screen cinema, Jumpin Gym USA amusement arcade and Snoopy's World, a children's playground themed around everyone's favourite beagle and his friends. Parking is plentiful and fairly cheap, or free depending on how much time and money you spend there ($200/$300 gives one hour free Monday to Friday/weekends and public holidays; $400/$500 gives two hours).

Other outlets include: Broadway, City Chain, D-Mop, Esprit, Fortress, I.T, K-Swiss, Levi's, Marathon Sports, Mirabell, Miss Sixty, Morgan, Pedder Red, Swarovski, Timberland.

Btn Des Voeux Rd &
Chater Rd
Central
Central
Map 16-E2

Prince's Building

2430 4725 | www.centralhk.com

The Prince's Building is synonymous with imported luxury. It's a prime hunting ground for upmarket international jewellery, exquisite antiques, men's clothing and tailors, and children's designer wear. For jewellery, there's Georg Jensen, Adler, Chen's, Baccarat, and Chopard to name a few. There are many tailors for men's and ladies' shirts and suits, all of which are in the highest of price brackets but provide a top quality service. The Kow Hoo Shoe Co is Hong Kong's oldest custom-made shoe shop.

325

Each pair tends to cost over $2,000 but they are made with care, and large sized men's and ladies' shoes can be hard to find in Hong Kong. The third floor of the mall has many shops for children, from Mothercare to educational toy shops. It's also home to some of the most respected antiques and art shops, including Alisan Fine Arts for contemporary Chinese painting, and Altfield Gallery for Chinese antiques.

The mall also has Central's only branch of the exclusive delicatessen, Oliver's. Head there for high quality imported food, freshly baked breads and an outstanding charcuterie counter. There's also a Frigidaire home centre selling their branded electrical appliances and a few kitchen and tableware shops.

The mall is easily accessible via taxi, the network of elevated walkways from Central MTR station, or one of the multitude of buses that come down Des Voeux Road into Central. Shops are generally open from 10:00 to 19:00 daily.

33 Wai Yip St
Kowloon Bay
Kowloon Bay
Map 10-D2

Telford Plaza

2750 0877 | www.telfordplaza.com.hk

The large mall is located directly above the Kowloon Bay MTR station. It's also easily accessible by bus and there are 500 parking spaces.

Divided into two sections (Phase I and II), it has all the usual high street fashion, health and beauty, jewellery and electronics shops. It's divided into handy zones, so you don't have to walk miles to compare prices if you're looking for something specific. Most of the mobile phone service providers have shops here in the Podium. For fashion, shoe, jewellery and beauty stores, head to Phase I ground and first floors, and Phase II third floor. There are quite a few children's clothes shops on the fourth floor of Phase II, home furnishings are centred on the fifth floor and travel agencies are on the sixth. Besides the 250 shops, there are also a lot of facilities like the Kowloon Bay Post Office, medical services, a Towngas customer centre, two 7-Eleven convenience stores, a ParknShop and a Wellcome. There is also a UA cinema.

There's a variety of local restaurant and cafe chains and a few western restaurants, mainly just catering for shoppers after a quick bite.

Department Stores

Most of Hong Kong's department stores can be found either inside or adjacent to malls, to maximize convenience and passing trade. Most stores sell a broad range of items, which almost always includes fashion, cosmetics, home furnishings, jewellery and gifts. Japanese-style department stores, such as Sogo, Seibu and UNY, are particularly popular, while both ends of the spending spectrum are well represented, from the dollar-stretching bargain shopping of Jusco to the credit-card-straining luxury of Harvey Nichols. The grand old lady of Hong Kong department stores, however, remains Lane Crawford, which has strengthened its position at the top thanks to recent big-money facelifts.

The Landmark
Central
Central
Map 17-E1

Harvey Nichols

3695 3388 | www.harveynicols.com.hk

There was a great deal of excitement generated by the 2005 opening of a Harvey Nichols in Hong Kong, the British department store's first branch in Asia. With such high expectations, it was bound to disappoint. While the design is a tasteful blend of hip and high design, it's nothing spectacular. The store takes up five

Get Personal
Harvey Nichols offers a free personal shopping service (by appointment) to help you hunt down the perfect gift or give advice on the season's hottest looks. Call 3695 3288.

floors, but each floor space is small and oddly shaped and it's difficult to find things. Waiting for the lift or hunting down the correct escalator to change floors regularly is frustrating. What sets it apart from other department stores however, is the cosmetics department. Perfumes and make-up tend to be 'cult' brands. Its Organic Pharmacy counter is impressive, and the neon Beyond Beauty counter sells ranges not available anywhere else in Hong Kong, including Ren, June Jacobs, This Works, Carthusia and Robert Piguet. It also stocks high-end fashion for men, women and children. If you spend over $3,000, the restaurant on the fourth floor will serve you a complimentary high tea for two. The store has an entrance on Queen's Road and is accessible via The Landmark. It's open Monday to Saturday, 10:00 to 21:00, and 10:00 to 19:00 on Sundays.

2 Kornhill Rd
Quarry Bay
🚇 *Tai Koo*
Map 17-E1

Jusco

2884 6888 | *www.jusco.com.hk*

Jusco is probably Hong Kong's most authentic Japanese and moderately priced department store. Besides an array of eastern and western groceries in its supermarket section, this huge store sells a range of lifestyle goods, from cookware to bed linen, electronics to children's shoes. It also has a bakery for fresh bread and a warm food counter for beef skewers, roast chickens and sushi boxes. The main branches are in Kornhill, Whampoa, Tseung Kwan O, Lok Fu, Tseun Wan, Tuen Mun and Tai Po, and there are other small branches dotted around the territory. See the directory on p.338. The Kornhill Road store is open from 08:30 to 23:00 daily.

IFC Mall
Central
🚇 *Central*
Map 16-E1

Lane Crawford

2118 3388 | *www.lanecrawford.com.hk*

T.A. Lane and Ninian Crawford established the first Lane Crawford store in Hong Kong way back in 1850 and the store has been a bastion of luxury shopping ever since. Today, there are four Lane Crawford stores (none of which are on the original site), each with its own distinguishing features and particular draw. The store in IFC Mall, for example, features conceptual designs by contemporary artists, one of which resembles a flock of birds composed of thin strips of paper. The Pacific Place branch has a quite hypnotic revolving shoe wall from which you can pluck styles as they ferry past, while the Times Square store has curious escalators that curve skywards rather than going straight. Whichever store you visit, you will find an excellent selection of high-end cosmetics, fashion, shoes and homeware. Prices may be high, but the service is generally first-rate, with personal shopper services on offer as well as cafes in which to take a break. For serious shoppers, The IFC Mall and Harbour City branches offer the most extensive ranges. For branch details see the directory on p.338.

> **Mall Martini**
>
> There's a small but perfectly formed Martini Bar hidden away on the first floor of the IFC Mall Lane Crawford store. Be warned: once you settle into its soft leather seats you may not want to leave.

Queen's Rd Central
Central
🚇 *Central*
Map 16-E2

Marks & Spencer

2921 8059 | *www.marksandspencer.com*

A little reminder of home for Brits around the world, Marks & Spencer has eight stores in Hong Kong in which you will find the brand's clothing, footwear, toiletries and foodstuffs. This is a popular place to pick up the basics such as underwear and nightwear in western-friendly sizes, and the lingerie section is popular. Unlike M&S stores in some other countries, the food on offer is limited to pre-packed items, such as biscuits, preserves and snacks, so anyone hoping to buy their tasty oven-ready meals will be disappointed. M&S really comes into its own at Christmas time, however, with Christmas puddings, mince pies and brandy butter just some of the hard-to-find products on offer to enhance your festive feast. One big selling point is the fact that

327

Marks & Spencer has far and away the most generous returns policy in Hong Kong. Goods in a saleable condition and with a receipt can be returned for an exchange or refund within a whopping 90 days of purchase; without a receipt, they will still give you an exchange or gift vouchers. For other branches, see the directory on p.343.

Seibu

Pacific Place
Admiralty
Admiralty
Map 16-F2

2971 3888

One of the largest department store chains in Japan (its Tokyo store is the third-largest department store in the world), this was the first Seibu store to open outside Japan. It's a chic department store that tempts affluent yuppies with top designer men's and women's clothing, shoes and accessories, cosmetics, and home furnishings. The fashion tends to be hip rather than classic. They have a good range of women's jewellery, from ornate Victorian-style chokers to girly silver pendants and earthy bracelets. Two-thirds of the store's merchandise is European and about 25% is Japanese. The Loft section carries stylish houseware, greetings cards and gifts. It's open from 10:30 to 20:00 Sunday to Wednesday and 10:30 to 21:00 Thursday to Saturday. There's also a branch in Langham Place and a small one in Windsor House. See the directory on p.338.

Sogo

555 Hennessey Rd
Causeway Bay
Causeway Bay
Map 17-B2

2833 8338 | www.sogo.com.hk

Sogo was founded in 1830 in Osaka by a Japanese businessman who was a retailer of used kimono. The company rapidly expanded into a major department store. Hong Kong's first branch opened in 1985, and it's now the biggest Japanese-style department store in the territory. If you're looking for something in particular, think of Sogo first. It

carries everything from massage chairs and mattresses to branded and everyday clothes, shoes, stationery, perfumes, tableware and digital cameras – all at competitive prices. It's a popular store, so expect to see lots of other shoppers, no matter what time you go. Its 12 floors are conveniently arranged into levels of similar goods. There's a food court and supermarket in Basement 2 and fashion, perfume, jewellery, watches and accessories for ladies and men spread over four floors. There's also a men's-only fashion level on Floor Five. Young ladies' and men's fashion has its own floor, as does sports clothing and equipment, and children's and babies' goods. The homeware and electronic goods sections offer a diverse selection and range of prices. The store connects directly to the Causeway Bay MTR station. The Tsim Sha Tsui branch of Sogo focuses only on designer fashions. See the directory on p.338 for contact details. Both stores are open from 10:00 to 22:00, seven days a week.

UNY

Cityplaza
Taikoo Shing
Tai Koo
Map 17-E1

2885 0331 | www.unyhk.com.hk

Of all the big Japanese department stores in Hong Kong, UNY retains the feel of its country of origin most closely, thanks largely to a superb food hall in the basement. Here you will find a huge selection of Japanese foodstuffs, from sweets and bottled drinks to freshly made delicacies such as yakatori and soba noodles. There is also an extensive sushi and sashimi counter, while a bakery is one of the many attractions at the reasonably priced sit-down food court on the same floor. UNY is a good place to shop for Japanese homeware, including professional quality kitchen knives, bedding and furniture (such as futons and massage chairs). This is not to say the products are exclusively Japanese; local and western brands sit next to their Japanese counterparts throughout the store. There is a fair-sized cosmetics area, featuring the likes of Lancome and Lush, while their footwear and toy departments also feature a broad range – although the clothing department is not the trendiest in town. The store is open from 10:00 to 22:30 (food hall and court till 23:00). There is free parking and free delivery on offer when you spend $300 or more.

Wing On

211 Des Voeux Rd
Central
Sheung Wan
Map 16-E1

2852 1888 | www.wingonet.com

Wing On is one of the more local of the large department stores dotted around town. Its five branches – in Central, Cityplaza, Tsim Sha Tsui, Jordan and Discovery Bay – offer a wide selection of modestly priced clothing, footwear, home furnishings, electrical goods, gifts and more. This is unlikely to be your shopping destination of choice if you are looking for designer labels, but it is a practical and cheap place to purchase home basics such as bedding items and kitchenware. Indeed, if you want to kit out your kitchen in one fell swoop, there are few places that have a better range of cooking and small electrical items to meet practically any budget, particularly the flagship store in Central. For other locations, see the directory on p.338.

Yue Hwa

301-309 Nathan Rd
Jordan
Jordan
Map 15-C3

3511 2222 | www.yuehwa.com

This old fashioned and inexpensive store gives an interesting glimpse into traditional Chinese culture. Many types of tea and traditional medicines are on sale, as are bamboo crafts, Chinese oil paintings, mahjong sets, rosewood furniture, tennis table bats, woollen underwear, cheongsams, shoes, men's suits and cute children's Chinese outfits. It's also a good place to buy an everyday Chinese tea set as there is a diverse range of styles and prices are reasonable. The staff don't tend to be fluent in English, but they are very helpful and will call a manager over to help you if necessary. The other main department store branch is at 1 Kowloon Park Drive in Tsim Sha Tsui and 257-273 King's Road, North Point, but there are other smaller branches that specialise in Chinese medicine. See the directory on p.338 for details.

Independent Shops

This is an area of the Hong Kong shopping scene that has burgeoned recently. In addition to designer boutiques bringing together the best in local and international fashion, there are many retailers who have elected to fill a gap in the market by importing merchandise from the United States, Japan and other countries, or by designing their own creations. Here are a few of the most notable.

329

G/F, 34B Staunton St
SoHo
⊞ Central
Map 16-E2

Chocolate Rain

2975 8318 | *www.chocolaterain.com*

Chocolate Rain is a quirky jewellery and accessories company set up by award-winning local designer Prudence Mak, who left the field of advertising in 2000 to follow her dream of being a fashion and accessories designer. Chocolate Rain has three branches within a one-minute walk of each other in SoHo. The Staunton Street branch sells handcrafted long, beaded drop earrings, flamboyant rings and delicate necklaces, fabric dolls, pin cushions, tote bags, cushion covers and other personal and home accessories, as does the branch at 63 Peel Street. You can also sign up there for a number of creative courses. You can learn to decorate fabric using jade, pearls, semi-precious stones, wire, beads and needlework, or make individual hats also decorated with a number of different objects. The branch at 18 Elgin Street called Art in Progress – Dessert is a cafe bar and restaurant specialising in desserts. They also sell jewellery and run jewellery-making and cookery classes. They host jewellery and cooking classes for groups for bridal showers and birthday parties.

Bartlock Centre
3 Yiu Wah St
Causeway Bay
⊞ Causeway Bay
Map 17-B2

Evergreen

2581 9763

Skateboarding may not be a crime, but you would be forgiven for thinking it was, given the lack of shops catering to skaters in Hong Kong. Evergreen, tucked away in the nondescript Bartlock Centre close to Times Square in Causeway Bay, is therefore a boon for budding Tony Hawks – or those that merely enjoy American skate fashion. Head to the third floor for an awesome range of boards, decks, trucks and protective gear by many of the most popular skate companies. The first floor is dedicated to skate fashion. Here you will find baggy jeans, hoodies, T-shirts, caps, belts, wallets and ski-hats by the likes of LRG, Lithium and Carhartt, as well as a great selection of skate trainers from brands such as Etnies, Lakai and DVS Shoe Co, including often difficult to find larger sizes. The shop assistants are extremely friendly and genuinely enthusiastic about the clothes, making this one of the best store atmospheres in Hong Kong.

> **Cheap Sneaks**
> Last season's trainers are frequently discounted or sold as two-for-the-price-of-one to make way for new collections in Evergreen. Check out the far left corner of the first floor for special offers.

Leighton Centre
Sharp St
Causeway Bay
⊞ Causeway Bay
Map 17-B2

G.O.D.

2890 5555 | *www.god.com.hk*

Don't be fooled by the divine-sounding acronym – G.O.D. has more to do with helping you create a heavenly home than achieving spiritual salvation. Standing for Goods of Desire, G.O.D. is many a Hongkonger's first choice for stylish furniture, home accessories and kitchenware. Its four stores sell a range of items, from shower curtains to cutlery to sofas, and many designs are inspired by Hong Kong and Chinois chic. This is a particularly good spot to pick up stylish linen, cushion covers and glassware, although it is rare to stroll through without at least one item from their alluringly arranged shelves convincing you to part with some cash. G.O.D. has also branched out with a high-quality clothing range, while the Causeway Bay store features a lifestyle restaurant, Home Cooking, which serves international cuisine and superb desserts at very reasonable prices.
Fittingly, G.O.D. is the phonetic sound for a Cantonese slang phrase that means 'to live better'.
For other branches, see the directory on p.338.

29-31 Gough St ◄
Central
🚇 **Sheung Wan**
Map 16-E1

Homeless
2581 1880 | *www.homelessconcept.com*

North of Hollywood Road, but downhill from it, is a scattered collection of restaurants, independent shops and a nightclub or two. The area, sometimes called NoHo, is undergoing a revival of sorts, although it is still very peaceful. Homeless, on Gough Street, is a treasure trove of funky accessories for the home. It stocks furniture, lamps, lovely wooden toys, unusual projection clocks, gorgeous (but expensive) Christmas decorations, quirky handbags, greeting cards and much more. Many of the brands are imported from overseas (Europe, Japan and Thailand, mainly) but some local designers are represented too. It's a great place to head if you're looking for a gift for someone who appreciates design. There's also a branch at 9 Hau Fook Street, Tsim Sha Tsui (2780 1363), which stocks a range of gift items. The Gough Street shop has a bigger range of furniture to choose from.

16 Queen's Rd ◄
Central
🚇 **Central**
Map 16-E2

Joyce
2522 7402

A favourite with Hong Kong label-lovers, Joyce stocks an enviable range of designer wear, shoes and cosmetics in its three stores. Among its effortlessly stylish racks you will find creations by the likes of Yohji Yamamoto, Issey Miyake, Marc Jacobs and John Galliano, while the cosmetics department features many luxury brands that you won't find anywhere else in Hong Kong. What sets Joyce apart from other designer boutiques – in particular its flagship store on Queen's Road central, opposite the landmark – is the mix of old-world charm, evoked by antique-looking furniture, books, trophies and ornate picture frames, and modern design. The faultless service is also a throwback to a more relaxed age, while the store's striking window displays add a touch of stylish humour to the shop's appeal. For other branches, see the directory on p.338.

Streets/Areas to Shop

Hong Kong's main shopping areas – Central, Causeway Bay and Tsim Sha Tsui – are easy to find and are packed with a multitude of retail options. There are, however, particular streets and areas within these districts (and, of course, outside of them) that are worthy of attention. Several of these more specific areas are largely dedicated to a particular product, such as Ap Lei Chau's furniture warehouses or Mong Kok's Trainers Street, while others offer something a little different to Hong Kong's often virtually indistinguishable malls.

Nr Aberdeen Harbour ◄
Map 14-A1

Ap Lei Chau

Ap Lei Chau's claim to fame is that it's the most densely populated island in the world, but for shoppers it has far more alluring charms. Situated just off the south coast of Hong Kong Island and connected by a road bridge, Ap Lei Chau (which means 'duck's tongue island') is perhaps the best place in the territory to shop for furniture or to grab a bargain at one of its many factory-seconds outlets. Horizon Plaza is the first (and often only) stop for most Ap Lei Chau shoppers as it features 26 floors of mainly furniture and carpet stores. Here you will find Asia's largest rug warehouse, Carpetbuyer, as well as stores selling indoor and outdoor furniture, barbecues and anything else you might need to beautify your home. There are also toy stores (Toys

331

Club and Bumps To Babes), a bookstore (Pollux) and a piano specialist (Piano One Two Company), and prices are often significantly discounted. In and around Horizon Plaza there are many factory-seconds stores and clearance warehouses, such as the Joyce Warehouse, Lane Crawford Warehouse Outlet and Space, where you can pick up last season's designs at a fraction of their usual cost.

Tsim Sha Tsui
Tsim Sha Tsui
Map 17-B2

Nathan Road

Nathan Road is the main commercial artery of Tsim Sha Tsui, running north from the Peninsula Hotel towards Mong Kok. Nicknamed the 'Golden Mile', this crowded thoroughfare is crammed with brightly-lit shops selling cameras, electronics, jewellery and watches. Buyers should definitely beware though, as the area has a reputation for rip-off merchants just waiting to sting gullible tourists. If you do buy a camera or electronic device, check that it has a warranty (valid in your home country, if necessary) and make sure you know exactly what you're paying for – it has been known for unscrupulous retailers to remove vital components from the box when you're not looking and then expect you to pay for them when you return later to complain. You're advised to avoid shops which do not display prices, and stick to those displaying a QTS (Quality Tourism Services) sign. Nathan Road also suffers from annoying touts who will try to flog you a new suit or fake Rolex. That said, it's still considered one of Hong Kong's tourist essentials – just remember the motto 'buyer beware.'

Nr Victoria Park
Causeway Bay
Causeway Bay
Map 17-B2

Paterson Street

Hong Kong may not be short of designer stores, but for hip locals in the know, there are few places more popular than trendy Paterson Street. This unusually wide boulevard close to the Causeway Bay MTR exit for Victoria Park brings together some of the coolest designers from Asia and beyond, with the emphasis on youth fashion. Replay, Camper, Y-3 and Tsumori Chisato all have boutiques here, as does local heartthrob Edison Chen: his Juice store stocks achingly hip imported labels from Japan, many of which are impossible to find elsewhere in Hong Kong. There is also an entrance for mini-mall Fashion Island, where you will find a number of local designers and a couple of cool cafes. The Island Beverly, popular with female teens, is also nearby.

Pedder St
Central
Central
Map 16-E2

Pedder Building

The unassuming doorway entrance may not look like much and the interior may be less than refined, but the Pedder Building is home to a plethora of second-hand fashion shops, local designers and children's stores. Step through the doorway next to Shanghai Tang on Pedder Street and you may get the feeling you are entering a derelict building until you reach the first floor, where you will find, among other stores, vintage-style clothing shop Once Upon A Time, as well as the old-world charm of the China Tee Club (p.373), the perfect place to set down your shopping bags and enjoy some refreshments. Peruse the other five floors and you will find such highlights as esteemed women's tailor and clothes shop Blanc de Chine, second-hand designer wear store Ty Treasures (which is a frontrunner for the dubious honour of having the surliest staff in town) and one-stop children's toy and clothes shop Bumps to Babes.

Nr the Escalator
Central
Central
Map 16-E2

Pottinger Street

It may never rank as a likely shopping destination for the city's glitterati but Pottinger Street, between Queen's Road Central and Hollywood Road, more than makes up for in usefulness what it lacks in style. Characterised by its sloping, cobbled surface and a line of stalls enclosed in green wooden shelters, Pottinger Street is particularly useful for anyone looking for a fancy-dress costume and those who enjoy creative pursuits. Among its many stalls and shops you will find outlets devoted to feather boas, wigs, thread, zips, buttons and all manner of novelty items. Partyland, just below Wellington Street is a particularly rich source of costumes, masks and other dressing-up necessities, while Saturn, a little further up, sells a distinctive collection of jewellery pieces. Pottinger Street also has stalls specialising in traditional Chinese ornaments and paintings, flip-flops, light bulbs, plants and hair accessories, as well as several inexpensive eateries.

Lower Mid-Levels
Central
Map 16-E2

SoHo

SoHo or 'south of Hollywood Road' is the perfect place to head on a Saturday or Sunday afternoon for a couple of hours of shopping and a light lunch or glass of chardonnay at one of the open-fronted restaurants. You're bound to bump into at least one person you know, as the two main streets of SoHo, Staunton and Elgin Streets, are cut by the main Central to Mid-Levels thoroughfare, the Mid-Levels Escalator link. Many of the shops are small and sell quirky, locally designed goods, like handmade jewellery, funky handbags and dresses, home furnishings and candles. Look out for Maymayking (2445 5655), Spy Henry Lau (see directory on p.338), Morn Creations (2869 7021) and Indigo (2147 3000) for hip clothing and accessories. There are also a few florists and some of the best art galleries in Hong Kong. Hollywood Road is famous for its antique shops and trinket stalls. The area is a great place to pick up a unique gift – for a friend or yourself – in more relaxed surroundings than one of the city's impersonal malls or the bustling shopping areas of Causeway Bay or Tsim Sha Tsui.

Fa YuenSt
Mong Kok
Mong Kok
Map 15-D2

Trainers Street

Technically, it's the area of Fa Yuen Street between Argyle and Dundas Streets, in Mong Kok, but its more common name is Trainers Street – and with good reason. Almost every store in this area, including many of the smaller streets that branch off from Fa Yuen Street, are devoted to footwear, with sports shoes being perhaps the best represented. Here you will find a range of brands and styles that puts the majority of sports shops to shame, and prices are a good deal lower than you will pay on Hong Kong Island or in Tsim Sha Tsui. It is also a godsend for those with larger feet – UK 11 or above for men, or UK 7 and above for women – as most sports and shoe shops in other areas usually have limited or no stock in these sizes. This is also a good area to shop for sports equipment, from shinguards to fishing rods, as well as camping equipment.

Markets

Other options **Bargaining** p.282

Hong Kong has a great variety of markets, from ones selling souvenirs and trinkets that cater to tourists, to traditional wet markets selling live seafood, vegetables and fresh meat. While some markets like the Flower and Goldfish Markets are specialised, the biggest markets, such as the Ladies' Market in Mong Kok or Stanley Market, sell anything from table napkins to clothing, handbags (fake and original) to small electronic gadgets. Markets are generally the cheapest places to shop in Hong Kong, but this reflects the quality of the goods on sale. Gone are the days of snapping up incredible bargains – you get what you pay for. You can bargain in most markets, but the price shouldn't drop too much unless the stallholder was charging you for a real antique when it is actually fake, or for high quality jade when it is garden variety. If you are looking for costly jewellery, antiques or anything else that requires a guarantee of authenticity, head to a shop with a QTS mark, the Hong Kong Tourism Board's assurance of quality.

Bird Market

Nr Yuen Po St
Mong Kok
🚇 **Prince Edward**
Map 15-D1

At the end of the Flower Market Street where it turns right to become Po Yuen Street, you'll see a sign for the Bird Market. Go through the red wrought-iron gates. You can buy birds prized for their plumage, singing or fighting skills from all over the world. You can also pick up ornately carved birdcages and bird food like live grasshoppers. Although it remains open, the threat of bird flu has left the Bird Market practically empty of visitors.

Cat Street Bazaar

Upper Lascar Row
Central
🚇 **Sheung Wan**
Map 16-D2

This market is located on Upper Lascar Row, which is also known by locals as Cat Street. There are many stories behind the affectionate nickname, one of which harkens back to the days when shoppers would crouch like cats and sift through wares displayed on rugs on the street. Another claims that, in the old days, if something was stolen, it would turn up on Cat Street, where thieves were no better than rats and the dealers that bought the stolen wares were the cats that fed off them. Nowadays, the market has shops selling high-quality antiques, and others offering – by their own admission – reproductions. It's also jam-packed full of stalls offering fun Mao watches and memorabilia, 'lucky' Chinese coins and other trinkets.

Flower Market

Flower Market St
Mong Kok
🚇 **Prince Edward**
Map 15-D1

The Flower Market is really a street lined with flower shops that have their blooms in buckets neatly arranged to cover half the pavement. There is a fantastic range of flowers and plants, from the ordinary to the exotic. You can find curving canes of bamboo, carnivorous plants and potted plants here too. There are also shops selling the usual flower arranging equipment and a variety of vases. The market is favoured by the catering and hotel industries because of the range, but also because it's probably the cheapest place to buy flowers in the territory. Most of the flowers are brought in from mainland China's flower centre, Kunming, and, compared to their European counterparts, they are sold at a fraction of the price. Open from 07:00 to 19:00, and if you go first thing in the morning, the birds will be singing and the flowers will be at their freshest.

Gage Street Wet Market

Central
🚇 **Central**
Map 16-E2

Roughly bordered by Queen's Road Central to the south, Hollywood Road to the north, Aberdeen Street to the west and Cochrane Street to the east, lies an area of narrow roads, some closed to traffic, but each packed with market stalls specialising in different food products or cooking utensils. If you take a wander down Gage Street, one of the central axes of this maze of market stalls, you will see local shoppers from all walks of life buying meat, fish and vegetables. Fish swim around in plastic buckets while housewives haggle over the price of dried cuttlefish. The Gage Street market is one of many such fresh food markets that can be found in residential areas of the city. Some of these wet markets have come under fire for being unsanitary, so while you may choose not to buy produce (especially fish, seafood and meat) here, they are certainly interesting places to look around.

Goldfish Market

Tung Choi St
Mong Kok
🚇 **Prince Edward**
Map 15-C1

Less a market than a street lined with small, open-fronted shops, many of which display bright fish of all kinds swimming in oxygen-inflated bags on stands that jut out onto the pavement. If you want an aquarium, this is the place to come. There's tanks of every size, pumps, filters, fish food (dry and live), as well as aquatic plants. You can also find terrapins, snails and frogs. There is great variety of goldfish breeds, as well as other freshwater and saltwater species. You can also find a few shops selling puppies, kittens, rabbits and other fluffy creatures but pet shops in Hong Kong are

notorious for not vaccinating their animals properly. Check out the SPCA instead, and only buy from a pet shop as a last resort. The shops are open 10:00 to 21:00 daily.

Jardine's Cresent
Causeway Bay
🚇 **Causeway Bay**
Map 17-B2

Jardine's Cresent and Bazaar

The market on Jardine's Cresent is frequented mainly by locals. It offers a wide range of women's apparel, from evening gowns and sweaters to stockings and accessories. Behind the stalls are shops selling discounted clothing for the young and hip and conservative and stylish. Jardine's Bazaar is one street over, parallel to the Cresent. It is usually lined with waiting minibuses, but the shops are worth a look if you're after designer outlet shops. Around this area of Causeway Bay you'll also find lots of small DVD, VCD (the precursor to DVD) and CD shops that sell incredibly cheap movies and music. Most of the music is Cantopop, but there's a good range of US blockbuster films, sometimes as cheap as $20. Take Causeway Bay Exit F.

Fa Yuen St &
Tung Choi St
Mong Kok
🚇 **Mong Kok**
Map 15-C1

Ladies' Market

Despite the name, this large and busy market sells goods for both sexes. You can find a plethora of fake designer bags, watches, sunglasses, silk pyjamas, boxers, cigarette cases and silver jewellery, as well as items for the home like towels and napkins, and fresh fruit and vegetables. Nothing is of top quality, but it's decent enough. This market is exclusively a street stall market permanently set up and running between Dundas and Argyle Streets. It's open from 12:00 to 22:00. Many of the vendors move to this market at 12:00 from the Fa Yuen Street market, which opens at 09:00 and runs between Mong Kok Road and Prince Edward Road. It's a busy market, but the best deals are in the shops behind the market stalls, many of which are clothing discount shops. Further down Fa Yuen Street, you can find sports shops a-plenty (see p.333). The nearby Sai Yeung Choi Street South is also worth a look as it's lined with electronics shops of varying standards.

Li Yuen St East &
Li Yuen St West
Central
🚇 **Central**
Map 16-E2

Lanes of Central

These narrow parallel lanes run between Queen's Road and Des Voeux Road Central. They are crammed with stalls that will appeal to tourists, but they are handy for locals too as you can pick up a gift, a cheap handbag or fabric for a new frock. There are a few discount clothing (adults and children) and shoe shops, and quite a few stalls sell thin pashminas (to brighten up an outfit rather than keep you warm) for about $40. You can also find cute children's outfits in Chinese silk, fake watches, low-grade jade jewellery and underwear. George and Me, one of the few vintage clothing shops in Hong Kong, can be found on Li Yuen Street West. The market is open from 09:00 to 19:00.

336

When you're lost what will you find in your pocket?

Item 71. The half-eaten chewing gum

When you reach into your pocket make sure you have one of these miniature marvels to hand… far more use than a half-eaten stick of chewing gum when you're lost.

Hong Kong Mini Map
Putting the city in your pocket

Abu Dhabi · Amsterdam · Bahrain · Barcelona · Dubai · Dublin · Geneva · Hong Kong · Kuwait
London · New York · New Zealand · Oman · Paris · Qatar · Shanghai · Singapore · Sydney

EXPLORER
www.explorerpublishing.com

2C Computer Mong Kok Computer Centre (2332 8127), New Town Plaza (2699 2028), Sham Shui Po (2725 9861), Tsim Sha Tsui (2730 4382), Wan Chai Computer Centre (2882 3377), Windsor House (2504 0126)

Abebi Festival Walk (2265 7388), Harbour City (2377 3844), The Landmark (2530 2560), Lee Gardens (2882 1793)

Aluminium Causeway Bay (2577 4766), Lyndhurst Terrace (2546 5904), Wan Chai (2577 4066)

American Nutrition Central (2542 2213), Discovery Bay (2987 0811)

Armani Exchange IFC Mall (2234 7462), Harbour City (2629 6388), Causeway Bay (2881 8200), Festival Walk (2265 8233), Cityplaza (2967 6632)

Ascot Chang IFC Mall (2295 3833), InterContinental Hong Kong (2367 8319), Prince's Building (2523 3663), The Peninsula (2366 2398)

Avante Garde Designs Festival Walk (2777 5798), Pacific Place (2840 1268)

Aveda Spa & Salon Harbour City (2110 0881), Hong Kong Hotel (2730 9368), Cebu Pacific (2737 3020)

b+ab Cityplaza (2884 4231), Telford Plaza (2750 3818), Paterson Street (2881 1090), Times Square (2506 0202), New Town Plaza (2681 2801), Harbour City (2175 3882), Festival Walk (2265 1723), Mong Kok (2388 6026), Tsim Sha Tsui (2368 1802), Grand Century Plaza (2628 3003)

Baleno Whampoa Garden (3125 9888), Pok Fu Lam (3125 9888), Quarry Bay (3125 9888), Tsim Sha Tsui (3125 9888), Central (3125 9888), Causeway Bay (3125 9888), Dragon Centre (3125 9888), Olympian City II (3125 9888), Queensway Plaza (3125 9888), The Peak Galleria (3125 9888)

Bang & Olufsen Causeway Bay (2882 1782), Central (2526 8800), Festival Walk (2265 7860), Harbour City (2730 6844), Pacific Place (2918 0007)

Baron Kay's Tailor Central (2521 0668), Tsim Sha Tsui (2723 2839)

Benland Shoes Stanley (2813 8327), Star Ferry Pier (2723 1513)

Body Shop Pacific Place (2537 7072), Windsor House (2576 2246), Prince Edward MTR Station (2391 1854), Festival Walk (2265 8236), Causeway Bay (2572 3378), Central (2522 8824), Mong Kok (2380 7134), Telford Plaza (2799 2171), Central MTR Station (2868 3013)

Bookazine Central (2521 1649), The Peak (2849 2995), Jardine House (2501 5926), Tsim Sha Tsui (2724 0431), Admiralty (2866 7528), Wan Chai (2802 4932), Prince's Building (2522 1785)

Bose Tsim Sha Tsui (2688 6887), Times Square (2836 3181)

Bossini Dragon Centre (2728 8742), Cityplaza (2560 1213), Whampoa Garden (2365 6405), Times Square (2111 1168), Grand Century Place (2398 2355), North Point (2590 6198), Tsim Sha Tsui (2368 5866), Causeway Bay (2895 4155), Central (2524 9313), Festival Walk (2265 7817)

Broadway apm (3148 1296), Times Square (2506 1330), Telford Plaza (2753 7309), Paterson Street (3427 9819), New Town Plaza (2606 7762), Harbour City (2736 7733), Cityplaza (2884 0324), Tsim Sha Tsui (2366 3032), Mong Kok (2783 9828), Grand Century Plaza (2392 8632)

Bumps to Babes ◀ Horizon Plaza (2552 5000), Central (2522 7112)

Bunns Diving Equipt. ◀ Causeway Bay (2574 7951), Mong Kok (2380 5344)

Burberry ◀ Alexandra House/Chater House (2868 3511), Harbour City (2377 3031)

Calvin Klein Underwear ◀ Harbour City (2116 0602), Queensway Plaza (2865 4315), Prince's Building (2973 0345), Lee Gardens (2577 5133), Festival Walk (2265 8891), Cityplaza (2915 3230), Central (2526 8113), New Town Plaza (2697 4776)

Castello del Vino ◀ Central (2866 0577), Wan Chai (2555 8946)

Chanel ◀ Pacific Place (2918 1108), The Peninsula (2368 6879), Prince's Building (2810 0978), InterContinental Hong Kong (2722 6030), Hong Kong International Airport (2261 2030), DFS Galleria (2723 4639), Lee Gardens (2576 0696)

Chevignon ◀ Mong Kok (2771 7644), Tsim Sha Tsui (2377 0527), apm (3148 9017), Cityplaza (2513 0682), Diamond Hill (2110 9172), Festival Walk (2265 7618), Grand Century Place (2628 3113), Langham Place (3514 4201), Times Square (2506 2155)

Chinese Arts & Crafts ◀ Nathan Hotel (2730 0061), Pacific Place (2523 3933), Wan Chai (2827 6667), Star House (2735 4061)

Chow Sang Sang ◀ Mong Kok (2171 4842), Causeway Bay (2891 2422), Tsim Sha Tsui (2730 3241), Central (2526 2009), Cityplaza (2569 6083), New Town Plaza (3104 0491), Silvercord (2735 4622), Telford Plaza (3105 9558), Times Square (2241 4008)

Chow Tai Fook ◀ Harbour City (3188 1381), Telford Plaza (2130 1618), Times Square (3102 9980), New Town Plaza (2699 1389), Tsim Sha Tsui (2735 7966), Mong Kok (2780 1351), Causeway Bay (2573 3888), Central (2523 7128), Olympian City (2151 1602)

Christian Dior ◀ The Landmark (2524 8277), The Peninsula (2724 8337), Lee Gardens (2907 4055), Hong Kong International Airport (2261 0460), Tsim Sha Tsui (2269 5000), Pacific Place (2522 7938)

City Chain ◀ Central (2259 9020), Tsim Sha Tsui (2368 1805), Causeway Bay (2576 0295), Pacific Place (2395 5837)

City'super ◀ Harbour City (2375 8222), Times Square (2506 2888), IFC Mall (2234 7128), New Town Plaza (2603 3488)

Columbia ◀ Tsim Sha Tsui (2376 2816), Yuen Long (2470 7287), Cityplaza (2569 8200), Festival Walk (2265 8680), New Town Plaza (2698 4181), Telford Plaza (2799 8066), Times Square (2506 0830)

Cosmos Books ◀ Tsim Sha Tsui (2367 8699), Central (2866 1677)

Cova ◀ Pacific Place (2918 9648), Quarry Bay (2811 9877), Prince's Building (2869 8771), World Trade Centre (2576 4233), The Landmark (2501 4760), Festival Walk (2265 8178), Harbour City (2907 3881), Lee Gardens (2907 3066)

Crabtree & Evelyn ◀ apm (3148 1348), Cityplaza (2567 6088), Festival Walk (2265 8883), Grand Century Place (2628 3198), Harbour City (2735 6683), The Landmark (2530 2518), New Town Plaza (2698 8922), Pacific Place (2523 8668), Times Square (2506 1168)

CSL	Central (2918 1010), Tsim Sha Tsui (2910 1010)
D&G	Pacific Place (2801 6827), Harbour City (2730 7900)
D-mop	Silvercord (2808 2825), Times Square (2715 4881), New Town Plaza (2602 2625), apm (3148 1360), Tsim Sha Tsui (2722 0072), Central (2840 0822), Causeway Bay (2203 4130)
David's Shirts Ltd	Central (2524 2979), Tsim Sha Tsui (2367 9556)
Davidoff	The Landmark (2525 5428), Regent Hotel (2721 5520), The Peninsula (2368 5774)
DKNY	Times Square (2506 3838), Lee Gardens (2377 9900), Festival Walk (2265 7982), Cityplaza (2970 2006)
Dr Martens	Harbour City (2377 9387), Sino Plaza (2892 1832), Sogo (2831 8561), Tsim Sha Tsui (2369 6881)
Dunhill	Festival Walk (2265 7806), Harbour City (2730 7608), Hong Kong International Airport (2261 0822), Hyatt Regency Hotel (2311 4448), Pacific Place (2537 1009), Prince's Building (2524 3663)
Dymocks	Admiralty (2156 2023), Central (2851 8030), Discovery Bay (2987 8494), IFC Mall (2117 0360), Peak Galleria (2849 8782), Prince's Building (2826 9248), Stanley (2813 8070), Wan Chai (2511 8080), Wan Chai (3527 3560)
Ecco	Harbour City (2377 1488), Telford Plaza (2758 6789), IFC Mall (2234 7007), Tseung Kwan O (2628 4528), Tsim Sha Tsui (2410 9809), Wan Chai (2808 1961), New Town Plaza (2697 0369)
Elegant Watch & Jewellery	Central (2868 1882), Harbour City (2735 8481), Times Square (2506 3663)
Emphasis	Mong Kok (3586 0022), Grand Century Place (2628 3166), New Town Plaza (3104 0491), Times Square (2241 4008), Central (2757 3726), Cityplaza (2915 3808), Festival Walk (2122 9088)
Emporio Armani	Causeway Bay (2891 6118), Alexandra House/Chater House (2532 7777)
Esprit	apm (3148 1088), Cityplaza (2907 0022), Causeway Bay (2890 4390), Central (2523 1900), Festival Walk (2265 8222)
Essential Spa	Kowloon Tong (3188 1919), Mid-Levels (3102 9333), Central (3106 0303)
Eugene Group	Tsuen Wan (2628 3268), Causeway Bay (2628 3777), Mong Kok (2628 3228)
Flow	Sai Kung (8207 6828), Central (8104 0822)
Fortress	Festival Walk (2121 8393), Times Square (2506 0031), Melbourne Plaza (2121 1077), Harbour City (3101 9205), Cityplaza (2568 2280), Quarry Bay (3150 8250), Admiralty (2866 2461), Central (2544 4385), Tsim Sha Tsui (2368 0937), Hopewell Centre (2866 3138)
Fotomax	Harbour City (2175 0819), Central (2530 5298), Telford Plaza (2795 1004), Times Square (2882 0496), New Town Plaza (2698 8609), Cityplaza (2560 4569), Mong Kok (2397 5832), Wan Chai (2866 2236), Aberdeen (2553 4811), Festival Walk (2265 8993)
French Connection	Festival Walk (2265 8110), Pacific Place (2918 1760), Times Square (2506 2373)

G.O.D SoHo (2805 1876), Harbour City (2784 5555), Langham Place (2816 5555), Leighton Centre (2890 5555)

Gallerie du Vin Wan Chai (2591 9028), SoHo (2854 2987)

GigaSports Cityplaza (2918 0028), Harbour City (2115 9930), Pacific Place (2918 9088), Paterson Street (2915 0918), Tsuen Wan (2940 0040)

Giordano Admiralty (2922 1141), Aberdeen (2921 1089), Central (2921 2556), Capitol Centre (2923 7111), Cityplaza (2922 7126)

Golf House New World Centre (3113 1211), Times Square (2506 2522), Festival Walk (2265 7293), Cityplaza (2915 9390), Tsim Sha Tsui (2377 0110)

Green Concepts Central (3113 5848), Jardine's Cresent and Bazaar (2882 4848)

Gucci The Landmark (2524 4492), Times Square (2506 4262), Lee Gardens (2576 6918), Hong Kong International Airport (2261 0538), Harbour City (2199 7728), Pacific Place (2524 0412)

Hallmark Cards Quarry Bay (2562 7312), Sheung Wan (2541 2312), apm (3148 1234)

Havana Express SoHo (2110 9201), The Peak (2849 8198), Tsim Sha Tsui (2366 2537)

HMV Central (2739 0268), Admiralty (3692 4178), Windsor House (2504 3669), Tsim Sha Tsui (2302 0122)

Homeless Tsim Sha Tsui (2780 1363), Central (2581 1880)

Hong Kong Book Centre Central (2522 7064), Cityplaza (2539 6822)

Hong Kong Optical Mong Kok (2381 3312), Tsuen Wan (2407 2687), Central (2523 3711), North Point (2560 6039), Causeway Bay (2576 2669), New Town Plaza (3110 3254), Quarry Bay (2134 1522)

Hong Kong Records Festival Walk (2265 8299), Pacific Place (2845 7088)

HP Cars Sai Kung (2791 4145), Chai Wan (2558 0222)

http://www.izzue.com Tsim Sha Tsui (2311 9286), apm (3148 1060), Cityplaza (2907 0108), Festival Walk (2265 7955), Harbour City (2992 0631), Island Beverly (2890 3560), Langham Place (3514 9037), New Town Plaza (2698 3217), Telford Plaza (2758 0496), Whampoa Garden (2356 7063)

Hugo Boss IFC Mall (3188 1171), Pacific Place (2918 1833), Central (2868 3122), Prince's Building (2110 1818), Harbour City (2735 1962)

I.T. Harbour City (2114 0268), Times Square (2506 0186), Sino Plaza (2834 4056), Silvercord (2992 0235), Silvercord (2730 8076), Pacific Place (2918 9522), Langham Place (3514 4150), Festival Walk (2265 1770), Causeway Bay (2504 0032), Tsim Sha Tsui (2736 9152), Causeway Bay (2881 6102), Mong Kok (2388 1676), New Town Plaza (2697 0510)

IKEA Causeway Bay (3125 0888), Kowloon Bay (3191 1188), Sha Tin (3125 0888), Sheung Shui – Warehouse (3125 0888)

Il Bel Paese Wan Chai (2804 2992), Mid-Levels (2549 8893), Happy Valley (2868 2818)

341

Inside ◄ Repulse Bay (2812 6685), Discovery Bay (2987 8337), Horizon Plaza (2873 1795), Prince's Building (2537 6298)

Japan Home Store ◄ Sheung Wan (2819 6408), Plaza Hollywood (2955 9091), Dragon Centre (2958 1126), Jordan (2736 3105), Central (2524 8734), Mid-Levels (2525 2402), Stanley (2813 8571), Wan Chai (2838 2441), Happy Valley (2573 1070), Tsim Sha Tsui (2723 5641)

Joyce ◄ Pacific Place (2523 5944), Harbour City (2367 8128), Central (2522 7402)

Jumbo Grade ◄ Grand Century Place (2264 3011), IFC Mall (2295 0008), Pacific Place (2526 3873), Cityplaza (2569 9063)

Jusco ◄ Tseung Kwan O (2703 2888), Whampoa Garden (2627 6688), Quarry Bay (2884 6888), Tai Po (2662 8888), Tuen Mun (2452 7333), Tsuen Wan (2412 8668), Lok Fu (2339 3388)

Kelly & Walsh ◄ Central (2810 5128), Pacific Place (2522 5743)

L'Occitane ◄ Causeway Bay (2591 1681), IFC Mall (2234 7198), The Landmark (2523 4111), Pacific Place (2522 1033), Cityplaza (2568 6860), Harbour City (2730 5020), Festival Walk (2265 7511)

Lancome ◄ Langham Place (2269 1801), Sogo (2831 8482), New Town Plaza (2698 7822), IFC Mall (2869 7518), Harvey Nichols (3695 3121), Festival Walk (2265 8665), Tsim Sha Tsui (2317 7236), Pacific Place (2971 3784)

Lane Crawford ◄ Times Square (2118 3638), Harbour City (2118 3428), IFC Mall (2118 3388), Pacific Place (2118 3668)

Lanvin ◄ The Peninsula (2368 1216), The Landmark (2525 3337), Pacific Place (2523 9512), Hong Kong International Airport (2261 2611), IFC Mall (2234 7686)

LensCrafters ◄ Central (2840 0621), Pacific Place (2848 9442), Prince's Building (2523 8385)

Lingerie Philiosophy ◄ Tsim Sha Tsui (2722 5922), Sha Tin (2603 0933), Lee Gardens (2577 0408), Queensway Plaza (2294 0480), Sogo (2831 8699)

Links of London ◄ Pacific Place (2918 9727), Times Square (2118 8888), Prince's Building (2525 1598), Tsim Sha Tsui (2317 1613), Festival Walk (2265 8982), IFC Mall (2295 3328)

Log-On ◄ Cityplaza (2560 0833), Festival Walk (2265 5333)

Louis Vuitton ◄ Harbour City (2736 6100), The Landmark (2736 6100), Lee Gardens (2736 6100), Pacific Place (2736 6100), The Peninsula (2736 6100)

Luk Fook ◄ Mong Kok (2394 8298), New Town Plaza (2698 2768), Yuen Long (2360 1228), Central (2606 0323), Causeway Bay (2838 8844), Tsim Sha Tsui (2770 6238), North Point (2566 1816), Jordan (2782 1777), Telford Plaza (2707 4480)

Magazzini ◄ Central (2521 3282), Horizon Plaza (2562 0671)

Mandarina Duck ◄ Tsim Sha Tsui (3188 4778), The Landmark (2845 4898)

Mango ◄ Cityplaza (2513 6019), Times Square (2506 1130), Pacific Place (2918 9313), New Town Plaza (2915 9313), IFC Mall (2295 3262), Festival Walk (2265 7137), Harbour City (2314 7395)

Directory

Mannings
Mid-Levels (2530 9258), Central (2537 2243), East Tsim Sha Tsui KCR Station (2311 3629), IFC Mall (2523 8326), Wan Chai (2598 7342), Quarry Bay (2561 0436), Tsim Sha Tsui (2724 4605), Causeway Bay (2241 4641)

Manolo Blahnik
The Landmark (2845 1575), Pacific Place (2918 0822), The Peninsula (2722 1298)

Marathon Sports
Telford Plaza (2798 9712), Times Square (2506 3139), Pacific Place (2524 6992), New Town Plaza (2699 1289), Langham Place (3514 4192), Cityplaza (2885 8409), apm (3148 9162), Tsim Sha Tsui (2367 9689), Central (2810 4521), Festival Walk (2265 7988)

Marc Jacobs
The Landmark (2868 9782), Pacific Place (2918 0812), Festival Walk (2113 1001)

Marks & Spencer
Diamond Hill (2927 6494), Times Square (2923 7970), Telford Plaza (2148 6012), Queen's Road Central (2921 8059), New Town Plaza (2929 4332), Festival Walk (2928 2213), Cityplaza (2922 7234), Harbour City (2926 3346)

Mirabell
Harbour City (2736 1076), Quarry Bay (2567 1834), Times Square (2506 2361), Whampoa Garden (2334 9711), Telford Plaza (2753 6483), Festival Walk (2265 7700), Dragon Centre (2708 2639), Causeway Bay (2504 3939), apm (3148 1165), Grand Century Place (2390 3544)

Mon Bebe
Harbour City (2628 3393), Windsor House (2904 8833)

Mothercare
Grand Century Plaza (2380 1832), Harbour City (2735 5738), New Town Plaza (2698 5533), Prince's Building (2523 5704), Windsor House (2882 3468)

Muji
apm (3148 9086), Langham Place (3514 9088), Causeway Bay (2808 1306), Mong Kok (2377 3293), New Town Plaza (2692 6406)

Nature's Village
Tsim Sha Tsui (2770 5098), Central (2121 1637), Mong Kok (3188 5183), Causeway Bay (2575 0188), Taikoo Shing (2117 2373)

New Balance
Times Square (2506 0896), apm (3148 1003), Harbour City (2367 6663)

Nike
Tsim Sha Tsui (2377 9660), Central (2526 7620), Harbour City (2895 5912)

Nine West
Festival Walk (2928 2080), Pacific Place (2921 2009), Central (2921 2628), IFC Mall (2926 7336), Harbour City (2926 3010)

o/3 Collection
Tsim Sha Tsui (2110 9036), Tsuen Wan (2499 8230), Tseung Kwan O (3194 4721)

One2Free
Sheung Wan (2854 1123), Telford Plaza (2798 5123), New Town Plaza (2602 0123), Hong Kong International Airport (2261 0818), Tsim Sha Tsui (2739 2123), Causeway Bay (2882 9039), Wan Chai (2591 5123), Mong Kok (2148 1123)

Optical 88
apm (3148 1068), Wan Chai (2893 3106), Cityplaza (2569 5902), Whampoa Garden (2994 8182), Causeway Bay (2891 7316), Central (2259 5188), Mong Kok (2783 0539)

Page One
Central (2536 0111), Festival Walk (2778 2808), Harbour City (2730 6060), Times Square (250 6028)

Papyrus
Prince's Building (2868 8788), Harbour City (2175 4888), IFC Mall (2295 3313), Lee Gardens (2907 2808), Pacific Place (2918 9711)

343

The Complete **Residents'** Guide

ParknShop — Olympian City II (2740 4159), Tsim Sha Tsui (3525 0200), Telford Plaza (2243 5892), Hopewell Centre (2121 8346), Diamond Hill (2955 9215), Stanley (2813 4419), Aberdeen (2873 4105), Central (2877 8785), Discovery Bay (2987 7486), Windsor House (2881 5527)

Patagonia — Harbour City (3188 2400), Times Square (2506 0677)

PCCW — Langham Place (2883 3380), Mong Kok (2394 8131), New Town Plaza (2883 9808), Causeway Bay (2881 8898), Central (2543 0603), Wan Chai (2575 6829), Jordan (2736 7331), Tsim Sha Tsui (2739 3992), Tsuen Wan (2439 0931)

Pedder Red — apm (3427 3288), Cityplaza (2886 9500), Harbour City (2118 0130), New Town Plaza (2696 5525), Times Square (2118 3581)

Pens Museum — Sha Tin (2681 0301), Telford Plaza (2305 1955), Tsim Sha Tsui (2368 7977)

Prada — Harbour City (2368 9662), IFC Mall (2234 7211), Lee Gardens (2907 3505), Pacific Place (2918 9233), The Peninsula (2369 1169), Alexandra House/Chater House (2522 2989)

Pricerite — Dragon Centre (2928 7006), Whampoa Garden (2926 5200), Olympian City II (2740 4551), Kennedy Town (2818 1160), Hollywood Plaza (2782 2710), Aberdeen (2554 0180), Sha Tin (2693 3731), Causeway Bay (2923 7010), Wan Chai (2893 0514), North Point (2117 7068)

Prince Jewellery & Watch — Tsim Sha Tsui (2369 2123), Causeway Bay (2776 0688), Harbour City (2311 1878), New World Centre (2301 1112)

Prints — Prince's Building (2523 9811), Queensway Plaza (2527 1191)

Protrek — Wan Chai (2529 6988), Tai Koo (2885 3566), Tsuen Wan (2413 9922), Sheung Wan (2850 7900), Ma On Shan (2695 9622)

Puyi Optical — Tsim Sha Tsui (2366 0199), Causeway Bay (2890 7070)

Quicksilver Boardriders Club — Grand Century Place (2628 3962), New Town Plaza (2895 5596), apm (2895 5038), Tsim Sha Tsui (2895 5891), Causeway Bay (2895 5948)

Rockport — Cityplaza (2560 0743), Pacific Place (2521 9323), Tsim Sha Tsui (2317 1147)

Royal Sporting House — Diamond Hill (2110 9166), Times Square (2506 2522), Olympian City II (2273 4431), New Town Centre (2698 9982), Festival Walk (2265 7293), Pok Fu Lam (2506 0112), Tsuen Wan (2405 2690), Tsim Sha Tsui (2377 0110), Tai Po (2662 2488), Cityplaza (2915 9775)

Samsonite — Causeway Bay (2573 0293), Cityplaza (2881 7872), IFC Mall (2295 3055), New World Centre (3113 1208), Prince's Building (2522 5368), Windsor House (2736 1936)

Sasa — Wan Chai (2146 1333), North Point (2566 3262), Grand Century Place (2628 9696), Mong Kok (2770 1311), Causeway Bay (2577 2286), Jordan (2359 3111), New Town Plaza (2688 0772), Tsim Sha Tsui (2311 7118), Central (2521 2928)

Seibu — Langham Place (2269 1888), Pacific Place (2971 3888), Windsor House (2890 0333)

Shanghai Tang — Hong Kong International Airport (2261 0606), InterContinental Hong Kong (2723 1012), Pacific Place (2918 1505), Pedder Building (2525 7333), The Peninsula (2537 2888)

Shoe Box
Cityplaza (2884 1685), Harbour City (2736 1053), Lee Gardens (2890 2329)

Shu Uemura
Harvey Nichols (3695 3117), Causeway Bay (2506 4283), Pacific Place (2918 1238), Sogo (2572 1694), Langham Place (2994 0487), Festival Walk (2265 7582), apm (3148 1022), Cityplaza (2513 5622), Harbour City (2735 1767)

SmarTone-Vodafone
North Point (2281 8888), Telford Plaza (2281 8888), New Town Plaza (2281 8888), Diamond Hill (2281 8888), Causeway Bay (2281 8888), Mong Kok (2281 8888), Tsim Sha Tsui (2281 8888), Wan Chai (2281 8888), Jordan (2281 8888), Central (2281 8888)

Sogo
Tsim Sha Tsui (3556 1212), Causeway Bay (2833 8338)

SoHo Wines & Spirits
Mid-Levels (2525 0316), SoHo (2530 1182), Sai Kung (2791 6283)

Spy Henry Lau
Tsim Sha Tsui (2366 5866), SoHo (2530 3128), Causeway Bay (2893 7799)

Staccato
New Town Plaza (2696 3428), Telford Plaza (2799 8459), Causeway Bay (2572 4211), Queensway Plaza (2865 0068), World Trade Centre (2882 8981), Cityplaza (2967 8399), Central (2530 0646), Langham Place (3514 4267), Harbour City (2175 3883)

Sunday
Central (2113 8383), Telford Plaza (2113 8383), Langham Place (2113 8383), Diamond Hill (2113 8383), Jordan (2113 8383), Aberdeen (2113 8383), Wan Chai (2113 8383), Tsim Sha Tsui (2113 8383), Sha Tin (2113 8383)

The Swank
Pacific Place (2521 4105), Tsim Sha Tsui (2735 0842), Alexandra House/Chater House (2810 0769), Harbour City (2175 4228)

Swarovski
Central (2530 9133), Causeway Bay (2972 2198), Tsim Sha Tsui (2736 0076), apm (3148 1018), Festival Walk (2265 7828), Harbour City (2175 5123), IFC Mall (2234 7126), Langham Place (3514 4115), Times Square (2111 0078)

Swatch Watches
Harbour City (2175 5218), IFC Mall (2376 3909), Sha Tin KCR Station (2699 5383), apm (3148 1012), Times Square (2506 1698), Mong Kok (2770 0046), Causeway Bay (2577 8479), Festival Walk (2265 7996)

Swindon Book Co
Tsim Sha Tsui (2366 8001), Harbour City (2735 9881)

Tech Easy Computer Pro Shop
Central (2522 8313), Wan Chai (2522 8313)

Three
Telford Plaza (2759 7974), Whampoa Garden (2773 1459), North Point (2807 1631), New Town Plaza (2696 2242), Langham Place (3514 9251), Tsim Sha Tsui (2367 6630), Causeway Bay (2882 5991), Wan Chai (2574 7726), Central (2187 2080), Diamond Hill (2321 4124)

The Tie Rack
Hong Kong International Airport (2810 8937), Central (2525 3083), Queensway Plaza (2866 8913), Festival Walk (2265 7272), Cityplaza (2567 1146), Sha Tin (2681 2883), Mong Kok (9877 7091), Telford Garden (2997 2066)

Timberland
Mong Kok (2391 9838), Festival Walk (2265 7723), Harbour City (2730 0772), New Town Plaza (2367 6422), Pacific Place (2868 0845), Times Square (2506 3808)

TimeZone
Tseung Kwan O (3194 4030), Peak Galleria (2849 6318), Mong Kok (3152 3778), Tsuen Wan (2414 0138), Central (2526 5288), Yuen Long (2479 8809)

345

Tom Lee Music	Tseung Kwan O (2493 4181), The Westwood (2542 7077), Cityplaza (2569 6111), Causeway Bay (2831 0133), Tsing Yi (2458 9110), Wan Chai (2519 0238), Aberdeen (2555 7808), Sha Tin (2602 3829), Tsim Sha Tsui (2723 9932), Telford Plaza (2997 2088)
Toni & Guy	Central (2801 7870), Lee Gardens (2890 1900)
Towngas	Tsim Sha Tsui (2880 6988), Mong Kok (2880 6988), Whampoa Garden (2880 6988), Telford Plaza (2880 6988), Cityplaza (2880 6988), North Point (2880 6988), Sha Tin (2880 6988), Tseung Kwan O (2880 6988), Causeway Bay (2880 6988), Tsing Yi (2880 6988)
Toys 'R' Us	Causeway Bay (2991 6222), Tsing Yi (2991 6222)
Toys Club	Central (2167 8474), Horizon Plaza (2836 0875)
Triton Fishing Equipt.	To Kwa Wan (2714 6262), Sha Tin (2632 7879), Kwai Fong (2615 2628), Tseung Kwan O (2512 9816), Jordan (2388 7229), Wan Chai (2866 8551), Tuen Mun (2618 3181)
Triumph	Causeway Bay (2890 5933), Central (2259 9081), Kwai Fong (2410 1339), Kwun Tong (2172 6262), Mong Kok (2625 1878), Tsim Sha Tsui (2316 2996), Tsuen Wan (2490 9785), Wan Chai (2573 9932), Yuen Long 2479 8070)
TSL	Causeway Bay (2838 6737), Central (2921 8800), Yau Ma Tei (2783 0191), Quarry Bay (2628 5708), Tsim Sha Tsui (2332 4618), Tsim Sha Tsui (2926 3210)
Ulferts	New World Centre (2628 3355), Hung Hom (2333 6281), Cityplaza (2567 8370), Festival Walk (2265 8181)
Ultimate PC & Mac Gallery	Windsor House (2881 6320), Central (2899 2239), Mong Kok (3591 8901)
United Optical Comp.	Tsim Sha Tsui (2893 6889), Wan Chai (2895 4311), Admiralty (2529 1136), Cityplaza (2567 7308)
Universal Audio & Video Centre	IFC Mall (2801 6411), Pacific Place (2801 6422)
Vilebrequin	The Landmark (2522 6286), Pacific Place (2918 0263)
Vivienne Tam	IFC Mall (2868 9268), Causeway Bay (2881 0006), Festival Walk (2265 8381), Harbour City (2117 0028), Times Square (2506 0098), The Peninsula (2721 1818), Pacific Place (2918 0238), The Landmark (2868 2826)
Watson's Wine Cellar	Stanley (2813 0173), Discovery Bay (2987 0268), Lee Gardens (3151 7628), IFC Mall (2530 5002), SoHo (2869 2210), Central (2147 3641), Happy Valley (3151 7130), Sai Kung (2792 6233), Wan Chai (3169 3150), Harbour City (2522 8893)
Watsons	Discovery Bay (2987 4089), Happy Valley (2833 6269), Star House (2730 2803), Melbourne Plaza (2523 0666), Dragon Centre (2360 0923), Sai Kung (2792 4319), Wan Chai (2294 0120), Mid-Levels (2540 7701), Mong Kok (2396 6637)
Wellcome	Causeway Bay (2577 4958), Telford Plaza (2758 6159), Wan Chai (2893 0215), Sai Kung (2791 1841), Aberdeen (2814 0612), Repulse Bay (2812 0340), Tsim Sha Tsui (2723 4982), Harbour City (2175 5513), Pok Fu Lam (2524 7174), Central (2529 1357)

346

Wing On	Discovery Bay (2987 9268), Tsim Sha Tsui (2196 1388), Jordan (2710 6288), Central (2852 1888), Cityplaza (2885 7588)
Wise Kids	Prince's Building (2377 9888), New World Centre (2368 7283), Pacific Place (2868 0133)
Wolford	IFC Mall (2234 7306), Prince's Building (2526 8078)
XGame	Tsim Sha Tsui (2366 9393), Causeway Bay (2881 8960), Langham Place (2264 3088)
Yue Hwa	Central (2522 2333), Jordan (3511 2222), Tsim Sha Tsui (2317 5333)
Yue Hwa Chinese Medicine Store	Sha Tin (2782 6622), Kwun Tong (2357 5172), Mong Kok (2395 7951), North Point (2578 0332), Wan Chai (2611 9622), Tsuen Wan (2614 6033)
Yves Saint Laurent	Harbour City (2377 2608), Alexandra House/Chater House (2868 0092)
Zara	Harbour City (2629 1858), IFC Mall (2234 7305), Pacific Place (2918 1099)

More than 15 Million hits per month
Over 170 User Nationalities
123 Countries Covered

CONNECTING
EXPATS
WORLDWIDE

@llo'Expat

www.alloexpat.com
www.hongkong.alloexpat.com

Your Online Journey Begins With Us
Country Guide • Classifieds • Forums • Real Estate

Going Out

Going Out

Local magazines and
newspapers carry
plenty of restaurant
advertisements, some
of which offer special
deals, discount
vouchers or a free
welcome drink. Many
restaurants offer
special deals on
Mondays, so it can be
good to eat out on this
otherwise painful day.
Credit card companies
occasionally offer
discounts for using
their card to pay for the
meal on top of the
credit card points
earned. Some
restaurants offer
privilege or
membership cards,
which may cut up to
10% from the bill on
subsequent visits, and
many cafes and coffee
shops have loyalty
cards, along the lines of
'buy 10, get one free'.

Going Out

Hong Kong is a city of hedonists and Hong Kongers pride themselves on being a cosmopolitan bunch who expect the best. Consequently Hong Kong offers world-class nightlife on a gleaming platter. Here you can find some of the best food, the swankiest bars and the hippest clubs in the world. And because variety is the spice of life, there are also plenty of earthier venues for those who like their nightlife gritty. Many of Hong Kong's restaurants, bars and clubs are found in the following areas – Knutsford Terrace in Tsim Sha Tsui, Lan Kwai Fong and SoHo in Central, and the infamous Wan Chai. Bars start to fill up after work at around 18:00, but things don't really get going until late. It's not unusual to have dinner at 21:00 and hit the bars after that. Then you can party all night.

Eating Out

Eating out is a national pastime in Hong Kong. The range of restaurant styles and cuisines available is mind-boggling. You can eat in cheap and cheerful streetside stalls, or in spectacular fine dining establishments, and everything in between. Chinese, Thai, French and Italian are among the most popular cuisines here, but you can also try Korean, South African food, Scandinavian food and much more. Many of Hong Kong's restaurants are on the swanky end of the scale with prices and a dress code to match. However, there are plenty of casual family-style eateries as well. In short, there's a restaurant for everyone, even the kids. Local children often stay up late and it's not unusual to see them out and about in the evening.

Delivery

Long working hours and hectic social lives mean that not many people in Hong Kong have time to cook. Many dine out almost every night, but when it all gets too much, home delivery is another option. Once again Hong Kong shows that it is a true service society and delivery services are not limited to pizza restaurants and the odd curry house. In fact you can pick up delivery catalogues containing delivery menus from a couple of dozen restaurants. Pick one restaurant or mix and match. Be warned, the prices are elevated and there is also an added delivery charge. As with everything here, convenience comes at a cost. To get your copy of a catalogue, log on to any of the following: www.ringadinner.com, www.sohodelivery.com.hk, www.dialadinner.com.hk.

Drinks

Other options **Alcohol** p.283

You must be at least 18 years of age and if you're driving you shouldn't have more than a glass of wine or half a pint. Other than that there are no rules. Alcohol is available everywhere - in corner stores, supermarkets and bottle shops, on ferries, in bars, restaurants, pubs and clubs. Beer from Belgium, arak from the Middle East, schnapps from Germany and wine from the Napa Valley to Naples. Martinis, Mojitos, Slippery Nipples and a Long Slow Comfortable Screw: you name it, you can probably find it in Hong Kong, at a price. Bars, especially in popular areas, charge elevated prices for booze in order to cover elevated rents. Even the price tag on a bottle of plonk from the supermarket may surprise you, due to high import duties. Soft drinks are also expensive in restaurants and bars, and that includes water. You can try asking for tap water but some places have a no tap water 'policy'. Please feel free to kick up a stink.

About 'Going Out'
The reviews in this section aim to give you an idea of the food, service, decor and ambience of a venue. Those that really impressed our reviewers earn the coveted 'Explorer Recommended' tag. Restaurants are categorised alphabetically by cuisine. If you're looking for somewhere with a particular quality, such as great alfresco dining or a romantic setting, see the Top Picks table on p.352. To avoid confusion, any non-English names retain their prefix (El, Il, Le) in the alphabetical placement, while English names are listed by actual titles, ignoring the prefix 'The.'

Hygiene

Restaurants in Hong Kong are generally hygienic. All outlets are spot checked annually by the Food and Environmental Hygiene Department. If a restaurant is deemed 'higher risk,' (eg, they serve raw meats) the department may visit them monthly. Most food in Hong Kong is stored for a short time and cooked at high temperatures which keeps the bugs at bay.

Special Deals & Theme Nights

With over 30,000 restaurants in Hong Kong you can eat almost any kind of food available on the planet. Not content with their normal menus, many restaurants hold promotions, either to showcase national specialities, or to bring in famous chefs from overseas as 'guest' cooks. For example, in May 2006 Hong Kong was visited by celebrity chefs from France, California, Italy and Australia. There were food festivals and themed menus from Goa, India, France, the South Pacific, New Zealand and Mexico. Then there were at least seven 'wine and food' nights featuring offerings from Australia, New Zealand, California, Italy and France. Nearly all the western restaurants offer special menus for Christmas Day, New Year's Eve, Valentine's Day, Halloween and any other holiday you care to think of. On top of all this, wine distributors often have promotional offers on selected wines at selected restaurants.

Local Cuisine

The local cuisine is Cantonese and most food is steamed or stir-fried. The emphasis is on fresh ingredients. Vegetables are bought from the market daily and meat is often freshly slaughtered, with no body part wasted. The dishes are usually lightly flavoured with ginger, garlic, spring onions and soy sauce. Bean paste and chilli are used as dipping sauces.

A popular Cantonese speciality that you mustn't miss is Yum Cha (literally 'drink tea'). There are numerous tea houses and restaurants serving a variety of Chinese teas along with Dim Sum. These are small steamed or fried snacks often served in bamboo steamers stacked one on top of the other. You choose the dishes you want to eat, and at the end of the meal the empty steamers are counted and you are charged accordingly. Although Yum Cha is usually a lunchtime occasion you can find restaurants serving Dim Sum through the night. It's a great way to sample Cantonese food and culture and is very reasonably priced.

Other styles of Chinese food are also well represented in Hong Kong, such as Szechuanese (hot and spicy), northern Chinese (wheat noodles, bread and mutton) and eastern Chinese (a mish mash of styles).

Making Friends

Making friends in Hong Kong is pretty easy. Expats are often here on short-term contracts so people come and go, sometimes with alarming frequency. The down side of this is regularly having to say goodbye to friends, the upside is that people have learnt to make friends quickly and everyone is pretty welcoming towards newcomers. Most newbies are scooped up and promptly introduced around town. However, meeting someone you want to date (and who wants to date you) isn't always so simple. It's perfectly acceptable to strike up a conversation with someone in a restaurant or bar, but it seems this rarely results in a long and fruitful relationship. For those seeking the fast track to loved-up bliss, personal ads can be found in *HK* magazine and on www.asiaxpat.com. Another very active online personals site is www.wheresmydate.com.hk. Meeting on the internet is very 'now'. Of course, not everyone in Hong Kong is looking for a relationship and there's plenty of room to manoeuvre for those who just want to have fun.

351

Tax & Service Charges

Most restaurants will add a 10% service charge on top of the cost of the meal. If there is a service charge you will see it written at the bottom of the menu. If you eat out during Chinese New Year you may find a couple percent more added to the total to cover the extra staff costs. Otherwise there are no hidden surprises when you ask for the bill.

Tipping

Tipping is customary in most restaurants with waiting staff, with anything from 5-15% being the norm. The general practice for tips is that any cash tips are pooled together and shared at the end of the night or week. Credit card tips are shared at the end of the month and companies quite often skim a little off the top. If you want to tip an individual server for good service put the money in their hand and say, 'this is for you.'

Hidden Charges

When eating in a Chinese restaurant it is quite common for waiters to bring snacks and tea to the table, which you will be charged a small amount for. A lot of restaurants offer free Chinese tea with a meal so it's best to ask the waiter at the time. The western restaurants usually offer bread with a meal and this is free of charge. If you find a bottle of mineral water on the table and drink it you will be charged for it.

Restaurant Timings

Most of Hong Kong's restaurants are open for both lunch and dinner, from around midday until 15:00, and again from around 18:00 until 23:00. Other restaurants are late-night or even 24 hour operations. There is always somewhere to eat and drink in Hong Kong. Opening times are generally unaffected by public holidays. The only possible exception might be Chinese New Year. Chinese New Year falls on different dates every year, between February and April. This is the only time when some businesses in Hong Kong close their doors, usually for three days.

Quick Reference Icons

🏆	Explorer Recommended!
👶	Kids Welcome
🍃	Alfresco Option
😊	Have a Happy Hour
🎵	Live Music
🍷	Serves Alcohol
🚚	Will Deliver

Vegetarian Food

Hong Kong people are not renowned for their vegetarianism (according to one survey less than 1% of the population refrain from eating any meat or fish) but every restaurant has at least a couple of vegetarian options. Chinese cuisine relies heavily on meat, fish and seafood but there are many delicious vegetarian friendly dishes. Check out any Buddhist Chinese restaurant for vegan options. Many Indian restaurants also have a great choice of vegetarian cuisine. If you want western food and can't face another cheese omelette, try the Bookworm Café on Lamma Island, or Life in Shelley Street, SoHo for great organic vegetarian cooking. For Japanese vegetarian food try the Fortune vegetarian restaurant on Leighton Road, Causeway Bay. For an exhaustive list of veggie restaurants go to www.ivu.org/hkvegan/gb/hkrest.html.

Top Picks

Alfresco		Good Cheap Eats		Romantic Evening		Cultural Experience	
Bebek Bengil 3	372	Good Luck Thai	385	Felix	356	City Hall Maxim's Palace	358
Cococabana	380	Jim Chai Kee Noodles	356	Isola	376	Habibi Cafe	355
Isola	376	Khana Khazana	370	La Kasbah	353	Nepal	382
Peak Lookout	375	Masaka	379	Pierre	368	Nzingha Lounge	398
The Stoep	353	Woodlands	371	Tutto Bene	377	Watermargin	361

African

Basement
17 Hollywood Rd
Central
🚇 **Central**
Map 16-E2

La Kasbah ───────────────────────

2525 9493 | *www.kasbah.com.hk*

The small entrance to La Kasbah is like a portal to another world. A few steep steps and a heavy wooden door transport you from Hollywood Road to Marrakech. Inside, the walls are draped in rich fabrics, there are lanterns, wooden chests and silver artwork. Lighting is low and the tables are small and intimate. This is definitely a place for romance. The dishes on offer are from the Magrhreb and are generally light and packed full of flavourful herbs and spices. Popular choices include the mixed mezze platter and any of the couscous dishes. A small wine list and some tasty cocktails are available. After your meal the aromatic mint tea will help to ease any symptoms of overindulgence. Alternatively you may wish to take your tea in the bar upstairs, where you can also enjoy a post dinner shisha.

32 Lower Cheung Sha
Village
Lantau Island
Map 12-E2

The Stoep ───────────────────────

2980 2699

If Lantau is your destination, there's no finer place to eat than The Stoep. It's South African-owned, so expect authentic native dishes. The legendary home-made bread is perfect to mop up tasty dips before moving on to the meaty mains. Step off the sand onto the covered terrace, and prepare to lounge away the hours in wicker chairs. The atmosphere here is strictly casual – you'll feel overdressed in anything but shorts. Indeed, many of the diners have just swum in from junks moored in the bay - sopping wet is a perfectly acceptable style at The Stoep.

American

15 Yuen Yuen St
Happy Valley
Map 17-B3

Alfred's Grille ───────────────────

2575 1322

Alfred's Grille is a little hard to find, but definitely worth the effort. Considering its quality, the food is very decently priced. Although the menu proclaims itself American, 'European' might be nearer the mark - with ingredients such as foie gras and Scottish salmon. As the name suggests, the kitchen's grill sees a lot of action – meat, fish and vegetables are all flamed to perfection. Muted tones and simple lines create an understated decor. Unfortunately, the small tables are a little close together, so lovers must censor their conversation. Still, it helps keep the focus on the food!

G/F 49 Elgin St
SoHo
🚇 **Central**
Map 16-E2

Bizou ────────────────────────────

2147 0100 | *www.diningconcepts.com.hk*

A custom-built rotisserie creates the centre-piece of this Californian-style bistro. The smell of slow-roasting suckling pig and crispy duck, as it drifts out of the open kitchen, would surely tempt even the Dalai Lama. Even so, Bizou's compact menu boasts a selection of non-spit-prepared dishes, leaving diners torn. But thanks to the typically Californian emphasis on fresh, high quality ingredients, all dishes are consistently good. Like most SoHo restaurants, Bizou is small, but the tables are far enough apart for diners to swing their elbows, while high ceilings and low lights give a sense of intimacy that doesn't feel cramped.

353

California

California Tower
30-32 D'Aguilar St
Central
🚇 **Central**
Map 16-E2

2521 1345 | www.lankwaifong.com

This 1950s American diner-themed restaurant and bar can take some credit for inventing Lan Kwai Fong as a nightlife hotspot. In business since 1983, it's best known for its dance floor – DJs spin tunes for a cosmopolitan weekend crowd. It also serves West Coast, Mexican and Italian dishes. When it comes to portions, California takes its American theme seriously: even the salads come piled high on huge square plates. Window-side booths give a great view of partying street life. Its location comes at a price however, and this restaurant is firmly in the upper 'Lan Kwai Fong' cost bracket.

Dan Ryan's Chicago Grill

Pacific Place
Admiralty
🚇 **Admiralty**
Map 16-F2

2845 4600 | www.windy-city.com.hk

This Pacific Place branch of Dan Ryan's is wildly popular with expats and locals partial to all-American fare. Menu classics include buffalo ribs, burgers and reuben sandwiches, all served with fries, coleslaw and a gherkin. Not a place for vegetarians or calorie-counters, this is somewhere to satisfy cravings for good, simple American food. The front bar gets filled with middle-aged beer-cradlers, while the dining section offers comfortable booths and walls covered with bits of Americana, such as a stuffed buffalo head. Kids are provided with a helium balloon and crayons to scribble on the paper table cloths with.

Inn Side Out

Sunning Plaza
10 Hysan Ave
Causeway Bay
🚇 **Causeway Bay**
Map 17-B2

2895 2900 | www.elgrande.com.hk

An American-style restaurant and bar, this is a popular post-work hangout. In the alfresco dining area, tall palm trees tower over the tables, while patrons munch on the peanuts provided then toss the shells on the floor. First-timers will soon start to enjoy the whole casual, messy experience. The bar offers one of the most extensive selections of beer (including imported microbrews)in Hong Kong, plus the usual tipples. The food is American and portions are generous. As well as offering pizzas, pastas, burgers and sandwiches, the menu has a whole section dedicated to sausages. Bang on.

Main St. Deli

Main St. Deli

Langham Hotel
Tsim Sha Tsui
🚇 **Tsim Sha Tsui**
Map 15-C4

2375 1133 | www.langhamhotels.com

Islanders regularly cross the harbour just to sample this New York-style deli's American fare. Choose from burgers, bagels and hot sandwiches, including the house speciality – a Reuben: a hearty feast of corned beef, pastrami, sauerkraut and melted Swiss cheese on toasted rye bread. There are also a few rarer dishes, such as the matzoh ball soup. This is the real deal. Ingredients are flown direct from New York and portions are big enough for three. With its black and white floor tiles, art deco fixtures and chandeliers, everything is sparkling clean and welcoming (rather unlike a real US deli).

Santa Fe

8 Observatory Court
Tsim Sha Tsui
🚇 **Tsim Sha Tsui**
Map 15-D3

2316 2818 | www.mhihk.com

A new addition to Hong Kong's dining scene, Santa Fe is a bright, terracotta-coloured restaurant offering a south-west American menu with lots of seafood, as well as some European dishes with 'tex-mex' twists. Rattan chairs, bright yellow window shutters and plenty of plants and flowers all add to the feeling that you're sitting in sunny California rather than hectic Hong Kong. Staff are welcoming and extremely eager to help, and food arrives fast. Thanks to its casual vibe and spaciousness, Santa Fe is a great place for large groups who enjoy eating fun food without being rushed.

Arabic/Lebanese

Winner Bld
27-37 D'Aguilar St
Central
🚇 *Central*
Map 16-E2

Beirut

2804 6611

Beirut is one of the few Lebanese restaurants in Hong Kong. The entrance is on Lan Kwai Fong, where the ground floor is taken up almost entirely by the bar. The decor has a Middle Eastern theme, with orange and green tiles and minaret-shaped plastering. Most visitors drink or suck on shishas instead of sample the mezze menu. Upstairs, however, is a different realm. Rich materials and lanterns create a calmer, more exotic atmosphere where diners linger over light offerings such as hummus, tabouleh and lamb shawarma. Vegetarians in particular fare better here than in many of Hong Kong's eateries.

112-114 Wellington St
Central
🚇 *Central*
Map 16-E2

Habibi Cafe

2544 3886 | *www.habibi.com.hk*

This fantastic Egyptian-owned eatery is as close as you'll get to ancient Cairo in modish Hong Kong. Step from Central's market bustle into this long restaurant and you'll find old Arab films playing above the bar and photographs of Cairo's vanished 'beau monde'. The food is irreproachable, including mezze, grilled meats and bowls of the koshary street-staple (lentils, rice vermicelli, macaroni, spaghetti, fried onions and chickpeas). Try the excellent value 'Mediterranean Magic' mezze combo with a glass of iced kharkadee (hibiscus) tea. Round everything off with home-made sweets or an apple-flavoured shisha if you fancy it. Divine.

Argentinean

32 Staunton St
SoHo
🚇 *Central*
Map 16-E2

La Pampa

2868 6959 | *www.lapampa.com.hk*

It's all about the meat at this Argentinean restaurant in Hong Kong's SoHo district. While the interior is simple and homely with pale yellow walls and caramel-coloured chairs, the menu is a carnivore's paradise. Steaks feature prominently – the menu offers cuts of your choice, cooked as requested. This is a rare treat at such reasonable prices in Hong Kong. In addition, the portions are generous and come with various vegetables. Other options include salads, native sausages and fish dishes. A reasonably priced bottle of Argentinean wine is the best way to wash down your meal.

Asian Subcontinent

Murray House
Stanley Plaza
Stanley
Map 14-D2

Chilli N Spice

2899 0147 | *www.kingparrot.com*

This restaurant is located in Murray House, a grand stone building first erected in Central in 1843, then dismantled and rebuilt in Stanley a few years ago. In a city with so few historic buildings, Chilli and Spice is worth a visit for this reason alone. The restaurant itself is large and airy, with wood panelling and high ceilings adorned

355

with ceiling fans. A balcony wraps itself around the restaurant and makes a very pleasant place to sit and gaze out to sea. The menu offers a host of Southeast Asian favourites such as Singaporean chilli crab and Indonesian chicken satay. Everything is tasty enough, if not exceptional. It's a good idea to order a selection of dishes to share, and don't worry about the bill, the prices are very reasonable. Chilli N Spice is popular with local families as well as tourists and daytrippers.

The Peninsula Hong Kong
Tsim Sha Tsui
🚇 **Tsim Sha Tsui**
Map 15-D4

Felix
2315 3188 | *www.peninsula.com*

Although a little dated now, Felix still attracts the cool crowd and those with guests to impress. From the moment you step out of the lift, you know you're somewhere special. If you're not wearing Armani, you'll suddenly wish you were. The indescribably glamorous Philippe Starck-designed dining area lies before you in all its uber-chic glory. Deep-pile carpet in the lower dining room prevents your conversation being interrupted by the clatter of stilettos. Upstairs the glass floors are lit from below and the long frosted glass bar is the perfect place to position yourself if you want to see and be seen. Unparalleled views of Hong Kong Island and Tsim Sha Tsui are visible through floor-to-ceiling windows. The dainty portions of Pacific Rim food do not quite live up to the surroundings, but are still pretty good. Oh, and don't forget to visit the toilets.

Jade Ctr
98 Wellington St
Central
🚇 **Central**
Map 16-E2

Jim Chai Kee Noodles
2850 6471

This famous noodle shop is a firm favourite of office workers, broke backpackers and bankers trying to get in touch with their roots. Jim Chai Kee was recently renovated for the better. Gone are the chipped formica table tops and plastic stools. Now modern, wood-veneered tables and benches are crammed with diners squeezing in wherever they can to sample one of the three dishes on the menu: prawn wonton, beef or fish ball noodles. The charm of the place is that, although simple, the food really is very good and you never know who you are going to sit next to, be it a couple of ancient grannies, the neighbourhood weirdo or your boss' daughter. Expect to queue, to be served within minutes and turfed out as soon as you've finished. However, for the price you won't find a better meal in HK and the management know it.

109 Repulse Bay Rd
Repulse Bay
Map 14-C1

Spices
2292 2821

Spices maintains the colonial feel of the building that houses it. The interior is elegant with high ceilings and lots of dark wood. However, the real draw is the large terrace. Here, round tables look out over the bay and accommodate couples, friends and young families. The extensive menu offers a range of dishes from South East Asia, so it can be a little difficult to choose and most customers end up sharing. The lengthy drinks list boasts fresh juices and cocktails. Everything on the menu is tasty, attractively presented and reasonably priced.

Kam Sing Mansion
Tai Fung Ave
Taikoo Shing
🚇 **Tai Koo**
Map 17-E1

That Little Town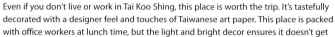
2513 8886

Even if you don't live or work in Tai Koo Shing, this place is worth the trip. It's tastefully decorated with a designer feel and touches of Taiwanese art paper. This place is packed with office workers at lunch time, but the light and bright decor ensures it doesn't get

---

Parking

Some of the more expensive restaurants and almost all five-star hotels offer valet parking for their customers. This can be a complimentary service or they may charge up to $60. If the service is not offered there are numerous carparks in Hong Kong costing $15 to $30 per hour. Leaving your car overnight can be done but will leave a large dent in your wallet. Better to take a taxi.

---

oppressive. The food is excellent and very reasonably priced. It is a Taiwanese restaurant but a few pieces of Shanghainese dim sum and a couple of spicy Szechuanese dishes have snuck onto the menu. Sticky dumplings with sesame paste, soup noodles with sesame sauce, honey duck and the white flower dessert are all specialties. There's also an interesting list of Taiwanese soft drinks which are definitely worth a try. Efficient and friendly staff completes an enjoyable experience.

Australian

Fenwick Pier
1 Lung King St
Wan Chai
🚇 *Wan Chai*
Map 16-F2

Quarterdeck Club

2827 8882

The Quarterdeck Club is one of few restaurants to offer comfortable outdoor seating by the harbour – in spite of the blighted view from the land reclamation work site. Inside, it's spacious, child-friendly and relaxed with a maritime theme. The menu has a distinctly American bent, despite claiming to be Australian. Expect standards such as sandwiches, pizzas and burgers served in big portions. Best to take a cue from the setting and stick with fish. The extensive seafood platter is enough to share. The bill takes a bite out of the wallet, so wait for a clear day and hearty appetite.

Knutsford Steps

Brunch

There are hundreds of places offering weekend brunches in various forms. Many restaurants and bars offer pub-style brunches at the weekends, but the most popular option is the hotel buffet. Some hotels offer a seafood-oriented brunch and some come with unlimited bubbly. Others put on entertainment for the kids and provide goodies to keep them occupied. The one thing all hotel brunch buffets have in common is that they are all totally gluttonous and over-the-top. You couldn't possibly sample everything on offer but most people give it a good go! Café Deco (p.372) is particularly good for kids, the champagne brunch at ToTT's (2894 8888) is good value and Top Deck (p.375) is a great alfresco option. Another popular choice on a sunny Sunday is brunch at the beach. The Blue Room at Big Wave Bay (p.372) has a good brunch menu.

Caribbean

35 Elgin St
SoHo
🚇 *Central*
Map 16-E2

Havana Bar and Grill

2545 9966 | www.eclipse.com.hk

Enter this SoHo restaurant and palm trees combined with strains of salsa instantly transport you to a sultry night in Cuba. Inside, the bar offers a range of daiquiris, mojitos and batidas (a Brazilian working man's drink) mixed by top-class bar staff. In the dining area, tables are a little cramped, but the atmosphere is lively. Socialist ideals scream out from the walls. The menu offers twisted classics, as well as unusual offerings such as the 'Collaloo' – a spinach and okra soup with crabmeat. Come on a Sunday for the 'Buena Vista Social Brunch' and live band.

357

Chinese

20 Lockhart Rd
Wan Chai
Wan Chai
Map 16-E2

American Peking Restaurant
2527 1000

This place is an institution. In the 50s it attracted American GIs looking for tasty Chinese food and cheap beer, hence the name. The food is delicious and the Beijing-style food is the perfect introduction to Chinese cuisine - it's not too heavy on the sea slugs. The sizzling prawns, chilli beef and peking duck especially stand out. The decor is basic and the atmosphere casual, with noisy chatter coming from diners at the large round tables. Waiters are brisk and sometimes a trifle brusque in true Hong Kong style.

51A Graham St
SoHo
Central
Map 16-E2

Chilli Fagara
2893 3330 | www.chilifagara.com

The red wooden flames at the front of this cosy, 18 seat eatery give a good clue to the spiciness of the food served within. With its authentic Szechuan cuisine, dim lighting and deep reddish walls, this place will send temperatures soaring during an intimate meal. While some dishes suit the more spice-loving of palates, such as the sirloin beef in chilli oil and Chilli Fagara crab, there are plenty of options for those wanting to keep their taste buds unsinged. Service is superbly attentive, so you'll always have a cold beer on hand to douse the flames.

City Hall
Central
Central
Map 16-E2

City Hall Maxim's Palace
2521 1303

Deservedly one of the most popular places in town to eat dim sum, so you'll need to arrive early to avoid waiting in line for too long. The steamed or fried snacks are served 50s style from passing trolleys pushed by old ladies, who'll happily show you each basket's contents if you can't read Chinese. Floor to ceiling windows reveal a superb harbour view. Maxim's Palace offers not only tasty food but an authentic cultural experience - the noise, the frenzied service and the nagging suspicion that you've just wolfed down a steaming bowl of pig's tripe and loved it.

63 Sing Woo Rd
Happy Valley
Map 17-B3

Dim Sum
2834 8893

This is one of Hong Kong's best dim sum restaurants. Tastefully decorated with cream walls, dark wood furnishings and 50s advertising posters, it's popular with both locals and expats and can get crowded at weekends. There are no trolleys, just a menu with picture aids for the hard of Cantonese. You can't go wrong with the dim sum. Many of the dishes come topped with shark's fin so be sure to specify 'no shark's fin' if you're concerned about the slaughter of the seas.

35-45 Johnston Rd
Wan Chai
Wan Chai
Map 17-A2

Fook Lam Moon
2866 0663 | www.fooklammoon-grp.com

You'll spot FLM by the Porsches and Ferraris parked outside. Once you've been sent up in the lift a hostess will ask your name (if she doesn't already know it) before rapidly weaving you through the feasting crowds to seat you. The spacious interior and understated beige and gold decor promote a relaxing atmosphere, and the food is traditional Cantonese of the highest order. Specialities include shark's fin, abalone and bird's nest together with a range of more standard dishes. Of course this kind of quality comes at a cost, so visit after a successful night at the races.

358

InterContinental
Grand Stanford
Tsim Sha Tsui
Ⓜ **Tsim Sha Tsui**
Map 15-D4

Hoi King Heen

2731 2882 | www.hongkong.intercontinental.com

Expats often complain Cantonese cuisine is oily. Not so at Hoi King Heen. The fare is interpreted in a lighter way with unusual ingredients, such as asparagus and pine nuts. This refreshing take has been recognised: the head chef was honoured at the 2005 'Best of the Best' culinary awards. Decor is typical hotel style - cherry wood round tables cater to small groups and couples, while private rooms accommodate larger parties. The glass-walled kitchen reveals chefs preparing the evening's food. A specialist tea server attends tables in the traditional manner: a fine way to round off your meal.

Hoi King Heen

Metropole Hotel
75 Waterloo Rd
Mong Kok
Ⓜ **Mong Kok**
Map 15-D2

House of Tang

2761 1711

If you're in Eastern Mong Kok and looking for a typical Chinese restaurant experience, then look no further than House of Tang. The restaurant seats around 250, and has the same standard features as many of Hong Kong's Chinese eateries: one large dining area, round tables, bright lighting, carpeting and a rather functional feel. Service is fast and the fresh, tasty dishes arrive quickly. The menu offers choices from all regions of China, and there is enough of a selection to keep both the cautious and adventurous happy. Good, but not ground-breaking.

IFC Mall
Central
Ⓜ **Central**
Map 16-E1

Lumiere / Cuisine Cuisine

2393 3933 | www.cuisinecuisine.com.hk

The experience justifies the cost in this phenomenal Chinese restaurant. The high-ceilinged space is separated into both a Szechuanese bistro and a more formal Cantonese restaurant, while Hong Kong harbour views are complemented by a beautiful bronze and blonde wood decor. Here, traditional Chinese food is transformed into haute cuisine – the sauteed prawns marinated in lemongrass and rose-blossom are particularly incredible. All the seafood is delivered fresh daily and they make their own soy sauces (crucial for good Chinese food). Go with at least three others to get the most out of the experience – great food is best when shared.

Four Seasons
Central
Ⓜ **Central**
Map 16-E1

Lung Hing Keen

3196 8888 | www.fourseasons.com/hongkong

This top-class Chinese eatery is one of the most stylish and contemporary in town. With its rich brown wooden walls and floor, dark wood tables and brushed steel ceiling, it's a chic blend of old and new, and the view across the harbour to Kowloon waterfront makes a spectacular backdrop for a spectacular meal. It has a vast menu, featuring traditional delicacies, such as bird's nest soup, as well as modern seafood dishes and desserts. Even tried and tested staples of Chinese cooking such as barbecued pork take on new meaning here.

Langham Place
Mong Kok
Ⓜ **Mong Kok**
Map 15-C2

Ming Ya Fe

2782 2200

Ming Ya Fe is one of the more popular options in the plethora of Langham Place eateries and attracts a crowd of regulars. It serves tasty Shanghainese fusion style food and there is also a lively bar. Although the restaurant is of an open design, the careful lighting and rich red tones lend a comfortable and intimate feel. The menu has plenty

359

of choices for all palates, and though serving sizes are generally modest, flavour is plentiful and the presentation appealing. There is live music every night from around 21:00. If you have to wait for a table, take advantage of the well-stocked and inviting bar area just inside the entrance where you'll have a ringside view of the band.

Food Restrictions

There are very few restrictions on food available in Hong Kong. There are certain exotic dishes which are available in mainland China, such as civet cat, rat, dog, owl and pangolin, which are banned in Hong Kong. You can still eat snake meat in Hong Kong if you so desire, but you can forget the urban myth of the monkey brains!

Grand Hyatt
Wan Chai
🚇 *Wan Chai*
Map 17-A2

One Harbour Road

2584 7930 | http://hongkong.grand.hyatt.com

This upscale Chinese restaurant in the Grand Hyatt Hotel has an air of affluence and business-like efficiency. However, this does not mean the atmosphere is subdued. In true Cantonese style noise levels are high and animated discussions can be heard from each table. The menu features such pricey delicacies as bird's nest, abalone and shark's fin. Other specialities include the famous beggar's chicken, camphor tea smoked peking duck and suckling pig. Typical Chinese desserts such as sesame fritters and fresh mango pudding round off the feast. The decor is understated with carpeting and chairs in soft hues of beige. Views of the harbour and Kowloon's ever-changing skyline can be enjoyed from every table. A generally polished experience is completed by impeccably dressed, charming and efficient waiting staff.

China Resources Bld
26 Harbour Rd
Wan Chai
🚇 *Wan Chai*
Map 17-A2

Quanjude

2884 9088

Impress friends with your local knowledge and take them to Quanjude. With no outdoor sign, few have heard of it - particularly in the expat community. However, it's possibly one of the city's most authentic, delicious dining experiences. As you walk into the vast, gaudily decorated room, the clatter of crockery and Cantonese chatter greet you. The roast peking duck is the main draw - imported from Beijing and roasted 'imperial style'. Carved up at your table within minutes, roll a few succulent morsels in a pancake with some crispy cucumber, spring onion and sweet plum sauce. Heaven.

The Peninsula
Hong Kong
Tsim Sha Tsui
🚇 *Tsim Sha Tsui*
Map 15-D4

Spring Moon

2920 2888 | www.hongkong.peninsula.com

Recently revamped to recreate the original 1928 setting, the results are elegantly excellent. Secluded in the hotel's west wing, its small size (100 seats) lends an air of intimacy. The understated interior is hardwood heavy, with wood panelled walls, stained glass features, and calm lighting. The food is fantastic, but be warned - this is serious Cantonese cuisine. Dishes include chilled pig trotter slices with jellyfish and bird's nest. Those with more timid taste buds can opt for various more standard seafood, meat, rice and noodle dishes. If you do brave the exotic, expect your bill to be equally outlandish.

Miramar Ctr
132 Nathan Rd
Tsim Sha Tsui
🚇 *Tsim Sha Tsui*
Map 15-D4

Tsui Hang Village Restaurant

2376 2882 | www.miramar-group.com

It's easy to see why Tsui Hang has a loyal following. This Tsim Sha Tsui branch cleverly combines modern and traditional decor, with lattice screens, sleek wooden furniture and contemporary Chinese artwork. The restaurant is spacious and sprinkled with extra touches, such as the silk jacket covers adorning each chair. The menu offers basic Cantonese fare, along with some fancier dishes. Favourites include deep-fried crispy chicken with steamed garoupa. At weekends, this place teems with families treating themselves. The prices reflect the quality at Tsui Hang – but it's money well spent.

Times Square
Causeway Bay
🚇 *Causeway Bay*
Map 17-B2

Watermargin

3102 0088 | *www.aqua.com.hk*

Watermargin's apothecary drawers, red lanterns, antique woodcarvings and dark, rich wooden furniture exude the magic of old Northern China. The atmosphere is hip but welcoming and staff will explain the ingredients of each dish or suggest complementary combinations. The northern Chinese food is occasionally spicy – best washed down with one of the restaurant's recommended signature drinks. As in most Chinese restaurants, order a few things to share. Each dish is beautifully arranged and the standard is high. Delicious Chinese tea, delicately scented with rose petals, is served throughout the meal at a small (but worthwhile) charge.

InterContinental
Hong Kong
Tsim Sha Tsui
🚇 *Tsim Sha Tsui*
Map 15-D4

Yan Toh Heen

2721 1211 | *www.hongkong.intercontinental.com*

To experience 'double happiness' in the form of an HK dining experience, try Yan Toh Heen. While the position of the restaurant allows superb views over Victoria Harbour to Hong Kong Island, the spacious layout, thick carpets and comfy chairs create a relaxed and cosseted indoor atmosphere. Popular with locals and visitors alike, it's best to book ahead at busy times. Brave traditional favourites such as bird's nest and shark's fin, or enjoy roast meat, seafood and vegetable dishes. Round off with a selection of desserts, as, surprisingly for a Cantonese restaurant, the portions are rather modest.

32-40 Wellington St
Central
🚇 *Central*
Map 16-E2

Yung Kee Restaurant

2522 1624 | *www.yungkee.com.hk*

This award-winning restaurant first opened its doors in 1942 – so it's practically ancient in Hong Kong years. It's since expanded its premises and menu, although the roast goose remains the house speciality. You can dine on any of the three opulently decorated upper floors, or opt for the more boisterous ground floor. Although the roast goose with its crispy skin and sweet plum sauce is always a winner, there are other tempting options, such as roast sucking pig, cold steamed chicken and thousand-year-old eggs with ginger. Expect to see a huge hungry clientele, including secretaries, A-listers and tourists.

361

Dinner Cruises

Other options **Boat & Yacht Charters** p.211, **Junk Trips** p.212

A dinner cruise is a novel way to see the sights while enjoying good food and the company of friends or family. A popular option is a trip around Victoria Harbour, with evening cruises timed to catch the Symphony of Lights. Another cruise heads north-west from the piers of TST and North Point and passes under the impressive Tsing Ma and Kap Shui Mun bridges, and Jaspas operates a junk that sails from Sai Kung. Many companies offer charters, so you can book a whole boat to yourself – even a Star Ferry – for parties or special occasions. While it doesn't actually sail anywhere, a meal aboard the Jumbo floating restaurant in Aberdeen is also a must for many visitors and residents during their time in Hong Kong.

Dinner Cruises		
Harbour Cruise – Bauhinia	2802 2886	www.cruise.com.hk
Jaspas Party Junk	2869 0733	www.jaspasjunk.com
Jumbo Kingdom	2553 9111	www.jumbo.com.hk
Star Ferry Company	2118 6120	www.starferry.com.hk
Water Tours of Hong Kong	2926 3868	www.watertours.com.hk

European

Other options **Mediterranean** p.380, **Pizzerias** p.382, **French** p.366, **Spanish** p.383, **Russian** p.383, **Italian** p.376

Oxford House
Taikoo Place
Quarry Bay
Quarry Bay
Map 17-D1

Belgo's East

2250 5020 | *www.elgrande.com.hk*

With its plump-cushioned sofas, soaring ceilings and Spanish or modern pop music, the glass-walled ground floor of Oxford House makes a laidback lunch or after-work hangout. The busy staff may not be overly welcoming, but by the time you're seated on the brown leather banquettes in the dining area you'll have forgotten any lack of ceremony. The Magritte-inspired mural of bowler hats and floating bottles emphasises the European feel. The signature dish – mussels and frites – is delicious. The mussels are perfectly complemented by a white wine sauce and the hot, crunchy frites come with the traditional European accompaniments: ketchup and mayonnaise.

15 Elgin St
SoHo
Central
Map 16-E2

Culture Club

2127 7936 | *www.cultureclub.com.hk*

Culture Club is a relaxed, yet multi-tasking restaurant-cum-art gallery-cum-tango bar. The venue is long and airy with high ceilings and casual decor. It's generally a little sleepy, but on the second and fourth Saturday of the month, local Tango enthusiasts sashay onto the dance floor to the beat of Argentinean music. The walls display local artists' paintings and drawings, which are available to buy. They have a limited but pleasant menu of European food and offer good value three or four course dinner sets. Dishes tend to be healthy and are all creatively presented. Food is art too you know.

Jumbo

Lan Kwai Fong Tower
Wyndham St
Central
Central
Map 16-E2

Finds

2522 9318 | *www.finds.com.hk*

Finds takes its name from the five countries whose cuisine it represents - Finland, Iceland, Norway, Denmark and Sweden. The innovative dishes both look and taste like masterpieces. The large, airy space has a separate bar area which gets buzzy by early evening. Dining tables are well-spaced, and there's also al fresco seating available. The whole establishment is awash in shades of white and cool blue, with hanging crystals, fairy lights and mirrors lending an icy Nordic atmosphere. A trendy restaurant with reasonable food, an upbeat atmosphere and well-groomed, attentive staff – what a find.

California Tower
30-32 D'Aguilar St
Central
🚇 *Central*
Map 16-E2

Lux Restaurant and Bar
2868 9538

With windows framing the crowds outside, a huge busy bar and massive speakers set in the walls, Lux is no place for a special dinner date. You're more likely to get distracted by the office workers misbehaving around you. Always bustling, the restaurant offers bar food with fancy twists, such as wagyu beef pie served with chateaux pomme fondant. Portions are hefty, and a pre 21:00 Happy Hour helps defray the cost of such luxurious eating. Ideal for unsure first dates or a pick-me-up, you'll want to join drinkers at the bar after your meal.

Fringe Club
Central
🚇 *Central*
Map 16-E2

M at the Fringe
2877 4000 | www.m-atthefringe.com

M at the Fringe is a survivor in Hong Kong's fickle restaurant scene. The small venue has a romantic feel with earthy orange and green walls, low lighting and a huge central floral bouquet. The food has influences from all over Europe, Turkey, Morocco and The Lebanon. Ingredients are wonderfully fresh and the sweet of tooth will love the Grand Dessert - a sample platter featuring six desserts, including the legendary M pavlova. Much of the eatery's charm lies in the details: the Moroccan glassware, the handwritten menu, and the little piece of Turkish delight accompanying your Turkish coffee.

32 Staunton St
SoHo
🚇 *Central*
Map 16-E2

My Place
2527 5223

My Place's window onto the street doubles as a tropical-fish tank. The fish are eye-candy rather than dinner, and the effect is calming. The seven candlelit tables are snug, and light blue walls give an underwater feel. The modern European dishes are made with rich, quality ingredients. Warmed appetizers include black truffle angel hair and foie gras, and the stuffed cornish hen main course is a favourite. Desserts range from strawberry tart to warmed chocolate pudding. My Place may be easy to miss, but you shouldn't - it's one of the best on Staunton Street.

9 Star St
Wan Chai
🚇 *Wan Chai*
Map 16-F2

One Fifth Grill
2529 6038 | www.elite-concepts.com

Forget the hype surrounding OFG, the reality is you will be served quality European food prepared by world class chefs. The restaurant's design is a modern take on a medieval banquet hall with reddy browns and candle-inspired lighting. The chic eatery attracts a trendy, self-conscious crowd who know good food when they see it. Chef Daniel Brolese insists the crispy duck leg is directly imported from France, and the dark, rich flavours of the 'Chocolate Fantasy' will truly dazzle. As you would expect from such a place, the wine menu is first class and handpicked to complement the food.

Theme Nights

There are countless theme nights in Hong Kong. Ladies nights can be found on Tuesdays at Joyce Is Not Here, Wednesdays at Carnegies, Thursdays at Stormies and Saturdays at Red. There are salsa nights on Tuesdays at C Club, Wednesdays at Club 97 and Thursdays at 1/5. And for something more cerebral, check out the quiz nights on Tuesdays at Bulldog's and Thursdays at The Chapel.

363

Orange Tree

17 Shelly St
Mid-Levels
🚇 **Central**
Map 16-E2

2838 9352 | www.orangetree.com.hk

This Dutch restaurant just off the Central – Mid-Levels Escalator is small and simply and elegantly decorated. There are wooden floorboards, wood panelled walls, gold ceiling fans and black and white photos of Amsterdam. Those who might not put Dutch high on their list of favourite cuisines will be pleasantly surprised here. The food is excellent, hearty and flavourful. Specialities include 'bitter ballen' – deep fried beef dumplings with Dijon mustard, and lamb fillets and eggplant baked in puff pastry on a creamy mash with rosemary jus. There are also grilled seafood and meat selections as well as monthly specials such as white asparagus and truffles. If you make it to dessert, try the dessert platter. Reassuringly the restaurant attracts a mainly Dutch crowd, along with some adventurous locals. The service may be a little slow, but the waiting staff are friendly and knowledgeable. There is a cellar-like private room available for parties.

Phoenix

29 Shelly St
Mid-Levels
🚇 **Central**
Map 16-E2

2546 2110

Heading up the Mid-Levels Escalator, the Phoenix is the last restaurant before you reach the top. It's another SoHo-style restaurant - small, cosy and warm with a no frills interior. The plain wooden chairs and tables and soft lighting bring to mind a farmhouse kitchen. There are two tables outside for the alfresco minded eater. Filled with young professionals and trendy locals, it's an excellent place for people watching. The menus are written up on chalkboards on the walls, tempting you with a choice of gastro-pub grub and classic European dishes. The food is simply presented with very generous portions and after three courses all you can do is sit and watch faces glide by on the Escalator. The service is friendly and relaxed. The Phoenix is open every evening with happy hour from 16:00-20:00. It's also open for an English roast lunch from Friday to Sunday, making it a great venue for homesick Brits.

Shining Stone

452 Shek O Village
Shek O
Map 14-F2

2369 3718

An oddity occupying a townhouse in the middle of Shek O village, Shining Stone sits right by the beach. An intimate, rustic little gem, this is the perfect place to unwind after a day by the sea or too many months spent in the manic city. The European food is good, but you're ultimately paying for the location and the sound of surf overlapping your conversation. A colourful blackboard details the various daily dishes, such as roasted red pepper soup and moussaka, divine tiramisu and saucy sangria. On weekends it pays to book in advance, especially in summer.

The Swiss Chalet

12-14 Hart Ave
Tsim Sha Tsui
🚇 **Tsim Sha Tsui**
Map 15-D4

2191 9197

Tucked away on Hart Avenue in busy TST, The Swiss Chalet is a real gem of a restaurant. When you walk in you're met by Max, the master chef and owner who greets you like an old friend and shows you to your seat. As the name suggests, the restaurant is kitted out like a Swiss Chalet with lots of wood and faux windows with net curtains, and even the odd alpenhorn on the walls. The clientele is an unusual concoction of Swiss, Germans and Austrians and local Chinese. There's an extensive menu featuring Swiss classics, as well as a specials board. Fondue is a favourite and there's a good selection, including one with red wine. The Swiss Chalet also serves Swiss wine, which is rare in Hong Kong and surprisingly good. The whole place is spotless and great care is taken with the food and service. A must do.

Fine Dining

Amber

The Landmark Mandarin Oriental
Central
Central
Map 16-E2

2132 0066 | www.mandarinoriental.com

Amber is the main restaurant in the Landmark Mandarin Oriental Hotel and it's seriously swanky. The decor is a mix of classical and contemporary, with high ceilings, wall to wall carpeting, sleek leather chairs and plush banquettes. The tones are earthy with plenty of burnt amber and an enormous sculpture dangling from the ceiling makes a striking centrepiece. The chef offers up modern, European haute cuisine with an Asian touch. Dishes are so beautifully presented here that you may be reluctant to ruin the effect by tucking in. An extensive wine list is made less daunting by a computerised sommelier which will recommend wine according to your particular criteria; for traditionalists, a real live sommelier is also available. There's no doubt that a meal here will impress your guests (the prices alone will make one swoon). However, serious foodies may decide to take their dollars elsewhere as it's really more show than substance.

Bo

T M Leung Bld
16 Gilman's Bazaar
Central
Central
Map 16-F2

2850 8371

A private kitchen turned legit, this Ice House Street restaurant has promptly earned a hot reputation among food cognoscenti. The cuisine is innovative Chino-Japanese, including bold but triumphant pairings, such as cucumber jelly and pumpkin rice pudding. Portion sizes are bang on and the bouji bar at one end of the restaurant offers a tantalising wine list. Dim lighting and gentle contemporary sounds create a cosy ambiance. The modish decor includes glass, dark stone and walnut. Expert staff will gladly guide diners through the menu. Here lies the undiscovered Hong Kong grail of eating establishments.

Caprice

Four Seasons
Central
Central
Map 16-E1

3196 8888 | www.fourseasons.com/hongkong

Caprice sets out to deal in superlatives and delivers on every count. As you are escorted to your table the old style opulence of the decor takes your breath away. Think deep velvet seats, plush carpets, glittering chandeliers, cut glass and gilt-edged crockery. The waiting staff take pride in their work, and are extremely knowledgeable, without a hint of snobbery. However, Caprice's real triumph lies in the food. From the homely bread basket, the foie gras, the lamb with sage jus, through to the best cheese plate in town, this is contemporary French cuisine at its best. Ingredients are fresher than fresh and delicate flavours are perfectly balanced. Naturally the wine list is monumental and there is a friendly sommelier to guide you

through it. Caprice also boasts a chef's table, private rooms and a cigar bar. Just when you thought Hong Kong's fine dining scene couldn't get any finer…

365

The Peninsula Hong Kong
Tsim Sha Tsui
🚇 *Tsim Sha Tsui*
Map 15-D4

Gaddi's
2315 3171

Although Gaddi's has long been considered one of Hong Kong's finest restaurants, young trendies tend to find it a bit fussy and old-fashioned. Instead it's popular with a slightly older crowd, who appreciate the blue and golden hued decor, the grovelling service and above all, the fine French cuisine. Food is taken very seriously at Gaddi's and the emphasis is on authenticity. All the ingredients are imported from France, right down to the lemons. Most dishes are traditional, hearty fair, with a few lighter options available. The marinated goose liver, lobster bisque and Bresse pigeon are all recommended. Needless to say, there is a suitably lengthy list of wines and a sommelier to guide you through it. Ageing Francophiles looking for a little indulgence are bound to enjoy this restaurant, so gentlemen, brush up on your schoolboy French and ladies, practise your pout. Bon apetit!

Smoke-Free

January 1, 2007 heralded more designated no smoking areas across Hong Kong. You can visit www.tobaccocontrol.gov.hk to check on any new sites. The fine can be up to $5,000 so it's best to be informed. Indoor areas in restaurants, karaoke establishments, cinemas, concert halls and theatres are now smoke-free, but some bars have been able to defer the classification until 2009. If you like to smoke while having a drink, enjoy it while you still can.

InterContinental Hong Kong
Tsim Sha Tsui
🚇 *Tsim Sha Tsui*
Map 15-D4

SPOON
2313 2256 | www.hongkong-ic.intercontinental.com

For a restaurant conceptualised by Alain Ducasse, one of the world's most Michelin star-decorated chefs, the staff here are surprisingly down-to-earth. Without any of the chilly manner common to many high-end eateries, they go out of their way to ensure your experience is exquisite. And it will be. Once you have marveled over the adventurous Asian-tinged French menu, you may decide to opt for one of the tasting menus. Between courses, languish in the lounge-like atmosphere and neutral-toned decor, absorb the breath-taking Victoria Harbour view, and contemplate the 554 glass spoons suspended from the ceiling. A sensory phenomenon.

French

Amigo Mansion 79A Wong Nai Chung Rd
Happy Valley
Map 17-B2

Amigo
2577 2202

At 40 years old, Amigo is an institution in Hong Kong. Located in a white-washed Spanish style villa and fronted by the Happy Valley racecourse, this restaurant was serving high-class French food and fine wines back when Hong Kong was a culinary backwater. Reassuringly, it has clung to its traditions – which are those of a bygone age of European splendour and formality. Waiters in black-tie cluster to uncover silver dishes from heated trolleys, the wine list is strictly Old World and the food is rich and luxuriating. From filo bags of lobster simmered in white wine and garlic and served with caviar, to beef tenderloin topped with foie gras and served in a truffle gravy, this is serious food that is seriously good. The surroundings match the food perfectly, with intricately carved chairs and expensive, classical paintings. Unfortunately none of this comes cheap, but there are reasonable lunch deals available.

13-13A Knutsford Terrace
Tsim Sha Tsui
🚇 *Tsim Sha Tsui*
Map 15-D3

BB's Bistro
2316 2212 | www.mhihk.com

BB's Bistro is modeled on a 1920s Parisian eatery. And, with the dark wood bar, blue leather banquettes and art deco light fittings, they've certainly achieved a distinctively French setting. The menu offers generous French fare, including moules marinieres and

366

coq au vin. While the dishes have been adapted slightly to suit the Hong Kong palate, they are still wholesome, rich and tasty. Jazz from the 40s and 50s bebops in the background and the clientele, mainly HK Chinese, all seem contented – perhaps even more so than if they were waiting to be served in an authentic French bistro.

Cafe de Paris

23 Elgin St
SoHo
Central
Map 16-E2

2810 0771

Cafe de Paris is a cosy little French bistro in the centre of the food mecca of SoHo. With its dark wooden walls, large mirrors and black and white checked floor it brings to mind a Parisian brasserie. The food is classic French cuisine - foie gras, moules marinieres, escargots, bouillabasse and sole meuniere. There is a good selection of fine French wines as well as quality house reds and whites. The clientele consists of young, local professionals and a melange of European food enthusiasts from all walks of life. Conversations in French, Spanish, English, Cantonese and Mandarin can all be heard here. The service is relaxed, attentive and friendly and you are made to feel at home as soon as you walk in the door. The unhurried atmosphere means the hours can easily slip away. A good choice for a romantic dinner or for a gathering of friends.

Cafe des Artistes

California Tower
30-32 D'Aguilar St
Central
Central
Map 16-E2

2526 3880

Cafe des Artistes is a popular choice for those looking for authentic Gallic food in a chic setting. The medium-sized restaurant looks like a smart French bistro with its understated decor. There are wooden floors, pristine white tablecloths and chairs upholstered in muted tones. There's a small bar and some club chairs for pre or post dinner drinks. The restaurant's first floor location above Lan Kwai Fong and its floor to ceiling windows make it great for people watching. The comprehensive menu features all the French classics, including endive salad, lobster bisque, warm goat's cheese, cassoulet and frozen nougat. Everything is tasty and beautifully presented and there is a good selection of French wines to complement the food. To round off the meal there is a wide choice of premium coffees and fine cigars.

Chez Moi

Arbuthnot House
10 Arbuthnot Rd
Central
Central
Map 16-E2

2801 6768 | www.chezmoihk.com

As the name suggests, Chez Moi has such a welcoming interior it feels like you're in someone's much-loved front room. Quaint ornaments decorate shelves, leather armchairs sit by the window and a rocking chair wobbles by the reception desk. A pastoral mural, complete with grazing cows, stares out from one wall, while you can spy chefs at work via the open kitchen. Each table is scattered with rose petals, making it popular with romantic Romeos. The menu boasts typical high-calibre French fare, including escargots, foie gras and veal chop - the chef's speciality.

Chez Patrick

26 Peel St
Central
Central
Map 16-E2

2541 1401

The area just off Hollywood Road is home to a growing number of interesting eateries and watering holes. Chez Patrick stands out however, as it's large and rather posh. The decor is what you'd expect in an upmarket bistro – leather chairs, pristine white tablecloths and sparkling chandeliers. The menu also has all the ingredients required in any self-respecting French restaurant. However, some of them are combined in rather unusual ways. Have you ever had your foie gras in a profiterole or your king prawns soaked in pastis? The service here is excellent. Bow tie clad waiters are always on hand and there's a good chance you will be visited by chef Partick Goubier during your meal. The only down side is the price, which seems cheekily high for the area.

Le Bristol French Restaurant

Marina Magic
Shopping Mall
Tuen Mun
Map 4-F4

2430 9929

Overlooking the Mediterranean style marina, both indoor and outdoor seating is available at this choice little place. Inside, the restaurant looks like a classy French bistro. But don't be surprised to hear 1980s British chart toppers every now and then. Comfortable booth seating is ideal for a tete-a-tete between lovers or old friends. The menu focusses on fresh, quality ingredients and sumptuous flavours. Classic French appetizers such as pan fried foie gras and frogs legs get things going. Then choose from rich red meat or seafood mains. France has come to the Gold Coast.

Le Parisien

IFC Mall
Central
🚇 **Central**
Map 16-E1

2805 5293

Le Parisien is wonderfully located with a phenomenal harbour view. The design is clean and modern with wood panelling and windows the length of the restaurant. Dishes of note include the traditional haute cuisine apogee of canard au sang, in which chef Pascal Breant pays homage to his apprenticeship at the Tour d'Argent, as well as the rustic crispy pig's trotter galette in white turnip vinaigrette and shallot vinegar jus. For the less adventurous, there's a broad choice of more mainstream dishes on offer – the sliced rack of Australian lamb in lavender jus is particularly good. All of this is backed up by a fairly extensive but very well-chosen wine selection offering a good range of price points. Open for both dinner and lunch, Le Parisien is a pleasantly unstuffy restaurant of supreme quality that lets the food speak for itself.

Le Tire Bouchon

B/F 45 Graham St
SoHo
🚇 **Central**
Map 16-E2

2523 5459 | www.hkdining.com

Amidst SoHo's circus of showy eateries, you could easily miss the discreet entrance to Le Tire Bouchon. But find it, and you'll enter true Gallic territory, complete with cheek-kissing patrons and horn-heavy French music. An archway from the dark-wood bar area leads into the large, open dining room reminiscent of a vaulted wine cellar. The menu leans towards the traditional with a choice of seafood and meats, plus vegetarian options. If unfamiliar with French cuisine, take advantage of the chef's six-course tasting menu, best washed down with their large stock of wines.

Pierre

Mandarin Oriental
Central
🚇 **Central**
Map 16-E2

2522 0111 | www.madarinoriental.com

This restaurant, which replaced Vongs on the top floor of the hotel, is named after Pierre Gagnaire, the three-star Michelin chef behind the contemporary French cuisine. The menu shows off fresh takes on classical French dishes, and changes regularly to focus on seasonal foods. The modern decor, dark colour scheme and rich textures provide a luxurious and intimate atmosphere, and the striking view of Victoria Harbour can be seen from all over the restaurant. Seats by the windows are the most romantic – and it seems that's exactly what most of the guests here are in the mood for. A private room is also available for those wishing to host an exclusive soiree. There's really no need to mention the prices – you probably already have an idea.

The Press Room

G/F, 108 Hollywood Rd
Central
🚇 **Sheung Wan**
Map 16-E2

2525 3444

The Press Room is one of the more upmarket venues to open its doors on thriving Hollywood Road, amid much hype. It's a bistro style restaurant with high ceilings, an oversized chalk board occupying one wall and simple furnishings. In keeping with the no-frills theme, the short menu is printed on a single piece of card. Unfortunately, the service also seems to be no frills. While wait staff are well meaning, they don't quite get it right, and it's easy to feel rushed. Fortunately, uninspired service is saved by great food. There are classic starters such as smoked salmon and foie gras, mains such as coq au vin and rack of lamb, a selection of salads, along with daily specials. Do try the cheese plate or else pop next door to the wine and cheese place run by the same owner. A small word of warning: noise levels here are almost as high as the prices.

33 Sharp St East
Causeway Bay
Causeway Bay
Map 17-B2

W's Entrecote

2506 0133 | *www.wsentrecote.com*

This restaurant is located behind Times Square in Causeway Bay making it convenient for a business lunch or a quick dinner after work. The decor is faux French with red, checked tablecloths, cafe-style chairs, framed sketches on wood panelled walls and French music. On each table a bottle of wine awaits you. The signature dish here is charbroiled ribeye steak served in herb butter sauce with a pile of French fries on the side. Other choices include escargots, veal chops and lamb, so not many options for vegetarians. The dessert list is long and what's on offer is tasty, if a little inauthentic. This isn't the best French restaurant in town but the service is efficient, prices are reasonable and it would certainly do in a Gallic emergency.

Fusion

Other options **International** p.372

Kimberley Plaza
15 Knutsford Terrace
Tsim Sha Tsui
Tsim Sha Tsui
Map 15-D3

La Cuisine de Mekong

2316 2288 | *www.mhihk.com*

Overlooking lively Knutsford Terrace, this restaurant claims to offer a 'culinary journey through south-east Asia'. With low lighting, well-spaced tables, booths and an open terrace, the decor is spacious and peaceful. South East Asia filters into the interior in the form of wooden latticework and benign buddhas, while ceiling fans and wicker chairs give a French colonial feel. Appropriately for a MeKong-inspired restaurant, the emphasis is on seafood. Familiar Thai and Vietnamese dishes sit alongside offerings from less well-charted Laos, Cambodia and Myanmar (ever tried a tea leaf salad?). Sweet, sour, spicy and salty – you'll find it all here.

G/F 40 Cheung
Sha Lwr Village
Lantau Island
Map 12-E2

NEWS Bistro

2980 2233 | *www.newsbistro.com*

This small restaurant in Lower Cheung Sha Village provides day trippers with an alternative to the other popular restaurants in the area. NEWS Bistro is housed in a brightly painted old village house on the beachfront. On days when the weather is just too nice to go inside, a terrace provides shady outdoor seating. This is a casual place with basic furnishings, friendly staff and reasonable prices. The menu is succinct but aims to appeal to everyone with a mix of simple Chinese, Thai and Western dishes. Veggie options are available and all the vegetables and herbs are grown in the restaurant's garden. NEWS Bistro pride themselves on using only natural ingredients - so no MSG here. It's usually only open on weekends, however you can book the restaurant for parties any day of the week. Call to discuss party packages.

32 Elgin St
SoHo
Central
Map 16-E2

Olive

2521 1608 | *www.diningconcepts.com.hk*

By offering dishes from between the Middle East and the Mediterranean, Olive capitalises on cuisines previously under-represented in Hong Kong. The exotic and tantalising main courses range from rabbit and leek pie to rich seafood tagines, while the dessert menu includes treats like yoghurt and honey panna cotta with toffeed

369

strawberries. Other pleasant surprises include a high quality wine list and staff ready to make informed, affordable recommendations. The restaurant itself has an intimate feel with subdued lighting, dark wood interiors and a modern full-service bar. If you're here for romance, ask for one of the tucked-away tables.

TRU

Grand Progress Bld
15 Lan Kwai Fong
Central
Central
Map 16-E2

2525 6700

TRU is another successful newcomer to Hong Kong's restaurant scene. The food is modern Thai-Vietnamese fusion and this is reflected in the tasteful decor. There is not a gaudy gold statue or a picture of a girl in an ao yai in sight. Instead there is a subtle nod to Asia in the form of bronze plated walls, comfy blue and purple seats and bronze Buddha heads on the bar. An open kitchen allows you to watch the food being created. The menu is short but well thought out, offering fresh takes on traditional dishes. Dishes are light and blend fresh ingredients with delicately balanced herbs and spices. Vegetarians are well catered for and everything is beautifully presented. There is a good wine list as well as some interesting cocktails. The restaurant is popular with groups of colleagues giving the company credit card a workout. Not too much of a workout though, as prices are very reasonable for the area.

Indian

Bombay Dreams

Carfield Commercial Ctr
75-77 Wyndham St
Central
Central
Map 16-E2

2971 0001

The aromas alone that waft out of Bombay Dreams are enough to make your mouth water. Not quite your average curry house, the Central branch has an upmarket feel. Sleek furniture and pale tones provide a modern look. However there are nods to tradition as seen in the patterns on the walls, scattered bright cushions and brassware. These touches complement the cuisine, which is proudly traditional. Dishes are drawn from the entire continent, from Kashmir to Goa, and ingredients and cooking methods are authentic. Particularly recommended are the aloo chat, a tangy potato and chickpea dish with tamarind chutney, and the tandoori platter which includes succulent pieces of meat and seafood marinated and cooked to perfection in a tandoor oven. As you would expect, the prices aren't quite your average curry house either, but there is a very popular lunchtime buffet when you eat your fill for just $98.

Khana Khazana

Dannies House
20 Luard Rd
Wan Chai
Wan Chai
Map 17-A2

2520 5308 | www.G5.hk

Tuck into your korma while watching international cricket at this cheap and cheerful Indian Vegetarian restaurant, frequented by the Indian community. One floor above the busy streets of Wan Chai, the airy interior is simply furnished in yellow fabrics with pink splashes. Tasty dishes come served on silver platters while Hindi music bleats in the background. The daily $88 lunch buffet is a great bargain, offering salads, starters, vegetables and dal. Bizarrely, there is a small selection of Asian, Italian and Mexican dishes on the menu, but you're best sticking to the southern Indian specialities.

Koh-i-Noor

Cityplaza
Taikoo Shing
🚇 **Quarry Bay**
Map 17-E1

2568 8757

Koh-i-Noor in Quarry Bay is your run of the mill curry house. It's cheap and no one could accuse the fluorescent orange walls of being less than cheerful. There are plastic flowers, sticky specials menus and of course, a giant statue of Ganesh.The incongruously tasteful and heavy, copper water goblets and postcard-sized, traditional Indian paintings must have come from a different creative mind. The food here is fairly average, with the usual curry house offerings, along with a smattering of more exotic chef's specials. The main attraction is the $88 lunch buffet which draws in the office workers from the surrounding buildings. There's cheap beer too. This may not be haute-cuisine, but you can certainly satisfy a craving, and the friendly staff make sure any meal here is a relaxed experience.

Private Kitchens

Private kitchens are a growing trend in Hong Kong. Basically these are small, quasi-legal eateries in residential blocks, in some cases consisting entirely of three or four tables in someone's sitting room. Many of these private kitchens are labours of love and standards tend to be high while prices are low. The usual set-up is that customers arrive at a fixed time to enjoy a set menu. The menu usually has at least five courses and customers can bring their own wine, although a corkage charge is often applied. Some of these places don't last long while others go on to acquire legal status. Some current favourites are Le Blanc (3428 5824) which serves French food, Ingredients (2544 5133) which offers international fare and Xi Yan (9020 9196) which dishes up Asian delights. Reservations are essential.

Veda

8 Arbuthnot Rd
Central
🚇 **Central**
Map 16-E2

2868 5885 | www.veda.com.hk

Often crowned Hong Kong's top Indian restaurant, the city's elite flock to Veda. The medium-sized restaurant offers contemporary twists on regional cuisine. The interior is harmoniously decorated in neutral chrome with mirrored mosaic designs. Food is expertly prepared and the open kitchen allows you to spy on the process. Dishes are subtle in flavour, with tasty appetizers such as the crisp quail samosas. The curries with aromatic spices are unusually zesty. There's also an eclectic wine list with new and old world offerings. If you find the price tag high, try the value lunch menu for $108.

The Viceroy

Sun Hung Kai Ctr
30 Harbour Rd
Wan Chai
🚇 **Wan Chai**
Map 17-A2

2827 7777

Master of reinvention, The Viceroy has survived for years. The quintessential Indian restaurant, on the harbour front of Wan Chai, has a large outside area to make full use of its gorgeous harbour views. The cavernous interior is full of polished woods, while outside boasts lush tropical plants, Hindu statues and wooden decking. The clientele is mainly well-to-do Indian families, with a few Europeans and local Chinese filling the gaps. The scrumptious food is Indian, with the recent addition of a small Middle Eastern menu. The Viceroy is also a premier stand-up comedy spot, with shows on Fridays or Saturdays.

Woodlands

Mirror Tower
61 Mody Rd
Tsim Sha Tsui
🚇 **Tsim Sha Tsui**
Map 15-D4

2369 3718

Woodlands is a firm favourite among the Indian community, as well as a handful of long-term expats and local Chinese. The simple restaurant has no decor but a couple of posters declaring vegetarianism ideals. People come to Woodlands for the food. The authentic vegetarian food from the subcontinent is tooth-suckingly good. Central to the restaurant's enduring success are the thalis – choose from Bathura, Puree or Chapatti. Woodlands doesn't hold an alcohol license, but it does a mean mango lassi and selection of Indian soft-drinks. You'd be hard pushed to find a better dish for your dollar.

371

Indonesian

Bebek Bengil 3

The Broadway
54-62 Lockhart Rd
Wan Chai
🚇 *Wan Chai*
Map 16-F2

2217 8000 | *www.elite-concepts.com*

With its fantastic outdoor lesehan (raised floor seating), traditional teak wood interior, running fountains, servers in traditional garb and evocative gamelan music, this is as close as you can get to the magical island of Bali without getting on a plane. Then there is the food: a collection of traditional Balinese dishes prepared and served in creative ways. For example, the fish skewers are served on a tiny barbecue with hot coals. All the food here is good, but nothing beats abandoning cutlery to get stuck into their signature crispy duck with your hands.

International

Other options **Fusion** p.369

The Blue Room

Big Wave Bay
Shek O
Map 14-E1

2809 2583

When you want to get far away from it all without leaving the island, Big Wave Bay is about as far as you can get and the Blue Room is the last pit-stop before plunging into the surf of a typhoon swell. This place is a simple beach-side cafe with a vaguely surfy theme that caters equally well to surfers, expat families and flirting teenagers. The 'Dawn Patrol' menu is available from 08:00 and features various breakfast standards, from a full fry-up to pancakes with strawberries. The lunchtime menu is a mix of salads, wraps, and pasta dishes and on weekends they serve a surprisingly good pizza with the thinnest of crusts. Good coffee, smoothies, juices and ice-cold bottled beers are all available to help quench your thirst. The staff are very friendly but prepare to be patient – in the summer the place gets so crowded that the service tends to melt faster than the ice in your drink.

The Boathouse

88 Stanley Main St
Stanley
Map 14-D2

2813 4467 | *www.igors.com*

The Boathouse is arguably the best of the seafront restaurants in Stanley and is usually packed to the gills. The restaurant is spread over three floors, including a balcony and roof top terrace. In fair weather the windows are flung open making the place bright and airy. Pale blue and white walls and photographs of boats create a yachting theme and the whole place has a touch of the East Coast about it. The Boathouse is known for its seafood and the enormous seafood platter is excellent. There are also plenty of other options including fresh, tangy salads, overstuffed sandwiches and flavourful pastas. The delicious desserts are also recommended. They do lunch specials too and you can enjoy a meal at the bar for just $88. This place attracts tourists, day trippers and regulars. Everyone's in a holiday mood here and many linger over glasses of Chardonnay or a chilled beer.

Café Deco

The Peak Galleria
118 Peak Rd
The Peak
Map 16-D3

2849 5111 | *www.cafedecogroup.com*

Café Deco is a huge two-floor restaurant on the Peak, with a grand spiral staircase and floor to ceiling windows. Its main draw is the view over Hong Kong, best enjoyed on a clear evening. Decor is art deco (obviously) with some original memorabilia pieces. Despite Café Deco's efforts, the sheer size of this place detracts from the atmosphere, although they excel at serving a huge range of dishes to a huge number of people. All your favourites are on the menu and they don't disappoint. Look out especially for the popular brunch buffet on Sundays.

Café Too

Island Shangri-La
Admiralty
Admiralty
Map 16-F2

2877 3838 | www.shangri-la.com

Floor-to-ceiling windows overlook Hong Kong Park's greenery at Café Too, a coffee shop-style restaurant in the Island Shangri-La hotel. Don't bother looking at the menu – everyone's here for the fantastic value buffet ($258 Monday to Saturday, and $298 on Sundays). For that reason it's always packed, so bookings are essential. With its seven different kitchens headed by 30 chefs, you'll find it difficult to choose between Japanese, Indian, Chinese and Western cuisine. Fortunately, you don't have to. Don't miss the dessert station either. Here you can dip squidgy marshmallows into a flowing chocolate fountain. Bring friends and an appetite.

Chilli N Spice Seafood Market

Marina Magic Shopping Mall,
Hong Kong Gold Coast
Tuen Mun
Map 4-F3

2430 1166

This restaurant is part of a chain that has adopted 'spicy' as its culinary theme, taking fiery flavours from around the globe. That said, when the food arrives it's not actually that hot. However, the main appeal is its marina promenade setting - plus the reasonable prices. Indoor seating is in a large Spanish style 'cantina'. Expect rather gaudy decoration in a faux Mediterranean style. If the weather is favourable, head outside for the quieter area of seating overlooking the marina, where you can linger over your meal and enjoy the view. The 'seafood market' in the title means you can choose your own fish from a market-style stall, then have it cooked to your specifications. This may not be top-notch grub, but it's all good fun.

China Tee Club

Peddar Bld
12 Peddar St
Central
Central
Map 16-E2

2521 0233 | www.chinateeclub.com

A firm favourite of ladies who lunch, the twee China Tee Club instantly transports one back to yesteryear. It has been serving well-prepared HK favourites for years - Laksa and nasi goreng rub shoulders with ploughman's lunches and char-grilled salmon pittas. Portions are feminine in size for dainty nibbling. Whether you prefer scones and clotted cream or dim sum, this is one of the best places in town to do afternoon tea - even if you don't have big hair. Potted palms, ceiling fans, Edwardian furniture and little songbirds dotted about make for a tranquil oasis in which to break-up a hard day's shopping in Central. The staff are whisper quiet and the service is good. Artwork by local artists is often displayed on the walls. The China Tee Club is not open for dinner as it closes at 20:00, but it can be rented out in the evening for private dos.

Jimmy's Kitchen

South China Bld
1-3 Wyndham St
Central
Central
Map 16-E2

2526 5293 | www.jimmys.com

A poster at the door declares that Jimmy's has been 'Moving With The Times Since 1929'. It's a lie. From the food, to the decor, to the music, Jimmy's is most definitely stuck in a time warp. The result is an almost surreal experience which you'll either love or hate. The large basement restaurant features wood panelling, wall to wall carpeting, brassware on the walls and faded photos of old Hong Kong. There's a small bar area where they serve a mean Martini. The supposedly European menu seems to draw its inspiration from British school dinners and seventies cocktail parties, from Oxtail and barley soup, to mushroom vol-au-vents and corned beef hash, bread and butter pudding and trifle. It's all served up by professional and courteous staff, who may not have realised that Hong Kong is no longer a colony. Inexplicably, this place attracts a local crowd along with groups of American businessmen. Go figure.

373

The Lobby

The Peninsula Hong Kong
Tsim Sha Tsui
Tsim Sha Tsui
Map 15-D4

2920 2888 | *www.hongkong.peninsula.com*

If you're feeling nostalgic and fancy somewhere colonial, don't miss the Lobby restaurant of the Peninsula Hotel. This world-famous, 1920s styled restaurant dominates the ground floor, with chandeliered ceilings, thick rugs and white marbled floors. Conversations are moderated by the buzz of hotel guests coming and going and the strains of a live string band from the balcony above. The restaurant is open all day and offers an international list of light meals, most diners come here for the traditional high tea. Scones, sandwiches and dainty cakes arrive on a tiered platter and tea is served in heavy silver teaware. Simply spiffing!

NoHo Cafe

24 Gough St
Central
Sheung Wan
Map 16-E2

2813 2572

Hong Kong's only bed cafe is an extremely relaxing place to hang out. Beds are lined up down one side of the restaurant and are intimately sealed off by silk curtains, so it's fabulous for a date. If you really want to get close, there's a sealed-off VIP bed chamber complete with TV and a wide selection of international films. The food comes from around the globe with enticing appetizers such as meaty oven-baked mussels with crispy bacon in crumbly filo pastry. The set lunch is a bargain at $78. So don't be shy, kick back and enjoy.

Nutmeg Grill

37 Elgin St
SoHo
Central
Map 16-E2

2522 3850

Located off what's fast becoming SoHo's busiest entertainment street, The Nutmeg Grill is just waiting to be discovered. You'll either love or hate the psychedelic purple and yellow interior with squidgy seating, groovy music and wavy patterns. Although Nutmeg Grill doesn't boast a large menu, the food is fabulous. Tasty appetizers include freshly-caught steamed clams in white wine sauce and tuna served with buffalo mozzarella. For the main course, deliciously tender veal stuffed with parma ham and succulent pork loin chops with creamy whole grain mustard sauce both come highly recommended.

One

The Rotunda
8 Connaught Place
Central
Central
Map 16-E1

2522 2246 | *www.cafedecogroup.com*

One screams power lunch. The place has a slick look with dark wood, clean white lines and light columns. The large place is divided in two, the noodle bar and the restaurant proper. The former offers a range of noodle dishes from around the world and is perfect for a quick lunch. The restaurant proper has a more formal feel and is ideal for talking shop. Most diners in this section opt for the antipasti buffet - the $150 price tag is surprisingly reasonable for the location, making One a must-do for any hungry exec.

Peak Cafe Bar

9-13 Shelly St
SoHo
Central
Map 16-E2

2140 6877 | *www.cafedecogroup.com*

Despite its new location in the centre of SoHo, Peak Café Bar manages to maintain a touch of its former peak-top location with plenty of plants and a fountain. The decor is Asian colonial with old prints of Hong Kong, ornate mirrors and some genuine antiques. Rather incongruous touches of leopardskin remind you the new Peak Cafe is meant for the funky, not the frumpy. The menu offers the usual South East Asian fare, from papaya salad to nasi goreng and there's a good booze list. Peak Cafe's great location and easy charm ensures a steady stream of diners.

121 Peak Rd
The Peak
Map 16-D3

Peak Lookout

2849 1000 | *www.thepeaklookout.com.hk*

Nestled in foliage next to the Peak Tram, the Peak Lookout occupies a charming colonial building. Seats on the terrace under the banyan trees offer fantastic views of Pok Fu Lam Country Park, over to Lamma Island and beyond. Inside there are oyster and drinks bars as well a spacious dining area. Gentle live music and the sound of the trickling fountain are perfect accompaniments to the impeccable food and Asian service. The cuisine is international, with a huge choice of Asian and European dishes, barbequed treats and tea time goodies.

Lan Kwai Fong
Central
Central
Map 16-E2

Post 97

2810 9333

Post 97 is a Hong Kong institution. People come here before a big night out in The Fong - or for breakfast following a big night in The Fong. Since most people are getting drunk or nursing a hangover, it doesn't seem to matter that the interior's a little dark and dingy. It's hard to describe the bizarre decor: there's a lot of red, a few gold cupids and a bird's nest. An eclectic crowd chatters and lingers over their meal. The international dishes are tasty and there are even healthy options if you hope to atone for your sins.

Kimberley Plaza
Knutsford Terrace
Tsim Sha Tsui
Tsim Sha Tsui
Map 15-D3

Q Club

2312 1168 | *www.mhihk.com*

The large and luxurious Q Club is reminiscent of a gentleman's club in London, with chandeliers, heavy curtains, large mirrors and 17th Century paintings adorning the walls. A pianist adds the final touch. The comfortable benches that curve round large tables are mainly occupied by successful local businessmen looking for a touch of prestige. Although Q Club is supposedly for members only, non-members are also welcome. The menu here is enormous and you can order from any of the groups various outlets. Expect locker aged steaks, jet fresh oysters, Vietnamese salads, Thai curries and much, much more. There is also a fine wine list. The service matches the surroundings and is impeccable. You can dine late into the night as the doors only close at 03:00. The restaurant also caters to private parties.

The Sanlitun
Causeway Ctr
28 Harbour Rd
Wan Chai
Wan Chai
Map 17-A2

Sens

2511 7311

Sens' outdoor seating is round the back of the Causeway plaza building - where the sun doesn't shine. Unfortunately, the decor inside is a little uninviting too. The restaurant sign is lit from behind in red neon and the rattan chairs are made of plastic. The menu offers a bizarre selection – sort of fusion without finesse. However, once the food arrives it is tasty enough. The prices are reasonable, especially if you order the set menu. If you work in the area, there are worse places you could eat than Sens - probably.

Jumbo Kingdom
Wong Chuk Hang
Aberdeen
Map 14-D2

Top Deck

2552 3331 | *www.cafedecogroup.com*

Elaborately decorated in red and gold, Top Deck is impossible to miss on top of the Jumbo floating restaurant in Aberdeen Harbour. Catch the Jumbo ferry from the quayside and arrive in style. Dine in a wood-panelled restaurant under a dramatic three-storey Chinese pagoda roof, or go alfresco - the outdoor wicker furniture and large couches are great to sink into while enjoying a cocktail. The menu focuses on fresh seafood cooked by Australian, Thai, Indian and Japanese chefs. Come for the live Jazz on Wednesdays or the seafood brunch on Sundays.

375

Italian

Other options **Pizzerias** p.382, **Mediterranean** p.380

Baci

1 Lan Kwai Fong
Central
🚇 **Central**
Map 16-E2

2801 5885

Though Baci's space is compact, the decor is elegant and the dishes do not disappoint. Selections of salads, thin-crusted pizzas, fresh pastas and risottos are all comforting and authentic. Similarly, classic Italian entrees include favourites such as chunky veal chop and nourishing Osso Bucco. The wine list is varied and reasonably priced by local standards, and diners can start the evening with a drink at the bar. Non-smokers be warned however - the restaurant allows smoking throughout, and you will notice this at some point during your meal.

Cine Citta

G/F 9 Star St
Wan Chai
🚇 **Wan Chai**
Map 16-F2

2529 0199

With the freshest pasta in Hong Kong, Italian movie star glamour, and waiting staff who talk you through the menu, Cine Citta is uber-cool. It's ideal for a business lunch, a date or a meal with friends. Sample the antipasto with some wine from the enormous glass cellar, the restaurant's centrepiece. The cuisine is modern Italian, featuring a wide range of meat and seafood mains, risottos and original pastas. Food is served against the backdrop of red velvet curtains, stills of Italian movie stars and Italian cinema classics screened to club-beats and chillout tunes. No carbonara or bolognaise here.

Gaia

Grand Millenium
Plaza
181 Queen's Rd
Sheung Wan
🚇 **Sheung Wan**
Map 16-E2

2167 8200 | www.gaiaristorante.com

Gaia is just off the beaten track in Sheung Wan. A welcoming, red lounge area to the left of the entrance is ideal for an aperitif. The main dining room has floor-to-ceiling windows and large sliding doors leading onto the terrace. The food has the freshest imported ingredients and there are a fine selection of pastas, thin-crust pizzas and fuller mains. An extensive wine list is also available - ask the Maitre d' for recommendations. Gaia attracts its fair share of celebrities, and no wonder, it's the best Italian in town.

Grappa's Millenio

Lincoln House
Tong Chong St
Quarry Bay
🚇 **Quarry Bay**
Map 17-D1

2219 0288 | www.elgrande.com.hk

Warm and inviting with floor to ceiling windows, Grappa's Millennio is perfect for a business lunch or quiet dinner. Busy at lunchtime, this eatery is quieter and more intimate in the evenings. Located in Taikoo Place, the lunchtime clientele is comprised mainly of nearby office workers and a few 'ladies who lunch'. Food is home-style Italian with bread baked on the premises. Specialties include fettuccine blackened with cuttlefish ink, homemade minestrone and tiramisu. The bar area with its high wall of wines and spirits is ideal to chill after work over happy hour drinks.

Isola

IFC Mall
Central
🚇 **Central**
Map 16-E1

2383 8765 | www.isolabarandgrill.com

In a packed city, Isola (which means 'island' in Italian) is space and light. Flanked by the harbour, the restaurant is divided between an in vogue, all-white interior, a broad patio for outdoor dining and a leafy roof-top bar offering spectacular views of the city. The food, created by Italian chef Gianni Caprioli, is fresh and wide-ranging, from succulent roasted scallops wrapped in pancetta to very thin crust pizza dressed in toppings such as black truffle, crescenza cheese, mozzarella and mache leaves. The pasta is homemade and there is also a range of oven-cooked and grilled dishes, such as baked

376

whole sea bass. Delicate without being fussy and beautifully presented, eating the food here doesn't feel sinful. The service is attentive and the dishes, which are all made fresh to order, don't take long to arrive. For atmospheric fine dining by the harbour, Isola is hard to beat.

Milano

Sun Hung Kai Ctr
30 Harbour Rd
Wan Chai
◉ *Wan Chai*
Map 17-A2

2598 1222

This rather large Italian restaurant curves around a long bar. The outer windows overlook the harbour, but the view is inexplicably masked by semi-sheer drapes. The decor is faux Italian with plaster columns, turquoise tiling and large jars of fake pickled vegetables. Caramel leather chairs are comfortable and the lighting is pleasantly subdued with plenty of candles. The menu features the usual pizzas, pastas, meat and fish mains. The food is all rather average with the exception of the desserts, which are deliciously decadent. It attracts mainly a local crowd and at lunchtime it's packed with office workers (the evenings, however, are often very quiet). They presently have a policy of not rushing the guests and only approaching when summoned – a nice thought that's taken just a little too far.

The Mistral

InterContinental
Grand Stanford
Tsim Sha Tsui
◉ *Tsim Sha Tsui*
Map 15-D4

2731 2870 | *www.hongkong.intercontinental.com*

Buried beneath the InterContinental Grand Stanford in Kowloon lies The Mistral, a restaurant decorated to resemble a rustic Italian country home with tiled floors, stucco walls, and low wooden beams. Photographs of famous Italian sportspeople adorn the walls, low lighting and well-spaced tables ensure a cosy atmosphere. A talented troubadour wanders between the tables, serenading guests with folksongs and hits from the 1950s. The Mistral's menu features ample portions of various classic Italian dishes and an extensive wine selection. The music creates a fun atmosphere suitable for a group night out or relaxed date.

Papa Razzi

2 Knutsford Terrace
Tsim Sha Tsui
◉ *Tsim Sha Tsui*
Map 15-D4

2312 6668 | *www.mhihk.com*

Italian restaurant Pappa Razzi has plenty of outside seating for people-watchers. However, the interior provides a welcome respite from the summer heat, with enough air-con and ceiling fans to ensure no hot seats. The walls are covered in old film posters and memorabilia, while tables range from two to six seaters and there are two large cushioned benches. The menu is predominantly Italian, with a few French dishes thrown in. As with most Italian restaurants you need to turn up with an empty stomach to do it justice. Service is efficient with enough waiters to cope with the lunchtime rush.

Tutto Bene

7 Knutsford Terrace
Tsim Sha Tsui
◉ *Tsim Sha Tsui*
Map 15-D4

2316 2116 | *www.mhihk.com*

Couples whisper sweet nothings to each other across the little tables and small groups practice the fine art of conversation at this relaxed, romantic Italian restaurant. The walls are warm yellow and dotted with black and white photographs. With seating for around 100, both indoors and outdoors, the candlelit restaurant still seems cosy. The menu is traditional Italian, with soups and salads through to risotto, pasta, fish and meat mains, on to a selection of exquisite desserts. Presentation has a rustic simplicity, with the focus on freshness, texture and flavour. Dishes here out-class those of the more expensive restaurants.

377

Va Bene

2845 5577

Va Bene screams sophistication. The modern entrance bar tempts you to stop for an apertif, even if that wasn't the plan. The largish dining area is all dark woods and pristine white table cloths. The silver cutlery, crystal glasses and chandeliers all sparkle away. The menu lists fine South Italian cuisine prepared with high quality ingredients. Unfortunately, the small tables are too close for romance. Instead it attracts groups of friends from the older, moneyed set. After years of service, Va Bene remains a place to be seen. Indeed, it's hard to shake the feeling you're on display here.

Japanese

Langham Place
Mong Kok
🚇 *Mong Kok*
Map 15-C2

Funky Fish

2782 6886

Funky Fish is one of a number of restaurants in the Langham Place development in bustling Mong Kok. It offers cheap and decent Japanese food and a fairly pleasant environment in which to take a break from shopping. The design is fairly minimalist, with light wood and soft tones. The atmosphere is relaxed and the service is excellent. The extensive menu features all the usual favourites from sushi to ramen and tempura. All the dishes are fresh, tasty and come in decent portions. The lesser known Japanese dessert 'banana split' is also available. OK, it's not authentic, but it's good. Funky Fish is a cut above the conveyor-belt variety of Japanese restaurants and a good choice for those who want a comfortable, unhurried meal without paying a premium.

Knutsford Terrace
Kimberley Plaza
Tsim Sha Tsui
🚇 *Tsim Sha Tsui*
Map 15-D4

Hibiki

2316 2884 | *www.mhihk.com*

Hibiki is a restaurant that combines classical and contemporary Japanese cuisine, all washed down with Japan's most famous alcoholic export, sake. The restaurant offers over 100 different types of this delicious rice wine to suit every taste and budget. The food menu boasts a large selection of sushi and sashimi, including some innovative dishes such as goose liver and fresh mango sushi. Meat options include the lamb chops with plum miso or the duck breast with hot apple sauce. There are also a range of tempura items on the menu along with various skewers. Finish with Japanese ice creams and sherbets and you won't need to eat again for a week. The decor is very Japanese - lots of clean lines and elegant, minimalist furnishings. The atmosphere is friendly and relaxed. An all-round good choice for a Japanese meal.

The Plaza
21 D'Aguilar St
Central
🚇 *Central*
Map 16-E2

Kyoto Joe

2804 6800

Kyoto Joe offers contemporary Japanese cuisine at realistic prices. The upper floor features a laid-back sake bar and a robabatayaki counter where you can watch the chefs cooking up a storm. Downstairs, dark-wood furnishings and vertical plasma screens blend traditional and modern Japanese decor. The sleek sushi bar offers a wide range of sushi and sashimi dishes, balanced by salads, appetisers and main dishes that run the gamut of Japanese cuisine. Beef Kyoto fumi and spicy inaniwa udon are considered house specialties, but the sushi, seared tuna and seabass dishes are particularly recommended. Smart yet relaxed.

Masaka

2264 4881

Paper place mats set the tone in this canteen-style restaurant. The 'no frills' decor includes dark floors, cream walls and small pieces of art on the walls. However, Masaka defies it's design and remains a popular lunchtime destination. Why? Because the food is tasty and cheap. The menu features modern and traditional Japanese tit bits. Try a flavourful hot pot with soup or the soft shell crab tempura. Service here is fast and furious – you'll be in and out before you know it. Not ideal for a leisurely lunch, rather somewhere to fill your belly without emptying your wallet.

Grand Century Place
193 Prince Edward Rd
West
Mong Kok
🚇 *Mong Kok*
Map 15-C1

Robatayaki

2996 8438 | *www.harbour-plaza.com*

Robatayaki offers traditional Japanese barbecue – you choose the delicacies you want and expert chefs grill them for you. The decor has a rustic Japanese feel with wooden beams suspended from the ceiling by rope. Most of the action happens around the central barbecue where there's room for a dozen people to watch chefs do their thing. The menu offers an array of ingredients to throw on the grill, including crab, snapper and kobe beef. There's also superb sushi and sashimi. Robatayaki is popular with the well-heeled and prices can climb to dizzying heights, but the quality makes it all worthwhile.

Harbour Plaza
Whampoa Gardens
Hung Hom
Map 15-E3

Tokio Joe

2525 1889 | *www.lankwaifong.com*

Tokio Joe is a tightly-packed restaurant with small tables surrounding a sushi bar. Consisting mostly of sashimi and sushi, the menu offers a range of innovative rolls. Fresh fruit appears automatically after you have eaten, and explains the limited desserts. Tokio Joe's fish pulls the punters, so reservations are recommended. This does however mean that service can seem rushed. Don't confuse this restaurant with its trendier sister Kyoto Joe (round the corner at 21 D'Aguilar Street). If you like good Japanese food with a modern twist, this is the Joe for you.

16 Lan Kwai Fong
Central
🚇 *Central*
Map 17-B2

Wasabisabi

2506 0009 | *www.aqua.com.hk*

You enter Wasabisabi via a 'catwalk', uplit and lined with dangling silver beads. The dining area has a sushi bar and several round booths which can be turned to face the bar and Lipstick Lounge. There's a lot of food choice but the signature sushi platters are recommended for their variety of flavours and textures. Platters include quality fresh fish flown in daily from Toyko's Tsukiji market. Expert wait staff are dressed all in black. A VIP room, called the Mirror Room, is available for private parties. This hangout is for the young and trendy – exclusively.

Times Square
Causeway Bay
🚇 *Causeway Bay*
Map 17-B2

Korean

Sorabol

2881 6823 | *www.sorabol.com.hk*

Don't be put off by the functional space, this Causeway Bay Korean restaurant serves authentic, tasty food. At each table you will find a small grill as cooking your own food is all part of the experience here. Flavourful dishes include the seafood and spring onion pancakes. However, if you're not sure, go for one of the set menus. These include marinated meats to throw on the grill, a couple of Korean specialities and side dishes. You're bound to have fun at Sorabol but be prepared to leave wearing eau de barbeque – despite the supposedly smoke-free grills.

Lee Theatre Plaza
99 Percival St
Causeway Bay
🚇 *Causeway Bay*
Map 17-B2.

Mediterranean

Other options **Italian** p.376, **Spanish** p.383

Beach Bld ◄ Cococabana
Island Rd
Deep Water Bay
Map 14-C1

2812 2226 | www.toptables.com.hk

A 15 minute taxi ride from town through the Aberdeen tunnel, Cococabana is rapidly establishing itself as one of the top al fresco dining options in HK. Set right on the beach and commanding a view over the bay, this simple but elegant restaurant is a marked contrast with the public changing facilities on the floor below. Beautiful white sofas and tables combine with candlelight and the shimmering sea to create an irresistibly romantic mood, which only heightens once the food arrives. The available dishes change regularly but the standard is consistently high. The owner, Jean Paul Gaucci, ensures the rotating menu has a Mediterranean twist, with norms such as foie gras, lamb tagine with couscous, or fresh tomato salad. One word of warning – the sound of the surf lapping just metres away can lull diners into a dreamlike trance which makes it almost impossible to get up and leave.

34 Gough St ◄ Lot 10
Central
🚇 *Central*
Map 16-E1

2813 6812

Lot 10 is situated in NoHo – an up-and-coming area hoping to rival SoHo. However, apart from the occasional art student, the area remains undiscovered. Lot 10 has a seaside villa feel. The restaurant features a tiny downstairs dining area, and a slightly larger room and terrace upstairs. The theme is Mediterranean with wooden benches, blue and white furnishings and soft amber lights. The French and Italian menu includes delicacies such as pan-fried foie gras and a tasty pasta and risotto section. Look out for the homemade chocolate cake which is just divine.

64 Stanley Main St ◄ Lucy's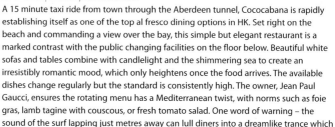
Stanley
Map 14-D2

2813 9055

This small restaurant has no windows, but it's cosy rather than claustrophobic. Decor is Mediterranean-inspired with warm orange walls and splashes of yellow and green. Apart from savvy tourists, the clientele are mainly regulars. If you're a lady who lunches then Lucy's is probably already your second home. The daily set menu is a bargain at $158 for three courses, or you can opt for a la carte. The menu is short but tempting, offering innovative takes on traditional Mediterranean fare. If you really like your meal you can buy the Lucy's cookbook.

112 Pak Sha Wan ◄ Pousada
Hebe Haven
Sai Kung
Map 6-F4

2335 5515 | www.pousada.com.hk

If you don't have time to pop over to Fernando's in Macau, Pousada is a pleasant alternative. The restaurant has a slightly unfortunate location just off the main road leading into Sai Kung. However, the charming lemon hued, Portuguese style villa helps you to overlook that fact, and the sound of chatter soon drowns out the noise of passing cars. The restaurant is open sided and simple, rustic looking tables and chairs are spread over two floors. There is also a roof terrace with a view out to sea. The menu is replete with the Portuguese dishes that most Hong Kongers have become so familiar with after their day trips to Macau. Specialities include fresh sardines, African chicken and roast suckling pig, with which you can sample some sweet Portuguese wine or some of their sangria. Various party packages are available, with the rooftop available for hire.

Mexican

Beverley House
93-107 Lockhart Rd
Wan Chai
🚇 **Wan Chai**
Map 16-F2

Agave Tequila Y Comida

2866 3228

With its colourful Mexican decor, Agave Wan Chai is a relaxed spot for post-work drinkies on Lockhart Road. From mild to spicy, from the well known to the unusual (such as frijoles, which are beer-soaked beans), there is something for everyone to eat. Authentic tapas are available as well as hearty mains. But Agave is famed for its tequila menu. A 'snifter' (not to be confused with a shooter) can set you back from $50 to $450, depending on how much of a connoisseur you are. But be warned – the drinks here are lethal.

26-30 Elgin St
SoHo
🚇 **Central**
Map 16-E2

Caramba

2530 9963

Caramba's Mexican decor includes sombreros, the skull of a Texas Longhorn, Mexican art, strings of garlic and chiles, and a wall decorated with Mexican matchbox designs. There's also a small glass-ceilinged back room which can be used for private parties. Of particular note is the 'Wall of Flames' – a large collection of hot sauces (including their own homemade concoction) available for both consumption and purchase. Latin music adds to the party atmosphere. The fairly standard menu is enhanced by monthly specials, and the drinks menu includes a list of margaritas and, of course, a good Tequila selection.

9 Staunton St
SoHo
🚇 **Central**
Map 16-E2

El Taco Loco

2147 9000 | www.diningconcepts.com.hk

Ah, Mexican, the ultimate comfort food! There is nothing more pleasurable after a hard day's work than to be sitting at a table surrounded by tacos, burritos and quesadillas, every possible type of chilli sauce with an ice cold bottle of beer in hand. Set right at the mouth of SoHo, it's a great place for a cheap and scrumptious meal, a couple of cheeky margaritas and some serious people watching. The menu is innovative and outlines a variety of different meat, fish and vegetable options which can be served in a number of different ways. The Carnitas (a deep fried pork burrito) comes highly recommended, but for the cholesterol conscious there are plenty of other goodies to choose from, such as pollo asade (chicken tacos) or baja pescado (grilled fish tacos). A great place for a quick lunch or a bite to eat at the start (or end) of an evening out in SoHo.

8 Observatory Court
Tsim Sha Tsui
🚇 **Tsim Sha Tsui**
Map 15-D3

Que Pasa

2316 2525 | www.mhihk.com

This small Mexican restaurant is reassuringly shambolic, with Mexican artefacts scattered at random, and half empty bottles crowding the central bar. Unpolished wood and a large saddle add a touch of the Wild West. You can expect the usual enchiladas and fajitas, but also some more inventive Mexican inspired fare, such as the spicy fowl broth with shredded chicken, green chilli, corn and avocado or the deep-fried jalapeno peppers stuffed with crab meat, onion and cheese. The food may not be strictly authentic, or even to everyone's taste, but this place is more about the atmosphere anyway. Cheesy Mexican style pop revs up the crowd and gets louder as the night wears on. Throw in a good dose of tequila and the odd bottle of Sol and you've got yourself a party. Ole – as they say.

381

Mongolian

55 Kimberley Rd
Tsim Sha Tsui
Tsim Sha Tsui
Map 15-D4

Nomads

2722 0733 | www.igors.com

Nomads is as much about fun as food. Budding chefs have the opportunity to test out their skills at this Mongolian barbecue style buffet. First choose from rice or noodles, then add bits of seafood, meat or vegetables and finish off your dish with a dollop of your desired sauce or a sprinkling of herbs and spices. Then hand your chosen ingredients to the chef who will cook them up on a hot plate before presenting your masterpiece to you at your table. You can eat as much as you like so have fun experimenting. For the less creative there are recipe suggestions. The fun at Nomads carries on into the decor which features 'ethnic' touches such as bows and arrows, raw-hide lampshades and sheepskin covered chairs. The restaurant attracts mainly locals and is popular with groups. Many visit to sample the regular specials which focus on different global cuisines.

Nepalese

G/F 14 Staunton St
SoHo
Central
Map 16-E2

Nepal

2869 6212

Just as the Himalayan kingdom of Nepal is sandwiched between two huge neighbours, this narrow restaurant is squeezed into place in the heart of SoHo. It serves a cuisine hard to find in Hong Kong, despite the city's large Nepalese population. The menu here has been developed from dishes served at the royal courts of Kathmandu. Similar to Indian food, it's a little lighter but no less spicy. Choose from curries, soups, salads and barbecued dishes, all seasoned with distinct combinations of Nepali herbs. Mountain specialities include yak cheese and Tibetan-style momocha dumplings. The restaurant faces buzzing Staunton Street and its crowds of window-shopping diners. Being a small space, the tables are close together, but the service is quick and efficient. Staff all hail from Nepal or thereabouts, and know the menu well. Their traditional dress is complemented by Nepalese carvings and kukris mounted on the walls.

Pizzerias

Other options **Italian** p.376

Since Pizza Hut opened their first pizza restaurant in Hong Kong in 1981, the pizza phenomenon has taken off in the hearts and mouths of the Hong Kong public. You can divide pizza restaurants into three different types. Firstly, you've got the restaurants selling American style pizza, eat-in or take-away, with outlets such as

Pizzerias	
Baci Pizza	2840 0153
Grappa's	2868 0086
Pepperoni's Pizza	2792 2083
Pizza Express	3528 0541
Pizza Hut	3810 0000
Wildfire (Stanley)	2813 6161

Pizza Hut, Pizza Express and Pepperoni's well-represented. Then you have the restaurants that serve pizzas as part of a much larger menu – many of which offer a delivery service as well as eat-in. And finally there are the Italian restaurants that only serve their pizzas in-house. If you do prefer to eat your pizza straight from the oven, there are literally hundreds of Italian restaurants all over Hong Kong. See p.376 for a selection of Italian restaurants.

Russian

Balalaika

10 Knutsford Terrace
Tsim Sha Tsui
Tsim Sha Tsui
Map 15-D3

2312 6222

This has a Russian peasant feel with wooden beams and folk art. Large tables accommodate groups of revellers. Food is hearty, with piroshki (dumplings), shashlik (kebab) and of course, caviar, on offer. It's just as well the food is solid as Balalaika's main attraction is the frozen vodka room. Inside this small space you can down a range of vodka shots at -20 degrees centigrade, the optimum temperature. Fur coats ease the pain. On most nights there's live Russian folk music and yes, the balalaika regularly appears. As you can imagine, the crowd gets rowdy as the evening rolls on.

Seafood

Dot Cod

Prince's Bld
10 Chater Rd
Central
Central
Map 16-E2

2810 6988 | www.dotcod.com

If you enjoy seafood, Dot Cod is the place for you – everything except the desserts involves the sea. This surprisingly spacious restaurant is located in the basement of Prince's building. Wander through the party atmosphere of the bar, which looks like a 1950s cruise ship with dark wood panelling and a brilliantly-lit aquarium full of (non-edible) fish. The crowd of senior-level professional expat men is loud, but friendly. In the dining area, art deco light fixtures and cast iron sculptures set the scene. A more mixed clientele enjoy elegant, but relaxed dining.

Oysters Bar and Restaurant

10 Wo On Lane
Central
Central
Map 16-E2

2877 9773

This is a venture by restaurant veteran Brian Dock, the force behind the famous (perhaps infamous) Joe Bananas, and a number of the city's other hotspots. Deep blue couches and blue-tinged lighting lend an aquatic ambience. There are generally oysters from five or six different regions on the menu which you can enjoy straight up or cooked with toppings. Six fresh oysters cost between $120 and $200. They also serve fish, steak, pasta and other international dishes. The service is friendly, and if Brian is about and the restaurant is quiet, he might knock you up a complimentary cocktail.

Spanish

Other options **Mediterranean** p.380

El Cid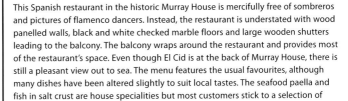

Murray House
Stanley Plaza
Stanley
Map 14-D2

2899 0858 | www.kingparrot.com

This Spanish restaurant in the historic Murray House is mercifully free of sombreros and pictures of flamenco dancers. Instead, the restaurant is understated with wood panelled walls, black and white checked marble floors and large wooden shutters leading to the balcony. The balcony wraps around the restaurant and provides most of the restaurant's space. Even though El Cid is at the back of Murray House, there is still a pleasant view out to sea. The menu features the usual favourites, although many dishes have been altered slightly to suit local tastes. The seafood paella and fish in salt crust are house specialities but most customers stick to a selection of tapas, which are tasty, if not outstanding. In the evening, you may be serenaded by the resident musicians. It seems no amount of looking in the other direction can keep them away. Just drink enough sangria and it'll be fine.

G/F 22 Staunton St
SoHo
🚇 *Central*
Map 16-E2

La Comida

2530 3118

La Comida is typical of SoHo restaurants in that it's small and intimate. Two rows of small tables with banquette seats run the length of the room. The warm colours of Spain feature heavily with yellow tablecloths, deep red cushions and orange walls. Sadly the pictures of flamenco dancers and bullfighters and sangria jugs don't quite transport you to Spain but it does deliver on its promise of authentic Spanish cuisine. There's a long list of delicious tapas, along with four different paellas and the obligatory sangria, as well as some authentic dessert options – the pears tintos (pears stewed in red wine) are recommended. La Comida attracts a mixed crowd. It fills up quickly even at lunch time, when they offer a set menu. It's at its best in the evening though, when the sangria merrily flows.

Steakhouses

Other options **American** p.353, **Argentinean** p.355

29 Elgin St
SoHo
🚇 *Central*
Map 16-E2

Craftsteak

2526 0999 | www.diningconcepts.com.hk

This is a steakhouse with a difference. Choose from steaks from Australia, Argentina or Canada, lamb or pork chops, poultry or seafood. Next, pick out your favourite sauce and vegetable dish. The meat is then cooked over an open flame. The interior of the restaurant is done out in dark woods and creams. The kitchen is open to the restaurant so you can see the team at work. The clientele is half western and half eastern, but all meat-loving. Be warned, however, the steaks here are so good you may never want anything else again.

Knutsford Terrace
Kimberley Plaza
Tsim Sha Tsui
🚇 *Tsim Sha Tsui*
Map 15-D4

Knutsford Steak Chop & Oyster Restaurant

2316 2381 | www.mhihk.com

There's no need to spell out the specialities at this New Orleans style eatery. Suffice to say they are the real deal – the steak is locker-aged and the oysters are freshly shucked. And fear not if neither tickle your fancy, because there are plenty of other all American favourites on the menu, from clam chowder to baby back ribs. Indeed, vegetarians might want to go elsewhere. For the thirsty, there's a large selection of bourbon whiskies and a late night happy hour. The restaurant itself is casual and cosy with wood panelling all around. A balcony provides outdoor seating and a view of Knutsford Terrace and everything going on below. Despite a valiant attempt at recreating the deep south in Kowloon, few Americans actually dine here, bar the odd tourist. The crowd is mostly locals out for a good time.

Sheraton Hong Kong
Hotel & Towers
Tsim Sha Tsui
🚇 *Tsim Sha Tsui*
Map 15-D4

Morton's

2732 2343 | www.mortons.com

Morton's is a swell American Steakhouse with ingredients flown in from around the world. One of the servers provides a short presentation of the menu's key features, such as the different beef cuts, the lobster and the vegetables. With a good view over Victoria Harbour, this long restaurant is split into mahogany bar, non-smoking section and larger smoking section. Tables are well-sized and spread out and swing music plays at an inoffensive volume. Popular with families, business folk and couples alike, a meal at Morton's is one of Hong Kong's finest dining experiences – justifying the fairly astronomical price tag.

The Steak House

InterContinental
Hong Kong
Tsim Sha Tsui
🚇 **Tsim Sha Tsui**
Map 15-D4

2721 1211

If the daintiness of Cantonese cuisine is not satisfying, get your fill of red meat at the InterContinental's popular Steak House. The menu is full of beef, lamb and other rich choices, with some steaks weighing in at 1kg. On choosing from the steak menu, waiters will present a selection of eight types of knife from all corners of the globe, with accompanying background information. A similar array of salt varieties is on hand. Although the portions are huge and nicely presented, don't expect the taste buds to receive a similar assault; the flavours are fairly plain. However, the selection of wines will not disappoint, with a walk-in cellar for those who wish to select a favourite vintage. A word of warning on the desserts; portion sizes are huge, suitable for at least three to share.

Thai

Auyuthaiya

Festival Walk
Kowloon Tong
🚇 **Kowloon Tong**
Map 10-B1

3105 5055 | *www.aqua.com.hk*

Ayuthaiya, is a surprisingly stylish Thai restaurant considering its mall location. Tables out front are suitable for business meetings or families, and inside holds a more intimate space and minimalist decor. Main courses are suitable for sharing. The baby lobster is succulent and mildly spiced , or try the crab dishes that Ayuthaiya specialise in. Desserts include various sticky rice sensations, as well as sweet Thai drinks. Service is brisk, orders arrive on the table in a flash. The tasty and reasonably priced food at Ayuthaiya makes a perfect break from a hard day's shopping.

Cafe Siam

40-42 Lyndhurst
Terrace
Central
🚇 **Central**
Map 16-E2

2851 4803

Ideally located next to the Escalator on Lyndhurst Terrace, Cafe Siam is great for people-watching and is always busy with locals, expats and tourists. The decor is basic but comfortable. Start off the meal with a fresh lime frozen margarita then order some dishes to share. Try the creamy eggplant hotpot, which is rich, but good. Service is erratic, but you can't fault the prices. For a real bargain, try the set lunch and dinner menus. It's not the best Thai food in town but if you're here for a cheap, tasty meal, you're sure to leave satisfied.

Good Luck Thai

13 Wing Wah Lane
Central
🚇 **Central**
Map 16-E2

2877 2971

Affectionately known as 'Rat Alley' among expats, Wing Wah Lane is an HK institution. Many an arduous night in LKF's bars begins in its restaurants, including Good Luck Thai. Staples such as tom yum goong, pomelo salads and curries of various hues abound. Washed down with chilled beer, everything is cheap and tasty. Most dining takes place in the alley, squeezed onto folding tables which merge with those of the neighbouring restaurants. To call this place relaxed would be an understatement – the owner permanently has a glass of wine in his hand. Look out for the infamous Indian Elvis.

Shek O Chinese and Thailand Seafood Restaurant

303 Shek O Village
Shek O
Map 14-F2

2809 2202

This restaurant is a stone's throw from the beach in the seaside village of Shek O. A favourite with beachgoers and hikers braving routes along the Dragon's Back, this is strictly a casual affair. It would be totally outdoors were it not for a smattering of concrete overhead, a bit of tin and some awning. Folding tables, a murky fish tank and

385

sticky menus set the scene. Nevertheless, cheery weekend diners wolf down the standard Thai food with gusto, then marvel at the modest bill. The main appeal of this place is its laid back, 'thank god it's the weekend' atmosphere.

Sukho Thai

Sun Hung Kai Ctr
30 Harbour Rd
Wan Chai
Wan Chai
Map 17-A2

2598 7222

The soft murmur of a Thai-style water fountain greets you as you enter this cosy eatery. Attractively furnished with brown wicker chairs, earthy fittings and Thai sculptures and paintings, it's divided into sections to make your experience more private. Food ranges from standard Thai to creatively-presented, outstanding Royal Thai. The food tends to be spicy, but there are milder dishes too. The vegetarian selection is large and the wine list is passable. Prices vary considerably – a three-course meal could cost anywhere between $250 and $450 per person.

Thai Lemongrass

California Tower
30-32 D'Aguilar
Central
Central
Map 16-E2

2905 1688

From the barman's green silk suit to the single malts and Cuban cigars he serves, Thai Lemongrass is immediately a step above many HK Thai eateries. For a decade the restaurant has served inspired, varied Thai dishes to couples and businessmen. It excels in seafood dishes, such as deep-fried sea bass with tamarind and chilli, and a range of curries, including roast duck in red curry with grapes and aubergines. Flavours are delicately balanced and dishes feel light. Thai Lemongrass is a perfect escape to a better Thailand.

Vegetarian

Harvester

Yardley Commercial
Bld, New Market St
Sheung Wan
Sheung Wan
Map 16-D1

2542 4788 | www.harvester.com.hk/veg

One of Hong Kong's few true vegetarian restaurants, this is pretty basic – think fold away tables which you share with other customers, plastic plates and paper napkins. However, it's also tasty and cheap as chips. The method of charging customers at Harvester will be intriguing to the uninitiated. You help yourself to rice and perhaps some soup, and then whatever you want from a small selection of dishes laid out buffet style. Your food is then weighed and you are charged accordingly. The dishes change every day but it's all Canto style veggie food with a large emphasis on tofu. The place is popular with locals who work in the area, along with a few more adventurous expats in the know. It's not somewhere to linger and you'll probably be in and out in under 15 minutes.

Life

10 Shelly St
SoHo
Central
Map 16-E2

2810 9777

This organic vegetarian restaurant is very popular with the health conscious set. The extensive menu offers a range of wholesome snacks and meals, along with revitalising juices and cleansing teas. Those with food intolerances and restricted diets are well catered to. The ingredients are fresh and according to Life's philosophy, everything is prepared with love. Most of it is pretty tasty too. The restaurant itself has a wholesome feel with natural tones and lots of wood, and there's a deli counter downstairs that sells salads and other foodstuffs. On the second floor the small roof garden is a pleasant place to sit on cooler days. Its main drawback is the service which is at times painfully slow. But perhaps that's part of the philosophy too.

Vietnamese

California Tower ◀
30-32 D'Aguilar St
Central
🚇 *Central*
Map 16-E2

Indochine 1929

2869 7399 | *www.lankwaifong.com*

For authentic Vietnamese cuisine, this place is hard to beat. In the hub of Lan Kwai Fong, IndoChine oozes French Colonial charm. Well established for the area (1993), it has a loyal expat clientele, so bookings are advisable. For something different, try the beef tenderloin with tomatoes or the braised duck with orange sauce. The Hanoi style fish also comes recommended. Regulars swear by the black sticky rice with red bean, coconut milk and roasted peanuts to complement the fresh mangoes. Definitely worth blowing the budget for.

75 Hollywood Rd ◀
Central
🚇 *Central*
Map 16-E2

Song

2559 0997

Song is an unexpected oasis of calm just off Hollywood Road. Drop down a few steps into the quaint Man Hing Lane and you will find the hidden entrance to this small restaurant. A white colour scheme, billowing sheer drapes and candles galore make the restaurant feel like a spa. The menu would not appear out of place in a health resort either. The modern take on Vietnamese cuisine sees a menu full of small, light dishes boasting expertly balanced flavours. Favourites include the obligatory rice paper rolls and caramelised chilli prawns. There are not many tables so the restaurant fills up quickly with couples and small groups of friends. Conversations are hushed and first time visitors will feel they've discovered a real hidden treasure.

Cafes & Coffee Shops

Hong Kong doesn't have a big cafe culture, probably because everyone's in too much of a rush. There a plenty of places to grab a bite on the run, including the usual fast food chains, sandwich shops, and Maxims which dishes up cheap rice dishes. For a more leisurely lunch, hotel coffee shops are a popular option, and many of these offer lunchtime buffets. If it's caffeine you're after, StarBucks and Pacific Coffee compete for worldwide domination on virtually every street in town, while Mix offers pseudo healthy smoothies alongside their coffee. If you're visiting any of these places at lunchtime, be prepared to queue or else push and shove with the best of them.

Afternoon Tea

A love of afternoon tea is a charming hangover from Hong Kong's colonial past. Various venues offer a truly traditional high tea, with dainty finger sandwiches, airy cakes and currant filled scones served up with a pot of earl grey or lapsang souchong. The Lobby in the Peninsula is renowned for its colonial atmosphere while the Clipper Lounge in the Mandarin serves the most delectable rose petal jam. Some of the five star hotels also offer tea buffets. Traditional treats are available alongside a host of other nibbles, from soup to sushi to spring rolls.

Coffee Shops		
The China Tee Club	Central	2521 0233
The Clipper Lounge – The Mandarin Oriental	Central	2522 0111
The Lobby – The Peninsula Hotel	Tsim Sha Tsui	2920 2888
The Lobby Lounge – The Conrad	Admiralty	2521 3838
The Lounge – Four Seasons Hotel	Central	3196 8888
Tiffin – The Grand Hyatt	Wan Chai	2588 1234
The Verandah	Repulse Bay	2292 2822

Internet Cafes

When it comes to technology Hong Kong is up there with the best of them. Internet access is available all over the territory, with very good wireless coverage in most urban areas. Many coffee shops offer free internet use to their customers and there are hundreds of restaurants offering wireless broadband coverage. In Central just one of the wireless service providers offers 39 locations in bars and restaurants. Another main service provider boasts 350 hotspots across the territory. For those without a laptop or pda try one of Pacific Coffee's many branches – most have two or three computers for customer use. For store locations, log on to www.pacificcoffee.com. If you prefer healthy juices while you surf the net free of charge, try The Mix. Most of their stores are on Hong Kong Island, but you can also find them in Sha Tin and Hong Kong International Airport. Visit www.mix-world.com for locations.

Bakeries

There are two different types of bakery in Hong Kong. Firstly, there are the shops which cater to the local palate. The breads on sale are much lighter than the European styles, as well as sweeter. They sell a lot of buns filled with a myriad of interesting flavours. They also sell a range of cakes, mostly variations of sponge, along with egg tarts – a delicious Hong Kong favourite. If you're after genuine European-style baked goods you should visit Great Foodhall in Pacific Place, or Citysuper in IFC, Times Square, New Town Plaza or Harbour City. Olivers Delicatessen in Prince's Building also sells a wide variety of excellent bakery products. Needless to say, the price point of the European style goodies is rather higher than the local stuff.

Fruit Juices

If you're after a freshly-squeezed fruit juice on a hot summer's day, you won't have to walk far to find a corner shop or fruit stall with a couple of blenders and a juicer. All the usual juices are on offer, plus a couple you may not have tried before, like dragon fruit juice. Whatever fruit you see on display will be juiced – you can even combine different flavours. Prices range from

$5 to $15 depending on the fruit and location. Then there are the fancy juice bars in shopping centres. Here staff will add ginger, wheatgrass, ginseng, beetroot and any number of other weird and wonderful things. Expect to pay up to $30 for a large glass. The Mix (www.mix-world.com) offers the widest selection of interesting juices and smoothies. Try the Liver Flush, a refreshing combination of Pink Grapefruit, Beet, Ginger, Lemon and Cayenne.

Street Food

Whether you're a church mouse or a tycoon, everyone in Hong Kong loves to eat out. For those who can't afford to go five star, Hong Kong has the Dai Pai Dong. This is street food Hong Kong style. The usual Dai Pai Dong will have a couple of greasy looking woks, boxes of uncooked food, an odd assortment of tables and chairs, a fan or two to cool down the patrons, and a whole lot of noise! They serve Cantonese-style rice and noodles, with seafood, meat or vegetables. They are very much social gatherings with big tables, regular customers and friendly stall owners. The standards of hygiene of most of these places has improved a lot over the years, and most stalls have been moved off the streets into the cooked food markets. Visit Temple Street night market to experience some authentic Hong Kong street food.

Ladies' Nights
Many bars have Ladies' Nights on Wednesdays, so as you'd expect, Wednesdays are popular with younger, cash strapped women, and the men who love them.

On the Town

Hong Kong, it is said, is a bit like New York sped up. This comparison rings particularly true when wandering around any of Hong Kong's nightlife epicentres after dark. Buildings are positively bulging with restaurants, bars and clubs and the pavements are overflowing with punters keen to try out the latest hot venue or visit an old favourite. Every night is party night, but some nights are busier than others. Friday nights, of course, are popular with everyone, and office workers begin to pack the bars at around 18:00. Most restaurants are open until 23:00. Few bars close their doors before 01:00 and many party on till dawn. Unfortunately, living the good life for all those hours will set you back a pretty penny. Drinks are expensive and even hopping from happy hour to happy hour will take its toll on your wallet.

Door Policy

A small number of Hong Kong bars and clubs claim to be 'members only'. Sometimes this is in order to appear exclusive and sometimes it is in order to get around alcohol licence laws. Rarely is it actually true. Beware bars or clubs who try to extract large sums of money in exchange for membership. Expensive membership seems to buy you no privileges at all, other than the right to air kiss the bouncers, thereby impressing people who are impressed by that sort of thing. Being smartly dressed, having an attitude, waving wads of cash around or looking like a Brazilian model should be all you need to get into even the most exclusive Hong Kong venue.

Dress Code

Although Hong Kong can be a hot and humid place in the summer, you won't find people strolling around in shorts and vests. The emphasis here is smart-casual. During happy hours, bars are a sea of suits as the weary executives stop off for a drink and a bite to eat on the way home. Later in the evening the designer labels come out to play. Although few bars have official dress codes, you're advised to dress up if you want to fit in. It's also a good idea to take an extra layer because some restaurants and bars like to keep their customers well-chilled.

Bars

Other options **Nightclubs** p.402, **Pubs** p.400

Al's Diner

39 D'Aguilar St
Central
🚇 **Central**
Map 16-E2

2521 8714

This small, 1950s American diner-themed bar is a Hong Kong institution. Every night is party night at Al's, but it's bursting on Fridays and Saturdays with revellers happily spilling out onto the streets of Lan Kwai Fong, suffering from lessening control over their limbs and moderate hearing loss. Eighties tunes scream out of giant video screens while the thirty-something crowd gyrate on tables. To get you in the mood, try the killer vodka jello shots – Al's speciality. The fun goes on until the early hours. By contrast Al's is quiet during the day, and a great place to enjoy an all-American meal (the burgers and shakes are known to be among the best in town).

Aqua Spirit

One Peking Rd
Tsim Sha Tsui
🚇 **Tsim Sha Tsui**
Map 15-C4

3427 2288 | www.aqua.com.hk

This place is an absolute must for anyone passing through or living in Hong Kong. Why? The view. It is surely the best in town and could not fail to impress even the most jaded Hong Konger. Add to that the super sexy decor, an extensive drinks list and great tunes and you're onto a winner. The drinks are a little pricey and it's all a bit poserish, but it's a small price to pay. If you have a date or an out of town visitor you want to impress, then this is the place to bring them. You can also enjoy excellent Italian and Japanese food in the restaurants Aqua Roma and Aqua Tokyo, just below the bar. For something a little different come on Bollywood Night when a bejewelled Indian crowd flock to shake their things to Bangra beats.

Baby Buddha

18 Wo On Lane
Central
🚇 **Central**
Map 16-E2

2167 7244

It may be less than a minute's walk from the bright lights and overflowing bars of Lan Kwai Fong, but Baby Buddha's relaxed vibe could hardly be further removed from that area's loud and brassy establishments. Located at the end of Wo On Lane, beside a large open courtyard and a tiny Buddhist shrine complete with incense sticks, this bar is easily spotted thanks to its proliferation of red fairy lights. The open frontage gives the bar an airy feel, allowing the chilled beats emanating from within to carry out into the night. DJs perform at weekends when the bar can become fairly busy, although never uncomfortably so.

Massage and Reflexology

In most of the western world someone in search of a massage at three in the morning might raise a few eyebrows. However, here in Hong Kong, a full body massage or an hour's reflexology at the end of a night out is common practice. Plenty of places provide the service round the clock but Sunny Paradise Sauna (341 Lockhart Rd, Wan Chai, 2831 0123) is one of the better known ones. Here you can have a 45 minute massage for $238. There's also a sauna and a lounge to relax in while staff bring you cigarettes, juice and tea. A true Hong Kong experience. If reflexology is more your thing try Big Bucket Footbath and Reflexology (G/F Hoi Kung Court, 264-269 Gloucester Rd, 2572 8611). A 45 minute treatment costs $138. If you request it, the staff will finish off with a shoulder rub.

Back Beach Bar

Back Beach
Shek O
Map 14-F2

The no fuss name says it all. This place is little more than a hole in the wall with a few tables on the walkway above the beach, and the decor is virtually non-existent, consisting mainly of photos of BBB regulars. But what it lacks in style, it makes up for in atmosphere. On a sunny Saturday afternoon, a chilled out

MOTORAZR maxx V6

Move faster with 3.5G HSDPA high speed mobile broadband, external touch music keys and a 2 mega-pixel camera with flash. **The new MOTORAZR maxx V6. Cutting-edge speed for cutting-edge style.**

hellomoto.com

crowd leans back and sips cheap beers whilst dogs and toddlers run around freely. The dress code is 'there is no dress code.' In the evening things heat up a bit, groups merge and parties often appear from nowhere. Don't be surprised if someone pulls out a guitar and starts strumming a tune. It's not hard to feel the love here and you will leave with a warm glow which may even outlast the taxi ride back to town.

4-5 Knutsford Terrace
Tsim Sha Tsui
Tsim Sha Tsui
Map 15-D3

Bahama Mama's Caribbean Bar

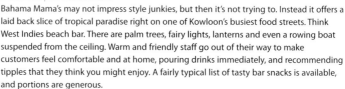

2638 2121 | www.mhihk.com

Bahama Mama's may not impress style junkies, but then it's not trying to. Instead it offers a laid back slice of tropical paradise right on one of Kowloon's busiest food streets. Think West Indies beach bar. There are palm trees, fairy lights, lanterns and even a rowing boat suspended from the ceiling. Warm and friendly staff go out of their way to make customers feel comfortable and at home, pouring drinks immediately, and recommending tipples that they think you might enjoy. A fairly typical list of tasty bar snacks is available, and portions are generous.

31 D'Aguilar St
Central
Central
Map 16-E2

Bit Point

2523 7436

A welcome retreat from the mayhem of Lan Kwai Fong, this relaxed, unpretentious German bar is named after Bitburger, one of the draught beers available on tap. Uncompromisingly German, you'll get some of the finest beers in Hong Kong as well as a great selection of German schnapps. The assorted snack platter includes typical fare such as sausages, cold cuts, cheese & gherkins. If you want a more substantial meal you can order a hearty German classic such as meatloaf. Functionally designed with plain wooden tables and cosy booths, Bit Point is dominated by the long spot-lit bar where patrons sit to drink and chat with the warm and welcoming bar staff.

Four Seasons
Central
Central
Map 16-E1

Blue Bar

3196 8888 | www.fourseasons.com/hongkong

If this place were a car, it would be a Ferrari – slick, expensive and popular with the rich and power hungry. Everything is finished and trimmed to perfection in true Four Seasons style. The aerodynamic leather chairs are softened by velvet cushions, a lit column of glass throws shades of blue across the room and plush carpeting softens the click, click of designer heels. There's a long list of cocktails as well as fine wines and champagnes, and a cigar menu featuring top of the range smokes. Dainty bar snacks are available, and there's even a buffet lunch during the week. Needless to say, none of this comes cheap, but that's probably part of the appeal.

65 Peel St
SoHo
Central
Map 16-E2

Blue Bar

Boca

2548 1717

Situated at the junction of three of SoHo's premier foodie streets – Staunton, Elgin and Peel – Boca is the perfect starting point for pre-dinner drinks or even a light meal. The brown leather sofas, dark wood interior and low lighting make it a sophisticated venue for a gathering of friends, but the thumping Euro-disco means it's not really suited to romantic dinners. Order a glass of the excellent Sangria (red, white or pink), and then dive into the eclectic but fairly pricy tapas menu. Incredibly fast (and sometimes over-enthusiastic) service means your hunger will soon be dealt with, so you can get down to the serious business of drinking.

3-5 Old Bailey St
Central
🚇 **Central**
Map 16-E2

Bohemian Lounge

2526 6099

If you're hoping to mingle with kaftan clad artists and writers discussing the virtues of free love and hallucinogenics, you may be a little disappointed. However, this is Hong Kong and The Bohemian Lounge doesn't do a bad job of offering an alternative to the usual trendy Central bars. The bar is casually decked out in rich reds and purples and is lit by Middle Eastern lanterns. There are plenty of low tables and chairs and many customers choose to grab a bite to eat from the tapas menu. The bar regularly features a variety of Jazz artists as well as hosting 'Mystic Mondays' when a tarot reader is available for short readings.

33 Tong Chong St
Quarry Bay
🚇 **Quarry Bay**
Map 17-D1

Cafe Einstein

2960 0994

Slap bang in the middle of vibrant Tong Chong, Einstein's is packed every Friday night with the straight-from-work media types, whose offices are just round the corner. There's a strong Eastern European theme going down, with Warhol inspired prints, mahogany wooden panelling, gigantic mirrors and comfy orange benches, and the atmosphere is unpretentious. Grab a beer at the bar and chat to the genuinely friendly staff who'll know your name before you leave. Or if the weather's nice, sit outside and chill under the yellow umbrellas. The drinks are good value, with happy 'hour' lasting from 16:00 to 21:00. There's a fairly decent international menu available, as well as a snack menu.

55 D'Aguilar St
Central
🚇 **Central**
Map 16-E2

The Cavern

2121 8969 | www.igors.com

Loud, brash and somewhat gaudily decorated, this live music venue cum bar/restaurant is not the place for a sophisticated bite to eat washed down with fine wine. Decorated in homage to the Swinging Sixties, with shag pile walls and psychedelic flourishes, The Cavern is best known for its live music, which is usually provided by tribute bands honouring rock'n'roll's greatest names. Go with a large group and you're bound to have some good, tacky fun. The menu is limited, but the dishes are tasty, well presented and more imaginative than in similar bars – although you will also find the ubiquitous potato skins and chicken wings.

78-82 Jaffe Rd
Wan Chai
🚇 **Wan Chai**
Map 16-F2

Chinatown

2861 3588 | www.chinatown.com.hk

This is a novel concept – a bar that's actually in China, but looks like a bar in New York pretending to be a bar in China. Chinatown takes faux Chinese to a new level. The deep green and bright red colour scheme is reminiscent of the rickshaws that now sit out of action at the star ferry. Plaster dragons, Chinese pop art and a giant fan decorate the walls while huge red lanterns hang from the ceiling. The drinks list is rather unadventurous and it's clear from the bellies walking around that most of the clientele are beer drinkers. Pub grub is served as well as a roast on Sundays, and on Tuesdays there's a quiz night.

9 Lan Kwai Fong
Central
Map 16-E2

Club 97

2186 1897 | www.ninetysevengroup.com

Club 97, also now calling itself Lounge 69, is a long-standing lynchpin of trendy Lan Kwai Fong. The classy decor includes plenty of marble and candles, and mirrored curtains frame the entrance giving a rather theatrical look. The menu is funky with drinks to match. Early in the evening drinkers prop themselves up on the stools to watch the world go by. Later on the dancing begins. The club's hot on the music scene and hosts top-notch local and international DJs. If you like house, you'll find it by the bucket load here. There are also special nights featuring latin, reggae and funk.

393

114-120 Lockhart Rd
Wan Chai
🚇 **Wan Chai**
Map 17-A2

Coyote Bar and Grill

2861 2221 | *www.coyotebarandgrill.com*

Coyote's colourful open frontage is a welcoming sight. Live entertainment, a busy bar area and a sunny, desert theme successfully impart a Latin fiesta vibe. A tasty Tex-Mex menu is available, as well as all the usual fare such as quesadillas, burritos and nachos and there are piquant daily specials of seafood and steak from the Mesquite Grill. On weekends, spicy Mexican brunches are served and portions are large enough to feed the hungriest of cowboys. A split-level layout means that diners in the upstairs section can watch the band downstairs, and also keep an eye on the bar where enthusiastic patrons lean backwards over the counter to receive direct pours of tequila. The bar claims to have Asia's largest selection of tequila and mezcal, and there are over 75 inventive margaritas on the drinks list. Latin band Azucar Latina play live music every Saturday night, making Coyote a great choice for a big night out.

76-84 Jaffe Rd
Wan Chai
🚇 **Wan Chai**
Map 17-A2

Dusk Til Dawn

2528 4689

The brightly painted yellow and purple frontage of Dusk Til Dawn has a Mediterranean feel. Inside there are a few tables but most customers prefer to lean against the bar or one of the wooden pillars. The bar attracts a typically mixed Wan Chai crowd of middle aged expat men, young ladies in short skirts, tourists and the odd drunken thirty-something. The main draw is the nightly live music when cover bands belt out convincing versions of classic rock and roll hits. Another attraction is the lengthy happy hour, which goes on until 22:00. Living up to its name, this place only shuts when the last customer goes home – usually at around 06:00.

38 Staunton St
SoHo
🚇 **Central**
Map 16-E2

Feather Boa

2857 2586

An open secret for those in the know, Feather Boa harks back to a forgotten era of decadent Eastern European coffee bars and glamorous Parisian night clubs. From the outside there are no signs to indicate Feather Boa's existence, but open the antique blue door and push through the heavy velvet curtains and another world awaits you within. Delightfully different with yellow silks, stately armchairs, elegant divans, and majestic candelabras, it attracts an eclectic mix of hardcore regulars and out of town first timers. Small and intimate it can get furiously busy as the night wears on. Arrive early to get a seat and relax with magical goblets of potent cocktails served by ethereal bartenders. The candles flicker, the crowd gets wilder as the evening goes on and you just won't want to go home.

Cigars

Although Hong Kong seems to be slowly coming round to the idea that smoking in public places is unpleasant, with campaigns for non-smoking bars and restaurants gathering momentum, cigar-smoking seems to retain a cyclical popularity. If you like the taste of a good Corona or Panatela and didn't procure enough at the airport duty free counter to last until your next holiday, you will find you are well catered for in Hong Kong. Davidoff has a handful of cigar boutiques stocked with the brand's full range, while there are a number of other specialist cigar shops dotted around town where you can find everything from a humble Hamlet to a majestic Montecristo. Red Chamber Cigar Divan beside the Pedder Building is a particularly popular spot to relax and enjoy a smoke with like-minded cigar-lovers. Failing that, you will find a few cigar options in 7-Eleven, some high-end supermarkets and at local tobacconist stalls.

The Fong

34-36 D'Aguilar St
Central
🚇 **Central**
Map 16-E2

2801 4946

The Fong is a relative newcomer to the Lan Kwai Fong scene and it remains to be seen whether it will survive the city's fickle moods. At the moment it's as good a place as any to enjoy a post work drink. The look is contemporary Asian with red leather banquette seating, wooden floors, large mirrors and carved wooden screens. The vibe is relaxed and it's usually pretty full with a mixed crowd. The drinks list is fairly extensive with a good selection of whiskies and the usual bar snacks are available. Go upstairs and the atmosphere is about five degrees cooler. The lights are dimmed with the latest dance tunes playing, as a sophisticated local crowd sip cocktails.

Fringe Club

2 Lower Albert Rd
Central
🚇 **Central**
Map 16-E2

2521 7251 | www.hkfringeclub.com

The Fringe Club is home to many of Hong Kong's artistic endeavours and occupies a historic building just a few metres from buzzing Lan Kwai Fong. The

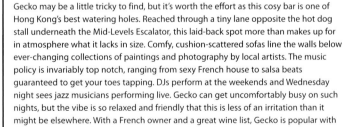

Lan Kwai Fong

relaxed rooftop bar makes a pleasant change from the more self conscious bars in the area and is also one of the few places in Central with plenty of outdoor seating. It's a pretty basic set up with aluminium tables and chairs dotted around on the Astroturf. Drinks are reasonably priced and there's a snack menu available, although offerings are mediocre at best. You may well catch an art or photography exhibition on display in the small, indoors part of the bar.

Gecko

Ezra Lane
Central
🚇 **Central**
Map 16-E2

2537 4680

Gecko may be a little tricky to find, but it's worth the effort as this cosy bar is one of Hong Kong's best watering holes. Reached through a tiny lane opposite the hot dog stall underneath the Mid-Levels Escalator, this laid-back spot more than makes up for in atmosphere what it lacks in size. Comfy, cushion-scattered sofas line the walls below ever-changing collections of paintings and photography by local artists. The music policy is invariably top notch, ranging from sexy French house to salsa beats guaranteed to get your toes tapping. DJs perform at the weekends and Wednesday night sees jazz musicians performing live. Gecko can get uncomfortably busy on such nights, but the vibe is so relaxed and friendly that this is less of an irritation than it might be elsewhere. With a French owner and a great wine list, Gecko is popular with the French crowd. Oh, and don't forget to try the absinthe.

Half Past Ten

10 Glenealy
Central
🚇 **Central**
Map 16-E2

2869 9089

As stylish as it is comfortable, Half Past Ten is a little-known gem in the Hong Kong bar scene. Located near the top of Glenealy, up the hill from the Fringe Club, its unassuming exterior gives way to a chic monochrome interior featuring low-slung tables and seats. The emphasis here is on chilling out, a fact reflected in the music policy, although the pace quickens somewhat at weekends. Even when busy, Half Past Ten feels intimate thanks to the clever seating arrangement, which includes a secluded alcove. For those in the know, this is a popular spot for pre-club cocktails, and the martinis come highly recommended.

395

35 D'Aguilar St
Central
🚇 **Central**
Map 16-E2

Hardy's Folk Club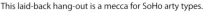

2526 7184

Hardy's is the black sheep of Lan Kawi Fong. The interior is grungy to say the least, with worn furniture, an exposed concrete ceiling and not much in the way of decor. Nevertheless, Hardy's is special. It caters to one of the most diverse crowds in Hong Kong and everyone is made to feel welcome. Come in black tie or a bin liner – nobody cares. Things really get going at about ten when karaoke kicks off. Karaoke with a difference that is. Instead of synthesised music and lyrics rolling across a screen, you get a song sheet and the talented resident guitarist to accompany you. Some of the people who come here to sing are genuinely talented, but even the most vocally challenged will draw wild applause from the crowd. Reasonably priced beers and jello shots help ease the nerves.

38-44 Peel St
SoHo
🚇 **Central**
Map 16-E2

Joyce Is Not Here

2851 2999 | *www.joycebakerdesign.com*

This laid-back hang-out is a mecca for SoHo arty types. If you want to chill out while talking art, film, music or poetry with like-minded souls, then this is the place for you. It's packed with quirky touches, from the endearing to the downright bizarre, including mannequins truncated at the waists and used to support tables, and menus that come printed on a series of floppy disks. One wall is taken up by shelves displaying a smorgasbord of magazines, books, paintings, objets d'art, photographs and various knick-knacks that range from arty to silly. All are available to buy. Drinks range from beers and spirits to alcohol-spiked coffees and house-speciality cocktails, while a thoughtfully created selection of snacks is also available. The bar is well known for its Wednesday night poetry readings and regular jam sessions, and films are shown on Sunday evenings.

The Broadway
54-62 Lockhart Rd
Wan Chai
🚇 **Wan Chai**
Map 16-F2

Klong

2217 8330

Klong is a largish bar overlooking Lockhart Road. The Thai influenced decor is chic and sleek. The bar is divided into several sections: in one – low tables, Thai cushions and sheer drapes invite you to lounge whilst in another, customers sip cocktails at high tables and watch the comings and goings in the street below. On the other side of the bar there is a popular pool table and finally the dance floor. Above the dance floor is a small platform and a solitary pole – presumably a reference to the infamous girly bars of Bangkok. With the growing popularity of pole dancing lessons, it's not unusual to see some lithe young thing pulling off professional looking moves to the delight of onlookers.

9 Lan Kwai Fong
Central
🚇 **Central**
Map 16-E2

La Dolce Vita

2186 1888

La Dolce Vita is the doyenne of the Lan Kwai Fong open-fronted bar. There's often a large wine-drinking fiesta spilling onto the street outside. Inside it's on the small side with just a couple of high tables – if you come on a Friday or Saturday night, don't expect to find a stool. The look is modern, with lots of black, white and red. The snack menu offers all the usual suspects and the generous portions are all fresh and tasty. There's a small but well-chosen selection of wine and the monthly specials occasionally turn up some real treasures. Classic cocktails and enticing shooters keep people coming back.

Drinking and Driving

In Hong Kong, the statutory limit for blood alcohol concentration is 50mg of alcohol per 100ml of blood, the same as in Germany, Australia and Japan. This compares with 80mg in the UK and Singapore. It works out at just under a pint of beer or a glass of wine. The maximum fine upon conviction is $25,000 and three years imprisonment. Taxis are plentiful, safe and cheap and are a much better option. Hong Kong also has one of the best public transport systems in the world with many buses and minibuses running all night to get you home.

35 Pottinger St
Central
🚇 *Central*
Map 16-E2

Linq

2971 0680

Linq is a cosy little bar off the cobbled Pottinger Street. It has a cellar feel to it with brick walls and low lighting provided mainly by small hanging lanterns. Linq attracts a slightly older expatriate crowd of regulars who start to arrive after work and often stay to chat into the early hours. Everyone here is very friendly, including the excellent bar staff. Another plus is that single women don't need to worry about unwanted attention, as friendly in this bar means no more than just that. The only oddity is the music which doesn't quite seem to match the crowd. A tiny booth houses the resident DJ who spins funky house. Apparently Linq has still got it.

37-43 Pottinger St
Central
🚇 *Central*
Map 16-E2

Lotus

2543 6290

Lotus is a newcomer to the restaurant and bar scene and has made quite an impression. The main draw is the excellent Thai food, dished up by infamous Sydney chef and master of modern Asian cuisine, Will Meyrick. However plenty of young hipsters come here just to drink. There's a mean cocktail list with inventive martinis, belinis and bartenders who shake their thingies. The contemporary Asian design matches the menu with plenty of modern lattice screens and red leather seats. The front section of the restaurant is for drinking only and is packed by 22:00. The back section houses the dining area and is a bit quieter – that is until the DJ gets going and hips start swaying later in the evening.

56 D'Aguilar St
Central
🚇 *Central*
Map 16-E2

Marlin

2121 8070 | *www.igors.com*

Marlin is something of an oddity. From the outside, the building is architecturally interesting, and somewhat reminiscent of the trendy hangouts in Venice Beach, California. Large neon letters proclaim the name of the bar and at night a kaleidoscope of colours runs up and down the walls. However, inside the bar is rather plain and very small. In fact, it's not really clear why anyone would visit, but visit they do. Perhaps it's the daiquitinis – Marlin's signature drink, made from fresh fruit infused rum and vodka. Perhaps it's the menu of tasty, US style snacks. Or more likely, it's the fact that in Marlin you can sit and watch the world go by without having to primp and pose.

83 Lockhart Rd
Wan Chai
🚇 *Wan Chai*
Map 16-F2

Mes Amis

2527 6680 | *www.mesamis.com.hk*

With its French name you might expect Mes Amis to be super chic and slinky. Its not exactly that, but in Wan Chai everything's relative. On most nights the room is filled with small round tables where customers relax and enjoy post work drinkies and snacks from a pretty standard menu. However, on Wednesday, Friday and Saturday nights the tables are cleared and the resident DJ plays the latest pop hits, while hot and sweaty bodies shimmy on the dancefloor. A certain level of inebriation is recommended. With that prerequisite fulfilled you're bound to have fun. However, ladies be warned, the men here are as free with their hands as they are with their compliments.

The Landmark
Mandarin Oriental
Central
🚇 *Central*
Map 16-E2

MO Bar

2132 0077 | *www.mandarinoriental.com/landmark*

Hong Kong has more than its fair share of swanky bars, but this one has the clout to out-glitz them all. Part of the terribly swish Landmark Mandarin Oriental and a short hop from Harvey Nics, MO Bar offers local fashionistas, tai tais and ladies who lunch

397

a chance to lay down their logo-emblazoned bags and enjoy a cocktail and a bite while their credit cards cool down. At night, the atmosphere turns sexy and seductive, with the giant 'O' that dominates one wall casting its warm red glow across the stylish furnishings. MO is large enough to accommodate the many style mavens, hotel guests and celebrities who descend here at weekends, and pricey enough to leave your wallet feeling considerably lighter after just one or two drinks. A smart-casual dress code is enforced.

Nzingha Lounge

48 Peel St
SoHo
🚇 *Central*
Map 16-E2

2834 6866 | *www.nzinghalounge.com*

Run by a lady from Cameroon, Nzingha is Hong Kong's first African bar and fulfils its promise to transport you there. It's welcoming and cosy with an earthy feel – low, mismatched chairs and tables are scattered around, all draped in rich African fabrics, and the walls are dotted with pieces of West African folk art. There's an unusual list of house cocktails, which are generally heavy on the rum as well as a small menu of authentic African nibbles. The bar has plenty of room to kick off your shoes and lounge, although most of Nzingha's clientele come here to get down to the African beats proffered by the resident DJ. Occasional live music draws an enthusiastic and energetic crowd.

Red Bar and Restaurant

IFC Mall
Central
🚇 *Central*
Map 16-E1

8129 8882 | *www.ifc.com.hk*

This slick bar in IFC is unique in that it features a large outdoor area overlooking the harbour. It's popular with the corporate types who work in the nearby offices, and gets pretty packed post work, but it does quieten down later as party animals move on and exhausted execs go home to bed. The interior is ultra modern with neutral tones, clean lines and no fuss. Customers are spoilt for choice on the drinks front, although prices are a little high. You can also eat here, choosing from a menu which is clearly aimed at the health conscious. With so many well-groomed and well-heeled bodies around there's plenty of eye candy, but most seem too stressed or too self-conscious to mingle, so don't expect to make any new friends.

Sahara Mezz Bar

11 Elgin St
SoHo
🚇 *Central*
Map 16-E2

2291 6060

Stepping into this cosy and relaxed North African/Middle Eastern restaurant and bar provides a welcome break from the sterile venues that dominate Central. Ornate wrought ironwork surrounds the shop front and the walls are painted an inviting shade of terracotta. Inside, pretty stained glass lamps and intricately painted plates decorate the ceiling and walls. Diners smoke shishas that leave the air scented with sweet tobacco. On weekends, the Egyptian owner is DJ and sometimes brings in a belly dancer to further liven things up. The music fits the theme – Arabian all the way. The menu offers a fine range of Middle Eastern meals, and they also stock some beer from the region, such as Casablanca from Morocco.

Soda

79 Wyndham St
Central
🚇 *Central*
Map 16-E2

2522 8118 | *www.soda.hk*

Soda is a colourful and well-designed spot in which to enjoy a drink or a bite at any time of the day or night. Retro furniture gives the bar a fun feel, while cool beats courtesy of in-house DJs enhance the relaxed vibe. Retractable doors make for an airy atmosphere, with the option to spill out onto the street when it gets busy, as it generally does at weekends. There's an impressive wine list, and Soda is also known for its excellent cocktails. Should you get a sudden attack of the munchies, Soda also offers a menu of reasonably priced burgers, pizzas, sandwiches and the like.

10-12 Staunton St
SoHo
🚇 **Central**
Map 16-E2

Staunton's Wine Bar and Cafe

2973 6611 | www.stauntonsgroup.com

Staunton's regularly gets 'Best People Watching' awards, and with good reason – its location right next to the Escalator in the epicentre of SoHo makes it a prime spot to grab a drink and spy on would-be-dates coming home from work. Chic and relaxed, it can nevertheless get deliriously frantic in the early evenings, with loyal patrons spilling onto the busy streets with their Happy Hour Sauvignon Blancs. And with over 28 wines to choose from, who can blame them? By day though, Staunton's emerges as a sun-lit chilled-out cafe bar where you can grab a paper and relax with a cappuccino. If you're feeling peckish, they've got a great bistro menu.

48 D'Aguilar St
Central
🚇 **Central**
Map 16-E2

Stormy Weather Bar & Grill

2845 5533 | www.igors.com

Affectionately known as Stormies, this bar and restaurant at the top of Lan Kwai Fong starts to fill up early and is overflowing by the end of the night. There's a vaguely nautical theme with small oars by the door, blue cushions on the seats and the odd porthole. Drinks are also named in a nautical fashion. Reasonable food is available in the dining area upstairs, with the emphasis on seafood. Fans of 80s and 90s pop and rock will love this place, and although there is not much room for dancing, plenty of toe tapping goes on, and cries of 'Oh, I love this song!' are regularly heard. Stormies attracts a sociable expat crowd and you're bound to make new friends before the night is out.

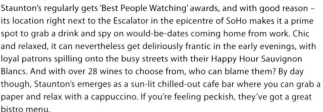

Gay & Lesbian Scene

The city's gay scene is confident and kicking. There are plenty of gay and gay-friendly bars and clubs in Central and NoHo (north of Hollywood Road). Propaganda on Ezra's Lane is a Hong Kong institution while Meilanfang at 14 On Wo Lane is a popular newcomer. Gay happy hours are listed in HK Magazine. Of particular note is Post 97 (p.375) on a Friday evening – a great start to the weekend.

For something a bit more risque, gay karaoke bars and saunas abound in Central, Wan Chai, Causeway Bay and Kowloon. For example, CE Sauna (37-43 Cochrane St, Central, 2581 9951) has a sauna, jacuzzi, massage chairs and play spaces. It attracts an international crowd and is sparkly clean. Free gay rags Gmag and Dimsum give the low down on upcoming happenings. And whatever you do, don't miss Gay Day at HK Disneyland.

Harilela House
79 Wyndham St
Central
🚇 **Central**
Map 16-E2

Yumla

2147 2383 | www.yumla.com

Yumla isn't so much a bar as a Hong Kong institution. In a city where many of the clubs are more concerned with looking stylish and having exclusive door policies than creating a welcoming vibe and fostering local DJ talent, this bar-cum-club is a glorious exception. Small in size but colossal in stature, Yumla has DJ nights every Friday and Saturday that sizzle through to the early hours, with playlists that boast an eclectic mix of sounds. Whether it be breakbeat, jungle, drum'n'bass or experimental electro, Yumla always has an up-for-it crowd and a superb atmosphere. It's not the biggest of spaces, so it can get incredibly busy at weekends, but the courtyard outside offers a welcome place to cool off and have a chat when it gets too hot and steamy inside.

399

Pubs

Other options **Bars** p.390

8 Observatory Rd
Tsim Sha Tsui
🚇 **Tsim Sha Tsui**
Map 15-D3

8 Fine Irishmen

2316 2133

There are two reasons to come to 8 Fine Irishmen – stout on tap, and traditional, hearty pub grub. Your favourite classic brews are all on the menu and you can tuck into large portions of fish and chips, shepherd's pie and the like for around $100. If you're planning to trawl the pubs and bars in the area you should make this your first port of call, as it's small and quickly gets packed and noisy. There are a few dining tables available, but they get filled quickly and you may have to stand or opt for the less comfortable high tables with stools. Sound familiar? Yes, 8 Fine Irishmen really feels like a slice of home to those from that part of the world.

38-44 D'Aguilar St
Central
🚇 **Central**
Map 16-E2

Bar George

2521 2202

This British pub lookalike is a cavernous place, divided into three sections. The first opens onto Lan Kwai Fong and houses a few tables and a bar. The vibe here is relaxed and sociable, perfect for a happy hour drink and an appraisal of the night's scene. The second, and arguably the most civilised, houses tables and booths where customers can grab a bite to eat. Carry on into the third section and things get more raucous. Here customers crowd around the huge bar downing beers or shots with amusing names, or shake their thing on the small dance floor. Bar George has acquired a reputation as a pick up joint and, on ladies night anyway, there are certainly plenty of scantily clad Asian woman being circled by salivating Western men.

17 Lan Kwai Fong
Central
🚇 **Central**
Map 16-E2

Bulldog's

2523 3528

If you're sick of slick, or just fancy a pint of bitter, then this place may tickle your fancy. It has a real English pub feel. That is to say it stinks of beer and fags and there are packets of crisps hanging from the wall. There are also sepia photos of old London and even an

The Smugglers Inn

old-fashioned, red phone booth. On the D'Aguilar Street side of the bar there's a nook named 'The Birdwatcher's Bar', which is generally full of expat men doing just that. Other customers gather round the large screens to watch the sport. The pleasant surprise at Bulldog's is the hearty and delicious traditional pub grub. Where else in Hong Kong can you have Jam Roly Poly with custard?

37 Cochrane St
Central
 Central
Map 16-E2

Dublin Jack

2543 0081

The Dublin Jack is what you might call a civilised pub. It's definitely a pub, but the walls are not nicotine stained and there are no crisps trodden into aging carpets.The simple decor, with plenty of dark wood, is homely but smart. A large bar stands in the centre of the main room. There is plenty of seating, including booths and the flat screen TVs dotted about cater to sports fans. The drinks menu is basic but comprehensive and the pub grub is hale and hearty, as good pub grub should be. The friendly Irish manager is simply charming and adds a touch of class himself.

39 Hollywood Rd
Central
 Central
Map 16-E2

The Globe

2543 1941

A quintessentially British pub patronised by a legion of loyal regulars, this traditional watering hole is renowned for its extensive selection of bottled ales, of which there are around 100. It also has a fine range of lagers and ales on tap, as well as British crisps and a hearty bar menu. It can get fairly busy on Saturdays (when live Premiership soccer is screened) and during its popular Tuesday night quiz, but if you get in early and secure a chair you'll be quite comfortable. Music comes courtesy of one of the city's best-stocked jukeboxes, where even the most discerning of audiophiles should find something to their liking. The down side to The Globe is that it can get quite smoky.

55 Elgin St
SoHo
 Central
Map 16-E2

McSorley's Ale House

2522 2646

With a traditional pub facade contrasting with the offices and apartments above, McSorley's is hard to miss. Open on one side to the street, this Irish pub is refreshingly free of 'Oirish' memorabilia – there's not a picture of Yeats or old Dublin in sight. Instead there's an attractive wooden bar on each of its floors, serving a wide variety of whiskies and several ales, and, of course, Guinness. The menu is not for the light stomached. From fish and chips to burgers and pies, this is good, straight food for drinkers. The pub also serves an all day brunch on the weekends, and there's a big screen for showing major sporting events.

90A Stanley Main St
Stanley
Map 14-D2

The Smugglers Inn

2813 8852

This small pub on Stanley's waterfront is named after the smugglers who used to inhabit the area. It's one of the oldest English style pubs in Hong Kong and possibly the most authentic. Dark wooden beams cross the ceiling and the tables and chairs are made from old barrels. There's a dart board and a juke box – both of which are regularly in use. You can forget fancy cocktails here, but there's a decent range of beers along with basic pub grub. Been longing for a ploughman's? You can get a good one here. The Smugglers Inn fills up alarmingly early in the day, and is a firm favourite with the expat crowd. The vibe is relaxed and everyone's friendly. It's definitely worth stopping by to sip a cold beer, chat to the regulars and gaze across the bay.

401

Nightclubs

Dragon-i

The Centrium
60 Wyndham St
Central
Central
Map 16-E2

3110 1222 | www.dragon-i.com.hk

Dragon-i is the favourite hang out of models, actors and wannabes. Everyone who enters must endure the scrutiny of the ultra discerning door hostess, so you'd better be beautiful or look like you have wads of cash. Inside, the club is divided into the VIP section and the sad nobodies section – otherwise known as The Playground. It's possible to eat in the VIP section (thereby securing entry) and the Chinese-Japanese fusion food is rather good. In both areas the lighting is moody and the decor glamorously modern. Everything here is designed to impress. Even the steel-doored unisex toilets are worth a visit. Unfortunately the music leaves a lot to be desired, except when a guest DJ visits. However, most people are not here to boogie. Dragon-i is all about show and the champagne quaffing expat men and East European models certainly make quite a spectacle.

Drop

On Lok Mansion
39-43 Hollywood Rd
Central
Central
Map 16-E2

2543 8856

This small club is wildly popular, mainly because of its legendary music policy. Any self respecting clubber visits Drop regularly to hear the best DJs in town. In fact it's so popular that the queues have become its main downfall. Once inside though, you'll find a pretty friendly crowd that gets more and more raucous as the night wears on. It also gets more and more crowded and can be a bit claustrophobic as sweaty bodies cram onto the tiny dance floor by the bar. The rest of the club has a bit of a padded cell feel with cream leather padding everywhere – perhaps to protect the customers who are bouncing off the walls. Drinks are suitably strong and the fresh fruit cocktails are delicious.

Hei Hei Club

On Hing Bld
On Hing St
Central
Central
Map 16-E2

2899 2068 | www.heiheiclub.com

This seven thousand square foot club is named after the Chinese character meaning double happiness. Its popularity has been growing steadily and it is now mainly frequented by the ABC crowd. There are various sections, including plenty of outdoor space. The decor has a Balinese resort feel to it, the highlights of which are the tiny pool and petal-strewn Jacuzzis on the terrace. Where else in Hong Kong can you enjoy a quick dip between trips to the bar? Unfortunately Hei Hei is not quite as relaxed as an Indonesian resort and you won't find many people wearing shorts and T-shirts. The music is a mix of hip hop and R&B. There are cocktails galore (with exotic prices), professional staff and plenty of beautiful people to look at. You could do worse.

Homebase

23 Hollywood Rd
Central
Central
Map 16-E2

2545 0023

Hongkongers like to party late and there are few places that cater to that desire with as much gusto as Homebase. Staying open until dawn and beyond, Homebase is the final stop for many people after a long hard night on the tiles. The club consists of a large metallic bar, on one side of which is a small dance floor and a DJ box that pumps out the latest house music. On the other side are large Thai-style mattresses, divided into booths by sheets of billowing white fabric. Here, you can flick off your shoes and recline in relative comfort with a bunch of your closest or newest friends. The club doesn't really get going until 04:00, which means you can often stay much longer than you intended.

Grand Hyatt
Hong Kong
Wan Chai
🚇 ***Wan Chai***
Map 15-D4

JJ's

2584 7662 | *www.hongkong.grand.hyatt.com*

Part restaurant, part bar, part club, the recently refurbished JJ's has something for everyone. The restaurant on the lower level serves 'six star Thai cuisine', with such innovative offerings as taro fritters (phuaek tord) with a tamarind dipping sauce, fluffy fried fish and shredded green mango (yam pla dook foo) and warm dark chocolate chilli tartelette with mango sherbet. Upstairs there are two bar areas and the legendary Music Room where a live band plays R&B nightly to a receptive crowd. Although JJ's is rather swanky and the drinks prices are on the high side, it's pleasantly unpretentious. One point to note – the air-conditioning is on overdrive, so bring an extra layer or you'll be obliged to wear one of the shawls offered to chilly guests.

23 Luard Rd
Wan Chai
🚇 ***Wan Chai***
Map 17-A2

Joe Banana's

2529 1811

For 20 years Joe Banana's has been the undisputed epicentre of Wan Chai nightlife. If you haven't pulled by 04:00, then this is the place to come. The mere mention of JBs makes most long term expats cringe as they remember bad chat up lines, unfortunate dance moves and ill-advised pick ups. It is done out with a beachy mood in mind – not that you'll probably notice. There are occasional live bands but at other times the DJ pumps out chart toppers and golden oldies that get the crowd going. Brave the dance floor only if you don't mind being groped. The crowd is mixed and includes tourists, air crew, US marines and ladies of questionable repute. It may be on the seedy side but it's all good fun.

32 Wellington St
Central
🚇 ***Central***
Map 16-E2

Kee Club

2810 9000 | *www.keeclub.com*

Kee Club is a private members club, although the rules can occasionally be bent if you look the part. There are two types of member – those who are well connected and are offered membership, and those who are prepared to pay for it (and it doesn't come cheap). Yes, Kee Club is as pretentious as it is exclusive. However, that's not to say you won't have fun here. It has hosted some happening private parties over the years and regularly has excellent DJs and club performers. Chef Gianluigi Bonelli creates truly inspired dishes with European flair and you can marvel at the original artworks on the walls as you dine. These range from works by Picasso to Tibetan antiques.

---

24 Hour City

Hong Kong truly is a 24 hour city with pretty much everything but sunshine available around the clock. That means nights out often really do last all night. If you're the kind of person who likes to party till dawn then here is a suggested itinerary for a big night out:

18:00 – Join the post work crowd in Staunton's SoHo for a pre-dinner drink.

19:30 – Move on to dinner in one of the many restaurants in SoHo. Caramba is a good place for those in the party mood.

21:30 – Wander down to Lan Kwai Fong, which is just hotting up at this hour. Stormies is great for making new friends.

01:00 – At around this time some LKF bars start to wind down and it's time to move on. Here the crowd divides. If you like your nightlife gritty head to Wan Chai for a boogie in Mes Amis or some live music at The Wanch. If hip and slick is more your style head to Drop to hear some of Hong Kong's best DJs.

04:00 – Your tired limbs may need a break at this point. If you're in the mood for another club, head to Homebase where you can recline on the leather beds. Otherwise opt for Sunny Paradise Sauna and a cheap massage followed by some reviving tea.

06:00 – It's getting light and it's time to top up the tank. Flying Pan serves great greasy breakfasts 24 hours a day, and with branches in Central and Wan Chai you're never too far from that essential fry-up fix.

403

9 Star St
Wan Chai
Map 16-F2

One Fifth Ultralounge

2520 2515 | www.elite-concepts.com

One Fifth is the venue that first put the twinkle in Star Street. Although it may be past its hey day, it remains popular and you may even have to queue on a busy night. Once inside, a narrow corridor with a mirrored ceiling opens into the large, uber-chic bar. The high ceilings and lashings of metal give an industrial feel, while chocolate brown velour lounge areas add glam. Behind the long bar drinks are stacked two metres high. You name it, it's on the menu, but cosmopolitans seem to be de rigeur. Resident DJs play funk and soul, a little too loudly at times, and although there's no dance floor, you'll see the occasional groovster get down wherever they're standing. One Fifth attracts the ABC crowd. They're young, they're beautiful and in a few years they'll be ruling the world – the financial world anyway.

38-44 D'Aguilar St
Central
Central
Map 16-E2

Volar

2810 1272 | www.volar.com.hk

One of the hottest clubs in Hong Kong, Volar strikes a fine balance between style and substance. For those who enjoy chic surroundings, the futuristic labyrinthe interior hits the mark. Audiophiles, meanwhile, will revel in the club's top-notch sound system and impressive list of resident and international guest DJs. All the big names play here and Friday nights, when techno dominates, are particularly popular. The club operates a fairly strict door policy meaning you generally need to be a member or on the guest list to get past the stony-faced doormen. Drinks are fairly expensive. They are also strong, making the many rooms and corridors even harder to navigate.

Tram Parties

The tram system is in good working order and public trams run regularly, cheaply and efficiently around North Point, Causeway Bay and the Happy Valley area. Hong Kong Tramways (2118 6338, www.hktramways.com) has antique and ordinary trams available for hire, meaning you and a maximum of 35 mates can ride around in your own private tram for an evening and see the sights and all the lights. They are all double deckers so you get a really great view. There is a music system on board to help the party atmosphere; the food and drink is BYO. Each tour starts and ends at the Western District Depot, and the minimum tour is two hours and maximum three and a half. Toilet stops on request!

Parties at Home

With so many entertainment options available, parties at home are not the norm in Hong Kong. When someone does decide to run the risk of cigarette burns in the carpet and red wine stains on the sofa, it's usually a casual, bring a bottle and a sausage or two, type of affair. However, if your heart's desire is to hold a lavishly catered dinner party for a few select friends, it can still be arranged. The grand exception to the 'not in my house you don't' trend, is children's parties. Taking little ones out en masse is just too daunting, so many parents choose to celebrate their birthdays at home. For such an affair you can outsource everything from the cake-making to the clowning. Indeed, in true Hong Kong style many a two year old's birthday bash has been known to turn into a grand and totally over the top spectacle. See the table below for a list of catering firms.

Caterers	
Bite Me!	2302 0097
Brown Catering	2881 5898
Complete Deelite	3167 7022
Gingers	2964 9160
Go Gourmet	2530 3880

Cabaret & Strip Shows

Despite the impression you might get walking around Wan Chai, the strip club scene in Hong Kong is pretty tame. So much so that most punters head to Macau for their fix of gyrating topless girls and cheap thrills. Here in Hong Kong the girls in most girly bars are merely scantily dressed rather than topless or nude. This doesn't stop owners charging hugely elevated prices for drinks though, and it's all still a little seedy. One possible exception to the rule is Goodfellas (2522 9218), a slightly better than average club on Ice House Street. There is a $5,000 membership fee and drinks are still pricey after that. However, the western girls do full stripteases and lap dances. And just in case anyone's interested, some of them really can dance.

Casinos

Floating Flutter
An alternative to a Macau trip is an overnight cruise. As soon as the boat leaves Hong Kong waters the tables open and most enthusiasts won't see the inside of their cabins that night.

The Hong Kong Chinese have a passion for gambling but it's illegal to operate a gambling establishment in the territory. That is with the exception of the government-sanctioned Hong Kong Jockey Club, which takes bets on horse racing and football, and also organises the Mark Six lottery. Of course, that's not to say gambling doesn't happen. Illegal dog fights are rife, and whenever you hear the deafening clatter of mahjong tiles, you can be sure money is changing hands. For an above-board gambling binge, many people make the trip to the Las Vegas style casinos in Macau. See p.217.

Cinemas

There are more than 40 cinemas in Hong Kong, ranging from small two-screen operations to multi-screen complexes. You can find a cinema in most areas, and in busy shopping areas like Tsim Sha Tsui and Causeway Bay you are spoilt for choice. The majority of films are English language or Cantonese. All English language films are subtitled in Chinese, and some are dubbed into Cantonese. If you're looking for films in other languages, such as French, German, Italian or Japanese, try Broadway Cinematheque in Yau Ma Tei or the Cine Art House in Wan Chai. Hong Kong films are usually censored for nudity or sex scenes while the swearing, violence and bloodshed remain untouched. Go figure. Most cinemas have a concession stand in the foyer selling the usual cinema snacks. All cinemas have modern sound systems which are usually a little on the loud side, and they also have powerful air-conditioning systems so take an

Cinemas

AMC Festival Walk	Kowloon Tong	2265 8933	www.amccinemas.com.hk	10-B1
AMC Pacific Place	Admiralty	2265 8933	www.amccinemas.com.hk	16-F2
Broadway Cinematheque	Yau Ma Tei	2388 0002	http://bc.cinema.com.hk	15-C3
Chinachem Golden Plaza	Tsim Sha Tsui	2311 3004	www.cel-cinemas.com	15-D4
Cine Art House	Wan Chai	2827 4820	na	17-A2
Golden Harvest Golden Gateway	Tsim Sha Tsui	2956 2003	www.goldenharvest.com	15-C3
Golden Harvest Grand Ocean	Tsim Sha Tsui	2377 2100	www.goldenharvest.com	15-C3
Golden Harvest Hollywood	Wong Tai Sin	2955 5266	www.goldenharvest.com	10-D1
Golden Harvest Mong Kok	Mong Kok	2628 9864	www.goldenharvest.com	15-D1
Golden Harvest New York	Causeway Bay	2838 7380	www.goldenharvest.com	17-B2
Golden Harvest Tsing Yi	Tsing Yi	2186 1333	www.goldenharvest.com	9-F1
MCL JP	Causeway Bay	2881 5005	www.mclcinema.com	17-B2
Olympian City	Mong Kok	2388 6268	www.cinema.com.hk	15-C2
Palace IFC	Central	2388 6268	www.cinema.com.hk	16-E1
UA Citygate	Lantau Island	2109 3568	www.uacinemas.com.hk	8-E3
UA Cityplaza	Taikoo Shing	2567 9669	www.uacinemas.com.hk	17-E1
UA Langham Place	Mong Kok	3514 9031	www.uacinemas.com.hk	15-C2
UA Telford	Kowloon Bay	2758 9997	www.uacinemas.com.hk	10-D2
UA Times Square	Causeway Bay	2506 2822	www.uacinemas.com.hk	17-B2
UA Whampoa	Hung Hom	2303 1041	www.uacinemas.com.hk	15-E3
Windsor Cinema	Causeway Bay	2577 0783	www.uacinemas.com.hk	17-B2

405

Film Hotlines
The UA ticket hotline is 2317 6666, and the Golden Harvest hotline is 2388 6268.

extra layer. Ticket prices range from $40 to $80, with cheaper deals for lunchtime showings and special deals on Tuesdays at some venues. For a premier cinema experience try the Directors Club in Cityplaza, Taikoo Shing or the Palace in Windsor House, Causeway Bay. These offer seats for couples, along with complimentary food and soft drinks, a bar and a state of the art screen and sound system. The Hong Kong International film festival held in April showcases hundreds of films in cinemas all across the territory. To find cinema listings check the English language newspapers or entertainment magazines.

Comedy

The Punchline Comedy Club is the main purveyor of stand-up comedy in Hong Kong. Shows take place in the Viceroy restaurant, Wan Chai (p.371) and feature comedians from the UK, Ireland, and North America. These nights are very popular and always packed. The Viceroy offers a dinner buffet before the show to make a night of it. Tickets are around $290 and you can expect to see three or four acts. Be warned, these shows are for a mature audience so don't bring the kids. For details of upcoming dates visit the club's website, www.punchlinecomedy.com/hongkong. Alternatively the Fringe Club in Central (p.395) has been known to present the odd comedy act. Visit their website to see what's on.

Concerts

Music Annual
The Hong Kong Arts Festival is an annual event which always features an excellent lineup, including classical, jazz and world music greats. See www.hk.artsfestival.org for details.

There are a number of concert venues in Hong Kong which play host to a growing list of international stars. Famous names from the world of rock and pop who've played recently include The Beatles (ok, it was 1964, but people still talk about it), The Rolling Stones, Prince, David Bowie, Oasis, The Black Eyed Peas and Coldplay. Classical artists have included Jose Carreras, Andrea Bocelli and Luciano Pavarotti. You can also see performances by leading Asian classical and popular artists, or listen to the strains of the Hong Kong Philharmonic or the Hong Kong Chinese Orchestra. There are the big venues, such as the Queen Elizabeth Stadium, City Hall and the Convention Centre, as well as a large selection of small and medium-sized halls. Listings can be found in *HK* Magazine.

Fashion Shows

Every major fashion designer seems to have at least one outlet in Hong Kong and fashion shows can be found taking place in large shopping centres or exhibition centres across the city. Hong Kong Fashion Week is an event held twice a year, in January and July in the Hong Kong Convention and Exhibition Centre in Wan Chai. You can see six or seven fashion shows at these events. Admission is free to most shows, although some are restricted to people working in the industry. There are shows held by designers of shoes, bridal wear, swimwear, handbags, accessories and anything else you could possibly wear.

Theatre

Other options **Drama Groups** p.240

Hong Kong is not exactly renowned for its theatre. In fact, for many years decent English language productions were almost completely lacking. However, efforts are being made to change that. The yearly Arts Festival brings in a host of world class acts, from performances of Shakespeare to offerings from top Chinese directors. On occasion a West End hit even graces our shores. Looking for something more intimate? There are a handful of local theatre groups, made up mainly of expats, who put on regular productions. Most of these are jolly good fun and are generally well attended by loyal supporters and would-be thespians. Probably the best known and loved group is the Hong Kong Players (p.241). Their annual Christmas pantomime is an integral part of any Hong Kong Christmas. Other upcoming shows are advertised on their website, as are audition dates. Ah, the smell of greasepaint.

Work Visas p.54
Weekend Breaks p.155

Written by residents, the Sydney Explorer is packed with insider info, from arriving in a new destination to making it your home and everything in between.

Sydney Explorer Residents' Guide
We Know Where You Live

Abu Dhabi • Amsterdam • Bahrain • Barcelona • Dubai • Dublin • Geneva • Hong Kong • Kuwait
London • New York • New Zealand • Oman • Paris • Qatar • Shanghai • Singapore • Sydney

EXPLORER
www.explorerpublishing.com

DIGITALGLOBE™

C L E A R L Y   T H E   B E S T

61 cm QuickBird Imagery is the highest resolution satellite imagery available. We offer products and resorces to both existing GIS users and the entire next generation of mapping and multimedia applications.

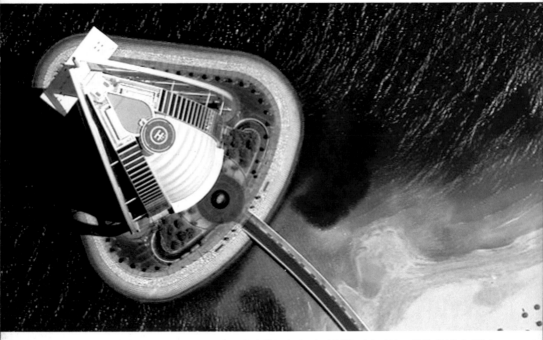

Burj Al Arab, Scale 1:2500, dated May 2003 © DigitalGlobe

MAPSgeosystems

DigitalGlobe's Master Reseller serving the Middle East and East, Central and West Africa

MAPS (UAE), Corniche Plaza 1, P.O. Box 5232, Sharjah, UAE.
Tel : +971 6 5725411, Fax : +971 6 5724057
www.maps-geosystems.com

For further details, please contact quickbird@maps-geosystems.com

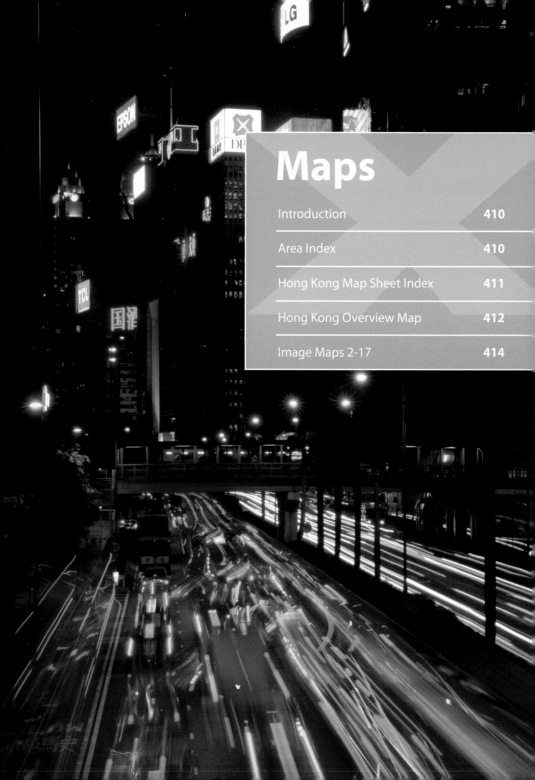

Maps

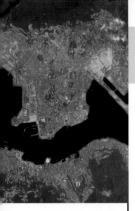

Maps

Introduction

The satellite image maps in this section cover the entire SAR, and allow you to pinpoint an exact location (and maybe even see your house). The map on the opposite page shows which areas are covered by the image maps, and map 1 overleaf illustrates the whole region. Maps 2 to 14 are at a scale of 1:50,000 and maps 15, 16 and 17 are 1:25,000.

Mapophobia!

Many people have an irrational fear of all things cartographical, but there's really nothing to be afraid of. The fascinating satellite images in this section are good for getting your bearings - main roads and landmarks are all superimposed to help you work out where you are. If you still can't tell your Sha Tins from your Stanleys, then turn to p.43 for a list of Hong Kong's taxi firms!

Map Legend

M	Museum/Heritage
E	Embassy/Consulate
H	Hotel
S	Shopping
+	Hospital/Clinic
✖	MTR Station
SHEK O	Area Name
(u/c)	Under Construction
▬▬	Expressway
▬▬	Main Road
▬▬	Border Line
[▬]	Tunnel
■ ■ ■	Under Construction

Area	Map Ref	Area	Map Ref
Aberdeen	14-A1	Pok Fu Lam	16-B3
Ap Lei Chau	14-A1	Quarry Bay	17-E2
Causeway Bay	17-B2	Repulse Bay	14-C2
Central	16-F2	Sai Kung	7-A3
Chai Wan	10-E4	Sai Wan	16-B2
Chek Lap Kok	8-D3	Sai Wan Ho	17-E2
Cheung Chau	13-B2	Sai Ying Pun	16-D1
Cheung Sha	12-E1	San Po Kong	10-C2
Cheung Sha Wan	10-A2	San Tin	2-D3
Clear Water Bay	11-A4	Sha Tin	6-C4
D' Aguilar Peninsula	14-E2	Sham Shui Po	15-C1
Discovery Bay	9-B3	Sham Tseng	5-D4
Fanling	3-A3	Shau Kei Wan	10-E4
Ha Tsuen	5-A1	Shek Kip Mei	10-B2
Hang Hau	10-F2	Shek O	14-E2
Happy Valley	17-A3	Shek Pik	12-B2
Ho Man Tin	15-E2	Sheung Shui	3-A3
Hong Kong Gold Coast	4-F4	Sheung Wan	16-E1
Hung Hom	15-E3	Shouson Hill	14-C1
Jardine's Lookout	17-D4	So Kon Po	17-B3
Jordan	15-C3	So Kwun Wat	5-A4
Kam Tin	5-D1	South Bay	14-C2
Kau Sai Chau	11-B1	Stanley	14-D3
Kennedy Town	16-B2	Sunny Bay	9-B1
Kowloon City	15-E1	Tai Hang	17-C3
Kowloon Tong	10-C2	Tai Kok Tsui	15-B2
Kwun Tong	10-D3	Tai O	12-A1
Lai Chi Kok	15-A1	Tai Po	10-A1
Lei King	17-F2	Tai Shui Hang	9-B4
Lei Yue Mun	10-F4	Tin Hau	17-C2
Lo Wu	2-F2	To Kwa Wan	15-E2
Ma On Shan	6-F2	Tsim Sha Tsui	15-C4
Ma Tau Kok	15-F2	Tsing Lung Tau	5-C4
Ma Tau Wai	15-E2	Tsing Yi	9-E1
Mai Po	2D2	Tsuen Wan	5-F4
Man Kam To	3-A1	Tuen Mun	4-F3
Mid-Levels	16-D2	Tung Chung	8-D4
Mong Kok	15-C2	Wan Chai	17-A2
Mui Wo	9-A4	Wong Tai Si	10-C1
North Point	17-C1	Yau Ma Tei	15-C3
The Peak	16-E3	Yau Yat Tsuen	10-B2
Peng Chau	9-C4	Yuen Long	5-B1
Po Toi	14-E4	Yung Shue Wan	13-F2

DIGITALGLOBE

Image courtesy of MAPS geosystems – Master Reseller for Digital Globe

© Explorer Group Ltd. 2007

This map is not an authority on international boundaries

3.5km

TUNG PING CHAU

TAI CHAU
TSIM CHAU

WONG NAI CHAU
KONG TAU PAI
WANG CHAU
PYRAMID ROCK

EAST NINEPIN ISLAND
SOUTH NINEPIN ISLAND

KUNG CHAU

PORT ISLAND

GRASS ISLAND

7

11

TOWN ISLAND
BAY ISLET
BLUFF ISLAND
BASALT ISLAND

NORTH NINEPIN ISLAND

ROUND ISLAND

FLAT ISLAND

JIN ISLAND
PING MIN CHAU
TRIO ISLAND

WAGLAN ISLAND

CRESCENT ISLAND

TAI TAU CHAU
KAI CHAU
KAU SAI CHAU

AP CHAU
CHEUNG SHEK TSUI
FUN CHAU

CROOKED ISLAND
YEUNG CHAU

FU WONG CHAU
DOUBLE ISLAND

YIM TIN TSAI

SHARP ISLAND

SHELTER ISLAND

STEEP ISLAND

TUNG LUNG CHAU

SUNG KONG

SHA TAU KOK

SAI KUNG

MA SHI CHAU

CENTRE ISLAND

MA ON SHAN

TAI CHIK SHA

TSEUNG KWANO
HANG HAU

TAI TAN

YAU TONG

D' AGUILAR PENINSULA

KAU PEI CHAU

BEAUFORT ISLAND

MAIN KAM TO

3

6

SHA TIN

10

NGAU CHI WAN

14

LO CHAU
PAK PAI

PO TOI

SHEUNG SHUI

TAI PO

KWUN TONG

15

SHEK KIP MEI

KOWLOON

17

STANLEY

FANLING

SHOUSON HILL

REPULSE BAY

STANLEY PENINSULA

KWAI CHUNG

16

HONG KONG ISLAND

ROUND ISLAND

MAI PO
SAN TIN

2

NGAU TAM MEI

KAM TIN

5

HA KWAI CHUNG

TSUEN WAN

TSING YI

STONECUTTERS ISLAND

POK FU LAM

WAH FU
ABERDEEN
AP LEI CHAU

SOK KWU WAN

YUNG SHUE WAN

SHAM TSENG

MA WAN
TSING LUNG CHAU

PEAKED HILL

GREEN ISLAND

LAMMA ISLAND

SHEK KONG

TAI LAM CHUNG

9

PA TAU KWU

SIU KAU YI CHAU
KAU YI CHAU

LAU FAU SHAN

TIN SHUI WAI

PING SHAN

SO KWUN WAT

TSING LUNG TAU

SUNNY BAY

CHEUNG SOK

DISCOVERY BAY

TAI LEI
PENG CHAU

13

SUNSHINE ISLAND
HEI LING CHAU

HA TSUEN

TUEN MUN

HONG KONG GOLD COAST

SIU MO TO

TAI SHUI HANG

MUI WO

PEARL ISLAND

4

8

TAI MO TO

TUNG CHUNG

CHEK LAP KOK

12

LANTAU ISLAND

CHEUNG SHA
CHA KWO CHAU

SHEK KWU CHAU

LUNG KWU CHAU

SHA CHAU

TAI O

SHEK PIK

SIU A CHAU

YUEN CHAU

CHEUNG MUK TAU

PEOPLE'S REPUBLIC OF CHINA

SHENZHEN SPECIAL ECONOMIC ZONE

LO WU

LOK MA CHAU

Deep Bay

MAI PO

SAN TIN

NGAU TAM MEI

LAU FAU SHAN

TIN SHUI WAI

KAM TIN

PING SHAN

HA TSUEN

YUEN LONG

SHEK KONG

TUEN MUN

LUNG KWU CHAU

SO KWUN WAT

TAI LAM CHUNG

SHAM TSENG

TSUEN WAN

HONG KONG GOLD COAST

PEARL ISLAND

TSING LUNG TAU

SHA CHAU

MA WAN

TANG LUNG CHAU

TSING YI

SIU MO TO

TAI MO TO

CHEUNG SOK

SUNNY BAY

PA TAU KWU

STONECUTTERS ISLAND

Discovery Bay

CHEK LAP KOK

SIU KAU YI CHAU

GREEN ISLAND

TAI LEI

PENG CHAU

KAU YI CHAU

TUNG CHUNG

TAI SHUI HANG

MUI WO

SUNSHINE ISLAND

LANTAU ISLAND

TAI O

HEI LING CHAU

YUNG SHUE WAN

CHEUNG SHA

Adamasta Channel

West Lamma Channel

SHEK PIK

CHA KWO CHAU

CHEUNG CHAU

Lantau Channel

SHEK KWU CHAU

LAMMA

SIU A CHAU

CHEUNG MUK TAU

YUEN CHAU MA CHAU

SOKO ISLANDS

South China Sea

TAI A CHAU

YUEN KONG CHAU

TAU LO CHAU

© Explorer Group Ltd. 2007

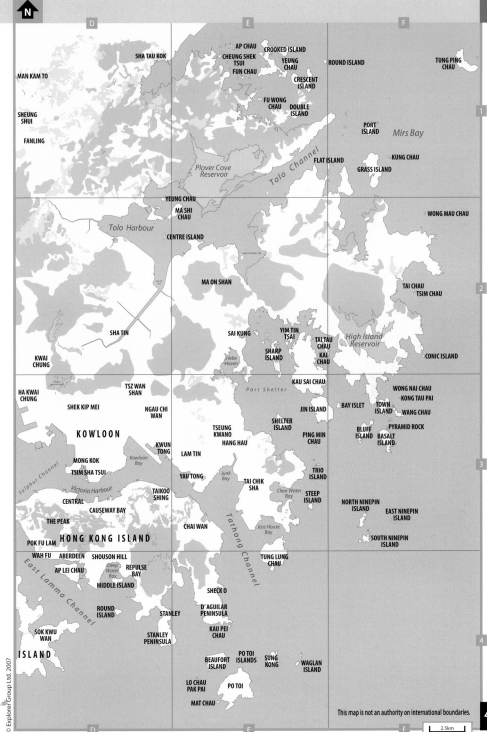

MAN KAM TO

SHEUNG SHUI

FANLING

SHA TAU KOK

AP CHAU
CHEUNG SHEK TSUI
FUN CHAU
CROOKED ISLAND
YEUNG CHAU
CRESCENT ISLAND
ROUND ISLAND
TUNG PING CHAU

FU WONG CHAU
DOUBLE ISLAND

PORT ISLAND
Mirs Bay

Plover Cove Reservoir

FLAT ISLAND

Tolo Channel

KUNG CHAU
GRASS ISLAND

YEUNG CHAU

MA SHI CHAU

Tolo Harbour

CENTRE ISLAND

WONG MAU CHAU

MA ON SHAN

TAI CHAU
TSIM CHAU

SHA TIN

SAI KUNG

YIM TIN TSAI

TAI TAU CHAU

High Island Reservoir

SHARP ISLAND

KAI CHAU

CONIC ISLAND

Hebe Haven

KWAI CHUNG

HA KWAI CHUNG

TSZ WAN SHAN

SHEK KIP MEI

NGAU CHI WAN

Port Shelter

KAU SAI CHAU

WONG NAI CHAU
KONG TAU PAI

BAY ISLET

TOWN ISLAND
WANG CHAU

JIN ISLAND

SHELTER ISLAND

PYRAMID ROCK

BLUFF ISLAND
BASALT ISLAND

KOWLOON

KWUN TONG

TSEUNG KWANO

HANG HAU

PING MIN CHAU

LAM TIN

MONG KOK
TSIM SHA TSUI

Kowloon Bay

YAU TONG

Junk Bay

TAI CHIK SHA

TRIO ISLAND

Sulphur Channel

Victoria Harbour

TAIKOO SHING

Clear Water Bay

STEEP ISLAND

NORTH NINEPIN ISLAND

EAST NINEPIN ISLAND

CENTRAL

CAUSEWAY BAY

THE PEAK

CHAI WAN

Joss House Bay

SOUTH NINEPIN ISLAND

POK FU LAM

HONG KONG ISLAND

Tathong Channel

WAH FU
ABERDEEN
SHOUSON HILL

AP LEI CHAU

Deep Water Bay
REPULSE BAY

TUNG LUNG CHAU

East Lamma Channel

MIDDLE ISLAND

SHECK O

ROUND ISLAND

STANLEY

D'AGUILAR PENINSULA

SOK KWU WAN

STANLEY PENINSULA

KAU PEI CHAU

ISLAND

BEAUFORT ISLAND

PO TOI ISLANDS

SUNG KONG

WAGLAN ISLAND

LO CHAU PAK PAI

PO TOI

MAT CHAU

This map is not an authority on international boundaries.

2.5km

© Explorer Group Ltd. 2007

N

Image courtesy of MAPS geosystems – Master Reseller for Digital Globe

MAPSgeosystems

SHENZHEN
SPECIAL ECONOMIC ZONE

Deep Bay

Mai Po Nature
Reserve

Border Rd

Border Rd

Tam Kon Chau

Wo Shang
Wai

Palm Springs

Bauhinia Rd

Lychee Rd

Golden Bamboo Rd

Mong Tseng
Wai

Fairview
Park

Chuk Yuen
Tsuen

Fairview Park Blvd

Deep Bay Rd

Tai Sang Wai

LAU FAU SHAN

Wetland Park Rd

Tin Shui Rd

Wetland Park Rd

Hong Kong
Wetland Park

Nam sang Wai St

Pok Wai

Route No.9

San Hing
Tsuen

Tin Sau Rd

Lau Fau Shan Rd

Ng Uk
Tsuen

Wai Loi St

Sha
Kong Wai

Tin Wah Rd

TIN SHUI WAI

Yuen Long
Industrial Estate

Mo Fan
Heung

414

© Explorer Group Ltd. 2007

Image courtesy of MAPS geosystems – Master Reseller for Digital Globe

LO WU

Lo Wu Station Rd

Liu Pok

Cemetery

Man Kam Toh Rd

Shun Yee San Tsuen

Fu Tei Au Rd

Border Rd

Ho Sheung Heung Rd

San Wan Rd

MAI PO

Border Rd

San Shun Rd

Border Rd

Wo Tso Lung Rd

LOK MA CHAU

Lo Wo Saddle Club

Ho Sheung Heung

Sheung Shui Heung

Po Wan Rd

Chau Tau

Pak Shek Au

Po Lau Rd

Po Shek Wo Rd

Mai Po Nature Reserve

Fanling Hwy

Kwu Tung

Kwu Tung Rd

Fanling Hwy

Castle Peak Rd

San Tin Tsuen Rd

Kwu Tung Rd

Kam Tung Rd

Tai Fu Tai

Kam Tsin

SAN TIN

Kwu Tung Rd

Castel Peak Rd

Hong Kong Golf Club

Kai Leng

San Tim Hwy

Shek Wo Wai

Fan Kam Rd

Mai Po Tsuen

Royal Palms

Barracks

Cemetery

San Tam Rd

Wai Tsai

Ngau Tam Mein Rd

Tsiu Keng

Fan Kam Rd

Lam Tsuen Country Park

Yau Tam Mei Tsuen

Lam Tsuen Country Park

Sai Wai Tsuen

NGAU TAM MEI

Ying Pun

Long Ha

Chuk Yau Rd

© Explorer Group Ltd. 2007

415

500m

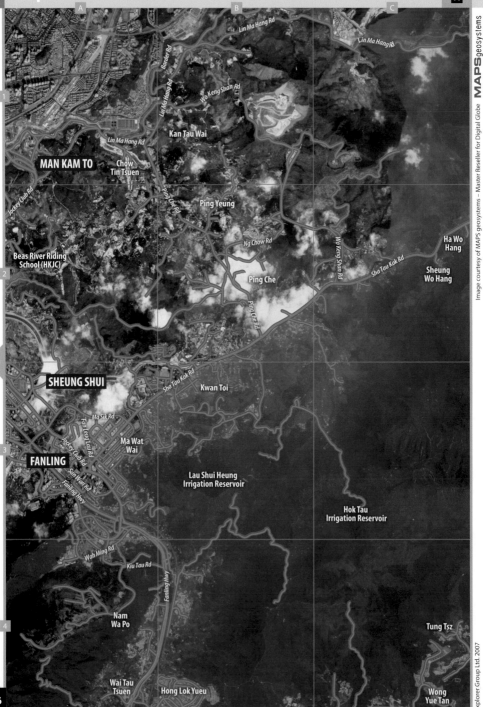

Image courtesy of MAPS geosystems – Master Reseller for Digital Globe

© Explorer Group Ltd. 2007

MAPSgeosystems

N

Lin Ma Hang Rd

Lin Ma Hang Rd

Border Rd

Lin Ma Hang Rd

Wo Keng Shan Rd

MAN KAM TO

Lin Ma Hang Rd

Chow
Tin Tsuen

Kan Tau Wai

Jockey Club Rd

Ping Kok Rd

Ping Yeung

Ng Chow Rd

Wo Keng Shan Rd

Ha Wo
Hang

**Beas River Riding
School (HKJC)**

Ping Che

Sheung
Wo Hang

Sha Tau Kok Rd

Ping Che Rd

SHEUNG SHUI

Sho Tau Kok Rd

Kwan Toi

Ma Sik Rd

Fan Leng Lau Rd

Ma Wat
Wai

Jockey Club Rd

FANLING

Sun Wan Rd

Fanling Hwy

Lau Shui Heung
Irrigation Reservoir

Hok Tau
Irrigation Reservoir

Wah Ming Rd

Kiu Tau Rd

Fanling Hwy

Nam
Wa Po

Tung Tsz

Wai Tau
Tsuen

Hong Lok Yueu

Wong
Yue Tan

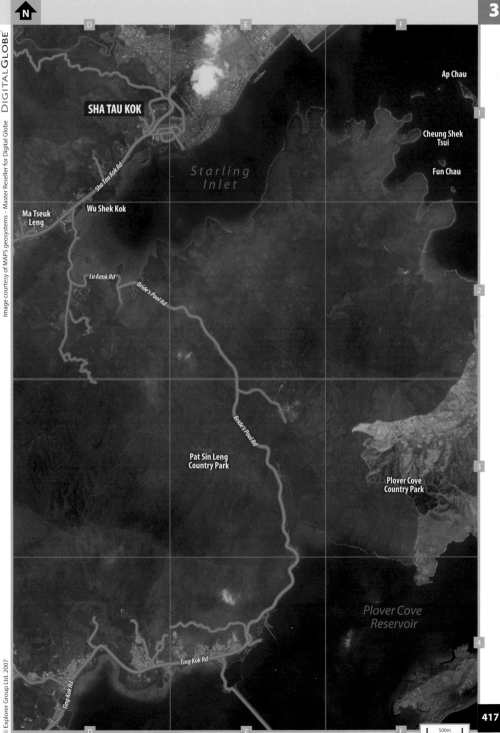

Image courtesy of MAPS geosystems – Master Reseller for Digital Globe

DIGITALGLOBE

© Explorer Group Ltd. 2007

500m

Deep Bay

Power Station

Black Point

Lung Kwu Chau

Image courtesy of MAPS geosystems – Master Reseller for Digital Globe **MAPS**geosystems

© Explorer Group Ltd. 2007

N

Image courtesy of MAPS geosystems – Master Reseller for Digital Globe

DIGITAL**GLOBE**

Ngau Hom Shek

Ngau Hom Sha

Deep Bay Rd

Sheung Pak Nai

1

Ha Pak Nai

Nim Wan Rd

Nim Wan

Tuen Tsz Wai

2

San Hing Tsuen

Po Tong Ha

Kei Lun Wai

Tsing Lun Rd

Tuen Mun Rd

Lingnan University

Ching Chung Koon (M)

5

Chung Wong Toi

Leung King Estate

Tsing Tin Rd

Sha Po Kong

Lang Kwu Sheung Tan

Shek Pai Tau Rd

Ho Pong St

Tsuen Wan Rd

San Hui Village

Lang Kwu Tan Rd

Tuen Mun Golf Centre

Pui To Rd

Tsing Wu Rd

Tsing Tin Rd

Tuen Mun Rd

3

Pak Long

Archery Range

Tin Hau Rd

Tuen Mun Rd

Castle Peak Rd

Sha Po Kong

Tuen Mun Public Riding School

TUEN MUN

Lung Tsai

Dragon Bowling Tuen Mun

Hoi Wing Rd

Tap Shek Kok

Hong Kong Pony Club

Lung Fu Rd

Wu Shan Rd

Lung Mun Road

HONG KONG GOLD COAST

Power Station

Wu Chui Rd

4

Lung Mun Road

Mong Fat St

Castle Peak Bay

Pillar Point

© Explorer Group Ltd. 2007

D   E   F

8

500m

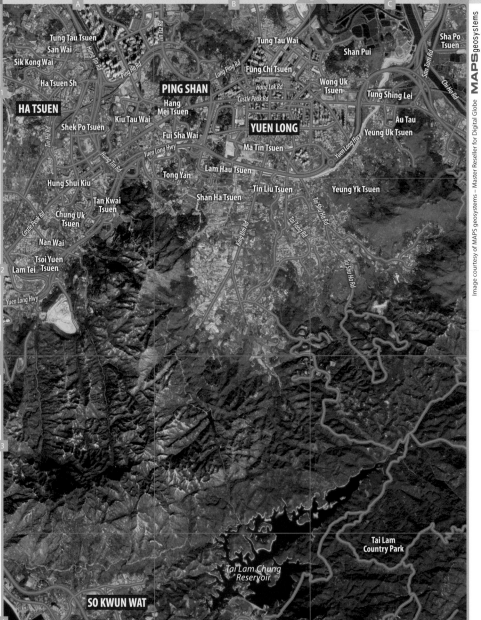

HA TSUEN

Tung Tau Tsuen
San Wai
Sik Kong Wai
Ha Tsuen Sh

Shek Po Tsuen
Kiu Tau Wai

Hung Shui Kiu

Tan Kwai Tsuen
Chung Uk Tsuen

Nan Wai

Tsoi Yuen Tsuen
Lam Tei

Yuen Long Hwy

PING SHAN

Hang Mei Tsuen

Fui Sha Wai

Tong Yan

Shan Ha Tsuen

Tung Tau Wai
Shan Pui

Fung Chi Tsuen

Hong Lok Rd
Castle Peak Rd

YUEN LONG

Ma Tin Tsuen

Lam Hau Tsuen

Tin Liu Tsuen

Wong Uk Tsuen

Sha Po Tsuen

Tung Shing Lei

Au Tau
Yeung Uk Tsuen

Yeung Yk Tsuen

Long Ping Rd
Hung Tin Rd
Ping Ho Rd
Tin Tsz Rd
San Tam Rd
Chi Ho Rd
Tin Ha Rd
Hung Tin Rd
Castle Peak Rd
Yuen Long Hwy
Yuen Long Hwy
Kong Uin Rd
Tai Shu Ha Rd
Tai Tong Rd
Tai Shu Ha Rd

SO KWUN WAT

Gold Coast Yacht and Country Club

Castle Peak Rd

Pearl Island

Siu Lam

Yuen Mun Rd

TAI LAM CHUNG

Tai Lam Chung Reservoir

Tai Lam Country Park

TSING LUNG TAU

Image courtesy of MAPS geosystems – Master Reseller for Digital Globe   **MAPS** geosystems

© Explorer Group Ltd. 2007

KAM TIN
Shui Tau
Kam Tai Rd
Kam Tin Rd
Walled Village
Kat Hing Wai
Barracks
Fan Kam Rd
Wang Toi Shan
Kam Tin Rd
Wong Chuk Yuen
Lam Kam Rd
Tai Mo Shan Country Park

Kam Shek Rd
Sheung Tsuen
Shui Lau Tin
Kam Sheung Rd
Yuen Kong
SHEK KONG
Kadoorie Farm and Botanic Garden

Yuen Kong San Tsuen

Ma On Kong

Ho Pui Irrigation Reservoir

Tai Lam Tunnel

Rte Twisk
Lo Wai Rd
Lo Wai

Tsuen Wan Adventist Hospital
TSUEN WAN
Cheung Pei Shan Rd
Castle Peak Rd
Tsuen Wan
Tai Wo Hau
Texaco Rd

SHAM TSENG
Ting Kau
Tuen Mun Rd
Yau Kom Tau
Tuen Mun Rd
Hoi On Rd
Tsuen Wan Rd
Sha Tsui Rd
Yeung Uk Rd

Tsing Long Hwy
Ting Kau Bridge
Ngau Kok Wan

500m

Image courtesy of MAPS geosystems – Master Reseller for Digital Globe
© Explorer Group Ltd. 2007

N

Image courtesy of MAPS geosystems – Master Reseller for Digital Globe

MAPS geosystems

Lam Tsuen
Country Park

Wai Tau Tsuen

Hong Lok Yuen

Fanling Rd

Tai Po Rd

Ting Kok Rd

Yuen Shin Rd

Dai Fu St

Dai Kwai St

Lam Kam Rd

Chung Uk
Tsuen

Tolo Hwy

Tai Po Tau

Tai Po Tai Wo Rd

TAI PO

Kwong Fuk Rd

Tai Wo Estate
Kam Shan

Tolo Hwy

Tolo Harbour

Tolo Hwy

Pan Chung

Tolo Hwy

Tai Po Rd

Ma Wo

Tai Po Rd

Tai Mo Shan
Country Park

Cheung
Shue Tan

Shing Mun
Country Park

Shatin College

Shan Mei St

Fo Tan Rd

Shatin Junior
School

Ten Thousand
Buddhas Monastery

Sheung Wo Che

Belair
Bowling
Centre

Shing Mun
Reservoir

Ji-Kiln
Studio

SHA TIN

Sha Tin Rd

Cheung Pei Shan Rd

Wo Yi Hop Rd

Shing Mun Tunnel

Shing Mun Tunnel

(S)

New Town
Plaza

Lion Rock Tunnel Rd

Mei Tin Rd

Che Kung
Temple

Shan Ha Wai

(E) Slovak Republic

Sha Tin Rd

Sun Chui Estate

(M)

Tsang Tai Uk

Kwai Chung Rd

Castle Peak Rd

Tai Po Rd

Che Lung Miu Rd

Hing Kong St

Tim Sam St

Kak Tin

ESF Bauhinia
School

Kam Shan
Country Park

Tin Sam

© Explorer Group Ltd. 2007

Yeung Chau

Plover Cove

Ma Shi Chau

Yim Tin Tsai

Centre Island

Whitehead Club

Cheung Muk Tau

Sia Sha Rd

Wu Kai Sha Village

Garden Farm Golf Centre

MA ON SHAN

Sai Keng

Chinese University of Hong Kong

Sha Tin Hoi

Heng On Estate

Ma On Shan Rd

Tolo Hwy

Kau T Village

Tate's Cairn Hwy

Tolo Hwy

Penfold Park

Sha Tin Race Course

Tate's Cairn Hwy

Shing Mun River Channel

✚ Prince of Wales Hospital

Shan Liu

Tai Chung Kiu Rd

Siu Lek Yuen Rd

On Sum St

Wo Tong Kong

Sha Kok Mei

City One Shatin

Cemetery

Sha Lek Hwy

SAI KUNG

Pak Kong

Ma On Shan Country Park

Wu Lei Tau

Tsiu Hang Lions Nature Education Centre

Hebe Haven

500m

Image courtesy of MAPS geosystems – Master Reseller for Digital Globe

DIGITALGLOBE

© Explorer Group Ltd. 2007

N

Image courtesy of MAPS geosystems – Master Reseller for Digital Globe

MAPSgeosystems

© Explorer Group Ltd. 2007

Three Fathoms Cove

Hot Ha

Ha Ha Rd

Long Harbour

Ko Tong Hau

Pak Tam Rd

Sai Kung West Country Park

Sai Kung East Country Park

Sai Sha Rd

Yam Yee Rd

Wong Chuk Wan

Tai Wan

Tai Mong Tsai Rd

Tso Wo Hang

Tai Mong Tsai

Tai Mong Tsai Rd

SAI KUNG

Wong Yi Chau

Cham Tau Chau

Yeung Chau

Yim Tin Tsai

Sai Kung Man Yee Rd

Kwun Cham Wan

Sharp Island

Tai Tau Chau

Inner Port Shelter

Jockey Club Kau Sai Chau Public Golf Course

Kiu Tsui Country Park

Kai Chau

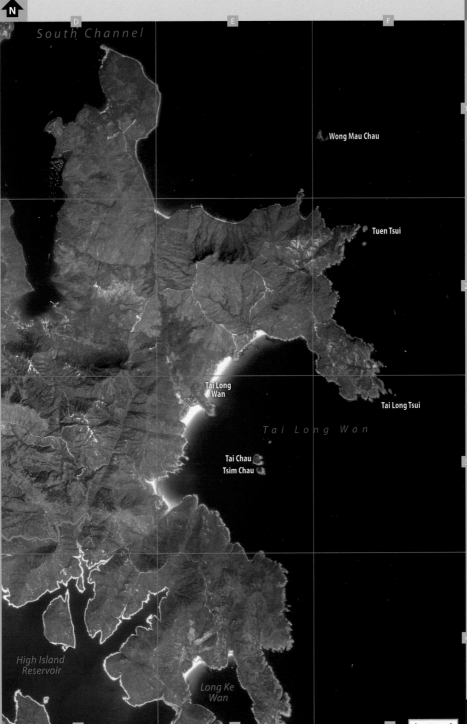

South Channel

Wong Mau Chau

Tuen Tsui

Tai Long Wan

Tai Long Tsui

Tai Long Wan

Tai Chau

Tsim Chau

High Island Reservoir

Long Ke Wan

Image courtesy of MAPS geosystems – Master Reseller for Digital Globe

© Explorer Group Ltd. 2007

500m

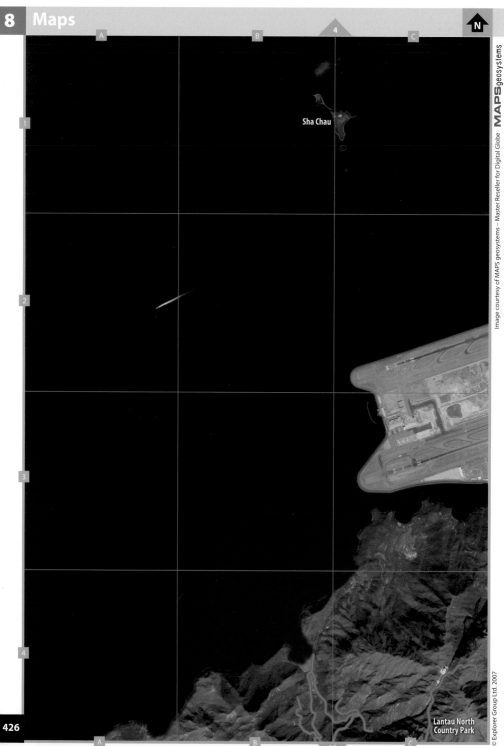

Sha Chau

Lantau North
Country Park

Image courtesy of MAPS geosystems – Master Reseller for Digital Globe

MAPSgeosystems

© Explorer Group Ltd. 2007

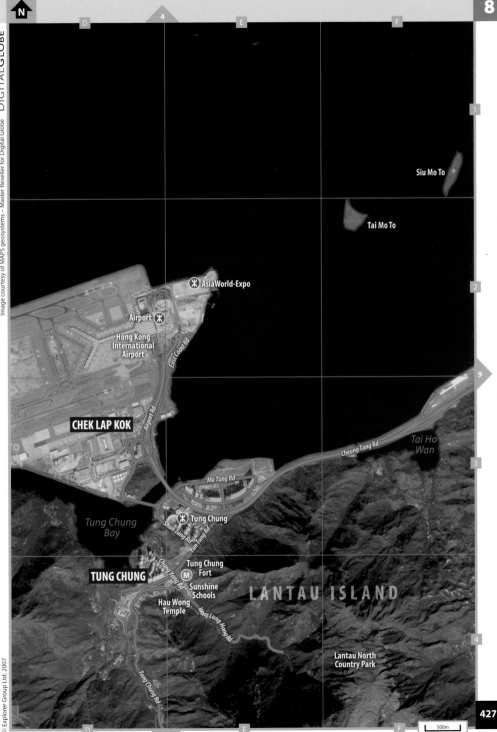

Image courtesy of MAP's geosystems – Master Reseller for Digital Globe

DIGITALGLOBE

N

Siu Mo To

Tai Mo To

AsiaWorld-Expo

Airport

Hong Kong
International
Airport

East Coast Rd

CHEK LAP KOK

Airport Rd

Cheung Tang Rd

Tai Ho
Wan

Ma Tung Rd

Tung Chung
Bay

Shun Tung Rd

Tung Chung

Yun Tung Rd

Tung Chung
Fort

Chung Yang Rd

Sunshine
Schools

Wong Lung Hang Rd

L A N T A U   I S L A N D

TUNG CHUNG

Hau Wong
Temple

Tung Chung Rd

Lantau North
Country Park

© Explorer Group Ltd. 2007

427

500m

N

Image courtesy of MAPS geosystems – Master Reseller for Digital Globe **MAPS** geosystems

5

Tuen Mun Rd

San Po Tsui

Lantau Link

SUNNY BAY

Tso Wan

Sunny Bay

Tsing Chau Tsai

Fa Peng

Luk Keng

Yam O Wan

PA TAU KWU

Cheung Tung Rd

CHEUNG SOK

Sham Shui Kok

Power Station

Sham Pak

Sze Pak

Disneyland Resort

Hong Kong Disneyland

8

Discovery Bay

Discovery Bay Rd

DISCOVERY BAY

**L A N T A U
I S L A N D**

Discovery Bay Intl School

Discovery Valley Rd

Nim Shue Wan Village

Pekip Nursery

Nim Shue Wan

Tai Lei

Tin Hau Temple

Discovery Bay Golf Club

Cheung Sha Lan

Trappist Monastery

PENG CHAU

TAI SHUI HANG

Silvermine Bay Beach

Tung Wan Tau

Kau Shat Wan

MUI WO

Silver Mine Bay

MAN KOK

Chung Hau

© Explorer Group Ltd. 2007

13

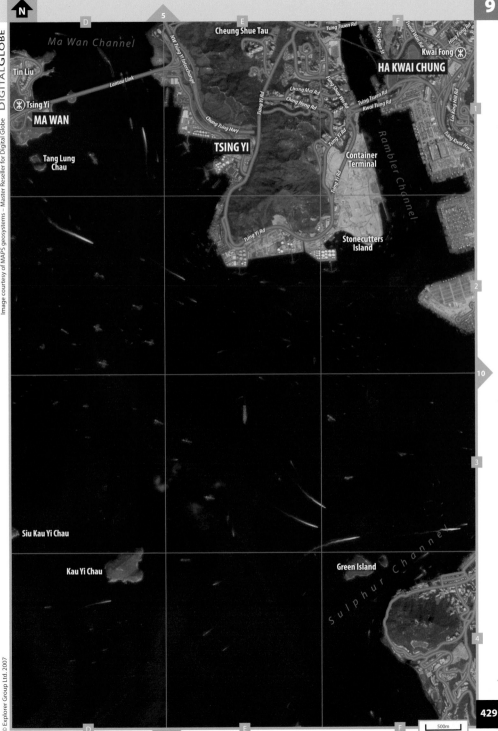

Ma Wan Channel

Tin Liu

Tsing Yi

MA WAN

Tang Lung
Chau

Siu Kau Yi Chau

Kau Yi Chau

Cheung Shue Tau

Tsing Tsuen Rd

Wing Shun St

Tsuen Wan Rd

Hing Fong Rd

Kwai Fong

HA KWAI CHUNG

Lai King Hill Rd

NW Tsing Yi Interchange

Lantau Link

Chung Mei Rd

Ching Hong Rd

Fung Shue Wo Rd

Tsing Tsuen Rd

Kwai Tsing Rd

Tsing Kwai Hwy

Tsing Yi Rd

Chung Tsing Hwy

TSING YI

Tsing Yi Rd

Container
Terminal

Rambler Channel

Tsing Yi Rd

Stonecutters
Island

Tsing Yi Rd

Green Island

Sulphur Channel

Image courtesy of MAPS geosystems – Master Reseller for Digital Globe

DIGITALGLOBE

© Explorer Group Ltd. 2007

5

D

E

F

1

2

10

3

4

13

D

E

F

429

500m

Image courtesy of MAPS geosystems – Master Reseller for Digital Globe

MAPSgeosystems

© Explorer Group Ltd. 2007

Hong Kong Explorer 1st Edition

Image courtesy of MAPS geosystems – Master Reseller for Digital Globe

DIGITAL GLOBE®

© Explorer Group Ltd. 2007

Ho Chung Golf
Driving Range
Centre

Trio Beach

Chuk Kok

Silverstrand

Tate's Cairn Tunnel

Tai Po Tsai

Choi Hung

Clear Water Bay Rd

The Hong Kong
University of Science
and Technology

Telford Plaza

Kowloon Bay

United Christian
Hospital

Po Lam

HANG HAU

Tseung Kwan
O Hospital

NGAU TAU KOK

Ngau Tau Kok

Kwun Tong

Hang Hau

apm

KWUN TONG

Sheung Tak
Estate

Laguna City

Lam Tin

Tseung Kwan O

Oriental
Golf City

Tiu Keng Leng

Cha Kwo Ling

Yau Tong

Junk Bay

Eastern Cross Harbour Tunnel

Devil's
Peak

TAI CHIK CHAU

Island Eastern Corridor

YAU TONG

Wan Po Rd

Quarry Bay

Tai Koo

Lei Yue Mun

Sai Wan Ho

SHAU KEI WAN

District Park

Shau Kei Wan

Island Eastern Corridor

SAI WAN HO

Lei Yue Mun
Holliday
Village &
Lei Yue
Mun Park

Heng Fa Chuen

LEI YUE MUN

Lei Yue Mun
Public Riding
School

Pamela Youde Nethersole
Eastern Hospital

CHAI WAN

Chai Wan

Ngan Wan

500m

Image courtesy of MAPS geosystems – Master Reseller for Digital Globe

MAPS geosystems

N

Kiu Tsui
Country Park

Sharp Island

Hap Mun
Bay

KAU SAI CHAU

Port Shelter

Kau Sai Wan

Rocky Harbour

Bay Islet

Shelter Island

Jin Island

Silverstrand

Pan Long Wan

Lung Ha Wan

Ping Min Chau

Sheung Yeung

Sheung Sze Wan

Lung Ha Wan Rd

Tai Hang Hau

Clear Water Bay
Country Park

Clear Water Bay Rd

Tai Au Mun

Trio Island

Tai Au Mun Rd

Clear Water Bay
Beaches

Clear Water Bay

CLEAR WATER BAY

Steep Island

Tai Au Mun Rd

Tin Hau Temple

Clearwater Bay
Golf & Country Club

*Joss House
Bay*

North Ninepin
Island

© Explorer Group Ltd. 2007

432

Conic island

Sai Kung Man Yee Rd

WONG NAI CHAU

Wong Nai
Chau

Kong Tau Pai

Town Island

Wang Chau

Pyramid Rock

Bluff Island

Basalt Island

© DIGITALGLOBE

Image courtesy of MAPS geosystems – Master Reseller for Digital Globe

© Explorer Group Ltd. 2007

N

TAI O

Ying Hing
Monastery

Tai O Rd

Keung Shan Rd

Ngong Ping Rd

**Big Buddha
& Po Lin
Monastery**

Tea Farm

Sham Wat Rd

Keung Shan Rd

A

B

8

C

1

Yi O

LANTAU ISLAND

Shek Pik
Reservoir

SHEK PIK

*Tai Long
Wan*

*Tung
Wan*

2

Wan Pui Rd

*Fan Lau
Tung Wan*

Ⓜ Fan Lau Fort

3

Lantau Channel

Siu A Chau

Yuen Chau

Ma Chau

Tai A Chau

4

A

B

C

Image courtesy of MAPS geosystems – Master Reseller for Digital Globe   **MAPS**geosystems

© Explorer Group Ltd. 2007

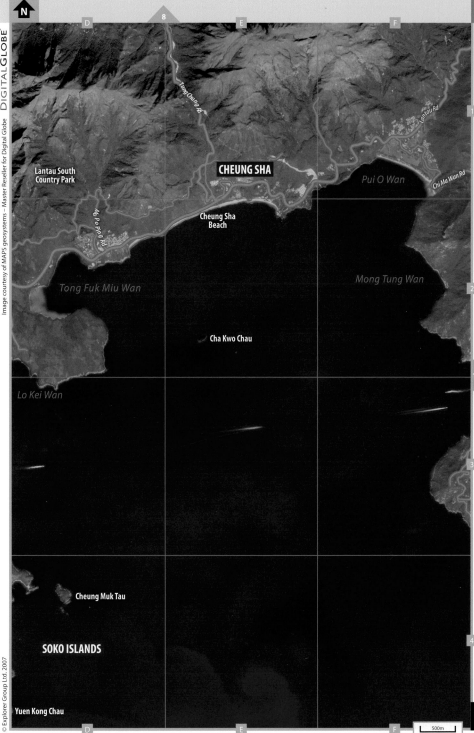

Lantau South
Country Park

CHEUNG SHA

Pui O Wan

Tung Chung Rd

Lantau Rd

Chi Ma Wan Rd

Mo Po Ping Rd

Cheung Sha
Beach

Tong Fuk Miu Wan

Mong Tung Wan

Cha Kwo Chau

Lo Kei Wan

Cheung Muk Tau

SOKO ISLANDS

Yuen Kong Chau

Image courtesy of MAPS geosystems – Master Reseller for Digital Globe

DIGITALGLOBE

© Explorer Group Ltd. 2007

500m

N

9

Sunshine Island

Hei Ling Chau

Lantau Rd

Shui Tseng
Wan

Ngau Kwa
Wan

Wang Tong

Shap Long
Kau Tsuen

Chi Ma Wan

Chi Ma Wan Rd

Shap Long
Chung Hau

Cheung Sha Wan

**LANTAU
ISLAND**

*Tai Long
Wan*

*Yi Long
Wan*

Adamasta Channel

CHEUNG CHAU

Tung Wan
Beach

Tung Wan

St. John
Hospital

*Cheung
Chau Wan*

Afternoon
(Kwun Yam)
Beach

*Pak Tso
Wan*

12

A   B   C

1

2

3

4

Image courtesy of MAPS geosystems – Master Reseller for Digital Globe   **MAPS**geosystems

© Explorer Group Ltd. 2007

Image courtesy of MAPS geosystems – Master Reseller for Digital Globe

DIGITALGLOBE

© Explorer Group Ltd. 2007

East Lamma Channel

West Lamma Channel

Luk Chau Wan

Yung Shue Wan

YUNG SHUE WAN

Hung Shing Yeh Beach

Ha Mei Wan

Picnic Bay

Lo So Shing Beach

Tin Hau Temple

LAMMA ISLAND

200m

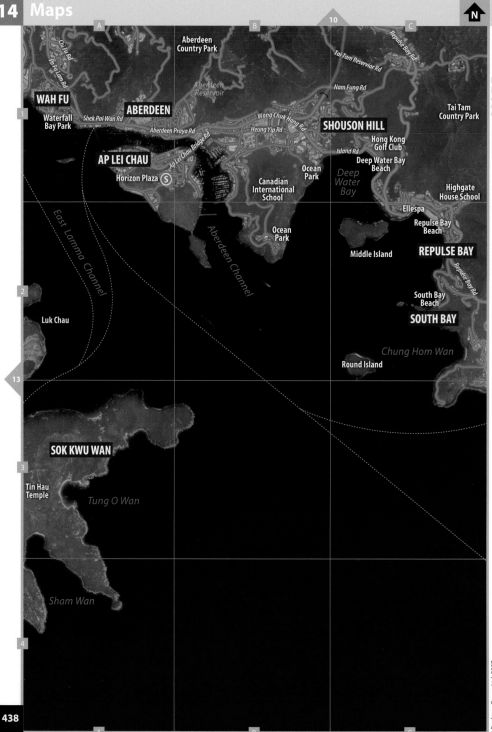

Image courtesy of MAPS geosystems – Master Reseller for Digital Globe   **MAPS**geosystems

10

WAH FU

Waterfall
Bay Park

ABERDEEN

Aberdeen
Country Park

Aberdeen
Reservoir

Tai Tam Reservior Rd

Nam Fung Rd

Repulse Bay Rd

Tai Tam
Country Park

Shek Pai Wan Rd

Aberdeen Praya Rd

Wong Chuk Hang Rd

Heung Yip Rd

SHOUSON HILL

Hong Kong
Golf Club

AP LEI CHAU

Ap Lei Chau Bridge Rd

Horizon Plaza (S)

Canadian
International
School

Ocean
Park

Island Rd

Deep Water Bay
Beach

Deep
Water
Bay

Highgate
House School

Ellespa

Repulse Bay
Beach

East Lamma Channel

Aberdeen Channel

Ocean
Park

Middle Island

REPULSE BAY

Repulse Bay Rd

South Bay
Beach

SOUTH BAY

Luk Chau

Chung Hom Wan

Round Island

SOK KWU WAN

Tin Hau
Temple

Tung O Wan

Sham Wan

A

B

C

© Explorer Group Ltd. 2007

DIGITALGLOBE

Image courtesy of MAPS geosystems – Master Reseller for Digital Globe

© Explorer Group Ltd. 2007

Chai Wan Rd

Mt Parker Rd

Tai Tam Rd

Shek O Road

Cape Collinson Rd

Ngan Wan

Tathong Channel

Tai Tam Reservoir Rd

Tai Tam Reservoir Group

Shek O Country Park

Big Wave Bay Beach

Hong Kong International School

Shek O Golf & Country Club

SHEK O

Shek O Wan

Tai Tam Harbour

Shek O Road

Shek O Beach

Stanley Gap Rd

Tai Tam Bay

Stanley Main Beach

Stanley Bay

St. Stephen's Beach

STANLEY

Tung Tau Wan

D' AGUILAR PENINSULA

Kau Pei Chau

Beaufort Island

Lo Chau Pak Pai

PO TOI

500m

Image courtesy of MAPS geosystems – Master Reseller for Digital Globe

MAPSgeosystems

© Explorer Group Ltd. 2007

LAI CHI KOK

Cheung Sha Wan Rd

Lai Chi Kok Rd

West Kowloon Expressway

Caritas Medical Centre

Tai Po Rd

Shek Kip Mei

Sham Shui Po

SHAM SHUI PO

Nam Cheong

Prince Edward

Prince Edward Rd

Goldfish Market

Ladies' Market

Waterfall Golf Driving Range & Gym

New Kowloon Plaza

Mong Kok

Argyle St

Langham Place

Olympic City

Olympic

TAI KOK TSUI

MONG KOK

Waterloo Rd

Yau Ma Tei

YAU MA TEI

Nathan Rd

Jade Market

Temple Street Night Market

Yue Hwa

Jordan Rd

City Golf Club

Bus Terminal

Jordan

Nga Cheung Rd

Kowloon

Wui Cheung Rd

JORDAN

Austin Rd West

Post Office

Kowloon Park

Harbour City

Hong Kong Heritage Discovery Centre

Western Cross Harbour Tunnel

TSIM SHA TSUI

Hyatt Regency

Langham Hotel

The Peninsula

Hong Kong Space Museum

Hong Kong Museum of Arts

Image courtesy of MAPS geosystems – Master Reseller for Digital Globe

© Explorer Group Ltd. 2007

DIGITALGLOBE

Beacon Hill
School

American
International
School

Kowloon
Tsai Park

Kowloon Walled
City Park

KOWLOON CITY

Waterloo Rd

Boundary St

Bird Market

West Prince Edward Rd

St Teresa's Hospital

Evangel Hospital

Former Hong Kong
International Airport

Flower Market

Argyle St

MA TAU WAI

Kadoorie Ave

Kowloon
Junior School

MA TAU KOK

Waterloo Rd

Fat Kwong St

To Kwa Wan Rd

Trainers
Street

HO MAN TIN

East Kowloon Corridor

TO KWA WAN

Kwong Wah
Hospital

Queen Elizabeth
Hospital

British
Military Hospital

Fat Kwong St

S Hung Hom
Square

Man Yue St

North East Kowloon Corridor

Open
University of
Hong Kong

Filipino
Club

Gascoigne Rd

United Services
Recreation Club

Kowloon
Cricket Club

Hong Kong
Polytechnic
University

Hung Hom South St

Hung Hom Rd

HUNG HOM

Hong Kong Museum
of History

M

M Hong Kong
Science Museum

Hong Kong
Coliseum

Hung Luen Rd

Bus
Terminal

Chatham Rd South

InterContinental
Grand Stanford

Tsim Sha Tsui

Peninsula

H

S Tsim Sha Tsui Ctr

Sheraton
Hong Kong
Hotel & Towers

H Kowloon Shangri-La

S Wing On Plaza

H

H InterContinental
Hong Kong

250m

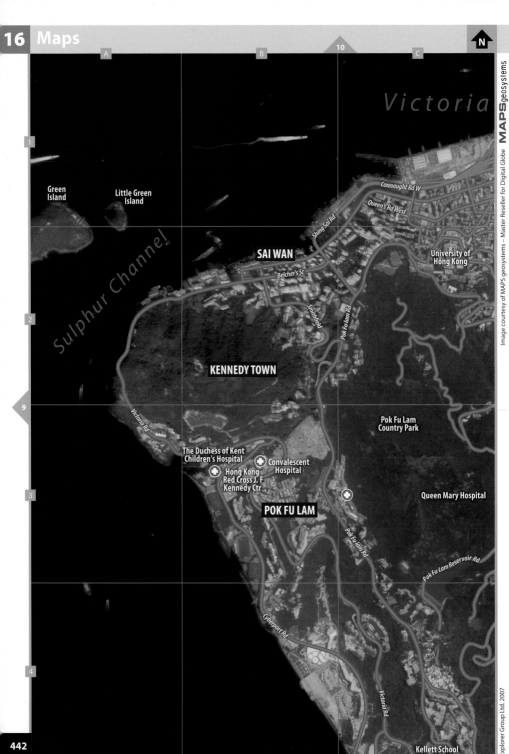

Image courtesy of MAPS geosystems – Master Reseller for Digital Globe

MAPSgeosystems

© Explorer Group Ltd. 2007

N

Victoria

Green Island

Little Green Island

Connaught Rd W

Queen's Rd West

Shing Sai Rd

SAI WAN

Belcher's St

University of Hong Kong

Sulphur Channel

Smithfield

Pok Fu Lam Rd

KENNEDY TOWN

Victoria Rd

Pok Fu Lam Country Park

The Duchess of Kent Children's Hospital

Convalescent Hospital

Hong Kong Red Cross J. F Kennedy Ctr

Queen Mary Hospital

POK FU LAM

Pok Fu Lam Rd

Pok Fu Lam Reservoir Rd

Cyberport Rd

Victoria Rd

Kellett School

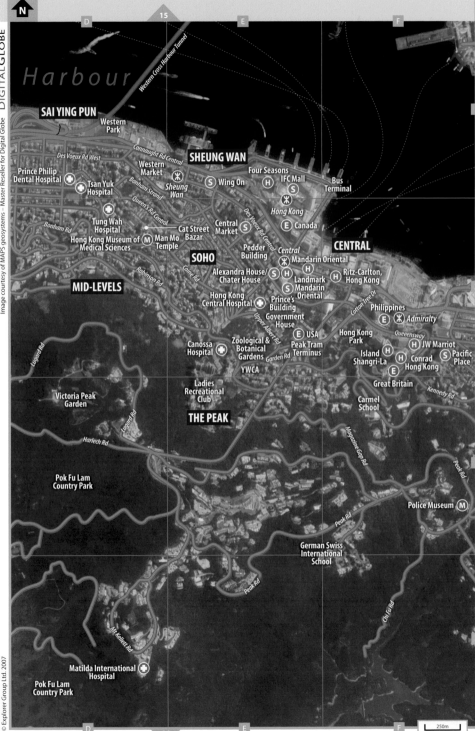

Harbour

SAI YING PUN

Western Park

Des Voeux Rd West

Prince Philip Dental Hospital

Tsan Yuk Hospital

Connaught Rd Central

Western Market

SHEUNG WAN

Bonham Strand

Sheung Wan

Wing On

Four Seasons

IFC Mall

Hong Kong

Bus Terminal

Queen's Rd Central

Tung Wah Hospital

Bonham Rd

Cat Street Bazar

Central Market

Des Voeux Rd Central

Canada

Hong Kong Museum of Medical Sciences

Man Mo Temple

SOHO

Pedder Building

Central

Mandarin Oriental

CENTRAL

MID-LEVELS

Robinson Rd

Caine Rd

Alexandra House/ Chater House

Landmark Mandarin Oriental

Ritz-Carlton, Hong Kong

Hong Kong Central Hospital

Prince's Building

Government House

Upper Albert Rd

Philippines

Admiralty

Cotton Tree Dr

Canossa Hospital

Zoological & Botanical Gardens

Garden Rd

USA

Peak Tram Terminus

Hong Kong Park

Queeensway

JW Marriot

Island Shangri-La

Conrad Hong Kong

Pacific Place

YWCA

Victoria Peak Garden

Ladies Recreational Club

THE PEAK

Great Britain

Kennedy Rd

Carmel School

Lugard Rd

Harlech Rd

Lugard Rd

Magazine Gap Rd

Peak Rd

Pok Fu Lam Country Park

Police Museum

Peak Rd

German Swiss International School

Peak Rd

Chi Fu Rd

Mt Kellett Rd

Matilda International Hospital

Pok Fu Lam Country Park

Image courtesy of MAPS geosystems – Master Reseller for Digital Globe

DIGITALGLOBE

© Explorer Group Ltd. 2007

250m

Image courtesy of MAPS geosystems – Master Reseller for Digital Globe

MAPSgeosystems

© Explorer Group Ltd. 2007

N

Cross Harbour Tunnel

Island Eastern Corridor

S Provident Centre

NORTH POINT

✻ Fortress Hill

Chinese International School

Braemar Hill Rd

Victoria Park Rd

CAUSEWAY BAY

Victoria Park

✻ Tin Hau

Hong Kong Convention & Exhibition Ctr

Grand Hyatt
H

South Africa
E **E**

Australia & New Zealand China Visa Office

Wan Chai Sports Ground

Causeway Bay

Paterson St

Percival St

✻

Jardine's Crescent and Bazaar

Causeway Rd

Tin Hau Temple Rd

TIN HAU

Hong Kong Central Library

Gloucester Rd

WAN CHAI

Hennessy Rd **✻** Wan Chai

Johnston Rd

S Times Square

S Lee Gardens

✚ St. Paul's Hospital

Ruttonjee Hospital **✚**

Queen's Rd East

Craigengower Cricket Club

Hong Kong Football Club

Hong Kong Racing Museum **M**

HAPPY VALLEY

Happy Valley Racecourse

Wong Nai Chung Rd

SO KON PO

SCAA Stadium

Olympic House

Hong Kong Stadium

✚ Tung Wah Eastern Hospital

TAI HANG

Stubbs Rd

Stubbs Rd

Black's Link

Hong Kong Academy

Hong Kong Sanatorium & Hospital **✚**

Sing Woo Rd

Tai Hang Rd

Adventist Hospital **✚**

French International School

Hong Kong Cricket Club

Wong Nai Chung Reservoir Park

Parkview

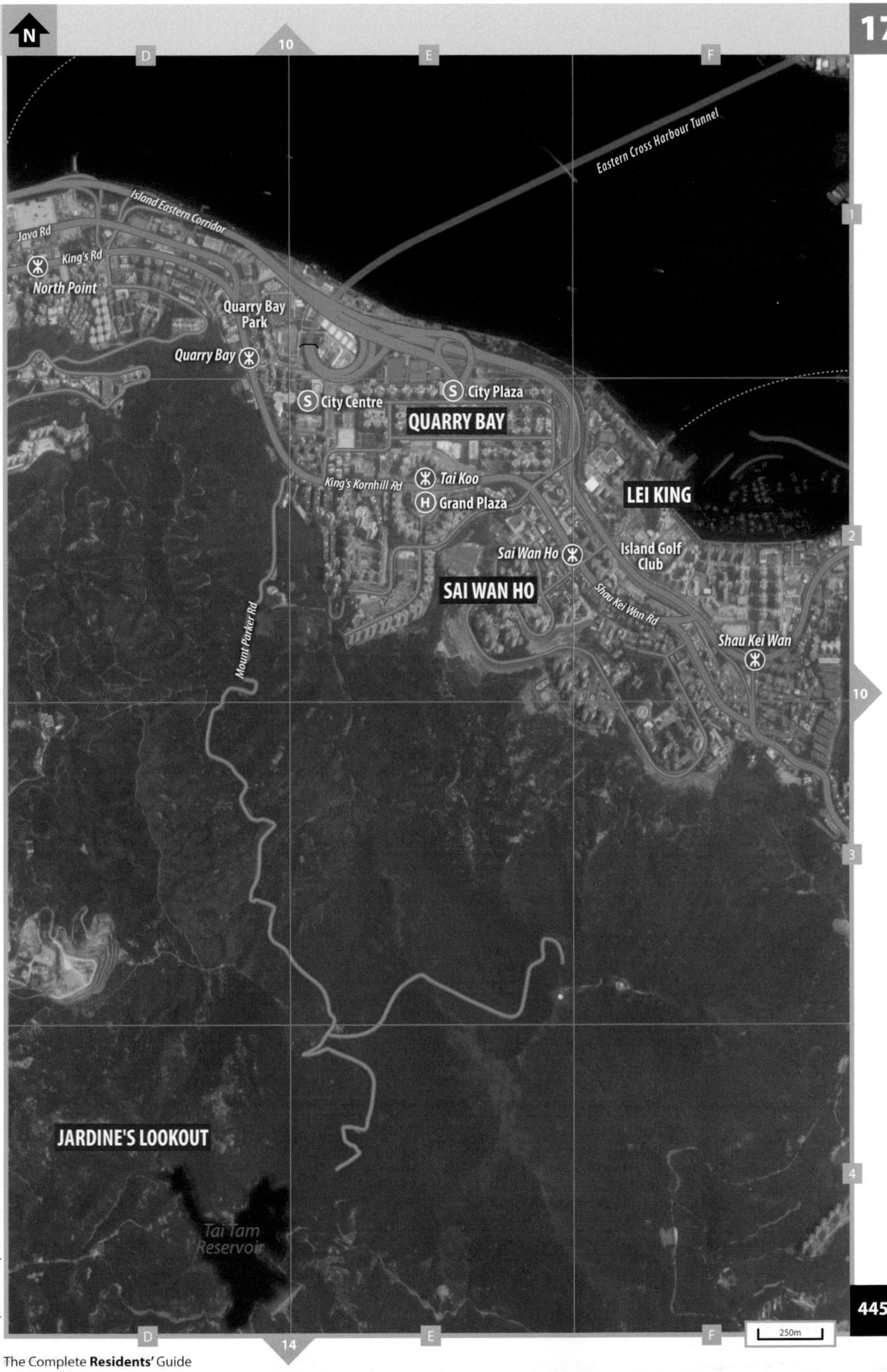
N
D
10
E
F
Eastern Cross Harbour Tunnel
Island Eastern Corridor
Java Rd
King's Rd
North Point
Quarry Bay Park
Quarry Bay
City Centre
City Plaza
QUARRY BAY
King's Kornhill Rd
Tai Koo
Grand Plaza
LEI KING
Island Golf Club
Sai Wan Ho
SAI WAN HO
Shau Kei Wan Rd
Shau Kei Wan
Mount Parker Rd
JARDINE'S LOOKOUT
Tai Tam Reservoir
1
2
3
4
10
14
250m

DIGITALGLOBE
Image courtesy of MAPS geosystems – Master Reseller for Digital Globe
© Explorer Group Ltd. 2007

Are you always taking the wrong turn?

Whether you're a map person or not, these pocket-sized marvels will help you get to know the city… and its limits.

Explorer Mini Maps
Putting the city in your pocket

Abu Dhabi · Amsterdam · Bahrain · Barcelona · Dubai · Dublin · Geneva · Hong Kong · Kuwait
London · New York · New Zealand · Oman · Paris · Qatar · Shanghai · Singapore · Sydney

EXPLORER
www.explorerpublishing.com

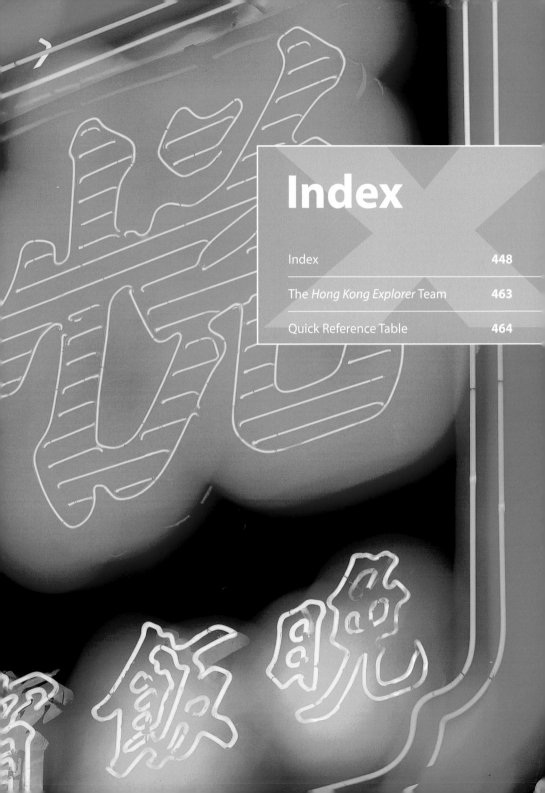

Index

Index

Hong Kong Explorer 1st Edition

Index

Index

Index

456

Index